Casebook for
Integrating
Family Therapy

Casebook for Integrating Family Therapy

An Ecosystemic Approach

Edited by

Susan H. McDaniel
Don-David Lusterman
Carol L. Philpot

American Psychological Association • *Washington, DC*

Published by
American Psychological Association
750 First Street, NE
Washington, DC 20002

Copies may be ordered from
APA Order Department
P.O. Box 92984
Washington, DC 20090-2984

In the U.K., Europe, Africa, and the Middle East, copies may be ordered from
American Psychological Association
3 Henrietta Street
Covent Garden, London
WC2E 8LU England

Typeset in Berkeley by EPS Group Inc.

Printer: United Book Press, Baltimore, MD
Cover Designer: Debra Naylor, Naylor Design, Washington, DC
Technical/Production Editor: Catherine Hudson

The opinions and statements published are the responsibility of the authors, and such opinions and statements do not necessarily represent the policies of the APA.

Library of Congress Cataloging-in-Publication Data
Casebook for integrating family therapy : an ecosystemic approach / edited by Susan H. McDaniel, Don-David Lusterman, and Carol L. Philpot.—1st ed.
    p. cm.
    Includes bibliographical references and index.
    ISBN 1-55798-749-1
      1. Family psychotherapy—Case studies. 2. Ecological family therapy—Case studies. I. McDaniel, Susan H. II. Lusterman, Don-David. III. Philpot, Carol L.

RC488.5 .C3696 2001
616.89′156—dc21

00-048529

British Library Cataloguing-in-Publication Data
A CIP record is available from the British Library.

Printed in the United States of America
First Edition

Contents

Contributors

Harlene Anderson, Personal and Professional Consultations, Houston, Texas

Sari Gilman Aronson, Department of Psychiatry and Internal Medicine, University of Illinois College of Medicine at Urbana–Champaign

Robert Bor, Department of Psychology, London Guildhall University and Institute of Family Therapy, London

Nancy Boyd-Franklin, Graduate School of Applied and Professional Psychology, Rutgers University, New York

James H. Bray, Department of Family and Community Medicine, Baylor College of Medicine, Houston, Texas

Douglas C. Breunlin, Family Institute at Northwestern University, Evanston, Illinois

Gary R. Brooks, Department of Psychology, Baylor University, Waco, Texas

Becky Butler, private practice, Atlanta, Georgia

Jebber J. Cozzi, Department of Psychology, Texas A & M University, College Station

Ronald M. Epstein, University of Rochester School of Medicine and Dentistry, New York

Catherine Weigel Foy, Family Institute at Northwestern University, Evanston, Illinois

Mary-Joan Gerson, Department of Psychology and Postdoctoral Program in Psychotherapy and Psychoanalysis, New York University

Wendy Greenspun, Counseling and Psychological Services, Columbia University, New York

Jami Grich, Department of Psychology, Texas A & M University, College Station

Jennifer L. Harkness, Department of Psychology, East Carolina University, Greenville, North Carolina

Jeri Hepworth, Department of Family Medicine, University of Connecticut School of Medicine, and St. Francis Hospital and Medical Center, Hartford

Susan H. Horwitz, Department of Psychiatry, University of Rochester Medical Center, New York

Jaime E. Inclan, Roberto Clemente Center, Department of Psychiatry, New York University School of Medicine

Barry Jacobs, Crozer-Keystone Family Practice Residency Program, Springfield, Pennsylvania

Nadine J. Kaslow, Department of Psychiatry and Behavioral Sciences, Emory University School of Medicine, Atlanta, Georgia

Anne E. Kazak, Department of Pediatrics, University of Pennsylvania, and Department of Psychology, Children's Hospital of Philadelphia

Deborah A. King, Department of Psychiatry, University of Rochester Medical Center, New York

Jay Lebow, Family Institute at Northwestern University, Evanston, Illinois

Ronald F. Levant, Center for Psychological Studies, Nova Southeastern University, Fort Lauderdale, Florida

Michael C. Luebbert, Department of Psychology, Texas A & M University, College Station

Don-David Lusterman, private practice, Baldwin, New York

Susan H. McDaniel, Department of Psychiatry and Family Medicine, and Wynne Center for Family Research, University of Rochester School of Medicine and Dentistry, New York

David J. Miklowitz, Department of Psychology, University of Colorado at Boulder

Riva Miller, Royal Free Hospital, London, University College London Medical School, and Institute of Family Therapy, London

David A. Moltz, Sweetser, Portland, Maine

Dana E. O'Brien, private practice, Rockville, Maryland

Carol L. Philpot, School of Psychology, Florida Institute of Technology, Melbourne

Robert Q Pollard, Jr., Department of Psychiatry, Deaf Wellness Center, University of Rochester School of Medicine, New York

Natalie C. Rinker, Northern Virginia Mental Health Institute, Falls Church, and Mental Health Center, Gallaudet University, Washington, DC

Thomas Russell, Bridge Family Center, Atlanta, Georgia, and private practice, Atlanta, Georgia

David Schnarch, Marriage and Family Health Center, Evergreen, Colorado

Carl D. Schneider, Mediation Matters, Silver Spring, Maryland

David B. Seaburn, Department of Psychiatry and Family Medicine, University of Rochester, New York

Sylvia Shellenberger, Department of Family Medicine, Mercer University School of Medicine, Macon, Georgia

Louise B. Silverstein, Ferkaut Graduate School, Yeshiva University, New York

Teresa L. Simoneau, Rocky Mountain Cancer Center, Denver, Colorado

Douglas K. Snyder, Department of Psychology, Texas A & M University, College Station

Thomas C. Todd, Adler School of Professional Psychology, Chicago, Illinois

Timothy T. Weber, Leadership Institute of Seattle, School of Applied Behavioral Science, Bastyr University, Kenmore, Washington

Foreword

Like many in the second generation of family therapists, I vividly remember the intellectual and emotional excitement, coupled with the trepidation and enormous sense of responsibility, that accompanied my journey into this field. Dissatisfied with approaches to psychotherapy that isolated individuals from their natural contexts, I knew three decades ago that I had found my professional home in family therapy. Reading this sweeping volume of clinical essays, *Casebook for Integrating Family Therapy*, imaginatively conceptualized and thoughtfully edited by Susan H. McDaniel, Don-David Lusterman, and Carol L. Philpot, reminded me of all the reasons I chose to be a family therapist. This book, with its focus on individual, couple, family, and larger system resources and strengths, its binocular view of human competence and struggle, and its insistence on an ecosystemic perspective, represents family therapy at maturity.

In keeping with the family therapy tradition of training and consultation from the unique vantage point of sitting behind the one-way mirror, this volume affords the reader a position behind a literary one-way mirror. Families come alive in these pages, and we are able to witness how seasoned therapists and families create a therapeutic system more encompassing than their separate selves and capable of healing and growth.

McDaniel, Lusterman, and Philpot and their talented array of authors have thought seriously about what it means to practice *ecosystemic* family therapy. One of the many joys in this book for me is that it eschews specific models of family therapy in favor of an integrated lens, at once broad and deep. Transcending earlier competitive struggles in the field over which model is "best," the authors in this volume demonstrate their own capacity to use that which fits well for each individual, couple, or family. The chapters demonstrate the many ways that ecosystemic family therapy is not simply a way of *doing* therapy, but foremost a way of *thinking* about human beings, their systems, their pain, and their triumphs.

The rich variety of work in this volume portrays a marvelous contradiction. Each therapy is a unique and tailor-made creation arising from the thoughtful presence of the therapist interacting with the profound needs of an individual, couple, or family, learning to improvise a never-before-seen dance. Simultaneously each therapy is embedded in a set of accepted systemic theories and beliefs. The reader has a passport allowing a journey at once unfamiliar and well-known. Work is presented not in ways to be repeated with the next family one meets, but rather in ways that fire one's own imagination, courage, humor, empathy, creativity, and humility.

The therapy brought to life in these pages is decidedly *not* magical. Unlike an earlier time in family therapy when reading cases left the reader feeling daunted and a bit skeptical, the family stories in this casebook help the reader to connect with the nonlinear progression, the fits and starts of real therapy, and the reflective process of the therapist. McDaniel, Lusterman, and Philpot have brought forth a model of case writing that empowers the reader to carefully contemplate his or her own work, to ask hard questions, and to refuse complacent reliance on someone else's answers.

In recent years, the family therapy field has struggled to truly attend to and integrate the critical dimensions of gender, race, ethnicity, and social class. Too often these key elements are either omitted or taught and written about as some kind of add-on. McDaniel, Lusterman, and Philpot clearly see these aspects of individual and family life as integral to each of us. They have given us a volume that does not paste gender, race, ethnicity, and social class on to families and therapists like poorly hung wallpaper, but rather weaves them into the fundamental tapestry of human existence.

I will use this volume with my students and discuss chapters with my colleagues. Thanks to Susan McDaniel, Don-David Lusterman, Carol Philpot, and all of their contributors for a gift to the field.

Evan Imber-Black, PhD
Director of the Center for Families and Health at the Ackerman
    Institute for the Family
Professor of Psychiatry at the Albert Einstein College of
    Medicine, New York

Preface

This book is the natural outcome of another book, *Integrating Family Therapy: Handbook of Family Psychology and Systems Therapy* (edited by Richard H. Mikesell, Don-David Lusterman, and Susan H. McDaniel; published by the American Psychological Association, 1995). In that volume we indicated that current conceptualizations of family therapy integrate individual, couple, and family issues. Leading family psychologists provided chapters that described their ecosystemic theories for treating the most common and persistent mental health, psychosomatic, and behavior problems of our time. We found the enthusiasm and cutting-edge ideas of these authors to be stimulating; they exceeded what we thought were our already high expectations. Gary VandenBos, PhD, at the APA, shared our very positive response and asked us to produce a companion book, one that would provide more in-depth case illustrations; take a closer look at the technical decisions required for this complex, fascinating way of conducting psychotherapy; and allow one to learn more about the therapist's own experience of the process. We quickly agreed, assembling a new team of editors—two old and one new. Susan H. McDaniel and Don-David Lusterman continued on with the new project, feeling that we still had much to learn about ecosystemic therapy and that somehow we would eke out the time to do so. Carol L. Philpot, a long-time colleague and author in her own right, joined the editorial team for the casebook. All three editors are active in the APA Division of Family Psychology (Division 43), which has provided inspiration and support as well as contributors for both books. Susan McDaniel is a pioneer in the evolving field of medical family therapy and is the current president of Division 43. Don-David Lusterman has had a long-time interest in multicultural and ecosystemic work and is a founder of the division. Carol Philpot has written extensively about gender issues in families and family therapy and is a past president of the division.

With the team of editors in place, we next contacted the previous book's contributors. We asked them, and several other family therapists, to contribute case descriptions illustrating the ecosystemic theories that they described in the first book. We wanted them to tell us not only what they *did* but also what they *thought* at critical decision points in the therapy. We believe that the results are both elucidating and entertaining. The contributors have made transparent the process of ecosystemic therapy. Which systems deserve assessment? How does one decide at which level of the system to intervene? What does one do at an impasse in therapy? The authors remain true to their own approaches and allow us to view the treatment and the decision making through their eyes. These case descriptions will allow readers to decide when and how often they might adapt such an approach to their own work.

ACKNOWLEDGMENTS

There are many people to thank when working on a project of this magnitude. First, we thank Gary VandenBos for initiating this project and for his ongoing encouragement and support. We also thank Margaret Schlegel, the development editor for this and the previous book—thank you, Peggy, for nurturing this project through to the end product. We are grateful to our contributors, who produced insightful, engaging chapters illustrative of their ecosystemic theoretical orientations in a timely manner, despite their own busy schedules. We extend a very special thanks to Jeanne Klee, Susan McDaniel's assistant, who provided administrative support (not to mention ecosystemic therapy) at crucial points of the project. Patricia Atkins and Julie Gonzalez provided critical clerical and administrative support in other aspects of Susan McDaniel's work so that she could focus on this book. The chair of the Department of Psychiatry, Eric Caine; and the chair of the Department of Family Medicine, Jay Dickinson; along with other University of Rochester colleagues, especially Cedric Alexander, Patricia Atkins, Tom Campbell, Barbara Gawinski, Susan Horwitz, Pieter leRoux, Sally Rousseau, Nancy Ruddy, David Seaburn, Cleve Shields, Jenny Speice, and Bill Watson, provide a stimulating environment in which Susan McDaniel works and develops her ideas about families and health. Judy Lusterman is the hidden editor of this book, and we all thank her for her contributions, her critical eye, and her continuing encouragement. Stacey Lusterman, in Don-David Lusterman's office, also provided useful insights and clerical support. Florida Institute of Technology graduate students Kim Gronemeyer and Jonathan Lehman made editorial and research contributions, and Jani McCray of Carol Philpot's office handled all of the mailing, faxing, and telephone calls and—most important—scheduled time away from Carol's duties to work on this project. We acknowledge the entire membership of Division 43, which serves as an extended professional family for all of us. Several colleagues in particular provided important reflections and support for the project, including Scotty Hargrove and David Seaburn. We thank them for having the courage to provide needed critical feedback while balancing it with support, which often seemed to come at just the right moment. Finally, we express special appreciation to our families for their support and endurance during this project. Thank you, David, Hanna, and Marisa Siegel; Judy Lusterman; and Tom Jensen.

Casebook for

Integrating
Family Therapy

CHAPTER 1

INTRODUCTION TO INTEGRATIVE ECOSYSTEMIC FAMILY THERAPY

Susan H. McDaniel, Don-David Lusterman, and Carol L. Philpot

No man is an island, entire of itself:
every man is a piece of the continent, a
part of the main.

—*John Donne, Devotions, XVII*

Psychology has experienced three distinct phases in its attempt to deal with human beings and their vicissitudes. The beginnings of psychology, of course, lie in the study of the individual. A second phase, family therapy, began in the early 1950s. Accepting the concept that we grow not in isolation but, for the most part, in families, a small band of pioneers began to study and treat families. These theorists focused not on individual pathology but on the structure and communications of families themselves. A third phase, ecosystemic therapy, emerged gradually. This parallel and sometimes intersecting interest, seldom even indexed in early writings about family therapy, concerned the interaction between families and still larger systems. Harry Stack Sullivan (1954), John Elderkin Bell (1975), and Edward Auerswald (1968) were among the first to address ecosystemic concerns. Harry Stack Sullivan (Havens, 1973) was an early American psychoanalyst whose work served as a bridge between individual and systems theory. His "interpersonal psychiatry" taught therapists to examine the individual in the light of familial and social history. Bell (1975) attempted to integrate the intrapsychic, interpersonal, and cultural elements in their attempt to treat people within a larger context. Auerswald (1968) was the first to describe this multileveled work as an "ecological systems approach."

Terms such as *ecology* and *ecosystem* have found

their place in such fields of study as biology and sociology over the past century. They derive from the Greek root *oiko-* or *oeco-*, which may be defined as a "home," often in the broadest sense—not an individual dwelling but a "habitat or environment, especially as a factor significantly influencing the mode of life or the course of development" (*Webster's Third New International Dictionary of the English Language*, 1986, p. 720). Like family therapy, ecosystemic therapy is more an attitude than a technique of therapy. A family therapist, whether treating an individual, a couple, or a family group, is collecting information and hypothesizing about treatment while taking into account a growing knowledge of that family's structure. The shift up toward an ecosystemic approach uses a still broader lens (Imber-Black, 1988). Work systems, health care systems, social services and legal systems, gender issues, religion, ethnicity, and culture may all require examination. This broad lens includes the therapy itself and sees the therapist as still another part of the ecosystem. In this chapter we examine what we see as ecosystemic elements in individual, in family, and in larger systems work.

In terms of technique, the ecosystemic approach is integrative or eclectic, in the best sense of the word. The *American Heritage Dictionary* (1991) defines *eclectic* first as "choosing what appears to be best from diverse sources, systems, and styles" (p. 473). The word *eclectic* went out of favor in family therapy circles in the 1970s because it was thought to connote a patchwork rather than a theoretically strong and homogeneous approach. However, by staying close to the actual definition of *eclectic* the practicing family therapist of the 21st century can create a flexible and effective way of conducting therapy. Such an approach targets the level or levels of the system that most need attention and uses the techniques most appropriate to that level.

We begin this chapter by describing seven principles that are common to most effective systemic therapies but particularly pertinent to integrative ecosystemic family therapy. Each plays some role in the cases presented in this volume, whether major or minor, and so deserves consideration. These principles include family competence, collaboration, neutrality, coaching, confidentiality, the use of power, and the therapist's use of self. After discussing these principles we introduce many of the concepts common to ecosystemic assessment and treatment at the same time we introduce the reader to many of the case studies in the volume that bring these concepts to life.

FAMILY COMPETENCE

Ecosystemic therapy is fundamentally a humanistic therapy. It is founded on the belief that the individual and family are essentially competent systems, if barriers to accessing that competence are removed. Similarly, ecosystemic therapists approach all larger systems as potentially healthy, no matter what their current functioning. This belief helps the therapist approach all parts of the system with respect and optimism while at the same time realistically appraising the barriers, dysfunctions, and difficulties that prevent the person or group from achieving goals. These goals may include dissolution or fundamental restructuring of some part of the system. Anderson, Goolishian, and Winderman (1986) pointed out that many problems are not so much solved as dissolved (or "dis-solved," as Anderson et al. termed it) as people arrive at a narrative on which they can agree.

At the individual level this assumption of competence may be operationalized by a thorough assessment of a patient's strengths as well as his or her psychopathology and intrapsychic struggle. Typically, individuals come to psychotherapy when they are at their worst, and paying attention to strengths provides the therapist with a more accurate overall as-

sessment of the person's functioning. It is also therapeutic for patients to discover this balance; they are usually overfocused on their pain and on the problem that resulted in the need for therapy rather than on their strengths.

A parallel process occurs at the family level. With a couple or family who is in pain and struggling, a group discussion regarding family strengths is an important aspect of a thorough assessment. Hearing about their strengths is, for the family, a therapeutic experience in and of itself. Often, the group members have not recently, or perhaps ever, told each other what it is that they feel their strengths are. This approach opens up meaningful communication on a topic that tends to be less threatening than the subsequent probing of painful issues.

Individuals and families are often taken aback by the assumption of competence and the listing of strengths by the therapist. When eliciting strengths, it is important for therapists to make clear their intent to investigate and listen fully to the patient's and family's concerns. An assumption of competence does not mean a lack of empathy for their pain or a naive approach to problem-solving; rather, it is an attempt to achieve a balanced assessment of strengths and weaknesses. This benefits both therapist and family.

Several traditional family therapy interventions are related to this assumption of competence: reframing, positive connotation, and symptom prescription (Minuchin & Fishman, 1981; Selvini-Palazzoli, Boscolo, Cecchin, & Prata, 1978; Watzlawick, Weakland, & Fisch, 1974). Although they are not entirely the same, these interventions draw on the assumption that the individual or family has positive intentions, however misguided, and that recognition of positive intentions will help the system to reorient in a more productive way.

The assumption of competence with regard to the ecosystem is more complex. Each larger system, whether it be a work group, an ethnic group, or an extended family, has infinite possibilities for human error, bureaucratic snafus, interpersonal difficulty, and leadership problems. The job of the ecosystemic therapist is to understand the culture of the larger system as it impinges on the patient and his or her problem. This assessment is conducted in a manner that is respectful of that system's beliefs, values, and necessary tasks. For example, when a child presents with a school problem, it is very common for the parents to blame the school for the difficulty (e.g., "If you handled my child appropriately, he or she wouldn't have this problem") and for the school to blame the parents (e.g., "If you disciplined and attended to your child appropriately, he or she wouldn't have this problem"). The job of the ecosystemic therapist is to understand both systems' perspectives and, eventually, to build a bridge between the two units that will allow for productive teamwork on the child's behalf. This requires understanding the competence that each system brings to the problem and their differing roles in the child's life, so that slowly both sides come to see the strengths in the child, the family, and the school system in order to more effectively work together.

COLLABORATION

Collaboration is the secret weapon of successful ecosystemic psychotherapy (McDaniel, Hepworth, & Doherty, 1992). What exactly do we mean by the term *collaboration*? We use it to mean respectful partnership and shared power. Power is distributed among patients, families, and professionals as we negotiate mutually acceptable diagnoses and treatment plans. One might think that collaboration is the opposite of assuming the "expert" role. This is an oversimplification. With collaboration, each player may have an area of expertise, whether it is biomedical, psychosocial, or a patient's understanding of his or her own problem. The point is that each person's expertise is respected. The exchange is characterized by a spirit of shared inquiry so that all members, including the patient, the family, and the larger system, participate in what Anderson (1996) called "generative conversation"—people talking *with* each other rather than *to* each other. A more complete definition of collaboration might be the sharing of information, meanings, and decision-making strategies with patients, families, and other professionals.

At the individual level a spirit of collaboration involves understanding and empathizing with each participant's phenomenology—his or her experience of the world. It means establishing a working partnership in which the therapist does not assume that he or she knows what is best. A collaborative relationship is a challenge to the traditional one-up position of professionals and the one-down position of patients. Instead, the therapist's expertise facilitates the exploration of each participant's experience, noticing patterns of coping and stress and arriving at the best decisions possible given the context, each system member's values, and his or her resources.

In ecosystemic family therapy the therapist also forms a partnership with family members whom the patient wishes to involve in treatment and whom the therapist agrees are important to involve. The patient and family are viewed as partners in care rather than treated as objects of care. The family is the first circle of health specialists to respond when a family member is sick or has a problem, and so they are the preferred context of care for many patients who seek help with life stresses, depression and anxiety, interpersonal difficulties, and serious mental illness. Effective collaboration at the family level often rises or falls on the capacity of the therapist not only to engage the family but also to identify, awaken, elicit, and use the patient's and family's own natural resources—their own strengths, competencies, and accomplishments.

In addition to collaborating with patients and families, the ecosystemic therapist also forms collaborative relationships with other professionals involved with the patient and the problem. These can range from attorneys to primary care physicians, from social services workers to ministers. The central skill for collaboration with these professionals, as with all others, involves building relationships. Psychotherapists are experts at building relationships; however, they do not always use that skill with their colleagues, where it is also needed. Professional collaboration requires clear communication and the development of a common mission.

Sometimes professional collaboration is as difficult, or more so, than the collaboration with a patient or family. Professionals may not share a common theoretical framework (such as a physician's biomedical focus vs. a family therapist's psychosocial systems focus). They may have different languages, working styles, practices regarding confidentiality, and expectations regarding communication with other professionals (McDaniel, Campbell, & Seaburn, 1995). The ecosystemic therapist must become aware of these differences and develop strategies that dissolve any barriers to effective collaboration with relevant professionals.

A joint session between two professionals, or a network session among many professionals, is often a way to bridge important differences. Convening the patient, family, and treatment team in one room allows all parties to state their perspectives and their wishes. It is a powerful vehicle for coordinating care, negotiating difference, and respecting and supporting the patient and his or her family.

NEUTRALITY AND ITS LIMITS

Psychoanalysts have traditionally prized neutrality as an essential principle of therapy. The psychoanalyst was expected to be a blank screen onto whom the patient projected his or her issues. As other theoretical models began to emerge, neutrality remained a highly valued concept, although its definition altered somewhat. *Neutrality* came to mean avoiding the imposition of the therapist's values onto the patient. The goal for the therapist was to facilitate the patient's problem-solving resources toward the patient's own goals, not those of the therapist.

In the 1970s feminist theorists pointed out that true neutrality was unfeasible. They produced evidence that existing theories, research, and practice were conducted through the lens of male experience and were not valid for women and girls. In fact, the unconscious imposition of the male value system on therapy and on research tended to place women and girls in a disadvantaged role (Philpot, Brooks, Lusterman, & Nutt, 1997). Since that time, psychotherapists and social sciences researchers have become aware of their inability to attain the ideal of complete neutrality. Instead, they are encouraged to become sensitized to their own value systems and to consider carefully when to use their values in therapy. For example, a nonjudgmental, accepting attitude on the part of the therapist is generally considered to be the best approach in most cases. However, there are situations in which therapists must openly advocate for change if their patients do

not seem to be able to do so for themselves. One such example is a case of physical abuse (Walker, 1984) in which the client's life may depend on the therapist's taking a more active and instructive approach.

Neutrality at the systemic level has been described as threefold: (a) neutrality with regard to values and beliefs, (b) neutrality regarding taking sides among family members, and (c) neutrality as to whether the family chooses to change (Tomm, 1984). The issue of taking sides is unique to systems approaches and causes some of the greatest dilemmas. The therapist struggles with the issue of who the client is—the family, or the individuals within the family. Most often the therapist will use multilateral partiality (Boszormenyi-Nagy & Krasner, 1986), connecting with and supporting each family member, empowering each in turn. However, occasionally what may appear to be the best resolution for the family as a whole may be detrimental to one family member; for example, when the mother sacrifices her plans and goals for the good of the family. The therapist must then decide whether to act as an agent of the social system (elevating the good of the family over the needs of the individual) or to act as an advocate for social change. Likewise, in couples work, when one partner, frequently the man, has more power than the other, the therapist must decide whether to balance the system by empowering the weak partner or to maintain neutrality. This dilemma arises often, especially in cases of divorce, extramarital affairs, and physical or mental abuse. The therapist is faced with difficult decisions regarding what to reveal and whom to support.

At the ecosystemic level, *neutrality* can refer to not taking sides among the larger systems but understanding and respecting each. This is certainly the case when one is working with larger systems, such as medical, work, religious, or school ecosystems. It is also usually the case when working with various ethnic groups that might have different value systems or expectations. However, neutrality at the ecosystemic level can mean supporting the status quo, such as acceptance of the role of women as primary caretakers of children regardless of the loss of power into which that position places women worldwide. At this level the therapist must sometimes decide between social action and neutrality. This is an individual decision.

COACHING

One of the most important roles of the ecosystemic therapist is that of coach. The therapist may often need to teach the patient new skills, which can then be practiced and modified both in session and between sessions. Coaching is a combination of psychoeducation, modeling, and role-playing that arms the patient with new techniques to deal with old problems.

At the individual level, the therapist is frequently called on to instruct patients in methods of self-care. For example, patients often suffer from cognitive distortions that interfere with their optimal functioning in life. The individual therapist can use cognitive–behavioral approaches or rational–emotive therapy to help such patients identify the faulty logic and negative self-statements and replace these dysfunctional thoughts with more realistic and positive ones. The therapist can assign self-affirmations to a depressed patient who suffers from feelings of worthlessness. He or she can teach assertiveness skills to a patient who is easily dominated and controlled and ask that patient to demonstrate those skills in a role-play in the session. Most important, the therapist can model self-care for the patient, by setting appropriate boundaries, asserting him- or herself when necessary, and taking care of personal needs for time and relaxation. Coaching at the individual level is like teaching golf or tennis: The therapist is providing the patient with tips on how to improve his or her game regardless of how the other players are doing.

Coaching at the family level, on the other hand, is more like coaching a team. Each player must learn the appropriate skills, but they must also work together toward a common goal. Coaching at this level involves the teaching of interactive skills such as communication, problem-solving, behavior exchange, conflict resolution, negotiation, and so on. Part of the process of coaching at the systemic level is motivating the patients to cooperate for the greater good of the family or couple as a whole. This involves a cognitive shift from "What's in it for me?" to "How can I contribute to the healthy functioning of this family as a whole without losing myself?" Couples must come to adopt a two-winner approach, recognizing the value of a healthy relationship to each individual's personal fulfillment. As when one is coaching a team, the therapist can have all the players in the room at the same time. The patients can practice in session, while the therapist can offer critique of performance, modeling of skills, praise for acquisition of new skills, and constant encouragement.

Coaching at the ecosystemic level requires the therapist to have enough knowledge of the larger system to teach the patient how to act within that system. Furthermore, the therapist will want to impart an attitude of respect, acceptance, and curiosity about the world of the other, which allows for positive and fruitful interaction. This could perhaps be likened to teaching someone how to scuba dive. In addition to providing education regarding the skills needed by the diver, the coach must also teach the student about the ecosystem that the diver will be entering so that the diver will know what to expect and how to behave while swimming with the fish in their undersea world. In a therapeutic situation, the therapist will coach the patient on the expectations, language, behaviors, belief systems, and values of the ecosystem, so that the patient can navigate that world with confidence. For example, a therapist might teach a patient how to talk to his or her doctor in a hospital setting and perhaps model such communication. Or the therapist might sensitize a patient to the differences to be expected and respected in a different culture or ethnic group. The therapist frequently must act as translator between the genders (Philpot et al., 1997) and coach patients in understanding the values, communications styles, and problem-solving approaches of the other gender. At the ecosystemic level, coaching incorporates a philosophical attitude of respect and curiosity with psychoeducation, role-play, and modeling.

LIMITS OF CONFIDENTIALITY

It is difficult to consider the issue of confidentiality without first defining an overarching value: privacy. Privacy and confidentiality are so closely linked that many authors (Canter, Bennett, Jones, & Nagy, 1994; Koocher, Norcross, & Hill, 1998; Schuchman, Foster, & Nye, 1982) have prefaced their discussions of confidentiality by first defining privacy. For example, Canter et al.(1994) defined *privacy* as "the right of individuals not to have their physical person or mental or emotional process invaded or shared without their consent" (p. 105). The definitions provided by Koocher et al. (1998) and Schuchman et al. (1982) also refer to privacy as an individual right—in fact, one protected by the Fourth, Fifth, and 14th Amendments to the U.S. Constitution. All agree that *confidentiality* guarantees that what is privately revealed will be protected. According to Canter et al., "psychologists are required by the Ethics code and by law to maintain the confidentiality of communications shared with them" (p. 105). For most individual therapists the issue of confidentiality is clear cut and is well defined by ethical codes. Only with informed consent may one, on a carefully defined and limited basis, share information, except where required by law.

A third concept, privilege, further enlarges one's understanding of confidentiality. Koocher et al. (1998) stated that "privilege and confidentiality are oft-confused concepts." He defined *privilege* (or *privileged communication*) as "a legal term . . . for certain specific types of relationships that enjoy protection from disclosure in legal proceedings" (pp. 463–464). Privilege belongs to the client, not the treating person. For this reason, if the client decides to waive the privilege, the treating person may be forced to testify.

With the introduction of film recordings of therapeutic sessions, such as the early work of Nathan Ackerman and Carl Whitaker and, later, the use of one-way mirrors and videotape in family and couples therapy training, the issues of both privacy and confidentiality required re-examination. If one refers back to the definition of privacy one will note that it is a privilege granted to the *individual*. From the moment that one begins to deal with couples and families, the private becomes public. Couples or families are invited to share their privacy with one another in the presence of one or more professionals.

As we consider confidentiality in the larger context of couple and family work, all sources cite the increased complexity of ethical issues, particularly of confidentiality. Gottlieb (1995) reviewed the ethical issues that surface as one moves from the individual to couples or family therapy, with particular attention to the issue of change of format. Gottlieb asked readers to examine the question "who is the client?" A therapist begins, for example, by seeing a woman alone, because the husband has refused therapy. After a certain number of sessions, the husband agrees to come. The therapist is now faced with a series of questions: Is the client now the couple? If so, how are the therapist's responsibilities to the couple best achieved? What, then, are the therapist's obligations to each member of the couple? In compliance with the current ethical guidelines of the American Psychological Association, Gottlieb noted, the therapist would have obtained a release from the woman at the outset of therapy that would permit him or her to share revealed information. He then pointed out that such an agreement might inhibit the initial patient from revealing important information to the therapist. Would the therapist better serve the system by knowing information and struggling with issues of confidentiality or by creating a situation that may almost guarantee that important information will be withheld?

Lusterman (1995) suggested one approach to this dilemma. He reminded readers that a systems-oriented practitioner never views a presenting problem as existing solely within the psyche of the "identified patient." Given this, he suggested that the presenting patient be told, "At some point others may join us. . . . Anything that is discussed in an individual session will be regarded as confidential. If you wish to discuss it with others, you may, but I will not." This often permits very important material, such as an adult's affair or a student's school truancy, to surface quickly. The therapist must, of course, point out that in certain circumstances there is a legal duty to report. Any time there is a further change of format, the question of confidentiality must once again be raised and a record made of the informing.

Live supervision is a juncture between family theory and treatment and larger systems interventions. Because it introduces an entirely new (and often unanticipated) element into treatment, the definition of who the client is, and the question of what the client's privileges and protections are, need to be addressed. Gottlieb (1995) concluded his discussion of change-of-format issues by stating that

> With adequate preparation of client systems for both change of format and live supervision, the systemic therapist may avoid a variety of potential problems. Treatment decisions cannot be totally driven by existing ethical principles; sound clinical judgment must also be used. (pp. 567–568)

Change-of-format issues multiply as therapists work with still larger systems. Therapists must work to define to each subsystem what will be considered confidential and how to protect that confidentiality. For example, a family therapist may be working with a family and a school in regard to the issue of a troubled child. The family requests that, because of economic danger, it is very important that the school not be informed that the father may have to close his currently shaky business. The school's principal, in turn, may ask the therapist to guard the information that a teacher who has acted inappropriately toward the family is soon to be fired. What can the therapist do at the very beginning of therapy to set the stage for dealing with such issues? Until guidelines are more clearly drawn, perhaps the best one can do is to be clear within oneself about how one views change-of-format issues and to routinely inform one's clients as one undertakes each new relationship.

USE OF POWER

What is *power*, and who has it? Neither question yields an easy answer. Simon, Stierlin, and Wynne (1985, p. 263) described the muddle surrounding power: "All authors on family therapy are of the opinion that questions of power are an essential aspect of family dynamics, and 'everyone knows what power is, until you ask them' (Cromwell & Olson, 1975, p. 3)." Individual-centered theories are no clearer. In general, when individually oriented theories touch on power they are dealing with the psy-

chodynamics of power or with how the power "drive," "need," or "motive" develops. Harry Stack Sullivan (1953), for example, described a "power motive," by which he meant the infant's struggle to develop increasing competence in handling his or her physical and social development. Sullivan compared this "normal" developmental event with its neurotic counterpart, the power *drive* (see Munroe, 1955, p. 360). In some individuals the self can achieve safety only in a hostile and insecure manner. When this happens, he explained, the power *motive* is replaced by the power drive, by which the individual "tends toward fulfillment at the expense of others" (Munroe, 1955, p. 360). Adler "saw man's problem as a struggle for power in an attempt to overcome a feeling of inferiority" (Thompson, 1950, p. 11). Freud placed the origins of the developing feeling of power in the struggle over bowel control, with its possible resolutions of either defiance or submission (Thompson, 1950, p. 31). Thompson (1950) noted that Freud, "in fact if not in intention," was describing "much more than the possible erotic pleasures connected with the anal zone." Rather, she noted, he was describing "a complex interpersonal situation."

All of the conceptualizations of power so far described deal with the patient's power issues and, to some extent, the family's as well. With rare exceptions, individually oriented therapists have placed little attention on the influence that the therapist has over the patient. The belief system of most individual therapies suggests that therapy, when properly carried out, enables the patient to change—it is the process, not the therapist, that motivates the change. Where there were problems, supervision often focused on the therapist's countertransference—defensive attitudes that interfere with the therapeutic process. It is ironic that one of the first psychologists to directly focus on the therapist's power was B. F. Skinner who, in a debate with Carol Rogers, pointed out that Rogers's so-called "nondirective" therapy was, in truth, very directive, although not by the therapist's conscious choice. Skinner insisted that the famous Rogerian response–"hmm hmm"–had strong value as a verbal reinforcer, as did the therapist's nods of assent and even changes of posture (Rogers & Skinner, 1956).

Early family therapists also paid scant attention to the therapist as a locus of power in the therapeutic process, but by making the process public, through film, video, and live demonstrations, it became impossible to ignore the powerful impact of the therapist's presence. For example, when one reads Nathan Ackerman's (1958) classic, *The Psychodynamics of Family Life*, one sees the workings of an "objective" thinker struggling to present the dynamics of family development and the impact of the therapeutic process. When one sees a film of Ackerman at work, however, one is immediately struck by the power of his presence and the use to which he puts this presence as he attempts to disrupt the family system. The same can be said for all the early masters: Satir, Whitaker, Minuchin, Haley, and others of great stature.

Although the masters seldom indexed the word, *power* is an ever-present force in much of their theorizing. For example, Minuchin (1974) wrote,

> *The therapist's skill at producing stresses in different parts of the family system will give him, and sometimes the family members themselves, an inkling of the family's capability to restructure when circumstances change. His input and his expert prodding produce new context, or changed circumstances, to which the family must adapt under his eye. (p. 147)*

(A note on gender and power: It was men who were seen as powerful therapists in 1974.) Hoffman examined the issue of power (and powerlessness) in an article entitled "Beyond Power and Control" (1985). After reviewing many family systems approaches to power, she proposed a "second-order" family systems therapy. Labeling it not so much a method of therapy as a stance, she suggested a cybernetic epistemology with the following characteristics:

1. an "observing system" stance and inclusion of the therapist's own context
2. a collaborative rather than hierarchical structure
3. goals that emphasize setting a context for change, not specifying change

4. a "circular" assessment of the problem
5. a nonpejorative, nonjudgmental view.

These principles provide a bridge from older, more "reparative" or "corrective" notions of family systems therapy to an approach that is inclusive, one in which the helping system has no "stars." "It is up to us," concluded Hoffman, "to find a noninterfering, nonpurposive vocabulary for change that respects this way of being organized" (p. 395). This bridge provides an elegant path to what might then be called a "second-order ecosystemic therapy."

McDaniel and Hepworth (in press) described a well-functioning system that includes the family and the helping professionals collaborating with them:

> *With regard to power and dependency, we want to suggest that the most effective way of using one's power . . . is to give it away—that is, to recognize the power of the patient and the power of the family as partners with us in healthcare.*

They then explained that "such a process encourages a functional interdependency between patients, families, and the healthcare team."

Let us return to Hoffman's examination of power. She noted (1981, p. 191) that many family theorists "posit power issues as the basis for family difficulties." "But power," she avers, "is never an absolute item; it always has to be 'power for what?'" What families can provide, she answered, is

> *an orderly access to intimacy. . . . It may also be related to an invisible systole and diastole of connecting and withdrawing shared by all the social animals. This unconscious but orderly arrangement can be a function of the nuclear family, but it can also extend to the borders of the face-to-face community in which the family lives. (p. 191)*

It is to this community and its interaction with families that ecosystemic theory and practice devote their attention. Within this context, it becomes increasingly clear that the belief that we, as therapists, possess power is more illusion than a reality. Pediatrician Ellen Perrin (1999) pointed out that "The difference between 'collaboration' and 'help' is that in a collaboration the participants have the same goal, relatively equal status and power, but different skills and knowledge that contribute to attaining the goal" (p. 58). As we move closer to a fully realized ecosystemic theory and practice the issue of power is replaced by the power inherent in the act of collaboration.

THERAPIST'S USE OF SELF

Therapist use of self has been an important component of therapy from the inception of psychoanalysis and Freud's concept of countertransference. Exactly what is meant by *use of self* differs depending on the theorist and the frame of reference the therapist uses to conceptualize a case. Thus, use of self is different for a therapist doing individual therapy than it is for a systemic therapist. Furthermore, use of self takes on even greater complexity when an ecosystemic paradigm is incorporated in the conceptualization.

For an individual therapist, use of self usually entails an awareness of one's own reaction to a patient in the moment, separation of that response from one's personal issues, and appropriate reflection of that reaction to the patient in order to help the patient gain insight into the effect his or her behavior might have on others. It might also mean the sharing of personal experience that could teach or model suitable behavior for the patient or offer the patient insight into motivations. At all times it is important for the therapist to understand his or her own countertransferential issues so as not to confuse personal concerns with those of the patient.

At the systemic level the therapist must be aware of the family-of-origin and marital issues that could color his or her perception and expectations in the therapeutic relationship. For example, a therapist who holds the position of oldest child in his or her family of origin may at times have difficulty supporting and empathizing with a youngest child who appears, to the therapist's standards, to be irresponsible. A therapist whose life experiences have taught him or her to value marriage more highly than individual fulfillment might work extra hard to save a marriage long after the couple has given up. A male therapist might find himself siding with the male in

the couple more often, whereas a female therapist may have more empathy for the female partner. Also, the expectations that a therapist brings to the case regarding a healthy family or marriage can influence the direction therapy takes, for better or worse.

Therapists can cautiously share familial or marital experiences that might offer suggestions for change or hope for successful outcome. For example, one exercise frequently used by couples therapists involves the generation of a list of nice little things a couple can do for one another to change the atmosphere of their marriage from negative to positive. A couple who is having difficulty thinking of these microbehaviors might find it helpful if the therapist says, "I like my spouse to bring me a cup of coffee while I'm putting on my makeup. Would that be something you would like?" When a couple feels discouraged regarding a commonly seen problem, the therapist can offer hope by acknowledging that in his or her experience, many couples have had similar problems and have been able to overcome them in different ways. Self-disclosure is a delicate issue that is hotly debated in therapeutic circles. When and how much should be disclosed must be carefully considered. The therapist must judge whether the personal disclosure will facilitate the therapeutic process and be certain that the disclosure is not the therapist's own attempt to resolve a personal struggle. This probably means that self-disclosure occurs only when issues are long resolved and no longer cause emotional responses. If unsure, the therapist should seek supervision or share his or her concerns with a trusted colleague. As in individual work, the therapist must be aware of the personal systemic issues that can affect the progress of therapy and allow the patients to come up with their own solutions.

At the ecosystemic level the therapist must be cognizant of the fact that perceptions, values, and expectations are influenced by the ecosystem in which the therapist is immersed, whether it be ethnicity; religion; gender; nationality; or the consequence of a smaller ecosystem, such as a profession or work setting. For example, female therapists will be less able to empathize with the dilemmas of manhood than will male therapists, unless they have learned to expand the female lens through which they have been socialized to see the world. White middle-class therapists will not be as attuned to signs of discrimination against minorities as will African American therapists, unless they have been thoroughly sensitized to these issues. In other words, the therapist must be aware of the effect of the ecosystem on his or her thinking and be trained to approach members of other ecosystems with curiosity and acceptance. On the other hand, a therapist cannot assume that just because he or she shares the same ecosystem with the patient that the patient's experience and solutions to problems will be the same as the therapist's. For example, a therapist who has suffered chronic illness will be more understanding of the issues involved in that existence than one who has not, but he or she must also be careful not to impose his or her method of dealing with illness on the patient. Nevertheless, the therapist can use his or her empathic knowledge of the ecosystem to facilitate the patient's movement toward healthy resolution. A therapist who sees that a patient is stuck in his or her gender role journey at the angry stage, for instance, can use personal knowledge of that stage to connect with the patient and move him or her toward change and integration. In order to sensitize themselves to the ecosystemic issues that affect their perceptions, therapists can take advantage of courses and continuing-education workshops on multicultural issues, gender, multisystemic approaches, and so on. Self-awareness is always vital to effective therapy.

At all three levels—individual, systemic, and ecosystemic—therapist use of self is a vital and integral part of therapy. It simply takes different forms depending on the size of the system.

ECOSYSTEMIC ASSESSMENT

Ecosystemic assessment, which by its nature is eclectic, can lead therapists to the "wise choosing" that is likely to produce theoretically sound and integrative treatment. At the individual level, the ecosystemic therapist may or may not explicitly consider the intrapsychic makeup and personality of the patient and relevant family members. Most ecosystemic therapists appraise individuals' strengths and

weaknesses in the context of a systemic evaluation. As we meet the individuals who compose the system, we seek information about each participant that will move the therapeutic process forward: What is the person's coping style? What are his or her strengths? What are his or her patterns of difficulty? Is the current problem one that has occurred before, or is it a new turn of events? What is the temperament of the patient? How does this temperament fit with the temperaments of the rest of the family? Have there been any serious illnesses, accidents, or disabilities in the family that may have had a profound effect on the intrapsychic and interpersonal processes of a system? A biopsychosocial history is an essential part of any comprehensive family assessment (McDaniel et al., 1992). Chapter 4, by David Schnarch, and chapter 8, by Mary-Joan Gerson, make particular reference to the intrapsychic lives of their clients even as they consider the role each plays in the couple system. In chapter 22 Becky Butler describes her treatment of an individual client by carefully examining the client's family and her gender systems and then connecting her to other systems in the 12-step community.

Depending on the therapist, the family assessment may be highly structured or relatively loose. Chapter 3, by Douglas K. Snyder, Jebber J. Cozzi, Jami G. Stevens, and Michael C. Luebbert, presents a fairly structured approach, as does chapter 32 by Catherine Weigel Foy and Douglas C. Breunlin. At the other end of the spectrum is chapter 9, by Harlene Anderson, who eschews any attempt to create an agenda for assessment and favors a conversation-generating approach to determine the direction of exploration.

ECOSYSTEMIC FAMILY TREATMENT

For many therapists the developmental stage of the family is of primary importance in both assessment and treatment. Indeed, it is at developmental transition points that families often present for treatment. In chapter 8 Mary-Joan Gerson describes a young couple faced with the decision as to whether to have a child. In chapter 19 Ronald F. Levant and Louise B. Silverstein describe a couple having difficulty renegotiating their previously egalitarian roles after their child is born. At the opposite end of the life cycle, in chapters 11 and 12, respectively, Timothy T. Weber and Deborah A. King describe two families, each dealing with an elderly widowed parent, under different but highly stressful circumstances. Gay individuals and couples have an additional developmental issue to negotiate: that of "coming out" to their families. As Thomas Russell illustrates in chapter 5, this coming-out process can precipitate a significant disruption in relationships. James H. Bray's research and clinical work show that the development life cycle of stepfamilies is different than that of first-marriage nuclear families; his case study in chapter 10 of a stepfamily with grown children nicely illustrates this. In chapter 2 Jay Lebow describes a family who visits and revisits therapy at various stages of the family life cycle, a phenomenon seen often in the practices of exosystemic family therapists.

A major decision that must be made at the beginning of treatment is who is to be seen, and when. Which individuals are most relevant to what Anderson et al. (1986) called the "problem-determined system?" Should the therapist work with the couple, the nuclear family, the friends, or include the extended family? What about the in-laws or a significant boyfriend, school personnel, religious advisors, and so on? Each of the cases described in this book reveals how the therapist went about deciding whom to see and why.

As we determine the treatment system, another question must often be answered: Are the identified patient and the "customer for treatment" the same person? The "customer" may be defined as the person who most desires change. If the patient is not the customer—the person most motivated for change—then it is useful during the assessment session to know that, and to know who is. For example, a parent or parents may be the customers seeking treatment for an unmotivated child. In chapter 24 Thomas C. Todd describes the identified patient in his case as an adolescent diabetic girl with an eating disorder but often finds himself thinking of her father as his customer. Carl D. Schneider and Dana E. O'Brien describe in chapter 7 the negative results that can occur when one assumes that both individuals in a couple are "customers" (in this case, in di-

vorce mediation) when in fact only one person has really bought into the working relationship. A school or court may require that a child or adolescent be seen when really the family is in need of services. In a case that reveals important racial and power issues, Barry Jacobs courageously reveals in chapter 13 his naivete as a new therapist in first excluding the sociocultural aspects of work with an adolescent who was court-ordered into treatment and his family. The active buy-in of social agency staff may greatly enhance the effectiveness of family intervention. In chapter 14 Wendy Greenspun shows how sensitive involvement of foster care and protective-services staff actually enhanced family intervention and paved the way for successful resolution of a potentially explosive child sexual abuse case. This case, like many others in this volume, illustrates that the ecosystemic therapist must work strategically to involve customers, patients, and any others who are significant in the problem-determined system so that the therapeutic process has the best chance of succeeding.

In actually working with a couple, whether in couples therapy or as part of family therapy, the ecosystemic therapist must consider the history of the couple and their repetitive patterns of interaction (e.g., communication, problem-solving, conflict resolution, intimacy). This includes their patterns of interactions with previous therapists, as David Schnarch aptly shows in chapter 4. What works well, and what may contribute to the ongoing problem? How strong is the marital subsystem? the parenting subsystem? What are their strengths and weaknesses as mates? As coparents? How can these be utilized to resolve the presenting problem?

At the family level, how does each significant subsystem work? the sibling subsystem? the grandparents or extended family? Are the boundaries between generations clear, appropriate, and functional? Are there significant cutoffs? Are certain members of the family routinely left out of communications? Would bringing these members back in be helpful in resolving the problem, or would it add more stress to an already-burdened system? Are there triangles that create problems in the family?

In terms of technique, most ecosystemic therapists now draw from the schools of family therapy that have evolved since the 1950s, whether they be structural, strategic, transgenerational, psychodynamic, cognitive–behavioral, or narrative, to name a few. Each of these approaches tends to emphasize certain aspects of content or process over others. For example, structural approaches tend to focus on family structure, boundaries, and hierarchy and favor here-and-now interventions such as blocking and reframing. Transgenerational approaches look for patterns of cutoff, triangulation, and unresolved grief and favor the use of genograms to trace how patterns have been passed on from one generation to the next. Cognitive–behavioral interventions focus on skills building in several areas, including communication, problem-solving, conflict management, and structured homework as core components of treatment.

How these approaches are combined depends on the particular therapist and presenting problem. For example, in chapter 12 Deborah A. King combines a transgenerational life review process with problem-solving and communications skills training in working with a widowed elderly depressed man and his grown children. Douglas K. Snyder and his colleagues describe in chapter 3 how they worked sequentially with a couple to strengthen boundaries between the couples and their families of origin (structural), improve communication and conflict-resolution skills (cognitive–behavioral), and examine the roots of their emotional reactivity in their families of origin (trangenerational) in order to begin to reduce their overreactions to one another. These integrated approaches are typical of most cases described in this volume. Some presenting problems, however, seem to lend themselves to a more focused approach. For example, family psychoeducational approaches to serious mental illness have been found to be highly effective and highly valued by families, as the cases described in chapter 29, by David A. Moltz, and chapter 30, by Teresa L. Simoneau and David J. Miklowitz, clearly show.

At the larger systems level, the ecosystemic therapist should consider many factors, including gender, race, ethnicity, culture, class, work, physical health, and religion. Because these issues are underrepresented in most general casebooks, we have chosen to include a number of cases in these areas.

In the area of gender, Gary R. Brooks examines in chapter 21 how he slowly came to appreciate the role of gender as a major organizing variable in families by reviewing the blunders he made in working with a family organized with traditional gender roles. He then was given a second chance to work with the family when he was more gender aware. In chapter 19 Ronald F. Levant and Louise B. Silverstein describe a structured approach to couples work that combines sharing an in-depth understanding of gender socialization with the couple with family-of-origin work. In chapter 20 Carol L. Philpot combines individual and couples therapy and a women's group to help women examine the gender messages they have internalized that are limiting their lives and their relationships.

Religion, another underrepresented variable, is explored by Don-David Lusterman in chapter 17, in which he describes his work with a Jewish family. Although his work with this family involved joining on many levels, his willingness to share the evolution of his own religious identity appeared to be a turning point in the therapy. In chapter 33 Nancy Boyd-Franklin describes her work supervising a young White therapist working with an African American family and emphasizes the role of spirituality as a resource in family therapy.

Work is another ubiquitous variable in ecosystemic work. Sylvia Shellenberger presents in chapter 6 a case of couples therapy in which the wife initially presents in crisis, her job threatened because of spotty performance in the context of a company in the process of downsizing. Although the case primarily focuses on the couple in terms of communication and support, the work nicely illustrates multiple levels of intervention, including work with the employee assistance counselor and the union representative and consultation with an organizational psychologist.

Culture and ethnicity are explored in several ways in this volume. In chapter 16 Susan H. Horwitz describes how a mother and her adult daughter had to negotiate three cultural transitions while negotiating unresolved grief from the past and the daughter's current marital crisis. Jaime E. Inclan describes in chapter 18 how the immigration experience affects relationship patterns and belief systems and explains how it is necessary to create a "cultural bridge" if family therapy is to be effective. In chapter 15 Robert Q. Pollard, Jr., and Natalie C. Rinker describe a different sort of culture, the culture of the deaf, and provide unique insights from their work with a deaf adolescent and her family. These principles are generalizable to families that are bilingual, those with intracultural differences, and families with different types of disabilities.

Perhaps nowhere is the ecosystemic model of family intervention more relevant than in cases of physical illness, where multiple systems are, by the very nature of the problem, involved. In this volume, seven chapters, each involving very different illnesses and stages of couple or family life, illustrate the various ways therapists work creatively with these systems to help patients and their families adjust to their illnesses and the illnesses' effects. In chapter 23 Anne E. Kazak describes the treatment of a couple with two young children (ages 2 and 8), the younger of which had just completed a long but successful treatment for cancer. Although the 8-year-old is initially referred for treatment, the therapist initially focuses on the overburdened couple, helping them strengthen their marriage before tackling parenting concerns. Thomas C. Todd describes in chapter 24 the family treatment of an adolescent diabetic girl who developed a life-threatening eating disorder, which forced him to add creatively to the structural model of working with families in which he had been trained.

In chapter 28 Robert Bor and Riva Miller present two case studies: In the first they describe how they set up a free-standing hospital-based HIV/AIDS counseling service, and in the second they tell of how they handled the ambivalence of a 33-year-old man to both tell and not tell his family he was dying of AIDS. In chapter 26 Jeri Hepworth shares how her individual and couples work with a chronic-pain patient changed radically once she herself experienced a stress-related health problem. David B. Seaburn, too, describes, in chapter 25, couples work with a chronic-pain patient, describing how the patient's change in attitude toward her own pain expanded his own understanding of treating illness. Susan H. McDaniel, Jennifer L. Harkness, and Ronald M. Epstein describe in chapter 27 how they

worked as a team to provide truly integrative family care to a 53-year-old man and his 82-year-old mother, who suffered from Crohn's disease and severe depression.

Self-of-the-therapist issues are vital for inclusion in an ecosystemic approach. Second-order cybernetics (Maruyama, 1963) resulted in systems psychologists' recognition that therapists are part of the system to be assessed. The therapist cannot be a distant figure, acting on a problem, a patient, or a system. He or she is a part of, not apart from, the systems they treat. As Don-David Lusterman is fond of saying to his supervisees, "You are your own violin. Make sure to be in tune, and know where you are in the orchestra." Each therapist must monitor his or her own individual and systemic issues and be aware of them and use them as part of ecosystemic treatment. This includes both what is currently happening for the therapist personally (e.g., a failing marriage, a sick child, own depression) as well as his or her own personal family history (e.g., an alcoholic father, an immigrant grandparent). It also includes the therapist's professional history—not just successes, but what he or she may consider real blunders as well.

Many of the chapter authors in this volume were willing to personally self-disclose in order to illustrate what this means in actual practice, so that others might learn how to do the same. In chapter 31 Nadine J. Kaslow and Sari Gilman Aronson describe a patient they treated as cotherapists, who later committed suicide. The description of their personal reactions provides a poignant example of such therapeutic use of self. Rather than suppress their feelings about the case, they courageously decided, 18 months after the patient's death, to visit her grave and to have a session with her family. In their chapter they candidly reflect about how this loss, early in their careers, affected them personally and professionally.

Although technique and content issues are presented in the cases in this volume, we want to stress that we believe that most of the therapist's effectiveness results from being an expert on the process, rather than the content, of ecosystemic therapy and from being open to continuous learning both from patients and from colleagues. This process focus includes making space for each relevant voice to be heard and recognizes that individuals are embedded in ever-evolving ecosystems that must be understood and valued by the therapist. The successful therapist is curious about each relevant subgroup and system and their interactions with one another and with the problem.

CONCLUDING WORDS

Readers familiar with the companion to this volume, *Integrating Family Therapy: Handbook of Family Psychology and Systems Theory*, are aware of the theoretical interests of many of the authors also represented in this book. In this chapter we have tried to examine the ecosystemic perspective from various points of view, taking into account each level of consideration, from that of the individuals, couples, and families; to the larger systems, such as schools, health care systems, social services agencies; and within the surrounding cultural context that encompasses distinctions such as gender, social class, ethnicity, and religion.

Because this volume is a casebook, the reader is allowed to go deeper into the therapist's experience of therapy as it unfolds. The reader is permitted to sit with the authors as they struggle to integrate theory with practice, self with system, ideals with realities. The reader will see the complexity of clinical work come alive as he or she faces, together with the authors, the many decisions that must be made about the direction that the therapy will take and the times that the therapist must surrender to the process of therapy itself. We invite you to join our authors now, as they take you on the journeys they have traveled.

References

Ackerman, N. W. (1958). *The psychodynamics of family life: Diagnosis and treatment of family relationships*. New York: Basic Books.

The American Heritage dictionary: Second college edition. (1991). Boston: Houghton-Mifflin.

Anderson, H. (1996). *Language, conversation and possibilities*. New York: Basic Books.

Anderson, H., Goolishian, H., & Winderman, L. (1986). Problem determined systems: Toward transformation in family therapy. *Journal of Strategic and Systemic Therapies, 5*, i–iii.

Auerswald, E. (1968). Interdisciplinary versus ecological approach. *Family Processes, 7*, 202–215.

Bell, J. E. (1975). *Family therapy*. New York: Aronson.

Boszormenyi-Nagy, I., & Krasner, B. (1986). *Between give and take: A clinical guide to contextual therapy*. New York: Brunner/Mazel.

Canter, M. B., Bennett, B., Jones, S. E., & Nagy, T. F. (1994). Privacy and confidentiality. In Canter, M. B., Bennett, B., Jones, S. E., & Nagy, T. F. *Ethics for psychologists: A commentary on the APA Ethics Code* (pp. 105–114). Washington, DC: American Psychological Association.

Cromwell, R. E., & Olson, D. H. (Eds.). (1975). *Power in families*. New York: Wiley.

Gottlieb, M. C. (1995). Ethical dilemmas in change of format and live supervision. In R. H. Mikesell, D-D. Lusterman, & S. H. McDaniel (Eds.), *Integrating family therapy: Handbook of family psychology and systems theory* (pp. 561–570). Washington, DC: American Psychological Association.

Havens, L. L. (1973). *Approaches to the mind: Movement of the psychiatric schools from sects toward science*. Boston: Little, Brown.

Hoffman, L. (1981). *Foundations of family therapy: A conceptual framework for systems change*. New York: Basic Books.

Hoffman, L. (1985). Beyond power and control: Toward a "second order" family systems therapy. *Family Systems Medicine, 3*, 381–396.

Imber-Black, E. (1988). *Families and larger systems*. New York: Guilford Press.

Koocher, G. P., Norcross, J. C., & Hill, S. S., III (Eds.). (1998). *Psychologists' desk reference*. New York: Oxford University Press.

Lusterman, D-D. (1995). Treating marital infidelity. In R. Mikesell, D-D. Lusterman, & S. McDaniel (Eds.), *Integrating family therapy: Handbook of family psychology and systems theory* (pp. 259–270). Washington, DC: American Psychological Association.

Maruyama, M. (1963). The second cybernetics: Deviation-amplifying mutual causal processes. *American Scientist, 5*, 164–179.

McDaniel, S. H., Campbell, T. L., & Seaburn, D. (1995). Principles of collaboration between health and mental health providers in primary care. *Family Systems Medicine, 13*, 283–298.

McDaniel S. H., & Hepworth, J. (in press). Family

psychology in primary care: Managing issues of power and dependency through collaboration. In R. Frank, S. H. McDaniel, J. Bray, & M. Heldring (Eds.), *Primary care psychology.* Washington, DC: American Psychological Association.

McDaniel, S. H., Hepworth, J., & Doherty, W. J. (1992). *Medical family therapy: A biopsychosocial approach to families with health problems.* New York: Basic Books.

Minuchin, S. (1974). *Families and family therapy.* Cambridge, MA: Harvard University Press.

Minuchin, S., & Fishman, G. (1981). *Family therapy techniques.* Cambridge, MA: Harvard University Press.

Munroe, R. L. (1955). *Schools of psychoanalytic thought: An exposition, critique, and attempt at integration.* New York: Holt, Rinehart & Winston.

Perrin, E. (1999). The promise of collaborative care. *Developmental and Behavioral Pediatrics, 20,* 57–62.

Philpot, C., Brooks, G. R., Lusterman, D-D., & Nutt, R. (1997). *Bridging separate gender worlds: Why men and women clash and how therapists can bring them together.* Washington, DC: American Psychological Association.

Rogers, C. R., & Skinner, B. F. (1956). Some issues concerning the control of human behavior: A symposium. *Science, 124,* 1057–1066.

Schuchman, H., Foster, L., & Nye, S. (1982). *Confidentiality of health records: The meeting of law, ethics and clinical issues.* New York: Gardner Press.

Selvini-Palazzoli, M., Boscolo, L., Cecchin, G. F., & Prata, G. (1978). *Paradox and counterparadox: A new model in the therapy of the family in schizophrenic transaction.* New York: Aronson.

Simon, F. B., Stierlin, H., & Wynne, L. C. (1985). *The language of family therapy: A systemic vocabulary and sourcebook.* New York: Family Process Press.

Sullivan, H. S. (1953). *Corruptions of modern psychiatry.* New York: Norton.

Sullivan, H. S. (1954). *The psychiatric interview* (H. S. Perry & M. L. Gawel, Eds.). New York: Norton.

Thompson, C. (1950). *Psychoanalysis: Evolution and development.* New York: Grove Press.

Tomm, K. (1984). One perspective on the Milan systemic approach: Part II. Description of session format, interviewing style and interventions. *Journal of Marital and Family Therapy, 10,* 253–271.

Walker, L. E. (1984). *The battered woman syndrome.* New York: Springer.

Watzlawick, P., Weakland, J., & Fisch, R. (1974). *Change: Principles of problem formation and problem resolution.* New York: Norton.

Webster's third new international dictionary of the English language (unabridged). (1986). Chicago: Encyclopedia Britannica.

PART I

COUPLES

CHAPTER 2

CONDUCTING INTEGRATIVE THERAPY OVER TIME: A CASE EXAMPLE OF OPEN-ENDED THERAPY

Jay Lebow

Even a cursory observation of recent writing and clinical practice suggests how completely the trend toward integration has transformed family therapy. Not only has a considerable literature emerged that is concerned with integration (Breunlin, Schwartz, & Karrer, 1992; Grunebaum, 1988; Lebow, 1984, 1987a, 1987b, 1997a, 1997b; Liddle, 1984; Mikesell, Lusterman, & McDaniel, 1995; Moultrop, 1981, 1989), and numerous integrative models been developed and widely disseminated (e.g., Feldman, 1985, 1990; Gurman, 1981; L'Abate, 1986; Pinsof, 1995), but also, and this is emblematic of a paradigm shift, the move to integration has become so much part of the fabric of therapists' work that it largely goes unrecognized.

I have practiced an integrative method for many years in which I combine elements of many schools of therapy. I became an integrative therapist early in my career because I was dissatisfied with the limited scope of various approaches to which I was exposed. Clients presenting for therapy seemed to vary enormously, to show very diverse processes in how problems developed, and to be likely to benefit most from different approaches and interventions. In supervision, lectures, presentations, books, and articles I was exposed to a wide array of effective therapists with noteworthy ideas, most of whom seemed to have a great deal to offer. I was impressed with the logic of integrative work of several colleagues and authors, most notably Bill Pinsof, Alan Gurman, Froma Walsh, Arnold Lazurus, and Clifford Sager. It seemed natural to me to combine ingredients, and so I did, ultimately developing my own integrative method.

The case I summarize in this chapter, that of the Zimmermans, brings into focus a key aspect of my integrative methodology: how therapy is organized over time. Schools of therapy typically suggest a very specific concept about how therapy is to be organized in time and who is to be involved in treatment. Therapy may be brief or long term. It may be conducted with a family, a couple, or an individual. Rarely, however, do approaches speak to the breadth of problems and goals with which clients present, a range with which I have found is more easily dealt through maintaining a flexible view of how therapy is organized.

There is no one ideal length of therapy. Research has shown that different lengths of therapy are appropriate to different problems and goals (Howard, Moras, Brill, Martinovich, & Lutz, 1996). High rates of recidivism for many problems are avoided only by clients returning for additional sessions at various points in the life cycle (Lebow & Gurman, 1995). These realities are particularly evident in couple and family therapy, because many family issues evolve and transform over time and cannot fully be dealt with at one point in the life cycle. For example, a family issue involving a couple and one of their parents might be prominent at the time of marriage, then quiet for many years, only to return at the birth of the couple's first child. Other family issues emerge only at particular points in the life cycle (e.g., issues about the care of children or of elderly parents).

Because of all these considerations, I and many other couple and family therapists have moved toward a practice that I term *open-ended* (Lebow, 1995), shaping the length of the treatment and who participates in various sessions in relation to what the therapist sees as most effective and as what their clients want and need. This approach creates a fluid view of therapy over time, doing different pieces of work as they emerge as most salient. Who is seen in the family also evolves over time, including perhaps a couple at one point, the couple and their children later, or one of the members of the couple alone.

I have chosen to describe my therapy with the Zimmermans because it was in my work with them and a few other families that I moved to an open-ended approach. My earlier view of time—that there should be a crisp beginning and clear ending, and clear boundaries around an "individual" or "couple" therapy—had little to do with the Zimmermans' view of what was useful. My therapy with the Zimmermans also more generally typifies my integrative approach to therapy. However, the combination of interventions described is uniquely tailored to this family.

THE ZIMMERMANS

When I first met Sally and Tom Zimmerman, Sally was a 32-year-old homemaker, and Tom was a 33-year-old associate in a very high-powered law firm. Both were of mixed European ancestry and Catholic. They had one child, Brian, age 4. My first contact with them was a telephone call from Sally in which she told me that she was despondent about how poorly her marriage was going. Sally let me know about the couple's marital problems and her considerable sadness. She said that she had talked with Tom about marital therapy and that, although he was not eager, he was willing to participate.

This brief telephone contact typifies how I begin with clients who are ready to engage in therapy. I have three simple goals: (a) to obtain the essential information I need about the situation so that I can decide whom to include in the first session, (b) to create the initial stage of the therapeutic alliance, and (c) to conduct the call in a way that reduces the possibility that other family members will believe that the therapy has already been stacked against

them. Because both Sally and Tom had already agreed to begin therapy, we set a time for the first appointment.

In this case, the decision about whom to include in therapy was simple, because Sally described a marital problem, and Sally and Tom had already discussed couples therapy. I do not typically include children in sessions when a marital problem is at issue. I believe it is part of the responsibility of therapists to help clients consider the ramifications for children but not necessarily to directly include them in the therapy.

The First Few Sessions

Sally and Tom presented for the first session on time. They were attractive, well dressed, and articulate. When we sat down, Sally immediately launched into a 10-minute statement in which she summarized a litany of complaints about Tom. She described how she felt abandoned by his constant attention to his budding career as a lawyer. She found him little help around the house and very unreliable in holding to commitments; he was habitually late, rarely calling to explain, and often failing to complete tasks that he said he would do. She raged and cried as she expressed her exasperation and showed a great deal of bitterness. She described feeling as if she did not matter to Tom. Tom responded in a highly defensive way, counterattacking by attributing Sally's feelings to her simply being an unhappy person. He complained about Sally's lack of energy, the amount of time she spent in bed, the way she attended to the house and Brian, her low self-esteem, and her frequent attacks on him. He used material that he had garnered from several books and television programs about depression as grist for the mill in attacking Sally, who he felt simply needed to get over her depression. When Sally countered that she was depressed because she did not have a partner, Tom argued that he only worked the same hours as his colleagues and that he was doing what he believed a man should do to support his family.

I have a few clear goals for first sessions. I want clients to be able to speak their minds so that they have a sense that their voices can be heard in the therapy. I want to gain a general sense of the range of problems and the strengths of the family. I want to build my alliance with each of the clients and with them collectively as a system and to instill a sense of hope that we can work in the direction they desire. I want the clients to learn something about me and about what we would be likely to do if we continue to meet. I want to discuss what the practical arrangements will be if the clients decide to move further with the therapy. I begin the session with little structure to see what emerges, then use the remainder of the time to complete the other first-session tasks.

I also try to envision in the first session the critical tasks for the beginning phase of the therapy and begin to work with these tasks. Couples therapy often begins with mutual complaints, and I see dealing with these complaints as a crucial early task. If clients fall into a habitual pattern of attacking one another, the therapy will be experienced as too painful (just like being at home, but worse), and the clients will be likely to end the therapy. Paradoxically, if clients do not feel that they have an opportunity to state their grievances, they will feel that they do not have voice in the therapy and also will be inclined to disengage. I see the therapist's task as allowing enough sharing to be productive yet being able to move the clients away from their habitual pattern, to keep the therapy from being overly noxious (and therefore not being therapy). When the anger between Sally and Tom began to escalate, I sought to establish control and interrupt the conflict. I let them know that they already had given me a clear sense of the difficulty they were describing and that we would have plenty of time to go into more detail.

To help create a sense of hope, I informed them I had seen many couples like them and that most had been able to work out their difficulties. At the same time, I let them also know that I recognized the seriousness of their complaints and that I could see how painful their present situation was. An important value I hold as a therapist lies in maintaining a balance between accenting hope as an antidote for despair and acting as a witness to the seriousness of the clients' situation. Grounded in a Rogerian notion of genuineness, I do not believe in distorting or

making promises I cannot keep but rather in looking for real signs of hope in the clients' lives. Because there seemed to still be a very palpable connection between Tom and Sally, and because they had little trouble recalling their better feelings for each other, I told them that I was optimistic and hopeful that we could work out their difficulties. However, I was particularly concerned with the power of those moments during which Sally became frustrated and attacking while Tom withdrew, moments when each seemed very despairing.

I also explained how I work. I told them that I would leave what we discussed at the beginning of each session to them and that they should bring up what was immediate for them at the moment. I told them that we would talk a good deal about what they were directly experiencing at the moment in our sessions or what they had experienced in the past week but that it was my hope that we would also learn about their individual histories and how these histories influence the present problem. I added that it seemed clear that their primary goal for therapy was to make their marriage more satisfying and that I thought we should meet until they either felt satisfied with the relationship or they had made a serious attempt to work the issues out without success and decided that it would be better to reach some other accommodation. I recommended scheduling weekly meetings, and they agreed. I added that we should commit to having a final session whenever they felt ready to end.

At the beginning of our second meeting I invited Tom and Sally to begin with whatever was on their minds. Tom launched into an example of a day during the week when Sally had been especially depressed and angry. He took out a notebook in which he had recorded what Sally had said and done and proceeded to list signs of Sally's inactivity and the critical statements she made to him. Sally's retort was that she thought anyone would feel the way she did if she had a husband like Tom, who was emotionally unavailable most of the time. She went on to describe how Tom had worked late several times during the week and how she felt abandoned.

I begin to construct a roadmap for therapy in the first few sessions. I form hypotheses that initially guide me, which I revise as I learn more. My first hypotheses typically focus on what is directly observable: the patterns of feelings, thoughts, and behavior that make for difficulties, how these are responded to by others, and the cycles that become repeated in the system. Later, I augment and revise these initial hypotheses on the basis of patterns that emerge, historical information that enlightens individual and interpersonal dynamics, and the way that clients respond to intervention.

It appeared that Tom and Sally set each other off in a cycle that was close to raging out of control. Tom and Sally had very different visions of marriage. Tom saw his task as working and earning the money that would allow them to have the kind of material life they both wanted. Sally valued closeness to a much greater extent and looked to Tom to be close, not only on special occasions but throughout the week. When Sally experienced Tom as unavailable she became distraught and very expressive of her disappointment and anger. When Tom experienced Sally as depressed and angry, he withdrew.

I also thought that the cognitions each brought to these experiences assumed a great deal of importance. Sally's thoughts appeared to typify those of people who become depressed. She would almost exclusively focus on the negative, would minimize positive experiences, had a profoundly negative view of the future, and blamed her own difficulties in functioning on her problems with Tom. Her depression seemed to be a mix of the intolerable situation with which she was presented, coupled with her individual way of cognitively and emotionally responding to these events.

Tom thought of himself as merely attending to the responsibilities that went with his role. He justified his behavior, placing his version of Sally's needs before her own. Tom seemed to be a classic example of a man with limited ability to empathize and connect, who used tuning out as a defense, so that when Sally seemed to need him most he became least available. I also noticed that for all of Tom's reading about depression, he seemed to understand depression poorly. Like some partners of depressed people, he used what he read about depression as a means of belittling her, a weapon in their conflict.

I also thought about Sally and Tom through the lens of gender (Philpot, Brooks, Lusterman, & Nutt,

1997). Their impasse represents a common conflict between men and women over the priorities assigned to work and financial security versus connection in relationship. Like many men, Tom saw himself as productive, a good provider, fighting the competitive forces in the work world. Sally saw him as preoccupied with his job and unavailable.

These ideas running through my head prompted thoughts about introducing more psychoeducation about depression, about probing the childhood meanings of closeness and withdrawal and of happiness and depression, about gender and marriage, and about explicating the cycle between them. However, at this point I held off. I felt that this was a time to appreciate Tom and Sally's degree of pain and defensiveness and to empathize with how difficult the problem felt to each of them. It was also the time to help them regain (or in Tom's case, perhaps, build) their abilities to listen to each other. I pointed out the research finding that couples need to have many more positive than negative exchanges to experience relationships as satisfying (Jacobson & Margolin, 1979). Drawing from behavioral couples therapy, I also suggested that they monitor their exchanges and see if they could move them to become more positive. Specifically, I asked what they liked to do together. They talked about exercising and going to movies, dinners, and music, all activities that they had stopped. They agreed to attempt to restore some of these more positive experiences to their life. I ended the session by letting them know that it was obvious to me that both had struggled positively to try to remain with each other despite a lot of pain. This was not a vacuous reframe but spoke to my experience of each of them as committed to each other despite this struggle. Tom and Sally appeared to respond positively to my comments, adding to my sense of hope. I felt we were building a good therapeutic alliance, and they seemed willing to try my suggestions.

Nonetheless, Tom began the third session with another litany of complaints, and Sally responded with a counterattack. In this couple, complaint was followed by defense and counterattack, making it impossible to get anywhere and presenting the distinct danger that sessions would only replicate the worst of their interactions. I decided that the useful life of this exchange in therapy sessions had been exhausted. Therefore, I intervened early in the session, interrupting the stereotypic sequence.

I assumed an interpretive psychoeducational stance toward what I saw happening. I first made it clear that I thought they both had valid viewpoints. I let them know I thought they both were trying to live as best they could with the life situation with which they were presented. Tom was trying to be a good provider, believing, as many men and women do, that filling this role should be his highest priority. Sally was trying to establish closeness and intimacy and had become the spokesperson for that part of their relationship. I labeled these positive intentions as degenerating into a struggle for control about whose agenda was more important. I pointed out that, although I had the sense that Sally also wanted financial security and Tom closeness, each acted as if the goals being pushed by the other did not matter. I let them know how common it was for couples to become caught in such conflicts about goals and expectations. Drawing from Sager's (1976) work on marriage contracts, I pointed out that couples have the difficult task of negotiating their differing expectations about their lives and their relationship, a task sometimes made more difficult by partners failing to share and discuss their expectations or even by having expectations about which they were not fully aware. I pointed out how often couples become polarized around issues such as these, given the many pressures in life and gender socialization.

I often assume this kind of interpretive psychoeducational posture early in therapy. A great deal of research has established the value of psychoeducation in almost every possible context, and my clinical experience has confirmed its value. I believe it is enormously helpful to clients to see that others have similar problems and to learn from how others have coped with them. With couples, I also use this information to defuse some of the power of the conflict and help them get a perspective from the outside about their difficulties so that they might be able to regain some empathy for each other.

I find the response of clients to interventions such as this one to be a crucial indicator of the likelihood that the therapy will be successful in chang-

ing the clients' feelings about the relationship. If the clients merely turn back to their complaints, I regard this as a very negative sign. Fortunately, Tom and Sally were able to listen, understand, and respond to my interpretation of their interaction. They recognized that they fell into negative patterns, and they expressed a desire to find a way out. I suggested that it would be useful to discuss further their core expectations in future sessions and make a greater effort to listen to each other and to see if they could agree to disagree when they could not find agreement outside of sessions.

At the beginning of the fourth session Tom and Sally reported having gone out and had a better time with one another. Each described having made some effort to try to listen to the other. Neither had substantially changed in their attitude or level of frustration, but the process signs remained positive. Because the signs were positive, I continued in the direction we had launched in the last session, zeroing in further on Tom and Sally's core expectations.

As we talked about what they each wanted, Tom again described his concern with financial security, and Sally described the value she placed on closeness. Although we could have simply negotiated their differences, I felt that it would be better to deal with this negotiation after we had an opportunity to better grasp what these issues meant to each of them. Therefore, I began to explore the intergenerational and psychodynamic aspects of these expectations. In my work, I always find this kind of exploration useful, but I also think the timing for it is vital. I use the natural opportunities provided by statements of beliefs to explore the sources of these beliefs. In couples therapy, being witness to one's partner's uncovering can also become an important source of empathy (Fishbane, 1998). Given the conversation we had been having, I felt that the timing was right, and I wondered aloud if Tom and Sally understood why these particular values had become so important to them in their lives. I was delighted when Tom immediately began to respond. I knew Sally would be open to looking at her history but had my doubts about Tom. Given his willingness to begin this process, I sensed that it would go well.

Tom explained that he came from a family in which his father had been a well-paid middle manager but lost his job when Tom was 6. His family had not been prepared to deal with this event. The family had to move to a smaller home and never financially recovered. Tom also saw his father become depressed and withdrawn and his mother become bitter and highly critical of his father. He vowed that he would not be like his father. His life became one of striving for success and security, defending against a catastrophic fear that he would be dragged into a situation in which he could become financially vulnerable. I underlined the clear connection between Tom's fears and the life script he had shaped for himself and how he seemed to regard Sally as a threat to completing this script because of her competing agendas. I also wondered aloud whether how he felt about his father's depression might affect his way of responding when Sally was down. Tom agreed that it was difficult for him to deal with depression.

Sally was thoughtful and supportive in listening to this conversation. Occasionally, she would add comments that were hypercritical of Tom's family and produced uneasiness in Tom, but mostly she was able to be empathic and connected. I asked her what she thought, and she related that as she heard Tom speak she could sympathize with what it meant for him to be successful in his work. She did remind him that she had other needs, but I regarded it as a good sign that she could begin to hear Tom's perspective.

I began the next session by commenting positively about Tom's exploration and invited Sally to add any stories from her own life that would inform our work. When one partner offers significant sharing from their family of origin, I believe it offers a propitious moment for opening up the life of the other. Sally described growing up as an only child with a father and mother who were very distant and a father who never was home. She felt very rejected by her father, who seldom spent any time with her. Both her parents were highly critical of her, and she remembered having been sad and depressed through much of her childhood. She described how important support and closeness were for her. She pointed to the time early in her dating relationship with Tom when they had been very close, how good this felt, and how terrible it was for her to live in an-

other family in which she received little in the way of connection. Tom was able to sit with what he heard and substantially stay supportive. When he drifted into some defensiveness about his behavior, I interrupted and refocused him on his more constructive responses to Sally's experience. I felt encouraged that each had been able to name some of the sources for their own behavior and to better grasp why the behavior of the other was so difficult for them. I was even more encouraged that we had spent two sessions in which there had been little blaming of each other.

Integrating Individual and Couple Sessions

Sally's sharing also provided the opening that I had been waiting for to discuss her depression without causing her to feel that I was siding with Tom and sharing in his criticism of her. I reviewed the signs of depression and suggested that she sounded a lot like a person who was depressed. However, I clearly separated my thought that she was depressed from the validity of her complaints about Tom. I told them it seemed to me that Sally had a problem with depression, but Sally's depression was not at the heart of their marital problem and that Tom should not make the error of dismissing what was at the center of Sally's unhappiness just because she had a tendency to become depressed. Sally was able to accept that she was depressed as well as that her depression had begun long before she met Tom. I asked if she would be willing to work on the depression, and she agreed. I proposed that Sally see a colleague of mine to talk about her feelings of depression. Sally responded by telling me that although she was willing to explore her depression further, she did not want to begin again with another therapist.

Before my therapy with the Zimmermans, I would not consider simultaneously seeing a couple together and one member of the couple alone. I regarded it as an inevitably fatal imbalance in my relationship with a couple to focus disproportionately on one person within our sessions or to meet with one party apart from those sessions. However, Sally's insistence moved me. Although I considered that the work with Sally might provide an opportunity to further pathologize her in Tom's eyes (i.e., that she was the problem) or to disturb the alliance I had with Sally and Tom as a couple, my instinct told me that it would be more useful to take the risk than miss the opportunity. Sally's idea that she found "one-stop shopping" much easier had an appeal. I decided to experiment to see if I could find a way to work both with Sally and with the Zimmermans' couples issues.

We considered the options available: to (a) do all the work together or (b) have some separate sessions with Sally. Sally preferred to meet alone to discuss her depression, and I favored this option as well because I thought the kind of work we would do, such as examining cognitions, would more easily be done in individual sessions. We therefore decided to try having separate weekly sessions with Sally as I might in an "individual" case, while continuing our schedule of sessions with Tom and Sally together, with each kind of session having a distinct purpose.

The therapy then assumed two distinct threads. In the conjoint sessions we further explored their relationship, primarily focusing on negotiating a shared set of expectations. These sessions mostly began with one or the other bringing up some difficult interchange in the past week, which would serve as a launching point for our work on building better communication and mutual understanding. In these discussions we also followed the trail of their individual anxieties, which, at times, caused each of them to distort what the other said or felt or to respond in ways that were provocative. When such dynamics came into play, I worked to identify what seemed to be happening out of awareness. I worked to get Tom and Sally to change enough about who they were so that they could live at peace with themselves and each other while also accepting one another's human failings. Tom came to understand his issues with closeness and to trust that he could be close and still maintain his career. He began to make decisions about his work life that allowed for greater connectedness. Sally, seeing that Tom was responsive to her desire for closeness and that he acted in a more reliable way, gradually became able to trust him more. Each diminished their criticism of the other, and even when problematic behavior reoccurred (e.g., when Tom stayed late at the office and failed to call), the arguments did not degenerate

to the name calling and sense of futility that were there earlier. Ultimately, we negotiated a contract of shared expectations about their marriage that worked for both of them.

In my sessions with Sally we directly addressed her depression, primarily using cognitive–behavioral interventions (Beck, 1976). First, we did some simple work with scheduling her time so that she would be more engaged in activity. Specifically, we looked at what Sally had liked to do in the past and tried to schedule her doing a few of these activities even if she did not feel like it. Sally responded well and began doing more. We spent the majority of the time in individual sessions examining the thoughts she had about herself and the world that clearly had a significant role in her depression. Through a range of examples that emerged, it became clear that Sally carried a core belief that everything would turn out badly and that she would inevitably be disappointed and criticized. The beliefs were strongly reinforced in her early experience and had received further support in the recent history of her marriage, so I pointed out that it was perfectly natural that Sally would develop a negative view. I helped Sally to identify her core thoughts and to challenge her belief in the absolute truth of her ideas. I helped her understand how these ideas helped create self-fulfilling prophecies, and we explored the alternative ideas that many things actually might turn out well and that she might be able to get the closeness she wished. I taught Sally a cognitive therapy technique (Ellis, 1962) for examining the relation of events (A) to feelings (C), looking for the thoughts (B) lying between event and action. Sally used this technique frequently to help her focus on her thoughts and question them. Sally's work in the individual sessions became very focused and determined. She followed the homework and began to transform her view of herself and others.

We carried Sally's belief that she felt she could not depend on anyone back to our meetings with Tom. Although it was clear that Sally needed to work with the pervasive way this thought interrupted her happiness, it also was clear that as long as Tom was substantially undependable and unavailable, Sally's belief would continually be reinforced. In fact, if Tom were going to engage in the kind of behavior he had, much of Sally's old thought pattern was functional: She could not depend on Tom. We established in the conjoint meetings how important it was for Tom to be dependable so that Sally could see that Tom could be dependable. Tom appeared to get the message and became much more reliable and available. When Tom did let Sally down, we examined how Tom came to do this and explored whether Sally now needed to return fully to her belief about Tom's lack of dependability. Tom became more dependable, and Sally became more trusting.

Tom and Sally also began to take up the difficult issues of how they would combine their respective conscious goals into what I termed "a family plan." In this process, Tom was able to uncover the difference between his conscious goal of being successful in his work and the driven state to which he could succumb. Tom and Sally agreed on a set of guidelines for Tom's work week, and for the time they would spend as a couple and a family, that included Tom working many hours but also clearly created boundaries around his work time.

Integrating individual and couple work was especially valuable here. A cognitive therapist working with Sally alone might well have Sally working to change a belief that continued to be reinforced daily in her environment. Not only would the result likely be unstable, but also this approach would have very important problematic consequences when the meaning in terms of gender in relation to depression and marital dissatisfaction is deconstructed. Working with Tom to help him be more reliable and with Sally and Tom to understand each other's needs allowed for the cognitive work with Sally to be much more productive.

The First Termination

After 12 weeks of sessions Tom and Sally clearly had turned the corner in their relationship. They were much more cooperative and described what was obviously a very real change in feeling. Without ever specifically "working" on their sexuality, they reported becoming more sexual and that their sexuality was again more enjoyable.

During the 13th week Tom and Sally had what had become a typical session for them, upbeat and

positive. However, in the middle of the session, Tom informed me that he and Sally had decided together that they had improved their relationship sufficiently that they had decided this would be their last session. I was happy that they were feeling so positive about their progress, but I was taken aback at the sudden way the decision was presented. I tried to dissuade them from ending at this point, but they were firm in their decision. I would have preferred the work to go on a bit longer so that the gains would have solidified and so that we would have an opportunity to see how they coped when a challenge occurred that might lead back to the old problems. I also liked meeting with them. However, they were doing well and wanted to end. In that moment, I tried to separate my own needs from theirs, and as I thought about their decision, it did seem the right one for them.

I suggested that they return for one further session, but it was clear that they had decided this session should be their last. In the little time left, I tried to do what I typically would do in the last few sessions when there is a planned ending, what I have called the *tasks of termination* (Lebow, 1995). I let them know that I thought they had worked very hard in the therapy to face some very difficult issues and that their hard work had resulted in their being successful at resolving their problems. I accepted their heartfelt thanks for my involvement but was careful to make sure they kept in focus that the outcome was their achievement. I emphasized the ways they could help prevent a reoccurrence of the problem, particularly by keeping the lines of communication open. I stressed the importance of their continuing to talk about the kinds of issues we had been discussing and suggested they continue to use the time of our sessions to do so. We also briefly reviewed situations that seemed likely to present themselves in the near future that might be particularly hard for them (e.g., Tom was about to have a case go on trial, which would demand his full-time attention for several weeks) and what they might do about these situations. I wished them well and left the door open for them to return at any time.

After the session, I was muttering to myself. The therapy had been going so well. Their withdrawal was so abrupt and seemingly final. I felt pleased about what we had accomplished but sad about losing the meetings that I, too, enjoyed. I wondered if I had done something that had brought this on or, as some suggest about therapy, that the closeness of the meetings was just too difficult. At the time, I did not grasp how natural this way of ending is for many people, even in therapies they value, when they no longer feel they need the therapy or do not want to expend any more of their resources of time and money. Ultimately, as I thought about the Zimmermans over time, I came to better understand how well the therapy, and even its ending, had worked for them.

Their Return Three Years Later

I did not hear from Tom and Sally for 3 years. Then I received a call from Tom, who told me he was having difficulties at work. I suggested that he and Sally come in to talk about the possibilities for our working on the issues about which he was concerned. Even though Tom's telephone call was about his own issues, I saw my relationship with Tom and Sally as a couple as being at the core of my alliance, and I wanted to be sure that Sally's feelings about Tom's issues had some forum for expression.

When they came in for the first meeting, I was especially glad that I had not chosen to meet first with Tom alone. Tom's issue had vast repercussions for them as a couple. Tom had received substantial negative feedback at work. Although he still was basically viewed positively, some of the partners in his law firm began to challenge him about the quality of his work. This, in turn, led to some reoccurrence of the old conflict between Tom and Sally. In the wake of this new work stress, Tom blamed much of his work problem on the time he devoted to his family. Tom had returned to extending his workday without communicating with Sally, and Tom and Sally had stopped communicating in a positive way about Tom's work.

In the first meeting, each again expressed feeling misunderstood and a great deal of anger. However, I found that in our first session we could draw on the earlier therapeutic relationship. I found myself reminding them of the lessons from our earlier therapy and was much more comfortable interrupting

their problematic sequences than I typically am at the beginning of therapy with new clients. I noticed an immediate effect. Not only were they willing to accept my directives about communicating and listening to one another, but also just being in the therapy clearly was a stimulus for communicating and calming down.

It took only a few sessions to fully restore the stability of the working relationship between Tom and Sally. Tom subsequently met a couple of times with me on his own to explore his work options. Again, termination was brief. At the end of our second individual session Tom told me that he had gained enough perspective to help him think through his problem and to consider the life decisions he needed to make and that he would call me when he wanted to meet further. I called a month later, not having heard from Tom or Sally. Tom told me that he had decided to stay with the firm, that they were doing fine, and that they had decided that they did not need to meet further. We again parted until some unknown time in the future. This time I took the sudden termination more easily. This obviously was their way of ending. It was not mine but, after all, it was their therapy. It was clear that this way worked for them, and I needed to accept it and learn to work with it.

Integrating Work With the Adolescent Son Six Years Later

Six more years went by. Tom and Sally had a second child, and Tom became a partner in his law firm. When I heard from them, it was with a concern about their elder child, Brian, who had recently turned 13. Brian was having trouble adapting to early adolescence, was at times sad and not performing as well in school as the standardized tests indicated he should, and had begun to have a series of conflicts with Sally about her authority. This, in turn, had set off some of Sally's old feelings of inadequacy.

Again, I first met with Tom and Sally. They identified that they wanted to find better ways to work with Brian, and I suggested our having a family session with Brian to discuss further what was going on. In scheduling the family session, I further scrambled some more of my traditional beliefs about maintaining clarity and clear boundaries in the structure of treatment. I knew Sally and Tom very well but had only heard about Brian. Brian was not even aware that I had seen his parents earlier. I decided to see in the session whether my earlier relationship with Sally and Tom helped or hindered my working with the family (see Gottlieb, 1995).

Because Brian was a willing participant, it was not difficult to make the transition to family sessions. I made a point of making a special effort to reach out to Brian so that we might form an alliance while at the same time making sure not to ally too much with him so as to diminish my alliance with Tom and Sally. We decided to meet further as a family. It also seemed clear that Brian needed to have a place to discuss his issues away from his parents, and so I suggested that Brian see another therapist alone. As before, Sally and Tom clearly did not want to have another therapist involved; neither did Brian want to see someone else. By this time, I had become more comfortable with seeing parts of family systems apart, so I offered to see Brian alone as well. Brian agreed, and we set a schedule of having one appointment per week, alternating sessions with the family and with Brian alone. Attending to the complex issues of confidentiality of communication in therapies in which the participants in sessions vary over time (Gottlieb, 1995), I established that all communications shared with me during therapy would remain confidential from family members who were not present at those particular meetings. This included what Brian told me in individual sessions and what Tom and Sally had shared over the years in couple and individual meetings. I also noted a couple of specific exceptions to confidentiality and, in the unlikely event these circumstances would arise, how these situations would be handled. I now was using the family as the base for treatment but making decisions about whom to see in a particular session more as a function of what I thought would be most effective and which arrangements fit best with what the clients wanted.

Brian was having some trouble, and presenting difficulties for his family, but clearly seemed more like an adolescent who was out of sync rather than

one who was very troubled. My work with Brian focused on helping him develop a more positive attitude about coping with adolescence and with his parents on developing more tolerance and their ability to empathically offer guidance.

A major part of my individual work with Brian consisted simply of my listening to his version of adolescence and providing a nonjudgmental figure with whom he could relate and problem solve. We also identified particular coping skills, such as managing his time, that he could benefit from mastering, and set about helping him learn these skills. I offered some psychoeducation about the struggles of adolescence, along with the message that I thought he had a lot going for him and that what he did with his life would ultimately be his decision.

In the family sessions we worked to create a set of shared expectations about Brian's responsibilities and the privileges and punishments he would receive in relation to his behavior. This work was enormously enabled by my earlier knowledge of this family. It was relatively easy to challenge Tom and Sally with some of the projections for success that they were placing on Brian, which Brian was rebelling against, and point out how intergenerational patterns were repeating.

I met with the family three times and with Brian alone four times. As earlier, there were fewer sessions in relation to the problem than I might have anticipated. As soon as behavioral patterns changed, the Zimmermans clearly indicated that they felt done. At the end of this therapy (or now what I see as this phase of a therapy I view as occurring over the life cycle), Brian was doing well in school, and Sally and Brian had established a level of closeness that was satisfying for each at this point in their lives.

CONCLUSION

I saw the Zimmermans one additional time. Sally's father had died. Tom and Sally came to talk about his death and its meaning for them. They did not schedule a further session. I have not seen the Zimmermans for some time, but I expect I will see them again. We have a good track record with each other for resolving difficulties. It is clear that the Zimmermans basically want to live their lives on their own, but at those nodal points when problems arise I am viewed as the therapist for the family.

The Zimmermans, and a few other families that followed a similar course, have had an enormous influence on my method of practice. I now see most therapy I conduct as open ended, both in terms of who will be involved and when meetings will occur. I expect to be available for therapy with families over the life cycle and explicitly offer them this option. Some take it, others come in with a more traditional view of a beginning, middle, and an end in which they say goodbye, never to return again. As I described in my chapter in *Integrating Family Therapy* (Lebow, 1995), I also now proactively deal with termination issues throughout therapy rather than waiting for an "end." The Zimmermans had a sense of the flow of treatment very different from that presented in any textbook. They called when they needed treatment, took time to digest interventions, and returned as desired. Although not all cases use therapy in the way that the Zimmermans did, I have found that most families prefer this way of thinking about therapy over time.

References

Beck, A. T. (1976). *Cognitive therapy and the emotional disorders*. New York: International Universities Press.

Breunlin, D., Schwartz, R., & Karrer, B. (1992). *Metaframeworks: Transcending the models of family therapy*. San Francisco: Jossey-Bass.

Ellis, A. (1962). *Reason and emotion in psychotherapy*. New York: Lyle Stuart.

Feldman, L. B. (1985). Integrative multi-level therapy: A comprehensive interpersonal and intrapsychic approach. *Journal of Marital and Family Therapy, 11*, 357–372.

Feldman, L. B. (1990). *Multi-dimensional family therapy*. New York: Guilford Press.

Fishbane, M. (1998). I, thou, and we: A dialogical approach to couples therapy. *Journal of Marital and Family Therapy, 24*, 41–59.

Gottlieb, M. (1995). Ethical dilemmas in change of format and live supervision. In R. H. Mikesell, D-D. Lusterman, & S. H. McDaniel (Eds.), *Integrating family therapy: Handbook of family psychology and systems therapy* (pp. 561–569).

Washington, DC: American Psychological Association.

Grunebaum, H. (1988). The relationship of family theory to family therapy. *Journal of Marital and Family Therapy, 14*, 1–14.

Gurman, A. S. (1981). Integrative marital therapy: Toward the development of an interpersonal approach. In S. Budman (Ed.), *Forms of brief therapy* (pp. 415–460). New York: Guilford Press.

Howard, K. I., Moras, K., Brill, P. L., Martinovich, Z., & Lutz, W. (1996). The evaluation of psychotherapy: Efficacy, effectiveness, patient progress. *American Psychologist, 51*, 1059–1064.

Jacobson, N. S., & Margolin, G. (1979). *Marital therapy: Strategies based on social learning and behavior exchange principles*. New York: Brunner/Mazel.

L'Abate, L. (1986). *Systemic family therapy*. New York: Brunner/Mazel.

Lebow, J. L. (1984). On the value of integrating approaches to family therapy. *Journal of Marital and Family Therapy, 10*, 127–138.

Lebow, J. L. (1987a). Developing a personal integration in family therapy: Principles for model construction and practice. *Journal of Marital and Family Therapy, 13*, 1–14.

Lebow, J. L. (1987b). Integrative family therapy: An overview of major issues. *Psychotherapy, 40*, 584–594.

Lebow, J. L. (1995). Termination in marital and family therapy. In R. H. Mikesell, D-D. Lusterman, & S. H. McDaniel (Eds.), *Integrating family therapy: Handbook of family psychology and systems therapy* (pp. 73–86). Washington, DC: American Psychological Association.

Lebow, J. (1997a). The integrative revolution in couple and family therapy. *Family Process, 36*, 1–17.

Lebow, J. (1997b). Why integration is so important in couple and family therapy. *Family Process, 36*, 23–24.

Lebow, J., & Gurman, A. S. (1995). Marital and family therapy: A review of recent literature. *Annual Review of Psychology, 46*, 27–57.

Liddle, H. A. (1984). Towards a dialectical–contextual–coevolutionary translation of structural–strategic family therapy. *Journal of Strategic and Systemic Therapies, 3*, 57–66.

Mikesell, R. H., Lusterman, D-D., & McDaniel, S. H. (1995). *Integrating family therapy: Handbook of family psychology and systems therapy.* Washington, DC: American Psychological Association.

Moultrop, D. (1981). Towards an integrated model of family therapy. *Clinical Social Work Journal, 9,* 111–125.

Moultrop, D. J. (1989). Integration: A coming of age. *Contemporary Family Therapy, 8,* 159–167.

Philpot, C. I., Brooks, G. R., Lusterman, D-D., & Nutt, R. (1997). *Bridging separate worlds: Why men and women clash and how therapists can bring them together.* Washington, DC: American Psychological Association.

Pinsof, W. (1995). *Integrative problem centered therapy.* New York: Basic Books.

Sager, C. (1976). *Marriage contracts and couples therapy.* New York: Brunner/Mazel.

CHAPTER 3

THE TAPESTRY OF COUPLE THERAPY: INTERWEAVING THEORY, ASSESSMENT, AND INTERVENTION

Douglas K. Snyder, Jebber J. Cozzi, Jami Grich, and Michael C. Luebbert

Couple therapists confront a tremendous diversity of presenting issues, marital and family structures, individual dynamics and psychopathology, and psychosocial stressors characterizing couples in distress. Given this diversity in couples' needs, effective treatment is most likely when the couple therapist works from a coherent theoretical framework, engages in extensive assessment of the marital and family system, and selectively draws on intervention strategies across the theoretical spectrum in a manner consistent with an explicit case formulation (Snyder, Cavell, Heffer, & Mangrum, 1995).

In this chapter we describe therapy with a couple exhibiting both individual and relationship issues that contribute to marital difficulties. Consistent with the model that Snyder et al. (1995) outlined, conceptualization of the couple's difficulties rests on comprehensive assessment across multiple domains and levels of the family system. We also present a model for organizing couple interventions ranging from crisis containment to exploration of relevant developmental experiences.

THEORETICAL UNDERPINNINGS

We have advocated a comprehensive model for assessing families in which assessment constructs are organized along five domains: (a) cognitive; (b) affective; (c) communication and interpersonal; (d) structural and developmental; and (e) control, sanctions, and related behaviors. Assessment data across these domains are gathered with multiple assessment strategies, primarily self-report and observational techniques, including both formal (i.e., more struc-

tured and psychometrically focused) and informal (i.e., less structured and more clinically focused) procedures. The assessment techniques across domains are used to evaluate each of five system levels: (a) individuals, (b) dyads, (c) the nuclear family, (d) the extended family and social support system, and (e) community and cultural systems. Implementing such a comprehensive family assessment model can be a daunting challenge. In our experience we typically scan across system levels and domains of functioning to identify the salient issues confronting the couple or family, generate hypotheses regarding any relation between presenting complaints and system dynamics, and test these hypotheses through further assessment and intervention (Heffer & Snyder, 1998).

We have found it useful to conceptualize the therapeutic tasks of couple therapy as comprising six levels of intervention (Snyder, 1999; see Figure 3.1). These include (a) developing a collaborative alliance, (b) containing disabling relationship crises, (c) strengthening the marital dyad, (d) promoting relevant relationship skills, (e) challenging cognitive components of relationship distress, and (f) examining developmental sources of relationship distress. Consistent with our belief that couple therapy often proceeds in nonlinear fashion, the model depicts flexibility of returning to earlier therapeutic tasks as dictated by individual or relationship difficulties. Similarly, individual differences in couples' strengths and concerns often dictate that different components of the model be given greater or less emphasis. For example, some couples require little more than sta-

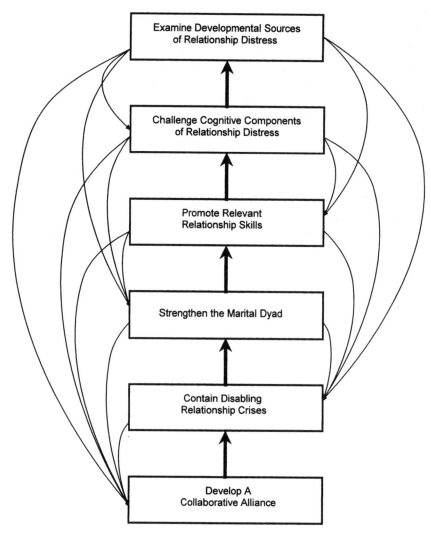

FIGURE 3.1.   A sequential model for pragmatic couple therapy. From *Casebook in Family Therapy, 1st edition*, by D. M Lawson and F. Prevatt, © 1999. Reprinted with permission of Wadsworth, a division of Thomson Learning.

bilization and crisis resolution to restore a positive relationship; others require extensive assistance in reworking enduring maladaptive relationship patterns established early in their individual development. With relatively higher functioning couples we have been able to implement the complete model in as few as 8 to 10 sessions; with other couples, exhibiting significant individual as well as relational impairment, successful therapy has required a year or more of intensive intervention.

The couple described in this chapter entered treatment in a state of crisis demanding prompt resolution before additional interventions emphasizing improved communication skills and relationship enhancement could be implemented. Although their

initial presentation suggested a somewhat fragile union that was vulnerable to dramatic variability in marital affect and conflict management, subsequent assessment revealed a couple with considerable strengths enabling intensive confrontation of long-standing individual issues in a brief pluralistic approach to intervention.

CASE EXAMPLE

Presenting Issues

Mark and Janice, ages 38 and 35, presented in a state of marital crisis precipitated by Janice's discovery of several men's magazines (e.g., *Playboy*) that Mark had left on their bed. Mark acknowledged using such magazines during masturbation in which he engaged while Janice attended school out of town during the week. Janice worried that their marriage might be in jeopardy, that Mark might be emotionally disturbed, and that their two sons might be at risk for sexual molestation by Mark because of his interest in pornography. The couple was referred to Douglas K. Snyder (DKS) after Janice demanded that Mark accompany her to the hospital emergency room for a psychiatric evaluation. Dissatisfied with the response from the emergency room staff, Janice contacted the community mental health center later that night. Mark feared that he had lost Janice's respect and trust and that she might leave him because of his interest in sexually oriented magazines and masturbation. Janice described a fear of her "life falling apart," anticipating that she might need to drop out of school to stay home full time to deal with this marital and family crisis.

Clinical Assessment

Background to Presenting Issues. Both Mark and Janice were engaged in the early stages of mid-level professional careers. Mark was employed as a physician's assistant at a federal correctional facility, but he felt isolated from his colleagues and had few friends outside of work. Janice had recently begun graduate study in occupational therapy at a university 2 hours from the couple's home and was home only on weekends. The couple had two sons, ages 6 and 8, with whom they both appeared to have good relationships. Janice had been married previously for 3 years but had had no children and no further contact with her first husband.

Mark reported that he had purchased sexually oriented magazines since age 20 and used these regularly during masturbation for about 8 years before his marriage. He insisted that he did not pursue any other forms of sexual pornography. Janice responded that she found such materials offensive to women, a threat to society, and a source of sexual violence against women and children. Until the past weekend, she had been somewhat tolerant of Mark having a few of these magazines, so long as neither she nor the children were exposed to them. However, her recent discovery of this material in the couple's bedroom reawakened long-standing concerns she

had regarding their sexual relationship. The couple ordinarily had intercourse several times weekly, but this had declined to once or twice on weekends since Janice had returned to school. Janice said she felt threatened by Mark's masturbation and that she felt guilty for not satisfying all his sexual wishes. She said she did not masturbate and did not experience the same sexual drive or frustration as Mark.

Janice acknowledged feeling somewhat insecure in their sexual relationship. She felt unattractive, having retained weight she had gained during her second pregnancy. She described a long history of dissatisfaction with her body. She had been thin when she and Mark first married and had undergone breast reduction surgery shortly thereafter because her disproportionately large breasts drew repeated, unwanted sexual comments from other men.

Family Histories. Janice's parents had divorced when she was 17. Her father, now deceased, had abused alcohol and been emotionally abusive to his wife and two children. Janice denied sexual abuse but recalled several instances during her adolescence when her father had made suggestive sexual remarks regarding Janice's physical appearance. Janice described her mother, age 65, as in poor health and excessively demanding. Her mother was harshly critical of time Janice spent with Mark and their two sons rather than with her, and Janice acknowledged feeling both guilty and resentful. She had an older brother but felt ambivalent toward him and stated that he neglected their mother.

Mark's parents were both retired. He had an older brother who was divorced and a younger brother who had not yet married. Mark's parents had a contentious relationship, and he described his mother as critical and unforgiving. His older brother had been particularly disruptive to their family life. Mark had learned to navigate family tensions by assuming an accommodating or nonconfrontive posture. Janice acknowledged feeling resentful about how much Mark's mother intruded into their lives. In particular, she felt hurt by his mother's criticisms of her "neglecting" Mark and the two boys while she attended school during the week. Mark was understanding of Janice's feelings toward his mother but resented the role of mediator that he felt forced to adopt.

Test Findings. Both Mark and Janice completed the Marital Satisfaction Inventory–Revised (MSI–R; Snyder, 1997), a self-report measure that assesses sources and levels of marital distress (see Figure 3.2). Although numerous techniques have been developed for assessing couple and family relationships, the MSI–R offers advantages of assessing specific domains of the partners' relationship as well as providing extensive documentation regarding scores' reliability and validity (Snyder et al., 1995; Snyder & Aikman, 1999). Responses to the MSI–R are scored on 13 scales and categorized as indicating low, moderate, or extensive distress in each domain.

Overall, both Janice's and Mark's test results indicated moderate levels of marital distress (Global Distress scale), although somewhat less than most couples entering therapy. Mark expressed significant dissatisfaction with his and Janice's inability to resolve relationship conflicts (Problem Solving scale). His distress regarding difficulties in communication were most apparent in their sexual relationship (Sexual Dissatisfaction scale), although Mark's profile also indicated concerns regarding the couple's disagreements about finances (Disagreement About Finances scale).

Both Mark's and Janice's approach to describing their relationship on the MSI–R stood in stark contrast to their interactional styles during the interview. Whereas Mark disclosed significant marital discontent in several domains on the MSI–R, in the interview he tended to adopt a passive and nonconfrontive style. By contrast, Janice tended to dominate initial sessions with complaints concerning their marriage and respective families but tended to minimize these when completing the MSI–R.

The MSI–R findings presented an opportunity to identify both specific areas of concern and enduring communication difficulties as well as a commitment to, and general positive regard each felt toward, the other. I (DKS) interpreted Janice's tendency to minimize marital difficulties as stemming from her fear about the marriage's fragility and as depriving her and Mark an opportunity to build on relationship strengths by collaboratively confronting long-standing issues. I framed Mark's acquiescent style in the marriage as a conflict containment strategy he had learned in his family of origin that paradoxically maintained rather than resolved tensions with Janice. Both spouses were able to use these interpretations as a basis for initiating more candid discussion of enduring relationship concerns.

Early Interventions

Establishing an Alliance and Containing the Crisis. It was clear from the outset that developing a therapeutic alliance with both partners and promoting their own collaboration would require a delicate balance between acknowledging the importance of Janice's concerns while remaining sensitive to Mark's feelings of embarrassment and resentment about the magnitude of Janice's reactions during the previous week. Both partners appeared wary of psychological intervention following their reception at the emergency room of the local hospital. Janice's concerns regarding Mark's interest in sexually explicit magazines and its implications for their sons had been dismissed by medical staff; with that response she lost hope in receiving assistance with more pervasive concerns regarding their sexual relationship. Mark felt shamed by the public disclosure of his use of men's magazines during masturbation and believed that the hospital staff had viewed him with derision. In their initial therapy session following their dissatisfying visit to the hospital, Janice gained obvious comfort when I acknowledged the depth of her distress regarding their sexual relationship and the role that Mark's masturbation played in her feelings of insecurity in the marriage. Similarly, my empathic inquiry into Mark's own views of his sexual behaviors provided critical reassurance regarding the nonjudgmental context in which we could discuss these issues.

FIGURE 3.2. Couple profiles on the Marital Satisfaction Inventory–Revised (MSI–R) at initial assessment. Material from the Marital Satisfaction Inventory–Revised, © 1997 by Western Psychological Services. Used by permission of the publisher, Western Psychological Services. Not to be reprinted in whole or in part for any additional purpose without the expressed, written permission of the publisher. All rights reserved.

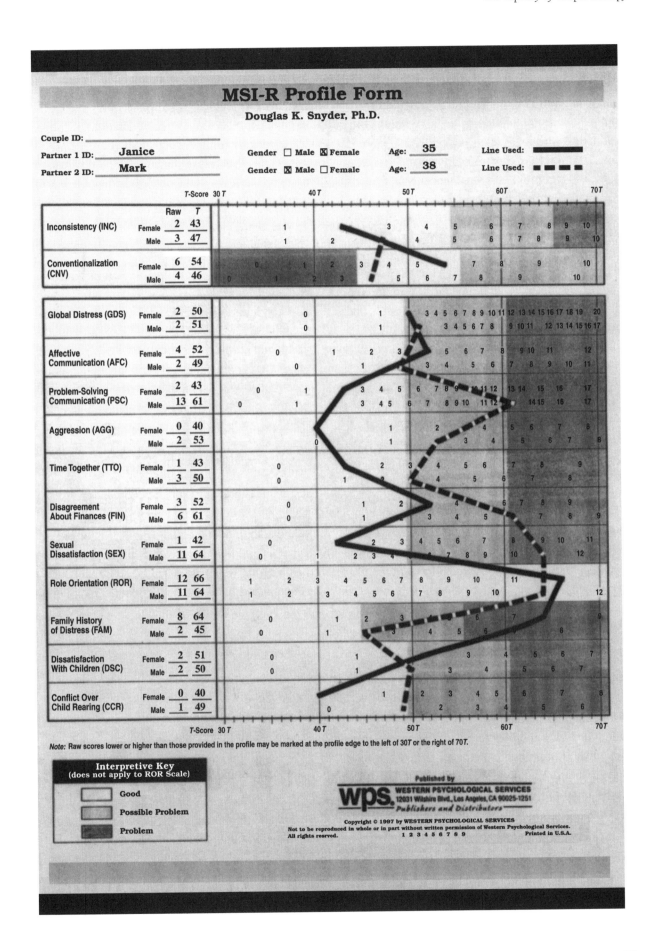

MSI-R Profile Form

Douglas K. Snyder, Ph.D.

Couple ID: _____

| Partner 1 ID: | **Janice** | Gender ☐ Male ☒ Female | Age: **35** | Line Used: ▄▄▄▄ |
| Partner 2 ID: | **Mark** | Gender ☒ Male ☐ Female | Age: **38** | Line Used: ▬ ▬ ▬ ▬ |

Note: Raw scores lower or higher than those provided in the profile may be marked at the profile edge to the left of 30T or the right of 70T.

Interpretive Key
(does not apply to ROR Scale)

☐ Good
◻ Possible Problem
■ Problem

Published by

WPS WESTERN PSYCHOLOGICAL SERVICES
12031 Wilshire Blvd., Los Angeles, CA 90025-1251
Publishers and Distributors

Copyright © 1997 by WESTERN PSYCHOLOGICAL SERVICES
Not to be reproduced in whole or in part without written permission of Western Psychological Services.
All rights reserved. 1 2 3 4 5 6 7 8 9   Printed in U.S.A.

Once I had heard both partners' views in an earnest and caring manner, each became more receptive to interventions aimed at stabilizing this initial crisis. Janice responded positively to my reassurance regarding her sons' well-being; by her own account, and by all other available evidence, Mark was a devoted and loving father. Similarly, once I allayed Mark's concerns about being identified as a potential child molester he became more receptive to Janice's broader concerns regarding their sexual relationship. Rather than constituting a crisis that demanded emergency intervention and jeopardized the marriage, Mark's interest in sexually explicit magazines became viewed as an indicator of communication difficulties exacerbated by situational stressors and individual concerns that predated the couple's relationship.

I made clear that I would respect each partner's feelings and attitudes toward his or her own sexuality and toward its expression individually and in their marriage. Mark and Janice were then able to negotiate an intermediate solution for dealing with their sexual relationship in which each spouse reduced pressures placed on the other. Mark temporarily suspended his requests for Janice to engage in greater frequency and variety of sexual behaviors, and she deferred her requests for Mark to eliminate his use of sexual materials for fantasy or masturbation. As each experienced greater acceptance from the other, they were able to rediscover the pleasure each had experienced previously in their sexual relationship; the frequency of intercourse increased, Janice felt more desired by Mark, and he felt less urgency for sexual stimulation through masturbation.

Strengthening the Marital Dyad. Mark and Janice both recognized that they needed to develop more effective communication skills for enhancing emotional intimacy and for resolving differences. However, two factors initially detracted from their ability to focus on developing these skills. First, the couple's fundamental friendship had eroded over the last several years; as a consequence, their marriage had become highly vulnerable to the situational stressors and inevitable strains of family life. The demands of child rearing contributed to this erosion, as did the pressures of Mark's work and Janice's return to school. Second, Mark and Janice had each failed to establish appropriate boundaries with their respective families of origin; the emotional energy that might otherwise be directed toward enhancing their own relationship continued to be drained by parents who demanded that Mark and Janice place higher priority on them rather than on themselves. I recognized that before the couple could pursue relationship skills they first needed to increase emotional autonomy from their families of origin and fortify a positive emotional platform in their marriage.

I encouraged Mark to talk with Janice about his needing more time alone for the two of them. He described his struggles to keep everything running at home during the week, cooking and doing dishes, cleaning the house, and keeping up with laundry so that Janice wouldn't have to contend with this on the weekends. At times he experienced her as being unappreciative or so caught up in her own academic struggles that they remained emotionally and physically separated even on weekends. He expressed a wish that Janice would be excited to see him on weekends and would express ways that she had missed him. Janice acknowledged her stress related to school and attributed this in part to her wish to achieve the same level of professional admiration from Mark as she felt toward him. She expressed her wish that Mark would plan more activities for their relationship, arrange for them to be alone together, and provide a relaxing environment. However, Janice also expressed concern for Mark and encouraged him to find ways of caring for himself better, even suggesting that he hire someone to help with housecleaning.

For several months Mark and Janice pursued various ways of strengthening their marriage. The couple focused on how they could better anticipate and manage stresses related to Janice's return to school. They planned a weekend away together, after which they announced strategies for reducing stress during the week and preserving both family and couple time on weekends. They also began to examine longer term strategies for promoting the family's well-being, including investing in a retirement fund, planning for the children's college education, and preparing to purchase a home of their own—all of which they achieved in the ensuing months.

Helping this couple to establish appropriate boundaries with their respective families of origin proved more difficult. Mark and Janice each continued to experience persistent anxieties regarding their roles in their own families, and they re-enacted many of these conflicts with their in-laws. The guilt that Janice experienced from her mother's complaints of neglect masked the resentment that she felt toward her mother's excessive demands and fueled the exaggerated anger she experienced toward Mark's mother when she criticized Janice's attention to her own career. Similarly, the discomfort Mark had experienced from the disharmony within his original family now generalized to conflict he perceived not only between Janice and his mother but also between Janice and her own mother. His efforts to broker a reconciliation between the contentious parties invariably aggravated the situation and deepened his sense of inadequacy.

With my support, Janice was able to discuss the conflict she experienced between feelings of loyalty for her mother and feelings of resentment toward her mother's demands and criticisms. When her mother became ill and required home-based nursing, Janice was able to facilitate these services and tolerate the modest guilt she experienced for not leaving school or her family to care for her mother full-time. She spoke with her mother by telephone daily but agreed with my suggestion to terminate these calls when her mother became excessively critical toward her. Janice's brother initially joined their mother in holding Janice responsible for their mother's care but subsequently assumed some of this care himself when Janice set limits on her own caregiving. Mark initially expressed considerable discomfort with the conflict in Janice's family as she redefined her role; however, with my encouragement he was able to refrain from intervening and instead trust Janice to negotiate these changes on her own. Mark's efforts at not mediating conflicts between Janice and her family resulted in her feeling greater support and confidence from Mark and in Janice having greater emotional reserves to invest in her marriage and children.

The couple's newly achieved confidence in negotiating boundaries eventually extended to Janice's relationship with Mark's mother. Mark became better able to distinguish between his wish for Janice and his parents to have a positive relationship and his general inability to produce this relationship himself. He accepted my directive not to engage in discussion with either party about the other—telling them instead that it was their relationship to work out, or not work out, on their own. In return, Janice agreed not to approach Mark with complaints about his mother. Gradually, Janice and Mark's parents found ways of talking directly with each other once Mark extracted himself from the role of mediator, and candid discussions of their respective wishes and disappointments slowly gave rise to a stronger alliance between them. Mark and Janice and their two sons subsequently spent a week at the beach with his parents and brothers, and they reported that the visit went surprisingly well.

Subsequent Interventions

Promoting Relevant Relationship Skills.

Throughout the beginning stages of therapy my interventions emphasized the importance of constructive communication skills, including emotional expressiveness, empathic listening, and problem solving. However, as is often the case with couples in crisis, Mark's and Janice's initial negativity interfered with their ability to develop or implement these skills successfully. As Mark and Janice strengthened their marriage by increasing positive time together and by establishing more appropriate boundaries with their respective families, they became more receptive to interventions that focused specifically on improving communication. Several sessions were devoted to process-focused communication skills, especially (a) identifying feelings and beliefs, (b) conveying these feelings and beliefs to one's partner, (c) paraphrasing (mirroring) feelings and beliefs expressed by one's partner, (d) checking out assumptions, (e) giving behavior–effect feedback, and (f) acknowledging differences in perspective (Snyder, 1999). Guidelines for teaching couples emotional expressiveness and listening skills have been described elsewhere (see Baucom & Epstein, 1990). Even after couples have acquired these skills, they sometimes find them difficult to implement during emotionally stressful exchanges; at such times it can be especially important to promote partners' exploration of feelings with the therapist before resuming efforts to do so with each other.

Mark and Janice used these communication techniques to explore their respective feelings regarding their sexual relationship. Mark was able to disclose the anxiety he felt about his own sexual adequacy, the affirmation he felt when Janice seemed to desire him sexually, and his own ambivalence regarding various sexual fantasies he had restricted to masturbation in order not to impose on Janice or elicit her rejection. Janice shared her own feelings of sexual inadequacy and described how these feelings were deepened by Mark's interest in men's magazines. She also disclosed her sensitivity about anything that reminded her of the abusive experiences in her first marriage. Mark became more understanding of Janice's reactions following this revelation and was better able to depersonalize her reactions and accommodate her limits. In turn, his increased acceptance of her sexuality encouraged Janice to initiate sexual exchanges more frequently.

Several additional sessions emphasized training in conflict resolution skills, including (a) identifying the problem, (b) generating and evaluating potential solutions, (c) selecting and implementing solutions, and (d) evaluating the solution's impact on the conflict and on the relationship. Consistent with their cognitive strengths and increased positivity in the marriage, Mark and Janice successfully applied these skills to a broad range of stresses in their family life, including finances, household management, and concerns regarding their sons' schoolwork and peer relations.

Challenging Cognitive and Developmental Components of Relationship Distress. While they struggled to establish more appropriate boundaries with their respective families of origin and to manage various stresses in their marriage, I was able to help Mark and Janice become more aware of the different styles for managing conflict they had observed growing up. Mark's parents were emotionally distant from one another; disagreements were rarely addressed directly between them, but resentment and conflict surfaced in their daily exchanges. Mark had learned a cautious approach to family interactions, avoiding potential triggers that might spark larger arguments and subsequent withdrawal and al-

ienation. By contrast, open conflict predominated in Janice's family. Her father's verbal aggression, exacerbated by his frequent alcohol abuse, had been contained only by reciprocal aggression by other family members. For Janice, rapid escalation of her own verbal aggression served a defensive function against anticipated criticism or emotional injury from Mark.

Early in their exploration of these dynamics, I encouraged Mark and Janice to challenge their own expectations regarding marital conflict. However, both partners continued to respond during arguments as they had in their families of origin. Over a period of several months, my efforts to promote new styles of communication required me to interpret Mark's and Janice's underlying anxieties regarding anticipated injury and rejection during these exchanges within session. A brief example of such an exchange is offered below:

Mark: I was wondering if maybe we could work today on something that came up this past week about our finances.

Janice: What are you talking about?

Mark: Well . . . you know, last Monday night.

Janice: [silence]

DKS: Mark, would you be willing to identify more specifically what your concern is?

Mark: Okay . . . well, this past Monday night I was paying bills, and Janice and I got into an argument . . .

DKS: Talk with Janice . . .

Mark: Okay . . . [looking at Janice] . . . *you* and I got into an argument. And it seemed like instead of being able to discuss the problem calmly, you blew up at me and were blaming me for the problem. . .

Janice: No, *you* were blaming *me* . . .

Mark: [long silence]

DKS: What's happening right now?

Mark: Well, it's happening again.

DKS: What's happening?

Mark: We just can't talk. If I bring up an issue, Janice gets all upset.

Janice: I'm *not* upset.

Mark: Just listen to your tone of voice.

DKS: [At this point the couple seemed stuck. I asked Mark to explore his feelings with me, anticipating that Mark could do so more freely and could then redirect his comments to Janice.] Mark, what are you feeling right now?

Mark: Frustrated.

DKS: What else?

Mark: Nervous, I guess.

DKS: Can you talk about that?

Mark: Well, I don't want Janice to be angry at me. Mostly, things have been going well between us. I don't want to upset the apple cart.

DKS: How's that going to work?

Mark: I know, I know. We've talked about this before. I know if I avoid it, we're going to have more problems later . . . because this money thing is important. We bounced two checks this last week. It just upsets me when Janice becomes angry, and then we don't talk.

DKS: [Mark's comments about his own apprehensions and concerns about the couple's communication process produced a softening in Janice's facial expressions and physical posture. I encouraged Mark at that point to redirect his comments to Janice.] Can you talk with her about those feelings?

Mark: Okay, look . . . [deep breath] . . . Janice, we need to talk about this. I don't want it to be a source of contention between us; I want us to be able to work this out together. It makes me nervous when I see us bouncing checks. . .

DKS: Talk with Janice about the nervousness you're feeling right now.

Mark: Well, it makes me nervous when I bring up an issue, and you right away snap back at me. I understand why you do that, that's how you protect yourself, but. (pause) . . . Okay, my own feelings . . .

well, I feel nervous. I'm afraid if we pursue this we'll get into a blaming cycle of who's at fault for the checks bouncing rather than how to fix it. I'm nervous about bouncing more checks. But mostly I'm nervous that we're going to enter another one of those cycles of being angry and not talking for days.

Janice: We're probably both to blame.

Mark: Well, I think you're probably right about that, but we can't get to that and figure it out if we right away launch into counterattacks. [pause]

DKS: [Janice had already acknowledged her own contribution to their communication struggles, and I prompted a more explicit response to Mark's anxiety.] Janice, what does Mark need right now?

Janice: Well, I think he needs me to listen to the problem first before telling him it wasn't my fault.

DKS: That's hard.

Janice: Yeah, it is . . . I know I screwed up on this one. I forgot to enter the cash I held back from my last paycheck to pay for the groceries last Friday.

Mark: Look, I should have recognized that something was wrong, too, before I wrote that check for the new tires.

DKS: [Janice's self-recrimination interfered with her ability to listen empathically to Mark's own anxiety about their finances. Helping her to gain insight into that pattern could potentially free the couple to explore their financial concerns in a less defensive and more constructive manner.] Janice, what happens when you think you might have screwed up?

Janice: Oh, God, it's awful. I get this panic. This time I'm really going to get it . . . there's no defense . . . it really is my fault . . . [pause]

DKS: Do you know where that feeling comes from?

Janice: Yeah, I do . . . [pause] . . . It's not from Mark. I mean we've talked about this before, right? I know that the best defense is a good offense . . . or that's what I learned. So that's what I fall back on with Mark. But it gets us in more trouble.

DKS: Is that what just happened in here?

Janice: I guess so.

DKS: What would it take for it to go differently?

Janice: I guess I have to remind myself that this is Mark, not Dad and not Mom. He's not going to attack me. [pause]

DKS: What does he need from you?

Janice: Well, he probably needs some reassurance that I'm not going to attack him . . .

Mark: Or pull back from me afterwards . . .

Janice: Yeah, that too . . . [pause] . . . Okay, you want to try again?

At this point Mark and Janice resumed their discussion using problem-solving strategies that they had acquired earlier in the therapy. Mark's anxiety regarding Janice's potential anger diminished, and he was able to identify problems related to their checking account and propose safeguards to ensure a more accurate accounting of their fund balances. Janice's defensiveness also declined, and she acknowledged her own contribution to their checking-account difficulties and collaborated with Mark in constructing strategies to reduce future problems. With time, both partners increased their ability to recognize their own contributions to the problems early in their disputes. Mark developed more tolerance for conflict, and Janice decreased her defensive anger. Although their respective maladaptive styles for managing conflict persisted at a reduced level, they were able to diminish the destructive effects of these patterns on their relationship.

CONCLUSION

Like most couples, Mark and Janice required interventions across multiple levels and domains of their relationship. Crisis stabilization regarding sexual issues commanded first priority. Strengthening the couple's relationship demanded intensive intervention emphasizing differentiation of the nuclear system from their respective extended families. Psychosocial stressors related to Mark's work and Janice's involvement in school required not only that the couple develop more effective management strategies at home but also that each increase his or her social support in the community. Honing communication skills dominated the latter half of therapy; however, reliable use of these skills required that I help both partners examine emotional overreactions having their roots in early family experiences.

Although Mark's and Janice's specific presenting complaints and respective individual histories are unique, the complexity of their concerns and their entanglement with early family experiences are common to many couples entering therapy. The tapestry of couple therapy demands the interweaving of theory, assessment, and interventions—selecting among diverse clinical techniques and implementing these in a strategic manner tailored to the couple's unique characteristics and needs.

References

Baucom, D. H., & Epstein, N. (1990). *Cognitive–behavioral marital therapy*. New York: Brunner/Mazel.

Heffer, R. W., & Snyder, D. K. (1998). Comprehensive assessment of family functioning. In L. L'Abate (Ed.), *Handbook of family psychopathology* (pp. 207–233). New York: Guilford Press.

Snyder, D. K. (1997). *Manual for the Marital Satisfaction Inventory—Revised*. Los Angeles: Western Psychological Services.

Snyder, D. K. (1999). Pragmatic couple therapy: An informed pluralistic approach. In D. M. Lawson & F. Prevatt (Eds.), *Casebook in family therapy* (pp. 81–110). Pacific Grove, CA: Brooks/Cole.

Snyder, D. K., & Aikman, G. A. (1999). The Marital Satisfaction Inventory—Revised. In M. E. Maruish (Ed.), *Use of psychological testing for treatment planning and outcomes assessment* (2nd ed., pp. 1173–1210). Mahwah, NJ: Erlbaum.

Snyder, D. K,, Cavell, T. A., Heffer, R. W., & Mangrum, L. F. (1995). Marital and family assessment: A multifaceted, multilevel approach. In R. H. Mikesell, D. D. Lusterman, & S. H. McDaniel (Eds.), *Integrating family therapy: Handbook of family psychology and systems theory* (pp. 163–182). Washington, DC: American Psychological Association.

CHAPTER 4

THE THERAPIST IN THE CRUCIBLE: EARLY DEVELOPMENTS IN A NEW PARADIGM OF SEXUAL AND MARITAL THERAPY

David Schnarch

When treatment goes well, I, like many therapists, never doubt that I have chosen the right career. In my case, getting treatment to go well required more than becoming more skillful—it involved radically changing how I conducted therapy. Along the way, my notions about the appropriate content, pattern, tone, and intensity of the "working-through" process —the yardsticks by which I gauged therapy and couples' marriages to be going well—shifted drastically. Ideas about what constitutes a "good" or "bad" (read: "difficult") client came undone. Ultimately, this cascade of changes altered my understanding of the nature and processes of marriage[1] and of psychotherapy. I thank and blame my clients for my professional and personal metamorphosis, which eventually led me to develop the Crucible Approach™ to integrated sexual and marital therapy.

Back in the early 1980s, I was dissatisfied with the "sensate-focus" mold of 1960s and 1970s sex therapy in which I had been trained. Seemingly sex-positive notions such as "sex is a natural function" spawned an inherently pathology-based therapy focused on removing blockages and inhibitions (believed to be interfering with spontaneous sexual function and desire). "Non-demand pleasuring" (a part of sensate-focus exercises) subtly pressured clients to feel relaxed, creating "performance-anxiety anxiety" (Apfelbaum, 1983).[2] Sexual desire was approached as a biological drive to be exhumed (e.g.,

inhibited sexual desire; Kaplan, 1979) rather than a capacity to be developed. Conventional sex therapy focused on symptom reduction rather than personal growth.

Eventually, I completely abandoned conventional sex therapy and the work of Masters and Johnson (1970, 1976, 1986) and Helen Singer-Kaplan (1974, 1979). I felt I should and could be doing more to help my clients. Sex therapy was (and often still is) practiced as a separate clinical discipline unto itself, a narrow subspecialty focused on sexual behavior. I always seemed to be dealing with "parts": body parts, sex as a part of people, and sex as part of a relationship. Urologists and marital therapists asked me to deal with the "sex parts" of their cases. I was looking for a more holistic psychotherapy.

Thirty years ago (and still today) sex therapists patched together a conglomerate of behavior modification, sensory awareness "exercises," communication skills training, individual psychotherapy, and marital therapy, strung together with conceptualizations from psychodynamic, object-relations, and attachment theories. Unfortunately, this "grab bag" eclecticism was not a virtue, because the fields of sexology and marital therapy developed independently of each other, giving rise to separate literatures, practices, concepts, and theories. Conventional "broad-band" sex therapy often involved inelegant intervention strategies based on contradic-

---

[1] I use the term *marriage* to refer to an emotionally committed relationship, regardless of legal status or sexual orientation.

[2] *Performance-anxiety anxiety* (also called *response anxiety*) is anxiety about feeling performance anxiety in treatment oriented to reduce performance anxiety. Conventional sex therapy makes feeling performance anxiety about sensate-focus exercises seem inappropriate.

tory ideologies that escaped clinicians' awareness. For example, common marital therapy strategies (e.g., encouraging compromise and negotiation) can create low sexual desire. Likewise, Singer-Kaplan's strategy for treating low sexual desire ("bypassing"; Singer-Kaplan, 1987) was inherently antithetical to intimacy.[3]

Within conventional sex therapy, performance anxiety was the paramount issue. However, actual understanding of and focus on anxiety per se was extremely limited, both regarding its pervasiveness in relationships as well as ways couples customarily cope with it. Treatment focused on anxiety reduction rather than on helping people increase their anxiety tolerance. Emphasis on anxiety reduction limited conventional sex therapy's utility in resolving sexual problems and limited its applicability to other aspects of marriage in which anxiety tolerance (rather than anxiety reduction) is key (e.g., having children and parenting).

In addition to performance anxiety, sexual problems were thought to be caused by the four "I's": ignorance, ineptitude, inhibition, and ineffective technique. The proposed solution involved therapists giving clients information, "permission" to be sexual, and telling them what to do and not do sexually. Sexual prescriptions (e.g., take turns giving and receiving) and proscriptions (e.g., "bans" on intercourse) were more than standard procedures; such homework assignments were defining hallmarks of modern sex therapy. These clinical strategies and the therapist's stance in treatment were never scrutinized through the lens of differentiation; in the same way, differentiation was absent in conceptualizing clients' difficulties or possible benefits of treatment. In many instances, standard sex therapy practices (e.g., prescriptions and proscriptions) positioned the therapist in an undifferentiated clinical stance and prompted boundary setting and rebellion (resistance) by clients.

In the 1980s I became fascinated by Murray Bowen's (1978; Kerr & Bowen, 1988) theories of differentiation. Bowen never actually applied his brilliant ideas to working with couples' sex and intimacy; however, I found his writings helpful in both organizing my observations about couples' sex and intimacy and developing new powerful clinical interventions. I began to suspect that differentiation was at the core of the ebb and flow of sex, love, and intimacy in emotionally committed relationships. In hindsight this may seem obvious, but at that time thinking this way was antithetical to both theory and practice of sex therapy.

Differentiation theory provided a basis for an entirely new paradigm of sex therapy, isomorphic in theory and practice.[4] For example, the ability to regulate one's own anxiety and willingness to tolerate discomfort for growth (i.e., differentiation) turned out to be far more important to maintaining sexual passion and emotional intimacy in ongoing relationships than communication skills, "safety and security," and receiving validation from one's partner. I found I could help clients resolve sexual problems in ways that enhanced their differentiation, making them more capable of tolerating intense intimacy and more resilient to performance anxiety in and out of bed. Their whole lives changed in the process. My therapy increasingly focused on self-validated intimacy and self-soothing, whereas traditional sexual and marital therapies emphasized reciprocal validation and "give to get" strategies. Often I found myself breaking up the very interactions between couples that traditional therapy encouraged.

Ultimately, my clinical approach departed from conventional sex therapy in four specific ways: One was the absence of standardized "exercises," structured activities, prescriptions and proscriptions, and homework. Another involved a shift away from sensation-based approaches (i.e., rooted in sensate-focus exercises) in favor of one rooted in intimacy

[3] Dr. William Masters was well aware of the intimacy-incongruent nature of sensate-focus exercises, which is why he attempted to compensate by having the "receiver" give feedback to the "giver" (personal communication, March 3, 1997).

[4] *Isomorphism* refers to similarity or congruity between different levels of operation. Isomorphic clinical practice occurs when various parts of an intervention strategy create cofacilitative desirable affects on multiple levels (e.g., both individuals, their relationship, and family system)—even when apparently aimed at one partner or one level of the system. For optimal clinical effectiveness, elements of theory and intervention strategy must each be internally consistent as well as consistent with each other.

and developing intimacy tolerance.[5] This allowed the third change: approaching clients' spontaneous sexual behaviors as meaningful and purposeful communication (i.e., an *elicitation* approach) rather than reflecting ignorance, individual pathology, or relational dysfunction.[6] A fourth change was a shift in the focus of treatment away from analyzing clients' resistances and toward using common sexual difficulties to create personal and relationship growth (Schnarch, 1995).[7]

These (and other) changes led to two important developments: One was developing a nonpathological model of how emotionally committed relationships evolved, including partners' interaction patterns and subjective experiences that lead to emotional gridlock, all driven by the natural unfolding of human differentiation (Schnarch, 1991, 1997/ 1998). The other development involved creation of a multisystemic[8] marital and sexual therapy that harnesses differentiation as it plays out in sex and intimacy within marriage: the Crucible Approach™ (Schnarch, 1991).

Progress toward this new approach did not really take off until I started to focus on working with difficult clients, especially those who were considered "treatment failures" in their prior therapies. These were the cases that made me throw away my teachings and listen with a fresh ear. They provided incentive to do things differently, because the tried-and-true ways had not worked for them. Clients who were considered "difficult" because they had not responded well to conventional sex therapy often proved most helpful (and taxing) in this regard.

In all honesty I can say this was not something that I was always eager to do. It is hard to practice your profession while giving up the tools of your trade. The tough cases also challenged my own differentiation. I knew the theory that differentiation had four main facets: (a) maintaining a clear sense of yourself while remaining close to your partner, (b) self-soothing your anxiety, (c) not getting "infected" with your partner's anxieties, and (d) tolerating discomfort for growth. It was "killer clients," however, who showed me how differentiation—developing a "self" by maintaining oneself in a relationship—operates as a real world process in therapy as well as in the bedroom.

Let me tell you about one such couple, who went from being every sex therapist's nightmare to one of my most warmly remembered cases. When I encountered them I was at mid-career, experienced in conducting and teaching sex therapy and ready for a change. I did not know it at the time, but the clinical dilemma they presented would change the way I subsequently did therapy with all of my clients.

CASE EXAMPLE

Mrs. Z and Mr. Z, both in their early 40s, consulted me about their long-standing sexual and marital difficulties. From the time of his initial adolescent sexual experiences, Mr. Z had had almost unrelenting erection difficulty during intercourse, which continued over the course of their 14-year marriage. For her part, Mrs. Z resented repeatedly being "left hanging" and frustrated when Mr. Z lost his erection shortly after intromission. In the past 4 years she had become less receptive to Mr. Z's initiations and increasingly reactive when Mr. Z lost his erection during intercourse.

Mr. and Mrs. Z had been in treatment twice before. First they worked with a marital therapist who said their bedroom problems were a reflection of

---

[5] The notion of intimacy tolerance is antithetical to conventional sex therapy's view that couples suffer from lack of intimacy. Based on this flip in perspective, the Crucible Approach™ focuses on helping couples tolerate the intimacy inherent in intimate relationships (and reduce emotional fusion) rather than producing exercises to create intimacy (and increase "communication" and "attachment").

[6] Sensate-focus exercises interfere with using clients' sexual interaction as an elicitation window.

[7] See Schnarch (2000) for elaboration on the Crucible Approach™'s paradigm shift from the work of Masters and Johnson and Singer-Kaplan, especially with regard to conceptualization and treatment of sexual desire problems.

[8] A true multisystemic (ecosystemic) approach not only recognizes and intervenes in multiple systems (e.g., object relations, unconscious processes, family-of-origin issues, current family and social systems), but it also organizes the interaction of these systems in a consistent and effective way. The Crucible Approach recognizes all of these systems but organizes them around differentiation rather than making any one of them the primary conceptual or clinical focus.

problems elsewhere in their relationship. However, initial improvements in "communication" disappeared when their sexual difficulties also failed to improve. They subsequently tried conventional sex therapy, using sensate-focus exercises. This was, by their estimate, "a complete catastrophe." Mrs. Z often argued with the therapist over "homework assignments" after which she fought with her husband about siding with the therapist instead of with her. On a number of occasions, Mr. and Mrs. Z did not follow the therapist's "rule" to refrain from intercourse or touching each other's genitals. When the therapist interpreted their behavior as resistance, Mrs. Z refused to continue treatment. Two years later, Mr. and Mrs. Z were ready to try again with me.

Session 1

In our initial meeting Mr. Z looked apologetic and ashamed, falling all over himself in attempts to say the right thing. As it turned out, this mirrored his style of trying to please his wife in bed and please everyone else in his life. Mr. Z's slight build and occasional stammer made it easy to treat him like an awkward boy—the same way Mrs. Z did.

From the outset of treatment Mr. and Mrs. Z demonstrated what I later recognized as *emotional gridlock* (Schnarch, 1991), the same deadlocked emotional fusion of needs and issues that created their worst sexual fiascos. In bed Mr. Z tried too hard to do his "duty." His anxiety and desperation to please his wife—and prove himself—made him lose his erection during intercourse. Mrs. Z compounded things by accusing him of not trying hard enough to satisfy her.

I could tell the inherent paradox was lost on them when in our initial session Mrs. Z accused Mr. Z of sexual incompetence and emotional indifference. Embarrassed, Mr. Z countered by claiming that Mrs. Z was argumentative and afraid of intimacy. Within a few minutes both were emotionally bruised, sitting in silence, with little soothing or understanding to offer each other. Neither could validate the other's perceptions without feeling invalidated in the process or worse, having to confront himself or herself in some unacceptable or intolerable way.

As if that were not enough, Mr. and Mrs. Z added another layer of gridlock to the therapeutic processes. Mrs. Z broke the silence by turning to me and demanding that I give her some idea of how long treatment would take and what I intended to ask them to do. Her tone said she was not volunteering to do whatever I suggested. She was inviting me to defend my competency by submitting an effective plan of action and, moreover, one that she liked.

In retrospect it was as though Mrs. Z was asking me to commit to a position so that lines of battle could be drawn—and engagement could therefore occur. We were simply negotiating the terms of treatment, in the same way every couple negotiates during foreplay the depth and meaning of the sex that follows. In the moment, however, it was hard to see this, because I felt like I was being trapped.

Sooner or later I knew I would get around to assigning fairly standardized "homework"—exactly what Mrs. Z wanted to sniff out. I thought Mrs. Z had a consumer's right to ask these questions—only I did not want to give her an answer. I knew this was the battleground on which their prior therapy had died, and my gut sense of the moment said that Mrs. Z's questions were not simply about informed consent and consumer advocacy.

I began trying to sidestep Mrs. Z's request. She appeared to recognize what I was doing and seemed to enjoy my discomfort. As I felt myself "twisting in the wind," searching for a way out, Mr. Z added another layer to the dilemma: He said he was worried that I *wasn't* going to give them specific instructions and sexual assignments. My attempts to dodge Mrs. Z triggered his fears that nothing would change sexually for him. Mr. Z joined with his wife in requesting my treatment plan and a statement of planned sexual exercises.

Part of what made this situation particularly difficult was the manner in which Mr. Z offered himself as my obedient student whom I was to instruct. Mr. Z was too willing, for the wrong reason, to place himself under my tutelage. I did not want to participate in Mr. Z subjugating himself in a deferential role with me. Approached the way Mr. Z was offering, therapy might do nothing to free him from being a perpetual "wimp" even if he developed better erections. The more Mr. Z did what he thought a good client should do, the worse my clinical dilemma became.

There was also the problem that Mrs. Z was not willing to do likewise. Mrs. Z said she had refused to do the prior therapist's assignments "as a matter of principle and autonomy." She offered other examples of rebelling when she felt she was being told what to do. Mrs. Z's notion of autonomy particularly applied to possible suggestions from me that might involve doing anything novel, anxiety provoking, or requiring effort and practice. Although she said that she felt some responsibility for their lack of progress, she was no more willing to follow my dictates than she was those of the previous therapist. To top things off, Mrs. Z declared that she was fed up, tired, and emotionally spent. She demanded quick results while simultaneously declaring herself unwilling to do much.

All told, Mr. and Mrs. Z looked like a "difficult pair" on their way to another treatment failure. Part of what made their treatment so difficult was that both partners' individual issues were pushing in directions where sex therapy—and sex therapists— were paradigmatically vulnerable. Knowing that sex therapy (of the day) involved prescriptions and proscriptions made it harder to see my way out of the dilemma this couple presented. Initial bans on intercourse and prescriptions for "non-genital, non-demand pleasuring," for example, were standard parts of erectile dysfunction treatment. Finding a new solution involved, for me, the same four aspects of differentiation couples face when seeking a new equilibrium in their marriage: I had to abandon familiar trappings and an identity that is no longer satisfying, calm my anxieties and misgivings (triggered by this challenge to my sense of self), and tolerate the ensuing discomfort as the price of growth. Appreciating the systemic elegance of it all does not make a therapist much better at doing it in the moment.

Mr. and Mrs. Z presented a complex set of dynamics with which conventional sex therapy could not cope. Mrs. Z outright refused to do the backbone activity of sex therapy: sensate focus. Mr. Z needed some assignment to feel secure. I knew how to resolve erectile dysfunction only through sensate-

focus exercises. Moreover, the breathtaking acceleration and velocity of issues surfacing in treatment through their respective demands was more than I —and probably most therapists—could comfortably handle.

Without realizing it this couple was, once again, stretching my differentiation. Bowen had observed that it is easier for a therapist to function when things are calm; when anxiety is high, clinical decisions are often based on a therapist's attempt to reduce his or her anxiety rather than well thought out therapeutic principles (Kerr & Bowen, 1988, p. 141). I had to remind myself many times that it was Mr. and Mrs. Z, and not I, who were stuck in an apparently untenable set of contradictory demands for therapy. The fact that my own professional and personal anxieties blended so nicely with their issues made it hard to remain nonreactive to Mrs. Z's repeated prodding to tell her what activities I might assign.

I tried out a number of possible strategies in my mind. I dimly recognized that Mrs. Z was pressuring me to accommodate to her comfort level. The fact that it fit perfectly with Bowen's description of attempted anxiety regulation through accommodation did not help much. I did not think that teaching Mrs. Z differentiation theory would offer much protection from her questioning. I also briefly considered giving an interpretation linking Mr. and Mrs. Z's respective positions as a collusive attempt to triangulate me and make me carry their anxiety.

Although these observations certainly fit Bowenian theory—and might have been true in this case to some degree—I decided against this course of action. I could not get around the fact that this might sound like a "resistance" interpretation, just like the one that had been the finale of Mr. and Mrs. Z's prior therapy. I was sure that suggesting Mr. and Mrs. Z were colluding unconsciously to raise my anxiety and immobilize me would bring a swift end to our meeting. No, interpretation was not the vehicle—even if Mr. and Mrs. Z were triangulating me, Bowen's proposed solution involved (the therapist's) differentiation rather than interpretation.

Moreover, I was not convinced that our situation arose because of collusion by Mr. and Mrs. Z. I knew part of the problem came from my knowing how to conduct therapy only in the ways I did. It also seemed that each spouse was driven by his or her individual anxieties in ways that created an emotionally gridlocked system with which I—and they—had to cope. Each wanted to take a position that was blocked by the position his or her partner wanted to take (to reduce his or her anxiety). Neither partner seemed able to accommodate the preferences of the other.[9]

That is not to say that I naively assumed these clients had no idea of what was happening for me. Mrs. Z was tenacious in pushing for an answer she sensed I did not want to give. She reminded me, for example, that I was a sex therapist and that she knew sex therapists gave homework assignments. I did not want to struggle with Mrs. Z about prescriptions and exercises, but at the same time I knew that backing down when she pressured me was a bad general strategy. When Mr. Z feared I would cave into his wife's terms for treatment, he indeed joined with his wife in demanding to hear about my treatment plan. However, this joining was superficial at best—they were really at odds with each other over an issue, and they both demanded clarification from me. I myself was not overjoyed that they could finally agree on something.

Baffled and perplexed by what to do next, I said the only thing that came to mind: "I'm sorry, I can't tell you what I'm going to do. I don't know. Only good sex therapists give homework assignments."

Mrs. Z laughed and asked, "Then what are you?"

"I'm a bad one," I said tongue in cheek. "You've already seen a 'good one.' Would you like me to refer you to another good one?"

"No," she responded; "We've seen one of those, and he was useless. Besides, I'm not a good patient, either! I ask for help, and then I won't take it."

Suddenly, I found myself charmed by Mrs. Z's wit and candor. What moments earlier had seemed combative and oppositional had suddenly changed to a reasonable, even jocular, interaction. I was struck by how quickly the tone and the alliance could change. In the past I might have offered Mrs. Z an interpretation, linking her rebellious "resistance

to treatment" to her family-of-origin issues. Now I saw how this would have only locked us into the very reality I thought I was trying to ameliorate.

In the past I might have discussed with Mrs. Z the difference between her husband's physical readiness for sex and his psychological readiness for sex and explained that touching him might be pleasing and arousing to him (and her) and might increase his psychological readiness for intercourse and feelings of intimacy between them. In this case, however, trying to convince Mrs. Z to do sensate-focus exercises as a way to ultimately get the sex she wanted just was not going to work.

Instead, I reassured Mrs. Z that I would not give her any homework assignments. I would not presume to tell her what to do, in part, because she had convinced me that this was a foolish thing to do with her. Moreover, I said that she should not follow any suggestions on the basis of my authority. Mrs. Z had an absolute right to decline to do anything, even if that precluded getting the results she wanted.

Mrs. Z looked relieved and triumphant, but Mr. Z appeared deflated. My recognition of Mrs. Z's control and authority made her beam, but it also scared her husband. Mr. Z now feared I would just "sit there passively and listen," never suggesting anything new. He was afraid I was capitulating to his wife and abandoning his interests. I reassured Mr. Z that I would offer suggestions when I had them; how they used my input was up to them. Mr. Z was not convinced. To him, sensate-focus exercises were the magic technique he needed—and I was supposed to convince his wife to do them. Mr. Z thought I was buckling under pressure from his wife and withholding from him the secret solution he was desperate to find.

Remember, I was searching for a workable position that would establish a productive alliance with *both* spouses (i.e., an isomorphic stance). I really did not think the exercises I knew would help Mr. and Mrs. Z, although I was not sure what would. When Mr. Z asked why I was declining to prescribe sensate focus, I acknowledged that it might seem that I

---

[9]Emotional gridlock is not reducible to unconscious processes, family-of-origin issues, or communication problems.

was bowing to his wife's terms for treatment. Although his wife might be delighted with my decision, I proposed, my stance was in accord with his own best interests. I offered Mr. Z two reasons why prescribed activities were unlikely to succeed, starting with the fact that they had already been tried previously without success. As I began to mention my second point Mrs. Z rose to defend herself, apparently thinking I was referring to her noncompliance in their prior therapy. She was as surprised as Mr. Z was when I continued to talk to him as if she had not moved at all.

I took what felt like a tremendous therapeutic gamble: I suggested that the second reason prescribed activities were likely to fail was because Mr. Z was *too* willing to do them. Mr. Z was desperate to maintain his erection to prove to himself and his wife that he was not as inadequate as he felt or appeared. He was running scared, frantically seeking a solution on the basis of feeling inadequate and unworthy rather than believing he really could do better. I said that I feared we could go about treatment in ways that might improve his erections but leave intact his feelings of inadequacy and his need to measure up to other people's expectations. I proposed that Mr. Z might be too eager to take my suggestions and perhaps could benefit from a touch of his wife's attitude. I concluded by saying, "I don't think your penis is going to work the way you want until it's clear that it belongs to *you*."

I waited to see what happened next, but the explosion I feared did not come. I had unwittingly practiced what has become a basic principle in the Crucible Approach™: *Always talk to the best in people*. The outcome of my gamble, in retrospect, was fairly predictable. Rather than being insulted or more anxious, Mr. and Mrs. Z settled down. The tension in the room dropped markedly. Mr. Z seemed sobered and more grounded but not unduly crushed and asked me what I had in mind to help him. I said I did not know specifically, but I knew one thing: We had to find a way to work together that involved Mr. Z "running his own penis instead of turning it over to someone else," including *me*.[10]

Mrs. Z seemed genuinely interested in the conversation in a whole new way. To my surprise, she nodded in agreement. She did not like the allusion that Mr. Z had a hard time holding onto himself with her, but she disliked even more the pitiful ways that Mr. Z tried to placate her and everyone else. It killed her respect and sexual desire for him. She liked my straight talk. In an unusual way, it treated Mr. Z with respect—more respectfully than either of them had anticipated. He certainly did not seem emasculated by our interaction—in fact, he acted as though he was just a tad more adult.

All three of us left the session feeling a little surprised. Although Mr. and Mrs. Z had moments of contention later on, the content and tone of our initial meeting veered away from the debacle they were anticipating and creating. Twenty minutes into our first session, none of us would have predicted we would end on a positive note. They both commented that they had never anticipated our meeting would go down the path it did; on this point, I certainly had to agree. In addition to the issue of genital function we now had the self-image and interpersonal aspects of Mr. Z's lack of phallicness on the table. I left feeling absolutely drained, intellectually stimulated, emotionally moved, and very much alive.

Session 2

In the following week Mr. and Mrs. Z were front and center in my reveries about my clients. I had done more than get myself off the hook with Mrs. Z. The struggle over "exercises" dissolved into a more relevant holistic focus and a more workable alliance. I had a vague notion that we were on a path that might lead Mr. Z to become more differentiated, more solid in his sense of himself, less riddled with anxiety, and less reactive to his wife. Not only would this be beneficial in itself, but also it could reduce his difficulties with erections during intercourse. What I greatly liked about this stance with Mr. Z was that it also aligned me with Mrs. Z in a less combative manner than she anticipated—I even

---

[10] This position corrected the undifferentiated clinical stance created by a therapist giving sexual prescriptions and proscriptions, which was the downfall in Mr. and Mrs. Z's prior treatment.

saw something admirable in her. I still was not clear about how we would focus on reducing in-the-moment performance anxiety during sex, but I was still excited. I had stumbled on a clinical stance about behavioral prescriptions that worked for both spouses simultaneously on multiple levels (i.e., what I now call *multisystemic isomorphic intervention*). It served both partners' goals, focused on intimacy (rather than sensation) and personal growth (rather than symptom reduction), created a well-balanced alliance with each spouse, and reorganized treatment in ways that encouraged each spouse's ability to hold onto himself or herself (rather than relying on me). As I began to consider how my new stance on behavioral prescriptions lined up better with my growing understanding of differentiation, I began to wonder about two ideas which, years later, now are certainties: First, what may appear to a couple as irreconcilable differences—and appear to a therapist as irreconcilable demands and impossible terms for treatment—often resolve if the therapist can maintain a well-differentiated stance. Second, resolving couples' sexual problems often requires and permits resolving long-standing unresolved developmental tasks. The more I considered these ideas, the more I could not wait for Mr. and Mrs. Z to come back.

However, all was not glorious. The new position I had taken now presented a novel situation in Session 2: I really didn't know what to do next. I had just shelved the homework activities that defined treatment as I knew it. Moreover, standard sex therapy focused on anxiety reduction, and I had gone in the other direction. I had raised the ante—and the meaning—of treatment by talking frankly about anxiety-provoking topics rather than pacifying and containing the situation. Now I was feeling my way, trying to apply what I knew about erectile dysfunction in a whole new package that fit this particular couple's dynamics.

Having given up trying to "lead" Mr. and Mrs. Z, I decided to "follow" them instead. Forgoing the laborious sexual histories I usually obtained, I asked them to describe in detail how they went about having sex. I wanted to understand what they did and did not do, and how they did (and did not) do it. I was looking for something—anything—that might offer a new point of intervention.

At first, Mrs. Z was aghast. She challenged my need and right to know such intimate details, particularly because neither of the other therapists had asked for them. My pointing out that I'd already said I wasn't a good therapist brought a smile back to her face. I reinforced her right not to reveal anything she wished, even if it diminished the likelihood of getting the results they sought. I left the prerogative and responsibility with Mr. and Mrs. Z, and it obviously made them anxious. Once again, the anxiety reduction paradigm of conventional sex therapy pulled one way, and anxiety tolerance and differentiation pulled another.

Mr. Z then volunteered to describe how they "made love." Although it felt like I was interfering with my own request for information, I had an urge to stop him. If this was Mr. Z's attempt to please me, I did not want to hear what he was about to say. I also did not want to trigger a control fight with Mrs. Z about the details of their sex life. On the other hand, if this was Mr. Z standing on his own two feet, then I was eager to listen. I shared my thoughts with Mr. Z, who took a moment to reflect on where he was coming from. In that moment, something I would normally gloss over—how the dynamics of differentiation played out in the data-gathering process—suddenly seemed laden with significance.

Mr. Z decided his best judgment prompted him to continue his description, and Mrs. Z did not object, whereupon there emerged a picture of foreplay I had heard many times from couples struggling with erection problems. Mr. and Mrs. Z typically lay in bed with the lights off. His wife lay on her back with her eyes closed. Mr. Z hovered over her, perched on one elbow, stroking her breasts and then her genitals with his other hand, scanning her impassive face for some reaction. When she would permit him to continue, he would bring her to orgasm by rubbing her clitoris before they attempted coitus. On most occasions when Mrs. Z was close to orgasm, she would stop his hand and pull him on top of her, signaling that she wanted to have intercourse. This usually culminated in Mr. Z losing his erection and Mrs. Z pushing him off of her in anger. At this point Mr. Z usually offered to bring her to orgasm with his hand or tongue, which Mrs. Z often declined as a second-class substitute for the "real thing." Mr. Z would then stimulate himself to a second erection and bring himself to orgasm manually or "finish himself off inside her" when his ejaculation was imminent.

I was struck by how Mr. and Mrs. Z's pattern of sex revealed so much about them as people. Mr. Z acted as if he had no right to ask or expect his wife to touch his penis.[11] There was no thought that he had the right to decline having intercourse when his wife told him she was ready. He believed his job was to do what his wife expected, even if it led to repeated disappointment and failure. When I asked what he liked about doing it this way, Mr. Z commented "I like that she does not reject me when I touch her. I like pleasing her, and I like it when she has orgasms, too. It feels very warm and close with her."

For her part, Mrs. Z said she liked the closeness but that she didn't need the constant frustration during intercourse. On the other hand, Mrs. Z acted like there was no choice but to play out this pattern of deprivation—and then get angry about it all over again. When I asked Mrs. Z why she never touched her husband's penis, she replied that "he didn't need it" because he always got an erection sufficient for intercourse (at least at first). I stopped assuming that this resulted from inhibitions and ineffective technique and began to wonder what kinds of experiences Mr. and Mrs. Z might have gone through that would make this pattern acceptable and reasonable to them.

We did not cover a lot of ground in that session, but how we got to what we talked about seemed as important as the actual content of what was said. I offered no suggestions to Mr. and Mrs. Z about what they should do or not do—mainly because I was not sure myself. I needed time outside the session to think. I did manage to comment that they must be very lonely while they had sex. In my mind's eye I could see Mr. Z lost in his anxiety and anticipating her anger. I imagined Mrs. Z hoping against hope and feeling set up to get angry one more time. My

comment seemed to take them by surprise. Mr. and Mrs. Z left my office in a somber mood.

Session 3

In between sessions, I kept trying to put the emerging pieces of their picture together. At first I could not understand how Mr. Z could possibly feel warm and close to his wife during sex, given how they described going about it. Then I realized I could square his subjective experience with his behavioral report—but only if I also made certain assumptions. One assumption was that Mr. Z was not used to very much intimacy with his wife—or, for that matter, with anyone. Second, he could report feeling close to her in the sex they had if he had relatively little tolerance for intimacy as well. Finally, his report of "good feelings" probably came from how others saw him rather than how he saw himself. Hypotheses about differentiation issues in their families of origin were starting to come to mind. I looked forward to our next meeting and checking out if these were true.

Mr. and Mrs. Z opened our next session by announcing that it was high time I laid out my game plan. Mrs. Z said she was not interested in therapy if I had no idea where we were going. I said I still was not sure about what to do but that their description of their sexual interactions gave me a much better understanding of what was going on. Mr. Z apparently thought I was about to talk to him about improving his technique. Instead, I suggested that he probably came from a family where he never felt secure enough to say, "Is it me you really love, or just what I do for you?"

Mr. Z acted like my statement took him totally by surprise and asked me to explain what I meant. I said he acted like a man still trying to live up to his parents' expectations, attempting to please them to make himself feel acceptable and worthwhile. I proposed that he probably never got a chance to relax with—and be with—the people he loved. His behavior screamed, "Please give me a chance to prove myself! I'll be whatever you want. Just love me."

---

[11] If I had instructed Mrs. Z to stroke his penis I would have destroyed the opportunity for Mr. Z to eventually work up the courage to ask for this, removing an important opportunity for him to increase his differentiation.

Mr. Z did not know quite what to say. At first he started to argue, "What does this have to do with sex?" Then he simply stopped and said, "How did you figure this out? You're describing my relationship with my father." I said it was encoded in his sexual behavior. By not prescribing non-demand pleasuring and sensate focus, I could see him through what he was already doing.

Mr. Z began to describe his family of origin, and the picture was not pretty: a highly successful but abusive and alcoholic father known outside the house as a pillar of the community, an explosive-tempered and image-conscious mother still denying her childhood of poverty. Rather than exploring his childhood at length, however, I brought the focus back to Mr. and Mrs. Z's sexual interaction. Given his developmental experiences, it was quite conceivable—if not likely—that Mr. Z could be functioning within my three hypotheses about how his sexual style and his self-report fit together.

I think all three of us were a little surprised that we did not dwell on Mr. Z's childhood experiences at greater length. Just a short time ago, I would have tended to see this as the "real stuff" I was after. Mr. and Mrs. Z, like many clients, also thought so. However, family-of-origin issues, rather than being our primary focus, became one of many lenses we used to look at their sexual interactions. I kept our focus on the patterns etched in their sexual routine, because I was fascinated by what was emerging—and because I felt some responsibility to pursue a solution to Mr. Z's erectile problem.

Not fully realizing what I was doing at first, I began to work back and forth between Mr. and Mrs. Z's current sexual interactions and their unresolved differentiation issues. I used their sexual style to make educated guesses about the kind of developmental experiences they might have had, and I used the details they provided to make sense of their sexual interactions. Gradually, I began to realize just how out of touch Mr. and Mrs. Z were when they had sex.

Mr. Z was totally isolated in his desperation and anxiety, anticipating failure and rejection, preoccupied with the referendum on his adequacy as a man and a lover and focused on how his erection was doing. Even as he slavishly tried to satisfy his wife,

he really wasn't *with* her. A sex therapy approach that reduced sex to "friction plus fantasy" (Singer-Kaplan, 1974) was not going to help.

Beyond deliberately tuning out to keep herself from being disappointed, Mrs. Z's isolation was a little harder to see but, like many people, Mrs. Z tuned out her partner and focused on sensations in her loins in order to be able to achieve orgasm. This allowed her to get her genitals functioning while simultaneously allowing her to keep their intimacy to levels she could tolerate. (Sensate-focus exercises would have reinforced this pattern.) Lights-out sex helped her avoid seeing what she feared "wasn't there" between them. As I understood their pattern of sexual interaction better, Mr. and Mrs. Z made more sense to me as people, and the drama regularly unfolding in their bedroom became more poignant, meaningful, and painful to me.

As I pursued this in our sessions, Mr. and Mrs. Z protested that I was making their sex out to be worse than it was. I, myself, wondered if I was being judgmental. In a final attempt to address the issue, I asked Mr. and Mrs. Z, "Are you so used to being out of contact with the people you love that you can successfully ignore being out of touch with each other during sex?"

Mrs. Z said nothing, but her emotional radar bristled. Mr. Z looked away to choke back his tears, acknowledging that he could tell the difference. Mr. Z's acknowledgment opened up a whole new level of discussion in our session. Not only was the topic of "who knows what about emotional contact and deprivation" now on the table, but also so were the many ways Mr. and Mrs. Z tried to cope with it.

I asked Mr. Z why he was willing to attempt intercourse repeatedly when he anticipated such a negative outcome. Without hesitation, he replied, "I want to please my wife. I want to please everybody. I'm a *pleaser*."

I thought about Mr. Z's statement and then flashed on the image of him trying to "please" his wife. Suddenly, I had a different picture from the one Mr. Z was painting. "You want to please your wife, and everybody, or you want them to be pleased with you?" I asked.

Mr. Z hesitated. "I want them to be pleased with me."

I decided Mr. Z's frankness deserved the same in return:

> *Your notion of "pleasing" other people involves measuring up to their standards and expectations so they'll love you or like you. I think you're describing your difficulty holding onto yourself when you're dealing with the people who matter to you. Really pleasing people is a virtue. What you're doing isn't. In some ways, it's quite selfish.*[12]

At first, Mr. Z was taken aback by my comment and, in his impulse to defend himself, he jumped to the conclusion that holding onto himself involved *not pleasing* Mrs. Z and taking an adversarial stance toward her. He thought I was encouraging him to "stand up to her" (and other people like his father) and become indifferent to what pleased others. I probably was not too helpful here because I, myself, was not clear on this point. I should have been encouraging him to stand up to himself—his own fear (e.g., of rejection, etc.). I had not yet recognized that self-confrontation lies at the heart of differentiation. It would be some time before I could help someone else see that holding onto yourself—maintaining a clear sense of self when dealing with others, soothing your own anxieties, not overreacting to others, and tolerating discomfort for growth—obviates the need for an adversarial stance.

Mr. Z began a productive personal struggle over the difference between confronting others versus confronting himself in relationship to them. I did not help him with this critical distinction as much as I might have, because I was still learning the difference between being confrontive versus being directive with clients. Given my training in Rogerian counseling and nondirective psychodynamic psychotherapy, realizing that confrontation could be collaborative as well as nondirective came as a revelation. I generally did not talk frankly with clients (as I do now). Still, confronting Mr. Z's jargonish self-label as "a pleaser" had enough impact to start a healthy cycle of self-confrontation into motion.

Rather than blaming his wife for not making him feel like more of a man, Mr. Z began to confront himself about letting his wife determine when they had intercourse—even when he was not ready for it. Rather than just berating himself, Mr. Z began to look at himself in ways that seemed to increase his stature and shore up his resolve.

Several days later during sex Mrs. Z gave Mr. Z the signal to mount her for intercourse when she was close to reaching orgasm. Mr. Z declined and instead continued to perform oral sex on her. Momentarily there was a hard edge between them. But Mr. Z persevered, and Mrs. Z eventually relaxed into his touch. In effect, he took charge of himself—and their sexual interaction—in a way he never had before. In the process, Mr. Z impressed himself and his wife with his resilience and patience in the face of her protestations, fidgeting, and nervous laughter. He had seen what needed to be done, and he did it. That single interaction seemed to have a remarkably positive impact on them as individuals and as a couple. It was Mr. Z's self-defining act of differentiation.

Session 4

In our next session I pointed out that Mr. Z did not seem to need instructions from me about what to do. At best he might want some help about where he might apply himself. When it came down to it, Mr. Z had acted as "his own man" rather than as "my boy." This had a lot of meaning to Mr. Z and his wife. He seemed to conduct himself with more respect. Once Mrs. Z saw how I worked with her husband, it made her more willing to do the same. She eventually asked me what I saw in her sexual style.

It would have been easy to give Mrs. Z a jaundiced interpretation about stopping her husband from bringing her to orgasm manually and urging him to have intercourse. "Fears of losing control" and "wanting to frustrate her husband" readily came to mind. But neither interpretation really held up in the face of what I had recently seen them accomplish in their sexual interaction. And neither notion

---

[12] In conventional sex therapy Mr. Z would have been encouraged to be "more selfish" by focusing on his own "pleasure" while receiving during sensate-focus exercises.

had the poignancy, vulnerability, and power of talking to Mrs. Z about "hungering" for her man.

I told Mrs. Z that I was struck by her lack of sexual desire. She was quick to point out that anyone whose partner repeatedly lost his erection would have low desire for sex, too. I clarified that I was not referring to sexual frequency. Rather, I pointed to how she never touched her husband's penis in an attempt to pleasure him. Moreover, she invited Mr. Z to "finish himself off" inside her vagina, but never with much enthusiasm or emotional contact. Her sexual style reflected little indication of passion or wanting.

When I did not back away from her, Mrs. Z once again transformed from being intimidating and adamant to being accessible and resilient. She talked about the years of disappointing sex and of feeling deprived and inadequate. When Mrs. Z described being afraid to get her hopes up after 14 years, of not wanting to want sex to be better because it hurt too much, her pain was palpable. Yes, there was a part of her that wanted to reach orgasm with her husband inside her to prove she was not "less" than other women. But there was also a healthy part of her that longed for more emotional union with her partner than she could bear. I had a much more tender and vulnerable picture of Mrs. Z than had previously occurred to me. I did not trivialize her struggles by proposing sensate-focus exercises to instill greater desire in her (as was typical in conventional sex therapy.)

It was a short leap from there to discussing other lessons Mrs. Z had learned about "not wanting to want" (Schnarch, 1991). Mrs. Z disclosed how her father's compulsive gambling eventually forced her mother and her to take control of the family finances. But as her history emerged in the course of discussing their sexual interactions, it seemed like it was more meaningful to her. Rather than just telling me her life story, it was as though she finally appreciated its impact on her. For my part, I loved the benefits of this departure from the structured roundtable history-taking approach (Masters &

Johnson, 1970). Contextualizing their sexual interactions as a concrete way to "resolve the past in the present" made their physical relationship and our therapy more meaningful.

Subsequent Developments

Mr. and Mrs. Z's relationship improved, but Mr. Z continued to have difficulty with erections when they attempted intercourse. I liked the new way therapy was going, but I wondered how we were going to improve his sexual function. Eventually Mr. and Mrs. Z provided the direction: In one particular sexual encounter they achieved an unusually (for them) positive, quiet, and peaceful emotional connection as they lay in bed. Mr. Z got an instant erection that lasted for some time. Neither he nor Mrs. Z was eager to lose the wonderful moment in a desperate rush to use the erection before he lost it. Mrs. Z was particularly struck by the palpable sense of emotional connection and realized in retrospect how isolated they had been. They took this as a positive sign of things to come.

For my part, I became more hopeful we could get symptom change without prescribed activities. Although I often engineered something similar to this in conventional sex therapy, what Mr. and Mrs. Z were doing was fundamentally different. This turning point came about as a result of each partner soothing himself or herself and confronting himself or herself rather than from mutual reassurances or reduced situational demands (e.g., bans on intercourse). The benefits they derived were more solid and tractable than what I saw other couples accomplishing.

Eventually, the sense of peace and quiet they increasingly experienced in bed carried over to oral sex. It took months, but Mr. and Mrs. Z managed to do it without any prescriptions from me. I also did not have much to prescribe when it came to making emotional contact during sex—my work with eyes-open sex (Schnarch, 1991) and "hugging 'til relaxed" (Schnarch, 1997/1998) was yet to come.[13] As they were increasingly able to remain intimately con-

---

[13] Eyes-open sex is often antithetical to sensate focus (because the former interferes with the latter), and "hugging 'til relaxed" is predicated on self-soothing rather than depending on your partner to make you feel safe or soothed.

nected during sex, Mr. Z became less likely to lose his erection. The first time Mr. Z maintained an erection long enough for him and his wife to achieve orgasm during intercourse was a watershed experience for them both. This carried over to the point that, eventually, erectile dysfunction was rarely a consideration. Mr. Z wrote letters to several old friends describing the profound impact this had had on him.

As Mr. Z and Mrs. Z realized whole other levels at which they were not in touch, they developed more respect for intense intimacy. I have since found almost half the couples who attend the Passionate Marriage™ Couples Enrichment Weekends cannot *feel* each other while they are touching. All they feel is physical sensation—with no sense of their partner's (or their own) emotional presence or absence. Becoming capable of greater emotional connection during sex is a personal challenge and a source of growth for many couples.

Eventually I learned to facilitate this process with couples like Mr. and Mrs. Z in several sessions, to the point that their sexual changes and self-disclosures challenged both spouses' self-definition and self-validation. This result requires and promotes self-soothing to handle the shakeup of established personas in a relationship. This process challenges both partners to maintain a clear sense of self. While physically and emotionally close to each other they must self-soothe, not get overwhelmed with the partner's anxiety, and tolerate discomfort for growth. These are the same core processes that promote differentiation. The client experiences more of a "relationship with himself or herself" in the context of a better relationship with the partner.

It took me years to understand the ramifications of the paradigm shift taking place in my work with Mr. and Mrs. Z and other couples. We did not just de-emphasize intercourse, reduce performance anxiety, and create symptom relief. Intercourse, genital function, and fear of failure ceased to dominate their encounters as we focused on something far more meaningful: the meaning of their lives. Being truly together became far more important. We shifted from looking at sex as a natural function to using it as a vehicle for intimacy, personal growth, and an adult capacity to love.

Now I realize that an emotionally committed relationship is a people-growing machine and that the processes of differentiation drive the mechanism through the ebb and flow of intimacy, eroticism, and sexual desire. This process involves recognizing how sex is a language rather than a collection of behaviors and skills. I now assume that clients' sexual patterns are purposeful and rich in meaning, no matter how painful those meanings may be and no matter how severe or long-standing their sexual and marital difficulties. No longer do I dismiss their sexual styles as faulty or inadequate, to be immediately replaced by my superior techniques. Thanks to couples like Mr. and Mrs. Z, I approach clients' sexual difficulties with greater respect—and my clients now get better results.

References

Apfelbaum, B. (1983). *Expanding the boundaries of sex therapy: The ego-analytic model* (2nd ed.). Berkeley, CA: Berkeley Sex Therapy Group.

Bowen, M. (1978). *Family therapy in clinical practice.* New York: Aronson.

Kaplan, H. S. (1979). *Disorders of sexual desire and other new concepts and techniques in sex therapy.* New York: Brunner/Mazel.

Kaplan, H. S. (1974). *The new sex therapy.* New York: Brunner/Mazel.

Kaplan, H. S. (1987). *Sexual aversion, sexual phobias and panic disorder.* New York: Brunner/Mazel.

Kerr, M. E., & Bowen, M. (1988). *Family evaluation.* New York: Norton.

Masters, W. H., & Johnson, V. E. (1970). *Human sexual inadequacy.* New York: Little, Brown.

Masters, W. H., & Johnson, V. E. (1976). *The pleasure bond: A new look at sexuality and commitment.* New York: Bantam Books.

Masters, W. H., Johnson, V. E., & Kolodny, R. (1986). *Masters and Johnson on sex and human loving.* Boston: Little, Brown.

Schnarch, D. S. (1991). *Constructing the sexual crucible: An integration of sexual and marital therapy.* New York: Norton.

Schnarch, D. M. (1995). Family systems approach to sex therapy and intimacy. In R. Mikesell, D-D. Lusterman, & S. H. McDaniel (Eds.), *Integrating family therapy: Handbook of family psychology and systems therapy* (pp. 239–257). Washington, DC: American Psychological Association.

Schnarch, D. S. (1998). *Passionate marriage, sex, love, and intimacy in emotionally committed relationships.* New York: Owl Books. (Original work published 1997)

Schnarch, D. M. (2000). A systemic approach to sexual desire problems. In S. R. Leiblum & R. C. Rosen (Eds.), *Principles and practices of sex therapy* (3rd ed., pp. 17–56). New York: Guilford Press.

CHAPTER 5

WHEN ROADS DIVERGE: A CASE STUDY WITH A GAY MALE COUPLE

Thomas Russell

Brad, a 24-year-old graduate student in the helping profession, called my private practice and requested an appointment for individual therapy. Initial telephone information indicated that Brad was very concerned about confidentiality, was gay, and was particularly interested in seeing a therapist who was also gay. The only additional information available was that he was feeling depressed and experiencing tremendous stress that was affecting his academic performance in his graduate work.

Although my practice does not solely consist of working with gay clients, I am "out" with my sexual orientation in the professional community and often receive referrals of clients wishing to see a gay therapist. It is also well known in the professional community that I work from a systemic, short-term clinical orientation and that I often request others involved in the system to participate at some point in the clinical conversation.

My early clinical development as a family therapist was through involvement with the Milan Group, particularly Luigi Boscolo. It was during this time that I became convinced that the conversation with the clients was in and of itself the most important intervention. In subsequent work with Lynn Hoffman and Tom Andersen I became less interested in strategic intervention and more interested in the evolving conversation. I find that minimizing an agenda is more helpful and respectful of the clients' ability to change in ways that fit their respective needs at the time. I have a deep, abiding faith in the clients' ability to reach their own solutions when helped in becoming "unstuck," as the Milan Group

espoused in their early work. I also believe that systemic intervention and change can occur when one is using this approach regardless of whether the conversation is with a single individual or collection of people (couples, families, etc.). Within the systemic frame are many lenses, such as narrative, structural, strategic, and so on. Earlier in my development, I found myself rigidly adhering to one frame in an almost obsessive manner. After several years of work in a reflecting team model introduced by Tom Andersen of Norway, I was able to free myself from this view, which I began to experience as constricting. Now, moving between lenses, focusing on the conversation, and minimizing an agenda has been very liberating, and I believe it has been helpful to the clients with whom I work. Some clients may have a very different need in terms of what they want from a therapist, and when this is the case then I am happy to assist them with a referral elsewhere and see this as empowering for them and for me.

SESSION 1

During the initial appointment Brad presented in an articulate manner, with a very sad affect. He stated that he was out in regard to his sexuality with his family of origin and his peers. He was at present in a relationship with William, a 30-year-old stockbroker. They did not live together but had been monogamous for approximately 2 years. Brad reported that the tone of their relationship was quite calm and a bit boring. He was adamant that he did not want this relationship to be a focus of our discussion; all was well in that arena. He described a very chaotic and unpredictable history with his family of origin and discussed in an animated manner how relieved he was to be living on his own with a roommate, free of his family.

When the discussion turned to his reasons for coming to therapy at this time, Brad seemed quite confused and unable to articulate what it was that he wanted to change. He merely said that he wanted to feel better and not feel so confused. When asked what the source of his stress might be, Brad expressed a plethora of self-negating explanations. These descriptions ranged from psychobabble labels, such as "maybe I am an adult child of an alcoholic" or "perhaps I am a child of a dysfunctional family," to a litany of diagnostic labels that ranged from possible dissociative disorder to major depressive disorder. On further discussion, it became quite evident that there was a very strong parallel between these evolving beliefs about himself and his current academic coursework regarding psychological theories, human behavior, and psychopathology. At this juncture in the clinical conversation I made a decision to use humor and respectful skepticism regarding his self-labeling. I did this for two reasons. First and foremost, I did not believe that these labels would create the possibility of a constructive conversation about new possibilities and solutions. Equally important, I was keenly aware that Brad might be experiencing "graduate student syndrome." I remembered with great clarity my own experience during graduate school of being convinced that I probably had every diagnosis within the *Diagnostic and Statistical Manual of Mental Disorders*. I also remember that this had created such angst for me during that time that I had sought out a therapist. I remember the great relief I experienced when that therapist normalized what I was experiencing. This was a conversation that Brad and I would continue over the next several therapy sessions.

Toward the end of the initial session, I pressed Brad again for what he wanted from therapy and from me as his therapist. He remained unable to offer anything other than a desire to feel better. He communicated with some naiveté that he thought perhaps I might hypnotize him or do some relaxa-

tion programming that would make him feel better. I told Brad that although those techniques might be possible with some other therapist, they were not something that I could do for him. I could be most helpful by exploring some of the themes he had raised—specifically, the labeling, the family-of-origin issues, and the current relationship with his partner. I told Brad that I was more interested in how these situations contributed to his current feelings and thoughts. I asked him what he thought would be different when things got better. I also cautioned Brad against placing too much emphasis on me as the expert, as opposed to his own ideas regarding changes that he might consider making. We agreed to continue working together.

SESSION 2

When Brad (B) arrived for the next session, I (Mr. R) proposed that we consider some of the issues he had raised in the first session.

Mr. R: Brad, why don't we revisit some of the issues you raised last time in the form of stories to be expanded upon?

B: What would be the point of that?

Mr. R: Well, these issues are areas of concern for you. They are part of your confusion and dissatisfaction. By looking at the experiences in your life that led up to your present circumstances, we can discover new ways to think about what has happened to you. It may be helpful to think about your experiences as stories that are unique to you. However, these stories are still being written and therefore have the potential for revision, changes, and rewrites which might prove helpful.

Looking relaxed, Brad expressed curiosity.

Mr. R: If we discussed some of the themes you raised we might also clarify where you might hope to make changes in your life, your way of thinking or your way of feeling about past and present experiences.

Brad responded by sitting up and assuming a more active posture.

Mr. R: OK, which of the themes would be most pertinent to your current situation, your reason for entering therapy?

B: Well, right now I am feeling a lot like I did when I came out to my family. That set off a chain of events I couldn't have predicted.

Mr. R: Good . . . what about that time seems parallel with your current situation?

B: Really it started out by accident. I was 15 years old and had been fooling around for about a year with this guy. My mom was out of town. My friend and I were enjoying a blissful weekend together at my folks' place. So late Saturday night Mom came home unexpectedly and caught us in bed making love.

Mr. R: Oh my! Then what happened?

B: The family went into a world-class uproar, unlike anything that happened before. Prior to this I had a very close relationship with my mom, but Dad was very distant. He was an alcoholic and a pretty passive parental figure. After this happened, I couldn't deal with the rejection, so I withdrew from my family and started getting pretty heavy with drugs. But after all the shouting matches that followed getting caught that Saturday, Dad got more assertive. He shocked me by declaring that efforts to "fix me" should stop. Maybe he had some understanding of what I might be going through because I was using drugs and he drinks. In fact, maybe he drinks to get away from his problems, like I was doing. I don't know.

Mr. R: Now what is the time frame we're talking about here?

B: Dad rose up about 3 months after my boyfriend and I were caught *en medias res*.

Mr. R: How did things change after your dad's shift in roles?

B: Well, before this all happened, Mom was the person who supported me, and as I said, we had a really close relationship. I could always count on her to be there for me. In fact, I kind of served as Mom's confidant. After the discovery of my homosexuality, Mom no longer saw me as perfect and in fact, wanted to save me from myself. Dad, on the other hand, essentially told her to lay off. So it was weird. It's like what used to be so predictable, Mom and I together and Dad in his own world, suddenly got all stirred up. It's not that they reversed roles, exactly. It's just that both of them supported me in some ways and criticized me in some ways. I felt closer to my dad than ever before and a little more distant from my mom. My drug use ceased with this change because Dad seemed to be saying it was okay for me to be gay and that he'd be behind me, no matter what. I felt happier about myself and my unfolding sexuality than ever before. For the first time, I felt truly accepted by my dad.

Mr. R: Sounds great! So what happened next?

B: Well not too much later my parents got divorced, for which I felt responsible and very guilty.

Mr. R: Why guilty?

B: It seemed like they fought over my sexuality, which is what broke them up.

Mr. R: Tell me more about that.

B: Prior to finding out about me, conflict had been basically unspoken. Yeah we all knew they disagreed on issues, but no one talked about it. I guess you would say they each tried to manipulate the other, but neither risked saying what was really on their mind. When Dad asserted himself in order to support me, the picture changed. Issues and conflicts were addressed more openly. Then they broke up. [somewhat mournfully] So you can see why I feel responsible.

Mr. R: So your situation motivated your father to take a stand and that opened a whole Pandora's box of disagreements?

B: Yes and that's what made them divorce. It would have been better if they had just kept quiet about it.

Mr. R: You think so? It seems to me a pile of shit smells just as bad with a blanket over it. Maybe this way, instead of being in an unhappy relationship for the rest of their lives, your parents have a chance to find a more compatible companion. Maybe they've learned that not talking about conflict doesn't work. Maybe you did them a favor.

B: Well that is another way of looking at it. I just know that one good thing that came out of all this was that for the first time I felt aligned with and supported by my father.

Mr. R: And what about your mom?

B: After the divorce Mom began to reluctantly accept my sexuality.

Mr. R: So what about Brad in all this? Have you accepted your sexuality?

B: I continued to date guys, but they have always tended to be older than me.

Mr. R: Any idea why you prefer older men?

B: I just feel more secure with older guys, you know, more special.

Mr. R: Okay, let's get back to the present. What similarities are there between then, at age 15, and now?

B: I feel very much the same as I did then. And very sad, stressed out just like the time when Mom caught us fooling around. I feel very much adrift, no focus, no purpose

Mr. R: If the feelings you are experiencing now resemble those you felt back then, it might be helpful to look at how you resolved the problem in the past. Then we could look at what solutions worked then that might apply to your current situation.

Brad look excited, puzzled, and curious all at once. Because we were running out of time, I didn't want to dive into something without having the opportunity to fully explore the issue. It seemed like an appropriate time to wrap up the session and suggest an agenda for our next one. I then said, "Why don't we focus on that at our next session?" Brad replied, "OK, that will give me a chance to think over some of the things we've talked about today. You know, I feel like we have made some real progress, and I like the way this seems to be going."

SESSION 3

Our next meeting was scheduled in 2 weeks. However, about 5 days later Brad called, very tearful and in a panic. We agreed to meet that evening at my office. The session began with Brad sobbing in his chair. "I'm scared. If I tell you what's going on you might not want to see me any more," he said through tears. I replied, "That will not happen. Just take your time and fill me in as best you can." Brad took a deep breath and began by saying, "I thought a lot about the connections between my family situation and the present." His tears increased as he went on.

B: The honesty in my family relating to my sexuality and my parents' relationship is really pertinent to the current situation. I am so sorry, but I haven't been honest with you. I told you my partner and I are monogamous. That's not true . . . I have been unfaithful to him several times even since our last meeting. William is totally unaware of my liaisons.

Mr. R: So why is it you think I'll reject you?

B: Well, therapy is based on being totally honest and I haven't been . . . I thought you might get mad and cut me off for being dishonest.

Mr. R: We are in a process. As therapy unfolds we will peel back the layers of honesty and establish trust. That is a natural process and this incident tonight is part of that process.

Brad seemed to relax, and his tears slowed. I continued.

Mr. R: The information you have shared presents me with two dilemmas. First, it forces me to introduce a new agenda into our conversation, something I usually try to minimize. Second, it leads towards involving your partner in our process, and I'm not sure how hard to push that idea, whether you're ready for that. Can we deal with these two issues separately?

Brad nodded cautiously, so I went on.

Mr. R: We need to talk about AIDS and safe sex. First, though, I have recently lost three close friends to AIDS, so that you will understand why I feel strongly about this. AIDS brings many things into our dialogue, mostly questions. For example, are you engaging in low-risk/no-risk sexual behavior? What is the relevance of these liaisons to your life with your partner? Can you be honest with him? Have you ever been tested for HIV? Let's take these one at a time, starting with the last.

B: We were both tested 2 years ago, and we were both negative then. We haven't been tested since. As for low-risk sex, yes, we are smart enough to protect ourselves, but it doesn't help any when I have these other contacts from time to time.

After a brief but sincere lecture on the importance of safe sex, I moved into questions regarding Brad's relationship with William. In the ensuing discussion it became clear that Brad used affairs with other men as a way of getting some passion out of William. Most of the time William operated in a logical, rational, unemotional manner, and Brad wanted emotion. The only way he had found to stimulate emotional response in William was to make William insecure in their relationship by seeing other men. Once Brad saw this as a systemic rather than intrapsychic issue I engaged him in a discussion of the pros and cons of having affairs and keeping secrets—that is, what worked in favor of their relationship, what damaged their relationship.

Toward the end of the session, Brad said, "Now I see why I will need your help both for myself and in dealing with my partner." As the meeting ended, it was clear that the HIV issue would need to be addressed further in a later session.

As our conversation about honesty in relationships continued, I realized that I was becoming perplexed and uncomfortable. These feelings were emerging from my own lack of honesty with my current partner about the nature of our relationship. Brad and I discussed the need for him not only to find a way to discuss the HIV and monogamy issues with William but also the need for Brad to be honest. He needed to ponder the issue of commitment

and what he did and did not like about the relationship. Essentially, he needed to decide if the relationship would survive a revelation of infidelity. As I continued to push Brad to consider the need for such honesty, I realized that a different course of action would also be required in my own personal relationship with my current partner of several years. There were many unspoken conflicts in my own relationship that needed addressing.

All in all, this session with Brad was particularly meaningful in focusing our therapeutic contract. Brad had introduced the agenda of honesty, I had introduced the agenda of HIV and safe sex, and we had mutually agreed that it was time to involve William in the conversation. We spent some time discussing ways that Brad might consider the conversation with William when they came for the next session. Brad and I agreed that, in addition to a discussion of the issues of honesty, monogamy, and HIV, the conversation might also encompass a discussion around issues of mutual goals for the relationship, current pleasures and dissatisfactions in the relationship, and future goals for the relationship. I suggested that he might want to consider one more individual session to prepare more for the couples session. Brad reported that he did not think that was necessary. His partner, William, was aware of the work we were doing and was already eager to participate. I agreed to serve as a guide for the next session, which both Brad and William would attend.

SESSION 4

At our next session Brad brought William. I started.

Mr. R: William, Brad initially sought me out for depression and its negative impact on his schoolwork. In our work together we have uncovered some similar patterns from his family of origin recurring in the relationship between the two of you. In particular, Brad's relationship with his father may influence the way he relates to you. It may also shed some light on Brad's expectations and needs regarding your relationship. I think your involvement in this process will be of value to Brad, to you, and to your relationship. Are you willing to participate in the work we're doing here?

William (W) was right with us. He said in a very businesslike manner,

W: I'd be very happy to be involved if you think I could help. Brad's problems with his family and some of our problems as a couple stem from Brad's inability to approach things logically and his reluctance to choose or decide on a logical course of action. I am, quite frankly, confused and impatient with Brad's inability and hesitation. I don't understand why he makes things so difficult.

B: Why do you have to be so logical, so boring? Don't you have any feeling at all?

Mr. R: Is this a familiar scenario, this kind of exchange between the two of you?

They both nodded emphatically as the conversation picked up steam.

W: This will eventually drive us apart.

B: It's always the same . . . we have a big fight, we hardly talk for awhile, and then we reconcile. Things are great for a short while, our relationship coasts until the next blow-up.

Mr. R: Who usually initiates the reconciliation, and how does it go in terms of a script?

B: It's usually William who initiates things . . . he's warmer, more open and fun and less rigid than he usually is. Oh, and sexually it's always great during these times.

W: Brad is more connected to me; he seems more willing to be close and accept my advice.

B: [recoiling] You don't get it do you? I don't want your fucking advice.

W: Without my advice you make poor decisions. You party too much. If you did things your way I'm afraid you'd be partying all the time and that would lead to becoming sexually involved with other men.

I asked William which of these things he feared most. He responded, "Getting involved with someone sexually, of course!"

Mr. R: Brad, what do you think about what William has just shared?

B: You might as well know that there have been a few incidents like that, usually during our angry times. But you must understand that I never wanted to hurt you. I felt I had no choice . . . it's just that you are so rigid and bossy.

Mr. R: So you are saying William is responsible for the choices you make?

B: [in a far less accusatory manner] No, I made the choices . . . I have always felt guilty about these things, and I am truly sorry because I know, William, that I have hurt you."

W: [looking rather flat and stoic] I'm not surprised by all this. I even suspected it might be happening. And it really makes me angry.

Although I pushed William to expand on his feelings, he was unwilling to share more intimate thoughts on the topic. It was evident that he was uncomfortable with emotions and preferred to keep discussions at an intellectual level. Brad became frustrated at William's unwillingness to share his feelings. He interrupted by saying, "This is so typical of you. You never display any emotions. You're just so rational."

I felt some feedback was necessary at this point, so I interjected:

Mr. R: Your relationship seems to be divided between very passionate times and more businesslike times. The more passionate times follow extrarelationship liaisons engaged in by Brad. You seem to be in a sort of a dance: On one hand Brad respects and needs your abilities, William, to make decisions, provide structure in the midst of seeming chaos, and to create a sense of security. This helps you to feel needed and helpful. On the other hand, Brad has the ability to introduce playfulness and spontaneity into the relationship. So, you both have strengths to bring to this union. But this kind of interdependence also introduces vulnerability. Does any of this resonate with you two?

Essentially, I was framing the infidelities in a systemic manner that led naturally to exploring more constructive ways for each of them to get their needs met within a monogamous relationship.

They both agreed to my interpretation, although Brad was more fervent in his acceptance of it. I forged on, saying, "I'd like to suggest an assignment for the two of you to work on until our next meeting. On even days, Brad, I would like you to act as you think William would like you best. On odd days, William, could you act in a manner you think is pleasing to Brad?"

Even as they started nodding in an intrigued manner, I went on, "But I don't want you to discuss the assignment, your reactions, or even your feelings until our next meeting."

They both agreed, and we set up an appointment for 1 week later. We agreed also to touch on the nonmonogamy/HIV issue as it related to them both. I really didn't need them to complete the assignment to the letter. This was merely a probe to determine how adaptable and empathic both partners were based on their own view of the wants and needs of the other. Any results at all would be helpful in the next session. A scheduling conflict lengthened the assignment to 2 weeks.

SESSION 5

At our next session I began, "So, how did it go?" Brad was animated, while William was rather bland and emotionally flat. Brad shared first.

B: On my even days I acted calmer, more thoughtful and logical. I felt less anxious and more laid back at home than I ever have before.

W: He really did seem calmer and more mature, but my reaction was that I began to feel sad and detached from Brad.

Ignoring this, Brad chimed in animatedly,

B: On William's odd days he seemed more interesting and spontaneous. He initiated sex. He arranged social outings like dinner with friends and dancing at bars afterwards. This is completely new—William's initiating fun stuff. That was great during the

first week but the second week was, well . . . not as good.

William picked up the description:

W: I was puzzled by Brad's behavior. He was so enthusiastic at these outings that I began to feel I might lose him to someone else.

B: I can't believe this. I was feeling hopeful we could use this assignment to create a new relationship that would be more fun and exciting for both of us, you know, dump the old one that's so full of child–parent conflicts.

W: I don't exactly know how I feel, but when we went out Brad was so outgoing that I had this nagging thought like "Why would Brad choose me over someone else?" and I just couldn't shake the feeling. That's when it started to break down for me.

B: [becoming vehement] What do I have to do to convince you that I love you? I've always been committed to you and to this relationship . . . I wanted it to be good for both of us, a growth experience, a new way of living for you and for me. I wanted to be accepted into your life by you and your family.

William had still not come out to his family, and they didn't know of Brad and William's relationship, although they did know Brad socially. William described his feelings about the past 2 weeks:

W: I could tell how well Brad responded during the first week, but I felt insecure and like I had lost control and that changed to a feeling of sadness. So, during the second week, I fell back into the old patterns. That made Brad angry, and I guess that's why he's being so assertive now.

I interrupted and offered a reframe with several suggestions.

Mr. R: First, it is unreasonable to expect William to change overnight. Second, giving up old patterns for new ones will take time and practice for both of you. Third, you both need to practice respecting each other's challenge in setting up these new patterns of interaction. Fourth, for this week's assignment I'd like both of you to keep a notebook. In it I want you both to record times when you see the other partner practicing these new behaviors. Also, I want you to record your honest emotional response to these behaviors. Fifth, I would like you, William, to give thoughtful consideration to the desires Brad has expressed. We can discuss your thoughts and feelings in our next session.

The couple then said that they wanted to let me know that they had both decided to take an HIV test since our last session. They had done this together by going to the gay center, where the test results would be anonymous. They thanked me for having shared my personal concerns and my personal experiences of having lost several friends to AIDS. They said my comments had made them feel as if I really cared about them as human beings and fellow gay men rather than just as clients. I thanked them and suggested that, whatever the results of the test, I did care about them and that we could certainly discuss the results together if they wished.

I also informed them that they had been helpful to me, too. Working with clients to increase honesty in their relationships and express their likes and dislikes always encourages me to be more honest in my own relationships. They responded positively to this sharing of information. We scheduled our next appointment for 2 weeks later.

I have made several references during this narrative to my own personal relationship and my increasing awareness of my need to be more honest with my partner at the time. During the time I was working with Brad and William and with several other couples, there was an emerging theme in each of the therapies of a need for greater honesty in terms of contractual arrangements in the relationships. An argument could be made that this theme was emerging from my own personal developing lens. The point could also be made that the timing of work with these couples was of sufficient synchronicity for this theme to emerge. I do believe that to some extent a person always constructs his or her theories and therapeutic approaches on the basis of his or her own lenses of the world at a particular time. In my view this is neither good nor

bad. It does, however, demand that clinicians accept responsibility for their lenses and exercise great caution when they interject those lenses into the therapeutic conversation. As a result of this convergence, my partner and I initiated therapy to begin reviewing changes in our own relationship. This was certainly no coincidence.

SESSION 6

Brad showed up for our next session alone. "Where is William? What's going on?" I asked. Brad seemed weighed down.

B: Well, a lot has gone on in the last two weeks. One night William and I went out to a bar together. Before we went out William told me that my gregarious nature in these situations made him anxious. I assured him that I was being social, not sexual. While we were at the bar, William tried to set up a *ménage à trois* with three different guys. None of the guys took him up on it. The attempts surprised and angered me. I felt like William was manipulating me and testing me. It's like he doesn't trust me, and he is trying to challenge my commitment to him and to the relationship. That really makes me mad! On top of that, I joined the gay/lesbian student alliance at school and then went to a rally. There was quite a scene, and the media showed up. William was livid that I would do something so public. He feels like it threatens his secrecy with his family and his father in particular, regarding his sexual orientation. See, his dad controls William by manipulating him with money. Anyway, William demanded that I resign from the gay/lesbian student alliance.

"So," I asked, "how do you feel about all this?" Brad's response was clearly from the heart:

B: Tom, I love William, I really do. But I'm confused. I've never seen this side of William before. Sure, I know about his secrecy and his fear his dad would cut him off, but I really didn't see this coming. Honestly, I'm having serious doubts about whether I can continue in this relationship with William.

Just then the receptionist broke in on the intercom. William had shown up. I asked Brad what he wanted to do, and he said he wanted to bring William in.

I welcomed William: "I was surprised when you didn't show up at first, but I'm glad you made it. Brad said that he wanted you to join us when you did show up."

Brad then recapped the information he had shared with me thus far. When he finished, I asked William if he agreed with what Brad had said and if he had anything to add. William had been rather stoic up until now, and he started off rather calmly, saying, "That all sounds pretty accurate." He became more intense as he added, "You cannot continue being such a visible queer with your rallies for queer rights and whatnot. I will not tolerate such behavior, and I'm here to make a proposition."

Brad responded angrily.

B: Why don't you just go fuck yourself! And while you're at it, why don't you tell Tom what else happened since our last meeting?

W: You brought it up, you tell him.

B: OK, I will. After we got home the night of the failed attempts at arranging a *ménage à trois*, we were both upset and angry. William kept needling me about my lack of support in these attempts. He kept accusing me of not cooperating even though, according to him, "you know you wanted it." At that point I told William to leave. He then hit me. Then I told him he would either leave, or I would have the police come and get him. So, William left. During the rest of the week, William was sorry, apologetic, and filled with remorse. In between his remorse and apologies we had great passionate sex. So that's it, that's what happened.

I jumped right in:

Mr. R: This development causes me grave, serious concern. I've worked with violent couples, and this turn of events follows a classic pattern, especially the remorse and intense sexual passion in the aftermath. This is what I have come to call "dangerous love," and at this point if your relationship is to continue, the primary issue must be one of safety.

W: That's why I came today. I have a proposition. I promise never to be violent again and to *always* trust you Brad. I will buy you a condominium. You will own the condo completely, but in return you must promise to resign from the gay/lesbian alliance and be quiet about your sexual orientation. In addition, you must promise never to bring up the issue of coming out to my family. I feel that these demands are reasonable since my professional and financial success is tied to my father's approval. I think this is a small price to pay for financial security and the lifestyle we can continue to enjoy.

B: [tearfully] It's over . . . you treat me as if I'm a whore you can buy. You never have understood that all I wanted from you was love, not money. I am proud of who I am and that includes my sexual orientation. I won't change that for anyone or any amount of money.

I turned to William and asked him to respond to Brad's comment. William coldly replied that this was his final offer: If Brad could not accept those terms, then the relationship would indeed be over. He waited a moment for some sign of reconciliation from Brad. When it did not come, William rose to leave.

I attempted to prevent this abrupt ending to our session.

Mr. R: It's been my experience that it is best not to make such far-reaching decisions in the heat of anger. I would suggest that the two of you evaluate the pros and cons of your relationship at a calmer time and decide what to do based on that evaluation. After all, you have a lot of time and emotion invested in one another.

William appeared stoic. "I don't think that will be necessary. We have enough data to make a decision." But he did sit back down.

Mr. R: So, where does this leave us in your counseling as a couple?

B: I would like to continue individual counseling. As to couples therapy, it's over, and I don't see any need to continue with that. I hope, William, we can still be friends, but our relationship has ended.

Mr. R: [to William] You might consider individual therapy. I would be glad to refer you to someone who can help you sort through things. Your intense loyalty to your father and your willingness to sacrifice significant relationships, as well as your violent outbursts, might be wakeup calls for further exploration in individual therapy.

W: I don't see any real need for that.

Before leaving, they shared with me that they had gone together to be tested for HIV and had both tested negative. It was a tearful ending to the session. Brad scheduled an appointment for the following week.

When Brad and William had left my office, I shut the door and sat in tears. I remembered the many times I myself had anxiously awaited test results for HIV. Unlike now, with the promise of the protease cocktails for treating people with HIV, years ago a positive test result was almost like receiving a death sentence. I remembered sharing tears of joy when the test results would be negative. I remembered trying to answer the proverbial question "Why am I negative when so many others are not?" I remembered the many efforts of trying to find meaning when there was no answer to that question. Most painfully, I remembered the many friends who had been my family of choice who had not survived. The loneliness that accompanies these thoughts can sometimes seem unbearable. Once again I can rejoice and move to a less painful place when I work with clients who, in the midst of a painful split, can also find hope for continued life.

SESSION 7

Brad returned the following week for an individual session. He described a very painful, lonely week. Nevertheless, he remained steadfast in his belief that he had made the correct decision regarding William. He had begun to use his newfound emerging support system in the gay/lesbian student alliance. He had even informed his parents of recent events and found them to be rather neutral in their response,

something that, compared to past responses, he experienced as positive. We discussed at great length his continuing concern for William's current inability to seek help. He had had no contact with William since our last session and remained concerned about what he referred to as William's "depression."

Brad also discussed ideas that he had regarding why he had allowed himself to be involved in the relationship with William, which had resulted in such a disastrous outcome. For the first time since he had initiated therapy he began again the negative self-labeling behavior that had been present when he initiated treatment. I reminded him of this problem and suggested more constructive explanations, which he seemed eager to accept. He seemed most willing to accept the notion that what at one time had been mutually beneficial to both him and William had run its course. He spoke of his changing needs and his expectations of both himself and of a relationship. Sadly he spoke of William's inability to extricate himself from his family and their financial baggage.

Then I asked Brad to think back on his reasons for initiating therapy. We remembered together his initial concerns regarding his sadness, depression, and inadequate academic performance. As we discussed each of these issues Brad expressed, with a sense of triumph, how these had changed for the positive. He noted the irony of his current sadness for the loss of William residing right alongside the comfort and joy he felt at having made what he considered to be the right decision. Brad seemed willing and able to accept the ambiguity that often seems to accompany all of us as humans.

SESSION 8

Brad and I got together for one final session. During that time he was able to solidify his gains and remain firm regarding his decision to terminate the relationship with William. We discussed and made a decision to end our therapeutic relationship at this time with the caveat that he could return at any time if he felt "stuck." According to my way of thinking, this seemed appropriate, and Brad seemed empowered by his success. It was during this last session that I shared with Brad a telephone call that

I had received from William. In that call William had discussed his depression and his acceptance of some responsibility for what had occurred and had requested a referral to a therapist. I provided him with that support and information and asked for his permission to share this information with Brad, to which he consented. Brad seemed comforted by this information.

EPILOGUE

Two years went by with no further word from either Brad or William. Then one day I received a telephone call from Brad requesting that I join him for lunch in order to discuss some issues relating to his professional practice. Also, it was his way of wanting to say thanks for the work we had done when he was my client. Normally I am extremely cautious about socializing with former clients outside of the therapeutic context. However, because of the length of time since he had been my client, and because we could now have a discussion as colleagues, I agreed. I was also acutely aware of the need for positive professional support from fellow gay colleagues.

During that meeting we discussed some issues related to ethics and integrity in professional practice. Brad also shared that he and William had been able to establish a casual, nonsexual friendship and that he was pleased with this achievement. He believed that this was possible because of increased honesty between them. The lunch was for me a pleasant closure to our work together.

This case study illustrates some themes pertinent to gay male couples. The issue of HIV, safe sex, and monogamy are all focal points that gay male couples must negotiate. Often these issues are resolved for periods of time only to be renegotiated when each partner's commitment or circumstance may change. The impact of these changes can be major and sometimes serve as an operating premise in the relationship. Another important issue illustrated in this case study has to do with family of origin, the process of coming out to that family and whether such revelation is greeted with support or emotional cutoff. These decisions are not easy ones to make, and the consequences are far reaching. Coming out to

one's family of origin can be an emotionally healthy decision and should be viewed as an ongoing process and not a singular event. Every effort should be made to empower the client with adequate information and support to make his or her own individual decision. In this decision the client is the ultimate expert. Within a couple's relationship the decisions made by each partner regarding this issue will have significant impact both on each partner's individual development as well as on the development of the relationship as a couple. Couples may need additional help as they negotiate this terrain in their developing partnership.

This case study also serves to illustrate some issues that I believe are germane to all couples work, not only gay men. In all couples cases there are differences between the individuals in terms of personalities, needs, family-of-origin issues, developmental stages, and so on. In this case study, family-of-origin issues and personality differences had a major impact, as did the developmental issue of revealing one's homosexuality to one's family. Another issue that affects all therapy relates to the temptation, based on the content a client or couple may present, for the therapist to cocreate unnecessary psychopathology or problems that may impede the client's achievement of what actually brought him or her to therapy. I have often described myself as a minimalist in terms of trying to hear what clients are really asking for in therapy. Probably one of the most difficult tasks facing a therapist is to avoid imposing his or her own lens when defining client issues. This case serves to illustrate and reaffirm my belief in a self-healing tautology present in all living systems. The difficult task is not getting in the way of emerging solutions that fit within the client's logic system. This case study also illustrates the approach of viewing clients as "stuck." Our primary task as therapists is to find ways to help our clients become "unstuck" so as to go about the business of living their lives without us.

I am grateful to the many clients who have reaffirmed my belief in the notion that our clients have far greater wisdom than we, as therapists, may have at any point in time. I am grateful to my gay clients who have helped me develop the belief that we will survive well in spite of overwhelming odds.

CHAPTER 6

"OUR COMPANY IS DOWNSIZING": COUPLE AND INDIVIDUAL THERAPY FOR WORK-RELATED AND SYSTEMS ISSUES

Sylvia Shellenberger

In our chapter of the book *Integrating Family Therapy* (Mikesell, Lusterman, & McDaniel, 1995), called "The Changing Family–Work System," Sandra Hoffman and I described the major changes in the family and work system, including the expansion of women's work roles, the increase in dual-earner families, and the changing work environment (Shellenberger & Hoffman, 1995). Stressors associated with each of these changes affect marital and other family relationships. I chose the case described in this chapter because it illustrates how the individual's functioning in work situations is intimately related to systemic issues of relationship patterns and stress within the family, to family-of-origin issues as well as to issues inherent in large corporations that are in the throes of downsizing.

Numerous writers have influenced my thinking about families and larger systems. Theoretically, my understanding of family functioning draws from Bowenian family systems principles (Bowen, 1978; Kerr & Bowen, 1988). The clinical processes I use derive from the theoretical and clinical model proposed by Hendrix (1988, 1999) of Imago Relationship Therapy (IRT). My clinical thinking about this case is informed by many other writings. Some of these include the stages of family development (Carter & McGoldrick, 1998; Gerson, 1995), the usefulness of the genogram for understanding and tracking families (McGoldrick, Gerson, & Shellenberger, 1999), the effects of emotional reactivity in family relationships (Gerson, 1994), the need for balance in attending to family members (Boszormenyi-Nagy & Krasner, 1986), and the importance of focusing on

strengths in families (Walsh, 1995, 1998; Wolin & Wolin, 1993).

MAY 1

"I feel like I'm in prison," Jackie began.

> *They monitor me all the time, trying to catch me making mistakes. Both me and my husband may lose our jobs. The company is downsizing, and I've had to change jobs eight times. And now they are trying to fire me. I have just 4 years 'til retirement, and they are doing everything they can to force me out. Yes, I admit I have a temper with the customers, but who wouldn't in that place?*

Jackie became tearful as she talked about the problems that overwhelmed her. I felt somewhat overwhelmed and angry myself, knowing that Jackie was here because she would lose her job if she didn't change her attitude. She told me on the phone when she requested the appointment that she had 3 months to show the company she was doing something to improve her attitude or she would lose her job. Pulsing through my mind were similar stories I had heard from other clients at this company. I couldn't imagine that all these employees I'd seen were paranoid and dysfunctional. Could it be that the company was wronging its employees by demanding too much or, worse, seeking evidence to build a case for cutting loyal employees loose before their retirement? I began to question my own philosophy for consultation when two sides are at odds. I have always believed there are two sides to the story, that both sides will make sense if they can be completely understood, and that my work is to help both sides understand and validate (although not necessarily agree with) the other side. To me, this meant trying to see facets of this problem from the client's perspective and from the work perspective. Thinking back to my conversation with Jackie's in-house employee assistance counselor, I recalled that he told me major changes were underway in their company. He predicted that there would be more people in crisis, indicating he might be coming to me with more referrals.

I realized I had already taken Jackie's side, and I pulled back a bit. Jackie said she had a temper, and I chose to move gently in that direction. First, I mirrored the content of what she said, then I validated her experience with her company by saying, "It makes sense that you would feel trapped and angry at a company that seems to be hurting, not helping you." She responded, keeping us on the subject of the negative workplace.

> *I started working for this company right out of high school. I used to go in early, work on my lunch hour and feel good about the work I did. I loved helping customers. Now they want us to spend precious little time with customers, make a sale, and get off the phone. It's so impersonal now. And they have all of us there at each other's throats because only a few of us will be kept.*

I empathized with Jackie's feelings of despair and disillusionment. She said she had not felt fully supported by her union, but neither had she talked with her representative about this recent complaint.

Jackie's depression and anxiety needed further evaluation. She used to sew and go fishing with her husband, but she had no energy for those activities or the basic tasks around the house. She hadn't balanced her checkbook in 5 months. She said she had difficulty getting to her office. She had periods of uncontrollable anxiety and took a benzodiazepine prescribed by her doctor. She experienced insomnia; when she finally fell asleep, it was a fitful sleep. She

"unloaded" on her husband more than either of them would have liked. I called her family physician while Jackie was in my office, and we discussed medication options. The physician asked for Jackie to come in to see her and said she was thinking of prescribing Jackie an antidepressant that would help ease her symptoms of depression, anxiety, and fitful sleep. The doctor said she would taper the benzodiazepine, which could be negatively affecting Jackie's sleep.

I contemplated whether to see Jackie individually to deal with the specific work-related issue or to bring in Jackie's husband. I chose the latter, believing I needed to assess the quality of Jackie's primary support system as she faced this major hurdle of working in a system that had judged her to be below performance standards. In addition, I believed that, for the most part, partners are the best resources for supporting their spouses through difficult times. Couples who support each other through difficult times can deepen the intimacy and connection they feel with each other, and this enhanced relationship can be curative. Researchers and clinicians have documented improvement in marital communication and marital adjustment from training couples to support each other (Baucom & Epstein, 1990; Christensen, Jacobson, & Babcock, 1995; Collins, 1977; Ginsberg & Vogelsong, 1977; Guerney, 1977; Halford & Markman, 1997; Jacobson, 1978; Markman, Renick, Floyd, Stanley, & Clements, 1993; Snyder & Guerney, 1999). Hendrix proposed a model for teaching couples to deepen their relationships through verbal expressions and behaviors demonstrating empathy for one another (Brown & Reinhold, 1999; Hendrix, 1988, 1996, 1999; Luquet, 1996; Zielinski, 1999). IRT is based on an integration of psychodynamic, behavioral, interpersonal, and systemic therapies. The major assumption of the clinical model is that couples choose each other for reasons related to their childhood upbringing with significant caretakers. They select a partner who has characteristics like their caretakers, primarily like the caretaker with whom they had the most significant struggles. Childhood experiences lead to the formation of an unconscious image, or *imago*, which is used in mate selection. The unfinished struggles from childhood are then re-created in the marital relationship. The couple relationship provides the context for healthy individual growth. When partners act with empathy, in contrast to the lack of empathy the person obtained during parts of childhood, healing from past hurts and a deepened relationship with the partner are accomplished. Many couples will benefit from education about how to provide empathy to their partners. Psychoeducation and interpersonal processes form the cornerstone of the therapeutic process. The therapist acts as a coach to teach and guide the couple through these experiences. The Intentional Dialogue provides the basic structure for communication and empathy development. The three parts of the IRT dialogue are *mirroring, validation,* and *empathy.* The dialogue is then used as the basis for other imago therapeutic processes.

For reasons of assessment of the support system and building the structure for healing through the interpersonal relationship of the couple, I decided to encourage Jackie to bring her husband, Anthony, to the next session, and we closed the first session with this suggestion. She eagerly agreed to invite him. Along with believing his presence could be helpful to her, she suspected he, too, could derive great benefit from therapy and predicted he might be willing to come. He worked for the same company and had his own difficulties with the administration of the organization. In addition, I suggested Jackie talk with her union representative about her need for support from the union.

MAY 15

Jackie's husband, Anthony, came with her to the next session. He said he would not always be able to come but that he wanted to support her as much as possible. I thanked him for coming and told them I wanted to teach them a tool for talking with each other using the Couples' Dialogue (see Appendix A; Hendrix, 1999, p. 27). I explained the basic philosophy of IRT, emphasizing the positive outcomes that were possible, including a deepened relationship for the two of them.

After some practice with the structure, I invited Jackie and Anthony to talk about a frustration using the dialogue. Jackie wanted to go first. She spilled

out her anger at the company as if she had been waiting for the opportunity. The management introduced new expectations that week, lowering once again the average amount of time the sales operators were to spend with customers. Also, one of her coworkers had been fired, and Jackie was on pins and needles. She desperately needed to keep her job. I asked Anthony to mirror, validate, and empathize with Jackie's perceptions and taught him how to do that. He said,

> *She doesn't want to lose her job. It makes sense she doesn't want to lose the job because we have depended on the money she earns. I can imagine she might feel worried about how it would affect me if she lost her job.*

Jackie affirmed that he was absolutely right about her concerns.

It was now Anthony's turn to respond. Anthony said they could survive without Jackie's salary and that he didn't want her to feel pressure to stay there. But then he began to reveal his own story. He had his own difficulties with management at work. Last year when his father was very ill, before his death from heart disease, Anthony wanted to spend time with his father in the intensive care unit. He explained to the management that his father was terminally ill. His supervisor, Mr. Jenkins, told Anthony that everyone was going to die sometime and that he would not be allowed to take the time off from work. Since his father's death, Anthony had been angry and out of sorts at work. The loyalty he used to have for the company was gone, and his former eagerness to please Mr. Jenkins turned to complacency. Jackie mirrored, validated, and empathized with her husband:

> *You resent Mr. Jenkins for not caring about your situation with your dad. That makes sense to me because you have given a lot to the company and the least they could do is give something back. I can imagine you might feel bitterness towards Mr. Jenkins.*

It was Jackie's turn to respond. Jackie said she was concerned about Anthony. He was preoccupied and sometimes unavailable to her. He withdrew when there were problems. Anthony mirrored, then validated her by saying, "You make sense because I have been preoccupied and sometimes not responsive to you. And I don't talk to you very much about what is on my mind."

Anthony had the floor. As he thought about what he wanted to say, his body flinched with emotion. He began to explain his fears about his mother. After his father died, his mother became depressed, going often to visit the emergency room for help with her anxiety, because she had no regular doctor. She seemed to be in a daze on the medication she was taking. Jackie mirrored and validated Anthony, saying, "You're worried about your mother. It makes sense that you'd worry about her because she has changed so much from the independent, loving person she used to be. I imagine you might feel scared and burdened."

Jackie revealed her own sense of loss with the big changes she and Anthony had seen in her mother-in-law. Jackie used to have a strong connection with her mother-in-law, sharing their loves of gardening and sewing. Anthony validated Jackie by acknowledging the loss both he and Jackie were experiencing as a result of his mother's decline. Anthony, haltingly, and with tears, divulged another deep-seated fear. "I didn't want to burden you with my problems. My worst fear is you won't be able to handle hearing about my problems and you'll become like my mother—dependent on me and drugs." Jackie mirrored his words but then stopped. She admitted she was stuck. She couldn't find any way to validate what he had said, because she didn't agree with it. I mirrored Jackie's concern, then said that validating Anthony's experience was different from agreeing with him. I asked her where the grain of truth was in what he said. She validated him then by saying "It makes sense you'd worry about me—I do take things to heart more than I should, and I have taken medication for my anxiety." The IRT clinical approach is for the therapist to mirror a member of the couple if the therapist believes the partner doing the mirroring is having a strong emotional reaction that prevents him or her from responding effectively to the partner.

I celebrated with Jackie and Anthony their ac-

complishment of putting their own agendas on hold temporarily to be there fully for each other. I asked their reactions to their conversation with each other. Jackie said she felt calmer because Anthony was exposing what had been weighing heavily on his mind. Anthony admitted he felt some relief and surprise that this structure gave him the space and the nudge to explain himself more openly than usual. He acknowledged that his openness was probably good for him. We talked about gender differences in communication and the specifics of their communication style. Jackie commonly told all, whereas Anthony was quiet. I mentioned that each of us has an emotional button, a sensitivity. When the button gets pushed, each person reacts automatically. The reactions may be sadness, anger, rage, or withdrawal. For example, if I have an invisibility button that gets pushed when my partner or coworker ignores me, then I am going to react. I may become angry or withdraw. Or, if I have an inadequacy button, and I feel my partner is criticizing me, I might react with rage or sadness. I gave each of them an instruction sheet naming various buttons (see Appendix B; Gerson, 1994, p. 28) and asked them to begin writing about their buttons.

I collected some basic information for constructing a family genogram and drew the genogram graphic on the computer for them (see Figure 1; Shellenberger & Gerson, 2000). Each was invited to complete a Family Pattern Analysis Questionnaire (Gerson & Shellenberger, 2000), which they both agreed to do.

Anthony asked if there were any physicians in the center where I worked who specialized in geriatrics who could see his mother. I referred them to a geriatrician in the department who was very skilled and very careful about the medications he prescribed. I sent the couple home with the assignment to talk with each other using the dialogue format. They were to practice this structure with each other at least 15 minutes each day.

As I dictated my notes for the day I reflected on the complex issues that had emerged in this case, including the complementary relationship patterns in the couple, family life cycle issues, gender issues, and the larger system issues of work stress. At first, work issues seemed most prominent to each of

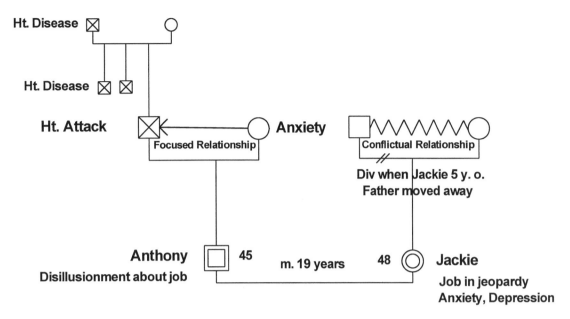

FIGURE 6.1. Genogram of Jackie and Anthony

them; however, their mutual job dissatisfaction was part of a larger picture of several losses. Fear of more loss compounded the problem.

Jackie and Anthony were both feeling the loss of their former intimate connection. They were in a covert power struggle, polarized over the issues of closeness and separateness, dependence and independence. Jackie wanted more openness, emotional connection, and interdependence. Anthony was preoccupied with family and job concerns. As he withdrew, Jackie became more anxious. As she became anxious, she took more drugs to calm herself. This exacerbated one of Anthony's worst fears—that Jackie would become dependent on drugs and on him. He brooded even more.

The couple's losses related to family life cycle issues (Carter & McGoldrick, 1998; Gerson, 1995) contributed to their sense of alienation, loneliness, depression, and anxiety. One life cycle issue related to the death of Anthony's father. Anthony continued to harbor resentment toward Mr. Jenkins for his lack of understanding when Anthony's father was ill. This may have kept Anthony from experiencing the grief in a way that would have helped him resolve his feelings of loss. He decided not to burden Jackie with his emotions for fear she would overreact. Regrettably, he sacrificed the opportunity to have her, his major support person, console and comfort him.

A second life cycle issue was that Anthony and Jackie lost their warm, satisfying relationship with Anthony's mother. A third life cycle issue related to Anthony's fears that he might be called on to care for his mother as she aged.

Another area of loss for Jackie and Anthony was the erosion of good feeling they had about their work lives. Their corporation had historically been oriented toward collaboration and teamwork. They viewed the corporate focus as having moved from loyal employees to ledger profits.

I reflected on my own experiences and what I had learned about healing from loss. My mother died when I was 19. Slowly, over the years, I healed from that loss. When my husband died 1-1/2 years ago, I used those hard-learned coping skills to make it through that trauma. I believed what I discovered could also apply to the losses experienced by this couple. I learned that coping with and healing from loss are facilitated through connections with others (Shellenberger, 1997). As many theoreticians, clinicians, and researchers have shown, intimate couple connections can buffer the effects of stress (Edwards, Nazroo, & Brown, 1998; Franks & Stephens, 1996; Kennedy, Kiecolt-Glaser, & Glaser, 1988; Kiecolt-Glaser et al., 1987; Pasch & Bradbury, 1998; Weiss & Heyman, 1997). Enhancing current relationships can lead to a more solid base for facing past losses and preparing for future losses. If the primary relationship of the couple could be improved so that both were getting more of what they needed from each other, they would have a strong base for supporting each other through challenging times. I considered options for addressing the presenting problem of Jackie's work difficulties. We would need to fully explore the complaints made by her employers. Getting the perspective of the administrators seemed important, but difficult, to achieve. Jackie needed someone who was an ally in order for her to feel safe to expose her true behaviors. I decided to attend to this dilemma at our next session.

MAY 29

As Jackie and Anthony came into the next session, I detected a pall of anxiety in their countenances. I stuck with my plan of beginning each couple session with an expression of appreciation for something the partner had done. I believed that beginning the session on as positive a note as possible would maximize opportunities for growth. Anthony began. He expressed appreciation to Jackie for being there with him when he saw his cardiologist the week before. She mirrored his words of appreciation and thanked him for allowing her to know his deep fears related to the terrifying symptoms he had had. He mirrored her appreciation. I asked them to fill me in on what happened.

Anthony explained that he had begun having cardiac symptoms (chest pain and dizziness) a few days after their visit with me. Anthony's father died in his early 60s, and two uncles and his grandfather died in their 40s and 50s from heart disease. Anthony and Jackie were very worried. He underwent a stress test and wore a heart monitor to further evaluate his problem.

My fears for them were aroused. My husband died in his early 40s, Anthony's age. I knew what serious illness and untimely death could mean for both of them. I expressed my compassion for their difficulties. I made a mental note to take extra care of myself as I worked with this couple.

In the midst of these dramatic developments, Jackie and Anthony were able to name some posi-

tive happenings. His mother had seen the recommended family physician, who began weaning her from the many medications she was taking. She was already showing signs of her old self. In addition, Anthony and Jackie had done the assigned dialogue, albeit with difficulty, several times since our last visit. They described being much more hopeful about their mutually supportive abilities.

They struggled, then, with how to handle the upcoming diagnostic procedure (cardiac catheterization) Anthony was to have. Jackie wanted to take time off to go with Anthony, but she knew she would risk a reprimand letter being placed in her file at work. She said she didn't care, that Anthony was more important. Anthony mirrored her but stopped when asked to validate her. I asked him what was going through his mind, and he told me that he wanted Jackie to go on to work. He could handle this minor procedure without her, and they shouldn't risk losing her job. Her job stability was more crucial now that his health was unstable. Here again were the issues that had so polarized them in the past—separateness and independence versus togetherness and interdependence. I realized I was having an emotional reaction to Anthony's health problems, and I found myself thinking back to the time of my husband's illness and hoped this couple would not have to endure the trauma I did. Although I wished for them that they would choose for Jackie to be present during the procedure, I realized my reactions were related to my regret at not always accompanying my husband during some of the difficult times of his illness. I decided to keep my own experience out of the room for the moment until I had more opportunity to explore my reactions and how they might influence this couple if I were to reveal them. I knew that if I shared my feelings at that moment I might not be able to contain my grief. The spotlight may have changed from them to me, and they might feel the need to take care of me in my grief. I decided I would discuss this case with a close friend and colleague to make sure my own issues did not interfere with the therapy. I mirrored Anthony's preference that Jackie not attend the procedure and reminded him that he would have a chance to fully explain his side later. He validated Jackie by saying, "It makes sense you'd want to be with me to support me and to help with your own fears." Jackie looked relieved to know that Anthony understood. He empathized by saying, "I imagine you might also feel worried that something bad might happen and you won't be there." She looked even more relieved to know he fully sensed her terror.

Now it was Anthony's call. He described to Jackie his fears of becoming disabled and not working. She mirrored and invited him to say more. With his heart problem and the possibility that he might have to take a lot of time off work, he was more worried about Jackie losing her job. He wished she would pay closer attention to what her supervisor said she needed to do to keep her job. She mirrored and then validated him by saying, "What you are saying makes sense to me because we would be in trouble without our jobs. And I imagine you might also be irritated with me for not paying closer attention to my supervisors."

Jackie was on the defensive. She revealed that she had not yet had the courage to discuss the work complaint with Sarah, her union representative. She wanted Sarah's support but didn't want to admit she needed it. Anthony mirrored and validated her hesitation, saying, "It makes sense you would hesitate. This complaint is not a pretty thing to talk about, and you would just as soon ignore the whole thing." This was the opener I needed to present an idea for expanding this system to include the work setting. I asked Jackie if she would like to have Sarah meet with her and me to more fully explain Jackie's work difficulties and devise a plan for meeting the management's requirements for Jackie to keep her job. Jackie and Anthony brightened at the idea. Jackie expressed excitement about the possibility of having me assist her in securing the union's support for her case. Anthony was clearly relieved to hear Jackie express interest in attending to what he saw as her fragile work situation. The color started to come back into his cheeks for the first time. He mirrored and validated Jackie, saying

It makes sense to me that you would want to do what it takes to keep your job, for your sake and for mine. And I imagine you might feel glad you've come up with a

plan that will please me and possibly make the situation better.

We planned to meet the next week with Sarah. Together Jackie and Anthony decided that Anthony would not be present for the session. He was already missing quite a bit of work for his tests, and he believed Jackie would be able to handle this meeting on her own. Jackie agreed, seeming to find some new confidence about her abilities to do what she could to secure her job. She expressed appreciation to Anthony for believing in her. I asked him to mirror that appreciation so that the good things that happened between him and Jackie could be reinforced. I offered to be available for telephone consultation during this critical period. They committed to continuing their dialogue at home in order to decide whether Jackie would take time off work to be with Anthony during his heart procedure.

After the session, I called a colleague and scheduled lunch so we could talk about my personal reactions to this case. As I dictated my notes, I thought about the therapy session. I saw several positive factors emerging in this case. I believed doing the couple's work was building the strong support base Jackie would need to tackle her work problem. The covert power struggle that had kept this couple dissatisfied, desperate, and distant was now beginning to ease. Both partners' needs were becoming the focus of attention. They were celebrating their own and each other's strengths. They were solving their own problems. Coming from a family systems background, I hold in high regard the tenet of paying attention to both sides of the couple so as to keep the work balanced (Boszormenyi-Nagy & Krasner, 1986; Kerr & Bowen, 1988). I did not want one member of the couple to appear to be the weaker or needier one.

I took note of the ingredients I believed were contributing to these positive developments in this couple. First was the belief that the best solutions emerged from within the individuals and the couple. Second was providing a structure from which to dialogue. The dialogue structure had multiple benefits for me and for the couple: It kept us on task, maintained a balance in addressing both partners' needs and thoughts, required each person to validate the other's perspective, facilitated empathy, and required modulation of negative reactions that could inhibit the process. The structure also kept the focus squarely on the members of the couple, not on the therapist.

I thought about the next session, when Jackie and I would meet with Sarah, the union representative. The goal was for Jackie to garner support in this larger system of the workplace. I thought about how our therapy sessions were laying the groundwork for Jackie to feel supported to do what she needed to do at work. She seemed to be feeling support from me and her husband. We would add this other prong of support from someone at her work setting. I pondered the possibility of moving to individual sessions for Jackie to focus on her responses to difficult customers. The couple sessions were helping Jackie become calmer and contain her automatic reactions while she listened to the other person, but we also needed direct discussion and practice of her response skills.

During the next week, I talked with my friend and colleague about my feelings of regret for not having been with my husband during all of his illness. My friend reminded me that while my husband was ill, neither he nor I believed he would die. We lived our lives as if we would continue to be together. She reminded me that I had tried to balance my needs for being with him and upholding my work responsibilities. I expressed more of my grief about my loss. Some positive benefits came from talking: I experienced a closer connection with my friend, who understands my feelings. I was also conscious of some resolution of another part of my grief. I was relieved to have a clearer understanding of my regrets about my husband's illness. In addition, this new clarity renewed my motivation to assist Jackie with her dilemma, and I looked forward to my next meeting with her.

JUNE 12

Shortly before my session with Jackie, her employee assistance counselor, who had referred her to me, called with another referral from their company. He mentioned that more changes, including downsizing, were imminent. I felt more pressure to work more

intensively with Jackie, knowing that she was vulnerable to losing her job. I asked what the company was doing to address the effects of the changes on the employees. He said they were assisting displaced workers with finding new jobs but little else. He also said they had been trying desperately, without success, to lure some high-level technical people to their corporation but that these potential employees were somewhat hesitant to sign on with the company. He said he had decided to talk to the administration about the need to have a stellar record of treating employees well in order to recruit the people they wanted.

Jackie introduced me to Sarah, her union representative. Sarah revealed guarded optimism about Jackie's situation. Jackie had a previous citation in her record that would not be revoked even if Jackie met current expectations. Sarah expressed some disappointment that Jackie had waited so long to talk to her about a plan for eliminating the current citation. She said that the company wanted a detailed plan submitted by Jackie describing how she expected to change her attitude and work performance. I asked Jackie to mirror and validate Sarah. Consonant with IRT principles (Hendrix, 1996), I believe that whenever possible it is important to show respect for the other person by expressing validation for his or her perspective. Familiar now with the validation process, Jackie easily responded, saying, "That makes sense to me because I have been ignoring the problem, pretending it does not exist, and the problem hasn't gone away."

Jackie explained to Sarah that until recently she had felt hopeless about the situation but that now she was ready to undertake the difficult task of developing a plan to satisfy the administrators. I asked Sarah if she understood why Jackie felt hopeless. Sarah said she could, especially because some of Jackie's coworkers had been fired in the midst of attempts to remedy problems the administration had with their performance.

Sarah revealed more. She said she had learned that Jackie's supervisor was monitoring her twice as often as her coworkers. Jackie was to submit a plan of remediation to be approved by her supervisor and appear before a panel of supervisors in 3 months to assess her progress. It was hoped that at that time they would eliminate the most recent citation from her record.

Jackie, more naturally now, mirrored what Sarah told her. She was tearful as she exposed to Sarah the turn of events in her life: her husband's illness. Sarah expressed surprise and support for Jackie's situation.

Sarah and Jackie discussed the plan of remediation Jackie was to present to her supervisors. Sarah told Jackie that the company would look very favorably on her participation in therapy. The goals they decided to list to be accomplished in therapy were: facing her personal issues that were getting in the way of a pleasant attitude at work, building support in her personal life so she felt strong and capable, and evaluating her impulsive reactions to customers who were complaining. Beyond this, Jackie would complete some correspondence courses on customer relations that were promoted by her corporation. Jackie and Sarah were pleased with the plan. I thanked Sarah for coming. Sarah left, and I closed with Jackie by scheduling an appointment for her and her husband. I also suggested we meet for some individual sessions to deal with the goals we had outlined in the session. Jackie agreed, and we scheduled six sessions over the next 3 months.

JUNE 26

At our next visit, Anthony and Jackie handed me their completed Family Pattern Analysis Questionnaire to be analyzed on the computer. They expressed mutual appreciation for each other. Anthony appreciated Jackie's attention to the performance requests of her supervisors. Jackie appreciated Anthony's willingness to dialogue with her the previous week. Believing it is important to focus on success and strengths in their endeavors and relationships (Walsh, 1995, 1998; Wolin & Wolin, 1993), I asked them to state one personal success that had occurred since the last time we all met together. Jackie said she was surprised how well she handled the most irritating customers this week. Anthony said he was pleased about overriding his tendency to withdraw from Jackie, talking with her instead.

They updated me about Anthony's health situation. His exploratory heart procedure had gone well. The doctors found a blockage and eliminated it with angioplasty. The doctors were hopeful this would ease Anthony's heart problems, but they strongly recommended Anthony adopt a more healthful lifestyle.

Jackie said she had some frustration about this that she wanted to discuss with Anthony. He said he was available to discuss her frustration. Jackie said she believed Anthony was dismissing the seriousness of his health situation. His doctors asked Anthony to control his diet, and he had not followed their recommendations. Anthony mirrored, then validated what she said: "You're right, I haven't changed my diet. And I can imagine you might feel worried about what could happen." Jackie told Anthony that he was on target—she was worried. She added that she also felt helpless to try to influence his eating patterns. Anthony said he would rather not think about his heart problem and that dieting was a constant reminder. He was not enjoying much else in his life and wanted at least this small pleasure of eating according to his preferences. Jackie appeared frustrated but simply mirrored him and said, "It makes sense you'd want to avoid this problem. It's not pleasant to deal with, and I know how much you enjoy eating what you like."

Jackie was invited to ask Anthony if his way of coping with this problem reminded him of anyone else in his past. He flinched, as I had seen him react before; he told Jackie that his father never admitted he had a heart problem, never complied with his medication regimen, and never changed his diet. His mother often was frustrated with her husband because he wouldn't pay close attention to his precarious health. Anthony remembered wishing his mother would back off from nagging his father, but now he realized that his father may have died prematurely because of his lack of attention to his health. Jackie mirrored all that Anthony said and validated him, saying,

> *It makes sense; nagging is not pleasant to watch. And it makes sense you are wondering how much your father's choice not to pay attention to his health problems affected how long he lived. And I can imag-*

ine you might feel worried about what this means for you.

I was surprised about how little I was intervening with this couple. I was even more amazed about the positive effects their behaviors were having on each other. They were providing their partner with a mirror so that even the unrecognized or unacknowledged parts of themselves could come to light, supporting each other through the tough and the blind spots, and validating each other so that each came away with the belief his or her perspective had merit and that their feelings made sense.

Jackie talked about how she felt like "the nag" in her relationship with Anthony. She realized she tended to provoke Anthony until he became angry. She felt frustrated and hopeless when things got to this point in their relationship, just as she felt frustrated and hopeless when dealing with her customers who wouldn't pay attention to what she said. She wanted to change her behavior toward Anthony and talked with him about how to do this. Anthony mirrored and validated her experience by saying,

> *You have tried hard to make me change my behavior, and the result is that now you feel like a nag in our relationship. It makes sense you'd want to do what you can to keep me healthy. And I can imagine you might feel desperate sometimes as you try to find the right way to help me.*

Anthony talked about wanting Jackie's help and support but wanting to find a better way for them to talk with each other about this difficult subject. I suggested we do another IRT process called the Behavior Change Request but realized we had come to the end of our allotted time for the day. We planned this activity for our next meeting. I gave each of them some information to read about the Behavior Change Request format.

JULY 10

At the next session, Anthony and Jackie began, knowing that they would be asked to describe an appreciation of the other person and a personal success. Jackie seemed quieter at this session. She thought awhile and then expressed appreciation to

Anthony for his help around the house this week when she had such a difficult work schedule. Anthony appreciated Jackie being more amorous this week. Jackie could not think of any personal successes. I waited with silence for her to think of something. Finally, she remembered pulling out her sewing basket to see what she might want to tackle on the sewing machine. Anthony reported success at paying more attention to his health risk factors this week.

Jackie asked to have the floor first. She felt devastated by what happened at work this week. She became angry at a customer, who then asked for her name and threatened to report her to her supervisor. Jackie was terrified she might lose her job because of this one incident. I asked Anthony to paraphrase what Jackie said. When he invited her to tell more about it, she blurted out that she felt like a failure to herself and to Anthony. She told Anthony she stayed as calm as possible but could no longer contain her irritation with the irate customer. Anthony mirrored everything and attempted to validate her by saying, "You make sense because you got upset, and you just lost it." Jackie shrugged and lowered her head. I could tell she did not feel validated by Anthony. I asked Anthony to mirror Jackie's nonverbal response. He said, "You feel even more like a failure because I said you lost it." Jackie looked up at Anthony, clearly relieved that he understood her reaction. I asked Anthony to talk with me about what he was considering saying as a validation of her. He said,

> *She's trying so hard, and she wants me to understand how difficult it is to be civil to problem customers. I know how hard her job is. I couldn't be nice to the customers when they get so angry, especially with all Jackie has on her, with the company on her back and all.*

I asked him to validate Jackie with those ideas. He said to her, "You tried your best to be nice to the customers, even with the company making it so hard for you." He empathized by saying, "I imagine you felt unsupported and scared." Jackie held her head up this time. Anthony took her hand and held it. She said she felt better.

I asked Jackie and Anthony if they were aware of what buttons of theirs were pushed. Jackie said her catastrophe and her helplessness buttons were pushed this week. She began to see her work situation as impossible and that she could never change her reactions to the customers. Anthony said he began to realize his control button was getting pushed, wanting to stimulate Jackie to shape up on her job.

We reviewed where we were last visit. Jackie desperately wanted to talk with Anthony about his health risks and not taking care of himself but felt like a nag when she did. Although Anthony wanted her support, he wanted them to find a better way to talk about his diet and other issues related to his health.

Both Anthony and Jackie had read the material I gave them about how to make requests. I told them I would help them first come up with an ideal they wanted to accomplish, then three specific behaviors that would meet the change they wanted. Next, I would help them describe the behaviors in specific, measurable, time-limited terms. The other partner was to mirror the requests, choose one of the requests, and give this behavior change to the partner as a gift. The reason for listing three possible changes of behavior was so the giving partner had a choice and did not feel he or she had to do all of the changes at once (see Appendix C; Hendrix, 1999, p. 29).

I asked the couple to decide who would be the first to ask for changes. Anthony invited Jackie to request first. Jackie said she backed off from mentioning anything to Anthony about his health situation because she didn't want to be seen as a nag. She said her worst fear was of driving Anthony away. Her nonverbal gestures of white face and wringing hands suggested she felt more strongly about this situation than her words revealed. Anthony mirrored her. Remembering material from their family genogram and Family Pattern Analysis Report, I asked Anthony to ask Jackie if these feelings reminded her of any similar feelings from her childhood. Jackie revealed that her parents divorced and her father moved away when she was 5 years old. The only interaction she could remember her parents having before that time was conflict. In her current relationship with Anthony, she feared her

nagging might result in conflict that would drive Anthony away. Anthony mirrored her fears. He hesitated, but thought for a minute and validated her, saying, " It makes sense to me that you'd be scared I'd leave. That's what your father did when your parents couldn't get along. And I can imagine you are scared about what could happen to us." I asked Anthony to ask Jackie what she needed from him the most. She said she didn't want him to leave her. He mirrored her hope. I asked him to ask her what three specific things he could do to help her feel he was committed to the relationship. With coaching, she was able to name three things she wanted. He mirrored her three requests to (a) tell her twice in the next 2 weeks he wanted to stay married to her, (b) talk with her about her feelings twice for 5 min each time in the next 2 weeks, and (c) bring up the issue of his diet one time in the next week. Anthony believed he could do all three of these but, after some coaching from me, chose the third to give her as a gift. He said this one would be harder for him but important for them both. He pledged to give her that request as a gift to her. I asked Anthony to make a list of these three requests, starring the one he agreed to do. When I asked for their reactions to our discussion, Anthony said he never realized her parents' conflicts and their divorce led to fears the same thing would happen to Jackie and Anthony if they had conflict. Jackie felt reassured that Anthony more fully understood her concerns about their relationship and his health.

Jackie invited Anthony to make his requests. Anthony said he became frustrated when Jackie told him he shouldn't eat certain foods or suggested he exercise more. This was exactly what his mother did to stir up trouble with his father. His mother would then complain to Anthony about what, in her opinion, his father was doing wrong. Anthony felt caught in the middle. He tried to convince his mother to retract from meddling, but he couldn't. Jackie mirrored, then validated what Anthony was saying:

> *You make sense to me. It was very hard*
> *for you to be caught in the middle of your*
> *parents' arguments. And I can see why*
> *you wanted to get your mother to stop*

saying negative things about your father. I can imagine you felt resentful.

Anthony acknowledged she was right about his feelings.

I asked Jackie to invite Anthony to say what would help this situation in their current relationship. He said that ideally he would like for Jackie never to bug him about his diet but to support his own efforts to be careful in what he eats. She mirrored his request. I asked Anthony to think of three specific behaviors Jackie could do to help this situation. She mirrored his requests to (a) notice twice each week for the next 2 weeks when he had been faithful to the diet prescribed by his physician; (b) call and chat with a friend of hers whenever she felt critical of what he was eating, for the next 2 weeks; (c) buy healthful foods for them to keep on hand, instead of high-fat choices she often bought. He wanted for her to do this for the next 2 weeks. Jackie told Anthony that, as a gift to him, she would call and chat with a friend whenever she felt critical of what he was eating. She put all of his requests on her list of things to do for the future and starred the one she committed to do now. Jackie was surprised by the requests Anthony made and pleased that she now had some ways of supporting his efforts without "nagging" him. Anthony was hopeful these efforts would calm the underlying tension they had been feeling with each other.

I told Jackie and Anthony I was pleased for them because they were finding ways to be supportive of each other. We talked about the importance of giving gifts freely, not for the giving to be tracked or observed by the partner. Then we talked about what they had learned about their own emotional buttons. Jackie said she had learned she has a button related to fears of abandonment—Anthony might leave if they had conflict. Anthony identified his button of feeling overwhelmed by Jackie, as if he'd lose his own identity when she nagged and tried to make him do what she wanted. They were asked to dialogue that week with each other about those particular buttons.

As I reflected on our session, I noted the progress we were making with each individual, the couple, and the larger system. Both individuals were learning more about themselves, taking responsibility for their own actions and reactions. For the couple, the quality of their connection seemed to be changing. There was less polarization around the issues of separation and connection. In the face of major life upsets and crises, the members of the couple supported each other and attended to the desires of each partner as well as to personal desires. In the larger systems of extended family and the workplace we were making headway as well. The relationship with Anthony's mother improved for him and Jackie. In regard to her work difficulties, Jackie had what she described as a setback. On the positive side, she took responsibility for the negative encounter with a customer. She was garnering support and validation from Anthony as she made the difficult changes in the face of pressure from supervisors.

JUNE 19, JULY 3, JULY 17, JULY 24, AUGUST 7, AND AUGUST 14

Jackie and I met to talk about her goals for improving her reactions to difficult customers. I suggested several books to read, including the *Dance of Anger* (Lerner, 1985) and *Feeling Good: The New Mood Therapy* (Burns, 1980). Jackie had already begun her coursework for the company. Although she believed the coursework was necessary to fulfill the contract she made with her supervisors for improving her handling of difficult customers, she was not finding the studies very helpful for her personal needs. She found our couples and individual therapy much more helpful in learning how to think through her responses before she made them. With irritated or irate customers, she used the mirroring and validation tools she learned from our couples sessions. Often, this dialogue took place in her mind, and sometimes even with the customers. She believed this helped her to respond with calmness.

In our sessions Jackie practiced new ways of reacting to customers who were difficult for her to handle the previous week. We talked about Jackie's reactions at work and her emotional buttons that were pushed. They were similar to the buttons pushed with Anthony. When customers were upset, she panicked and retorted with a sharp tone of voice. Her catastrophe button was frequently pushed, and she admitted she saw the situations as hopeless. We looked at Jackie's genogram and family patterns from her childhood. Before her parents divorced, there was a lot of conflict that included yelling and occasional hitting between her parents. Jackie remembered panicking and yelling to try to stop her parents. The conflict continued. When Jackie was 5 years old her parents divorced, and her father left their community. Jackie admitted that the intensity of her reactions to upset customers might be related to the vulnerability and helplessness she felt as a child. We looked at ways for her to soothe herself, such as imagining herself at her ideal placid place—in a boat at her favorite fishing lake. She also told herself that the situation was not a catastrophe and that she had some control over the outcomes of the interchanges. She practiced mirroring and validating customers' complaints the way she had her husband's in our couples therapy sessions. She found this gave her a way to automatically react to customers that was not offensive. It also forced her to see alternative ways of viewing the interchanges with customers. Furthermore, Jackie was able to see what might have led the customers to react the way they did. Jackie acknowledged her customers had their own sets of emotional buttons and family patterns from their childhoods and that she did not need to react to their issues.

AUGUST 28

At our next couples session, Jackie seemed brighter. She told Anthony she appreciated the reassurances of his commitment to their relationship and his paying more attention to his diet. He mirrored her and then thanked Jackie for starting her correspondence course on handling customer complaints. She mirrored his appreciation. I asked them to name one personal success since our last meeting. Jackie said she accomplished making it through 2 weeks without a major confrontation with a customer. Anthony said his success was not overreacting once when Jackie started to confront him about what he chose to eat.

Jackie and Anthony updated me about the current status of their lives. Anthony's doctors believed

they had finally found a medication to keep his arrythmias under control. They were pleased with his progress but still asked him to begin gradually a program of exercise and weight loss and to be careful about his diet. Jackie and Anthony had had some enjoyable get-togethers with his mother. Jackie took one correspondence course at work on handling customer complaints. Although she barely passed it, the work was sufficient to satisfy her agreement with her supervisors. They scheduled a meeting to review her progress at the 3-month interval after her suspension. Jackie was nervous but confident this would go well.

Neither Jackie nor Anthony had a current frustration they wanted to discuss. I suggested we engage in another IRT process: creation of a shared vision for their marriage (Hendrix, 1988). I believed the more solid the foundation of their relationship, the more confidence they would have for dealing with individual struggles—Jackie with her work situation and Anthony with his health issues. They were to list separately the positive qualities and behaviors they had now and those they wanted in their relationship, stating these qualities and behaviors in present terms, as if they were already happening. After they completed this step I asked them to dialogue about an ideal relationship. Some of the qualities they listed included the following: (a) We express appreciation for and praise of each other, (b) we are special to each other, (c) we are supportive of each other, (d) we have fun together, (d) we work out finances easily, (e) we respect each other's separate interests, and (d) we enjoy our love life together.

In their dialogue, they talked about the difficulty they had with two of these items: working out finances and respecting each other's separate interests. As homework for the next week they were asked to dialogue about one of these items. Then they were to list the desired goal, the specific behaviors to accomplish the goal, a strategy or action plan for completing the objective, and a description of the ideal outcome.

SEPTEMBER 11

When Jackie and Anthony returned in 2 weeks, they appeared less stressed than before. Jackie was wearing brighter colors; when I complemented her, she mentioned she had made by hand the dress she was wearing. Anthony appeared slimmer, and his posture indicated more confidence than on previous visits. He said his posture was helped by the weights he was lifting at the health club.

Anthony said he appreciated the time Jackie spent with his mother. Jackie mirrored him and expressed appreciation for his support during the 3-month ordeal with her work. She delightedly related her recent success in meeting with her supervisors: The citation was removed from her file. Anthony's success was regular attendance at the health club's cardiac care program.

Jackie gave the details of her work situation. Her supervisors removed the citation but cautioned her that her old citation was still in the records and that any new citation could lead to automatic dismissal with no remedial process. She thought the supervisors were genuinely pleased by her efforts. She was not sure whether to really trust this new interest in her but was hopeful she could do what was necessary to keep her job until retirement. Anthony was hopeful this new program at the health club, designed especially for heart patients, would be just what he needed.

As assigned, Jackie and Anthony had dialogued about one vision statement on their shared list: supporting each other's separate needs. I recalled their earlier struggle and polarization around closeness and separateness. A new air of confidence emerged to grapple with this divisive issue. They shared with me the objectives and plan for accomplishing the goal of validating their separate needs. Their objective was to make statements of support for the other person's separate needs at least once each day. The strategy was for each partner to perform at least one separate activity each week and for each partner to make validating and supportive statements about those separate activities each day. The ideal outcome would be a relaxed feeling while undertaking their separate activities. Then they would share with their partner what they experienced during their time apart. It appeared to me as though Jackie and Anthony had already begun that process—Jackie was sewing again and spending time with Anthony's mother. Anthony was visiting the health club regu-

larly. We discussed several other vision statements and their strategies for accomplishing the objectives.

Jackie and Anthony exhibited newfound confidence about their relationship, their work, and their extended family relationship. They suggested less frequent therapy visits. I agreed that they had learned many tools for keeping their relationship strong. We set up another visit in 1 month.

ONE-MONTH FOLLOW-UP

When Jackie and Anthony returned for their visit, Jackie ashamedly told me that she had been fired from her job. Even though humiliated and upset, she thought she handled the event with surprising equanimity. She learned so much in therapy and garnered lots of support from her husband, me, and her union, all of which helped her through the dreaded event. She had begun to compose a resume and was in touch with several people who had job leads. Her union was appealing the dismissal. Anthony reacted to Jackie's firing with surprising calmness. He was eager for her to find a job and wished now that he had been supportive when she said 2 years ago she wanted to go back to school. Anthony was doing well and exercised regularly. They continued in therapy with monthly visits, for a reduced fee because finances had become an issue.

I was shocked and saddened by Jackie's news but glad she handled the event so well. I committed myself to following her situation for any renewed signs of depression and Anthony's to make sure he stayed on a salutary course. I believed part of the reason Jackie was fired was because the company was eager to let go of employees with many years of service where there were reports of problems on the job. This would result in a financial savings for the company, because Jackie would not now be eligible for any retirement benefits. Furthermore, Jackie had become known as someone who was short tempered with clients. Although she had changed her manner of responding, the recent complaint against her, which under ordinary circumstances would have resulted in an opportunity to have her side heard, was not given appeal because of Jackie's history of problems. Jackie could not identify a specific interchange that led to the complaint. She believed it was possible the complaint against her might have been from an earlier period before she made significant changes in her response style, or she may have reverted to old patterns when under pressure. It is difficult to say what would have happened if we had worked more intensively or more directly on the work problems in the first month of therapy.

The future looks bright for Jackie, although she fears for her former colleagues who may suffer the same fate. Jackie called 1 week later to change the time of their next appointment because she had gotten another job. She described the new position as having much less pressure but also less wages. She felt relieved about becoming employed so quickly. She heard from previous coworkers that another former colleague was under pressures similar to those experienced by Jackie. I committed myself to do what I could to influence the work system to do whatever possible to assist employees identified as having difficulties.

LEARNINGS

There are several aspects to this case that were new or renewed learnings for me. This case heightened the respect I have for relationships and therapeutic work on relationships. I found that an important first step in moving ahead with individual issues is to first make sure the partnership relationship is strong. I believe that in most couple relationships people are drawn to partners who have things to teach them. When there is the potential for abuse or harm, a therapist's trust in the relationship would be misguided. This case provides evidence that, in most couples, the greatest learning will come from each other. The synergism created in the coming together of this couple carried them through difficult times and enhanced the functioning of each. The strength and support Jackie experienced in her relationship with her husband became the springboard from which Jackie was able to face her part in her work system.

I believe it took courage for Jackie and me to expand our therapeutic system to include Jackie's union representative, Sarah. We took a risk: Sarah could have misunderstood our intent; however, we trusted her good will. As it turned out, she became

an important support person for Jackie. I believe she will be a strong advocate as Jackie's case is appealed by the union.

My personal loss could have negatively influenced the direction of therapy with this couple. Instead, learning to manage my own vulnerabilities strengthened my capabilities in helping Anthony and Jackie with their own pain. Privately attending to my own grief issues with a friend and a colleague and writing about my experience (Shellenberger, 1997) enabled me to keep the focus on the needs of the couple. Furthermore, I was able to apply what I learned about loss and reconnection to the work with this couple. That is, after all, the primary therapeutic responsibility.

References

Baucom, D. H., & Epstein, N. (1990). *Cognitive–behavioral marital therapy.* New York: Brunner/Mazel.

Boszormenyi-Nagy, I., & Krasner, B. (1986). *Between give and take: A guide to contextual therapy.* New York: Brunner/Mazel.

Bowen, M. (1978). *Family therapy in clinical practice.* New York: Jason Aronson.

Brown, R., & Reinhold, T. (1999). *Imago Relationship Therapy: An introduction to theory and practice.* New York: Wiley.

Burns, D. D. (1980). *Feeling good: The new mood therapy.* New York: Morrow.

Carter, B., & McGoldrick, M. (Eds.). (1998). *The expanded family life cycle: Individual, family and social perspectives* (3rd ed.). Boston: Allyn & Bacon.

Christensen, A., Jacobson, N. S., & Babcock, J. C. (1995). Integrative behavioral couple therapy. In N. S. Jacobson & A. S. Gurman (Eds.), *Clinical handbook of couples therapy* (pp. 31–64). New York: Guilford Press.

Collins, J. D. (1977). Experimental evaluation of a six-month conjugal therapy and relationship enhancement. In B. Guerney (Ed.), *Relationship enhancement program* (pp. 192–226). San Francisco: Jossey-Bass.

Edwards, A. C., Nazroo, J. Y., & Brown, G. W. (1998). Gender differences in marital support following a shared life event. *Social Science and Medicine, 46,* 1077–1085.

Franks, M. M., & Stephens, A. P. (1996). Social support in the context of caregiving: Husbands' provision of support to wives involved in parent care. *Journals of Gerontology, Series B, Psychological Sciences and Social Sciences, 51,* 43–52.

Gerson, R. P. (1994). *The emotional buttons.* Unpublished manuscript.

Gerson, R. P. (1995). The family life cycle: Phases, stages, and crises. In R. Mikesell, D. Lusterman, & S. McDaniel (Eds.), *Integrating family therapy: Handbook of family psychology and systems theory* (pp. 91–111). Washington, DC: American Psychological Association.

Gerson, R., & Shellenberger, S. (2000). Family Pattern Analyzer for Windows and Macintosh [Computer software]. Macon, GA: Genoware.

Ginsberg, B. G., & Vogelsong, E. (1977). Premarital relationship improvement by maximizing empathy and self-disclosure: The PRIMES program. In B. G. Guerney, Jr. (Ed.), *Relationship enhancement* (pp. 268–288). San Francisco: Jossey-Bass.

Guerney, B. G., Jr. (1977). *Relationship enhancement.* San Francisco: Jossey-Bass.

Halford, W. K., & Markman, H. J. (1997). *Clinical handbook of marriage and couples interventions.* New York: Wiley.

Hendrix, H. (1988). *Getting the love you want: A guide for couples.* New York: Henry Holt.

Hendrix, H. (1996). The evolution of Imago Relationship Therapy: A personal and theoretical journey. *Journal of Imago Relationship Therapy, 1,* 1–17.

Hendrix, H. (1999). *Getting the love you want: A couple's workshop manual.* New York: Institute for Imago Relationship Therapy.

Jacobson, N. S. (1978). Specific and non-specific factors in the effectiveness of a behavioral approach to the treatment of marital discord. *Journal of Consulting and Clinical Psychology, 46,* 92–100.

Kennedy, S., Kiecolt-Glaser, J. K., & Glaser, R. (1988). Immunological consequences of acute and chronic stressors: Mediating role of interpersonal relationships. *British Journal of Medical Psychology, 61,* 83.

Kerr, M. E., & Bowen, M. (1988). *Family evaluation.* New York: Norton.

Kiecolt-Glaser, J. K., Fisher, L. D., Ogrocki, P., Stout, J. C., Speicher, C. E., & Glaser, R. (1987). Marital quality, marital disruption, and immune function. *Psychosomatic Medicine, 49,* 13–34.

Lerner, H. G. (1985). *The dance of anger.* New York: Harper & Row.

Luquet, W. (1996). *Short-term couples therapy: The Imago model in action.* New York: Brunner/Mazel.

Markman, H. J., Renick, M. J., Floyd, F. J., Stanley, S. M., & Clements, M. (1993). Preventing marital distress through communication and conflict management training: A 4- and 5-year follow-up. *Journal of Consulting and Clinical Psychology, 61,* 70–77.

McGoldrick, M., Gerson, R., & Shellenberger, S. (1999). *Genograms: Assessment and intervention.* New York: Norton.

Mikesell, R., Lusterman, D-D., & McDaniel, S. (Eds.). (1995). *Integrating family therapy: Handbook of family psychology and systems theory.* Washington, DC: American Psychological Association.

Pasch, L., & Bradbury, T. N. (1998). Social support, conflict, and the development of marital dysfunction. *Journal of Consulting and Clinical Psychology, 66,* 219–230.

Shellenberger, S. (1997). Losing one's match: A proposed model of Imago grief therapy. *Journal of Imago Relationship Therapy, 2,* 37–54.

Shellenberger, S., & Gerson, R. (2000). Genogram-Maker Plus for Windows and Macintosh [Computer software]. Macon, GA: Genoware.

Shellenberger, S., & Hoffman, S. (1995). The changing family–work system. In R. Mikesell, D-D. Lusterman, & S. McDaniel (Eds.), *Integrating family therapy: Handbook of family psychology and systems theory* (pp. 461–480). Washington, DC: American Psychological Association.

Snyder, M., & Guerney, B. G., Jr. (1999). The power of shared subjectivity: Revitalizing intimacy through Relationship Enhancement couples therapy. In J. Carlson & L. Sperry (Eds.), *The intimate couple* (pp. 359–380). Philadelphia: Brunner/Mazel.

Walsh, F. (1995). From family damage to family challenge. In R. Mikesell, D-D. Lusterman, & S. McDaniel (Eds.), *Integrating family therapy: Handbook of family psychology and systems theory* (pp. 587–606). Washington, DC: American Psychological Association.

Walsh, F. (1998). *Strengthening family resilience.* New York: Guilford Press.

Weiss, R. L., & Heyman, R. E. (1997). A clinical–research overview of couples interactions. In W. K. Halford & H. J. Markman (Eds.), *Clinical handbook of marriage and couples interventions* (pp. 13–41). New York: Wiley.

Wolin, S., & Wolin, S. (1993). *The resilient self: How*

survivors of troubled families rise above adversity. New York: Villard.

Zielinski, J. (1999). Discovering Imago Relationship Therapy. *Psychotherapy, 36,* 91–101.

APPENDIX A

The Couples' Dialogue

Purpose: This tool provides couples with a structure for communication that allows both partners to feel fully heard by one another. At the same time, the tool provides safety for revelation of important information by the partners.

Sender: Ask for appointment: "I would like to dialogue about something. Is now okay?"

Receiver: Grant appointment as soon as possible: "I am available now. What's going on?"

Sender: Send message.

Receiver: *Mirror* (paraphrase what he or she has heard)
    (a) If I got that right, you (said, think, feel). . ."
    (b) "Is there more about that?"

Validate (say how what the partner has said makes sense)
    (a) "I can understand you would think. . ."
    (b) "That makes sense to me because. . ."

Empathize (say what he or she imagines the partner might feel about his or her issue)
    (a) "I can imagine that you may feel. . ."

Adapted from *Getting the Love You Want: A Couple's Workshop Manual* (p. 45), by H. Hendrix, 1999, Winter Park, Florida: The Institute for Imago Relationship Therapy. Copyright 1999 by Harville Hendrix. Adapted with permission.

APPENDIX B

Emotional Buttons Worksheet

Decide which buttons are yours. Give examples of when the buttons have been triggered in your relationship and how you protected yourself.

Rejection button (sensitive to being rejected, not wanted or unloved)
Control Button (sensitive to being dominated, coerced, smothered, overprotected)

Abandonment Button (sensitive to being deserted or abandoned, fear being left alone)
Rescue Button (sensitive to the needs of others, rescuing those who are weak and helpless, telling them how to live their lives, complaints about being overburdened)
Invisibility Button (sensitive to being ignored, neglected, unattended to, or unappreciated)
Helplessness Button (sensitive to being overwhelmed by difficulties, becoming confused, irresponsible, submitting to others, withdrawing from life's problems)
Catastrophe Button (sensitive to signs of difficulty, expect the worst, worry about what will happen, feel responsible to prevent disasters)
Injustice Button (sensitive to inequity, unfairness, the wrongful injury of self or others)
Inadequacy Button (sensitive to possible failure, criticism, blame, put-downs, or signs of disapproval).
Other (Describe)

Adapted from *The Emotional Buttons* by R. Gerson, 1994. Unpublished manuscript. Reprinted with permission.

APPENDIX C

Behavior Change Request

Purpose: All frustrations contain a hidden desire. This exercise helps partners discover the hidden desire in the frustration and assists in translating the frustration into a request.

Sender: Ask for appointment for Behavior Change Request

Receiver: Grant appointment as soon as possible

Sender: State frustration in one short sentence

Receiver: Mirror

Sender: State frustration fully

Receiver: Mirror

Receiver: After frustration has been fully explained and mirrored, say "Tell me what these feelings remind you of in your childhood."

Sender: State hurt from childhood

Receiver: Summarize, validate, empathize. Then ask, "What is it that you desire of me?"

Sender: State global desire

Receiver: Mirror, validate, empathize, and then ask, "What could I do specifically to help meet your desires?"

Sender: State three behaviors that would help to meet that need

Receiver: Mirror each and offer one as a gift

Sender: Thank the partner for the offer of this gift

Adapted from *Getting the Love You Want: A Couple's Workshop Manual* (p. 55), by H. Hendrix, 1999, Winter Park, Florida: The Institute for Imago Relationship Therapy. Copyright 1999 by Harville Hendrix. Adapted with permission.

CHAPTER 7

OPPORTUNITIES FOR CLARITY, UNDERSTANDING, AND CHOICE: THE PRACTICE OF DIVORCE MEDIATION

Carl D. Schneider and Dana E. O'Brien

The challenges for divorce mediators are twofold. The most easily recognized one is the task of working with people at the most helpless and stressed time of their adult lives. The less obvious challenge is actually more demanding: to resist the temptation to rescue people who seem so in need of our help. The zen of being a mediator is to intervene, yet not control; to offer information, not advice; to identify options for clients without pressuring for a particular solution; to clarify choices without inserting judgments about the "right" choice; to care passionately about outcomes yet not be invested in any particular outcome.

As mediators we are challenged throughout the process: Do we truly believe in this ascetic practice, which abjures advocacy and advice? Can we hold to the simple faith that clients, if they will, can make their own decisions? However, these subjective challenges arise only in the context of our objective work as mediators with the clients who opt to mediate, so let us first address the way the field deals with the challenges our clients face.

A couple who enters marital therapy has reached an impasse in their relationship. Nevertheless, a hope remains of rebuilding the relationship. Often, therapy involves identifying patterns of interaction that are no longer effective for the couple. By helping them recognize these patterns and teaching what may be new skills in communication, the therapist helps the couple develop new ways of relating to one another.

Although couples who enter marital therapy may maintain a tenuous hope for rebuilding the relationship, couples approach divorce mediation with a very different set of attitudes and concerns. At least one party in mediation has reached a point at which he or she has decided to end the relationship and move on without the other. It is a unique moment in their lives. They may feel a sense of shame and failure, anger, or fear as they approach the mediation. And now they are being asked to sit in the same room and negotiate with the person whom they feel has caused these negative feelings. Many people in their lives may well have taken sides in the couple's conflicts, and they wonder if the mediator will do the same. In addition, they have heard stories about the adversary system of divorce and are wary and defensive. Will they give too much away, or make an uncorrectable mistake? Often they feel a sense of loss—loss of the many dreams and hopes with which they entered the relationship and the loss of the financial partnership they may have had. They are no longer interested in learning about the problems in their communication, neither are they interested in learning new ways to communicate. Well aware of those problems, they have already concluded that the problems are insurmountable.

The mediator, then, must commence by creating an environment that feels both safe and hopeful. These qualities can be transmitted in a variety of ways, including by means of the structure of the mediation, the mediator's approach, and the underlying philosophy of mediation. Ultimately, the process of divorce mediation helps the couple face the end of their marriage with a sense of mutual participation and, thus, ownership, in the decisions to be made. In this chapter we present a case that reflects an amalgam of a number of actual cases. We hope to illustrate how a focus on the principles of separation and individuation within a structured process enables a couple to move to a sense of closure about the past. This in turn opens each person's future.

ORIENTATION AND THE CONTRACT

The Mediators

We are two mediators who are also licensed psychologists. One of us still maintains a major clinical practice; the other, after a decade as a full-time therapist, has shifted into doing full-time mediation and training of mediators nationwide. We are capable of working individually; we offer clients the option of a comediation team. Sometimes this team is interdisciplinary, with a therapist–attorney pair. In the case we describe next, we had decided to comediate as an opportunity to give further experience to the newer mediator. We have found that clients find comediation valuable for its male–female gender balance as much as for its disciplinary balance.

The Case

Marital mistrust was apparent even before our first meeting with Michael and Fran. The original contact with us was made through their attorneys, who intended to accompany the couple to the first mediation session. Both attorneys had some knowledge of mediation; they had agreed to encourage mediation because both were concerned about their clients' anger. The attorneys expected that complicated legal issues around inherited property were going to be crucial in this case. They were concerned that client anger would precipitate an extended legal battle that would quickly dissipate the limited funds that this couple had. Although it is not unusual for attorneys to refer clients for mediation (in some jurisdictions an attempt at mediation is required by the courts), it is unusual for attorneys to request that they accompany their clients.

In the first session, then, in addition to joining with the couple and telling them about mediation, we had to work to keep the session from being framed in an adversarial way by the attorneys. We

had to help the couple feel safe enough to risk talking directly and to be able to present their own interests without feeling the need for their attorneys' continued protection.

Michael arrived first, dressed in a three-piece suit. He was clearly a "Michael," not a "Mike." Fran arrived a short time later—a "Fran," not a "Frances" —dressed casually and on the verge of tears. Both attorneys, briefcases in hand, were ready to inform us of the issues they each felt were most important. We tried to keep the atmosphere informal. Rather than allowing the attorneys to state their cases, we chatted with them and the couple about traffic and mutual acquaintances. Michael and Fran said little, staring at us and not looking at each other.

We opened with the seminal question that parses whether someone belongs in divorce mediation or therapy: Turning to Michael and Fran, we asked, "Do we understand that there has been a decision to divorce?" Both Michael and Fran looked a little surprised by the question. Michael answered with a curt "yes"; Fran nodded in agreement. The issue is whether there has been a *decision* by at least one party to divorce. If so, that decision determines that there will be a divorce. The question is not how people feel about getting a divorce or whether they both want to get a divorce. Typically, it is not a mutual decision: One party is leaving, one is left.

We went on to ask about the current living situations for each. Michael explained that he had moved out of the family house and into an apartment 8 months before. He went on to state that Fran and two of their three children were still living in the house, that he was paying both his rent and the mortgage, and that this was becoming quite difficult. Michael seemed ready to expound further about the burdens he was experiencing. We knew that allowing each person to start arguing his or her position not only would be unproductive but also would give each the impression that the sessions were not safe. We therefore gently broke in:

Mediator: Michael, we do need to hear more about these issues, but before we get too deeply into all that we want to tell you a little about how we work. First, we want to be sure you both know that this is a voluntary process. While your attorneys thought this was worth a shot, it is entirely up to each of you whether we proceed. Either one of you may decide at any point that you don't want to go on with this process. Here, you have both *control* and *choice*. We will make no decisions and have no power over you. No decision will come out of here unless each of you agrees to it.

The process of ending a marriage, as you've indicated, Michael, is draining financially and emotionally. To end this marriage in a nondestructive way you each need to know you'll be okay. To make sure that is the case we'll have each of you fill out budget forms and will work with you to assure that you each have what you need. Our goal in working with you is to help the two of you reach an agreement that each of you feels is *fair*. One way to make sure you both feel the agreement is fair is for you to agree to *full disclosure*. Full disclosure means you will each provide full information and documentation of your assets and debts. It is important that each of you know that all the cards are on the table.

We also want you to know this process is *confidential*. That means we will not discuss anything that happens in our sessions with anyone else. We will ask you to agree not to subpoena us if this process breaks down and your case is adjudicated. We think this is important so that you know that there is no benefit to trying to sway or to win us over to one side or the other to help if you do go to court. Obviously, you each may discuss what happens here as you wish. There will be times that we encourage you to talk to people, such as your attorneys, to get information that may be helpful in making a decision.

Michael: So, we can talk to our attorneys? What if we don't like something that is suggested here?

Mediator: Well, there may be suggestions about the mediation process that we might make, and there will be proposals that most likely will be made by either you or Fran. You may like some; others will not be acceptable to you. You absolutely will not have to agree to something you don't like, and you certainly can talk to your attorney. If you do reach agreement, we will draft a memorandum on your decisions at the end of this process, and we will ask each of you to review it with your attorneys before finalizing it.

As we addressed some of the fears both Michael and Fran were experiencing, we could see them relax a little. And as we acknowledged the attorneys' competence and value as resources for their clients they, too, sat back in their seats.

We asked each party if they had questions. Whereas Michael had been assertive, Fran had been quiet. When we turned to her she became openly tearful, apologizing and saying that this was difficult. However, she wanted to go ahead and give it a try. When Michael did not respond we asked him specifically if he also wanted to proceed. He agreed, noting that he didn't have much choice.

We could not let that go by: Our core belief as mediators is that clients do have choices.

Mediator: Michael, you say you don't have a choice. There are no victims in mediation; no one has to do this. You do have choices, the first of which is how you wish to proceed. You can work out this divorce through settlement negotiations with attorneys, by way of decisions by the court, or you, yourself, can keep control of the process by mediating. Being in mediation is a choice, and we want to be clear you are making that choice.

Michael seemed taken aback that his comment had been heard. He indicated that in fact he thought it was a good idea and, as it might cut down on expenses, he would give it a try.

Michael asked how long this was going to take. We noted that each situation is different but generally the issues could be resolved in 6–8 sessions. We then queried whether Michael and Fran wanted their attorneys to attend future meetings. Both were comfortable meeting without their attorneys. We then put all this in writing and had the clients sign an agreement to mediate. We gave Michael and Fran asset and budget forms to be completed for the next meeting.

As we all were gathering up papers, however, Michael's attorney interjected to say that he wanted to emphasize a financial issue regarding monies that Michael had inherited and funds that he had received as a buyout by his company. Michael had accepted a lump sum from his company in lieu of continuing to work when the company was downsized. The attorney declared tersely that some of those funds were unaccounted for and that there was an issue of dissipation of assets that needed to be addressed.

Our first session thus ended on a note of tension, foreshadowing the conflicts to come.

THE PROCESS OF MEDIATION

Mediation is a process with identifiable stages. As couples move through stages, knowledge is gained that aids the couple in reaching decisions together about how to "get apart." This is of primary importance, because people often enter divorce settings with strongly held positions about what they will or should get as they leave the marriage. It is a recurring problem throughout the mediation process. What the couple must learn is that the who-gets-what decisions are made only late in the game (Stage 5; see subsequent list). Different mediators punctuate the process differently. However it is punctuated, all mediators need to have a clear understanding of the process and to trust that it works. They need to be aware constantly of the step-by-step stages and be clear where they are in that process. The model we have found helpful focuses on the following six stages:

1. *Initiating the process.* First, mediators must join with the parties by establishing an emotional connection. Then the parties must buy into mediation and choose to work out their conflicts and issues through this process rather than the alternatives of either ignoring the issues or pursuing an adversarial solution.
2. *Gathering information.* Next, both hard and soft information is gathered concerning finances, needs, and interests. Often, outside experts are used in this stage in a way that is quite different from the typically isolated work of traditional individual or marital therapy.
3. *Framing issues.* The mediators must help the parties identify the problems and issues. They frame the issues in language that is neutral, future-

oriented, and involves the needs and interests of both parties. The issues are not solved here!

4. *Developing options.* Once a problem is identified, options are explored that might deal with that problem. People regularly come to mediation with their own preferred solution—an approach that often immediately locks parties in unresolvable argument. By encouraging the couple to slow down and consider options "outside the box," the mediators can assist them in developing alternatives that they may not have considered. This is the parties' mediation: We encourage them to come up with their solutions rather than giving them our solutions. The goal is to empower parties rather than rescue them.
5. *Negotiation.* Here, finally, parties negotiate and make decisions based on the options available to them.
6. *Finalizing the process.* The decisions reached are finalized in a written Memorandum of Understanding.

Some mediators begin by discussing parenting, others start with finances, but all full mediations (i.e., mediations that are not simply custody mediations) must sooner or later deal with three major areas: asset division, support (maintenance), and parenting. We personally choose to begin with finances because we find it helpful to have a database to ground the discussion.

Mediation addresses very concrete issues: budgeting who will pay for the children's clothes, whether Dad will take the children to church on Sunday morning when he has them, whether the present value of the pension is calculated on the basis of its maximum value, or how the number of a child's overnight stays will affect child support. Issues such as missing funds are often an area of concern. Whereas marriage counselors approach each session with their eyes on intimacy and communications skills, mediators must also have the child support guidelines and a calculator.

HE SAID, SHE SAID: GATHERING INFORMATION

We began the second session by asking how Michael and Fran had done with their homework, gathering their financial information and records. Michael quickly started in on what funds he felt were missing and demanded that they be repaid. He complained that he was paying the majority of the household bills and bearing the heaviest financial burden. Fran, meanwhile, became more and more withdrawn, her eyes filling with tears.

In the language of mediation Michael was "locked into his position"; he not only had a concern but also insisted on his solution. He was ahead of the process. Michael, pushing for a particular outcome, was really at Stage 5. We were increasingly aware of his anger and desire to push his position. This often occurs at the beginning of the process, and we assured Michael that his concerns would be addressed but suggested that we had found it most helpful first to gather concrete information about their assets (Stage 2, Asset Identification and Valuation) prior to negotiating who gets them (Stage 5, Asset Distribution).

We then spent some time discussing their work and financial history. Michael and Fran had married soon after Michael left the military service, during which he had seen action in Vietnam. Their marriage had lasted 27 years; their three children were all older than age 18. Michael had gone on to work for a large corporation while Fran maintained a secretarial position. She had left that job when she was pregnant with their first child. Both, they acknowledged, had agreed that Fran should not work outside of the home after their children were born. Their youngest child, now 20 and in college part-time, was living at home and not working. Their middle child also attended college while living at home. Their oldest was living on his own and working. Meanwhile, Fran had returned to work as a part-time teacher's aide. Since their separation, she had been able to increase her hours to a full-time but low-paying position.

Michael had worked for the large corporation for 20 years, moving into a management position. Five years ago, the company downsized and offered Michael a buyout package, which he accepted. He had planned to develop a consulting business but had not started the business immediately.

Fran revealed that Michael really felt he had been let go by his corporation and was seriously de-

pressed after his termination. She found him unavailable and near impossible to communicate with during this period.

Michael protested that his feelings were understandable. He went on to say that his last remaining aunt had become terminally ill during this period and that he had cared for her and had continued as the executor of her estate.

As Michael spoke, Fran noted quietly that she had helped with his aunt. When the aunt's health declined, she had moved in with the family, and Fran had reduced her hours at work to help care for her.

As we listened to this history, we both became aware of and commented on the stress both Michael and Fran had experienced in recent years. Perhaps because she felt that her feelings had been recognized, Fran began more actively to participate in the discussion. Thus, while we had moved to information gathering (Stage 2), we also continued the process of joining with them.

After gathering this narrative history we put onto a flipboard the financial data each had gathered. The goal here was to take the separate fragments from each party and knit them into a *consensual* document. The rhythm of divorce mediation is a constant dialectic between separating people and bringing them together—one or the other movement always going on. In mediation in which the parties are mainly focused on getting apart, the first task, paradoxically, is to bring them together in agreement about their assets. They must come to an agreement about what they consider marital property and what it is worth. Only then do they proceed to an orderly and fair division of assets. In the adversary system this is a contentious process that can involve lengthy and expensive, formal, *coerced* discovery (e.g., depositions, interrogatories, subpoenas). In mediation the rubric is *voluntary* full disclosure. Although voluntary, however, it is not a process simply or primarily of trust: It is a process of disclosure that includes both documentation (e.g., tax returns) and a set of checks and balances (e.g., signed contracts for full disclosure, including consequences for nondisclosure).

Fran, frightened at the time of separation about being able to pay household bills, volunteered that she had withdrawn money from a joint account and opened a savings account in her name. Michael and Fran had not been able to talk about this except with mutual recrimination. Now, Fran voluntarily shared critical information as well as supporting documentation of what had happened to the money.

As Fran shared the financial figures, Michael became increasingly angry. Michael felt that the sum Fran had taken was higher than she reported. Fran retorted that the couple had used much of the money Michael was referring to to pay household expenses while Michael was getting his consulting business started. She asked that he bring in the bank records to review. Michael balked. He feared, as do many people, that just to share the information threatened to give the other party an advantage.

This clearly was a hot issue. Fran pushed the issue further, asserting that Michael had inherited some family money and that he would also receive more funds when his aunt's estate was settled. Michael did not respond to her statements. Prompted by us, Michael agreed to bring in both a current bank statement and a history of transactions on that account.

This often occurs in mediation. Parties protest that the other has hidden assets. Mediation has a fundamentally different approach to the process of Gathering Information (Stage 2) than the adversary system. The adversary system does this by formal discovery and a series of consistently coercive measures—for example, depositions, interrogatories, subpoenas—that carry a high transaction cost for the parties. Mediation addresses the same issue without coercion but with a series of checks and balances that includes a formal agreement for full disclosure, the use of financial Asset and Budget forms, voluntary documentation of assets, the clients' use of attorneys, and a commitment to informed decision making.

We continued to gather information and now focused on their income. Fran's income was low but had been steady. Michael's income had varied as he established his consulting business but had risen steadily. We raised the question of the value of the business. Michael protested that he was the primary asset of the business; it was his knowledge that

made it work. We asked that he bring in copies of the tax returns for the last 3 years. Michael reluctantly agreed.

By the end of our second session we and, more important, the parties, had a good picture of their finances. Each had assignments to complete for the next session. Assigning homework is a major role for the mediator. People come to us saying they want a divorce but are bogged down and stuck. Researcher Ken Kressel (1985) said that the job of mediators is to help clients orchestrate their divorce. We help them move forward.

Michael and Fran, for example, agreed to talk to a real estate agent to find out what would need to be done to the family house to prepare it for sale and what its fair market value was. They were not committing to selling the house but were gathering information so they could later consider options (Stage 4) and make an informed decision about how they wished to proceed. The assumption in divorce mediation is that the parties got into their marriage without lawyers making that decision for them. Similarly, if provided with proper information so they can make informed decisions, they can work out the end of this partnership themselves.

In addition, we asked both Michael and Fran to complete individual budget forms for their future as they separated. Much of divorce mediation is reassurance about fears: the budgeting task is structured to help reassure clients who are understandably and predictably anxious about the future. Mediation offers clients the opportunity to plan concretely for the future beyond the divorce. It can reassure them that they will be able to cope financially.

The identification and valuation of assets is a consensual task, requiring agreement on what each person has and what it is worth in order to divide them up and to separate. Divorce mediation consists of an alternating rhythm of bringing people together and separating them. There is much work couples need to do *together* in order to separate nondestructively. The budgeting process has a different dynamic. It is not a consensual task. The marriage is ending, and the parties are planning for what each will need individually for the future. Here, the task is to help them gain separation–individuation as each concentrates on his or her own budgetary needs and lets go of his or her long-ingrained desire to criticize the other's lifestyle and values.

NEGOTIATION: FROM SHORTFALL TO DIVISION OF ASSETS

At the beginning of our third session we followed up on the assignments Michael and Fran had agreed to complete. Fran had brought the requested bank statements and her budget; Michael had brought only part of his budget and had not brought the bank statements that he had agreed to bring. The dynamics of our mediation increasingly centered on the issue of voluntary full disclosure. At this point Fran interrupted and said nervously that she had something she needed to discuss. She had contacted one bank for current balances on some of the accounts and had been informed that one account, which was jointly titled but which Michael had taken over, had a much larger balance than Michael had reported. This statement led to a moment of tense silence. Michael finally commented that he would look into the discrepancy.

As we talked together after the session, we realized that each of us felt more concerned about Michael possibly hiding assets or attempting to avoid full disclosure. We each also felt the impulse to warn Michael of the consequences of nondisclosure. We held our counsel, however, recognizing that although this issue needed to be addressed doing so here would likely break an already fragile relationship.

Because Michael had not completed his budget, we returned to working on assets. Michael had a coin and stamp collection started by his father that he had continued. It was actually now quite valuable. Fran said that she felt that it was Michael's, regardless of its monetary value. Michael quickly agreed.

As Michael and Fran talked, we increasingly confronted the mediator's key dilemma. We are committed to remain neutral and to allow the couple to reach their own agreement, regardless of whether we believe it meets our standards of fairness. Our role is not to attempt to control the content of the negotiations; our commitment is to the integrity of the process. We increasingly felt the strain of maintaining that commitment as Michael seemed to stonewall and Fran seemed repeatedly to be getting the short end of the stick. Michael blamed Fran for "dissipating assets" that she reported were easily accounted for. While complaining that he had less money than he should, it appeared that Michael might actually have more money than he was reporting. He also was withholding records that would clarify these issues.

This, of course, is the major critique that has been levied at divorce mediation by both the legal profession and sectors of the women's movement. It appears to them that mediation does not have adequate safeguards and that women are often disadvantaged in the negotiations. They need protection. They need an advocate. Mediators abjure the role of advocate. Our commitment is to self-determination and to the *empowerment* of both parties to negotiate effectively with one another. As Gary Friedman (1983) put it, "I will help you do it, if you have something you wish to say, but I am not going to be able to do it for you." If mediators succeed in the process of empowerment, they believe they can get out of the way and allow the parties to negotiate their own interests.

This is the existential encounter about mediation truly being a *choice*—not only for parties involved in the divorce but also for professionals. The question becomes, Do people need rescue or empowerment?

Not only is this commitment to empowerment in mediation often an offense to the legal community, but it also is a deeply divisive issue within the mediation field itself. The field has for 20 years organized itself around needs-and-interests-based negotiation, best articulated by Fisher, Ury, and Patton's (1991) classic work, *Getting to Yes: Negotiating Agreement Without Giving In*. Here, the focus is on outcome.

That theory has been challenged by the work of Baruch Bush and Joseph Folger (1994) in their book *The Promise of Mediation: Responding to Conflict Through Empowerment and Recognition*. Bush and Folger argued that mediation's fundamental commitment is to self-determination, which requires the mediator to focus not on outcome but on process and the empowerment of the parties. When the mediator is invested in outcome (i.e., getting an agreement), inevitably the mediator is no longer fully present. He or she begins to get involved in the substantive agreement—that is, is it fair? He or she begins to push in the present while focusing elsewhere —on the future.

For Bush and Folger (1994), the challenge in mediation is truly one of *trust:* Can the mediator truly trust that the process will work, even with difficult clients? When Fran stated that the stamp collection was Michael's we found ourselves biting our tongues, increasingly nervous about her ability to assert herself. The temptation for us to abandon the process and try to advocate—at least a little bit— for Fran and her future needs was increasingly hard to resist.

However, Fran's offer to give Michael the collection seemed to have helped him relax. Michael stated that he thought most of their property could be readily divided if they met outside the mediation session. They agreed to try this and to get comparable estimates for items such as the boat and the piano.

At our fourth meeting both Michael and Fran reported that they had met and had successfully agreed on most of the property. We asked about the bank statement that Michael had agreed to bring in. He told us that he had had time only to finish his budget. We found ourselves increasingly frustrated with what clinicians would identify as Michael's passive–aggressive style. However, we attempted to maintain our bond with Michael by reiterating one of his goals, which was to reach an agreement as quickly as possible in order to reduce costs; we noted sympathetically that the more work he accomplished between sessions the faster the process would go.

He again agreed to bring in a copy of the statement, and we turned to the process of examining the prospective budgets. Mediators have to struggle to remain neutral here. Parties often inflate figures, trying to position themselves more advantageously for an anticipated support discussion. Again, the process is very different from the adversary system, in which budgets are often used as a position for requests to increase or reduce support. In mediation we truly are using the budget for purposes of planning for the future, to allay clients' fears. Until clients can deal effectively *together* with their shortfall and eliminate it, mediation recognizes that there will never be anything but a fight over support. Although a party may need support, support is an internal transfer of money. If there are not enough resources between the parties in total, then it is premature to negotiate support. Again, clients must come together in order to separate nondestructively.

It quickly became clear that Fran expected to shoulder a great deal of the expenses for their children, whom she assumed were going to continue to live with her. She included in her budget the costs of their car, health insurance, and tuition.

Michael, in contrast, had projected his ideal budget. He had budgeted for vacations of the sort he had never taken before, for expensive hobbies not yet undertaken, and so on. His projected house payments were larger than the mortgage on the current family home. Michael was quick to justify all of these as needs.

At the end of the process we added up the total budget of each party and then put their income next to their projected needs. The difference was dramatic, as it often is. At this stage each couple often experiences a surge of anxiety and despair. It seems impossible to them that they will be able to find a way to manage this financial shortfall. As Michael and Fran looked at the numbers, Fran announced that she would have to find a way to lower her expenses; Michael sat silently. We asked that each of them take time before the next session to look at ways not only to decrease their expenses but also to increase their income.

Before the next meeting, we discussed the couple's mutual concerns. Fran had spoken during one meeting about how her role in the family had been that of peacemaker and caretaker of people's emotional needs. It was difficult for her to disagree with Michael. We were aware of her having strong reactions to Michael's budget, yet she had not challenged his figures. Michael also seemed increasingly tense. We decided to *caucus,* that is, to meet separately with each party in the next session.

Caucus is one of the most controversial techniques in mediation. Many mediators, especially in community mediation settings, use it routinely. After opening statements mediators go directly into caucus. Others, who appeal to the family systems roots of mediation, object to its use at all. Going to caucus, for them, is to open oneself to inappropriate alliances and triangulation. They view their client as the couple. Anything that needs to be said can be said in joint session. We acknowledge this split in the field, although we have ourselves found caucus to be an invaluable tool among other things in clarifying interests, protecting client vulnerability, saving face, and empowering parties.

Thus, in the fifth session we caucused and met with Michael first, as he seemed most resistant to the process of mediation. We asked his reactions thus far. He quickly launched into a tirade about the expenses he had to pay toward his children, feeling that they should be sharing more of those expenses because they were over 18. He also spoke again of the amount he had to pay for the mortgage and rent. Michael went on to note that he felt the children could start working part-time jobs as one way to increase the family income. He had not had time, he reported, to try to address his budget and the deficit between his projected expenses and his income. His income was variable, because he was self-employed. He then complained about how long and costly this process was. The mediators tried to acknowledge his concerns; we noted that much of the control over how long this process took was actually in the parties' hands. The more work, such as gathering financial information, they were able to do between meetings the less time the mediation was likely to take.

When we met alone with Fran, she quickly became tearful. She spoke in a rush of her outrage over Michael's budget and her fears that she would be left destitute. We acknowledged her fears and her role in the family of always working to keep others happy and smooth over problems. We wondered aloud if this were a situation that could simply be brushed under the rug. Might there be some benefit to Fran in addressing these issues, both in terms of reaching an agreement with which she would be comfortable and in terms of learning a new way to approach problems as she prepared to move on alone? Fran sat silently for a moment and then laughed, telling us that we sounded just like her therapist.

Indeed, there are moments that mediation can be therapeutic, as it gives individuals the opportunity to explore new possibilities. In this regard, much of mediation is psychoeducational in nature, teaching people how to negotiate effectively. The agreement is most likely to be sound and lasting if each individual has participated fully in reaching the decisions made, not only by sharing information but also by sharing in the problem solving.

We returned to our joint meeting and their budgets. Michael began to speak about his feeling that the children should share more of the expenses. Fran, taking a deep breath, said that she wanted to review both projected budgets. She had, she said, found some ways to cut her budget, and she wondered if Michael had done the same. Michael began to argue. Fran quickly interrupted. She stated firmly that she felt many of the figures given by Michael were inflated and could be cut with a little effort. She also went on to note that she expected Michael was concerned about her getting "his" money and that she was willing to negotiate that. She said it would be impossible to negotiate if they did not start out with more realistic figures. Michael sat in silence for a moment and then asked what Fran had in mind. Fran went on to suggest ways she could cut her expenses and then turned to his budget with a similar approach. Michael hesitated, then said he could not commit to her proposals until they had reached some decision about the assets. It became clear that this continued to be a prime concern for Michael, so we turned to that area.

The first step in that process was to review the list of assets, so this was a natural moment to follow up with Michael about the bank statement he had agreed to bring. Michael somewhat hesitantly offered the statement, saying tersely that the balance was larger than he thought, and he was not sure why. He seemed hesitant to discuss it further, but Fran did not accept his nonexplanation. She began to question him more actively, finally asking if the deposit was connected with his aunt's estate. Michael said he thought that was a possible explanation adding that, if so, it was his inheritance, he thought it should not be included in our discussions, and he believed that the law would support him.

Fran said that she wasn't sure and added that she

had actively helped care for his aunt. Fran felt that what the aunt left to Michael was intended to go to both of them. As they squared off we encouraged them to talk with their attorneys about how the courts, were they to make a decision about this matter, would handle the grey area of inheritance. This would enable Fran and Michael to make an informed decision after becoming aware of the alternatives.

We then asked Michael about his concern regarding the "missing funds." It turned out he had also brought those statements, and we reviewed them together. Fran pointed out that each of the withdrawals had occurred before they had separated. She reminded him of how the money had been used—for household expenses and for children's tuition. She acknowledged the withdrawal she had made at the time of the separation, and she provided Michael with the current statement for the savings account she had opened. Most of the money she had withdrawn from their joint account remained. Michael acknowledged Fran's statements. Through a simple review of the records, the issue of "dissipated funds," which the attorneys claimed was the heart of the case, had disappeared.

Soon after this session, Michael called to cancel the next session, saying that he was too busy to meet then and would have to call later to reschedule. He again expressed vague dissatisfaction with the progress of mediation and, as the mediator acknowledged his concerns, expressed more open frustration. We had been neither listening to him nor sufficiently understanding of his concerns, he offered. The mediator spent far more time than he normally would on the telephone with a client in an effort to try to find some way to connect with Michael. The effort was thoroughly unacknowledged by Michael.

DEVELOPING AN AGREEMENT

As our next meeting opened, Michael said that he had thought of some ways to decrease his projected expenses. We reviewed those changes with him and then moved to assets. We asked if they had spoken to their attorneys. Fran reported that she had gotten some information suggesting that those assets would

be considered marital property. Michael indicated that he thought she was wrong but had not spoken to his attorney. Nevertheless, we thought we would try working through the assets to see if there was ground on which they both agreed. Indeed there was. They quickly made decisions to cash in their whole life insurance policies. They also readily agreed to allow each of them to keep the full amount in the checking accounts each had established after their separation, to add up the amount of money that was in their various joint savings and checking accounts at the time of their separation and to divide the amount evenly. Michael also indicated that he understood Fran was entitled to 50% of his pension and agreed to that plan. Michael also proposed that the money he had received and invested during his company's buyout should be split equally because he believed it would be considered a marital asset.

We then addressed spousal support, the most polarizing issue in divorce mediation. Fran stated that she felt she was going to need support for awhile. To increase her income she realized that she needed to further her education. She looked tearful and anxious as she explained this to a stony-faced Michael. When asked his thoughts, Michael said he had none. It was Fran's turn to become angry. She stated that she could not believe that he had never thought about spousal support in all the time they had been separated and in mediation. Hooray Fran! In our next session Fran, having spoken to her attorney, said she had some ideas about how much support she might get. Her attorney had also informed her that the laws about inheritance were complicated but that she might well be entitled to half the funds in dispute. Michael became more tense. Fran said she had a proposal. Given an even split of the marital assets, she proposed a decreasing schedule of spousal support that would give her increased short-term aid to finish her schooling. Michael did not respond.

We asked Michael if he had a proposal to make. He indicated that he did not, that he knew only that he could not continue paying what he was paying now. We took that as a starting point to explore Fran's proposal in more detail, breaking down the numbers so that both could see how they added up.

Michael again raised his suggestion that perhaps the children should begin to assume responsibility for some of their own expenses. Although Fran was hesitant at first, she responded to his suggestion, and they proceeded to discuss options for the expenses for the children in a more cooperative spirit. Both seemed relieved as the size of the shortfall between their income and budgets decreased. The session ended on this positive note. We began to feel hopeful.

Before our next meeting, we received a call from Michael's attorney, who expressed concern about whether we were making progress. Therapy as traditionally practiced has frequently been a very private activity. Mediation, in contrast, is inextricably involved with other professionals. Mediators must work with other cognate professionals, including accountants, actuaries, and attorneys. However, this collaboration can be a double-edged sword, as other professionals at times apply pressure on the mediation. Mediators, who are subject to peer pressure from colleagues, are not at liberty to discuss the content of the mediation sessions. Mediators are not unlike therapists, who are unable to talk to third parties about the case when family members call and complain about "how long this mediation is taking." But mediators must be able to work with attorneys. We encouraged Michael's attorney to speak with his client and help him develop some options for support.

By our eighth meeting both Michael and Fran had completed all their assigned tasks. The figures provided by the real estate agents regarding the market value of their house were quite close to each other and gave Fran and Michael solid numbers with which to work. We again worked through the numbers and found that the difference between their two proposals was lessening. We encouraged them to brainstorm options, including alternate ways to finance Fran's education and to handle the expenses involving the children. When we can actually get clients to this point, we can largely get out of the way. Clients have largely stopped blaming each other as the problem and have begun to problem solve together.

Michael and Fran were clearly at an impasse on many parenting issues. Now, however, they agreed

that their children could begin to assume more responsibility. They developed a plan that brought their numbers closer to each other. Each time we recalculated, they both looked somewhat relieved. It seemed to make them more eager to find a way to bridge the gap and come to a resolution.

At this point we returned to the question of support. Michael clearly was resistant to paying support of any amount. He was more open to increasing Fran's share of the assets. He still had a question about how much of his aunt's estate he would consider marital. We reminded him that, even if it were not considered marital, the courts could count it as part of his income in determining support. Michael paused and offered another option: to give Fran more of the proceeds from the sale of the aunt's house. Fran brightened. We gave them a draft of their agreement and gave them homework to explore options for financing Fran's education.

To summarize our progress to date, we joined with Fran and Michael (Stage 1) and facilitated their gathering of information (Stage 2). We developed a shared definition of the problem (Stage 3). The parties began to develop options (Stage 4). At our next meeting, Fran reported that a portion of her tuition could be covered by a grant and that she would be eligible to obtain a student loan. Michael continued his concern about committing himself to pay support if his income dropped. Fran countered that he might do significantly better in his business and that she would be left struggling. We suggested that they could deal with these uncertainties with a contingency agreement, simply adding those conditions to the agreement. We went on to explain that they could modify support if either party's income changed more than a certain percentage in either direction. Both appeared pleased that this was fair and responsive to possible changes in their circumstances.

Whereas therapy is present oriented, mediation develops agreements that bind the future in spite of major unknowns and uncertainties. Here again, the mediators interrupt interminable arguments about unknowns with contingency agreements that protect and reassure both parties. A large part of divorce mediation involves reassurances of parties' fears. What was so difficult for us in dealing with Michael was how defended he was about ever acknowledging the fear behind his anger. By the end of that meeting we had a fairly detailed agreement worked out. Again, we agreed to send each party a draft to review both alone and with their attorneys. We scheduled what we thought might well be our final meeting.

CONCLUSION

Whenever possible, we have found it helpful to include the children in a final meeting so that they have the opportunity to hear from their parents and us that their parents have committed themselves to be there for the children in spite of, and after, the divorce. The children also have an opportunity to ask questions about the arrangements. With Michael and Fran, their children had clearly been affected emotionally by all the events in the family, even though they were not minors. We offered the opportunity to have a family session to Michael and Fran but, after a brief hesitation, they declined. We do not force this issue on couples. For clients who do meet together with their whole family, it is often a ritual time of closure on the marriage.

We scheduled our last meeting for a few weeks hence. We sent both Michael and Fran a draft of the Memorandum of Understanding; they were to review it with their attorneys. Shortly before what was to be our final meeting, however, Michael called and canceled the session, saying he was busy and would reschedule "later." As weeks went by, we attempted to contact him, without a response. We began to believe that Michael was making himself unavailable, effectively ending the mediation.

After the weeks of work we had put into this mediation, we felt simultaneously frustrated and concerned that perhaps we had made an error in the process. On reflection, we recognized that as Fran became stronger in the mediation, Michael pulled back. There is debate in the field as to whether mediators should advocate for "fair" agreements or make decisions about the substance of agreements. Here, although tempted, we had resisted this and had trusted the process. We felt good that we had not rescued Fran but helped empower her. We also felt good that we had resisted the temptation to control Michael and had focused instead on supporting them both.

It seemed, however, that Michael could not accept making concessions to his wife. In the face of the requirement for full disclosure, Michael dropped out. By empowering each party, a system of checks and balances is operative in mediation. Fran found a voice and was increasingly able to assert her concerns and wishes. Michael had been unwilling or unable to voice his fears and pain; however unsatisfying, he felt safer holding onto his perception of himself as the victim in the marriage and the mediation.

As we discussed our work with Fran and Michael, we had many mixed feelings. Fran's growing sense of self-confidence was rewarding to see. She had grown individually. However, we were frustrated by our inability to truly connect with Michael and to create an atmosphere in which he could give fairly. Our inability successfully to join with Michael, the very first task of mediation, signaled what we feared was the fatal flaw of this mediation.

We had begun to accept this state of affairs and were drafting a letter to formally end the mediation when we received a telephone call from Michael, who asked to schedule the final meeting. We were surprised and cautious, but we set a date. Shortly before we met with Fran and Michael we received a telephone call from Michael's attorney, who informed us of events in the intervening weeks. Michael had been prepared to go to court, believing the judge would declare him right. His attorney, however, in looking over the draft of the Memorandum of Understanding, had been quite candid with Michael about the possible outcome if he did go to court. He pointed out that he Michael might well have to pay substantial alimony and court costs. Apparently, this conversation prompted Michael to reconsider the mediation.

Michael grimly entered the final meeting. After welcoming them both back, we asked them to update us, including telling us what response they had each gotten from their attorneys to the Memorandum. Fran spoke first, noting that her attorney told her it was possible that she could get more alimony if they went to court. However, when Fran sat down and calculated the potential financial and emotional costs of such a choice, she felt that was not the option she wanted to pursue. She turned to Michael and said,

> *Michael, I know you're angry about giving me anything at all. For years, I avoided making you angry in any way that I could, and it's very hard for me to know how angry you are now at me. But that's not the reason I'm not going to fight with you in court. I want us to accept this agreement because, for all the problems we've had, we deserve to end this with as much respect as we can. I mean, respect for ourselves and our kids, even if you don't respect me.*
>
> *I think this is fair and I'll be OK with the way we've worked it out. I also know you'll be OK, and believe it or not, that matters to me. I hope you can accept this too.*

Michael was silent. Then he said his attorney had told him he could fight it out in court but that he decided he would spare Fran that stress.

We were silent for a moment and we later realized that, as mediators, we were stunned. Michael had found a way to accept the agreement while saving face and seeing himself as the stronger one once again. Although this might not have been a satisfying outcome if we were conducting therapy, it was a very satisfying way to bring the mediation to a close. Fran and Michael signed the Memorandum.

Fran thanked us and left somewhat tearful but looking relieved. Michael shook our hands and left without a word.

We would have wished for more connection and a greater sense of closure, yet ultimately the process of mediation worked to the degree that we resisted the temptation to rescue someone who seemed so in need of our help. Mediation may indeed be transformative, but it often is transformative with a small *t*. Clarity and understanding frequently enable people to make choices when they thought they had none. Fran was able to care for herself and yet still provide an opening for Michael, allowing him to give something. Because we resisted the temptation to advocate, there was an opportunity for empowerment. But it is an opportunity only. We can only create the space; people still have the choice of whether to move into it. Here one person availed herself of that choice, and one resisted choosing. In the end, we were brought back to our beginning place: that this is truly about not the mediator's wishes but about the couple's choices.

References

Bush, R. A. B., & Folger, J. P. (1994). *The promise of mediation: Responding to conflict through empowerment and recognition.* San Francisco: Jossey-Bass.

Fisher, R., Ury, W., & Patton, B. (1991). *Getting to yes: Negotiating agreement without giving in.* New York: Viking.

Kressel, K. (1985). *The process of divorce.* New York: Basic Books.

Part II
FAMILIES IN TRANSITION

CHAPTER 8

A BABY, MAYBE: CROSSING THE PARENTHOOD THRESHOLD

Mary-Joan Gerson

Robin and Bob called me because they could not reconcile their conflict about having a child. They had been struggling over this decision for more than 2 years and finally decided that they needed help in coming to some closure soon. They wanted to talk to a therapist because they were frightened about the consequences of their choice. In other words, the continuation of their marriage depended on whether they decided to have a child. This case held great interest for me.

Why young people want and do not want to have children has fascinated me as a psychological question since I was a graduate student. Entering my PhD program with two young children in tow, I was something of an anomaly to my classmates. Moreover, I spent some of my time in between studying wondering whether I should have a third. I found a way to "sublimate" my indecision: I chose to focus my dissertation on parenthood motivation—why young unmarried women in college want or do not want to have children. I found surprising answers. The second most common reason for wanting a child was "to participate in the miracle of birth." The first reason—"to experience the honesty and freshness of children"—was less surprising (Gerson, 1980).

Today the world is witnessing an explosion of radical possibilities in the fertility arena. Women can freeze their eggs and wait for a suitable mate. Improved in vitro procedures are creating new and uncharted relationships among birth mothers, surrogates, sperm donors, and so on. Human cloning is no longer a science fiction fantasy. If I was interested

before, I am now riveted on why and just how much some people want to have children.

Because I am a clinician as well as a researcher, I have been consulted by and have treated many couples who are struggling with the choice of parenthood. I am a two-hatted, if not two-headed, therapist, formally trained both as a psychoanalyst and as a family therapist. In my training and teaching experiences I enjoy building bridges of integration between these approaches and eventually wrote a book to describe these bridges (Gerson, 1996). Often, however, the sharpest challenges to my thinking occur in my private office. In the therapeutic moment, I am called on to choose a particular focus or direction. I know that this choice—although occurring in a microsecond—has clear consequences for the scope, flow, and outcome of the consultation or treatment.

There used to be a strained tension between systemic and psychoanalytic theory. Today many psychoanalysts are interested in what they call a "two-person psychology," the systemic relationship between analyst and patient, and many family therapists are committed to understanding individual psychology, often from a psychodynamic perspective. For me, working back and forth between systemic and psychoanalytic models is facilitated by my interpersonal orientation, rooted in the work of Harry Stack Sullivan. Sullivan began challenging Freud's ideas in the 1930s, insisting that family attitudes and cultural expectations shaped individual character. Salvador Minuchin, with whom I did advanced supervisory training, is best known for his structural theory and deft interventions, but I have always been impressed by Minuchin's deep respect for individual differences. I think this is partially due to Minuchin's psychoanalytic training at the William Alanson Institute in New York—an institution founded in part by Sullivan.

What I deeply believe is that the link between systemic and psychodynamic practice is one of figure and ground. Each perspective offers a different set of explanations and constructs of how relationship difficulties come to be, how they can be examined, and how they can be expanded and resolved. But I think one clinical approach must dominate in any given treatment relationship and provides a "frame" for the therapy.

For me, psychoanalysis and family therapy provide different frames. Family therapy is fitted to the psychological reality of family life, which is structured around familiar and repetitive patterns of interaction. How could it be otherwise? Each family shares a history, secrets, loyalties, and myriad activities and purposes, which, if not organized in some predictable pattern, would feel chaotic. For troubled families, the patterning is overly rigid or unsuitable to current developmental needs. The experience of therapy—for both the therapist and the family—is necessarily kinesthetic and dramatic, for it must carry the family across what Minuchin and Fishman (1981) called the "threshold of redundancy." It is a therapy of enactment of new patterns, new possibilities.

In contrast, psychoanalysis is a therapy of re-enactment; the patient brings into the treatment relationship ghosts from the past and fuses them onto the person of the analyst. The power of psychoanalytic treatment derives from an exploration of how the patient transfers past experience onto the person of the analyst as well as how the analyst participates —through her own psychology—in the treatment relationship. It is this mutual exploration that decodes the unconscious life of the patient.

My psychoanalytic and systemic work feels different. In my psychoanalytic work I feel an intense intimacy with one person. In family therapy, I often feel somewhat outside the circle of intimacy of the family (Gerson, 1996). Always attempting to track my participation and how the family or couple is

organizing me, I nevertheless feel more playful, more directive, more experimental with families. Because families are so cued to each other—and dysfunctional families are overly so—I often feel that it takes dramatic and visual, as well as a verbal medium, to expand experience.

I hope to illustrate my figure–ground schema in the case I describe in this chapter, which basically shows how I grapple with the complexity of individual history and individual dynamics while maintaining a focus on intense couple conflict. I chose to write about Robin and Bob because they arrived so neatly split on parenthood motivation—and thus provide a challenge to both individual and systemic perspectives.

THE BEGINNING

Robin was 31, worked in the health professions, and was a therapy believer. She had been in thrice-weekly psychoanalytic treatment for the past 2 1/2 years, working through her sense of being emotionally neglected by her parents and her anxiety about maintaining intimate relationships. Bob, who was 33, worked for a nonprofit organization in a creative position. He had been in brief family therapy with his parents and younger siblings (sister and brother) when his parents had difficulty accepting Robin into their family because she had been raised in a different religious faith. For the last 2 years Bob had been in once-weekly therapy, coupled with group therapy. Bob felt that a serious relationship commitment was something he had both feared and deeply desired and found his therapeutic work useful in resolving this conflict. He made it clear that his therapy group unanimously supported his decision not to parent.

How were they divided on childbearing? Robin said that she could not envision marriage and life without children. She was the second of four children in a "cold" Irish Catholic family, from whom at an early age she had detached herself, particularly from her "icy" father. She said she hoped to offer a child the love and security that she had never experienced.

Bob could not imagine life with children, certain that they would deprive him of his freedom to work as well as the pleasure of his avocational interests.

Bob felt that his mother had used him—her first-born—for comfort and for distraction, because she found his father unavailable. Essentially he felt that he had been psychologically exploited as a child. Bob was certain that he could not love a child enough, but he was concerned that rejecting father-hood would cost him his marriage to Robin.

They both claimed that they had absolutely no marital tensions or difficulties, that their individual therapy had largely resolved their conflicts about intimacy. Their single therapeutic goal was to resolve the baby conflict.

My Participation and Thinking

What struck me most about this couple was their claim to utter harmony. Why couldn't they admit to some—if only minor—tensions or dissatisfactions? Moreover, where was Robin's ambivalence, or at least minor concern, about making this irrevocable life choice? I speculated that the overly constricted boundary around this couple sealed them off from re-experiencing aspects of their childhood unhappiness but, most important, I wondered how could I begin to stretch the tightly guarded boundary around what could and could not be examined in their marriage.

Of course, dynamic formulations popped into my mind: Wasn't Bob an oedipal victor, that is, someone who had replaced his father in his mother's affection? If so, wouldn't the role of fatherhood be fraught with anxiety for him? On the other hand, would not his mother's psychological exploitation of him have engendered rage at her? Or a sense of specialness that would be threatened—in his current marriage—by a child?

Wasn't Robin trying to "thaw" Bob's coldness toward children, potentially succeeding with him as she had so abysmally failed with her "icy" father? Was her wish to change his mind an end in itself? Was she hoping to find in motherhood a kind of tenderness that Bob wasn't providing, or that she couldn't ask for from him?

I found their individual stories very compelling; their individual conflicts seemed palpable and invited exploration. But I intuitively felt that if I spoke to them as individuals their polarized positions re-

garding parenthood would be reinforced rather than dissolved.

- Addressing both of them, I said I wondered about other sore points between them. It seemed surprising that their relationship was conflict free with the exception of the parenthood struggle.
- I also reflected that Bob's reservations about parenthood might be masking Robin's. I suggested that couples often divide mixed feelings, or ambivalence, in a polarized way: She is "positive" and he becomes "negative," like magnet heads. It happens over time outside of awareness, masking truer feelings.
- Most important, I forged a link between their fantasies of child rearing stemming from their individual histories. My link was a "tragic" joining. It seemed to me, I said, that Robin's fantasy of healing her own past deprivations, through attentive nurturing, would enact Bob's worst nightmare; that is, he would witness his child being emotionally "used" for the mother's purposes.

With this proposal I was recasting the elaborate family-of-origin exploration each had done in individual treatment into a couple's frame. I ultimately believe that whatever individuals experience in their own history becomes reconstructed and refigured in their current relationships. Moreover, I think that personal historical narratives can become too familiar. What begins as one narrative version becomes, over time, frozen as historical truth and can actually limit self-understanding. But I wondered: Had I oversimplified?

SESSION 2

Robin and Bob reported that they had thought more about my "interlocking parenthood fantasy" thesis. Robin was noncommittal, and Bob outright rejected it. I expressed interest and curiosity about his response but didn't challenge it.

It is interesting that during the week Robin and Bob had mused about how they would manage parenthood. Their conclusion? That Robin would relentlessly nag Bob about child care and that he would feel resentful and imprisoned. At the end of the session Bob began talking about a conflict in his own family of origin, and Robin took over his description of the situation. At some length she explained why Bob was upset, how he was different from his parents and siblings, and how much he was misunderstood by them.

My Participation and Thinking

Robin and Bob began the session by dismissing my formulation from the previous one. However, my experience is that a formulation can take hold becoming part of a couple's preconscious experience even if it is consciously rejected. I hoped to encourage Robin and Bob to view their emotional lives as interdependent, and I knew that there would be other opportunities to suggest this.

When Robin took the trouble of explaining Bob's emotional reality, I perked up.

I chose the moment of Robin explaining Bob's feelings because I was trying to invite differentiation between them. My sense was that baby making had subsumed all the difference and conflict, and thus some of the vitality, in their shared experience. In psychodynamic therapy I often wait for a theme, such as overactive emotional caretaking, to unfold. I will hear about it in the past, and in the present, and will experience it in the patient's relationship with me. As a couples therapist, however, I more actively choose moments on which to focus. Partners do not readily see themselves as organized by significant others, except in the old familiar ways. New patterns of influence are even harder to come by in married life because the familiar patterns are so deeply etched in the relationship experience. I sensed that I could present an interesting challenge to this couple by highlighting a moment involving dependency, and possible emotional invasiveness, instead of the usual scripted "nagging," criticism, and deprivation.

Thus I asked Robin, "Why did you bail Bob out emotionally? Do you become uncomfortable when he becomes confused or anxious?" I urged her not to rescue him emotionally during the coming week. I recommended that if she noticed Bob's distress, that she inquire about it but to absolutely resist clarifying his feelings for him. From a psychoanalytic perspective, I had an intuitive feeling that Bob was re-enacting the special status that he experienced

with his mother but was reversing the action. He could be central to Robin, and she could serve his emotional needs! Also, I sensed that Robin was nurturing Bob as she hoped to nurture a child—to compensate for her own deprivation by "doing" for others. I was thinking psychoanalytically but working systemically by actively challenging Bob's unacknowledged dependency and Robin's collusion with it. I hoped to expose some other tension in their relationship besides baby making.

Psychoanalytic concerns occurred to me after the session. Would Bob's underlying rage at being emotionally used in the past now flare as I discouraged Robin from applying her soothing balm? Would Robin become frightened by facing how she avoids demanding her own emotional gratification by focusing all of her attention on Bob? Would intensifying these conflicts simply activate their defenses and thus further rigidify their positions about themselves and their marriage?

SESSION 3

Robin had "misunderstood" the task. She said she thought I had meant that she should not talk about her own concerns to Bob. Bob had understood my suggestion perfectly but had not corrected Robin's interpretation. This was a perfect example of individual plus systemic resistance—two heads are even better than one when it comes to avoiding a task assignment. I inquired about Bob's lack of interest in pursuing a "true" or "correct" enactment of the task. He said he felt their individual interpretations were most important.

Then Bob began to focus on Robin's "obsession" with the idea of having a baby, viewing her preoccupation as strange and almost pathological. Robin was dismayed. How could he so misunderstand her? I turned to Bob. Why did he personify her as possessed with this longing? Was this because he so valued his own rational, cerebral approach to life? After all, he had been so clear about my task assignment. Did he perhaps view Robin, and women in general, as overly emotional, irrational, "possessed" by their biology? I mused, Haven't women always been viewed this way in history?

My Participation and Thinking

I was aware here how differently I would have explored issues of gender stereotyping in an individual, psychoanalytically oriented treatment. Within that paradigm I would view stereotyping as defensive. I would invite an exploration that is open ended and reflective. However, with this couple I was focused on expanding conflict about parenthood. Questions about gender stereotyping often reveal less obvious power imbalances. In fact, I hoped that inviting Bob to consider his sexist attitude toward Robin might lead him to question all his assumptions about Robin.

With the issue of baby wanting now cast as a gender issue we had a new twist to freshen the old story of motivational conflict between Bob and Robin. I was aware from my own research results (Gerson, 1989) that there are striking gender differences in fantasies about future children. For example, when asked to "picture a future child," men imagine 5- and 6-year-olds whom they can teach; women imagine babies. Men intensely worry about issues of discipline and disobedience; women worry about becoming emotionally depleted. I was not including this information in our therapeutic conversation. I kept the couples work focused on stereotyping. In fact, I felt too single-minded in my inquiry: Had I substituted my own rigidity for theirs?

SESSION 4

Bob began this session by saying that he was thinking of ending couples therapy. It was interesting, he commented, but pointless. Yes, they talked to each other more openly, but that hadn't been their purpose in seeing me. We talked about the previous session. Bob absolutely denied feeling that Robin was "nutty" concerning motherhood. My hypothesis was misguided.

I spontaneously asked them to imagine a moment of parenthood right then and there in my office, as a way of uncovering any unusual images or stereotypes of each other they might be denying. I looked around for a baby prop and settled on Robin's cardigan sweater, which she promptly rolled up into a little ball. She tenderly held the "sweater baby" and handed it to Bob. He kissed it and

treated it lovingly. I was a bit shocked. This scene was altogether more tender than I ever would have imagined.

But Bob didn't act lovingly toward me. He dryly commented, "You know my therapist would have done exactly the same thing with that sweater." Once again I was taken aback but quite skeptical. I confronted Bob with my sense that this similitude was extremely unlikely and symbolized for me his reluctance to have me contribute to his self-understanding, to experience me as having a personal effect on him. I said I wondered if Robin felt that she had little impact on him. Carrying this gambit further, I asked both Robin and Bob to describe their mutual influence on each other. Bob offered a short list. Robin could think of no way she had affected Bob's life. She began to cry. Bob became visibly alarmed and reassured a weeping Robin about her importance to him.

My Participation and Thinking

In this session, I followed my intuition. I faced the limitations of rational conversation. One of the insights I have derived from working in a systemic model is an awareness of the limitations of verbal explanation and interpretation. Language is the fulcrum of psychoanalytic therapy. However, associations expressed by the patient and interpretations proffered by the analyst are reflective of the intense relationship between therapist and patient. In couples therapy, the intense relationship between the couple is maintained on a 24-hour-a-day basis, in the therapist's absence, and language, as Minuchin has said, often does not "cross the [couple's] threshold of redundancy." Because my psychoanalytic work has emphasized countertransference, or tracking my own reactions, I felt spontaneously comfortable in revealing my own response to Bob's dismissiveness. It seemed clear to me that he was being dismissive; I was sure that his therapist was not likely to fashion a sweater baby—a serendipitous invention of our session that day. When I look back on the moment, I think I was inducted into the dramatic experience I had created. It had released in me, as well as them, a sense of multiple relationship possibilities, the way that theatrical performance does.

In my individual work, if I experience a strong

personal reaction to the patient, I sit with it for awhile and then raise it in a fairly measured way. I don't want to intrude too much of myself into the treatment. Thus my direct objection to Bob's dismissiveness was different. I trusted my own unconscious process and followed it into a spontaneous drama, which included me as a player. I think a lot of things happened in that moment. I confronted Bob with his own contemptuousness toward me, a female therapist. I also challenged him with my full experience as an "other," as a person (albeit a therapist) with a unique and intense response to him. Over time Robin had muted her own responsiveness in their relationship. Bob had stopped recognizing what she needed and wanted. Of course all her longing had become represented by one wish: to have a baby.

Bob was stricken with a new awareness of his effect on Robin, specifically, that she felt impotent with him. It seemed to me that Bob could no longer hold his self-defensive, self-protective position and could no longer view Robin as his relentless accuser. She had revealed her impotence, and he had reached out to her with comfort and reassurance. Every aspect of the gestalt had shifted.

SESSION 5

Robin began the session by telling me how important she thought couples therapy was, how much our work had confirmed the dynamics that had been brought out in her individual therapy. Bob prompted her to tell me why else she thought it was important. She smiled sheepishly and asked him to tell. "We've decided to have a baby," he announced.

I told them I felt anxious and wanted to hear more. Bob said, "I took a leap of faith. I don't want to lose her." Robin then detailed all the practical problems of parenthood: division of labor, time demands, conflicts about these issues. I asked her whether she were trying to quiet Bob's anxiety, and moreover her own, by returning to their previous struggles.

My Participation and Thinking
My reaction of palpable anxiety, which I shared, was genuine. The change in motivation was a bit

alarming in its discontinuity. Had I maneuvered them into it? Psychodynamic theory usually conceives of change as a gradual process. I think I always have a micromoment of concern as a trained analyst when my family approach produces radical shifts. But my family expertise has proven to me that helping a couple expand rigidity and narrowness can be a powerful elixir, leading to serendipitous solutions.

However, my decision to share my concern about the shift in course was systemic and strategic. A tried-and-true axiom for couples therapists is that change is frequently undercut, usually because one member of the couple starts the old familiar struggle, and the other—so cued to the conflict—responds in kind. The therapist is left in the newly plowed field. I tried to bring into the room the quite expectable alarm about this dramatic turn of events, hoping thereby to dissolve reflexive resistance to it.

SESSION 6

Robin actually wanted to continue discussing potential conflict. She was worried that Bob wouldn't be sufficiently involved in child care. We pursued this for awhile, until the discussion wandered and diffused. At some point I noted that we were ill-advisedly trying to predict the future.

The rest of the session was spent talking about talents and strengths: Robin's playfulness, Bob's discipline. Robin talked about Bob's singing voice, how she fell in love with him hearing him sing at a friend's party. She hoped he would sing lullabies to their child. Robin couldn't make music, she said, but she loved playing board games with children. As in a freeze-frame ending of a film I witnessed their pleasurable recognition of difference within closeness.

CONCLUSION

Experiential shifts in therapy are really minibirths. Perhaps we become therapists to continually experience rebirth?

What were my concerns? I worried that this treatment went too fast and was too discontinuous. However, I reassured myself that the steep slope of change benefited from the concomitant individual therapy, past and present. These were two people who knew from whence they had come. What they needed was an expansion of who they were with each other.

Was my stance unduly pro-life, growing out of my own experience of self-healing through motherhood? I have comfortably worked with several couples who decided that parenthood was not their choice. I reassured myself that it was the rigidity of Bob and Robin's positions that I challenged. Bob could have taken a different decision-making turn when the knots loosened.

In the end, I can only hypothesize about why this outcome occurred. It may have been that Bob viewed Robin differently as a woman and as a potential mother. And she did indeed change, exposing her vulnerability. Perhaps I was an important transference figure, my analytic mind suggested. Did I allow Bob to defeat me, to resist being "pushed" by me to examine himself and then make his pointless victory ironically clear?

I think the therapy drew Bob and Robin to the realization that choice always involves renunciation. Bob realized that he could not hold onto Robin and continue to grow in her love. He had to give up something: his fear of repeating a traumatic part of his life. Robin came to accept the reality of flawed, less-than-perfect love, both in herself and in Bob.

They both had to view their past history as past, as a given, however hurtful or unfair it was.

John Kennedy once said in a speech that the Chinese character for the word *crisis* is composed of two characters—one represents danger, and the other represents opportunity. Psychotherapy operates in that Chinese idiom, following a path that is sometimes circuitous, sometimes uneven, and generally heads toward an unknown destination. What therapists can offer their patients, however, is the sturdy rail of our own clear thinking and a well-delineated "frame" to allow us to creatively participate in treatment. If we are clear about our underlying premises within any clinical interaction, then we can confidently expect to release new opportunities rather than new dangers for our clients.

References

Gerson, M. J. (1980). The lure of motherhood. *Psychology of Women Quarterly, 5,* 207–218.

Gerson, M. J. (1989). Tomorrow's fathers: The anticipation of fatherhood. In S. H. Cath, A. Gurwitt, & L. Gunsberg (Eds.), *Fathers and their families* (pp. 127–144). Hillsdale, NJ: Analytic Press.

Gerson, M. J. (1996). *The embedded self: A psychoanalytic guide to family therapy.* Hillsdale, NJ: Analytic Press.

Minuchin, S., & Fishman, H. C. (1981). *Family therapy techniques.* Cambridge, MA: Harvard University Press.

CHAPTER 9

DREAMS NOW AND THEN: CONVERSATIONS ABOUT A FAMILY'S STRUGGLES FROM A COLLABORATIVE LANGUAGE SYSTEMS APPROACH

Harlene Anderson

Mindy and Charles were high school sweethearts who shared a dream. Currently 30-something, married for 19 years, and the parents of four children—ages 11, 8, 6, and 4—they had orchestrated their lives in some uncommon ways: They worked hard; saved their money; bought a piece of land in the country; and, step by step, built their home with their own hands. Mindy stopped working outside the home when their first child was born, and Charles retired early so both he and Mindy could be family-focused full-time parents. The children, all born at home, were being home schooled. Charles described it as a "back-to-the-land homestead lifestyle." Having invested their savings wisely, and with Charles occasionally doing contract work, they were self-sufficient and, as Charles put it, "live modestly and frugally." In Mindy's words, "We do things non-traditionally."

In this chapter I narrate my experience of two conversations that I had with Mindy and Charles and with Mindy, Charles, and their children. I first met them 2 years ago when Mindy called for an appointment. I soon met Charles and over the 2 years had appointments sometimes with the two of them and sometimes with only one of them. We would meet intermittently, whenever one or both thought they needed to come. On this occasion it had been a few months since I had last seen them. I intertwine my narration with comments on the connec-

tions between our talking and my therapy philosophy and its central premises. I use their words and phrases in the narration, placing them in quotation marks. My narration is in chronological order, including the transcription excerpts—telling the story as it unfolds.

I selected these two conversations because they were videotaped and transcribed verbatim.[1] Mindy and Charles had agreed to the videotaping when they made the appointment, knowing that the agenda was to produce a learning tape for therapists. At both meetings there were three additional people in the room with us: Two operated the cameras; one was a visiting therapist who observed.[2]

A videotape transcription leaves a great deal up to the reader because it does not portray the uniqueness of voiced tones and inflections or of body postures and gestures. Excerpts reveal even less, missing the richness of stories as they unfold, intertwine, and transform. To help the reader have a multidimensional picture, I offer the following description: Mindy, Charles, and I were seated in a semicircle facing the cameras—I was to the left, with Mindy next to me, and Charles was next to her and across from me. Their conservative casual dress reflected their nonpretentious lifestyle. Mindy, who was of a medium physique, wore no makeup, and had abundant naturally frizzy hair, occasionally looked down. Charles, who had a close-cropped

---

[1] The family meetings discussed in this chapter were produced as teaching videotapes—*Separateness and Connectedness* and *City Clothes and Country Clothes*—available from MasterWorks, 10650 Kinnard Street, Suite 109, Los Angeles, CA 90024; 1-800-476-1619.

[2] Jennifer Andrews and Shelby Robinson were the camera operators. David Clark was the visiting therapist.

beard, wire-rim glasses, and was tall and lanky, occasionally paused to clear his throat. The atmosphere was one of quiet tension; both Mindy and Charles were articulate; and neither raised their voices, although each sometimes accentuated a point. They looked at me and at each other as they talked. Even in their frustrated exchanges there was a sense of respectfulness between them.

A PAUSE: INVITING CONVERSATION, NOT JUDGMENT

My philosophy of therapy has evolved over the past 20-some years, and its evolution has been a reciprocal process of clinical experience and theoretical discovery. Included in this process have been (a) a sustained interest in interviewing clients (mine and those of other therapists) about their experiences of therapy and what they would identify as the characteristics of successful and unsuccessful therapy and (b) a continuous journey searching for ways to understand these experiences and characteristics. The journey for understanding has led my colleagues and me, at least to this point in time, to postmodernism, including social constructionist versions. My philosophy centers on the concepts of language and knowledge as relational and generative (see Anderson, 1995, 1997; Goolishain & Anderson, 1987). Language—spoken and unspoken—gains its meaning through its use; is the primary vehicle through which we construct and make sense of our world; and "is the transformation of experience, and at the same time it transforms what we can experience" (Goolishain & Anderson, 1987, p. 532). Problems, for instance, can be said to form and dissolve in language (Goolishain & Anderson, 1987). Knowledge—what we know or what we think we might know—is linguistically constructed, its development and transformation is a communal process, and knowledge and the knower are interdependent.

This view of language and knowledge as relational and generative informs what I call my *philosophical stance*: the way that I prefer to think about the people with whom I work; be in relationship with them; and act and talk with them whether I am in a therapy room, a boardroom, or a classroom. This view also influences me to think about my

practices as involving dialogical conversations and collaborative relationships. *Dialogical conversation* refers to a conversation in which people are talking *with* each other rather than *to* each other. An active, in-there-together, back-and-forth, give-and-take, two-way process characterizes dialogical conversation. To invite another person into this kind of conversation requires that the therapist be a learner, a not-knower. In my experience I have found that being a learner, showing genuine interest in and curiosity about the other person, naturally and spontaneously invites him or her into a collaborative relationship and shared inquiry. Participants form a *conversational partnership* by which they connect, collaborate, and construct with each other. In this kind of client–therapist relationship and therapy community, valuing hierarchical organization and top-down expertise is replaced by valuing equal contribution and shared expertise. The conversation, or the shared inquiry, becomes a generative process in which the participants are mutually exploring the familiar and constructing the new. It is a polyphonic multivoiced conversation in which each voice entwines with the others, adding to the conversation, inviting opportunity for exploration, expansion, clarification, and erasure of the familiar and creating opportunity for newness in descriptions, meanings, thoughts, actions, feelings, words, or a combination of these. Put differently, in my experience the natural consequence of such conversations and relationships is transformation. Thus, my key question in all of my practices—clinical, research, teaching, and consultation—is, How can I create the kinds of relationships and conversations with others that allow all parties to access their creativities and to develop possibilities where none seemed to exist before? (Anderson, 1997).

Inherent in this philosophy is a bias against judging how others live their lives and claiming expertise on how they should be living. Neither is there a focus on problems or solutions. Instead, the focus is on what is important to the clients and an interest in learning more about their lives and the associated narratives in a manner that invites collaborative relationship and dialogical conversation and therefore invites generativity. These kinds of generative conversations and collaborative relationships invite uncertainty and ambiguity. Uncertainty and ambiguity should not be mistaken as nondirective and laissez-faire or as lacking structure and aim. Rather, when involved in collaborative, generative, and evolving conversations and relationships in which all participants equally contribute, problems dissolve, and the way in which they do so—the outcome or the steps toward it—cannot be predetermined.

THE FIRST CONVERSATION: MINDY AND CHARLES

When Mindy and Charles came into the room I first reiterated what I had told them on the telephone about the videotaping agenda. I then said that I imagined viewers would want to know something about them and that I had two curiosities, both of which centered on my philosophical stance of "being public." I wanted the viewers and readers to meet Mindy and Charles through their words and descriptions and in their presence, rather than through my summary with or without their presence. Also, I think that the reason a person initially seeks therapy does not remain the same over time.

Harlene: I'd be curious to hear what you would say was the reason that you sought consultation in the first place about 2 years ago . . . has that changed any, where it is now . . . what would be the reason you were coming [today]?

Mindy: When I first started coming, I thought I was going crazy. I had all kinds of things going on I just didn't know how to sort them out by myself. . . . Today . . . I have more focus on what's going on, so if you asked me what's wrong today I would say a lot of different things, but one thing is that I don't know much about me, who I am, what I'm about, what I like, what I don't like. . . .

I commented that during the 2 years we had met sometimes frequently (weekly) and sometimes infrequently (not for several weeks or months), saying "We kind of take one appointment at a time." I then turned to Charles.

Harlene: But what about you, Charles?

Charles: It's fairly simplistic in that I look at something, figure it out, and then figure a way to deal with it, and so I was, it seems to me . . . protecting Mindy and trying to give her the answers she was looking for. But my answers just don't work for Mindy. So when we first . . . it was with the idea of trying to resolve these dramatic differences between our operating styles and whole belief and value systems, and things like that. . . . But it's been beneficial because I've learned . . . that my ideas don't work for Mindy, that Mindy has a whole different way of being than I, and that Mindy has changed a lot and is doing a lot of processing-type work that is difficult for me to get a handle on. And, through our sessions here, I've got some insight . . . I have learned to be more sympathetic and supportive of that. Today . . . for me this is a safe place for she and I to be in conflict. And we do our best work here, which is a source of frustration to me because I want to be able to, you know, to work some of this stuff out without a referee.

Harlene: Absolutely.

When I first met Mindy she said she was on a journey, in her words, "to find me." She felt that as a daughter in a divorced family, as the eldest of eight children, and as a mother of four, she had spent most of her life "taking care of other people." She was seeking "my space" and "my dream," having decided that her and Charles's dream no longer worked for her and was now only Charles's. As part of her journey, Mindy was involved in a Quaker church, community-building groups, and courses at a Jung center. Both Mindy and Charles were, by my description, struggling with the issues with which many couples struggle—how to be individuals, a couple, and a family, in ways that work for each and for all.

Mindy made the original telephone call. In our first few meetings, much of what she talked about involved Charles, so I was curious to meet him. I asked her what she thought about my inviting him in so that I could hear his perceptions about her journey and their relationship. She said that she was eager for him to come but that he probably would not because he did not believe in therapy or that she should be coming. But, she said, she would ask him. I wondered aloud if perhaps Charles might see me as more sympathetic to Mindy. She thought that was a definite possibility, so I asked her if she thought he might be more amenable to a meeting with just him and me. Yes, Mindy said, she believed that would increase the likelihood of his coming. Within a few days, Charles called for an appointment.

At subsequent meetings the membership fluctuated: I sometimes met with Mindy, sometimes with Charles, and sometimes with the two of them. At Mindy's request, I met once with Mindy and their 8-year-old daughter and once with Mindy and her mother. I always took their lead about who should be included. I do not conceptualize therapy as individual, couple, or family therapy, or as any combination. Who is involved in any conversation and what the conversation is about is not determined ahead of time. Decisions about who talks with whom, when, where, and about what is determined on a meeting-by-meeting basis by the people involved in the conversation. If I have an idea about any of these I offer it and my reason, but the idea is always provisional, always offered as food for thought and dialogue. For instance, when I asked about meeting Charles, if Mindy had objected I would not have pressed the issue. Instead, I would have wanted to learn about her objection and alternative ideas. Perhaps I might have said more about my intention but would have left the choice to her. Neither would I have interpreted Mindy's objection or Charles's reluctance; rather, I would have taken them seriously, wanting to understand them and their interpretations. In a collaborative approach a client's expertise on himself or herself and his or her situation is invited, respected, and taken seriously. I want to include the client and take his or her lead in decisions about the therapy system, including who comprises the membership of each session and the frequency of sessions.

Still not sure why Mindy and Charles had made today's appointment or what they wanted to talk about, I began to summarize what I remembered about how things were when we last met, about 6 months ago, and what I remembered about a telephone call from Mindy since that time. In the call

Mindy told me that she and Charles had agreed on an "arrangement" for her to have some "space of my own" and how thrilled she was with the plan. She had leased an apartment in the city about an hour's drive from their home in the country. The children lived with Dad in the country and visited with Mindy in the city and in the country. Both Mom and Dad went back and forth between the two residences. Before I could ask more about today's agenda Mindy shook her head no, saying, "It's not working." "So that's different than when I last saw you," I replied.

Distinguishing "separateness" from "being separated," Mindy said that she did not have the separateness that she wanted. The children she said, "want connectedness." She maintained that connectedness was different for the children than it was for her and Charles. Charles was worried about how Mindy's separateness was affecting the children. These were the reasons for this appointment.

Mindy: I've been trying really hard for it to be us, but it isn't. It is that separateness that I need. And I've tried hard to say that. And there's a part of me that even wants more disconnectedness than there is right now. I've been talking to Charles about the pull . . . the pull is the kids. I have devoted my life to these children. I have given them every ounce . . . I'll go to tears again . . . I've given them every ounce of everything that I've had. And so it's like he said that he's [Charles] a big boy and that we'll work it between us. But the *kids* . . . I can't . . . the disconnection . . . they stayed connected to me with the heartstrings, and they want to pick up the phone and they want to call me. And they want me at home, and they want whatever they want. But they want that connectedness . . . I want to tell them that I'm going on a 2-week vacation, or you know, some amount of time that they can register in their mind or mark off on the calendar or do whatever they want to. . . .

I commented that I was thinking about their lifestyle—how they spend more time with their children than most parents do because they home school the children. I commented that Mindy seemed "really pulled" and that Charles was "trying to reassure" her that he and the kids can handle it. Charles disagreed with me.

Charles: What I am saying is: It's fine for me, that I can deal with it . . . she can go be separate, she can go to her place in Houston and stay for as long as she needs to stay. I can pull back off of that and be okay, but the kids cannot. The kids are in real distress about not getting to see her.

Charles continued to talk about the children's pain. Then they went back and forth, sharing different perceptions about how much time and when the children have, and should have, to spend with Mindy. I commented that it's "sort of a jagged transition, there's some unpredictability to it." Charles interrupted, wanting to know what I meant by *transition*—"transition to what?" he asked. "That's a good question," I replied. He continued to talk about how the arrangement had turned into something different and that he did not want it to be "open ended." "Mindy specializes in open-ended, no-pressure type situations," he charged. I clarified that I was using *transition* to refer to the back and forth shuttling between the apartment and the house and agreed that things had not turned out the way that either of them had planned. I turned to Mindy.

Harlene: How are you handling it with the children? I mean what are you saying to them when they ask questions . . . when they call you on the phone?

Torn and guilty, Mindy had spent the week in tears. She told about their 8-year-old daughter calling and announcing that she and her siblings "don't feel like we're getting enough family time." Mindy talked about how she tries to explain to the children that she needs some "alone time," "has meetings," and "I'll be back" and to reassure them that "No, we're not getting divorced." Mindy confessed her dilemma in trying to be "supportive of them" (i.e., the children) and at the same time "I'm so *me* oriented." She didn't want to perpetuate these feelings in her children. I wondered about this.

Harlene: So, how do you each think the children are understanding or making sense of, or not understanding or not making sense of what's going on with the two of you? What are your thoughts about that or what are your fears about that?

Charles was not sure about the younger children but thought that the older ones understood what their mother said on an intellectual level. He said he was sure that they see the separation as divorce.

Charles: Separation as a prelude to a more permanent kind of a separation. I'm sure it's like their fears, their worst fears, are becoming realized . . . a divorce kind of thing. But that's my own interpretation of their feelings . . . I have no idea whether that's accurate or not, but it seemed plausible.

I acknowledged that it could be plausible and asked Charles if his worst fear was that the children think the family is dissolving. He agreed and returned to the uncertainty of the situation for the children. Trying to better understand what he was saying, I wondered,

Harlene: So you think if there's some structure, some timeline, some predictability to it, that they would . . .

Charles: [Nodding] I don't think they can handle this unknown. . . .

Harlene: [To Mindy] And you're shaking your head "no." So, this is one of those things that the two of you find a real hard time to talk about?

Mindy: No.

Harlene: No?

Mindy: *No.*

Mindy said that no structure or limits had been specified in their original agreement about time spent with the children and with the family. I asked if she wanted things, using her and Charles's term, "open ended," moment by moment, or day by day. She was unsure. Charles strongly reasserted that "the children need some predictability."

Harlene: And so what are your ideas about how to get past this place? When you're [Charles] thinking there needs to be some predictability and structure and you're [Mindy] saying all I can say is where I am today? . . . As you said, there are lots and lots of differences between the way each of you are in the world, and this is just one of them.

My aim was to provide space for and promote a generative conversation, a storytelling process by asking questions, wondering, making comments, and offering ideas—all geared toward facilitating the retelling, clarifying, revising, and expanding of Mindy's and Charles's stories. I wanted both Mindy and Charles to have a voice and the space they each needed to tell their story at their pace.

People experience the same event in different ways. No one experience is more correct than another is; it is simply different. I want to show equal interest, take seriously, and respect each version. I do not want to act in ways that might indicate that I value one version over another or to take sides. Being interested in and respecting all views does not mean agreeing with or condoning. Often by the time a couple has reached a therapist's office, as I had learned from previous conversations with Mindy and Charles, others—friends and family—have already taken sides. Friends and family members had developed explicitly and implicitly expressed opinions about how Mindy and Charles as individuals, a couple, and a family, ought to live their lives. Not unlike these others, therapists who have viewed this tape expressed judgments, divergent opinions, and took sides concerning Mindy and Charles as a woman and a man and as a husband and wife.

Charles reiterated and elaborated his concerns about Mindy "not being in the kids' lives" and how upset they were. He said he wanted to be understanding of Mindy but feared that "when she gets an inch, she has a tendency to take a mile." Mindy again declared her need "to protect my space." Their different perceptions were highlighted as each recounted a recent telephone call between Mindy and the children. Charles did not understand how Mindy could get so "bent out of shape by a 5-minute telephone call." Mindy said that it was not just a 5-minute call, because "my guilt and grief about

what I'm putting the children through lasted a whole day." He said that "it's not that I'm unsympathetic to that," because he processes things also, but that he was "badgered" by seeing what was going on with the children and could not imagine a 5-minute call "shooting the whole day." I wondered if the telephone call experience, for him, was similar to what he said earlier that if he gives Mindy an inch, she takes a mile. It's a "grand illustration," he asserted.

Harlene: Oh, okay, you [Charles] were saying "I don't" . . . I don't remember exactly the wording . . . something like "I don't *want* that, this can't *be*, she can't do this". . . I'm not saying you should agree with her, accept her, understand her explanation, but it sounds like whatever her reasoning is behind this, meaning the 5-minute phone call turning into 5 hours of misery . . .

Charles: [Nods]

Harlene: . . . and pain and reflections, that whatever that is, that it's not something she's able to communicate to you in a way that makes sense, in terms of how come a 5-minute phone call [in his view] could do that to her.

Charles: Now, it's not that I'm unsympathetic to that. You know, I process things and deal with these kinds of thoughts, okay. Not the same way she does, but life . . . life forces certain compromises on us. . . . In one context what she's asking for is not outrageous. . . .

Harlene: [Nods]

Charles: Okay, it can be done.

I remarked about Charles's passion, how upset and angry he seemed. Without comment, he continued.

Charles: What I'm saying is if you need this, we can do it. But we've got to know . . . we've got to have a return date. We have [with emphasis] *got to have a return date*. If you want me to do this . . . this is not easy for me, and it's not going to be easy for them. We *need a return date*.

Mindy: You don't have to tell me it's not easy for them . . . and I know it's not easy for you.

Charles: Okay.

Mindy: But that doesn't mean I can give you a date.

Charles: Okay.

Harlene: [Referring to something that Charles had said earlier] This is one of those pieces where you're [Charles] wanting an answer or something, and you're [Mindy] over here [pointing in the other direction].

Charles: Yeah. What I would say to this is, "that's fine . . . if you're willing to do that," meaning . . . meaning in my weaker moments, "if you're willing to drag them through that kind of . . . *stuff* . . . if your conscience will allow that, then let it be on your shoulders!"

Harlene: Let me back up to something you said earlier . . . a moment ago or several minutes ago, Mindy said that you had recently described her to a friend as fragile.

Charles: Fragile and emotional.

Harlene: Fragile and emotional. Say more about that.

Charles: Just that right now she is, she is very much into this work, this internal processing that she's doing, and she's just very emotional. She cries easily, she gets upset easily she's just . . . just very fragile in her emotional state. She just . . . you know, it doesn't take much to undo whatever harmony she has kind of collected for herself.

Harlene: And is this, I mean is this a concern? Or you're saying this is the way she is? Or how . . .

Charles: I'm . . . it's just an observation. It's a different Mindy than the one that I'm used to, you know, seeing . . .

Harlene: [Nods]

Mindy: Heart work. I'm very much about. . . . and I am very much working with my feminine side . . . wearing dresses . . . fixing my hair . . . wearing makeup, and I'm associated with heart things. . . .

I've tucked it [the woman who does housework, takes care of the kids] someplace, and the other is what's coming out now . . . soul work.

Harlene: So you call it soul work and heart work, and you've described yourself before when we've talked as being on a journey . . . sort of a self-exploring journey.

Mindy: [Nodding] Journey to wholeness.

Mindy continued, talking of "trying to be" rather than "do–be do–be do–be," referring to taking on Charles's "likes and dislikes," her "parents' stuff," and taking care of everyone else. In the end she said, "I want the integration."

Harlene: The integration? I'm thinking that in terms of some of the things you're exploring and some of the ways that you're being, that all of those people that are intermittently connected to you in terms of your immediate family and your close network of friends are just *jarred*.

Mindy: Oh!

Harlene: Because you're so different than they're used to. And then, Charles, I think with you that it's like you're on one hand trying to be very supportive and understanding of it, and on the other hand sort of confirms this, also you use the thing of the "loose cannon on the deck." Is that the phrase you used?

Charles: [Nods]

Harlene: That in a way . . . it's like you're each in so many different places with all of this, and it's . . .

Mindy interrupted to give an example of a telephone call with her mother where she was crying and Charles walked into the room and declared [referring to the children's hearing her crying], "Enough is enough!" Mindy defended her crying, "because it's *real* . . . because it's where I'm at." Charles decisively questioned whether Mindy really wanted to put the children through "that," and wondered, "does she *care*?" I acknowledged that this is the real tension place, referring to the children and connecting back to why they were here this day; that is, their mutual concern for the children and whether those differences were affecting the children and, if so, how and what can we do about it?

At this point we had been talking for 50 minutes. I had not forgotten about our visiting therapist (David Clark), whom I had kept in my peripheral vision. Curious to know his thoughts as we talked, and with Mindy and Charles's permission, I invited David to join us and share his reflections. We had not planned that this would be his role. It simply seemed like an opportunity of which to take advantage. It was also in keeping with my bias toward being public. I wanted Mindy and Charles to hear David's comments if they wanted to rather than simply hearing David's private comments to me after the meeting. I wanted Mindy and Charles, not David or me, to select which of David's observations interested or disinterested them and with what they agreed or disagreed. I did not hold an idea about how David would share his reflections. I was open to what he might say and open to how Mindy, Charles, and I might respond.

David first remarked on listening from a male's point of view. He wondered if Charles's concerns about the children's pain in fact "reflects your own pain." Charles disagreed, and Mindy softly and conclusively joined in supporting Charles and summarizing her position.

Mindy: Charles and I have a deep commitment to each other. We have known each other for a very long time . . . been through talking about divorce, thought divorce was an option. I think we've come through all of that. . . . I think the relationship is going to have to change. . . . I think he's right. I think most of his concerns are for the kids.

David wondered if Charles might have any other concerns. Mindy continued, and then I asked Charles.

Mindy: Some concerns from him that I don't feel like he's facing, deep down. My assumption would be the dissolving of the marriage . . . not having me in his life as much as he would want. . . .

Charles: I think you [Mindy] should have, and this is a judgment, I think you should have an easier

time because some of this stuff we have talked about and I have shared some of my particular fears with you on that . . . I'm thinking that yes, I am disappointed that you're not there; however, we've had so much trouble the past couple of years and when you have been there [it] has been so painful that after a certain time of so many painful experiences that you come to realize that it's no good, this togetherness, if it's going to be a painful event. And so, you start backing away from it. So, yes, I'd like to have you there and I do miss her presence, but the angry Mindy's presence I don't miss.

I commented that even though they were struggling with difficult questions and had polarized positions, I was impressed with how they often seemed to go home and do something constructive. Mindy and Charles agreed. They believed that the two of them would get through this, yet they still expressed concern for the children. David wondered what the children might have said if they had been here today.

David's curiosity about what the children might have said brought to the forefront a nagging sense that had been in the background of my mind as we had been talking: I wanted to talk with the children. Although Mindy and Charles often talked about the children when we met, somehow this day it seemed different. More important, however, was what Mindy and Charles wanted to do. Even though I had met with Mindy and Charles off and on over the past 2 years, I did not assume that I *knew* them or how they wanted me to participate in their lives. I did not assume that they wanted another appointment. As with all my clients, I simply thought of myself as a visitor, a guest, who was invited to participate for brief moments in their lives, and in a setting and circumstance that are different from their everyday lives. So, I asked Mindy and Charles, "Where are we now? Where do we go from here?"

Once more they reiterated their concern for the children. I asked what Mindy and Charles thought about a meeting with the children in which they could share their concerns about the children and learn about any worries that the children might have. They believed it would be helpful for the children, so we made an appointment for the next day.

It just so happened that in this situation my suggestion for the appointment fit for them. If it had not, I would not have pushed but rather would have asked what they thought our next step should be.

THE CONVERSATION THE NEXT DAY: WORRIES

I had met and chatted informally with the children several times, because they usually came with their parents to my office. They were always well mannered, engaging, and self-disciplined as they read in the reception area or played on the porch. This day, as always, the children were captivating, articulate, and polite. They were attentive to each other as they talked; Mindy and Charles listened intently and joined in when invited or if they had something to say. We were seated in a semicircle, with the children in the middle, flanked by Mindy and Charles on the left and me on the right. Here is a glimpse of how the meeting began.[3]

Harlene: So I guess I would like to say, first of all, thank you for coming today. And I think our meeting today, in a way is an example of the way I work, because one of the things that I talk about in my work is that each conversation forms the next, so the ideas about all of us getting together and talking today came out of the talking that the three of us did yesterday. And normally we might have scheduled the session next week or in 2 weeks. We did it today so that we could videotape it in conjunction with yesterday's. So why don't we reintroduce the two of you, Mindy and Charles, and let people know who you are. [And then to the children who had already introduced themselves to the camera people and David:] So, you want to say your name one more time and maybe how old you are.

Each child readily and proudly introduced himself or herself by name and age, going around the room as they were seated (beginning on my right): 8-year-old Denise, 6-year-old Melissa, 11-year-old

Sylvia, and 4-year-old Joel. I welcomed each. Joel was last.

Harlene: Hi Joel, and good morning [to all]. Thank you guys for coming. What did your Mom and Dad tell you about coming today, because this is a little different than what we usually do? Usually when I talk with Mom and Dad or with your mom, you're playing on the porch, or in the yard, or doing something like that, so usually we don't talk this way do we?

Denise: No.

Harlene: Did you know I was going to be talking with you?

Denise: Mom and Dad told me when we were waiting.

Harlene: When you were waiting, okay. What did they tell you?

Denise: They told me that you probably would be videotaping, and that we were going to come in too, they might ask us a few questions, answer them as well as we could, that's pretty much all. [To her siblings] Anyone else have any comments?

Harlene: So you're kind of wondering what kind of questions I'm going to ask you?

Denise: Yeah.

Harlene: Yeah, I guess I would be, too, if I thought somebody was going to ask me some questions. Well, let me tell you why I wanted to talk to you. Because when your mom and dad and I were talking yesterday, one of the things we were talking about was some of the changes in your family . . . the change meaning the new apartment in town and your mom being, it seems like, more at the apartment than at home? Is that accurate?

Denise: Yes.

I summarized what I had said yesterday about them—the uniqueness of their family—including

---

[3] For an expanded discussion of including children in therapy and this meeting, see Anderson and Levin (1997).

home schooling and both Mindy and Dad being full-time at-home parents. I then was curious if they were worried about their parents, and if so, about what. I have been asked in a workshop why I choose to address the children rather than asking the parents to say why they wanted this meeting. I can only imagine that at the time it was a spontaneous choice with no intention intended other than to begin to talk about why we were here today. I certainly could have asked the parents to say why we were all here. However, I was the one who suggested the meeting, so I wanted to tell them why *I* wanted to meet with them.

Harlene: . . . so people know a *little* bit about you already. But we wanted to talk about some of these new arrangements, and I guess I also wanted to know what kind of questions that you might have or what kind of worries or concerns you might have, because your mom and dad think that you are worried about them.

Denise: In a way I am . . . sometimes when they have a big argument, I get kind of scared they're going to get divorced.

I acknowledged her fear and asked if the others were "scared" (using Denise's word) or had some questions about Mindy and Charles. Sylvia and Melissa said they were afraid that Mindy and Charles would divorce. Joel nodded his head in agreement. Denise inserted that her parents tell them that they "don't think they will get divorced," quickly adding "that they *hope* they won't at least." Mindy joined in.

Mindy: I remember telling you that we're working as hard as we can to work through a difficult time.

Harlene: So it sounds like though, when they try to reassure you, that maybe it's not very reassuring? You're still worried.

Denise: Well, sometimes when you're worried, it's kind of hard to stop, you know.

Harlene: Yes. Sometimes when you have a worry, it's kind of hard to let go of that worry.

I again acknowledged the children's worries about divorce. Before learning more about these worries, I was curious to know if there were other worries that were, using Denise's words, "kind of hard to stop." They talked about being worried that Mindy was gone a lot, that Mindy and Charles hardly saw each other, and that they go back and forth between Mindy's apartment in the city and the family's house in the country. Joel chimed in—"I have a worry"—and told about the electricity going out during a storm because icicles were on the lines (a very unusual experience for Texas Gulf Coast children). Denise remarked that Joel had favored talk about "things that we're doing rather than feelings."

Denise: I'd rather talk about my feelings, of course.

Harlene: Your feelings, of course. You're laughing Sylvia, what do you think?

Sylvia: I think she's being silly.

Harlene: You think she's being silly.

Mindy: I think she's being accurate.

I was intensely involved in talking with the children, attending to each child's words, trying to learn more about what each was saying or not saying, giving each story fragment a chance to develop. I allowed each child to be center stage as she or he talked. I equally respected and took seriously Joel's worry about losing the electricity and followed his concerns about the icicles just as I did his sisters' worries about a divorce. As each child spoke I responded to him or her, returning to asking more about the fear-of-divorce feelings, checking to make sure that I had heard what they wanted me to hear: "They're not going to get a divorce . . . that's what they say?"

> She [I] asks each of the children if they have comments they would like to share, offering an opportunity to participate, without requiring it. Entering the conversation does not commit one to a particular path, but is more like an invitation to test the water each person having the opportu-

nity to go deeper, or back out, if it does not feel comfortable. (Anderson & Levin, 1997, p. 266)

Denise: No.

Harlene: No, they don't say it that way?

Denise: They *plan* that they won't.

Harlene: They *plan* that they won't. Okay. So, is it the way that they word it that makes you doubt, as well as that Mom is gone a lot now?

Denise: I think yes. Kind of both.

Harlene: Well, do you know that Mom and Dad are very worried about the four of you? That they have a worry they can't get rid of either?

They gave a united "no." I asked, if they could "make any guesses as to what they're worried about?" Again, a unified "no idea." I turned to Mindy and Charles and asked them if they "want to say some of the things that the two of you are worried about." Charles responded first.

Charles: Well, my biggest concern is that y'all are feeling fearful and being upset because we've got some big changes in our life, and Mom is in town most of the time now, and is asking for a lot of . . .

Denise: Alone time?

Charles: Alone time, yeah. And I just see that y'all are sad about that, and uneasy with all of this.

Denise: Mother?

Mindy: I guess being the mother in the family, I've . . . each of you has always been with me all of the time. And so we've spent a lot of time together and gotten to know each other real well, and when Daddy came home, when Daddy retired and came home, I started feeling differently and felt like there wasn't a need for both of us to be at home at the same time. . . .

Mindy continued, referring to the change, or the arrangement, as a "switch." She expressed concern that the switch was made rather quickly and that

she was not sure whether—and, if so, how—it bothered the children.

I asked if there were other worries that Mindy and Charles had about the children. They said there were no others. I took them at their word and returned to what I had mentioned in the beginning to the children: what other people knew about them, noting the differences between their family and other kinds of families in which one or both parents work outside the home and the children go to school outside the home. I voiced a silent curiosity: Did they think that they noticed these kinds of changes more than other families might because they spent more time at home with each other than perhaps other families did? I did not pose it as a question to be answered just as I do not pose any question to collect information or expect any of my curiosities to be satisfied. Nor did I ask the question to seed an idea. Questions are simply to facilitate people talking about what is important to them and to help them talk about it in a way that invites dialogue. The children simply looked at each other. After an ample pause, in case one of them did want to speak, I left the question in the air and continued in another direction.

I often criss-cross back and forth, returning to something I remember from earlier in a conversation. I typically do not stay with any one curiosity too long, not wanting to skew a conversation in any one direction or inadvertently influence a focus on any one content area.

Harlene: [Addressing the children] And your mom says that she's afraid that she's making you worry more. [Addressing Mindy] Is that right? Is that what you're saying? That you're concerned about the effect of your not being there as much . . . what that effect is having on them?

Mindy: Correct.

Harlene: That they might be worrying more, that they might be hurting, they might be . . .

Mindy: Concerned that I don't love them.

Harlene: Oh, that they might think that you don't love them.

Mindy, to illustrate the children's concerns, told me that Denise wrote the "sweetest" note yesterday, in which she told Mindy that she loved her and missed her. I turned to Denise and wondered, "Is that something that you worry about, that your mom doesn't love you?" Denise said that she worried about it "a little." I noticed that Sylvia was nodding yes. I checked out her nod and learned that she also worried that Mindy did not love her. I then asked Melissa and Joel the same question. "No," neither had that worry.

The emotions in the room swelled, and the children were weeping. Mindy and Charles tried to comfort them. Joel was curled up in Charles's lap. Mindy moved across the room to sit with the girls —placing Melissa on her lap, holding Denise's hand, and giving Sylvia tissues. (Earlier, one member of the camera crew had given Denise tissues.)

Sylvia and Denise began to talk about how Charles is with them all day and how Mindy is hardly ever there and that they worry about the "hardly ever" part. I commented on their missing her and questioned if they worried that "maybe she's kind of on her way to being gone forever?" An immediate "yes" came in unison. I commented on how hard and sad it was and wondered what they thought "we need to do to help you feel a little bit better?" I tend to use collective language to promote a sense of equal contribution, to promote doing together rather than my doing for or to them.

All of the children started talking spontaneously. Joel and Melissa joined in as the conversation shifted to telephone calls and the difference between knowing and not knowing when Mindy was going to be where and for how long. Responding to what helps or could help, they proudly told me about their idea to have a weekly "family day," a day when Mindy would come to the house in the country and they would plan something for all six of them to do as a family. "That's the meaning of family day," Denise said, "we do everything together."

I wondered if anything else was helpful. I learned that each child had his or her own unique way of handling the "switch" and their fears. Denise said that writing notes helped. She wrote notes (sometimes letters, sometimes poems) to Mindy and Charles to let them know that she loved them and

"always will." She was especially pleased that she had written the first letter that her mother received at her apartment. Sylvia said that she draws pictures (cartoonlike figures with a "voice bubble" containing their words) to express her and her siblings' "scared, sad, and frightened" feelings. When she is "really mad" she folds the pictures into paper airplanes and "flings" them down over the balcony, always making sure to just miss her target (usually her mother). Denise and Sylvia joined to describe the pictures, some showing Mom and Dad fighting, some showing Sylvia and the others in tears.

I explored their stories from another angle, asking them if Mom and Dad were fighting more or less than they used to. They said "less" and gave some of the reasons why they thought this was so. As the children and I talked I wondered what thoughts their parents were having. I typically invite listeners to reflect on what they have heard, giving them an opportunity to voice silent thoughts.

Harlene: [To the children] Well, let me hear from [Mindy and Charles] for a moment, because I'll bet that while you have been talking that they've been having lots of things going on in their heads . . . lots of thoughts. What kind of thoughts are you having?

Charles: [Looking at the children, speaking with sincerity] I'm just really pleased that you are sharing so well . . . I hear that you're expressing what you really are feeling, and I hope that if you're holding back anything, or if you have anything else that you'd like to share with . . . that you've noticed, anything you want to say is okay with me. Anything that's really going on with you is okay to share. I just want to reinforce that I'm real concerned about your feelings and that I want you to have a good and happy and full life, and I'm just doing the best I can with trying to make that happen.

Mindy: [Also addressing the children] Okay, we've been talking for a long time. I try to keep you aware of what's going on as much as I can. Daddy and I started, I think yesterday, arguing a little bit in the morning . . . disagreeing on something . . . I wanted to catch a quick lunch before we had to do [take the children to a friend's house]. . . . and Daddy did not want to. Daddy wanted me to fix it there, and so Mother went into an uptight mode and Daddy had a reaction to it. And I watched both of your faces [referring to Sylvia and Denise], and both your faces saddened a bit, and were ready for . . . it's okay . . . it is *okay*, I think for Mommy and Daddy to disagree. I want you to think about the times that you as sisters argued. And then make up with each other. What happened yesterday morning was . . . it was quick. . . .

Harlene: It was quick.

Mindy: It was *quick*.

Sylvia: What it was, just because I was asking you, "Could you drop us off at Cher's or something?" But . . . it was quick.

Mindy: It was quick, but I saw the look on your faces, and I know that upset you. But you and I aren't always going to agree on everything, and *Daddy* and I aren't going to always agree on everything. And we're still working it out. We still try every day. I am far from perfect, but I keep trying to learn and learn about things. And Sylvia, the other day when I was at home and started taking my sewing machine with me? And I watched you, and I saw a reaction in you about me taking my sewing machine? Can you tell me what you were feeling when you crawled down underneath the desk?

Sylvia and Mindy talked about the sewing machine incident and their different perceptions and feelings. Sylvia said, which was not surprising to anyone, that she had thought that this was just another step to Mindy's being gone and never coming back. Mindy, however, saw it as a way to be nearer to the kids—meaning she can feel "connected with you without being home . . . all the time." Sewing was connecting. Therapists who have observed the videotape often comment at this point on the changed atmosphere in the room. Tears have left the children's eyes and worry has left their faces. They are at ease and energized and are spontaneously entering the conversation.

I returned to talking with the children, wondering if they had friends whose parents had similar arrangements or who argue. During the discussion

Sylvia said that she was no longer worried when her parents "fuss" because there is not as much "*intensity*." She was referring to what was said earlier about the morning argument being "quick." We then began to talk about the difference between "fussing" and "intensity." Each child had an idea. Joel declared that Mindy and Charles should get a babysitter. The older sisters agreed, advising that Mindy and Charles should go out and talk so that the children could not hear them. Sylvia offered to babysit; the parents said they appreciated her offer but thought that she was too young.

The children, all eager to tell another story, returned to family time. Then they shifted to making distinctions between "fights" and "disagreements." They said that Mindy and Charles sometimes argued over their differences. They gave an example of Mindy's and Charles's different rules about "city" and "country" clothes. Through their examples they struggled with their parents' rules and expectations, talking about who makes decisions about what, the changes that had occurred since Mindy had begun spending time in her apartment, and eventually returning full circle back to what helps. Joel enthusiastically suggested that an alarm clock would help Charles.

At this point the clock mandated that we stop. In closing I thanked them for coming and said that I hoped it had helped. This was a sincere closing comment, and I did not expect a response. I smiled as Denise exclaimed, "See, that's what I was going to say! This session has helped me a lot by being able to express without having a fear." I thanked them again for coming, and in a charming way they thanked me for "letting us."

Each therapy meeting is unique in how it begins, proceeds, and ends. I often take a moment at the beginning of each meeting to mention where we left off at our last meeting and give people a chance to tell me what they are occupied with this day and how they want to use the time. I do not assume that we will begin where we left off, as each of us has been in other conversations since with others and ourselves. I sometimes make a brief summary of what we have talked about at the end of a meeting, asking input on where to go from here and including whether and when to meet again.

"THE TALE GOES ON"

A therapy conversation is not singular and self-contained. It is a multiplicity of intertwining, overlapping present, past, and future conversations that people have with each other and with themselves. Each conversation is a collage of story fragments—some merge, some fade, some continue—emerging into something different for all. A conversation can have many directions: Any path can be explored, any path can be abandoned. The future paths that these family members' conversations would take, with each other and with themselves, were not predictable. The endings of our conversations would be beginnings for future ones, for silent and out-loud conversations, for out-of-therapy and in-therapy ones.

Continuing conversations and unforeseen outcomes are as likely for the therapist as for the client. Since the meetings described in this chapter, both immediately afterward and over time, I have continued to reflect on this family and my work with them. This reflecting process represents my bias that therapists should be lifelong learners, in continuous consideration with themselves and others, including their clients, students, and colleagues, about their therapy experiences (Anderson, 1997). Questions and comments by therapists who have watched the videotapes—for example, "Why didn't you ask about . . . ?" and "Why did you start talking with the children rather than ask the parents to state why they wanted the meeting?"—invite continuous thinking about my therapy philosophy and practice.

Most noticeable to me is that I saw the members of this family off and on for more than 2 years. This is more unusual than usual for a therapist whose experience is that therapy from a collaborative approach tends to be briefer. After these two meetings Mindy occasionally called for an appointment. Charles came in two times. Mindy's thoughts about the marriage shifted back and forth, at times being committed to it and at other times resigned that it no longer worked for her. Charles continued to want the marriage but respected, although painfully, that Mindy eventually did not. They divorced 18 months later. I say "they" because, although it was Mindy's decision, together they decided that it

would be best for Charles to file for the divorce. They maintained joint custody of the children, who still spend their time in the city and in the country and are home schooled by both parents. I met with the children a year after the divorce to do a follow-up interview. They were doing fine and were touching as they told of their dream that their parents would get back together. They smiled as they animatedly told me how they would draw "beautiful hearts," cut them in half, and give each parent a half.

This is the kind of family and life situation that pulls at therapists' values. I always have my own values in the therapy room with me, but I want to respect the family members' values. Although I have opinions about marriages, families, men, women, and children, I do not want to force my opinions on another person or manipulate people toward any outcome. I would not hesitate to share any idea that I might have about divorce and its effect on children—but again, this would be offered as food for thought and dialogue, something we can talk about, not something with which any family member is obliged to agree or do. This is not a position of therapist neutrality.

To the contrary, I do not believe that therapists can take a neutral stance. What is important to me is how I position myself with my values. I do not want my values to interfere with my ability to create space for, and facilitate, collaborative relationships and generative dialogue that will allow people to talk with themselves and each other in ways that they have not been able to do before and in ways that give each of them a sense of self-agency.

I still see this family on the videotapes when I teach and as I write these words. Every now and then therapists have a client for whom in fleeting moments they become part of each other's lives—or, should I say, each other's ongoing conversations. This family is one for me.

References

Anderson, H. (1995). Collaborative language systems: Toward a postmodern therapy. In R. Mikesell, D-D. Lusterman, & S. McDaniel (Eds.), *Integrating family therapy: Handbook of family psychology and systems theory* (pp. 27–44).

Washington, DC: American Psychological Association.

Anderson, H. (1997). *Conversation, language, and possibilities: A postmodern approach to therapy.* New York: Basic Books.

Anderson, H., & Levin, S. B. (1997). Collaborative conversations with children: Country clothes and city clothes. In C. Smith & D. Nyland (Eds.), *Narrative therapy with children and adolescents* (pp. 255–281). New York: Guilford Press.

Goolishain, H. A., & Anderson, H. (1987). Language systems and therapy: An evolving idea. *Psychotherapy, 24*(Suppl.), 529–538.

CHAPTER 10

THERAPY WITH STEPFAMILIES: A DEVELOPMENTAL SYSTEMS APPROACH

James H. Bray

Although stepfamilies are an old family form, there has been an exponential increase in their numbers because of the rise in the divorce and remarriage rates in the United States. It is estimated that there are between 15–20 million stepfamilies in the United States, and the number continues to rise each year. The most common type of stepfamily is the divorce-engendered stepfather family, in which a man, who may or may not have been previously married, marries a woman who has children from a previous marriage or relationship (Bray & Hetherington, 1993; Bray & Kelly, 1998). Most stepfamilies are created after a remarriage but, with the increase in cohabitation, many stepfamilies are formed without the legal sanction of matrimony. Most of the research and clinical writings are about stepfamilies with minor children (Bray, 1999; Bray & Kelly, 1998; Hetherington, Bridges, & Insabella, 1998). However, divorce and remarriage are not limited solely to adults with young children. Many middle-aged or older adults also remarry, after a divorce or the death of a spouse. Their adult children are also affected by the remarriage, and many of the same dynamics and issues arise in these families as well.

Professional interests sometimes originate from a personal experience or simply a chance question. My own clinical and research interests in stepfamilies grew out of several encounters with stepfamilies at a time when not much was known about them.

In 1979, as a young and somewhat naive psychology intern working on my PhD in clinical psychology, I was assigned the case of the Sampson family, a mother and her two children, Buddy and Jessica. Ms. Sampson came to the clinic because she feared that her children might be developing problems because of her recent remarriage. The visit was precipitated by a conflict over helping with the dishes. When Mr. Sampson asked his stepson, Buddy, to lend a hand, he refused: "I don't have to do what you say 'cause you ain't my real daddy." Until that moment Ms. Sampson had felt that all was well in her new family and that she had made the "right" choice for herself and her children. Somehow this incident called into question her decision, and she was afraid that she might be "ruining her children's lives."

Because I was inexperienced and uneducated about stepfamilies, I simply consoled her during the first visit. Then I went to the library to find out more about the subject. My search did not take very long, because there was very little in the literature about divorce-engendered stepfamilies, and there was a paucity of research. So I decided that I would treat the Sampsons like a "regular" (i.e., nondivorced nuclear) family, because there were now two parents and children.

Over the next few sessions I consulted with Ms. Sampson about her fears and her parenting. I

Preparation of this chapter was partially supported by Grant RO1 AA08864 from the National Institute of Alcoholism and Alcohol Abuse and Grant RO1 HD22642 from the National Institute of Child Health and Human Development.
The description of these families, their names and locations, have been changed to protect their identities and privacy.

worked briefly with the children around their problems with their family. Mr. Sampson, the new stepfather, did not come to therapy. The message he sent was that it was Ms. Sampson's problem and that she and the children had to take care of it. Ms. Sampson occasionally brought up issues about her ex-husband and the children. I usually brushed over these incidents to focus on the "real problems" in her new family. After several sessions Ms. Sampson stopped therapy. She seemed to be feeling better, and the conflicts had ceased. I assumed that they were doing OK.

In the clinic where I worked, two staff members —Carol Brady, PhD, and Joyce Ambler, MSW—noticed that children from divorced families and stepfamilies were overrepresented in the clinic. We decided to write a research grant proposal to develop a prevention program to help stepfamilies cope with their unique stresses and changes. The grant proposal was soundly rejected by the federal agency. The scientific reviewers thought the program was interesting and innovative; however, they said they could not fund a program when it was not clear that there was a need for it and when there had been no systematic research to study stepfamilies and demonstrate how they are different than other types of families. One reviewer asked, "Are there enough children in these kinds of families to warrant such a program and if so, why do stepfamilies need any different treatment than other types of families?" We shook our heads in disbelief. Our own experience had taught us that stepfamilies are unique and need special programs, but we did not have the time and energy to do the basic research without support.

About a year later, Ms. Sampson called me and requested an appointment. At this point I had completed my PhD and was a postdoctoral fellow in a family therapy training program. At the first session I was eager to find out what had happened to the family. Ms. Sampson was also quite eager to let me know what had happened and how my interventions had created all kinds of changes, both positive and negative, in her family.

The precipitating incident for consulting me was a lawsuit her ex-husband had filed because he now wanted to see his children, after not having seen them during the last year. Ms. Sampson had previously filed a lawsuit for nonpayment of child support of *her* children. Mr. Sampson, the stepfather, did not understand why his stepchildren were suddenly acting distant and more difficult to parent after he had developed such nice relationships, especially with Buddy, over the last 2 years. Ms. Sampson told me that she had tried to follow my advice and become a "regular" family and that if her ex-husband would just "leave them alone" everything would be A-OK. The children stated that they were excited to see their "real dad," but their mother and stepfather made it difficult for them to do so. Buddy said that he sort of liked the idea of having two dads and did not understand what all the problems were about. Sarah also wanted to see her father because she still wasn't too sure about Mr. Sampson.

Fortunately, at this time I had a supervisor who knew about stepfamilies and was also a family therapist. When I told him about the history of this case he just chuckled and told me, "Well, I guess you're ready to learn that there's lots of kinds of 'regular' families and what's 'regular' for nuclear families is certainly not 'regular' for stepfamilies." I read some new articles and a book by Emily and John Visher, pioneers in working with and writing about stepfamilies. I was amazed to find out what is "regular" for stepfamilies and how this can be very different than "regular" for other kinds of families (Visher & Visher, 1988).

In reading the articles, I learned that it was estimated that 20%–25% (it is up to 40% now) of all children in the United States would live in a stepfamily before they reached age 18 (Glick, 1989). During their childhood and adolescence, millions of children would be directly involved in the breakup and reorganization process as their family changed from a first-marriage nuclear family; to a postdivorce, single-parent family; to a stepfamily. Many children would be involved in repeated family changes because of their parents' multiple divorces and remarriages (Bray & Hetherington, 1993; Hetherington et al., 1998). Multiple marital transitions in stepfamilies remind me of the quote by Will Rogers: "I guess the only way to stop divorce is to stop marriage."

After I completed my postdoctoral fellowship, I

took a faculty position in the Department of Psychology at Texas Woman's University in Houston. In 1982 I again decided to study stepfamilies because of their increasing numbers following the "divorce revolution" in the United States. This time I worked with Joyce Ambler and Sandra Berger, both social workers. We all agreed that this type of research was sorely needed so that prevention and intervention programs could be developed for stepfamilies. Thus, we embarked on conducting basic developmental research on the nature of stepfamilies and how children grow and adjust within them. Using my research expertise and Joyce and Sandra's clinical experience, we designed a study to investigate how stepfamilies functioned during the first 5 years after remarriage. We submitted a grant proposal to the National Institute of Child Health and Human Development of the National Institutes of Health and, after a couple of revisions, we were funded to begin the project (Bray, 1988; Bray & Berger, 1993).

We examined what a "normal" stepfamily looks like and how it operates. Our goal was to understand and document the family life cycle of such families and how they differ from nuclear families. Furthermore, we studied the impact of life in a stepfamily on individual functioning, such as social and emotional adjustment, and how extended family relationships develop in stepfamilies. Finally, we wanted to know what factors determine whether a stepfamily succeeds or fails.

When we began the Developmental Issues in StepFamilies (DIS) Research Project in 1984, we made several naive assumptions about what we would find in our study. On the basis of our understanding of divorce and remarriage at that point, we assumed that life in a stepfamily would be initially stressful, involve several short-lived changes for children and adults, and that children would respond to these changes with increased behavioral problems. We were partially correct in this assumption, but we grossly underestimated the amount of change, both positive and negative, that families experience after a remarriage. Changes often included moving to a new residence, usually better than the previous one, because of the increased income available with two adults in the family. For children, this move was usually quite stressful, because it entailed losing old

friends, changing schools, establishing new peer and family relationships, and especially getting accustomed to a new stepparent in the home. We also underestimated the influence that children had on the remarriage. As Herbert Samuel stated, "It takes two to make a marriage a success and only one to make it a failure." In the case of stepfamilies it takes at least three, as the children had much influence on this.

We also naively assumed that within a year, or at most two, stepfamily relationships would settle down, adapt, and become quite similar to those in nuclear families. In addition, we believed that children's adjustment would improve and that there would be few differences between children in stepfamilies and those in nuclear families after a couple of years in a stepfamily.

We were wrong about several of our hypotheses. We found that it takes longer than a year for stepfamilies to adjust. There continue to be unique aspects of stepfamily relationships and marriages, different than those in nuclear families. Stepchildren continue to have more behavior problems than children in nuclear families, although these problems are not as pervasive as some researchers claim (Bray & Berger, 1993). The adults sometimes had a difficult time understanding the changes that occurred after the short-lived honeymoon wore off. As Peter DeVries said, "The difficulty with marriage is that we fall in love with a personality, but must live with a character."

We then began a longitudinal follow-up study in late 1988, which continued through 1992. In the meantime I had moved to the Department of Family Medicine at Baylor College of Medicine in Houston. There we refocused the project to examine how health and well-being are affected by the special stresses associated with stepfamilies' lives.

In following these families over time we found that stepfamilies change in unique ways compared to nuclear families. Children's adjustment continues to be affected by these particular stepfamily relationships. Stepfamily life is influenced by the developmental changes of children, especially during adolescence. Successful stepfamilies were good at making "lemonade out of lemons" or, as George Bernard Shaw said, "If you cannot get rid of the family skeleton, you may as well make it dance." We were particularly surprised by some of our findings, because they were different than what we had expected and different than some of the prevailing myths about the impact of divorce and remarriage. This chapter draws on the theory and research on stepfamilies from the DIS Research Project and my clinical experience in working with stepfamilies. A summary of the findings of the DIS Research Project can be found in Bray (1999), Bray and Berger (1993), and Bray and Kelly (1998).

DEVELOPMENTAL SYSTEMS FRAMEWORK FOR STEPFAMILIES

Stepfamilies are evolving interactional family systems that appear to have their own developmental cycle. There are unique normative issues and tasks that occur during the stepfamily life cycle that differ from those of first-marriage families (Bray, 1995, 1999; Bray & Berger, 1992, 1993; Bray & Kelly, 1998; McGoldrick & Carter, 1988; Whiteside, 1982). Relationships in stepfamilies change over time and are affected by previous individual and family experiences, developmental issues within the stepfamily, and developmental issues for individual family members. Marital and family experiences during the first marriage, separation, and divorce may have a great impact on the functioning of the stepfamily (Bray & Berger, 1992; Bray & Kelly, 1998; Hetherington & Clingempeel, 1992). Thus, the multiple developmental trajectories of family members and the stepfamily life cycle are important to consider in understanding the functioning of stepfamilies.

Forming a stepfamily with young children is likely to be different than forming a stepfamily with young adolescents, and different than forming a stepfamily with adult children, because of the discordant developmental needs of family members (Bray, 1995). The stepfamily life cycle and individual developmental issues may be congruent, or they may be quite divergent. The developmental issues are congruent in new stepfamilies with young children because both the children and the stepfamily need close, cohesive family relationships. The centripetal forces of stepfamily formation coincide with the need that young children have for affective in-

volvement and structure. In such cases, the stepfamily is moving to develop a cohesive unit, while adolescents are moving to separate from the family. Adolescents want to be less cohesive and more separate from the family unit as they struggle with identity formation and separation from the family of origin. In this case the developmental needs of the adolescent are at odds with the developmental push of the new stepfamily for closeness and bonding. Stepfamilies are usually less cohesive than first-marriage nuclear families, although their ideal level for cohesion is remarkably similar to that of nuclear families (Bray, 1988; Bray & Berger, 1993; Pink & Wampler, 1985).

A DEVELOPMENTAL SYSTEMS APPROACH TO TREATING STEPFAMILIES

A useful approach for working with stepfamilies is based on the developmental systems model described above (Bray, 1995; Bray & Harvey, 1995). Helping family members understand the context of stepfamily life through psychoeducation about divorce and remarriage is an effective intervention to normalize the experiences of family members and promote a context for change. The remarried family system comprises the current residential stepfamily and includes links to the nonresidential parent's extended family system and the stepparent's extended family system. In addition, relevant issues from the previous marital and divorce experiences—particularly unresolved emotional problems and attachments—and issues from the family of origin are central concerns. Differentiating the unique issues encountered by stepfamilies from the expectations based on a nuclear-family model is a frequent part of the normalization process in psychoeducation. In addition, it is useful to educate family members about developmental issues and sequences for all children so that their problems are not labeled as having been created by the stepfamily. Strategic–intergenerational interventions are also used to facilitate change in family patterns, interactions, expectations, and meanings (Bray & Harvey, 1995; Williamson & Bray, 1988). These interventions are designed to consider the interactions between the life cycle tasks of the stepfamily and the individual family members.

CASE EXAMPLE

Joe and Sarah Boyd are a remarried couple who were referred for family therapy by Sarah's lawyer. Sarah had consulted her lawyer because she had "had enough of Joe and his son and daughter-in-law, and was tired of playing second fiddle to them." The Boyds had been married for 10 years. The lawyer suggested that the couple try family therapy before proceeding with a divorce, because each spouse indicated that he or she would prefer to be married if the couple could work out their problems. This was the second marriage for each of them. Joe had been married to his first wife for 14 years and had two children from that marriage. One of his sons had died at age 8. Joe had been divorced for 5 years before marrying Sarah. He ran a small business and was quite successful, although it required considerable time and energy. He often had to work 6 or 7 days a week.

Joe's remaining son, Jerry, had returned to the area and had worked in the family business for about 6 months. The plan was for Jerry to take over the business, after his father retired. However, in a later session it became clear that this was an area of contention between Joe and Sarah. Jerry was married to Cindy, and they had a year-old baby. Cindy had grown up in another state, so she had no family in the area. Joe described his son as strong willed but somewhat immature. Sarah, however, described Jerry in much harsher terms, such as "bull-headed, stupid, childish, and manipulative." Joe reported that during his adolescence, Jerry had a drug problem and an unstable work history. His hope was that Jerry would now settle down, because he had a wife and child to support. Cindy was not employed but received financial support from her parents. She wanted to work in the Boyd's family business with her husband, and this too was a major point of contention for Joe and Sarah.

Sarah had been married to her first husband for 17 years, and they had a son and two daughters. Her son lived in the same city, and her daughters were away attending college. Sarah had been divorced for 2 years before meeting and marrying Joe. Her children had lived with her and Joe after their marriage. Jerry had spent significant time with the family but had resided primarily with his mother. Sarah had been a secretary for many years and seemed to enjoy her work, which occupied about 40 hours per week. Thus, she had more free time from work than her husband did. Sarah indicated that she had a cordial but distant relationship with her former spouse. Joe and Sarah described their relationship with Joe's first wife as distant and conflictual. They were both openly critical of her parenting of Jerry. Figure 10.1 presents a genogram of the family.

During the first visit I asked each member of the couple with what problems they wanted help resolving and how I could be of help to them. Joe said, "I am here to save my marriage." He continued, with a tear in his eye, "Sarah says that if I don't change some things with my son and daughter-in-law, she will leave and divorce me. I love Sarah, and I don't want to lose her." Joe indicated that this was extremely difficult for him because he felt caught between his wife and his son. He said that he did not understand why Sarah was so "worked up about everything." Jerry was his only surviving son, and he didn't want to lose him, too. His first son had died from a childhood illness. You could see the pain and grief in Joe's eyes when he talked about the loss of his young son and the possibility of losing the woman he loved. He did not understand why his wife was upset, neither did he appreciate the depth of her anger and resentment.

Sarah stated that she wanted help with "how to deal with Joe's insensitivity to me, especially about his son and daughter-in-law, and to improve our communication in our marriage. She continued angrily,

> I feel betrayed, used, and ignored by Joe. Joe, Jerry, and Cindy are the Three Musketeers and I am always the odd person out. I'm sick of it and won't stand for it anymore. Jerry and Cindy know how to play Joe like a well-tuned fiddle. They know all the right strings to play and Joe does whatever they want and whatever he pleases without considering my feelings!

Joe seemed startled by Sarah's strong statement.

Sarah added, "Dr. Bray, I don't want to force Joe to choose between me and his son, so if things can't

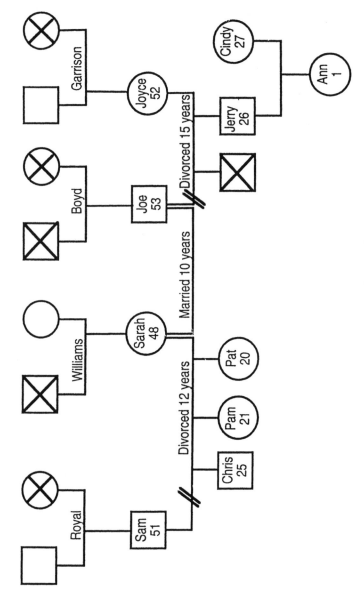

FIGURE 10.1. Genogram of the Boyd Stepfamily.

change then I will just leave." On the clinic intake form Sarah indicated that her satisfaction with the marriage on a scale of 1 to 10 was a 1, whereas Joe indicated that his satisfaction was a 7. Clearly, he was completely unaware of Sarah's level of unhappiness.

Later, when I asked Sarah what had attracted her to Joe, she said,

> I fell in love with him early in our dating and knew I wanted to spend the rest of my life with him. However, looking back I didn't realize that it was a package deal, and I would have to put up with his son, his crazy ex-wife, and now his manipulative daughter-in-law. It's just too much.

This stepfamily was unusual in that they had been married for 10 years and they had adult children who lived outside of the home. Yet their problems were similar to those of many newer stepfamilies that struggle with the stress of blending two families with minor children (Bray, 1995; Bray & Harvey, 1995). The family was undergoing a developmental shift that was due to the recent return of Joe's remaining son, which stimulated unresolved family issues. In addition, the patterns of relating that had developed during their early years of marriage were being challenged with the new problems. Each spouse had angry and hurt feelings left from earlier times when the children were younger and lived with them.

On the surface, Joe seemed to brush off his own concerns and hurt. After I scratched the surface a little, it became apparent that he was afraid that if he opened up the issues that bothered him, he would have another great loss—either his son, his wife, or both. This fear prevented him from facing and dealing effectively with these issues. The couple seemed to be caught in a thick fog of the past that kept them stuck in dysfunctional patterns and prevented them from creating a workable future.

Sarah felt that Joe had been disloyal to her after Jerry's return and entry into the family business. This loyalty issue had escalated considerably in the last 6 months. For example, when she and Joe saw Jerry and Cindy at a restaurant and Joe went to speak to them, Sarah saw this as yet another example of disrespect and disloyalty. She told Joe to ignore them and not speak to them. Furthermore, Sarah was very concerned about her husband turning over the family business to a son who could not manage it, which might affect their retirement. Both Joe and Jerry felt that this was not Sarah's concern, because the business predated Joe and Sarah's marriage and Joe had made other financial investments to ensure an adequate retirement for Sarah. However, Sarah countered that she did have a vested interest in the business, because her salary was being used to support the family and she helped out with the business when needed. She saw this as yet another example of how her husband was siding with his son against her. Although Joe had a strong commitment to save the marriage, Sarah was beginning to show signs of developing a pervasive negative perception of the marriage. She was highly critical and sarcastic with Joe. These types of interactions and "recasting" the marriage as totally negative are strong predictors of later divorce (Bray & Jouriles, 1995; Gottman, 1994).

I complimented the couple on dealing with these important issues and assured them that these were the types of concerns that typically arise in stepfamilies. I did this to normalize their concerns, provide information about stepfamilies, and set the context for making changes. Joe listened carefully, while Sarah tended to "yes, but" me about my attempts to normalize the situation.

At the end of the first session, I asked each of them to do homework. Such assignments continue the therapeutic process between sessions and speed the therapy. It was apparent that Sarah had significant emotional wounds from Joe's past behavior, that Joe was not aware of the hurts or how deeply Sarah felt about them, and that they did not have the skills or the context to productively resolve them. Their homework was to write a history of their marriage and to make a list of the hurts that each one had from the other. They were to independently prepare their marital histories and list of hurts and return next week prepared to discuss them.

At the beginning of the second session, they were visibly more relaxed, but not for long. Sarah stated that she had done her homework, and showed me many pages of handwritten notes. Joe said he "sort of" did his, to which Sarah responded, "See, he says he is interested in saving our marriage, but he won't do anything." Joe replied, "I just had too much to do this week at work." Sarah retorted, "You had time to go out to lunch with Jerry and Cindy, didn't you!" For Sarah, this was yet another instance of how Joe put his work and relationship with his son first and their relationship second.

I asked Sarah about her list. She said that, in writing it, she had learned a lot about their problems because she had written half a page of hurts about other family members and four pages about her husband. Joe was clearly taken aback by this. I asked her to highlight with an imaginary yellow marker the major areas of concern. As she related the incidents, many of them went back to the early years of their marriage. The issues reflected a combination of unhealed hurts and unrealistic expectations about stepfamily life.

The bulk of this session was used to explore Sarah's concerns. Because she had completed her homework, we started with her list. I asked her to describe her feelings about each of her issues. Then I asked Joe to acknowledge and mirror Sarah's concerns and inquire about anything he really didn't understand. I asked him to describe his view of the situation and to explain what actions he had taken and what his intention had been. For example, Sarah said that she believed that Jerry was just using Joe for money. She felt that when Joe took Jerry out to eat, he was not only excluding her but also permitting himself to be used. I asked Joe whether he saw this the same way. Joe said that it never entered his mind that Sarah might see his dining alone with Jerry as excluding her. It also seemed only proper to him to treat Jerry to lunch and to socialize with him. He had intended no harm to Sarah. However, he could acknowledge now how Sarah could see it differently. This enabled me to help them to explore some of their different views of the situation. I then asked Joe to review Sarah's list. Where he could see her hurt, even though he felt no intention to harm her, I asked if he could now apologize. Sarah was then able to forgive Joe for some issues, but she said there were others she could not. I added, "maybe not at this time, but in the future." The same process was now repeated with Joe's list.

Sarah also had very strong opinions and unrealistic expectations about many of the things that had happened. The struggle between her and Joe was over who had the "right" view about what happened. The problem was that they were confusing what had happened with their interpretations of what had happened, and they were locked into a "fight to the death" about having the "right" view. This struggle is a common one for couples, especially remarried couples. The struggle about being right becomes a struggle for survival, which deprives the couple of the love and positive aspects of having a thriving marriage (Bray & Kelly, 1998).

Later, when Joe and Sarah clashed about still another incident, I said,

> *I am impressed to hear how committed each of you is to being right about what happened. You each report a similar set of actions, but your interpretations of what happened and what the other meant is vastly different. I wonder what is more important, to be right or to get along with each other? You may need to choose.*

Joe responded, "I don't have to be right about it. I've told Sarah that I think her perceptions are valid and OK for *her*." I believe she heard this as, "your opinion is wrong or doesn't really matter."

Sarah responded, "See, that is just what I mean. He keeps saying that, 'It is just my perceptions', but they don't mean anything to him. He just discounts them."

I said,

> *This is exactly what I mean. You two struggle as if your lives depended on proving that your view is the correct one, but each of you confuses what actually happened with your own interpretations of what happened. But the price of needing to be right is losing the love and compassion you have for each other. Is it worth that price? Again, what is more important—to be right or get along? I suggest that you consider the possibility that it might be more important for you to get along than be right about everything.*

This frame helped the couple consider alternative views and particularly affected Sarah's ability to listen to some of my ideas about stepfamilies. It facilitated positive communication between the couple and interrupted their escalating defensive communication cycle (Alexander, 1973). Sarah became more able to express her concerns to Joe in a context and manner that permitted Joe to hear her without being overwhelmed by her negative emotional expressions.

Gottman (1994) reported that when there is highly charged negative emotion between a couple, men tend to shut down, both psychologically and physiologically, and do not attend to the cognitive message that accompanies the negative emotional message. This is a way of coping with the unpleasant arousal state triggered by the interaction. As Joe got beyond this defensive stance, he could help Sarah to understand that he was "on her side."

Both Joe and Sarah had unrealistic expectations about their stepfamily relationships. Like so many stepparents, Sarah expected Joe to feel exactly the same about her children as he did about his own. This is part of the "nuclear family myth" for stepfamilies: People expect stepfamilies to be just like nuclear, first-marriage families (Bray & Kelly, 1998). Holding onto these expectations makes it difficult to resolve stepfamily problems. Because Sarah was more overt and verbal about her concerns, she tended to be the initial focus of the therapy. However, I had to be very careful not to be perceived by Sarah as "on Joe's side." To do this, I had to deal with her concern about loyalty and being left out of her new family. When I tried to explore the history of this issue, Sarah said that although this might have been an issue in her first marriage and family of origin, she did not see it as causing her current problems. She wanted to focus on *this* marriage. To maintain a neutral stance, I asked Sarah to tell me if she thought I was siding with Joe and against her and told her that we could talk about it if she felt that such was the case. This seemed to allay her concerns.

Although this was a difficult session, it appeared that the couple had adequate communication skills to discuss these issues on their own. However, the unspoken hurt, unresolved issues, and need to be right were still interfering with their communication. They were each avoiding dealing with underlying issues. I suspected that it had something to do with their unconscious protection of Joe's feelings of grief at the loss of his son and his first marriage. Their homework was to schedule at least three meetings in which they would go over their list of hurts, as we had practiced in the session. If they completed this assignment, they were to tear the lists up and tell one another that they were forgiven. If they could not complete their lists, they were to bring them in for the next session. To promote positive interactions, they were also asked to invite each other to do something together just for fun. It could be something small, like listening to a joke, or something big, like having a date together.

The next session was to include Joe's son and daughter-in-law. There was considerable resistance to having all of the parties in the room at the same time. It was apparent that a context needed to be set before the session. This situation was similar to the loyalty conflict discussed by Carter (1989) in which an inappropriate triangle is created among the parent, stepparent, and child. The stepparent asks, overtly or covertly: "Is the biological parent more loyal to the children or to me?" This type of question actually generates the problem, because it presumes that the stepparent and children are at the same hierarchical level within the family (Bray, 1995). Adults and children are in different categories, and this question is like comparing apples and mangoes. Making this distinction explicit can detriangulate the situation and set a context for different relationships within the family.

To help Sarah and Joe prepare for this potentially difficult session, we discussed the need for family members to agree to treat each other with courtesy (Bray, 1995). We then discussed the difference between *courtesy* and *respect*. Respect cannot be demanded, it is earned, whereas courtesy is a given. I suggested that Joe tell his son and daughter-in-law that he expected them to treat "my wife" (not their parent or stepparent) with courtesy. The language is important. By not referring to his spouse as a stepparent, the expectations about parental roles and authority are subtly addressed. In addition, I recommended that Joe tell Sarah that he expects her to treat "my son" (not "our children") with courtesy. This process detriangulates relationships and sets the stage for resolution of other problems. He agreed to do this with his son and daughter-in-law during the next week.

Joe and Sarah also questioned whether Jerry would agree to attend the next session. Joe said that when he first mentioned the idea, Jerry said he didn't need to see any "shrink" and that Sarah was the one who had problems and needed help. Joe felt that he should simply demand that Jerry come and even threaten him with the loss of his job. However, I felt that it was important to develop a different context for the session. I suggested that Joe invite Jerry and Cindy to come to the session as my "consultants." He was to tell them that they would not be coming to receive help from me, but rather to help me help their father. I asked him to make it clear to them that this would be for only that one meeting.

All four attended the following session. All appeared apprehensive. The initial seating arrangement was quite telling. Jerry, Cindy, and Joe sat on one side of the room, and Sarah sat on the other side by herself. Before we started, I rearranged the seating to have Joe and Sarah together on a couch and Jerry and Cindy together.

I thanked Jerry and Cindy for coming and agreeing to help me help Jerry's father and his marriage. I told them that I appreciated their commitment. Because they had known Joe and Sarah much longer than I had, they could provide valuable information for me in my attempt to be of help. This seemed to relax them.

To create a productive context, I asked Joe to restate his request that everyone treat the others with courtesy. Several important issues were then addressed. Some of the hot, unresolved topics were openly discussed for the first time. This enabled me to get a better picture of what had happened, to start the process of improving communication, and to offer alternative views that might be more productive. Several things became apparent: Sarah was on the outside of the relationship with the others, very angry, and openly hostile to Jerry and Cindy. Jerry was very angry and hostile toward Sarah. Joe did indeed make many decisions and commitments

without consulting Sarah. He felt that this was not done in a malicious or power-oriented way, but as a style of just getting along and making decisions on the spot. He believed that Sarah did the same thing with her children and in their social relationships, so he thought it was OK for him to do it. This had been a major unspoken "rule" that they had never really negotiated.

The meeting was spent going over several incidents that had provoked conflict. This allowed each person to hear the others' perspectives and resolve their concerns. In addition, it enabled Joe to take a clear position of alignment with his wife. Several times he was coached to support his wife when she raised concerns, rather than defend his son and daughter-in-law. This helped restructure the triangle in the family.

A major issue for Sarah was how Joe had handled remodeling their kitchen and how he had helped Jerry and Cindy remodel their home. She felt that he had put his son's project over theirs and that Jerry and Cindy did not appreciate Joe's contribution, and certainly not her own. This issue had arisen when Joe insisted that he had not taken Jerry's side against Sarah. Sarah exclaimed,

> *What about when you had the workers leave in the middle of our remodeling job to go work on their house? What do you call that? Our kitchen was a mess for a couple of weeks, while the men worked on their house!*

Joe responded,

> *The reason they left was because the materials to finish our kitchen weren't ready, and our new appliances hadn't come in. There wasn't anything for them to do at our house, so I thought they could get started over at Jerry's.*

"I don't believe you," countered Sarah, "you just put it off to help Jerry and Cindy."

Jerry inserted: "There she goes again, always thinking Dad is against her and *for* us." Cindy added,

Come on Sarah, Dad (referring to Joe) was just trying to save us all money by having the workers stay busy. If I had known you were so upset about this, I would have had the workers not come, and waited 'til they finished with your house.

Sarah retorted: "Sure you would've, but your dad would never let you two go without, while I had to put up without a kitchen for weeks. See, Dr. Bray, how Joe takes their side and how Cindy plays up to him?"

At this point I stopped the process and thanked them for showing me how they interact. I said this was a good example of how our interpretation of events get in the way of getting along. I then asked Sarah to listen as Joe recounted what had happened. I asked Sarah to let me know if she had a question. When she raised the concern about not believing Joe, I asked Joe if he could show Sarah that the material and appliances were not available. He said that he would show her the dated invoices. Joe admitted that he should have consulted with Sarah before moving the workers and promised to do this in the future. This seemed to help her understand his point of view and made her feel included in the decision-making process.

I asked Cindy to describe her understanding of what had happened and for Sarah to listen and inquire about discrepancies. In the process, Cindy subtly indicated her appreciation for their help. I asked her to express her appreciation to Joe and Sarah in a much more explicit manner. Initially, Cindy balked. At that point I asked Joe and Sarah to explain their view, that help and gifts from Joe were really from both of them. After all, Sarah contributed to the family's income, and Joe and Sarah viewed all of these resources as "theirs," not as separate funds. Cindy indicated that she understood this. However, Jerry stated that the money his dad gave him came from the family business, which predated Joe and Sarah's marriage. For that reason, he felt that he didn't need to thank Sarah for it. I decided to leave this issue alone for the present, because some progress had been made, and there were other concerns with which to deal. Another goal was to get Joe out of the middle of the relationship be-

tween Sarah and Jerry and Cindy. To achieve this, they came to an agreement about how and when they would see each other and agreed that Joe would consult with Sarah before he made social commitments with them. They also began to examine how the money issues between father and son affected them all. Despite the productive changes made during the session, it was apparent at the end of the meeting that Sarah and Jerry were still very angry with each other. Sarah remained skeptical about the changes and still felt very hurt by what had happened in the past. Although on the surface the issue was about money, it in fact represented the arena in which Joe and Sarah's underlying battle over loyalty was being fought. This became even more apparent in the following session.

At our next meeting, Joe said that he felt things had gone "reasonably well," whereas Sarah appeared quite angry. I indicated that I felt that the session had gone well. Jerry, and especially Cindy, appeared willing to work to improve the relationship. But Sarah snapped, "She suckered you, too, Dr. Bray. That's the way she is with men, she always gets what she wants. I don't believe that you didn't see how she is." The triangle was reappearing in the therapy session.

I asked the couple if they had completed their list of hurts. They had not. Sarah angrily stated that Joe had continued to betray her and that nothing had changed. I asked what had happened and she said that Joe had lunch with Jerry twice this week. Joe asked Sarah, "What's wrong with having lunch with my son, everybody has to eat, don't they?" Sarah retorted, "Did you pay for the lunches? The only reason Jerry has lunch with you is so that you will pay. Can't you see he is just using you—using us?!" I thanked Sarah for bringing this up and stated that this was a perfect example with which to start the session. I acknowledged Sarah's strong feelings and asked her if she was willing to let go of her hurt and anger and move forward. She indicated that she could not or would not do that. It appeared that Sarah felt "wronged" by Joe. Sarah experienced Joe's relationship with Jerry almost in the same way that a hurt partner views a mate's extramarital affair. In such a situation the offending spouse must undertake some penance to help heal the wrong. The idea of penance was consonant with the couple's religious beliefs.

We spent most of this session discussing Sarah's concerns and clarifying the agreement between the couple about how and when Joe would see his son and daughter-in-law. I asked Sarah how she wanted Joe to make amends for the past. She wanted him to stop giving Jerry and Cindy any money for the next month and not to have any social contacts with them for that period. Joe agreed. This seemed to make a dramatic impact on Sarah. It helped her understand how committed Joe was to their marriage and to healing this situation. I also again normalized this situation as a typical stepfamily issue. I ended by complimenting them for developing a workable plan.

The next several sessions were spread out over a 2-month period. The couple continued to make steady progress. After the session in which Joe agreed not to see his son, there was a dramatic shift in Sarah. "Now," she said, "I can let go of the past and move forward." However, an issue arose that seemed to be a step backward. Without consulting Joe, Sarah had made some plans with her children. She had invited them over to the house on a weekend when Joe was planning some time alone with Sarah. She had also agreed to pay for some unexpected expenses that her daughter had incurred, again without consulting Joe. Soon after, Joe had dinner and a visit with his son and daughter-in-law, without first talking with Sarah. Sarah was very angry and concerned about this. I was concerned too, but for different reasons. Sarah felt it was a relapse: Joe was once again putting his loyalty to his son above his loyalty to her, willfully violating their agreement. I initially wondered if this was passive–aggressive behavior on Joe's part. Then, I began to consider the possibility that this was a return to their earlier escalating defensive communication cycle.

We used this session as a means to reclarify their agreement and to discuss Joe's concerns about Sarah and her children. Joe explained that his dinner with his son was not related to what Sarah had done, and he reminded Sarah that he had agreed not to have dinner with his son for a specific period of time, which had elapsed. He also stated that he felt he had a right to spend some money in any way he pleased and pointed out that Sarah did that with her

children. This led to a useful discussion about how the couple would allocate their money and that each needed the freedom to spend some amount of money without checking with the other. Furthermore, Joe was upset because he felt that, when it came to the children, Sarah held him to a much stricter standard than herself. The remainder of this session and the next explored how they could deal with their children fairly while still being considerate of one another.

The final session was used to review what had been learned in therapy and how to deal more effectively with future issues. The couple seemed very content with their current situation and were able to discuss issues as they arose. There were no longer "off-limits" topics for them. Sarah appeared to have let go of her anger and resentment toward Joe. Joe indicated that Sarah still did not have a close relationship with his son and daughter-in-law but was willing to have social events with the family and to continue working to improve the relationship. In addition, Sarah reported that, rather than dreading these social events, she could now enjoy them. I suggested that they might want to have another session with the four of them, but they declined and stated that they had made good progress on the issues and wanted to handle the rest on their own. We talked about warning signs to which the couple should attend that would signal approaching problems. Planning for dealing with future problems and how to handle relapses are important strategies for maintaining changes in couples (Bray & Jouriles, 1995). I agreed with their plans, and we concluded that we would have a final session in 6 months. I called the couple before the schedule final visit. Sarah said they were doing very well, enjoying each other, and didn't feel the need for a session.

FINAL THOUGHTS

This stepfamily exemplifies many of the issues that stepfamilies face during their development and over the course of their life cycles. Although this family had been together for some time, they encountered and re-encountered various issues concerning loyalty, triangles, parent–child conflict, and marital conflict that are faced by all stepfamilies (Bray & Kelly,

1998). What is striking about this family is how interactional patterns that developed during the early years of their marriage continued and evolved into problem areas for the couple. Their inability to discuss issues and maintain communication prevented them from resolving new issues and moving forward. Unresolved hurts and incomplete mourning of losses had a significant impact, even years after their occurrence.

Parenting issues, even with older children, tend to have a significant impact on stepfamily marriages. The direction of effects of parent–child problems and marital problems tends to differ in first-marriage families as compared with stepfamilies. In first-marriage families, problems in the marriage usually move downward and create problems with the children. However, in stepfamilies the problems tend to move upward. Conflict over how to meet the demands and needs of stepchildren is the frequent cause of problems in the marital relationship. This was clearly the situation with Joe and Sarah.

Money is often an arena of conflict for all families, but especially for stepfamilies. For Sarah and Joe, money represented loyalty and support. In stepfamilies with adult children the money issue is usually centered around inheritance and planning for retirement. Although adult children may be financially independent, they still have an interest in their inheritance, and this again adds to potential conflict and stress.

The developmental systems model I used with this family is typical of my work with stepfamilies. It addresses the developmental issues in stepfamilies and their intersection with individual life cycles. It informs both clinicians and clients about potential stress points or areas of conflict so that they can understand and, I hope, plan for them. A final point: Although we now know significantly more about how stepfamilies function and develop, we still need much more research, so that we can create effective prevention and intervention programs for these complex family systems.

References

Alexander, J. F. (1973). Defensive and supportive communications in normal and deviant families. *Journal of Consulting and Clinical Psychology, 40,* 223–231.

Bray, J. H. (1988). *Developmental issues in stepfamilies research project: Final report.* Bethesda, MD: National Institute of Child Health and Human Development.

Bray, J. H. (1995). Family oriented treatment of stepfamilies. In R. Mikesell, D-D. Lusterman, & S. McDaniel (Eds.), *Integrating family therapy: Handbook of family psychology and systems theory* (pp. 125–140). Washington, DC: American Psychological Association.

Bray, J. H. (1999). From marriage to remarriage and beyond: Findings from the Developmental Issues in StepFamilies Research Project. In E. M. Hetherington (Ed.), *Coping with divorce, single-parenting and remarriage: A risk and resiliency perspective* (pp. 253–271). Hillsdale, NJ: Erlbaum.

Bray, J. H., & Berger, S. H. (1992). Stepfamilies. In M. E. Procidano & C. B. Fisher (Eds.), *Contemporary families: A handbook for school professionals* (pp. 57–79). New York: Teachers College Press.

Bray, J. H., & Berger, S. H. (1993). Developmental issues in stepfamilies research project: Family relationships and parent–child interactions. *Journal of Family Psychology, 7,* 76–90.

Bray, J. H., & Harvey, D. M. (1995). Adolescents in stepfamilies: Developmental and family interventions. *Psychotherapy, 32,* 122–130.

Bray, J. H., & Hetherington, E. M. (1993). Families in transition: Introduction and overview. *Journal of Family Psychology, 7,* 3–8.

Bray, J. H., & Jouriles, E. (1995). Treatment of marital conflict and prevention of divorce. *Journal of Marital and Family Therapy, 21,* 461–473.

Bray, J. H., & Kelly, J. (1998). *StepFamilies: Love, marriage, and parenting in the first decade.* New York: Broadway Books.

Carter, E. A. (1989, October). Working with the remarried family. Workshop conducted at the Annual Convention of the American Association for Marriage and Family Therapy, San Francisco, CA.

Glick, P. C. (1989). Remarried families, stepfamilies, and stepchildren: A brief demographic profile. *Family Relations, 38,* 24–27.

Gottman, J. M. (1994). *What predicts divorce?* Hillsdale, NJ: Erlbaum.

Hetherington, E. M., Bridges, M., & Insabella, G. M. (1998). What matters? What does not? Five perspectives on the association between marital transitions and children's adjustment. *American Psychologist, 53,* 167–184.

Hetherington, E. M., & Clingempeel, W. G. (1992). Coping with marital transitions: A family systems perspective. *Monographs of the Society for Research in Child Development, 57*(2–3), Serial No. 227.

McGoldrick, M., & Carter, E. A. (1988). Forming a remarried family. In E. A. Carter & M. McGoldrick (Eds.), *The changing family life cycle* (pp. 399–429). New York: Gardner.

Pink, J. T., & Wampler, K. S. (1985). Problem areas in stepfamilies: Cohesion, adaptability, and the stepfather adolescent relationship. *Family Relations, 34,* 327–335.

Visher, E. B., & Visher, J. S. (1988). *Old loyalties, new ties: Therapeutic strategies with stepfamilies.* New York: Brunner/Mazel.

Whiteside, M. F. (1982). Remarriage: A family developmental process. *Journal of Marital and Family Therapy, 4,* 59–68.

Williamson, D. S., & Bray, J. H. (1988). Family development and change across the generations: An intergenerational perspective. In C. J. Falicov (Ed.), *Family transitions: Continuity and change over the life cycle* (pp. 357–384). New York: Guilford Press.

CHAPTER 11

WIDENING THE LENS: ENGAGING A FAMILY IN TRANSITION

Timothy T. Weber

Sue's voice was strained, urgent, pleading: "I really need your help. We've got some problems in our family. And I'm about to go crazy!" I wanted to be responsive and empathic, but focused. She continued, "We've gone through a lot of changes in our family, and it's all driving me nuts! I'm crawling out of my skin!" I was intrigued with her passion, but I did not want to engage in a lengthy story. How could I listen with heart yet elicit the necessary information and move us toward closure? "Briefly," I emphasized, "tell me about your situation." Sue then inventoried an exhaustive list of concerns: her husband's recent retirement from a large company, starting a new home-based business, mother-in-law now living with the family, a recent move from another state, new schools, new friends and the loss of old friends, smaller home, concerns about her son's developmental problems. As if she were alone in her worries, Sue insisted, "I know I have problems dealing with all this. I don't know about everybody else." "Who is in the family?" I asked. "My husband, my three children—19, 15, and 12 —and my husband's mother, who moved in with us when we moved here. I'm having trouble dealing with her."

Therapy begins at the first point of contact, often in the initial telephone contact. The therapist and the prospective client meet in a conversation at multiple levels—information, business, a mutual testing of the potential for a relationship, and some sense of direction for the work. This beginning conversation and the first few sessions underscore the central themes in the journey, begin to shape the therapeutic relationship, and establish the process through which the work will be accomplished.

In this chapter I unpack these beginning encounters between therapist and client by focusing on one case example—Sue and her family. Although the case study follows the general principles of engagement outlined in a previous chapter (Weber & Levine, 1995), this chapter is more pragmatic and personal, emphasizing the unfolding drama and the modification of theory and technique in the actual practice of a psychotherapeutic relationship. It is important to learn the basics of psychotherapy, but not in an absolute manner so that the novelty, mystery, suspense, and creativity inherent in the encounter with others are sacrificed for the sake of technical purity. A therapeutic approach that is built on basics but is also open to novelty and experimentation enhances "mindful learning" (Langer, 1997) and potentiates the possibility for change. In this chapter I also highlight the principle of respectful irreverence —accepting the client's initial presentation and slowly "widening the lens" of conversation and understanding toward greater complexity and imagination, irreverently defying a more reductionistic view. Finally, I take the point of view that the therapist and, more specifically, the therapeutic relationship, is the most critical instrument of change. The therapist's primary task is to embody and promote increasing self-definition, relatedness, and learning in a collaborative conversation with clients (Weber & Williamson, 1998). I tend to be active in using myself as an "interventionist" rather than taking a more restrained, minimalist approach (Minuchin, 1996). I involve family members in the action of conversation and relationship while also seeing individuals as part of the larger whole.

THE CALL

Desperate for help, Sue volunteered herself as the impaired family member, protecting herself and others in the family from more difficult conversations. She described her immediate family (see Figure 11.1): husband, James, 47 years old, recently retired from a full-time management position, now beginning a consulting business from a home office; Sue, 43 years old, with a master's degree in education, taught for the first 2 years of their 21-year marriage, raised children and volunteered in the schools since then; Amanda, 19 years old, home for the summer, soon to begin her second year of college; Adam, 15 years old, a 10th grader with a history of learning and social disabilities; Joshua, 12 years old, a seventh grader; and Martha, James's 80-year-old mother, who had been living with the family since their move 9 months ago. Sue described the family as living in tension, with "no talking . . . we're just going about our business." She increasingly was feeling uncomfortable with the "invasion," as she put it, of her mother-in-law. This newly blended intergenerational family was moving through multiple family transitions with minimal conversation and renegotiation of family roles and rules (Carter & McGoldrick, 1989). Would they be able to negotiate these "rapids" of family change openly and directly, with each other, or would Sue and other family members carry the family's pain through their symptoms?

Sue was eager to unfold the complexities and emotions of her family story. I was in the middle of a busy day, eager to complete the call without dismissing Sue in her distress and isolation. (Memories of my mother came:—beleaguered and worn down with so many family responsibilities, isolated, driven by tasks, innumerable changes in the family, little conversation, less collaboration, lonely, compelled to express her pain through the voice of somatic complaints, undaunted in her caring, relentless in her

devotion. We are often drawn to those encounters that give us fresh opportunity to rework an old family story.)

Typically, I ask both the complainant (Sue) and his or her partner to attend the first meeting. In this case, I modified this principle, at least for the first meeting, and invited Sue to set an appointment for herself. Why? Was I succumbing to Sue's emotional plea to be the family patient? Was I losing the "battle for structure" by not insisting on my way of working (Napier & Whitaker, 1978)? Was I caving into her desire to meet alone because I was tired and didn't want to argue the point? Did I simply want to settle into coziness of one-to-one therapy rather than the more challenging process of family therapy and multiple, often-conflicting realities? Was I invoking the principle of meeting with the "customer," the family member who carried the complaint and is interested in change (Fisch, Weakland, & Segal, 1982)?[1] (Sometimes, all things being equal, I accept and decline clinical opportunities and modify my way of working more on the basis of my individual tolerance level, prevailing mood and energy, and my own life circumstances as much as any elegant clinical theory or principle.) I added, "After we meet, we'll both be able to better understand how to proceed and who should be included." Sue seemed relieved that finally she would have a place to talk, to unravel all that she had carried. I wanted to respond to her most immediate and pressing desire— to find some momentary, safe haven for a conversation—while also making it clear that our first meeting was a "consultative session" (Wynne, McDaniel, & Weber, 1986) at which we would collaboratively shape the course of subsequent meetings. I am more inclined now than earlier in my career to begin with the client's framework rather than insisting on my own methodology. I want to respect what the client brings to the first conversation and invite, not insist, the client to move beyond the typically more individual framework of problem definition and membership ("I'm going crazy. It's me. I want to come in.").

These days in the health care environment, initial

---

[1] Probably some or all of these.

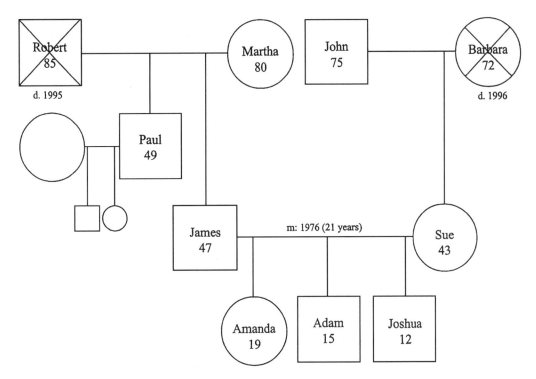

FIGURE 11.1. Family Genogram (1997)

conversations about therapy usually include some business pertaining to managed health care, insurance benefits, fees, and precertification. Sue and I concluded our telephone conversation with a cursory review of the precertification procedure before our first meeting. (I detest this part of the work—paper, calls, precertification, justification, third-party invasions, busywork in the midst of a busy day, appeals, etc. But I also want to get paid, and so I laboriously explain the procedures, offer my assistance, and make sure the job gets done before and throughout our work together. Therapy in the movies never includes the humdrum of this paperwork, but I know from the "war" stories of other therapists that I'm not alone.)

SESSION 1: SUE

As Sue entered my office for the first session, she sat down with a tired, deep sigh and began speaking over the glasses perched low on her nose: "I don't know what to do. Things have got to change. I have no time, no space; I'm crowded in. I want to pull my hair out!" she exclaimed as she thrust her arms high in the air with clenched teeth and a deter-

mined voice. She seemed firm, but helpless. Similar to many clients who enter psychotherapy, she uttered a litany of complaints with little sense of direction, solution, or hope in her ability to influence any substantial difference. As I attempted to elicit more specific information about her circumstances, I listened with patience and empathy, slowing the pace. (I do this as much to settle my own anxiety as I do to help the client. It is possible that the most beneficial impact of all theory and technique is to help the therapist with his or her anxiety so that the relationship gets the mindfulness it needs.) It is also important to build the "holding environment" as the fertile, therapeutic soil (Weber & Levine, 1995).

(My mother had been frequently distressed, overworked, isolated, and angry. She was so central in the family, and yet so marginalized; critical in managing the family, expresser of the family's passionate love and fury so that others could remain more constrained, and yet ostracized. My mother was a whirlwind who could not be harnessed, feared and imprisoned within the family while all of us benefited from her enormous care. These were some internal "flashes" as I recalled my role as mediator in the mix of the family's emotionality. No wonder I became a family psychologist! Sue's husband had to be included soon. I thought to myself that my own family's mistake was that my father, hardworking and benevolent as he was, was too afraid to include and sustain himself in the family fray.)

Doing psychotherapy includes this continual interplay between the therapist's personal history and the client's story (Framo, 1968). Being mindful of this interplay, even using this interplay as a resource (vs. interference) to expand and deepen the therapeutic conversation as the therapist's history and the client's story converge in the relationship, is one of the artistic strokes in therapy. The therapist uses himself or herself and all of his or her history while attending to the client's story as the story of concern. Mindful of my own history, I thought to myself, "I recall in my own family how, after we went through a lot of changes close together, it was difficult for us to talk about things. We wanted to be competent, avoid pain, just kept moving along, and my mother just kept working." Perhaps at some point in our work I would disclose some of my own personal associations. One of the arts of therapy is being mindful of the difference between the therapist's story and the client's story and knowing when and how to use the therapist's story as a resource.

I wondered about gender issues and role distribution (Walters, Carter, Papp, & Silverstein, 1988). Why was Sue here and not her husband? Why was she carrying the emotional load, or at least more willing to express distress in this public setting? Why was she volunteering herself as the client? How did her husband manifest his concerns? Were they in a complementary dance in which she overreported, and he underreported, concern? Was Sue attempting to recruit me as an ally to balance or move against the alliance between her husband and her mother-in-law? Individuals seek alliances in all organizations, especially when anxiety is high, in order to gain support and advance their cause. How could I support Sue's concern about Martha's presence without allying with her point of view against her husband? I responded by taking a more relational point of view (vs. an individual view), normalizing her concern:

I can understand how difficult it must be to include someone else in your family who has not lived with you before and who has particular habits that might be different from your way of operating. You care for her. (It helped to find within Sue's story small notes of care and commitment for Martha that I could amplify.) You are also frustrated, as most people would be under similar circumstances.

Repeatedly during the session, I reflected back to Sue concern for her personal circumstances but attempted to broaden the comments to family life, noting similar experiences of families in transition and the challenges of an intergenerational household with elders (Carter & McGoldrick, 1989). Sue appeared to relax more as the session continued, breathing with less strain and commenting that she felt less "psycho" than she had feared. I frequently accented her strengths, a primary task of a therapist who wants to increase hope, healing, and health: "In spite of these challenges, Sue, you seem to have an open heart to include James's mother in your family"; "It takes some skill to be at the center of all these changes and still manage the daily workings of the family." I wanted to accent her competency in the midst of her despair. For example, in response to Sue's heightened fright of "going crazy," I stated,

I suppose you feel that way, in part, because you are so eager to absorb into yourself the family's distress. That may be commendable and loving, but may also be overdone. Sounds like maybe you've had a lot of practice doing that. How far back does this skill go?

Sue briefly alluded to a pattern in her family of origin whereby she, an only child, had taken on the role of a negotiator between her distant parents. I then challenged Sue: "It seems that you grew up carrying the emotional load alone in your family, as you are doing now. I think it would be critical to include James as a partner in addressing these family transitions."

When conducting therapy I frequently insert what I call "synaptic questions," inquiring about the relation between the here and now and one's developmental and family-of-origin history. The lens is widened, and the parameters of the initial complaint and focus are stretched, increasing flexibility in thinking and reducing anxiety that is so urgently focused on the present moment. Initially, Sue seemed resistant to the idea of including James but progressed toward embracing this next step. There is a difference between attempting to convince clients and inviting them to entertain a different point of view. I did not want to take an extensive history from Sue, preferring to interview the couple together about their family history. Establishing a "beachhead" with Sue by eliciting a great deal of information would make it more difficult for me to include James later on. Furthermore, jointly interviewing the couple is also a partnership ritual that could enrich their collaboration as they come together around their multiple realities.

In this session I simply took stock of the multiple family changes, most of them in the past 12 months: James's early retirement from a job he had held for 20 years; the family's move to a different part of the country; Martha's joining the family household; Sue's termination of her part-time employment and move into a full-time household manager; James's new consulting business in the home and the "invasion" of Sue's protected space; Amanda, the eldest child, beginning her first year in college away from home; Adam's adolescent struggles; the "loss of innocence" with John as he was moving from a child to a preteen; and the death of James's father and Sue's mother within the past 2 years. Changes like these in any family system—expected developmental changes, transitional changes by choice, and unexpected changes (e.g., sudden illness)—may spark great emotional distress in families and challenge family members to adapt their way of thinking and relating to new, evolving realities. Sometimes simply listing the changes in the family heightens awareness of and appreciation for family strength and resiliency and pinpoints the adaptive challenges and the call for collaboration. I concluded the session with a conversation about inviting James to the next meeting with the framework of "coming together to work as partners as the family moves through these many challenging transi-

tions." This was not an invitation to do marital therapy, because that was not the request, even though this work would likely enhance the functioning of their marriage. A more innocuous and generally alluring request is for parents to come together to help the family face its challenges more effectively. Given this presentation, I also did not want to invite all the family members, preferring to work from "the top-down," beginning with the parental and spousal leadership and gradually incorporating other family members.

SESSION 2: SUE AND JAMES

I greeted Sue and James in the waiting room, especially welcoming James because of his absence during the first meeting. He rose from the chair, engaged me with a polite smile, and we began to lightly chat as we walked down the hallway to my office—the weather, the drive over, the logo on his sweater. I wanted to begin to incorporate James while not excluding Sue, attentive to the gender split (male–male . . . female) in the group.

As we seated ourselves in my office, Sue and James sat close together but appeared stiff and cautious, anxiously looking to me for direction. (I can easily take over a session when given the opportunity and must guard against shifting the balance of energy and initiative away from clients. How can I fully bring my resources to the moment and yet support the growing initiative of the clients so that we are in more of a creative, collaborative adventure?) It is important for me to respect the emotional tone in the room—seriousness and caution in this case—while also moving the conversation so that it becomes a more freewheeling, fluid give-and-take. (I work better in these kinds of conversations and believe that more of this style supports the movement of therapy. I do need to move in a direction that essentially works for me, or else I will not be of service to the client.) I asked James if he wanted to be called "James" or "Jim." He responded, "It doesn't matter." I asked, "Do you have a preference?" "Well, I suppose 'James'," he replied. Brief exchanges such as this undergird critical values in the therapeutic journey, such as the importance of conversation, caution about assumptions, declaring wants, and taking responsibility. I decided to test his flexibility and retorted, "You know, when I was called 'Timothy' at home, something seemed to be wrong! Sounds like 'James' didn't have that problem?" James chuckled a bit, loosened up, and Sue added with a serious smile, "Well, I guess I'll call him 'James' when he's in trouble." And we were on our way! I lobbed back a quick but critical editorial comment, "And our work is about working together, so let's go."

These seemingly trivial, ongoing exchanges in therapy are nonetheless critical building blocks in seeding the conversation and the unconscious, slowly building on the values that are instrumental in the work. At this point, a core theme was collaboration, not competition. Organizations in distress will prefer modes of relating that are laden with anxiety, blame, competition, reductionistic views, rigid responses, and numbness to multiple realities.

I also had more specific goals for this session. My belief is that helpful therapy is directed and intentional, having a direction that is shaped by the therapist's and client's goals and the client's initiatives. Leadership begins with the therapist taking some clear point of view about the direction for the work. In this meeting I wanted to (a) help this couple listen to each other's stories with empathy and compassion as the "holding environment" was being shaped (Weber & Levine, 1995); (b) underscore the competencies in the couple and family; (c) unpack their "multiple realities," acknowledging their divergent feelings and perspectives while emphasizing their mutual values; (d) shift the tendency to reduce and blame to a wider perspective that normalizes family transitions and adaptive challenges; and (e) develop greater clarity for the goals of our work in some plan of action. I am more active during the beginning sessions because I want to reinforce norms that I believe are fundamental to achieving satisfactory outcomes.

Looking at both James and Sue, I said,

I appreciate that both of you have been willing to come together to work on some of the challenges facing your family. I'm also imagining that you may have different points of view about the circumstances in your family and how best to deal with them. Before we move on, I'm curious, James, about what Sue told you of our previous meeting. How is it for you to be here now?

James reported, "Well, Sue said she talked about how things had changed for us, and especially how she had a hard time with my mother moving in. I do, too." (I've had some clients attribute statements to me that would only inflame others not present such as, "Well, the counselor agreed with me and said that your mother must move out . . . by next week!" I like to attend early on to any potential minefields and distortions.) James was less specific about his own concerns and turned to Sue for the story. Sue pressed on with her mother-in-law concerns (punctuating the story with, "And she is a wonderful woman; I love her.") as James dutifully listened, adding very little. I asked, "Do you talk with each other about your concerns and feelings?" Both stated that they periodically uttered concerns but did not have any sustained conversations. They both felt exhausted with all the changes and preferred retreating rather than conversing about difficult topics. They had grown more alienated from each other but now were beginning to unpack their experiences more fully with my support, inquiry, and perturbations of their patterned avoidance. Therapists often do not have to be too ambitious at these points.

Sue expanded her complaints with examples: Martha cleans up the house without Sue's request, often moving things around so Sue can't find them; Martha is always at home, never getting out (Sue adds, "I'm missing time alone in the house with no one around."); Martha gives the children lots of money for doing simple things, such as cleaning the room; Martha won't get a hearing aid and won't go to the doctor unless forced. As James passively listened to Sue's litany, nodding in agreement at times and toning down the intensity of Sue's complaint at other times, I wondered how they both could shoulder the distress. (I remembered my father listening to my mother's complaints, seemingly feeling helpless about how to take leadership in partnership with my mother.)

I noted to them, "Seems like you've been down this path before. It appears so natural—concerns, frustration, listening, agreement, and a fatigued conclusion like 'Nothing will change.'" They both nodded, and I continued,

> *It appears like your deep love for Martha and your willingness to invite her to live with you has sparked more challenges than you anticipated so that you easily could feel stuck. I'm believing that you both want to at least move toward some plan that will help make things more livable, even if it's only small shifts.*

(Establishing the goal of small changes, not global shifts, is more hopeful and relieving as well as pragmatic. I wanted to sow the seeds of some ideas, giving them opportunity to ferment without moving ahead too swiftly.) "Let's come back to this area of your family life, " I suggested. "I'm curious about some of the other changes you have been experiencing." (I wanted to broaden the scope beyond the anxious intensity focused on Martha.)

In this conversation about Martha, Sue and James appeared relieved that their care for Martha was acknowledged while, at the same time, their predicaments resulting from this decision were openly discussed. Woven into this conversation was the illumination of the basic values that had influenced Sue and James to take in Martha. This kind of moral-based inquiry, or "soul searching" (Doherty, 1995), deepens the therapeutic conversation, creating a more human experience and enhancing the resiliency that comes from living out of one's values.

In this case, where hardship in the family was at least in part a function of the decision to invite Martha to live with the family, I noted Sue and James's mutual willingness to consider the intergenerational community over individual needs and responsibility to others over personal selfishness. This decision, however, had spawned other challenges, which called them to work closer together and jointly assume leadership for solving new problems. (Challenges to clients also evoke challenges to ourselves. Would I make room for my 80-year-old father or my 45-year-old mentally handicapped brother? How far am I willing to go in service and care for family

members? What adjustments would I be willing to make? Would it be any different for a member of my wife's family?)

As I inquired about other changes in the family, the picture became more interesting and complex. Therapy is about the "here and now," the current landscape of family life on which the stories are being played out as well as what is immediately happening in the room as the drama unfolds. However, therapy is also about the historical context, the past and future of family life that give substance and texture to the immediate process. All these dimensions of therapy are alive in any one moment and are part of the therapist's consciousness and choices.

James was concerned that Sue had been more upset since their eldest daughter, Amanda, had left for college the previous fall. Sue and Amanda had been especially close over the years, paradoxically more connected as Amanda became older and more independent. Sue often imagined Amanda as a "substitute sister," frequently having chats and outings together as would two close friends. Amanda's departure for college had triggered Sue's feelings of loss, reminding her deeply of past regrets of being the only child in her family and her struggles in developing friendships. (Stories have many layers. Peeling back the layers of a client's presentation with compassion and inquiry will often uncover critical associations of vulnerability that build the emotional connective tissue between the couple.) Sue was now attempting to make new friends, paralleling in an interesting way the challenge she had posed to her reclusive mother-in-law: "How come you just sit around the house and don't go anywhere, like to the senior citizens' center!" (Usually in a family, a statement about one is also a statement about others. Sue, speaking about Martha's need for friendships, was also referring to her isolation.)

I acknowledged Sue's lament of not having a sibling and her partial loss of Amanda while also attempting to widen the lens by asking James, "And how do you feel about Amanda leaving; any feelings of loss for you, too?" (How is one person's voice also the voice for others? Reductionism increases as people are assigned restricted jobs—Sue will grieve Amanda's leaving, and James will comfort Sue—instead of distributing the job and asking, "How does

James grieve Amanda's leaving, and how does Sue comfort James?")

I wondered about this theme of companionship and asked, "James and Sue, I'm curious about how you've been companions for each other as all these people in your family come and go?" (Had Martha been invited to live with the family to take Amanda's place after her departure?) The subsequent discussion centered on how this family had been more family and child focused than couple focused, a common theme in many families. Sue added that since Martha's entry into the family home her companionship with James was less than before. She was bothered that James was attending more to his mother "as if she were his wife!" James stoically shook his head, turning to me—as if looking for support—as I replied, "James, sounds like you've got a challenge in loving too many women! How can you be your wife's husband and still care for your mother?" The seeds of couple work were being planted as James came back to the theme of losses in the family.

James said he had missed Amanda but more so his two sons, Adam and John. "They're growing up too fast," he sighed. "I'd like to put a brick on their heads. It's all moving too quickly." Sue leaned toward James, put her hand gently on his knee without comment as James continued. "I liked it when they were younger—kind, generally obedient, tagging along, playful," chuckling as he reminisced. Resuming a more ponderous look, he added, "now they're off with their friends, doing their own thing, although Adam still has some trouble making friends." (Did Adam struggle with friendships in part to mirror his parents in their loneliness?)

I was becoming less impatient with James's passivity as I experienced him as more disclosing, and I appreciated how Sue and James were using this occasion to create a more open system of conversation between them. They had not talked about these matters at home, preferring to conduct their lives, as many people do, as if they were caught in the grip of the comings and goings of corporate management. In the first session I had gathered some information about James's father's death and Sue's mother's death, both within the past 2 years, adding to their experiences of loss. So I asked, "I under-

stand, James, that your father died a couple of years ago and, Sue, your mother died last year. What have these deaths been like for you?" James immediately began to talk about how his father, Robert, had been closer to his older brother Paul, but then added that he had managed to get closer to his father during the past 10 years, often sharing stories about baseball, which both of them enjoyed. I emphasized James's capacity to change relationships that were distant—a capacity critical for the evolution of his marriage. His father had died at 85 of multiple health problems after a period of general deterioration. Although James felt relieved that his father was not suffering, he missed him greatly and now felt more compelled to take care of his mother. Turning toward James, Sue noted, "He misses his father more than he's admitting," to which James shrugged his shoulders, faintly tearing.

Sue had a more acerbic relationship with her alcoholic mother, Barbara and, with Barbara's death, felt sorrow for the relationship she never had with her mother. In part, her sorrow fueled her envy of James's closeness with both his parents, even further reminding her of her alienation as she was often on the outside of the triangle. James also admitted that he may have been more attentive to his mother out of envy of the historical closeness between his older brother and mother. Even now, James and Sue said that when they wanted Martha to get medical care they had to struggle with her, whereas James's older brother, with a simple directive, could get her to go to the doctor. Now that James had his mother in his home he was determined to rewrite this long-standing script. (How many problems in living come about when we are overly determined to compensate for previous life narratives?)

Sue continued her litany of concerns as she and James briefly reviewed Adam's problematic biopsychosocial history, concluding with "And we're very worried about him." Their story was a real part of the larger fabric of their lives and deserved respectful consideration. They had been anxious and occupied with Adam since his birth—premature, ocular difficulties, multiple surgeries, learning and social disabilities ("He's weird with his peers," James noted). Adam had visited several counselors over the years with minimal success. Since their move to the area, they had not sought psychological or medical assistance for Adam, in part because of the numerous changes, and had put both boys in public schools, working closely with Adam's teachers. Adam did have a flair for the dramatic and would tend to overdramatize his day-to-day contacts (e.g., going up to a girl, he would fully bow and announce, "Glad to meet thee, my fair maiden!"). This problem had turned into a resource, as Adam had been in several television commercials and drama clubs. Yet their worries superseded their pride and confidence in Adam and in his future.

As I listened to Sue and James talk about Adam, I asked myself, "How can I be most helpful now? I want to respect their anxiety, support them in expressing their many concerns, yet not get organized around Adam in a way that will add to the intensity around this litany of worries." I acknowledged their concerns, underscored their steadfastness as parents (adding a brief reference from my own experience as a father concerned about my children), and offered to assist them in accessing some resources for Adam. I agreed to meet with Adam and, in the meantime, referred them to a physician for medication consultations and a small group that worked on skills training for adolescents. They also agreed to pursue some theatrical opportunities for Adam as a way of helping him establish more confidence and connectedness with others.

Inundated with so many other concerns, Sue and James had been delaying conversations and decisions about Adam. Providing a space for their conversations and helping them move toward some decisions and resources helped shape their anxiety toward hope instead of despair. In their consultative role, therapists serve as "ecosystemic brokers," linking clients with community resources and collaborating with other professionals and clients to increase well-being. In my consultative role with James and Sue I worked to shift the initiative to them and emphasized their collaboration. One of the therapist's jobs is to shift both responsibility and anxiety back to the clients while linking them with resources. There is a critical difference between being helpful and overfunctioning.

As we moved toward closing the meeting, Sue and James referred to how they managed their money now compared to before the move. Sue said, "Now that he's not working for the company, he's more uptight about money. I used to take care of the money, and he didn't complain." James responded, "I'm consulting now. The money is less certain. We've got to be more careful." This was a common couple complaint—the management of money—attached to issues of gender, power, influence, and changes in the family system. James also brought up concerns about time. Now in this "retirement/consultant" phase of his life, he was spending more time at home. Sue said, "He's driving me crazy!" But James was also less emotionally available to Sue. James responded, "I've got my mother and a new business. What am I to do?" And so the list of concerns lengthened, as often happens in the beginning therapeutic encounter.

I acknowledged how the issues of money and time were critical to this couple and to most families these days and that we certainly had to come back to these matters. Emphasizing the concrete details of family life—such as time, money, and space—focuses attention on the stage on which the drama, roles, and rules of life are played out, including the values of justice, fairness, and the equitable sharing of burdens and benefits (Carter, 1996). I invited Sue and James to write down their concerns with money and time and especially how they would propose resolving these concerns, beginning with how each of them could take responsibility for creating a more satisfactory outcome.

I proposed meeting for the next session with the entire household—Sue, James, Amanda, Adam, John, and Martha. I said I wanted to meet everyone because they all were in the family and were being affected by family changes and, perhaps, had some ideas about how things should go. This is an innocuous frame that is usually quite understandable and inviting in spite of the anxiety often present when families come together to talk about what matters. I wanted to continue to move away from a more reductionistic, individual view of the problem and expand, open, and include more members of the family. It is also easier to work with family members later in therapy if they have been invited in the earlier sessions. I suggested a 2-hour meeting for the third session. With more family members, I wanted to ensure that we had enough time for conversation with all the family and subsystems if needed. I am flexible with both membership in sessions (mixing and matching individuals within a system according to the movement and focus of therapy) and time.

SESSION 3: THE FAMILY

James and Sue arrived for the third session with their three children—Amanda, Adam, and John—and James's mother—Martha. Having already worked with James and Sue, I initially emphasized engagement with Martha and the three children, using the typical ways of engaging family members already described in a previous chapter (Weber & Levine, 1995). I was struck by the family's overall politeness and general restraint. As I asked each of them questions about themselves, they seemed to be careful in answering, glancing at others out of the corner of their eyes as they conservatively responded, "Things are fine." (Would I be able to succeed in challenging the norm of protective togetherness, opening up the family so that they could converse about their full experience in the midst of all these changes and transitions while at the same time respecting their pace, style, and norms of family life? One of the arts of the therapist is being able to walk this "balance beam" with courage and not intimidation. How could I slowly shape the conversation in a different direction?)

Martha went on to say, "I know it's hard on them (glancing at James and Sue, who were seated together), having me at their home." Martha had been widowed for 2 years after a 55-year marriage in which she had assumed a more deferential role with a husband who had enjoyed being in charge. She said she had enjoyed being supported by him and missed him dearly but was thankful she had "two boys" to take care of her. "I can depend on them," she said confidently, "they're both wonderful." And just as I was beginning to wonder whether she included Sue in her network of care, she added, "And Sue is wonderful too; she really helps me a lot. I don't know what I would do without them. I love the kids." (With this kind of accolade, it's much harder to push back around the unsatisfactory parts of family life. Family life includes both the positives

of support and the challenges in dealing with changes. Helping move people from polarizations—good–bad splits—to the humanness of "mixed experience" is one of the arts of therapy.) Sue smiled as she rolled her eyes, faintly grunting. James said nothing, looking around the room as the children said, "And we love you too, Grandma." Amanda briefly talked about her first year at college and how she had missed her family, carefully not referencing her first year away as delightful. Adam was the most active, moving about restlessly, talking about his dramatic interests, and periodically inserting lessons about life. He seemed to be a bright, energetic teenager who loved to be "on stage," even in this family meeting. I could understand how his style would seem strange to his peers. His flair complemented the family's subdued presentation. John was more quiet than his siblings, noting how he was making some new friends.

Routinely I ask family members who join the session to talk about what they had been told of the purpose of the meeting, what they know of what had transpired in previous meetings, and how they feel about being in the session now. This inquiry begins to focus and deepen the conversation and grafts newcomers into the unfolding family story, highlighting any concerns that could be addressed to help the conversation continue. Amanda then disclosed that she had been concerned about changes in the family, especially with her mother. In response to these more global concerns, I attempt to elicit more specific behavioral descriptions. Amanda stated she had been concerned that Sue seemed less energetic, with less interest in outside activities, than she had before the move. Sue had been calling Amanda less and, when she called, she talked more about "how difficult it was to help Grandma." (I liked the way Amanda reframed "complaints" into "difficulty helping Grandma.")

To increase an interactional emphasis, in contrast to an individual emphasis, I asked about the impact of all this on Amanda—the meaning she created, her feelings, what she did in response to her observations. I then asked Sue about her reaction to what Amanda had said. I inquired about the experiences of other family members with Sue—how they were similar to or different from Amanda's observations and responses. These inquiries helped open up the family system around a critical issue about which all family members had concerns but had silenced for fear of upsetting each other and increasing the risk that Grandma would feel unwanted. I also asked family members how they felt about this here-and-now conversation, a meta-question about the process of talking with each other about issues at the center of this family's life. There seemed to be some overall caution but relief as "the cat was out of the bag," James remarked. This is a sample of the process I might use to shift the conversation from a more generalized, individual report into something that is more alive, interactional, disclosing, circular, and respectful of multiple realities. It is not enough to have family members simply report in circular fashion (Selvini-Palazzoli, Boscolo, Cecchin, & Prata, 1982) about interactions and experiences outside the session. That focus, in addition to conversations about immediate experience in the here and now (e.g., "How is it for you, Sue, right now to hear how Amanda has been concerned about you? Could you tell her?"), is what is critical in promoting more open and fluid relationships (Weber, 1994).

These increasing interactional conversations in the meeting helped open the system and generated relief that comes, sometimes slowly, when "secrets" (here, things known but not discussed) are disclosed and discussed. Respecting the multiple realities of experience as I inquired, affirming the strengths in the family, and normalizing the family struggles when possible all served to establish a context for describing the challenges and specifically stating what was and was not working in the family. I sometimes use newsprint or dry-erase boards to help magnify the family conversation. In this 2-hour family meeting, I used three visual interventions to amplify the dynamics of family life: (a) an inventory of family changes, (b) the family floor plan, and (c) family assessment.

Using a psychoeducational approach, I noted how changes—positive or negative—in a family can create distress, especially when they cluster together, as had happened in this family. I wanted to normalize their distress and spread it out among the family, away from individual containment. I had every member of the family individually write down

changes they believed had occurred within the family over the last 2 years, inviting them in a game-like format: "Let's see who can come up with the most changes . . . a prize awaits." (I have a stash of "cheap" trinkets in my office for such purposes.) A game format enhances participation and a more "mindful" means of learning and remembering (Langer, 1996). As we debriefed this exercise I noted the sequence of changes on the board linking them with the family life cycle and the genogram (Weber & Levine, 1995). Some of the changes identified were coping with the deaths of two grandparents, James leaving his company position, Sue quitting her job, the family moving to a new state, Martha losing her husband of 55 years, Martha moving into the family home, Amanda going off to college, Adam and John leaving old friends and having to make new ones and attending new schools, the family moving into a smaller home and having less money, and so on.

Macro changes (e.g., Martha moving in with the family) were broken down into smaller changes as I asked, "So what does this change specifically mean to all of you?" John, for example, responded, "Grandma gives us money for cleaning up our rooms." Sue said, "Martha cleans when I want her to and often when I don't want her to clean." Positive changes were examined for their cost (e.g., Adam: "Dad doesn't go to the office to work anymore, and he also is around more as the boss"), and negative changes were examined for any positive benefits (e.g., Amanda: "We've left some of our friends behind, and we have an opportunity to meet new people, although it's been difficult to start over"). Differences in reactions were highlighted (e.g., Adam and John liking Martha's payment for chores vs. Sue and James having a different point of view about compensation), leading to more mindfulness of multiple perspectives and less anxiety devoted to containment and fear. This more open conversation was inherently providing the resources for change and adaptation without the ambition of pushing change.

The second intervention, building on this conversation about change and points of view, was the family floor plan. Amanda, Adam, and John were invited to draw two basic floor plans—one of their previous home and one of their current home. They went to another room to work on this exercise while I remained with Sue, James, and Martha, demarcating the adult from the sibling subsystems. James spoke about how he had been more active in caring for his mother, in part because he had felt more peripheral in her life when she was living near James's older brother Gus. He told Martha that he felt guilty for being underresponsive but that he had been "bothered" because his mother had not sought his assistance as much as she had gone to Gus, leading James to believe his mother thought he was less competent. James recollected many years of competitive feelings with Gus. James was reviving old feelings of being marginalized in the family as the "younger brother" and spoke about how he just wanted to be "respected." His attention to his mother was at least partially driven by his search for her acknowledgment. Martha was generally reassuring with James, said she had not known about many of his feelings, and wanted him to realize that she always had respected him. Although James did not seem especially comforted by his mother's attempts to comfort, he did express relief that he had finally spoken about these concerns he had been carrying for years and that his mother did not die in the room. Sue also had not been privy to these matters. She had sensed that James was disturbed by these feelings of being marginalized but also did not want to raise his distress through any focused inquiry. She was finding new respect for James as he finally was having this conversation in front of his mother, not away from her. Sue needed to experience James in an intimate conversation with his mother that was more real and disclosing; she had been the receptacle for his discontent. Now, the focus in this triangle was shifting so that the relationship between James and his mother was being given the attention it truly deserved.

Amanda, Adam, and John returned with an elaborate set of floor plans as they had used the plans to dramatize family life and their feelings about some of the changes. Amanda, for example, had felt angry that her room had been converted to a study for her brothers but had silenced her laments because "the family had too much to deal with anyway . . . and it wasn't that important." I commended Amanda on her willingness to support the family but encour-

aged her to explore alternatives with her parents. James's new home office bumped Sue from the "office" that she had in their previous home. She had sacrificed her space with minimal conversation and negotiation. The women in this family tended to give way to James's, Adam's, and John's needs. This observation opened a discussion about gender and fairness and some reflection about Martha and her husband in the previous generation.

The family was invited to continue their work together between sessions by doing a family assessment with the following directions:

> I want each of you to think about your family—what's working for you, what you are grateful for, and what is not working for you, and what you would like to see changed. Schedule a meeting between now and when we all meet again and see if you can come up with some similarities and differences between your view of the family.

(Here is the challenge in all families: to understand separateness in the midst of togetherness and then to negotiate satisfactory and fair solutions.)

SESSION 4: JAMES AND SUE

"How have things been going?" I asked as James and Sue reclined comfortably in their seats, looking more at ease than in our first meeting together and bantering between them about the week's events. (These opening moments of the meeting are like a barometer of the emotional atmosphere. How open or closed are they? Do they seem more flexible or rigid today? Are they carrying more optimism or despair? Do they seem occupied with an urgent crisis, or will they be able to be more reflective? Do they want to be here with each other, with me? Where is the anxiety? Where is the initiative in the room?)

Turning toward me, James said, "Adam and John were both accepted into music camp this week. Adam was expecting to go, but we're real surprised about John. We didn't think he'd ever apply. We're delighted about it." Sue punctuated the report with a pleasing smile. "What do you think gave John the courage to apply to the camp?" I asked Sue and

James. James thought his more active encouragement with John may have helped. Sue agreed. (Then I wondered about how James's reflection about his competition with his own brother and regrets about feeling marginalized in his family may have influenced James to take a more proactive stance in encouraging John, the younger brother, as James was in his own family, to link with the older brother, Adam. Children give parents another shot at their own childhood.) I do spend time amplifying positive change, inviting clients to muse on the personal question: "How did you all pull this off?" (Whenever I hear a positive report about change, I inquire about the client's initiative and responsibility behind the change, expanding the client's consciousness about possibility and influence and de-emphasizing comments alluding to passivity and fatalism such as "It just happened"; Weber & Williamson, 1998.) Sue reported that she was able to focus more on her sons now that she and James were addressing the problems that had been binding them for months, especially the challenges with Martha.

James quickly added that he and Sue also had been talking about how to manage Martha's presence in the home. They had met with each other to determine what exactly they wanted Martha to do and not do in the home. This consultation and planning with each other was instrumental in decreasing anxiety and increasing clarity and focus. When the leadership of a system works collaboratively in this way, increasing confidence, with a lessening of symptoms, cascades through the system. Previously, Sue felt like the isolated complainant, fighting with Martha with little support from James. Now, in spite of some irresolvable differences of temperament, style, and expectations (e.g., James: "I don't care what she does in the home. She doesn't mean any harm. She's just trying to help."), they were functioning more like "cocaptains" and were confident in their commitment to forge a plan of action. The also were developing greater compassion for each other's positions, focusing more on the feelings behind the position than the position itself (e.g., James: "I'm not that bothered by Martha's tinkering around in the home, but I do see how Sue might feel shut out."). James was beginning to "liberate" Sue several times a week by transporting Martha to stores, physicians' ap-

pointments, and the senior citizens' center. James was more determined in defining how he wanted things to work in the home rather than accommodating his mother's ambivalence. Martha was now more willing to get a hearing device, which would enable her to more actively engage with others at the senior citizens' center. Still, James noted, "Mother likes to be by herself, just playing with her stamp collection. She doesn't like to get out that much."

Sue and James also had expanded the family-assessment assignment into a weekly family meeting, dedicated to reviewing the week's events, discussing what was working and not working in the home, and planning together. This ritual, they reasoned, would help them come together as they had been doing in family therapy and keep from going "underground," as Sue put it. Family rituals help families come together in a patterned manner, attending to values that are a core part of their identity.

As the "hot triangle" among James, Sue, and Martha cooled somewhat, the conversation turned more toward the couple—Sue said, "We rarely talk just about us. We're always talking about Amanda, Adam, John, Martha . . . What about us?" James nodded, agreeing in silence. Both were reluctant to deepen their exploration of their life together, but they pressed on with mild nudging from me: "Seems like you need oxygen masks on yourselves before you can give oxygen to others in the family." Their courage in disclosure increased. James said, "I worry about my consulting business. Will I make it? Maybe I shouldn't have left the company when I did. Now that Sue and I have more time together, what's going to happen?" Sue said,

> I don't have advanced training in art. But I've helped out in the schools. I'm looking for some opportunities. I want to do more with you, James, but you seem so preoccupied. I thought that your retirement would bring us closer together, but it seems we're struggling for time together as we did before.

James and Sue were now in an evolving conversation, more courageous in examining their individual lives and life together in this period of marital renegotiation (Carter, 1996).

FOLLOW-UP

I continued meeting with Sue and John over the next 4 months, about once every 2 or 3 weeks, focusing on strengthening the collaboration between them as cocaptains of the home, encouraging them to maintain an open system of conversation in contrast to the closed and overly anxious system of the past, helping them establish administrative clarity and follow-through in regard to decisions in the family (e.g., structuring Martha's visits to the senior citizens' center during specific days and times rather than having Martha indicate whether she "felt" like going out of the home) and exploring new developments in their individual and couple lives as they became less anxious (e.g., Sue finding a part-time job teaching art in a local school). Martha attended a couple of the meetings, and other members of the family attended only one meeting, during that 4-month period. The family was adapting effectively to their new challenges, primarily because the leadership of the family was in more open conversation, working collaboratively, more self-defined, less anxious, and detriangulated.

As anxiety decreases and symptoms become less apparent and urgent, other adventures of growth and development emerge, including working on the emotional process in problematic triangles (Kerr & Bowen, 1988). James became interested in talking with his older brother. They had been emotionally distant siblings, and James had often resented how his older brother had received special consideration from their father and seemed to have more influence over their mother. They had not talked about these things as well as the impact of their father's death on their lives. They had "gone through the motions" of being a family, encapsulating the heart and soul of their relationship.

Sue's reactivity toward James's tightness with his mother led her to reflect on how alienated she had felt with her father. She rarely spoke with him but had many internal, private conversations in her head about him, whom she would meet occasionally but did not know emotionally. She began to realize that her intense emotions toward James and his mother were a clue to the cutoff in her own family relationship. Although her ambition to deal with this cutoff was minimal, she began to shift more of the anxious energy from James toward her own life and relationships, including conversations with her father about his life and new developments in her life.

At this phase, family therapy was more "consultative" (Wynne et al., 1986), with periodic consultations on individual, couple, and family issues that would arise as this family evolved. I value this kind of relationship with a family over time when a consultative relationship develops after a more intensive, symptom-focused phase of therapy. The therapist is a resource for the family as it continues to move through the life cycle and helps the family access its inherent resources in dealing with their snags. In this process not only is healing crafted, but also greater hope can emerge.

References

Carter, B. (1996). *Love, honor, and negotiate: Making your marriage work.* New York: Simon & Schuster.

Carter, B., & McGoldrick, M. (1989). Overview: The changing family life cycle—A framework for family therapy. In B. Carter & M. McGoldrick (Eds.), *The changing family life cycle: A framework for family therapy* (pp. 3–28). Boston: Allyn & Bacon.

Doherty, W. J. (1995). *Soul searching.* New York: Basic Books.

Fisch, R., Weakland, J., & Segal, L. (1982). *The tactics of change: Doing therapy briefly.* San Francisco: Jossey-Bass.

Framo, J. (1968). My families, my family. In *Explorations in marital and family therapy: Selected papers of James L. Framo* (pp. 282–292). New York: Springer.

Kerr, M., & Bowen, M. (1988). *Family evaluation.* New York: Norton.

Langer, E. J. (1997). *The power of mindful learning.* Reading, MA: Addison-Wesley.

Minuchin, S. (1996). *Mastering family therapy: Journeys of growth and transformation.* New York: Wiley.

Napier, A. Y., & Whitaker, C. (1978). *The family crucible.* New York: Harper & Row.

Selvini-Palazzoli, M., Boscolo, L., Cecchin, G., &

Prata, G. (1982). Hypothesizing–circularity–neutrality: Three guidelines for the conductor of the session. *Family Process, 19,* 3–13.

Walters, M., Carter, B., Papp, P., & Silverstein, D. (1988). *The invisible web: Gender patterns in family relationships.* New York: Guilford Press.

Weber, T. (1994). *Response–ability axes in the learning group.* Unpublished manuscript, Leadership Institute of Seattle/Bastyr University School of Applied Behavioral Science, Bellevue, WA.

Weber, T., & Levine, F. (1995). Engaging the family: An integrative approach. In R. H. Mikesell, D-D.

Lusterman, & S. H. McDaniel (Eds.), *Integrating family therapy: Handbook of family psychology and systems theory* (pp. 45–71). Washington, DC: American Psychological Association.

Weber, T. T., & Williamson, D. (1998). *The leadership triad: Essentials of consciousness, competency, and well-being.* Unpublished manuscript, Leadership Institute of Seattle/Bastyr University School of Applied Behavioral Science, Bellevue, WA.

Wynne, L. C., McDaniel, S. H., & Weber, T. T. (1986). *Systems consultation: A new perspective for family therapy.* New York: Guilford Press.

CHAPTER 12

THE CASE OF THE "EXPENDABLE" ELDER: FAMILY THERAPY WITH AN OLDER DEPRESSED MAN

Deborah A. King

I am a middle-aged geropsychologist who grew up in the Midwest, the middle of three children. My mother died when I was nearly 4; my father remarried when I was 5. As unlucky as we were to have lost our mother, we were lucky to have had three sets of grandparents who played an influential role in our upbringing. My closeness with them is no doubt one reason why I am so fond of working with older adults. As well, I was influenced during my training years by the family described in this chapter. They taught me about the potency of the intergenerational relationship and the power of unspoken attitudes about old age. I will always be grateful for all that they revealed to me.

MEETING MR. V: "GO AWAY AND LEAVE ME TO DIE"

I was eagerly awaiting the opportunity to work with the first patient of my inpatient rotation during my psychology fellowship when I received this telephone call from the unit staff: "We've admitted a patient for you to work with, but don't hurry in. It's an old guy, and he isn't going anywhere. He had a stroke several months ago and never really recovered."

Arriving on the unit, I found the following information in Mr. V's medical chart: age 77, Hispanic, retired widower who had suffered a stroke 3 months previously. He had few if any cognitive deficits but was partially paralyzed in his right arm and leg, requiring him to use a cane. He had precipitously discontinued physical therapy 1 month ago because

he believed that it was of no use. His primary physician had prescribed an antidepressant in response to his frequent statements that he was "no good anymore" and "would be better off dead." His admission to the hospital was precipitated by a serious suicide attempt; Mr. V had overdosed on his antidepressant medication. Fortunately, his daughter-in-law had made a visit to Mr. V's home and discovered him lying unconscious in bed. A suicide note on the nightstand contained information about his bank accounts, along with a recently revised will. The note explained that he could no longer justify living because his disabilities prevented him from being of use to anyone: "I don't want to be a burden to my children. . . . I'm worth more dead than alive."

With this background I found myself feeling a curious mixture of eagerness (this was one of my first opportunities to work on an acute psychiatric unit) and dread (I was worried about the depth of Mr. V's despair). I entered his hospital room and found him in bed, sleeping soundly in the middle of the day. There was a faint smell of urine in the air, and I noticed a thin trail of saliva dripping down his chin. He was startlingly thin, with hollow cheeks and dark circles under his eyes. Immediately my heart sank. How on earth was I going to help someone who looked so frail and so sick? I made several unsuccessful attempts to awaken him, finally giving up to look around his room for some clue of with whom I was about to work. I saw very few belongings—just a shirt, trousers, and shaving kit. Then I noticed a picture frame lying face down on the nightstand. Picking it up, I saw the shining faces of a family of six: a proud-looking couple, perhaps in their 30s, standing behind four youngsters, two boys and two girls. Looking closely at the dashing young father, I struggled to determine if this could possibly be the same person as the gaunt old man snoring away in the bed.

Suddenly Mr. V awoke with a start and stared at me. I introduced myself and attempted to shake his hand, but he turned away muttering: "Go away and leave me in peace. I don't want any help. I just want to die." After several more vain attempts to make a connection, I left the room. Feeling dismayed and rejected, I decided to see if Mr. V had any family who could shed light on his situation. (In addition to needing more information in order to get the treatment started, I had been exposed to family systems and interpersonal models of depression that underlined the critical role of family in making and maintaining treatment gains.)

THE FIRST FAMILY MEETING

The hospital record listed the telephone number of a son, Henrique, as next of kin. Dialing the number, I reached the patient's daughter-in-law, Carmella, who apologetically explained that her husband worked very long hours in a new job as a department store manager, although he would be willing to come to the hospital later that evening. I inquired after other family members who could help us understand Mr. V's situation. She explained that Mr. V had three other children: Rosita, who lived with her family in a neighboring city; Juan, with whom the family had not had contact for "several years"; and Evita, who worked in Henrique's store. I explained the importance of getting family together to get information and the need to work quickly because of the seriousness of their father's condition. I suggested that we set up several family meetings over the next 2 weeks during which we would work together to help Mr. V. She agreed to call her sisters and invite them to the meetings, although she refused to call Juan, stating that things were "just too tense" between her husband and his younger brother.

Later that evening, my cotherapist (a psychiatric resident) and I met with the available family members: Henrique, Carmella, and Evita. Rosita said she

was unable to come to the first meeting, and Mr. V refused to attend. In our rush to arrange the meeting, we had not developed a plan or formal agenda other than simply to get as much information as possible about Mr. V, his family, and possible reasons for his depression.

Mr. V's oldest son, Henrique, was a dapper, middle-aged man who resembled a younger and more vigorous version of his father. With downcast eyes he explained that he hadn't realized how serious his father's condition had become. He was working hard to succeed in his position at the store and had little time to check on Mr V. His wife Carmella chimed in, explaining that she had been accustomed to visiting her father-in-law every week or so, although this had become more difficult since their youngest daughter gave birth to twins 2 months ago. Evita, who had remained sullen and silent to this point, looked up and said,

> He hasn't wanted any help! He's turned
> me away more times than I can count,
> and I'm sick and tired of it! At this point
> it's best if we leave him to do as he wishes.
> He won't even try to get better. . . . There's
> not a damn thing we can do about it!

Immediately, Henrique leapt to his feet, shouting,

> How can you give up on your own father
> who worked so hard for you and for all of
> us? He deserves your respect and your pa-
> tience! He is sick and he needs our help. . . .
> If you won't help we don't need you here!
> Get out!

Shouting behind her in Spanish, Evita stormed out of the room and off the unit. Dumbfounded, I started after her but stopped after the elevator door closed in my face.

THE SECOND FAMILY MEETING: ASSESSING "THE TIES THAT BIND"

The next day my cotherapist and I found ourselves watching the wall clock as the hour of our proposed second family meeting came and went. We began to realize that we had overestimated the family's ability and perhaps willingness to work together on behalf of their father. As is typical on a busy hospital floor that is focused on efficient, acute care, we had "jumped in" without assessing the family's strengths and vulnerabilities, including their emotional resources and whether there were solid bonds of attachment that would support positive communication and problem solving (Shields, King, & Wynne, 1995; Wynne, 1984). We had wrongly assumed that all family members were ready, willing, and able to work together toward a common goal, that is, helping Mr. V. Yet the level of charged interaction between Evita and Henrique, as well as Mr. V's cutoff from Juan, were indications that we needed to address the family relationships at a deeper level. Were there strong, positive bonds of attachment among family members that would support intergenerational caregiving, or were the relationship bonds weak, ambivalent, or negative? What were the developmental challenges or crises facing the adult offspring, and how might these help or hinder their ability to work together on behalf of their father? How much of the negative interaction and cutoffs in this family were fueled by unresolved grief or despair over the loss of Mrs. V so many years ago?

After about 20 minutes we received a breathless telephone call from Carmella, explaining that she was waiting for her husband to return from a meeting so that they could come to the hospital, but he hadn't appeared. She agreed to attempt another meeting the next morning, prior to her husband's typical working hours. After several telephone calls to Evita, appealing to her importance in the family and the need to "get all the help we can," she agreed to come to a second family meeting. We were able to reach Mr. V's oldest daughter, Rosita, who also agreed to come. She was willing to give us Juan's telephone number, but we were able to reach only his answering machine to let him know we were meeting.

In order to avoid another "blowup" and to maximize our chances of helping the family have more positive interactions, we decided that the second family meeting would be more structured and focused on gathering important history by constructing a family genogram. In this way, we began a process of family life review (Hargrave & Anderson, 1992; Shields et al., 1995) that would help us un-

derstand the history of Mr. V and his family while at the same time helping them view him and each other from more positive perspectives (see Figure 12.1). To start, we welcomed each family member (everyone came except Juan) and spent a few minutes commiserating with Rosita about her long drive to the hospital in the midst of bad weather. Mr. V was still refusing to participate in individual or family sessions but, interestingly enough, gave us full permission to talk with his children. We told them that we would be sharing the content of our meetings with Mr. V along the way. We also explained that we needed lots of input from them in order to understand Mr. V, his history, and the nature of stresses that he and the family had been facing. In this way, we underlined the importance of their role on the "treatment team" and acknowledged that their ability to share as much as possible would be very helpful. They each agreed to this approach, although Evita did so with visible reluctance.

With this background, we gained the following information: Mr. V immigrated to the United States in the late 1940s. He left his native Puerto Rico and a life of farming to seek a better future for himself and his children after his wife died suddenly from a heart attack at the age of 40. In this country he obtained employment as a janitor in a local hospital. Working long hours, he gradually worked his way up to supervisory and managerial positions in the housekeeping department. He was active in civic affairs, especially as a leader in the local Catholic church. He was described by Henrique as a very firm but loving father who always wanted the best for his children. With tears in his eyes, he explained,

> Until he got sick, I could always feel him by my side, encouraging me to do my best. From the time I was a little boy I could always count on him to be there to help.... Yes, he could be strict at times, but I always knew he cared about me and that I could count on him to take care of me through any trouble.... Now with the store, I miss his guidance, his business sense. He had always been an advisor to me.

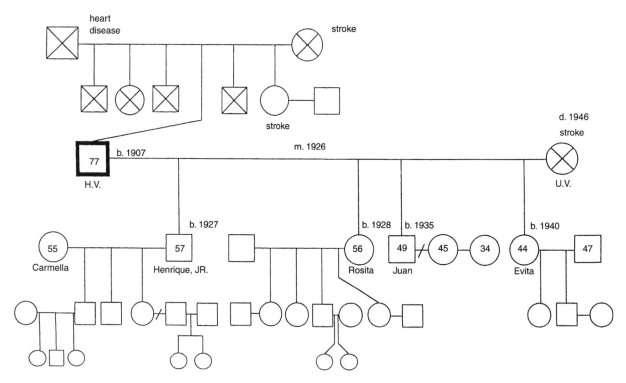

FIGURE 12.1. The Genogram of the V Family.

From comments such as this, we knew that the attachment between Henrique and his father was strong and positive. In contextual terms (Hargrave & Anderson, 1992), Mr. V had "credits in the bank" with his eldest son and, therefore, we could expect Henrique to be an important source of support for his father. This discussion was also important in that it helped the adult offspring view their currently enfeebled father from the vantage point of his past strengths (e.g., bringing the family to this country for a better life).

The oldest daughter, Rosita, generally agreed with her brother's assessment of her father, although she noted sadly that he had changed after the death of their mother. In her view, he had become more angry and harsh, frequently arguing and punishing Juan for "running" with his friends. At this point, Evita spoke up angrily:

He took all of his frustrations out on Juan, and as for this devoted father . . . I never knew him! He was always at work or yelling about something. Sometimes I think we're talking about two different people!

Juan should be here. . . . He knows what I'm talking about!

She further indicated that the history of conflict between Juan and his father dated back at least as far as Juan's early teenage years, when he had purportedly fallen into the "wrong" crowd and suffered harsh punishment at his father's hand. The two of them broke off all contact about 10 years ago when Juan married a woman outside of the Catholic faith.

It was clear that the bonds of attachment were weaker between Mr. V and his two younger children. Our working hypothesis was that the early caretaking relationships between father and children were damaged by Mrs. V's sudden death. This family crisis had impaired Mr. V's ability to be available to his younger children, who were developmentally more vulnerable at ages 11 and 6 than were the older offspring at ages 19 and 18. It seemed as if Mr. V's characteristic authoritarian stance had become angry and critical after his wife's death. We thought it likely that he had been depressed since that time, now more than 40 years ago.

After more discussion, it was agreed that Evita

would approach Juan about joining the next family meeting. In the event of his refusal, she would at least share with him the family genogram and the history we had been discussing.

"THIS PATIENT ISN'T GOING ANYWHERE": RECOGNIZING OUR OWN AGEIST ATTITUDES

Prior to the next meeting, I sat with Mr. V and told him about what I had learned from his family. Although he refused to respond, he did not protest or turn his back. I noticed his jaw tighten when I mentioned inviting Juan to the next meeting, and he simply muttered, "He'll never come."

As I sat with Mr. V, I marveled at how such a previously vigorous and productive person could be reduced to so much hopelessness and misery. I was well aware of the devastating impact of severe clinical depression but was unprepared for the degree of self-repulsion and loathing that Mr. V projected. In fact, I felt ashamed of some of my own thoughts while sitting with him. . . . At times the smell of urine or unwashed skin became so strong that I would find myself dreading entering his room. Uncharacteristically, I would pass up opportunities to comment on the negative effects of his poor hygiene or his rejecting interpersonal stance, imagining that he was either too fragile or too impervious to change. In retrospect, I know that I was acting out some common ageist attitudes, for example, that older adults become fragile, like children, and should be treated like children (the "role-reversal" myth; see Butler, Lewis, & Sunderland, 1991) and that older adults cannot or will not change (the myth of "you can't teach an old dog new tricks"). I now see that I was having difficulty communicating with Mr. V on an adult-to-adult level, alternating between an infantilizing stance (viewing him as fragile or childlike) and a pessimistic, hopeless one (identifying with the helplessness and hopelessness projected by him and the family). Once, while sitting with him after a family meeting, I even caught myself looking at him and thinking: "He looks like death warmed over!" These types of fleeting thoughts or images were indications of the common but extremely destructive "contagion" attitude about

older adults, an attitude that can be difficult to recognize because, like many of our attitudes about death, it is often deeply unconscious. According to this mythical belief, association with older adults somehow zaps us of our own vitality, bringing us one step closer to our own death and demise. (See Myers, 1984, for unique types of transference and countertransference that may be encountered when working with older adults.)

Once I was able to recognize and acknowledge some of these negative and hopeless feelings about working with Mr. V, I began to wonder whether other unit staff were having the same reactions. I noticed them offering fewer interactions or encouragements to participate in unit activities, as if they were starting to avoid him. It seemed as if on some unspoken level, we were all beginning to give up on this man, a feeling that no doubt applied to his family members, who were already taxed by the demands of their work and family-of-marriage responsibilities. Horrified, I wondered if we were all starting to collude with Mr. V's morbid self-perceptions —that he was a burden, expendable, somehow not worth the effort it would take to keep him alive.

At this point it was extremely helpful to give voice to these "forbidden" thoughts and compare notes with my cotherapist. We began to review each of our own family experiences with elders, including my feelings about my own critically ill grandparent who was failing in a nursing home. I realized that there were ways in which Mr. V reminded me of her and triggered some of the same painful, helpless feelings. Although this process opened up a new wave of sadness about my grandmother, it enabled me to see Mr. V more objectively and break through some of the pessimistic feelings that I was having about his prospects.

At the same time, my cotherapist and I wanted to share some of our concerns and insights with others on the unit staff who were unaccustomed to working with elderly patients. We were eventually able to do so in the context of a unit staff meeting, at which we offered a brief, experiential "in-service" on understanding the role of older adults in one's family of origin (see Shields et al., 1995, for a similar exercise). Additionally, we recognized that all involved in Mr. V's care were more likely to unwittingly join in his hopelessness and negativism about himself if they had no opportunity to view him from the perspective of his past strengths and accomplishments. Therefore, with the family's permission, we made arrangements to include more of the relevant staff in the family meetings. Because we did not want to overwhelm the family, we worked out a system whereby a representative from nursing, social work or activities therapy would rotate in, one by one, to participate in the family meetings and pass on useful information to staff who were unable to participate.

THIRD MEETING: JUAN RETURNS TO THE FAMILY

We started the meeting by getting an update from Evita about Juan. She revealed that he was unsure about whether to attend and that he had a distinct fear of hospitals. (Although we were yet to meet Juan, we viewed this fear as further evidence that he had been profoundly affected by his mother's death.) Evita agreed to keep him informed of our meetings and to let him know that it would be helpful if he joined us. As well, we agreed that I would seek Mr. V's permission to send Juan brief summaries of what was discussed in our meetings, starting with the current one. (We wanted to maintain some contact with Juan in the hope that, at best, he would decide to participate in our meetings and, at least, not sabotage our efforts.) We then reviewed important information about Mr. V's diagnosis, possible treatments, and side effects; that is, that he had a severe major depression that could profoundly influence his personality and judgment and that we would attempt treatment with antidepressant medication, supportive individual psychotherapy to address his personal concerns, and family meetings. (So far, Mr. V had refused to consider the antidepressant medication. I had been meeting with him on a daily basis to attempt individual psychotherapy, but at this point he was unwilling to share much about himself or his feelings.) Hoping that the adult offspring would eventually be full-fledged collaborators in his care, we reviewed the possible risks and benefits of the somatic treatment. When Henrique and Evita began a characteristic disagreement about the appro-

priateness of antidepressant treatment, we stopped the interaction and explained that we needed more information before deciding on a comprehensive treatment plan. We added that depression stresses the entire family and that we would do our best to provide them with whatever information and support we could through the treatment process.

At this point the door opened and in walked a dark-eyed, middle-aged man who I assumed must be Juan. A silence fell over the room, and Henrique settled back in his chair with a sigh. I welcomed Juan, thanked him for coming, and explained that we had been reviewing his father's condition, the medication we were proposing, and the possible side effects. Proceeding on this track for a few minutes, I noticed that the tension in the room felt palpable. I was tempted to observe this aloud and encourage the family to talk about their feelings of being together in the same room for the first time in years. Yet I could see that no eye contact was being made between the two sons and, given the previous stormy interactions between family members, I was concerned about their ability to communicate in anything but negative terms (see Shields et al., 1995, regarding levels of family intervention). I decided to stick with the strategy of focusing on Mr. V's needs and history for now, with the hope that we could work toward a deeper, more positive level of communication as we continued to construct the family genogram and engage in a process of family life review.

Directing the family's attention to the genogram we had started in the previous session, we asked them to fill in the names and ages of Mr. V's siblings or, if the siblings were deceased, the approximate dates and causes of death. In this way, we began with a concrete task that would eventually bring our discussion to issues of loss. Aware of the fact that no one was volunteering information about the death of Mrs. V, we focused for the time being on a less threatening issue: what the offspring knew about Mr. V's early life and upbringing. Henrique and Rosita, who had the clearest memories of their paternal grandparents, described how Mr. V had to stop his schooling at the age of 10 in order to help support his family. This always had been a painful topic for him and the origin of his fierce insistence that his children be educated and do their very best in school. Henrique further revealed that their grandfather was an alcoholic who had physically abused their grandmother and Mr. V as a boy. Juan looked up at this point and admitted sullenly that he had not known this part of his father's history. Evita was surprisingly quiet throughout this discussion, and we could see that she, too, was viewing her father from a different perspective. For the first time in her life, she was able to see him in the context of his history as a vulnerable young boy rather than viewing him solely as the angry father who fell short of meeting her needs. There was a long silence in the room that seemed to come from thoughtful understanding rather than from the angry tension we had come to expect with this family. Realizing that we were nearing the end of the meeting, we thanked the family for their participation and underlined the importance of piecing together more of the family history in our next meeting.

The next day, armed with new information about his early history, I entered Mr. V's. room and was shocked to find him sitting up on his bed, clean shaven for the first time since I had known him. He spoke up immediately (another first), saying that he had learned from his nurse that Juan had been in the night before. I showed him the genogram, and he took it in his good hand, immediately beginning to correct some of the ages and dates pertaining to his family of origin. He remained silent when I reviewed the information that Henrique had shared about his early hardships, but I could see a glimmer of tears in his eyes. Were these tears of sadness about his past, or were they tears of happiness that his children had gathered together on his behalf? I could not answer this question, but I knew we had turned a corner in the treatment. Mr. V agreed to attend the next family meeting.

FOURTH FAMILY MEETING: BRINGING MRS. V TO LIFE

For the next meeting we added the newly obtained information to the genogram and displayed it on a large easel for all to see. Using standard genogram notation, we had darkened the symbols for deceased family members, a visual effect that was striking and

no doubt helpful in directing the course of the session. All family members gathered at the appointed hour, except for Juan; we wondered if our hopefulness had been premature. Mr. V sat quietly in a chair next to Henrique Jr., having offered only a silent nod in response to the greetings and queries of his children about his well-being. After a few minutes, Juan entered the room, saying quietly "Hello, Father." For what seemed like an eternity, Mr. V sat frozen in his seat, staring without expression at his youngest son. Then, he very slowly rose from his chair and solemnly shook Juan's hand. Rosita and Evita wept quietly, while Henrique looked on, silent and tight lipped.

Caught up in the drama of the moment, I was surprised when the family turned toward me and my cotherapist for direction. Taking a deep breath in an attempt to gather my thoughts, I was thankful for the structure of the genogram and asked the family if it would be agreeable to proceed with the family history.

Sensing more of a willingness to talk than had been present previously, I asked Mr. V why he had not shared the hardships of his early history with his younger children. He replied that he had never wanted to be weak in the eyes of his children, so he had never shared aspects of his harsh upbringing with any of them. In fact, it was his wife who once told Henrique these "secrets" when Henrique was a teenager battling some of his father's strictness. It was useful for Juan and Evita to hear about this period of conflict between Henrique and Mr. V, as they believed that Henrique had always been on good terms with his father. This discussion also gave us an opening to bring Mrs. V back into the family:

Therapist: Your wife wanted Henrique to understand what you had been through . . . . She thought that was important to share.

Mr. V: I don't know. . . . Maybe so.

Therapist: Why do you think she told him?

Mr. V: That was her way, to try to make things OK. To try to make us get along better. . . . She would be, you know, softer about things. Me, I did not want my sons to be soft or to see their father as soft. . . . But a mother can do these things.

Therapist: What kind of a mother was your wife? What was she like?

Mr. V: (noticeably softer) She was a very good mother. The best . . . (He falls silent, tears in his eyes.)

Therapist: You loved her very much. . . . Perhaps more than you can express . . . (Mr.V nods slowly, quietly weeping). You miss her very much, even after all these years?

Mr. V: (loudly) I am ashamed of my feelings, my weakness!

Therapist: You want to be strong for your children, as you had to be when they lost their mother. But what would your wife say about this? How would she want you to help them . . . even now?

Evita: (interrupting, shouting) Papa, you would not let us talk about Mama! . . . It's as if she died all over again because we could not know her through your memories!

Therapist: (interrupting) Evita, are there still things you would like to ask about your mother? Things you would like to talk about?

Evita needed help framing her questions in less angry terms, so that her father could respond. Eventually, she triggered a review of the day Mrs. V developed chest pains and was taken away to the hospital, a day that Evita herself had great difficulty remembering. It emerged that the three younger children had returned from school to find their aunt babysitting at home with no explanation of the whereabouts of their mother. Late that night some of them heard their father come home, but they dared not leave their beds to ask questions. Henrique, who had started working by that time, did not even know anything was amiss, as he frequently returned home after all other family members were in bed. The next morning their father appeared drawn and would only say "Mama has gone to the hospital." Mr. V now explained that she had died that same day, although he could not find the strength to tell

his children that she had "gone to the angels" for more than a week.

Through this discussion, we continued to frame Mr. V's lack of communication and distance during this period as his attempt to be strong for the children in the face of losing his beloved companion. Although initially very quarrelsome and angry, Evita's anger eventually turned to tears, and the session was no longer punctuated by her harsh comments. Juan was conspicuously silent during this important recounting of what had happened more than 40 years ago. Eventually, we asked what his experience had been during that time.

Therapist: Juan, it almost seems like you're sitting outside the family listening to this. . . . What do you remember?

Juan: I don't think you want to know what I remember.

Henrique: Don't start this, Juan.

Therapist: Henrique, you are worried about what he might say?

Henrique: This is the time to help Papa. We don't need to go into anything else.

Therapist: (turning to Mr. V) It seems that you need to help your children now. One thing that we have noticed is that it's been much harder to talk about things since your wife died. When she was alive, you could give them the stronger side of things, and she helped with the softer. Maybe part of her job was to share information, and you could attend to other things. Now, even after she's been gone so many years, they still need direction as to what's OK to talk about. Otherwise they will fight about what is best for you, what you can take and what you can't. Even though you are the patient here in this hospital, they still need direction from you as their father, the head of this family.

Mr. V: (nodding, speaking softly) It's OK. . . . Go ahead and talk, Juanito. It is important for you.

At this juncture, it was critical to underline the patriarchal, advisor role that Mr. V still had in the family, by pointing out that his children still needed his help and direction. Richman (1993) and others have written about the isolation and loss of meaningful social roles experienced by suicidal elders who become estranged from their families for a variety of reasons, including the conflicting developmental needs of the adult offspring or the tendency for elders to be painful reminders of unresolved loss in the family.

What ensued next was a discussion between Juan and his father about Juan's adolescent years, including Juan's account of harsh beatings and Mr. V's view that Juan had needed a stern hand to "keep him in line." It was important that we maintained structure throughout this interaction to keep other family members from interrupting the important exchange between Juan and his father. At the same time, we reframed the discussion in terms of the difficulties they all had in adjusting to Mrs. V's death, for example,

Therapist: Juan, now that you're hearing more about your mother's death, do you think it is possible that you scared your father when you would not return home at night? Do you think he might have been afraid of losing you, too?

THE FIFTH FAMILY MEETING: ADDRESSING MR. V'S FEELINGS OF EXPENDABILITY

Mr. V's appearance and behavior continued to improve after the fourth family meeting. He agreed to resume physical therapy and began accepting antidepressant medication. At the end of his third week in the hospital, we were preparing for his discharge home. In individual meetings with me he was more open to discussing his feelings about his disability and his suicide attempt. As a man who had capitalized on his physical strength and endurance throughout life, he was now challenged to find other ways to derive meaning from life. Because of the partial paralysis, he was ashamed to resume his previous social involvements, including his active participation in church. At the same time he questioned whether he could ever be of use to others in his weakened physical condition, noting as an example that he was not able to make toys for his new great-grandchildren. Over the months preceding his sui-

cide attempt he had become convinced that he was expendable and that his family would be better off, financially and emotionally, if he were dead. I told him that I thought this was the last issue we had to discuss with the family before he left the hospital. The entire family came to the last family meeting.

Therapist: (after reviewing Mr. V's progress and seeking responses to the previous meeting) We have been impressed with the strength of this family and your ability to tackle some very difficult and painful topics. Yet one thing we've yet to talk about is Mr. V's attempt to take his life. Is this difficult for the family to talk about?

Mr. V: My behavior was a sin against God. It was shameful.

Henrique: Papa, you were ill. We know that it was the depression.

(Many families with depressed or suicidal elders have family members who seek to "protect" the older adult by shutting down any negative or upsetting communication. Although well intentioned, this type of closed communication leaves the elder feeling isolated and gives the message that they are too fragile or sick to be fully involved in important family business.)

Therapist: Henrique, are there any other feelings you had about your father's overdose?

Henrique: What do you mean?

Therapist: It's normal for family to have all kinds of feelings about such a serious and dangerous act. Would you talk to your father about your reactions to what he did?

Henrique: (doubtfully) I don't know . . .

Therapist: (turning to Mr. V) Once again I have the sense that your family is trying to help you by holding back their discussion of difficult things. How would you feel about Henrique speaking his mind on this matter?

Mr. V: Go ahead, son. It's OK with me.

Eventually, Mr. V's children were able to express anger that their father would consider "leaving" the family so destructively. This kind of discussion might have been too difficult in the earlier family meetings, when Mr. V was more depressed. Now, however, it was important that we help the family treat Mr. V as a full-fledged family member who could engage in adult-to-adult discussions, even when charged with difficult feelings. Otherwise, they (the adult offspring and Mr. V) might be prone to falling back to their recent view of him as simply a stereotypically helpless and enfeebled old man.

Henrique: Papa, you wrote in the note that you were worth more dead than alive! How could you say that?

Mr. V: I did not want to be a burden to my family. I know that money has been tight for you and the others. . . . I thought it was one way that I could still help.

Rosita: Papa, how would it help us to have you gone like that?! How would that help?

Mr. V: There is the trust money that you will get after my death. . . . Maybe also life insurance if they didn't find out what I did.

Henrique: But we don't need that kind of money! And to think that you would leave us like that . . . not knowing your great-grandchildren! What would Mama say?!

Mr. V: One of my dreams is to be with your Mama again. When you kids were little, you needed me and you needed your mother. And when your mother was alive, she needed me, too. After she died it was hard, yes, but you still needed me. And even grown up I could help you build things for the house, for the grandchildren. Now what can I do? Grow old in some home where I will rot like old vegetables? (Mr. V's only living sibling, a younger sister, had recently been placed in a nursing home following a stroke.)

Henrique: Papa, we would not put you in a home . . . even if you needed it. I've told you before that we have room for you.

Mr. V: Yes, you say these things, but I don't see you anymore. I don't know what's going on with you!

Henrique: I'm sorry, Papa, it's been hard for us with the new job, and Camille (his daughter) needs our help . . .

Mr. V: (interrupting) I know! I know these things! You have many other people to worry about besides me.

Henrique: Papa that's not what I mean. I get involved with my work, and I lose track of other things. Heaven knows, you should remember what that's like! But I miss your help . . . someone to talk to about the business, you know. You never come over anymore, and you stopped coming for Sunday dinner after the stroke.

Mr. V: I did not want to be in the way.

In this way, Mr. V shared his feelings of expendability with the family and received reassurance about his role as a valued advisor with experience in business and other aspects of living. We were able to capitalize on the strong bonds of attachment between Henrique and his father by encouraging them to resume Sunday dinners, in part so that Mr. V could counsel Henrique about his new managerial role. In some families, where such strong bonds are nonexistent, it is more difficult to help elders find a meaningful role in the family. In these cases, and even in those with strong intergenerational bonds, it is important to attempt to help the elder build or re-establish connections with church, civic organizations, social clubs, or other volunteer groups. All of these involvements work against individual, familial, and cultural tendencies to view older adults as expendable individuals without a meaningful place in society.

CONCLUSION

I continued to work with Mr. V as an outpatient on and off for several years following his hospitalization. For the first year we met approximately once a month, typically in individual meetings to monitor his progress and encourage regular participation in church or community activities. These sessions also included a good deal of reminiscence and grieving about his wife. Periodic family meetings were also an important part of the posthospital treatment, as the family members were inclined to become more closed and distant in the face of ongoing normative crises, such as the terminal illness of Rosita's husband and further strokes suffered by Mr. V. In the months following his psychiatric hospitalization, he resumed involvement with his church and even became a deacon. His depression did not return, and he maintained good relationships with three of his four children. Sadly, he and Juan were never able to completely resolve their difficulties. In the language of Shields et al. (1995; see Table 12.1), this family had a mixture of relational features indicative of both positive bonds of attachment and caregiving (Levels II, III, and IV) and weak, ambivalent, or negative bonds (Level V). On the one hand, Mr. V and his two oldest children exhibited positive attachment and caregiving but were overwhelmed by family crises so that they failed to communicate or engage in effective problem solving (Levels II and III). Building on the solid foundation of their positive bonds, the primary intervention with these family members was to actively encourage communication about affect-laden issues and, if necessary, help them frame negative communication in more positive terms. For example, I obtained Mr. V's permission to talk about "difficult things" and encouraged Henrique and Rosita to share their feelings about their father's overdose.

Despite these positive bonds of attachment, Mr. V was an ailing patriarch in a family that had not yet successfully traversed that stage of the family life cycle at which the adult offspring assume more responsibility for and caretaking of the older generation (Level IV; see also King, Bonacci, & Wynne, 1990). Mr. V was inclined to view himself as weak and shameful if he could not help his children, let alone accept help from them. Therefore, we used family life review to underline his past accomplishments and reaffirm his leadership role in the family. Only after this review could he accept the idea of finding new ways to "help" his children; for example, letting them share their feelings, providing business advice to Henrique.

In contrast to strong positive bonds of attachment with his older children, the bonds between

---

TABLE 12.1

Five Levels of Family Intervention

	Description	**Intervention**	**Example**
Level I	Positive, balanced attachment bonds; positive, clear communication; effective problem-solving	Provide education, information, referral, support	Educate the family about depression
Level II	As above except problem-solving is temporarily overwhelmed by crisis situation	Provide liberal support, encourage active communication and problem-solving, minimum structuring of communication	Help Henrique and Rosita share feelings regarding the overdose
Level III	As above except communication is negative and problem-solving ineffective	Improve communication skills, actively structure angry, negative communication	Set limits on Evita's comments and help her verbalize feelings of grief
Level IV	Positive but unbalanced caregiving bonds	Restructure roles and lines of authority in the context of family life review	Help Mr. V take less active "advisor" role while accepting more help from his children
Level V	Negative, weak, or ambivalent attachment bonds; negative communication; ineffective problem-solving	Actively challenge family members' negative perceptions of one another and induce intergenerational empathy through family life review	Help offspring view Mr. V more empathically by discussing his history of early physical abuse

Mr. V and his two youngest children were considerably more ambivalent (Mr. V and Evita) or negative (Mr. V and Juan), making it difficult to engage in positive communication or problem-solving (Level V). The family life review provided a context in which we could actively structure negative communications while at the same time identifying and challenging negative perceptions they had of one another. For example, Evita's perception of her father as a cold and distant man throughout this crisis was reframed as an image of a grief-stricken father attempting to be strong for his children. Although we were able to positively influence the relational bond between Evita and her father, the rift between Juan and Mr. V remained deep and impervious to our intervention. At a later family meeting, Evita ventured to guess that they would never be close because she believed Juan looked so much like his mother that Mr. V could not tolerate it. Despite considerable effort to address this issue in individual and family therapy, Mr. V never consented to meet Juan's wife and accept their marriage, so the relationship broke off again shortly after Mr. V's discharge from the hospital.

PERSONAL EPILOGUE

Prior to working with Mr. V and his family, I shared a common view that work with older adults was depressing. I'm embarrassed to admit that my first response to an invitation to do a postdoctoral fellowship in geropsychology was something like this: "Gee, I dunno. Older folks are always sick and then they die. . . . Can you really make an impact?"

Since I have grown older myself and gained more experience with elderly patients, I have encountered Mr. V in many families and in many forms. He is a familiar figure in my work with depressed older adults who are frequently lonely and harboring images of themselves as worthless, unlovable, expendable, or burdensome to others. Each one of these patients forces me to look at my own images and fears about getting older. Yet as I get closer to them and to their families, I see how much can be accomplished by helping them rediscover their common bonds and values in the course of weaving together their family stories across the generations. Rather than being depressing, this work has been a rewarding antidote to the pervasive ageism of our Western culture. I have been fortunate to witness the resiliency, strength, and wisdom of these elders and the devotion of countless family members who have been willing and steady allies in their treatment.

References

Butler, R. N., Lewis, M., & Sunderland, T. (1991). *Aging and mental health: Positive psychosocial and biomedical approaches*. New York: Macmillan.

Hargrave, T. D., & Anderson, W. T. (1992). *Finishing well: Aging and reparation in the intergenerational family*. New York: Brunner/Mazel.

King, D. A., Bonacci, D. D., & Wynne, L. C. (1990). Families of cognitively impaired elders: Helping adult children confront the filial crisis. *Clinical Gerontologist, 10*, 3–15.

Myers, W. (1984). *Dynamic therapy of the older patient*. New York: Aronson.

Richman, J. (1993). *Preventing elderly suicide: Overcoming despair, professional neglect, and social bias*. New York: Springer.

Shields, C. G., King, D. A., & Wynne, L. C. (1995). Interventions with later life families. In R. H. Mikesell, D-D. Lusterman, & S. H. McDaniel (Eds.), *Integrating family therapy: Handbook of family psychology and systems theory* (pp. 141–158). Washington, DC: American Psychological Association.

Wynne, L. C. (1984). The epigenesis of relational systems: A model for understanding family development. *Family Process, 23*, 297–318.

PART III
CULTURE, RELIGION, SOCIAL CLASS, AND ETHNICITY

CHAPTER 13

TAKING SIDES: A WHITE INTERN ENCOUNTERS AN AFRICAN AMERICAN FAMILY

Barry Jacobs

"I'm not signing," the middle-aged Black father declared to me in a gravelly tone. He stood close by me, cocked his head back, and squared his shoulders, as if daring me to start something with him. I knew his show of bravado was mostly bluff but found myself squirming nonetheless.

It was late one afternoon toward the end of my internship year of clinical psychological training, and I was a White, Jewish neophyte leaning nervously against a metal counter in this Black man's well-worn kitchen. He rocked back and forth before me on the cracked linoleum floor. His wife sat motionlessly at the pocked wooden table behind him, silently contemplating the two groups of papers I'd hastily drawn up and rushed to their home. In the pile to her right were release-of-information forms for them to sign to allow me to deliver a report to the county's juvenile court judge about my 6-month psychotherapeutic treatment of their 16-year-old son Jack. By sharing with the judge my clinical opinions as well as background information about the family, I hoped to help Jack get out of the juvenile detention center where he had been placed the day before for probation violations. In my report I concluded —with the overweaning surety that marked me as an earnest graduate student in those days—that his offensive actions were due to his father constantly scapegoating him.

His father, who had already read the copy his wife was perusing, was incensed. "I, I don't want them, those people to get the wrong impression," he stammered at me. "What you wrote is not true." I fumbled for words, trying to defend myself, when

Jack's mother cut in with a quiet, restrained voice, "Just sign the papers, Leonard." "But it's not true what's in there," he protested. She said with greater firmness, "We've got to get Jack out. Just sign the papers." Leonard stomped over to the table, grabbed the pen from his wife's hand, and signed rapidly. "Here," he said, whipping the papers toward me. "I'll be in touch with you soon," I replied with heart pounding as I stuffed the forms into my briefcase and scurried out the door to my car.

My memory of this scene, after a decade of seasoning as a clinical and family psychologist, still makes me wince. The father's seething look, the mother's voice of resignation, evoke guilt for me that I forced them to choose between their son and their pride. What I thought of as a kind of gallantry at the time—young clinician going the extra mile for an embroiled teenager—mostly strikes me now as hubris. Yet in my own development the case has provided me with an education through hindsight in integrating individual and family considerations with the impact of culture and race. It was only by proving to be a danger to the disadvantaged Black people I was attempting to help that I learned the wayward power of being a privileged White professional on a mission.

It was early in my internship year at a community mental health center in a White, middle-class suburb when Leonard first came to see me about Jack. A small, swaggering man, he looked like a fashion statement 10 years out of date with his Afro haircut, smoked glasses, and color-print polyester shirt, with a pendant around his neck. Like his clothes, his speech seemed oddly stylized, sprinkled with psychological phrases. "My son has disordered anger," he said. "He has always had inborn temper in him." He explained that Jack was forever picking fights with his older brother and sister. Recently, his son had been arrested for severely beating another teenager, who was a rival for a girlfriend. "I figured we get him a little counseling now before his court date, and it will look good to the judge," he reasoned, as if gaining judicial leniency were his main goal.

When I asked Leonard to tell me more about his family in order for me to better understand Jack's situation, he looked away momentarily, then said casually, in a tone meant to make light of their problems, "Oh, we have our troubles. My wife and I are both out on disability. Not much money coming in. My oldest son is slow and needs help. But that doesn't account for Jack's behavior. He's always had that temper." To prove his point, he related that one of Jack's first actions as a toddler was to wobble across the room and hit his older brother in the head with a glass ashtray. As he gazed at me for my reaction, I nodded slightly as if impressed but wondered inwardly about this father's need to present his son in so negative a light. I hadn't much clinical experience with adolescents but knew what it was like to chafe at a nay-saying dad from my own rebel teenage years. I told Leonard I thought I could relate to Jack and would be happy to work with him.

When Jack sauntered into my office a few days later, he looked the picture of cool, African American youth. Light-brown handsome with a lanky build, in a black-and-silver Oakland Raiders' T-shirt and black nylon runner's suit, he had a smooth, practiced style that exuded invincibility. He slid halfway down in his chair, slowly brushed the wrinkles out of his pants, and tilted his head to one side with a slight grin like a high school bad boy in the principal's office waiting to hear what he'd be charged with. His calmness revealed no signs of the anger his father had touted.

"What did your dad tell you about why we're meeting?" I asked him, uttering the opening question that my supervisor had taught me. He shook his head and shrugged. "I'm not sure," he replied softly. "Something to do with court." I responded, "I

heard his version of what happened. Can you tell me yours?" Jack scratched his nose in indifference. "There's nothing to really tell," he said blandly. "Some dude was messing with my girlfriend, and I had to defend her. He wouldn't back off, and I took him down." He made it sound as matter-of-fact as shaking hands. But I could recall that his father had said that Jack had dispatched the other teenager to the hospital with a concussion. Had he just defended a girl in distress, or had he lost control of himself? "You took him down and out," I commented to him. "It sounds like you really hurt him." Jack said nothing but looked at me coldly as if the guy's injuries weren't worth troubling over. Then he said in the same flat tone, "He lost the fight and then went crying to the police. He wasn't hurt so bad." He smirked as if showing his disdain for the dude's cowardice. I paused and then said slowly, "Well, what do you think the judge will say?" He blurted out, "I can deal with 'juvie'"—meaning the county juvenile detention center—"My friends say they'll bust me out."

I was struck by the absurdity of this last statement and felt sudden sympathy for Leonard; Jack's posturing was irritating me. Yet the fact that I was aggravated, I reflected to myself, was just an indication of how quickly we had assumed adversarial roles. Jack's callousness had provoked the authority figure in me to try to straighten him out. For him to ever share the fear that was probably just beneath the posturing, I'd need to try a different approach.

"When you defended that girl, it sounds like you were fighting for what you felt was right," I said, reframing his situation in heroic terms. "Have there been other times in your life when you've stood up like that for what was right?" Jack hesitated for a few moments before saying, "My dad is always after me, blaming me for things I didn't do. I stand up for myself with him, I guess . . ." His voice trailed off uncertainly, as if he were venturing into an area for which he had no polished patter. Sensing a trove of emotions in that direction, I followed his lead. "What goes on between you and your father?" I asked him. "Nothing," he said suddenly sullen. "I'm a little confused," I retorted. "Didn't you just tell me he's always blaming you?" He was silent for a few seconds as if deciding how much to reveal to me.

"It's no biggie," he finally said. "My father thinks I'm no good. Fine. I can deal." He put on the slight grin again that he'd worn at the beginning of the session. Having momentarily revealed a slight crack in his image, he was now clearly back in his cool mode.

I realized that if I pressed him I'd only be pursuing him as an adversary again. Besides, my supervisor had cautioned me to be respectful of clients' defenses, regardless of how self-defeating they may seem to me. I switched tacks again, keeping the conversation low key and concrete. When I asked Jack to tell me more about his family, he related that they had moved from the inner-city to the suburbs 8 years ago. His brother was moderately retarded and attended a day program. His sister was working in retail, saving money to move out on her own. When I mentioned that I'd heard that both of his parents were on disability and asked him about the nature of their injuries, he looked at me quizzically. "I'm not sure," he said. "I think my mom hurt her back. I don't know what's wrong with my dad." Neither could he tell me what line of work Leonard had been in before becoming disabled. I found this lack of basic information strange but said nothing.

At the session's end, I told Jack that his father had wanted me to meet regularly with him through his upcoming trial in 2 months in order to help him prepare for it. I also said that I thought it would be helpful for him if we spent some time examining the choices he made and their consequences. "I don't know too many 16-year-old guys who want to come to a psychologist," I said. "I also assume that if you're against meeting with me, you'll find some way out of it. What do you think?" I was encouraged when he replied with the face-saving line I've heard from many adolescents since: "If my dad makes me, I guess I'll be here." Later, when I called Leonard to go over his son's session with him, he said with some menace, "That boy will come see you. I will make sure of it."

Even as a dim novice I could recognize that this case needed to be approached on the individual and family levels. Viewing Jack as an individual, his actions and image could be perceived as signs of either budding sociopathy or mere teenage roughhouse and cockstrutting—how much of which was not as yet clear to me. His pummeling of his rival

was disturbing, but he had never committed an act of such violence previously, his father's stories of backtalk and ashtray wielding notwithstanding. He had no prior criminal record, and his school record, although middling, suggested he made at least some effort at his studies. He denied drug use other than a few weekend beers. If my textbooks on development were correct, then his posturing was prompted by a need to forge an identity for himself separate from that of his down-on-its-luck family. Perhaps through individual therapy sessions Jack could find his own voice—expressing his evident anger and even sadness—without hiding behind the cool trappings. At the very least, meeting one on one could help him think through to a greater extent the effects on others of what he said and did so as to better choose among the consequences for himself that resulted. All this, my supervisor and I surmised, would require meeting twice weekly through the trial and probably beyond.

Viewing Jack as an integral part of a family convulsed by injury and hardship, I could come up with a multitude of ideas from my family therapy readings that seemed to apply. Nathan Ackerman's concept of scapegoating within families appeared to fit Jack's circumstances like a Hollywood script: If his father felt diminished by incapacity and impoverishment, then he could retain some sense of power by riding herd on his youngest son. In fact, all the family members might find it easier to focus on Jack's "badness" than face the pileup of their own tragedies and failings; Jack would only be showing his loyalty when he helped divert their attention with his troublemaking. A completely different family approach, drawing on the more psychodynamic writings of Ivan Boszormenyi-Nagy and Helm Stierlin, would regard Jack's behavior as self-punishment for the guilt he was experiencing for having greater innate endowment than his retarded older brother and greater prowess than his disabled dad. Yet another family perspective would look at the system's relationship triangles à la Murray Bowen. Perhaps Leonard and his wife were unable to resolve their differences directly but instead were projecting them onto, and fighting them out through, Jack. That triangle would then have been replicated and played out among Jack, his girlfriend, and his rival, including Jack's socking the rival as a displacement of the anger he felt toward his father. (Another triangle was being formed among Jack, Leonard, and myself, but that wouldn't occur to me until later.) All of these possibilities, it seemed to me, cried out for family systemic assessment and intervention. I could address part of it during the individual sessions but agreed with my supervisor's recommendations to refer Jack, his parents, and his siblings to the community mental health center's home-based family services team for adjunctive family therapy.

What was missing from these considerations—missing, actually, from most psychotherapy work in those days—was the sociocultural piece: that this family had climbed out of the ghetto and deserved credit for still clinging to the rung it had achieved despite enormous forces pulling it down. That African American parents, Leonard among them, tend to be especially strict with their sons in order to protect them from the prevailing societal bias that views young Black males as thugs until proven otherwise. That dealing with a slew of powerful and paternalistic White institutions—the court, the school, and a mental health clinic manned by young didacts—would only make these family members feel negatively judged, straining their hold on their middle-class dream and their affections for each other.

Individual therapy with Jack quickly fell into a predictable pattern. He began missing sessions or showing up very late, always with some school-related excuse. I would reschedule him or keep him for the full 50 minutes regardless of what time he shuffled lackadaisically into my office with a blank, "what-me-worry" face. I could easily have come down hard on him with stern admonitions or repeated calls to his parents, but I'd only have been echoing his father's bluster and allowing Jack to continue playing the bad boy. I could also have taken a strict but dispassionate approach, informing him he'd be imminently discharged from treatment if the cancellations or latenesses continued. But I sensed that he needed some concessions from me as proof that I could be different than his dad or the no-nonsense deans at his high school. Instead, I'd bend but not break, taking his excuses at face value, treating his every pronouncement and action respectfully,

and assiduously calling him each time he missed a session in order to demonstrate that I was concerned and took our talks about his life very seriously.

This was all well and good so long as I also delivered something of concrete value to him. As our conversations gravitated toward the latest altercations with his father, there were ample opportunities for practical, war room strategizing. From Jack's perspective, Leonard treated him like a wild animal that had to be prodded, bullied, and restrained. His father was in his face every morning, warning him that he'd better not be late for school or act up in class that day. He was on Jack every evening for not getting his chores done or for fussing with his older brother. Jack knew only two ways of dealing with his father—"yes"-ing him or meeting his aggression with his own invective. The shouting matches were frequent, the slammed doors and physical threats becoming more so. I said repeatedly to Jack that we needed to think these situations through, considering the pros and cons for each possible response he could make to his father's provocations. What would happen if he didn't raise his voice when his father did? I asked him. What if he wrote a list of points he'd like to make to his dad? He regarded me dully at first, uninterested in or uncomprehending of what I was getting at. But as we went over situation after situation, I could see a look of understanding coming into his eyes as he became aware that he didn't simply have to react but had choices that he could exercise whose consequences he could predict. Whereas he'd at first snickered when I told him, "You don't need to take the bait your father dangles," he now seemed to be listening.

This didn't necessarily produce changes in his behavior, however. From Leonard's perspective, Jack was being more belligerent than ever. "He's got a big mouth," he said to me during one of our periodic phone discussions. "I have a good mind to talk with the judge and let him spend some time behind bars. But his mother won't have it." I came to expect Leonard's sweeping denunciations of his son, no matter how much progress I thought Jack seemed to be making. There was also always a challenging tone to his inquiries about my therapeutic approach that put me on the defensive. After every prickly conversation I had with his dad, I found myself more sympathetic to Jack's feelings of being beleaguered.

After 2 months we went to court for his hearing. Although we'd talked several times about it, it was clear that Jack was nervous about what I might say to the judge about him. I'd never testified in a case before and was nervous, too. The courtroom was a modern, impressive space, its blond wood veneers with brushed-steel trim glowing in the soft lighting. The judge was a vital, silver-haired man who sailed through the details of the long lineup of cases swiftly and penetratingly. As I sat toward the back, waiting for Jack's case to come up, I could see him and his parents perched silently on a bench to one side. Jack sat stiffly next to his mother, wearing a sports jacket likely purchased for the occasion. Leonard sat on her other side, looking outlandish in his smoked glasses and an ancient, plum-colored leisure suit. When his case was called, Jack stood respectfully before the judge and let his public defender do all the talking. In a few moments, I heard my name called. Before I even had the chance to approach the judge's bench, he called out to me across the room, "In your opinion, does Jack understand the seriousness of this incident?" I answered quickly, "Yes, I believe he does." "Is he likely to repeat this action?" the judge continued. I responded, "No, sir. He has made good use of psychotherapy to learn new ways of handling his anger and resolving conflicts." The judge was quiet for a moment while reading over the police report again. He then began writing and announced without looking up at either me or Jack, "One year's probation."

I walked down the aisle to where Jack and his parents were sitting to congratulate them. We were met there by a bailiff who handed each of us a copy of the court order. On it had been written the duration of Jack's probation, the name of his probation officer and, as a stipulation of his sentence, "continued counseling by Barry Jacobs." After reading it, I looked up, surprised, and was greeted by Jack's usual cool stare and Leonard's scowl. After an awkward silence, Jack's mother thanked me profusely. Leonard grunted, "Hmmph," and then added gruffly, "Thanks," before turning away. I said to Jack, "I'll see you at our regular time on Monday." He shrugged and nodded.

As I look back on the hearing, it strikes me now as a blow to this family. They must have found the process profoundly alienating. The judge had not even acknowledged the presence of Leonard and his wife—had barely even acknowledged Jack—let alone soliciting their opinions or gauging their degree of commitment for helping their son. Instead he turned to the professional—whose knowledge of this 16-year-old and adolescent psychology in general was at best slim—to provide him with the answers he needed. Little wonder the father scowled and turned away from me; I had superseded him. I never knew whether this had racial overtones in Leonard's mind, but it could well have. He and his family were the only Black people in a courtroom in which the White judge, White lawyers, and a White psychology intern held sway. Justice may or may not have been color blind, but the high-handed manner in which it was meted out struck chords of racial disparity. To compound this, the psychotherapy of his son, initiated at Leonard's request, was taken out of his control and made a court mandate. With a stroke of the judge's pen, I went from being an ostensible ally of the father's prerogatives to an embodiment of the power of White institutions over his family.

Under these new conditions, my relationships with both Jack and Leonard took decided turns. Whether because I'd now be reporting his progress to his probation officer, or because he trusted me more after I'd vouched for him in court, Jack wised up. The latenesses and absences ceased. He largely dropped the posturing and simply talked with me, mostly about how he handled himself with his dad. He was slowly beginning to stand back more and see the bait before he bit on it. Then he'd try out new responses in the hopes they'd help him avoid getting pulled into a fight. In only one area—the big question as to why his father was so hard on him—did he seem to make little headway. Whenever I asked him about it, he'd answer me with the throwaway line, "My father's crazy. He should be the one in here talking with you, not me." It was as if he didn't want to think too deeply on the question—perhaps afraid there really was something bad in him about which his father was not crazy, but right.

Having lost the power to fire me, Leonard now

viewed me warily, as if unsure how I might influence his son. When I'd ask him about Jack, he continued to complain about his behavior but generally volunteered few details. I found myself calling him less and less frequently, because I still felt defensive about his past criticisms and guilty for having usurped some of his power. Jack's stories about him also angered me. As Jack backed away from Leonard, he rode him harder than ever, seemingly intent on proving him incorrigible. I tried to counter this by alerting the family therapy team but learned that Jack, his parents, and his siblings had just dropped out of treatment with them. From the outset, the family therapy had gone badly because both Jack and Leonard resisted it; sessions had been sporadic and unproductive. When I called Leonard to tell him that I thought his family needed the services, he answered me pointedly, "The court order says Jack's got to see you. It don't say nothing about the family." When I talked with one of the family therapists about petitioning the court to include family therapy in the order, he told me that it was unheard of for a judge to require a family to undergo treatment for its child's criminal act.

Conditions were set then for an escalating pattern without reprieve or retreat. With my hand strengthened by the court, I no longer felt reliant on Leonard to maintain the therapy. It wasn't long before I'd lost appreciation for the system's dynamics and was openly and explicitly taking Jack's side. Emboldened by my advocacy and directed by my guidance, he was better able to pull away from his father, who responded by doing whatever he could to keep his son engaged with him in the fight. Observing the father's bullying only made me more determined to defend his son. Some breaking point in the mounting tensions was bound to be reached.

As a first move, Leonard tried to wrest his son back by siding with him against me. I received a call from the probation officer that Leonard and Jack had met with him to complain that the twice-weekly therapy schedule was too arduous. When I called Leonard about it, he told me, "I want you to only meet with him every two weeks or so. That'll keep the judge happy and give Jack more time for school." I told him I'd think about it, then decided to have Jack continue meeting with me at least

every week. I had my clinical reasons but knew even then that I wanted to demonstrate to Leonard that he wasn't going to push me around. It occurs to me now that I was also showing him the power I had over his son that he lacked.

Then, a month later, Leonard exercised what power he did have. He provoked Jack into a huge fight early on a Sunday morning. Jack shook his fist at him. Leonard called the police and reported that his son was threatening to strike him. Because Jack was on probation, a squad car came at once to haul him off to juvie. He'd be confined there until a hearing could be conducted in a few days.

I learned about this only after Jack didn't show up for his session on Monday. When I called his home, his mother explained to me in a tremulous voice what had happened. With a rush of anger, I concluded immediately that Leonard had been to blame. I hung up the telephone and sought out my supervisor to get his okay for me to convey my views to the court. We talked about what I might say, and then I dashed off a 3-page letter to the judge in which I stated in the strongest terms that Jack was the victim of his father's scapegoating and shouldn't be jailed. After I gave it to my supervisor to review, he suddenly raised concerns about confidentiality. How could we provide information about Jack and his family members without either a signed release or a judge's subpoena? Because I couldn't reach Jack in juvie, my supervisor went on, I'd have to get written permission from his parents or forget about sending the letter. I blanched at the thought of having Leonard read what I'd written about him but agreed anyway in order to rescue Jack.

If I were more experienced and less preoccupied as I followed the mother's directions to their home, I would have grasped the visible signs of what this family long had faced. They lived in a predominantly White, upper middle class neighborhood on a tucked-away and forgotten cul-de-sac. Amidst the trim lawns and neatly shingled homes, their old wooden house had a forlorn and ramshackle look, as if it had been carted from some poor country byway and dumped perversely into prim suburbia. As I walked its overgrown path, climbed its sagging steps, and knocked on the peeling front door I was too concerned about the impending confrontation to notice that the house's woeful state exuded despair. This family must have felt extremely isolated—culturally, racially, and economically. The turmoil that went on within their walls was likely a manifestation of the disdain they felt from without. I was coming to do battle for their son but couldn't see that in their minds I was just another recruit in a sociocultural war with the White forces that surrounded them.

Our meeting felt like it went on for an eternity but actually was over in 15 minutes, after his wife forced Leonard to give in. I fled the scene but felt myself brave for having even faced it. I sent my letter via overnight delivery and patted myself on the back.

The court hearing 2 days later was like an exaggerated version of the first one. It seemed like the judge and everyone else involved with the case had read my letter and embraced my opinions. "It appears that Jack's father has instigated the actions leading to this current complaint," said the judge. "Probation will be renewed under the previous terms." No one looked at Leonard or spoke with him. He was never given enough respect to be offered a voice in a process in which his actions were maligned. I could see him sitting silently, observing the proceedings with his arms folded tightly and head slightly bowed. Afterward, I went over to shake Jack's hand. He asked me if I'd drive him to his home, and I said yes. After talking with his parents for a moment, he came back over to me and asked if I would drive them, too. They had no working car, he explained, and taking several buses home would exacerbate his mother's injured back. I agreed, although with trepidation. Silence reigned during the half hour it took to drive back to their house. I glanced every now and then in my rearview mirror and caught sight of Leonard's face, impassive behind his smoked glasses. I couldn't imagine what was going through his mind, insulted publicly by a young White professional and then having to be the recipient of that man's magnanimity. I may have doubly trounced his pride, but he had enough of it left to not let me see his hurt.

The following weeks with Jack were uneventful. I would be leaving the community mental health center in 2 months to rotate to another internship site, so we spent our last sessions together consolidating the gains he'd made in preparation for saying goodbye and transferring him to another therapist. He was now adept at analyzing the various ways of handling conflicts. Because of it—or perhaps because Leonard had backed off since the last hearing—there were no further altercations between father and son. There was a warmth between Jack and me now. I was proud of him. We were each able to express sadness over the end of our time together. I hadn't spoken again with either of Jack's parents after I'd driven them home, so I asked Jack to convey my farewell.

When I returned from a 2-week vacation, I was surprised to hear the voice of one of the family therapists on my answering machine. I was shocked by the story he told me when I called him back. Leonard and Jack had had a terrible fight in the midst of which Leonard became "psychotic" and pulled a gun on his son, threatening to kill him. No shots were fired, but the police had removed Jack from the house afterward for his own protection. He was now staying with a foster care family with whom he might remain until he reached 18. "It turned out that Leonard had a history of mental breakdowns that he'd kept from us," the therapist told me. "It was the family's secret." We both could understand why Leonard's pride kept him from trusting us with the information, but we wondered why Jack hadn't told us. Was it possible that he didn't know? we speculated. Did certain loyalties make him protect the father whom he fought?

My first thoughts after this telephone conversation, I'm ashamed to say, were that I was right. I'd found the man aberrant and dangerous; I'd fingered him for what he was. But then my thoughts turned, with horror, to Jack's circumstance. Being right didn't make it any easier for him to be separated from his family and thrust into the care of strangers. I got his new telephone number from the probation officer and gave him a call. Jack sounded distant, almost embarrassed. He had little to say about what had happened except to describe it in the terms I'd already heard from others. He felt "fine" about being with a new family. Nothing was bothering him. It was as if we were back at square one and he was evincing invincibility once more. I gave him my telephone number and suggested he call me if I could ever be of help. I never heard from him again.

In the last decade, I have thought many times about the myriad mistakes I made in this case and wondered what I might have done differently to make some difference. Should I have taken over the family therapy myself once the home-based team had been fired? That may have been the only viable means available to involve the mother in the treatment in a more meaningful way to help unravel the triangle among her, her husband, and their son. But would Leonard have allowed it? Would Jack have stood for it without retreating into being cool?

What has most haunted me since is the feeling I have that I helped precipitate the breakup of a family by not being attuned to the sociocultural forces with which it struggled. Neither did I realize the part of young White intruder I was playing. What this family probably needed were discussions about the crushing external pressures it was under, the outsiders' judgments it felt. In that way, perhaps, some of its volatile internal pressures could have been explored and reduced in a safe way. Instead I took sides in the internal struggle, and the fragile system burst.

If experience is humbling, humility brings awareness. I think of Jack and Leonard often, not just when working with African American families but with any cases in which the family's internal life is roiled by the culture at large. Before I jump in now and do any more roiling myself, I strive to understand my part in the cultural war, too. Like Jack, I've learned to think through the consequences before fighting.

CHAPTER 14

USING CONTRADICTION: FAMILY TREATMENT OF CHILD SEXUAL ABUSE

Wendy Greenspun

My initial telephone call inviting the family to our first session was met by a terse, angry response. "Why do we have to go to family therapy?" asked Louise, the mother in the Walker family. "There's nothing wrong with us except having these caseworkers interfering in our lives." Louise's initial statement told me much about the family's perspective at this point in time. I knew that engaging a family for mandated treatment when sexual abuse is the presenting issue is generally not easy.

The Walkers, an inner-city African American family, consisted of a single mother (Louise), an adolescent daughter (Lenore, age 18), and three children in foster placement (Gordon, age 10; Tonya, age 8; and Maria, age 7; see genogram in Figure 14.1). Louise also had a fiancé, Thomas, who did not currently live with the family. The children's father had never been married to Louise. He had several young adult sons from a prior relationship.

The three youngest children had been removed from their mother's home and placed in foster care following the discovery that Tonya had been sexually abused. Evidence of the abuse emerged when a routine pediatric examination revealed that she had contracted gonorrhea, of which the mother was not aware. The other children in the family were examined, with no physical evidence of sexual abuse found. The pediatrician reported the case to child protective services (CPS).

CPS already had had dealings with the family. About 5 years previously, the oldest daughter, Lenore, had been sexually abused. At that time there were also strong suspicions that the other children

in the family had been sexually abused, although initial laboratory reports with findings of chlamydia in the siblings were reportedly "lost" by the hospital that performed the tests. Because of the previous history in this family, as well as Louise's lack of knowledge of Tonya's symptoms, the three youngest children were all removed from their mother's custody and placed in foster care.

I was asked to treat this family as a clinician working at the foster care agency with which the Walker children were placed. The foster care supervisor and worker who gave me the background history on the family described the Walkers as "quite difficult." They said Louise acted very suspicious and hostile, and they believed she told her children not to reveal any information to agency staff. She also did not openly acknowledge Tonya's victimization. Tonya would not disclose the identity of the perpetrator, and she would not talk at all about having been sexually abused. Gordon was starting to exhibit "acting-out" behaviors, including running away and stealing money from his foster mother. The supervisor said he wondered about the extent of sexual improprieties within the family system, and he believed that Tonya's perpetrator could well be a family member.

In hearing the negative attitude of the workers toward this family, I realized I had a tough job. My role as a staff member of the foster care agency meant that I was part of the team of helpers working to ensure the safety of children who had been abused. On the other hand, as family therapist I needed to empathize with and engage the family,

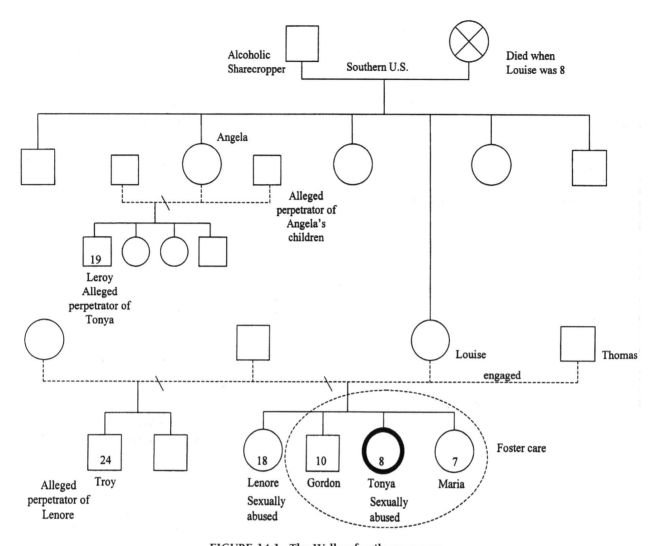

FIGURE 14.1. The Walker family genogram.

who seemed to mistrust the helping team of which I was a part. I could be walking a tightrope between seemingly conflicting loyalties.

Working with conflicting loyalties and contradictory ideas was a task befitting my theoretical orientation. In treating abuse in families, I value ideas and approaches from several schools of thought in order to address the many complexities present in this work (Greenspun, 1994, 2000). Family therapy approaches to treating sexually abusive families (e.g., Sheinberg, True, & Fraenkel, 1994; Trepper & Barrett, 1989) informed my choice to work with individuals, subsystems, and the whole family at various times in the course of treatment. From a systems perspective, I believed in focusing and building on

strengths in families in order to facilitate positive change. I also saw certain structural concepts, such as boundaries and hierarchy, as particularly relevant to this population. I looked at larger systems influences (Imber-Black, 1988) to understand the complex interplay between context and behavior, particularly in families involved with foster care and CPS systems. From psychodynamic theory I used my knowledge of defense mechanisms and internal sequelae of trauma to understand some of the feelings and behaviors of the victim and the family. Most important, I used countertransference responses as a tool to uncover parallels within the emotional worlds of my clients.

Before going into the first session with the Walkers, I found myself haunted by numerous negative thoughts about them. I wondered about Louise's culpability in Tonya's sexual abuse. At the very least, she did not seem focused on getting Tonya help following her sexual trauma. In fact, the help that was being offered was being actively resisted by family members. I dreaded facing the hostility that was aimed at me as both a therapist and representative of the "system."

My experience with sexual abuse in families allowed me to understand some of the dynamics contributing to their hostility. Often such families possess a rigid boundary between themselves and the outside world (Burkett, 1991). Once sexual abuse is disclosed, this protective barrier is violated by myriad representatives of the helping system, resulting in hostility toward the "helpers" and a tendency for family members to cling more tightly to each other. This certainly could apply to the Walkers.

My knowledge of larger systems also added a certain understanding to this case. A family that has been involved with the CPS system may feel disempowered when the "system" rightfully acts to protect the children but takes over parental functioning in the process. This "helping" act inadvertently leaves parents without authority over their children, exacerbating what may already be an ineffective hierarchy, one of the very factors that can contribute to sexual abuse.[1]

Armed with the understanding that this family was probably struggling with the trauma of its recent dissolution, I approached the initial consultation aware that I needed to engage the family around their current pain and mistrust of the system before we could address the sexual abuse.

INITIAL CONSULTATION

The entire family showed for the consultation, including Louise, Thomas, and all four children. Louise's sister, Angela, also was present. They all spoke excitedly to each other and seemed to roll their eyes when I tried to bring our session to order.

In asking the group their understanding of why we were meeting today, the two younger girls said they did not know. Louise said in an angry tone that she had been told by the caseworker they had to meet with a psychologist, but she did not understand the reason why. Gordon stated "we're not crazy," remarking that "only crazy people go to see psychologists." Angela responded that "the system just tells you what to do, and you have no choice."

With Angela's comment leading the way, I asked them about their experiences with "the system" so far, including the removal and placement of the younger children. Gordon and Maria said they did not like their foster mother because she was strict and that they wanted to go home. Tonya nodded her head in agreement but said nothing. Lenore remarked that she hated the caseworkers here, as they were so "nosy," trying to "get into [the family's] business."

Louise stated guardedly that she felt she was being punished unfairly, as were the children, but that she would do anything that was required in order to get the children back. Angela then remarked that "[CPS] always makes you jump through hoops," and "never believes your story." She said her own children had been placed in foster care, so she knew what Louise was going through. Louise asked, "Why are they doing this to us?" and began to cry.

I reflected back to the family what I had heard them say regarding their frustration, confusion, and anger at their situation. I then suggested that they might feel the same toward me as they did with the other members of the "system." Maybe they thought that *I* would not believe them, would be nosy, and would make them jump through hoops.

Gordon responded that a friend told him in advance of our meeting that I would be White and, on arriving at this session, he found this was true. I asked how he felt about seeing a White therapist, and he replied in a forthright manner: "I don't like White people, and I don't think you will be on our side." Thomas intervened with Gordon, telling him that was not a good attitude to have and that he shouldn't talk in such a manner.

---

[1] I want to thank Ellen Landau for the development of this idea.

I thanked Thomas for trying to help me but said I also really appreciated Gordon's honesty. I noted to myself that Gordon was probably the family member who would bring up the difficult issues in sessions. To the family I stated that Gordon was helping me to see that there were many levels at which they had good reason to be unsure about me. The fact of my color, in addition to my being part of the system, would understandably make them wary. They all seemed to noticeably relax.

Having broached the difficult topic of race, we were then able to talk more openly about the family's negative attitude toward therapy. I cautioned the family not to trust me too quickly, because they didn't know me and had not had positive experiences in the past with helpers. This restraining intervention assisted in the formation of an alliance.

The alliance seemed to go both ways. Toward the end of the session, I found myself feeling much empathy for what the family was going through, especially around the removal of the children. It seemed clear that this forced separation was the trauma with which the family was dealing at present. Louise's "resistance" to getting help seemed more like the fierce protectiveness of a lioness for her cubs, which I saw as a tremendous strength during this period of disruption.

Suddenly, I stopped in mid-thought. Was I now ignoring the other side? My initial negative reactions to the fact that several children in this family had been sexually victimized, and that the abuse had not been acknowledged, seemed far away as I focused on positives. Could emphasizing strengths become tantamount to colluding with a sexually abusive system? I started to worry.

I then knew that my varying emotional responses were relevant and that this countertransference could be used to form hypotheses about parallel experiences in the family. My vacillating between wanting to empathize, keeping a focus on strengths, and the need to remain constantly aware of the sexual abuse could allow me to understand analogous emotional oscillations within the family, even if they were unspoken at present. Very similar contradictory emotions are often present in the response of an abused child and other family members toward a person whom they love but who is also abusive.

Perhaps Tonya's perpetrator was someone about whom the family cared deeply.

Recognizing that I needed to keep the issue of the sexual abuse alive even as I engaged the family around their strengths, we ended the session by talking about possible treatment goals. The family's objective was for the children to return home, which coincided with the formal plan of the foster care agency. Yet the family did not know what they had to "do" in order to get the children back. I let them know that understanding and dealing with the issue of Tonya's sexual abuse would need to be part of what would happen in our therapy and could help promote the return of the children. I also emphasized that it would be important to help Tonya to deal with her reactions to the sexual abuse. I told them I would work in various modalities, including individual, subgroup- and whole-family sessions. In addition, I clarified my role as member of the foster care agency. I then suggested that I meet alone with the parents to talk about how to get further information regarding what was expected of them and of therapy, and we scheduled a session.

TREATMENT PLANNING: FAMILY AND LARGER SYSTEM

In my session with the parents, Louise vented much more frustration and anger at her children's removal and at "the so-called helpers" she had encountered so far. As I empathized with her experience, Louise began to talk openly about her extensive history with social services agencies.

She described her childhood experience as one of six children born in the South to a sharecropper, alcoholic father and a mother who died when Louise was 8. After the mother died, the father was either off working in the fields or on a drinking binge, leaving the children with no adult supervision. Louise spoke of how the "child welfare" workers would come around to their home, and the children would lie and say their father was taking a nap, or had just stepped out, for fear that the family would be broken apart if the workers knew their dire situation. So, even as a young child, Louise learned not to trust outsiders, who were seen as trying to interfere and cause harm.

Louise also detailed her experience around the discovery of Lenore's sexual victimization. After a weekend visit to her father, Lenore, who was then 13, complained of pelvic pain. Louise took her to the emergency room, where examination revealed physical signs of penetration, as well as "a sexual disease." CPS was called and asked that all the children be examined. Louise reported that Lenore's siblings were fine but that the CPS worker, Mr. Bailey, "lied and said that the other kids had sexual disease, too." Louise went to the hospital to get copies of the laboratory reports but was told that the reports had been misplaced.

Eventually, Lenore's older half-brother (the father's eldest son, Troy) was named by another child as the perpetrator. Lenore would not talk about what happened but did not deny Troy's role. Louise described being "treated like a criminal" by Mr. Bailey, who asked her why she had not been able to protect her daughter. She explained that Lenore's father had legal visitation rights, and she had no control over this. Mr. Bailey did not remove the children from Louise's home, given that the abuse did not happen there and because the laboratory "evidence" had been lost. However, according to Louise, Mr. Bailey said he felt that she should have known what was happening, and he still believed that all the children had been abused sexually.

Louise became quite tearful at this point in the session. "How could he have blamed me? I was so angry at my kids' father and so upset that my girl had gone through this." She told of refusing to participate in the recommended treatment for herself and Lenore. She believed it would "only make things worse," given the negative reaction she had to Mr. Bailey. She also thought that talking about the abuse might upset Lenore, because Lenore did not want to discuss it. Louise then acknowledged that Lenore continued to live with much unspoken pain, such that it now seemed that talking might have actually helped.

Mr. Bailey was currently the CPS supervisor on the Walkers' case. I now had a much clearer understanding of Louise's mistrust of the system at this point in time, given her previous experiences. I found myself questioning the motivation of the "helpers," feeling that Louise had been misinter-

preted and blamed. I felt somewhat disaffiliated from the helping team, believing that the agency workers were unable to see the experience from the Walkers' perspective.

With such a rift between the family and the helping system, as well as the family's uncertainty regarding how to facilitate the return of the children, I suggested having a meeting with the parents and all the involved helpers. In this family–larger system session (Imber-Black, 1988) the family could find out first hand about what was expected of them in order to get the children back home. I also hoped that such a session might promote a better working relationship between the family and the helping team. Thomas thanked me for suggesting the meeting, saying that they had not known how to approach Mr. Bailey and that he felt I had really understood their perspective. Louise said she thought she would feel safer with me at such a meeting.

Because I had seen the family alone without the workers, hearing their point of view, it seemed important to also get to know the helper perspective in a similar manner. I let Louise and Thomas know this, and I scheduled a larger system meeting, which the parents could then join halfway through.

The larger system meeting involved the workers and supervisors for both the foster care agency and for CPS. Mr. Bailey did most of the speaking, giving a lengthy, detailed description of atrocities he attributed to the family, including denial of extensive sexual abuse for several generations, lying outright to workers, various sexual perversions on the part of family members, poor boundaries, and out-of-control teenagers. He reported that all of Angela's children had been sexually abused by Angela's boyfriend and that Louise had actively interfered in their getting help. He said Louise and her family were the most disturbed family he had ever encountered in his work.

My heart began to sink. Had I been so naive as to believe the Walkers' "story" of being misunderstood by the system, blinding me from the very grim picture of victimization and denial put forth by Mr. Bailey? Was I just a "do-gooder" therapist who was ignorant of the dark side of family life? I found myself questioning my deepest convictions as a family therapist who emphasizes strengths, wondering whether a "pathologizing" approach was more accurate in such cases. I began to think I should never have invited the family to join this meeting.

As my thoughts and feelings began to swing so far from center, an internal red flag went up. I recognized that I had gone from one extreme to the other in my countertransference and that I needed to use this experience to understand what was happening in the case. I then realized that this tendency to "split" seemed to characterize the interactions in the family–larger system interface.

For the helping system, viewing the family in pathological terms was consistent with a child advocacy model, where ensuring the safety of children is paramount. The Walkers' resistance and denial lent credence to this perspective and did not leave much room for strengths to be noticed. In terms of the meaning for the family, I hypothesized that splitting allowed them to see the system as all bad, and to view themselves as all good. Consequently, the family did not have to look at painful issues within themselves, and responsibility for addressing the sexual abuse came from the helpers rather than the family.

This realization confirmed my belief that attending to countertransference reactions was key to understanding the complexities and contradictions inherent in working with sexual abuse in families. By being able to simultaneously tolerate and use my own positive and negative feelings, I could guide the family and larger system to a more integrated view and help the family begin to address their problems.

I was then able to listen openly to Mr. Bailey and the other workers regarding their negative opinions of the family while also presenting some information regarding my positive experience with the Walkers. Mr. Bailey and the foster care supervisor both sounded pleasantly surprised to hear about Louise's cooperation so far in the therapy process, bringing a bit more balance to their previously one-sided conceptualization.

When Louise and Thomas were brought into the room to meet with the helpers, there was an atmosphere of guarded, slightly hostile interaction. Agency workers all agreed that the stated goal was for the children to return to their mother, which appeared to be a relief to the doubtful Louise. Mr. Bai-

ley was able to commend Louise on her cooperation in treatment so far, stating that this was one of the requirements he had for the children to return home. He said it would be important for Louise to acknowledge the sexual abuse and to help Tonya in healing from her traumatic experience, as well as to learn how to protect her children so that no further abuse could occur. Mr. Bailey also said he hoped that the perpetrator would be revealed. Perhaps in part because strengths in the family had been noted, Louise and Thomas agreed that these were positive goals.

TREATMENT

With treatment goals of family and helpers more consistent, we were able to formally begin the therapy. My work with Tonya was aimed at beginning to address the trauma of her victimization. Involving her mother and the rest of the family in sessions could focus on the impact of the abuse on all family members, their relationships, possible obstacles within the family to disclosure of the perpetrator's identity, and ways to facilitate safety for the children.

For my first session with Tonya, I asked if she wanted to meet alone with me or to include her mother, in order to give her a sense of control in this process. She chose to involve Louise, and we met soon after the larger system meeting. Louise started the dyad session by thanking me for the meeting with all the workers, stating that it was the first time she felt she was able to talk to Mr. Bailey and the others without becoming very angry.

It occurred to me that her mention of the adult meeting during this session with Tonya could represent a blurring of boundaries between the subsystem components of the treatment. Did this boundary violation point to diffuse boundaries within the family, a frequent characteristic of incestuous families (Burkett, 1991)? Or was it a necessary part of a multilayered treatment that involved work with various systems and subsystems (Sheinberg et al., 1994)? As usual, I realized both were probably true and that this represented an integrated viewpoint. In addition, Louise's vote of confidence for me at the beginning of the dyad session may have signaled to Tonya that it was safe to open up.

Tonya began the session playing with various toys in the room, then drew a card that said "I love you, Mommy." I let Tonya know that we would talk and play like this in our sessions, in order to help her deal with all the different feelings she might have about the sexual abuse.

When I mentioned the abuse, Tonya made a disquieting face. Louise told her not to look like that, because this was "important." I commented that Tonya may have been telling us something that was also important with that face and that maybe we could try to find out what she was communicating. Tonya could not state how she was feeling until I introduced my "feeling cards," with figures depicting a variety of emotional states. After going through them all, she picked out "happy" ("to be with my mother now") and "sad" as well as "scared" ("to talk about the sex abuse") to describe her feelings. Louise told her she shouldn't be sad and scared because we were here to help. I gently suggested that whatever Tonya was feeling was okay, and helping her to express the feelings was part of how we would help. In this sense, I began to show Louise that contradictory emotions may exist simultaneously and that understanding them would be important for Tonya.

In the second dyad session, Tonya agreed to meet with me alone for half of the session. She drew a picture of her family and spoke about missing them. I then asked if she would like to read a book with me, which was about a girl, like herself, who had been sexually abused. She skeptically agreed but paid close attention as we read.

The story described a girl who had been molested by a family member but told no one about it (Jance, 1985). The girl in the book spoke about being scared to tell anyone because she thought they would blame her. She eventually told her mother, with another adult's help, and her mother lovingly told her that it wasn't her fault.

Tonya and I discussed the book thoroughly, talking about why the girl had worried that others would blame her and how the girl's mother was not mad at her after all. Tonya asked to read the book a second time, indicating its significance to her. Because Louise was coming in for the second half of the session, I asked Tonya if she would like to tell her mother about this book. Tonya said she would like to read it to her mother, and we did.

In the reading with Louise, I asked Tonya if she was worried herself that the sexual abuse had been her fault, and she slowly nodded in agreement. Louise spontaneously hugged her daughter, and said "It was *not* your fault, Tonya." Tonya held her mother tightly, then smiled, and asked to play something else, as if satisfied to move on. The strengths of this mother and daughter came through clearly as they began the journey toward Tonya's healing.

At the next week's whole-family session, Gordon continued to complain about his foster placement. Tonya interrupted and said she had read a book with the therapist and asked me if she could read it to her family. She got the book out, and they took turns reading parts of it aloud. Tonya ended the reading by saying, "So you see, it wasn't the girl's fault what happened to her." I asked her if she thought some people in her family might believe that her being abused was her fault, and she nodded affirmatively. This led to a discussion of how family members viewed what had happened to Tonya.

Again, Gordon was able to broach controversial feelings. He said that anyone could prevent abuse by "just saying no." Maria echoed his sentiment, stating she thought Tonya must not have wanted to stop it.

At this point, I felt extremely protective of Tonya and wondered if this discussion was damaging to her. When I asked how she was feeling, Tonya acknowledged that she already knew her siblings felt this way. Without my prompting, Louise and Thomas intervened, talking about the fact that children can't easily control the actions of someone older, because the adult is bigger and stronger. We discussed how scary this seemed and that Gordon and Maria probably wanted to know that they could keep themselves safe. I said that one of the things we would do in sessions is talk about how to ensure safety for all of them.

I recognized the importance of this difficult discussion. The children's ability to look at negative feelings felt toward one another represented a move away from maintaining the image of the family as all good. Gordon and Maria may also have been voicing a part of Tonya's self-blame for her, which could then be addressed, and the parents' capacity to intervene on Tonya's behalf suggested that Louise and Thomas truly did not fault her and could be protective. We continued by talking about the idea that a child can be abused by someone he or she loves, which makes it hard to prevent and to divulge. By the end of the session, Gordon and Maria seemed more understanding of Tonya's victimization.

Being able to confront negative feelings continued at the next family session. Gordon started out by angrily asking Tonya why she didn't just tell who abused her, so that they could all go home. Tonya got very quiet and merely shrugged her shoulders.

Somewhat dramatically, Lenore jumped out of her seat. "Leave her alone! Don't you understand, she *can't* tell right now. I know how she feels. I couldn't tell when it happened to me." She went on to describe how scared and confused she felt when she had been sexually victimized, leaving her incapable of talking about it or disclosing the perpetrator. Lenore asked Tonya if that was true for her, and Tonya began to cry, nodding in agreement. Louise looked at Lenore and said, "I never knew that's how you felt." Lenore said she hadn't wanted to upset her mother, so she had never talked about it before. Lenore then spoke in more detail about blaming herself and feeling confused, because the boy who abused her was her half-brother, and she liked him. Lenore and her mother agreed that they would continue to talk about Lenore's experience.

I felt very moved by Lenore's courage in talking about her own victimization in order to help her younger sister. Her action corroborated my sense of the tremendous strengths in this family. It also seemed to confirm the use of a multiple-modality approach in the treatment of child sexual abuse. Lenore's revelation gave voice to Tonya's unspoken pain, validating the experience, much as Tonya's recent abuse recalled Lenore's earlier trauma, which she could now begin to address. I started to see that work at one level of intervention could mirror and amplify what was happening at another level.

From that point on, Tonya began to slowly open up about what had happened. Over the next few months, she said the perpetrator was someone that she knew and loved, and she placed a paper with his initial on it into a "secret box" we constructed together in session. Louise was very supportive of

Tonya as she went through the process, not pushing her to disclose too quickly but instead seeming to understand that it was a painful experience that took time.

As I reveled in the family's strengths, I reminded myself that I still needed to remain aware of the other side of this family's story, the fact that several of the children had been sexually abused. In the next phase of treatment I focused more directly on what Trepper and Barrett (1989) referred to as a family's "vulnerabilities" to sexual abuse. These include social isolation and aspects of family structure, such as poorly delineated boundaries and hierarchy, which may leave a family at greater risk for sexual abuse of the children. In attending directly to these vulnerabilities, a family's future risk can be reduced.

With regard to social isolation, the Walkers had tended to be quite isolated from all but their own extended family, receiving little outside input, especially with regard to how to deal with sexual abuse. I was now able to refer Tonya to a group for girls who had been sexually abused and Louise to a group for non-perpetrating parents. They both became eager participants, talking with others who had been through similar traumatic experiences. Neither mother nor daughter had been ready for the groups at the beginning of our treatment, as they had not identified the sexual abuse as a primary problem to address. In sharing with others, their sense of isolation was dramatically decreased.

Parallel to the reduction in the family's isolation, my therapeutic solitude was lessened because I was now not solely responsible for the treatment of this family. I established regularly scheduled treatment review meetings, which included input from foster care, CPS, and group and family therapies. It is interesting that the co-therapists of Louise's group found her to be an "amazing" person, with tremendous strengths, including openness, an ability to examine her responsibility, and a capacity to help others in the group. I felt validated in seeing her strengths, and the agency workers continued to hear feedback about the family that contradicted their initial beliefs.

In relation to structural factors that were addressed in treatment, lack of clarity in boundaries and hierarchy became a big focus at this point. With regard to boundaries, the sharing of information across modalities was now always preceded by a discussion, such that the family started to see that options for privacy existed. For example, when Tonya began to tell me more individually about the sexual abuse, I would ask her at the close of a session how much, if any, she wanted to share with others, and why (see Sheinberg et al., 1994, for a discussion of this topic). She became more selective in her sharing, revealing information mostly to her mother.

We also looked at issues regarding the Walkers' skewed hierarchy. With Louise as a working single parent, she had often let the children have free rein in the home when she was not present. She had always valued self-sufficiency, favoring hard work over public assistance or dependence on a man. Because she needed to put in long hours to support the family, she often knew little about what occurred in her absence and left decision making to the kids. Through our discussions and in listening to other mothers in her group, she realized that this left her children vulnerable to many problems and that she needed to take control. Louise made the decision that she would work part time in order to devote more time to the children if and when they were permitted to return home.

In addition, 10 months into treatment Louise and Thomas got married, so they were beginning to address their role together as the "executive subsystem" (Minuchin, 1974) of a newly blended family. Louise began to reveal numerous problems with Lenore, who had moved into her own apartment but spent most of her time at Louise and Thomas's house, inviting friends over, making telephone calls, and eating their food. Eventually, the parents decided to change the lock on the door and not give Lenore a key but said she could come over whenever they were home. This demonstrated a very literal shoring up of a boundary that had been problematic when left wide open as well as representing the development of an intact hierarchy with the parents clearly in charge.

Discussions then ensued in family sessions about safety and protection, in order to prevent any further abuse. Louise talked to the children about what to do if anyone approached them sexually or in any other way that they did not like. Simultaneously,

Louise herself began to make changes in their home to make it "safer," such as insisting that the landlord install window guards (which had not been done previously) and rearranging the apartment so that her and Thomas's bedroom was in closer proximity to the children's, to assure better monitoring.

In her group and individual sessions with me, Tonya continued to address her feelings about being sexually abused. About a year and a half into treatment, with much supportive work, she finally told me the name of her perpetrator. She said he was her male adolescent cousin, Angela's oldest son, Leroy. Leroy had been staying with the Walkers periodically, baby-sitting the younger children in the evenings when Louise was working and Lenore went out.

I asked Tonya whom else she would like to tell, and she asked for her mother. Louise hugged Tonya when she revealed Leroy's identity and stated tearfully, "I'm so proud of you for being able to tell." Tonya asked if her mother was mad at her, and Louise loudly exclaimed, "No!" She said she knew Tonya loved Leroy, but it was not Tonya's fault; Leroy should not have ever abused her, and he had a "real problem." Tonya looked more calm and relaxed than I had ever seen her. We then spoke about how to handle this disclosure, including whom to inform and how to do so. Tonya was a part of this discussion and chose to have her mother tell the rest of the family. I would inform all the agency workers.

Tonya, her mother, and the rest of the family were able to process reactions to learning the perpetrator's identity. On a practical level, Louise handled dealing with Angela and their extended family. No one knew where Leroy resided at present; he was allegedly living in Europe after defecting from the military. Louise told me that Leroy was clearly a troubled young man. He had been sexually abused by his father when younger and had lived in group homes most of his early adolescence.

We talked about Louise's guilt with regard to letting Leroy stay in their home and trusting him with her children. She was able to look at how her fondness for Leroy, and perhaps her identification with his difficult past, may have clouded her judgment about his character. She said she also had believed that "family can always be trusted" and that only outsiders could pose a danger. This deeply ingrained premise had begun to be challenged when she had positive experiences with outsiders in our therapeutic work, allowing her to question her idealized beliefs about family as well.

TERMINATION PHASE

With the significant changes in the Walker family's ability to address the sexual abuse, and the work on their underlying vulnerabilities to further abuse, in conjunction with Tonya's disclosure of the perpetrator, CPS and the foster care agency both agreed that the children could start the transition of returning home to Louise and Thomas. This became the final phase of our treatment; my role as therapist would end when the children left foster care.

The children had been in care for more than 2 years now. Significant changes had happened, in terms both of each child's development and of who was now going to be living in the family. Gordon had gone from a latency-aged boy enamored with his mother to a rather rebellious early adolescent who tested limits. Lenore had moved out of the home, and Thomas had moved in. Obviously the family had to prepare for these changes in order to help ensure a successful reconciliation.

At this point in treatment mostly whole-family sessions were held, along with occasional parental dyad sessions and termination work individually with Tonya. Family and parent sessions focused a lot on Thomas's role as stepfather and the children's relationships with him. With Gordon acting out now, we also discussed rules for the household when the children returned, something that had never been made explicit before. These rules got tested and revised as the children started to go home on weekend trial visits.

Tonya was able to work with me around our termination. We created a book of pictures that covered the issues that she found most significant. Included were bringing her mother to sessions, the use of feeling cards, the secret box, and reading the book about the girl who had been sexually abused. At the end of treatment I gave her a copy of this book to continue to remind her that she was not to blame for the abuse.

Both Tonya and her mother opted to continue in their sexual abuse treatment groups, as they realized the need to address ongoing feelings. Tonya was also trying to decide whether to press charges against Leroy. Louise also asked for a referral for family therapy in her community, as she said she knew that the return of the children was likely to be rocky and that she had learned that outsiders really could help.

As the children were moving home, and in spite of the amazing amount of work that was done, I found myself having doubts and concerns. Had we gotten the name of the real perpetrator? Had other family members known all along about the abuse or even actively colluded in it? Would the family really follow through with treatment, or were they just saying what I wanted to hear? My questions seemed to hearken back to the pathological beliefs expressed at the beginning of treatment by the agency workers and, at times, by me. I puzzled over what this could mean.

It occurred to me that my negative thoughts again reflected the need to balance contradictory possibilities with this family. With such a strong emphasis during termination on the family's ability to change and grow, my doubts needed to emerge as well. Because the children were returning home, outside of the "protection" of foster care, the full responsibility for the safety of the children was now left to the family. My countertransference pointed out that continuing awareness of their vulnerabilities, much like an alcoholic's cognizance of the ongoing dangers of drinking even when sober, would help the family to safeguard the children. The family would need to continue to address these issues in their ongoing group and family treatments.

CONCLUSION

This case demonstrated an integrated family therapy approach to the treatment of child sexual abuse. In terms of theory, ideas from family systems, family sexual abuse treatment, larger systems work, and psychodynamic theory were integrated to address the myriad complexities inherent in this work. At the level of practice, interventions occurred across modalities, from the macro level (larger systems and whole family) to the micro (individual), in order to address and integrate relevant issues.

Embracing contradictions at the levels of both theory and practice set the stage for the important work that ensued. Using my internal experience of countertransference, I was able to see splits within my own reactions and hypothesize about parallels within the family and larger system. Focusing on the conflicts in the larger system–family interface assisted with uncovering similar problems within the family. Addressing contradictory reactions within the family helped bring out the confusing emotions of the sexually abused child. Working through the child's trauma aided the family in addressing their own vulnerabilities, and strengthening the family helped develop a positive foundation for the abuse victim to internalize.

Thus, this complex treatment seemed to occur as a kind of feedback loop, with each level of intervention mirroring and expanding on the other levels, and each theoretical perspective adding to the other theories. Only when such complexity can be welcomed can the healing of child sexual abuse begin to occur.

References

Burkett, L. P. (1991). Parenting behaviors of women who were sexually abused as children in their families of origin. *Family Process, 30,* 421–434.

Greenspun, W. (1994). Internal and interpersonal: The family transmission of father–daughter incest. *Journal of Child Sexual Abuse, 3*(2), 1–14.

Greenspun, W. (2000). Embracing the controversy: A metasystemic approach to the treatment of domestic violence (pp. 152–177). In P. Papp (Ed.), *Couples on the fault line: New directions for therapists.* New York: Guilford Press.

Imber-Black, E. (1988). *Families and larger systems.* New York: Guilford Press.

Jance, J. (1985). *It's not your fault.* Mt. Dora, Florida: Kid's Rights.

Minuchin, S. (1974). *Families and family therapy.* Cambridge, MA: Harvard University Press.

Sheinberg, M., True, F., & Fraenkel, P. (1994). Treating the sexually abused child: A recursive, multimodal program. *Family Process, 33,* 263–276.

Trepper, T., & Barrett, M. J. (1989). *Systemic treatment of incest: A therapeutic handbook.* New York: Brunner/Mazel.

CHAPTER 15

THE MISFIT: A DEAF ADOLESCENT STRUGGLES FOR MEANING

Robert Q Pollard, Jr. and Natalie C. Rinker

The case described in this chapter involves a young deaf woman, Kris, and the psychotherapy services that were provided to her and her family. The case illustrates common issues that arise in the treatment of families with deaf members: communication, education, Deaf[1] culture, and the interaction of multiple external systems with the "identified patient." However, the issues addressed and the therapeutic points illustrated herein are not unique to work with the deaf population. Families that have deaf members share commonalties with families that are bilingual, those with intracultural differences, and families that endure different types of disability. Regardless of whether a therapist has the occasion to work with deaf individuals, this case makes important points about diversity within families that all therapists are likely to encounter.

We specialize in services to deaf and hard-of-hearing individuals. At the time this was written, Natalie C. Rinker was a Fellow in the Program for Deaf Trainees at the Department of Psychiatry at the University of Rochester Medical Center, and Robert Pollard was her supervisor. This case example is written in the first-person point of view, from Dr. Rinker's perspective, to enhance readability. The material presented is an amalgamation of both authors' experiences with mixed deaf–hearing families, further enlightened by the experiences of our col-

leagues in the field. Although not representative of any one family, the events and issues depicted herein are, in our experience, common in families that include deaf children. The chapter is written in a style that alternates the factual aspects of the case with commentary drawn from our clinical supervision sessions.

FAMILY CONSTELLATION

The Clark family consists of George and Margaret and their three children: Trevor, Jason, and Kris. At the time my involvement with the family began, George Clark was an executive with a major manufacturing firm. Margaret Clark was a registered nurse but had been a homemaker since her first child was born. Trevor, age 20, was a sophomore at the University of California, Los Angeles (UCLA), which he attended on a basketball scholarship. Jason, age 17, was a junior at the local high school. Although not as athletically skilled as his older brother, Jason hoped to win a basketball scholarship to Cornell University the following year. Kris, age 15, had enrolled the previous September in the state school for the deaf after completing her elementary education in local public school programs. The school for the deaf was only a few miles from where I worked but more than 90 miles from the Clark family's home.

We acknowledge the assistance of Lee Twyman in conceptualizing this case study.

[1] In keeping with preferences in the deafness field, the uppercase "D" will be used when referring to this specific sociocultural group and the lowercase "d" when a more general reference to hearing loss is intended. While acknowledging the Deaf community's heterogeneity, the term is generally understood as referring to people who have hearing loss in the severe to profound range, communicate in American Sign Language (ASL), and otherwise demonstrate a sociocultural association with the American Deaf community.

I am hard of hearing[2] but fluent in American Sign Language (ASL) as well as English. I can hear moderately well when using bilateral hearing aids. My speech is understandable to most people.

RELEVANT HISTORY

Kris was born deaf, but her hearing loss was not diagnosed until she was 18 months of age. Her mother had expressed concern to the family physician about Kris's delayed speech when Kris was 13 months old, because the other two children had spoken their first words quite early. The physician told Margaret not to worry, emphasizing the variability in the pace of children's speech development and noting that younger children with assertive older siblings often are reticent to speak. George also downplayed Margaret's worries, attributing them to her medical background and sensitivities. Yet when Kris still had not spoken by 18 months, Margaret insisted on a hearing examination. An audiologist confirmed that Kris had a severe, bilateral hearing loss of approximately 80 decibels through the speech frequency range. No cause was identified, but the etiology of Kris's deafness was assumed to be congenital.

The diagnosis had a profound effect on the Clarks, most overtly on Margaret, who was tearful and depressed for many weeks thereafter. Her previous doting on infant Kris ended abruptly. George reluctantly stepped in to help with the caretaking of Kris and the other children while Margaret recovered slowly over the next few months. George was deeply shaken by the diagnosis as well but, as was his nature, he responded with a stoic, can-do attitude characterized by detailed plan making about Kris's future speech and educational training. He spoke frequently with the audiologist and family physician, both of whom urged him to counter Margaret's initial suggestion that Kris be enrolled in the state school for the deaf. The medical practitioners painted a bleak picture of Kris's future if she were

unable to read lips and speak intelligibly in "the hearing world." They warned that acquisition of sign language would come at the price of these critical oral skills. Worse, they warned that sign language use would relegate Kris to socialization only with other "deaf–mutes" and that the family would "lose her" if they allowed her to learn sign language.

Heeding this advice, George planned a rigorous course of speech therapy and early education for Kris with the local public school district's special education staff. One month after the diagnosis was made, Kris was fitted with bilateral hearing aids that were not covered by the family's medical insurance. Also not covered were the speech therapy lessons that Kris attended three times weekly from age 2 to age 4, until she was old enough to enter the school district's "handicapped preschooler" program. Kris was one of five children in the program and the only one with a hearing loss. The other children's disabilities included cerebral palsy, mental retardation, attention deficit disorder, and spina bifida.

As suggested by the medical professionals and most of George and Margaret's friends, the family embraced the "oral" communication approach for Kris. The audiologist instructed the Clarks to always keep Kris's hearing aids on and in good working order, to speak to her clearly and with good eye contact, and to instruct her as directly and frequently as possible in vocabulary enrichment and speech enunciation.

Margaret eventually recovered from her depressed state and began taking a more active role in Kris's education. George returned to the rigorous demands of his job, leaving the home and school responsibilities to Margaret. Margaret did her best to balance the demands on her time between Kris's educational and speech/audiology training and the boys' athletic, school, and recreational activities. Jason and Trevor seemed to take Kris's deafness in stride; their routine and behavior changed little after the diagnosis, although they often complained that Kris's needs seemed always to come before their own. The family

---

[2] At present, the preferred terminology to describe individuals with hearing loss is *deaf* or *hard of hearing*. The term *hearing-impaired* has lost favor because of its emphasis on the individual's "impairment." In contrast, *deaf* and *hard of hearing* are taken as assertive, unapologetic statements about one's auditory status, leaving open the more important issue of one's broader capacities. Terminology shifts such as this are common among minority groups and reflect important dynamics regarding majority–minority labeling and other social interactions.

tried to communicate with Kris as instructed, but the hustle and bustle of family interaction often precluded the slow, deliberate communication they were supposed to practice. Besides, Kris was not a great speechreader.[3] Although her own speech quality progressed slowly and steadily over the years, her good speaking skills caused others to underestimate the difficulty she had with *receptive* oral communication. As the years progressed, Kris lagged further behind her brothers both academically and socially. Things continued in this pattern throughout Kris's elementary school years.

Comments

The reactions of the Clark family are not uncommon when deafness in a child is diagnosed. While each parent copes in his or her own way, grief is experienced, future expectations are challenged, and the unknown presents myriad questions, all of which seem critical but inadequately answered by the "specialists." The Clarks's emotional and informational needs were not properly addressed by their physician and audiologist, who rendered narrow and definitive opinions on issues that are very complex. Passions in the deafness field run high, especially regarding communication and educational methodologies. Few specialists remain truly objective. Many thrust their opinions on parents before the parents are ready to digest them or consider the alternatives carefully. Parents often express consternation at how deafness experts disagree but seem so sure of their individual opinions. This is a fair assessment of an impassioned and divisive field.

Rather than being recruited to a particular corner of the various communication and education debates (e.g., sign vs. speech), the Clarks should have been comforted, encouraged, and set on a more empowering path of learning and independent decision making. Organizations for parents such as Tripod (1-800-352-8888) and books such as Marschark's (1997) *Raising and Educating Deaf Children* offer parents of newly diagnosed deaf children helpful information for making their own communication, edu-

cation, and other decisions. Additional information on deaf children and adults is available from the Alexander Graham Bell Association (202-337-5220), the American Society for Deaf Children (1-800-942-2732), the National Association of the Deaf (301-587-1788), and the National Information Center on Deafness at Gallaudet University (202-651-5051).

Margaret's initial withdrawal from Kris after the diagnosis was made, and George's rigorous pursuit of education and speech training services, are common parental reactions. Psychiatrist Hilde Schlesinger (Schlesinger, 1976, 1987, 1988, 1992; Schlesinger & Meadow, 1972) has researched parent and deaf child interactions for more than 30 years. Her findings indicate that some parents react to the deafness diagnosis from a position of powerlessness (which is often aggravated by professionals). Powerlessness, based in deep-seated feelings of inadequacy about raising the deaf child, can be manifested by extremes of withdrawal, overprotection, or a rigid focus on superficial aspects of communication. These behaviors discourage the child's psychological, social, and cognitive development. Schlesinger found that the academic success of deaf children is more accurately predicted by the cognitive stimulation and emotional comfort of the early parent–child bond than on the specific communication or educational approaches families choose.

THE TRANSITION

By the time Kris was in junior high school she had met a number of deaf youth through her school's special education activities, including students from the state school for the deaf. Despite her parents' urging to the contrary (and in part because of it), Kris acquired a considerable degree of sign language fluency from her social interaction with these students, especially one girl named Lorie, who was close in age to Kris. Lorie resided at the school for the deaf during weekdays but returned to her family's home, in Kris's community, on weekends and during the summer. The Clarks liked Lorie but were

---

[3] *Speechreading* is a term preferred over *lipreading*, because it emphasizes that there are important information sources beyond lip movements that are used by deaf and hard-of-hearing people in recognizing the meaning of observed human speech. These additional information sources include residual hearing, gesture and body language, and numerous aspects of the communication situation and environment.

concerned that her sign language use was "rubbing off" on Kris and might diminish her oral skills. On a deeper level, they were uncomfortable with the overt display of the children's "handicap" that signing seemed to represent, especially when the family was out with Kris and Lorie in public.

Throughout junior high school, Kris increasingly spoke of her desire to transfer to the school for the deaf. At first, the Clarks flatly refused, assuming that Kris simply wanted to be with Lorie and did not understand the consequences this would have on her communication, her functioning in the "hearing world" (of which the professionals spoke often), and the investment they had made for the last 12 years in her oral education. Yet the Clarks also perceived how unhappy Kris had become in junior high, as she was increasingly excluded from important school and social activities that they remembered fondly from their own youths. Kris had been branded a "special education student" and was unwelcome among the popular crowd. Although her speech skills were good, she struggled greatly to comprehend the speech of people who were not from her immediate family. She courageously tried, and failed, to win positions in competitive extracurricular activities, such as the school play and the cheerleading squad. The contrast of Kris's social struggles at school with the enjoyable time she spent with Lorie and other deaf youth stimulated the Clarks to reconsider their opposition to Kris's increasing demands to transfer to the school for the deaf.

At the deaf education program's summer picnic, the Clarks had an emotional conversation with Lorie's parents. It was the first time they had ever met. Lorie's parents shared their own struggles with grief, learning, and coping after Lorie's deafness was diagnosed. Although their educational and communication decisions differed from those of the Clarks, George and Margaret felt more support and understanding from Lorie's parents than they had ever felt

from deafness professionals. Meanwhile, Kris had a delightful time at the picnic, which heightened her resolve to transfer to the state school for the deaf. In a tearful and heated confrontation that evening, George and Margaret reluctantly agreed to allow Kris a 1-year trial at the school. She was elated; they were terrified.

Kris enrolled the following September. The 2-hour drive from the Clarks's home to the school was mostly silent; each family member (Trevor and Jason rode along) was deep in thought. Kris's imminent departure was meaningful for all concerned, but in different ways. George fantasized Kris's deterioration into an ill-defined "deaf–mute" existence. Margaret was newly regrieving the loss of this child she felt she had lost once before, when Kris's deafness was first diagnosed, feeling a peculiar mixture of sadness, distance, love, and guilt. Trevor was happy for Kris, having just experienced his own emancipation from the family at UCLA. Jason was envious, wishing that he, too, could live independently as both Trevor and Kris now would.

It was Jason who best understood the importance, and fear, of this transition for Kris. As the closest in age and personal demeanor, Jason and Kris shared a lot in common. Both stood in the shadow of Trevor, the accomplished one, and knew that they brought their parents less pride and more hassles. In their private time, Kris had taught Jason quite a bit of sign language. Thus, he was able to understand and discuss with her topics that the rest of the family never could. By this time in Kris's life, Margaret could fingerspell[4] and knew a number of individual signs, but she could not form long or complex sentences in Signed English[5] or ASL. When George was not around to criticize, she and Kris communicated through a combination of speech, gesture, and limited signing. George could fingerspell, slowly and arduously, but he rarely would, except to teach Kris a new English word.

---

[4]Fingerspelling refers to the use of a standard system of 26 handshapes to represent the letters of the English alphabet. Words are fingerspelled by making one handshape after another until each letter of the word has been presented.

[5]The term *Signed English* refers to a group of manual communication methods invented and used by educators to attempt to teach deaf children the structure of English more readily. Signed English systems borrow from the vocabulary of ASL but add, subtract, and alter many elements in order to mimic English syntactic and grammatical characteristics. The grammar and syntax of ASL are very different from that of English and the Signed English systems. ASL takes advantage of the visual modality of the language, which is difficult to re-create in an oral language or an attempted visual equivalent of an oral language.

After spending several hours at the school getting Kris settled into her dormitory room, and saying their good-byes tearfully, the hearing members of the family returned home to an environment that seemed quite different without Kris. Communication felt uncomfortably easy, almost inspiring a sense of guilt. Kris, who had long represented a center of family attention and effort, was now absent, and the family members' energies searched awkwardly for new topics of concern and usefulness.

At school, Kris found herself in an environment more fascinating, exciting, mysterious, and challenging than she had imagined. Although proficient in signing, she was not as fluent as most of the students. They welcomed her, but she felt "behind" in ways that were similar to how she felt among the hearing students at her junior high. Although she was happy to be at the school for the deaf, where she understood and felt accepted by her teachers and fellow students as never before, Kris didn't feel like she really fit in and began missing her family terribly. Her mixed feelings about her independence, her improved communication environment, her longing for the nurturance and protection she experienced at home, and her new concerns about identity (e.g., oral deaf vs. ASL Deaf) soon precipitated eating disorder symptoms. Kris began bingeing and purging, influenced by an older student in her dormitory who had similar problems. Kris was caught several times, tearful and sick in the bathroom, by her dormitory counselor. Kris's parents were notified (she was still a minor), and they were given my telephone number.

THE INITIAL CONTACT

George Clark was the first to call me. In a formal and hasty fashion, he described the problem and briefed me on Kris's history. Noting my imperfect speech (I can hear generally well on the telephone using an amplifier), he complimented me on my "good oral skills." He then queried me on my education, inquiring specifically if I had attended "regular schools" throughout. I had, but I emphasized to him that my hearing loss was of moderate severity and that I had had good support in my public school and college classes, which included sign language interpreters and notetakers. His final, most hesitant question was whether I could "talk with [my] hands." I assured him that I was fluent in both ASL and Signed English and that I worked full time with a range of deaf individuals. "That will be good for Kris," he said quietly, in a sincere (and unbusinesslike) tone of voice. I set an appointment time aside for Kris and asked her father to have Kris call me (by TTY[6]) to confirm.

Kris initially contacted me from her dormitory room. As we conversed on the TTY, Kris wouldn't reveal her name until she felt satisfied that I would respect her anonymity and not tell other deaf individuals that she was inquiring about therapy. She indicated that she was calling because her parents insisted on it. Her own feelings about initiating treatment were ambivalent. Nevertheless, she appeared for her first scheduled appointment the following week.

Before we delved into Kris's presenting concerns and psychosocial history, we discussed her communication preferences. Although she spoke well and was proficient in English, she said that she preferred that we communicate in ASL. I began to do so, but it was quickly evident that she did not understand ASL as well as she claimed. Without discussing it overtly, our signing style naturally gravitated toward a "pidgin" combination of ASL and Signed English with speech, which was clearly best for Kris's overall comprehension.

In describing her presenting concerns, Kris indicated that she had felt increasingly depressed since entering the school for the deaf 2 months earlier. She described the slow onset of her symptoms of bulimia, which had now progressed to several incidents of bingeing and purging per week. She no-

---

[6] TTYs (an abbreviation for teletype) or TDDs (telecommunication devices for the deaf) are devices deaf people use to communicate by means of telephone. They consist of a keyboard and visual display and some means of connecting to a telephone. As words are typed (in English), the TTY transmits special sounds over the telephone line that are translated back into letters or numbers by the TTY at the other end. People using TTYs can communicate with people who do not have one by calling a "relay service." Relay operators with TTYs vocally translate TTY communications to the hearing party and type the spoken portion of the conversation to the deaf party via TTY.

ticed that her anxiety and bulimic symptoms usually worsened a few days prior to going home on weekends. I asked her to tell me more about her weekend visits home and how she felt about them.

Her experiences of inclusive communication at school had markedly increased her resentment at being left out of conversations at home. She found herself more angry with each visit. Yet, she simultaneously feared that her parents would reject the "Deaf person" she felt she was becoming and criticize her failure to thrive academically and socially in the environment she had argued so vehemently to join. Her father's recent denial of her request to obtain a driver's permit had stimulated a serious argument the previous weekend. His stated reasoning, "It's too dangerous. Suppose you don't hear a fire engine coming?" angered Kris and hurt her deeply, causing her to have doubts about her ability to be loved and to live a normal lifestyle within the family regardless of her educational or communication achievements.

Kris's self-esteem had eroded steadily after an initial "high" on entering school. In addition to the family conflicts, the social skills on which she previously relied ("passing" as a normally hearing person and telling "hearing" jokes) were ineffective in the deaf school environment, where one's ASL proficiency, Deaf pride, and Deaf sociocultural characteristics were most valued. Kris didn't know with whom she could discuss these struggles (certainly not her parents), and she hardly understood them herself. By now, Kris had begun losing interest in making friends and maintaining good grades. Trips home only worsened her mood. However, because she maintained her weight and demonstrated no other noticeable changes in her behavior, her family members and peers were generally unaware of her bulimia and intrapersonal turmoil.

Before we ended our first session, I addressed issues regarding confidentiality, communication with her family, and how we would handle any situations where we saw one another outside the therapy office. This latter issue was important to raise at the outset of treatment, given the small size of the Deaf community in most regions of the country and the likelihood that a deaf therapist will see deaf clients at community events. When discussed in advance,

such occasions are usually not problematic and can even serve to strengthen community members' trust that the therapist is a part of, and in tune with, Deaf community issues and values.

Comments

The issues Kris and her family faced in her transition to the school for the deaf are not unusual, regardless of whether they take place in the deaf child's adolescence or earlier. It was the rigidity and narrowness of the Clarks's attitudes and perceptions, and Kris's own excessive prior investment in "passing" as a hearing child, that made her transition more difficult. There were also few sources of information or support available to or known by the Clarks during Kris's early education. Note that the stress the family experienced had more to do with unrecognized and unresolved psychological issues than with overt medical, communication, or educational issues regarding deafness. Note, too, the contribution and complexity of the multiple systems affecting the family, including the health care system, the deaf education system, networks of other families with deaf children, and the sociocultural Deaf community. These various systems have profound influence on families with deaf children and can help or aggravate the challenges these families face. Providers who render treatment to deaf consumers and their families must be informed about the nature and significance of these systems.

My initial contacts with George Clark and Kris reflected the importance of systems issues. George exhibited his role as director of medical, educational, and other services for Kris in his meticulous telephone conversation. His strong "oral" bias was immediately evident and important for me to bear in mind (and not challenge) in understanding and addressing family conflict around communication issues. His most emotive moment, in expressing his deeper recognition that signing was helpful to Kris, stimulated my empathy for the pain and ambivalence he must harbor, most likely created by value conflicts between the systems to which he had been exposed, without adequate opportunity to come to his own understandings and conclusions about communication issues.

The new school environment in which Kris

found herself was more complex and challenging than she had anticipated. It disrupted familiar patterns of being and coping, strongly challenged her delicate adolescent sense of identity, and left her with few immediate sources of support. Her hesitancy to reveal her name or acknowledge her need for help reflected the shame she felt at her latest "failure." It also reflected the reality that the Deaf community in most cities is small and closely knit and that seeking mental health treatment is unfortunately a stigma risk, just as it is for the general population.

My addressing communication as the first topic of business was critical; it declared a recognition that the deaf experience prioritizes clear communication above all else. Communication inadequacies, including those within families, are pervasive in the lives of most deaf people. Beyond the practical utility of such deliberate communication planning (because deaf people's communication preferences vary), this intervention immediately framed therapy as understanding and respectful of Kris's experiences as a deaf individual (as well as my own) and as a process that would be different and more comfortable than her typical intercourse with the outside world. I hoped this beginning would encourage further investment and disclosure in therapy. Harvey (1989) described the process of collaborating and connecting with deaf clients around the issue of communication as "linguistic matching."

Kris's unconscious transition from her stated ASL preference to a more English-oriented signing syntax was a powerful observation. It meant that she overtly wanted to portray herself as culturally and linguistically Deaf when in reality, her history—and, a short time later, her relaxed signing modality—was inconsistent with that. I needed to gravitate to a more English-like signing style (without calling attention to it), to keep the technical aspects of our communication at maximum comprehensibility, yet recognize that she had made an important statement about who she wanted to be, at least for the moment. Given what I'd already learned about her father, this set the stage for a critical deaf–hearing family conflict, one that is commonly observed when serving this population.

It is also common to observe a marked increase in family tensions regarding communication and independence demands when deaf individuals return home after experiencing new, immersionlike deaf environments. This is what the Clarks began to experience on weekends, further stimulating unresolved psychological conflicts within the family. (By the way, deaf individuals can and do drive, with better safety records than hearing people.) Kris's bulimia, of course, was not a deaf issue per se; neither is it typical of deaf individuals in her circumstances. This behavior needed to be understood in a mental health context, informed, of course, by the biopsychosocial and systemic issues related to it.

THE EARLY COURSE OF THERAPY

Over the next few sessions, I learned a great deal more from Kris about her family and her tumultuous emotional state. She harbored deep-seated feelings of guilt and inadequacy over her hearing loss. She felt like a burden to her family and was ashamed of her lack of social and academic success, especially in contrast to her brother Trevor. Kris envied the pride, comfort, and ease of socialization she saw in her brothers and many of her deaf peers, but she felt so different from them inside, doubting she could ever achieve security in her identity. Although I would have preferred to engage the family in treatment at this early stage, the 2-hour driving distance from my office precluded family sessions for the time being.

The message of Kris's inadequacies had been ingrained in her from her earliest years, not only by her parents (or so Kris felt) but also by audiologists and speech pathologists, who overtly expressed their disappointment with her hearing, speech, and speech-reading abilities, and by teachers at school, who frequently blamed her lack of comprehension, lower fund of information, and slower progress in language achievement areas on "inconsistent effort" or inaccurate perceptions of limited intellectual ability. In fact, these difficulties were the consequence of long-standing inadequacies in her communication environment.

Since enrolling at the school for the deaf, Kris perceived her parents as pulling away from her, just when the identity challenges of her new environment and the physical distance from her family were increasing her need for their approval and guidance. Kris's weekend visits home were disappointing in her realization that the family members' lives had "gone on" in her absence and that she was not suddenly the center of their weekends just because she was home. The foci of Kris's anger and yearnings vacillated among her parents, herself, and her past and current educational and social environments. Her binge eating and purging behaviors arose from these tumultuous dynamics of shame and anger and control and nurturance desires.

The school's Christmas vacation was soon to begin. In our fourth and final session before the break, Kris shared her dread at the thought of spending 3 weeks with her parents (although she missed Jason terribly) and returning to the communication and personal-affirmation inadequacies of her home environment. She only half-jokingly asked if she could stay with me through Christmas break, projecting and commenting on the wonderful family environment that must exist at my home, given my multiple communication abilities and my achievements as a hard-of-hearing psychologist. We discussed a number of coping and stress reduction strategies in preparation for her return home, but I was secretly worried that a crisis of some sort would arise.

THE CRISIS

I received a call from the hospital's psychiatric emergency department a day before the scheduled break was to begin. Kris had ingested about 15 headache tablets in the dormitory but told her roommate immediately. I was contacted by a psychiatry resident who requested a telephone consult to better understand Kris's current situation. (Kris had been cleared, medically.) When I asked if there was a sign language interpreter present, the resident said he did not need one because "she speaks fine." I asked him to consider if communication *for Kris* might go better through an interpreter. He acknowledged that he hadn't asked her (neither, however, had Kris asserted

her right to an interpreter per the Americans with Disabilities Act). After the resident discussed communication with Kris, an interpreter was called in. Kris was admitted to the hospital's psychiatric unit to assure her safety until her support system could be strengthened. Although she was no longer stating that she was suicidal, school was closing the next afternoon, and her parents could not arrive until then. (Her parents had been contacted by the hospital.)

George Clark called me a short time later, with Margaret on the extension telephone. They were both quite distressed. I was struck by the intensity with which they expressed their obvious love and concern for their daughter, in contrast to the picture Kris had been painting. The Clarks had been told by the attending physician that if Kris felt safe in the morning and spent an uneventful night in the hospital, she could be discharged to their care the next day. We planned for a session in my office the next afternoon. The Clarks indicated that Jason would attend as well, because he wanted to make the trip to pick up his sister from the hospital. Trevor had not arrived home from college yet.

THE FIRST FAMILY SESSION

Prior to the session, I had arranged for a sign language interpreter to be present. In my office, I had situated four chairs in a linear fashion, with one chair positioned directly across from the rest. Another chair was off to one side. The interpreter arrived a few minutes early so I could brief her on Kris's preferred communication mode and the nature of the session's objectives. I had worked with this interpreter numerous times. She not only was certified in English–ASL translation,[7] but she also was familiar and comfortable with the dynamics that often take place in family therapy.

We met the Clark family together in the waiting room and introduced ourselves. The family members' facial expressions spoke volumes when the interpreter was introduced. All were obviously surprised. George and Margaret appeared silently

---

[7] Professional sign language interpreters are certified by the Registry of Interpreters for the Deaf. They earn certificates that verify different linguistic competencies (e.g., English–ASL translation, English–Signed English translation) and knowledge regarding professional roles and ethics.

offended. Kris was wide eyed, clearly shocked, although I couldn't read her affect. Jason, who was wearing a baseball cap so low that it hid his eyes, raised his head when he shook the interpreter's hand, revealing quite a smile.

I had a strong internal reaction to George immediately on seeing him; he had a bushy moustache that made speechreading nearly impossible for me, even with my residual hearing ability. I could only imagine how much Kris must labor to understand him, with her more severe hearing loss. That it hadn't occurred to him, or been important enough to him, to shave it raised feelings in me that I had to monitor closely to prevent interference with my empathy for his own struggles and with what I knew was the importance of "joining" with this strong family leader in treatment.

We entered the office, and the family members chose their seats. From left to right sat George, Margaret, Kris, then Jason. Jason scooted his chair to the side, obviously to be in more direct visual contact with Kris. George pointed to the chair I had placed off to one side, which was closest to him, and suggested that the interpreter sit there, which she did, after she caught my eye for consent. I sat in the chair across from the family.

Before the interpreter had settled into her seat, I silently signed to Kris, "You're going to have difficulty seeing and understanding everyone." She rolled her eyes and used an ASL sign that means "same old thing." To my surprise, Jason laughed out loud. His parents quickly directed their anger toward him, although clearly they were mad at our ASL exchange: "What's going on; why are you laughing?" Again to my surprise, Jason responded with an accurate translation of what Kris and I had signed to one another. He appeared quite pleased with his ability to "one up" his parents and gave me an approving smile. I apologized specifically to George and Margaret, acknowledging that I was wrong and that "I know how it feels to be excluded from conversation happening right in front of you." I was confident they understood the deeper message, judging from how their facial expressions instantly lost their angry quality.

I further explained that the interpreter had not "voiced" our exchange because I began signing before she was seated and looking at me. "Why do we need her anyway?" Margaret asked. "We communicate just fine on our own."

"And you speak as well as Kris," George added, as he scowled at his daughter, who was leaning forward, nearly falling off of her chair in order to see the interpreter at the other end.

"I am glad you understand me and Kris well," I said (while simultaneously signing in English), but I cannot understand you well, especially with the way your moustache obscures your lips. What about you, Kris?"

"I want to understand," she said simply; "I want her to stay." With that, George and Margaret nodded their assent. Jason then tugged at Kris's chair, and the two of them moved so that Kris could easily view the interpreter, me, and her parents. The interpreter moved her chair slightly, leaving the family and me in a sort of circle, with the interpreter slightly on the outside but clearly visible. I smiled at her obvious experience that this was ideal, both for communication and for maximizing the bond between me and the family members.

The remainder of the session was focused on Kris's overdose, her bulimic behavior, and plans for ensuring her safety and mental health during the upcoming Christmas vacation. Kris vehemently denied current suicidal intent, explaining that she just felt "out of control" and frightened at the prospect of her 3-week vacation at home. This led to a discussion of the feelings that underlay her bulimic behaviors.

Kris's parents were aware of the seriousness and psychological complexity of eating disorders, based on reading they had done subsequent to the school's initial referral of Kris to me 6 weeks earlier. They also had some appreciation for the ambivalence Kris felt regarding her newfound independence. However, George and Margaret were genuinely surprised (and hurt) that Kris experienced returning home as unpleasant. As they expressed their love and concern for her in tender and articulate terms, Kris began to weep.

Margaret came to her daughter's side for a long embrace. George left his chair to kneel beside his wife, putting his hand on Kris's shoulder. Jason put his hand on Kris's other shoulder. The interpreter moved to a position near, but still behind, George and Margaret, signing "Oh, my sweetheart; I'm so sorry," and other such comments that Margaret was whispering but which Kris, of course, could not see or hear. Kris's eyes were riveted on the interpreter. George saw this and, turning to the interpreter, said "Please, we can talk to our own daughter!"

"Not like that," Jason interjected, in a biting comment that caught his father off guard. Kris nodded her agreement, and her tears intensified.

"Young man," George began, "you don't know the first thing about what we've tried to do for your sister."

"Please . . . !" Margaret implored, not finishing her thought. I asked the family and the interpreter to return to their seats. As they parted, Kris signed "I love you" silently to her mother, who understood this popular sign. "There's a lot happening here," I observed. We did our best in the time remaining to identify the many issues that had been raised, plan for a safe vacation, and set the stage for future sessions. The family agreed to return for another session in 3 weeks, when they would drop Kris off for school again.

Comments

Much of what transpired in this session is common in psychotherapy with mixed deaf–hearing families, although some events reflected unique aspects of the Clarks' relationships and interpersonal dynamics. The presence of the interpreter frequently draws powerful transference reactions, usually from the parents, and stimulates other therapeutically informative interactions. Countertransference issues, too, can be significant. I found myself recognizing strong and familiar feelings when observing how the Clark family's characteristics mirrored those of my own upbringing in an all-hearing family.

As I suspected, Kris relied heavily on the interpreter during the session, suggesting that communication at home was indeed inadequate—far poorer than George and Margaret realized. Like the psychiatric resident at the hospital, their ready comprehension of Kris's speech (and, just as likely, their history of educational and emotional investment in oral communication) biased their perception of Kris's own level of comprehension. Yet, over the course of

the session, they subtly recognized how much more they could talk about when signing was permitted. By the end of the session, the interpreter (and the modality of communication per se) had faded into the background, leaving the content of the communication in the foreground. This was a more effective lesson than could have been taught through a debate on communication methods or other awkward and defense-inducing approaches, such as me translating between Kris and the family or demanding that they sign, write, or rephrase until Kris understood. Harvey (1989) described how a child's hearing loss is sometimes "figure" (the focal topic at hand) and sometimes "ground" (a background issue) in family therapy sessions. He also described how therapists can use this figure–ground shift to further particular treatment objectives.

The interpreter's presence also stimulated dynamic events that were instructive to me. I judged George's anger at the interpreter's proximity during the embrace, Jason's verbal barb, and Margaret's whispered apologies to reflect deeper individual issues with which each of these people were dealing. It is common for the interpreter to draw powerful reactions from family members, in particular, parental feelings of guilt and resentment at the ease with which the interpreter communicates with the child they have loved and raised yet with whom they struggle to communicate. Transference reactions involving the interpreter are common and must be dealt with by the therapist without directly involving the interpreter, who must be left free to perform his or her professional duty, keeping the dynamic focus on the family.

I also learned about Jason in this session. He was acutely attuned to the above communication issues, had picked up a considerable degree of sign language from his sister (underscoring their closeness) and, for reasons I was not yet sure of, readily willing to confront his parents on Kris's behalf. I would come to understand this better in our next family session.

THE SECOND FAMILY SESSION

During her vacation at home, I monitored Kris's safety and touched base with George and Margaret through weekly telephone calls (using both voice and TTY). The family returned for a session at my office 3 weeks later, as planned. I immediately noticed that George's moustache was neatly trimmed and no longer obscured his lips. This was a small but important step that had both practical and dynamic significance, showing that he could listen and change. "Mr. Clark, you have a different moustache," I chose to say. "It was time for a change in style," he responded; "Big whiskers went out with the Civil War." Our shared laughter strengthened the bond between us, and I added as we all walked into the office how much easier it was to understand him. He nodded knowingly.

The selection of seats was also different than at the end of the prior session. George again took charge but arranged the chairs as they had been previously, with good visual contact among all present. He even placed the interpreter's chair beside and slightly behind his, as it was before. Jason again sat farthest from his father.

We began with a review of the intervening 3 weeks. Kris had remained safe throughout vacation and reported no binge or purge episodes. She complained that her parents were still against the idea of her obtaining a driver's license and stated that she was going to "get one anyway" by enrolling in driver's education at school this semester.

"You are so lucky," Jason said jealously. I asked him to explain.

He described his image of Kris's school as a place where you could have all the freedom you want, "with no one looking over your shoulder all the time, picking on every damn thing you do." In further discussion, he revealed his anger and jealousy at how Kris's (and Trevor's) departure to school had increased the time and attention his parents paid to him, which he did not welcome. "You are so lucky," he repeated to Kris (but really to his parents). "I wish I was deaf."

To my surprise, Kris took Jason on:

> *You think it's fun to be deaf? You think it's fun to live 2 hours from home in a stinky old dorm? Fine, you be deaf and I'll be hearing, and then I'll go back to Central High, and you can stay here.*

George and Margaret encouraged Kris to come home if she wished. She recanted, noting that she really wanted to attend the school for the deaf but wished that Jason would understand that "it's hard to be deaf." Jason scowled, and Margaret stroked Kris's shoulder. "I know, sweetheart," she said quietly. "I know."

Margaret's empathy and George's resistance to Kris obtaining a driver's license caused me to wonder how they had come to picture the lives of average deaf people. I had learned through supervision that exploration of parents' earliest recollected exposure to a deaf person often revealed useful therapeutic material. Margaret indicated that she had never met a deaf person in her youth but recalled how sorry she felt for the pitiful deaf character in Carson McCullers's novel *The Heart is a Lonely Hunter*, which she read during college. George shared that he had grown up in a small town where one deaf boy also lived. Poorly parented and uneducated (public education for children with disabilities was not mandated until 1973), this boy was the town hoodlum with plenty of time on his hands. When George was 12 years old, the boy was struck and killed by a car while evading the police in a foot-chase. "He didn't hear it coming," George said. After a pause, his thoughts returned to the present; "So I made sure we got one of those 'Deaf Child Area' signs for Kris as soon as we found out she couldn't hear."

"I hate that sign," challenged Kris. "I know how to cross a street by now! Do you think *she's* got a sign outside her house (referring to me) so that *she* won't get hit by a car?" I couldn't help snickering at that thought, and George smiled, too. I described how parents' decisions about raising deaf children are shaped by many things, by early childhood recollections of deaf people, by deaf characters in the media, and especially by physicians' portrayals of what life with deafness is like. Rarely, however, do such sources provide information that is positive or as extensive and diverse at it should be for yielding a valid picture of the lives of deaf adults. "It's hard not to do everything you can to protect your deaf child," I explained to Kris, "if the only deaf person you ever met was hit by a car."

"But that's unrealistic," Jason accurately observed.

"Deaf kids learn how to cross the street just like other kids do."

"I know," I responded, "but your father's feelings are loving and understandable. He did not grow up knowing as much about deaf people as you do." George then asked me several questions about driving and traffic safety with "other deaf people," which I was able to expand into a broader discussion about functional, educational, vocational, social, and other types of diversity in the deaf population.

With our remaining time we discussed plans for the immediate future, in light of what had been raised in today's session. A number of compromises were reached. Jason would pick up Kris at school on alternate weekends, allowing him some additional freedom from home. George or Margaret would pick her up the remaining weekends and participate in more of the school's parent–student activities that were organized for Fridays and Sundays.

In discussing this plan, which pleased Kris greatly, I could sense some trepidation from George and Margaret. "What concerns you about this?" I asked. They expressed fears of feeling awkward among the more ASL-oriented students and parents and being unable to communicate with them. "Lots of parents don't sign," Kris said encouragingly, "and Lorie's parents will be there; you like them."

"Yes," I said, "there are lots of different types of families, and all are welcomed. Besides, what's important is that Kris is *your* daughter; she doesn't belong to the school, and they wouldn't want it that way." This comment seemed to allay their anxieties, which I thought were based in long-standing competence fears and inaccurate images of "losing" Kris to an antagonistic Deaf world.

Comments

The moustache incident reinforced several important lessons. Although George had not shaved it completely, as I had wished at the time of the first family session, he had voluntarily made some accommodation to Kris's communication needs, and that was something to celebrate. He showed this new attitude again in his arrangement of the chairs. These events reminded me that progress in therapy must allow family members to "be themselves" as they simulta-

neously work toward growth, change, and conflict resolution. My fantasies of a clean shaven, sign fluent George Clark were unrealistic and based in my own countertransference. To push communication changes on George and Margaret too quickly would have risked severing the very relationship I was trying to develop.

The session's lessons about Jason were equally important. Too often, the deaf–hearing conflicts in a family can overshadow the presence of other, equally significant concerns that have nothing to do with hearing loss issues but may be played out through them. Jason had his own problems and conflicts with his parents. Fighting for his sister's rights provided the perfect "stage" on which to act out his own undeclared anger. Because of my countertransference feelings, this even fooled me for awhile.

I first thought that Jason's willingness to spar with his parents on Kris's behalf reflected his closeness to her and greater perceptiveness about her communication and identity needs as a deaf individual. He was saying things that part of me wanted to say to George Clark. But when we discussed his jealousy of Kris's geographic independence, I began to recognize that this was not simply a deafness issue, but a parent–adolescent independence conflict regarding Jason himself, being played out through the safety of deaf issues he knew about. In later sessions, I eventually learned that Jason had engaged in quite a bit of unruly and risky behavior when Trevor and Kris previously lived at home. Trevor's demanding and lauded schedule of sports, academic, and civic leadership activities drew much of his parents' time and positive attention. Kris's special education and other needs had drawn much of the rest of George and Margaret's available time (and negative attention), leaving Jason with little guidance and supervision—independence that he came to enjoy. He was now rebelling against the increased scrutiny (and overdue supervision) he was experiencing in Trevor's and Kris's absence.

Kris's ambivalence about attending the school for the deaf resurfaced in this session. The agreement George and Margaret made to attend more school functions helped Kris feel more bonded to her parents, whom she had missed since leaving home. The agreement would have the additional benefit of broadening George's and Margaret's exposure to diversity in deaf people and their families. Their formation of narrow, negative preconceptions of the lives and abilities of deaf people, stemming from lack of information and negative youthful influences, is a common phenomenon. It was aggravated by pressure from systems beyond the family, especially the medical–pathological perspective (see Pollard, 1996a, 1996b) on sign-language-using deaf people that influenced George and Margaret for so long. The unknown nature of the seemingly powerful Deaf community, about which the Clarks had only vaguely heard, further aggravated their hesitancy to explore this aspect of Kris's life. Their doing so through these school activities would assist Kris in resolving her own mixed feelings about her communication and socialization choices.

CONCLUSION

I continued to see Kris every 2 weeks for the remainder of the school year and somewhat less frequently thereafter. She had no further suicidal ideation and greatly reduced but did not eliminate her bulimic behavior. Gaining full control over these symptoms would require additional insights into their psychodynamic origin and further increases in her coping resources. Kris joined an Overeaters Anonymous group that employed a sign language interpreter. She found the support she received there very helpful and began to understand that the dynamics of eating disorders are complex and not solely related to the deaf–hearing issues with which she had to contend. She continued to struggle with her sense of identity and her ambivalent feelings about independence from her family. Slow but steady progress in these areas continued to be evidenced as we explored how common deaf–hearing issues versus unique Clark family dynamics influenced these developmental challenges.

I saw the other Clark family members every month or two; I even met Trevor. He was able to help both Kris and me understand that family conflicts were not unique to Kris and Jason. Trevor himself had his share of run-ins with George over issues of freedom and responsibility. Kris was not

aware of this because she had not been told about, nor had she overheard, their arguments. "I guess I'm not the only problem child," Kris said, in a freeing and insightful moment.

Jason and his parents began to deal with their own concerns more directly. I referred them to a family therapist colleague in their home town, and they had productive sessions with him. This further reduced family tensions and helped distinguish what were family issues, what were each member's personal issues, and what were unique deaf–hearing issues.

George and Margaret followed through on their agreement to become more involved in Kris's school activities. They saw her perform a number of roles in school plays. (Kris achieved considerable acclaim in theater at the school for the deaf, an activity that was not accessible to her in her former school.) George accepted a position on the school's advisory board, where his business acumen was greatly valued. Margaret befriended the school nurse and began consulting with teachers about needed improvements in the students' health care curriculum. She also became more proficient in sign language. George, always emphatic about the importance of oral communication skills, nevertheless learned to use a few common ASL expressions.

Deafness should not be viewed simply from a medical perspective. Focusing exclusively on amplification and speech training misses the larger picture. The onset of deafness, particularly when it occurs early in a child's life, can have a profound impact on family relationships, language, cognition, socialization, identity, self-esteem, and academic and vocational achievement. However, deafness itself does not impede development in these areas; rather, healthy cognitive and psychosocial development depends on how the hearing loss is perceived and dealt with by the individual, the family, the educational system, the community, and society as a whole. The impact and the outcome are interactive. There are no simple answers to the challenges of growing up deaf, raising and educating deaf children, or making our society accessible and equitable to people with hearing loss or other disabilities. Yet there is a rich history of Deaf culture, deaf achievement, and fulfillment in the lives of many deaf people that suggests that deafness in a family is best conceived as an aspect of human diversity to be understood and embraced, not a tragedy to be borne or simply a condition to be treated.

Suggested Reading

Dolnick, E. (1993, September). Deafness as culture. *The Atlantic Monthly,* 37–53.

Elliott, H., Glass, L., & Evans, J. W. (Eds.). (1988). *Mental health assessment of deaf clients: A practical manual.* Boston, MA: Little, Brown.

Glickman, N., & Harvey, M. (1996). *Culturally affirmative psychotherapy with deaf persons.* Mahwah, NJ: Erlbaum.

Harvey, M. A. (1985). Toward a dialogue between the paradigms of family therapy and deafness. *American Annals of the Deaf, 130,* 305–314.

Lane, H. (1988). Is there "a psychology of the deaf"? *Exceptional Children, 55,* 7–19.

Lane, H. (1992). *The mask of benevolence: Disabling the deaf community.* New York: Knopf.

Lane, H., Hoffmeister, R., & Bahan, B. (1996). *A journey into the deaf-world.* San Diego, CA: Dawn Sign Press.

Leigh, I. W., Corbett, C. A., Gutman, V., & Morere, D. A. (1996). Providing psychological services to deaf individuals: A response to new perceptions of diversity. *Professional Psychology: Research and Practice, 27,* 364–371.

Moses, K. L. (1985). Dynamic interventions with families. In E. Cherow (Ed.), *Hearing-impaired children and youth with developmental disabilities* (pp. 82–98). Washington, DC: Gallaudet University Press.

Myers, R. R. (1995). *Standards of care for the delivery of mental health services to deaf and hard of hearing persons.* Silver Spring, MD: National Association of the Deaf.

Padden, C., & Humphries, T. (1988). *Deaf in America: Voices from a culture.* Cambridge, MA: Harvard University Press.

Pollard, R. Q (1993). 100 years in psychology and deafness: A centennial retrospective. *Journal of the American Deafness and Rehabilitation Association, 26*(3), 32–46.

Pollard, R. Q (1994). Public mental health service and diagnostic trends regarding individuals who are deaf or hard of hearing. *Rehabilitation Psychology, 39,* 147–160.

Pollard, R. Q (1998). Psychopathology. In M.

Marschark & D. Clark (Eds.), *Psychological perspectives on deafness* (Vol. 2). Mahwah, NJ: Erlbaum.

Sacks, O. (1989). *Seeing voices: A journey into the world of the deaf.* Berkeley: University of California Press.

Steinberg, A. (1991). Issues in providing mental health services to hearing-impaired persons. *Hospital and Community Psychiatry, 42,* 380–389.

Trychin, S. (1991). *Manual for mental health professionals Part II: Psycho-social challenges faced by hard of hearing people.* Washington, DC: Gallaudet University Press.

References

Harvey, M. (1989). *Psychotherapy with deaf and hard of hearing persons: A systemic model.* Hillsdale, NJ: Erlbaum.

Marschark, M. (1997). *Raising and educating deaf children.* New York: Oxford University Press.

Pollard, R. Q (1996a). Conceptualizing and conducting pre-operative psychological assessments of cochlear implant candidates. *Journal of Deaf Studies and Deaf Education, 1,* 16–28.

Pollard, R. Q (1996b). Professional psychology and deaf people: The emergence of a discipline. *American Psychologist, 51,* 389–396.

Schlesinger, H. S. (1976). Total communication in perspective. In D. M. Luterman (Ed.), *Deafness in perspective* (pp. 87–116). San Diego, CA: College-Hill Press.

Schlesinger, H. S. (1987). Effects of powerlessness on dialogue and development: Disability, poverty, and the human condition. In B. W. Heller, L. M. Flohr, & L. S. Zegans (Eds.), *Psychosocial interventions with sensorially disabled persons* (pp. 1–27). Orlando, FL: Grune & Stratton.

Schlesinger, H. S. (1988). Questions and answers in the development of deaf children. In M. Strong (Ed.), *Language, learning, and deafness* (pp. 261–291). Cambridge, England: Cambridge University Press.

Schlesinger, H. S. (1992). Elusive X factor: Parental contributions to literacy. In M. Walworth, D. F. Moores, & T. J. O'Rourke (Eds.), *A free hand: Enfranchising the education of deaf children* (pp. 37–64). Silver Spring, MD: T. J.

Schlesinger, H. S., & Meadow, K. P. (1972). *Sound and sign: Childhood deafness and mental health.* Berkeley: University of California Press.

CHAPTER 16

GRIEF AND CULTURAL TRANSITION: A JOURNEY OUT OF DESPAIR

Susan H. Horwitz

Gwen, a beautiful Chinese woman in her 50s, settled in the United States with her second husband John. She recently returned to her birthplace, Hong Kong, to visit with her son Stephen. On the way, she decided to travel to Australia, where Anna, her 30-year-old Eurasian daughter, resided with her husband of 2 years.

During this visit, Gwen sensed that Anna was depressed. Although Anna was guarded with her, Gwen knew that her daughter was in serious trouble. Anna's husband was careful to put his best foot forward in Gwen's presence. Nonetheless, Gwen began to piece together Anna's painful situation. She could see that Anna, in her desire to be a "good wife," worked hard to cope with her husband's verbal and psychological abuse, trying to convince herself that her marriage would get better.

Gwen left Australia deeply concerned about her daughter's precarious situation. After a week's visit with Stephen, she could no longer contain her anxiety and decided she must return to Australia. Once there, she implored Anna to come to the United States with her for several months in order to gain distance from the abuse and to reassess her situation.

On arriving home in Rochester, New York, with Anna, Gwen made arrangements for her to enter therapy at Strong Family Therapy Services, Department of Psychiatry, University of Rochester Medical Center. Gwen accompanied her daughter to the first session. Anna's stepfather John chose not to attend the first meeting but agreed with Gwen that he would attend future sessions as needed. In the first session Anna described her goals as, first, to understand how she had allowed herself to be treated so poorly and why she had stayed in this abusive relationship for 2 years and, second, to gather strength to get on with her life, independent of this relationship. Gwen's goals were similar in that she wanted Anna to find purposeful work while maintaining herself economically, psychologically, and emotionally. Most of all, Gwen wanted Anna to feel safe and proud of her accomplishments.

I asked Gwen and Anna to share with me a bit of history about their mother–daughter relationship, as well as information about the family. At first they were reluctant to express their thoughts and feelings. When I asked about their hesitancy, Anna told me that she did not want to hurt her mother in any way. Gwen reported that Anna had been through so much disruption that bringing up the "old wounds" might be damaging. I encouraged them to share their feelings with one another and with me. I assured them that I would listen carefully and use their experience to help them reach their goals. I knew that if we did not work on the pain of the past, then we would not be successful in helping Anna. They agreed to talk about their extraordinary history.

As the two women recounted their story, I listened carefully, at times tearfully, while I organized the information in my mind. As therapists we train ourselves to think on several levels simultaneously. I worked hard to maintain some objectivity by drawing mental pictures of transitional maps for the first several minutes.[1] The multigenerational patterns of transition, sacrifice, devotion, loss, and pain experienced by the women in Anna's family emerged quickly and graphically.

Gwen grew up in Hong Kong, where her father and mother raised her with an older sister (see Figures 16.1 and 16.2). Her childhood was filled with tension between her parents. Gwen came to understand their discord when she learned that her father was simultaneously married to another woman—a custom permitted by Chinese culture but not easily accepted by Gwen's mother. He also fathered a son and four daughters with his second wife. Gwen's mother, a well-educated and intelligent woman whose father had taught her "the classics," was unhappy about her husband's dual life and imparted much of her anger and frustration to Gwen as the years went by. Even so, her mother remained in the marriage despite her feelings of rejection and sadness.

The painful commitments of obligation and loyalty in this family triggered deep appreciation in me for the freedom my father gave me just before he died. As the second daughter born to a 39-year-old father who was never to have the son for which he so desperately wished, I had always been confused about my role in my family. The mixed messages were constant. Should I strive to be "accomplished," like my father, or "a good housewife and mother," like my mother? There was no clear option to be both accomplished and a good housewife and mother. However, a few months before my father died, I went to him, at the suggestion of my supervisor, to discuss my confusion and ambivalence about my professional path. He was clear in his admiration for my accomplishments and his faith in me to do whatever I thought was important with my life. Several times during

our talk I asked permission to move in this direction or that. Unequivocally, he blessed everything I did and wanted to do. Somehow, he had grown beyond my childhood experience of him, which I discovered only during these life-changing conversations. I would have never been free to leave the narrow script imposed on me, and also self-imposed, had he not intervened. This personal experience helped me see that Anna was trapped by at least the two generations of female scripts that had preceded her. I knew, as her therapist, that I was powerless to free her. My first challenge was to find a way to free Gwen from her inheritance of pain and isolation so that Gwen could free her daughter. I decided to gather more information. The answer would be in their story. I just needed to be patient, listen carefully, and seize the opportunity whenever it presented itself.

When Gwen was 30 years old, she met her first husband Michael in a bar in Hong Kong. He was the only child of Russian immigrants who had experienced several cultural transitions prior to making their home in Australia. Michael's mother's family had fled Leningrad, Russia, in 1917 during the Bolshevik Revolution and escaped to China, where his mother Victoria, a brother, and a stepsister were raised. It was there that Victoria's brother died at age 17 from tuberculosis, a loss from which she never recovered. She met her husband in China, where in the early 1920s they married. In 1956, when Michael was 28, the family immigrated to Australia. Six years later, Michael's father died of a massive heart attack.

All the men abandon them through death or disloyalty. I was reminded of a book I read a long time ago, called Herland: The Lost Female Utopia, *by Charlotte Perkins Gilman (1979), in which a society of women had survived and spawned female*

---

[1]For a description of transitional mapping, refer to Seaburn, Landau-Stanton, and Horwitz (1995). A further explanation can be found in Landau-Stanton, Clements, and Associates (1993).

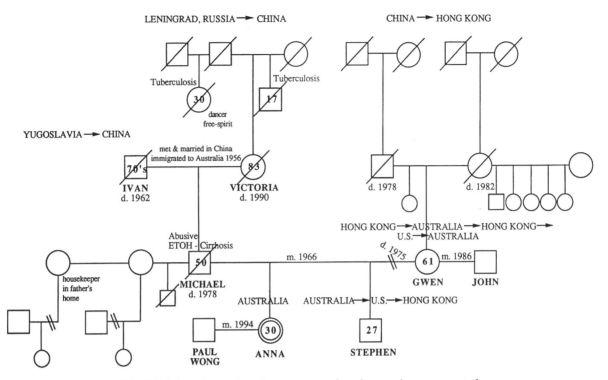

FIGURE 16.1. Anna's family genogram. d. = deceased; m. = married.

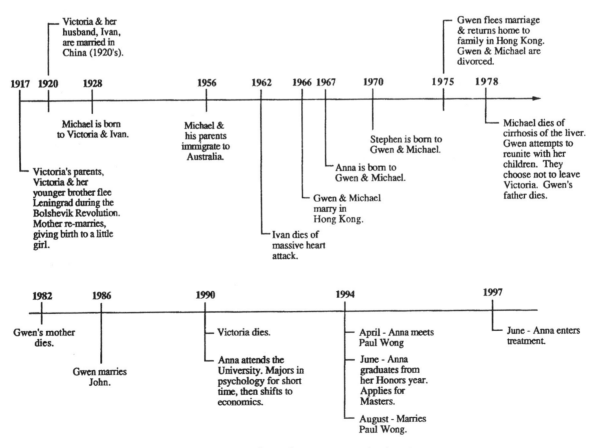

FIGURE 16.2. Timeline of major events in Anna's story.

children after their husbands, fathers, and brothers had left for war. The men could never return because the pass between the mountains had become blocked, destroying the only route back to their homes and families. In this all-female society the children were raised in full awareness of their competencies and expected to assume a role based on their natural talents and interests. The story revolved around three men whose airplane crashes inside the territory of Herland and how each of them both challenged and contributed new ideas to the society of women. In Herland, the women were comfortable and secure without male family members. In Anna's family, the difference was striking. The women suffered the losses of their men but could not move beyond the emptiness. Mired in this state of emotional paralysis, the women in Gwen's and Anna's family were frozen in their attempts to develop and realize their potential. Herland is a fascinating portrayal of women's strengths and competencies, in 1979 a timely contribution to the growing intensity of the women's movement. Although fictional, there was a message within the story for Gwen and for Anna: "Move beyond the grief and grow into the beautiful and capable women you can become." My second challenge became finding a way to create healing pathways despite feelings of abandonment and rage.

In 1966, 4 years after Michael's father's death, Michael and Gwen were married. Gwen gave birth to Anna the following year and 3 years later had Stephen. The marriage was fraught with tension because Michael was an alcoholic and physically and emotionally abusive to the stoic and shy Gwen. When Anna was 8 and Stephen was 5, Gwen, fearful for her life, fled Australia and her abusive relationship with Michael. She returned to her family in Hong Kong (Gwen and Anna began to cry at this point in the story). She tried to take the children with her, but her husband threatened to kill her if

she left the country with them. The pain of that separation for Gwen and for Anna was so intense that it created a wound that haunted them both until the end of the therapy and, perhaps, beyond.

I listened and watched as the tearful Gwen related this story. Imagine having to choose between motherhood and survival—a cruel ordeal! Anna also listened and cried. It was clear from the pained look on her face that she knew at least some of this story. I asked her what she was thinking as her mother spoke. Anna said that she remembered lying in bed at night, wondering if her mother left because of something Anna had done. Her father and grandmother never spoke about what led up to Gwen's leaving.

Having almost lost a daughter in a motor vehicle accident 2 years ago, my heart broke during this part of Gwen's story. I tried to imagine the fear and the depth of her pain. I found myself reflecting back to a moment in time when my daughter, still in a wheelchair and weak, but clearly on the mend, was asked to come before our religious congregation to recite a prayer of thanksgiving for her survival and recovery. Her child's thin voice came over the public address system, reciting an unfamiliar prayer in perfect Hebrew. I wept for the joy of her restoring health, her intact intellectual ability, and for the terror of what might have been. I could have been there that day saying Kaddish (the Jewish prayer for the dead). I deeply admired Gwen. Could I have survived such a separation? This woman was teaching me a lot about courage. I began to see a pathway that would lead to the ultimate intervention.

Gwen kept in contact with her children from Hong Kong through telephone calls, letters, and sporadic visits to Australia, as both opportunity and money allowed. Anna and Stephen were confused about their mother's role in their lives because their father was unkind in his descriptions of her and her presence in their lives was so sporadic. The children lived with their father during the week and spent weekends with Victoria, their paternal grandmother. According to Anna, Victoria doted on Stephen, infantilizing him and spoiling him, while she demanded that Anna take care of her little brother and be available to help with household chores.

Victoria's influence was very strong. She schooled the children on the ways of Russian living: customs, manners, gender expectations, and so on. She was clear about her disregard for Chinese people and would often tell the children they did not "look" Chinese; they looked European.

> *Anna interrupted her mother to tell me that she had always been confused by this idea; when she looked in the mirror she saw a Chinese face. She remembered the children at school calling her disparaging names and making slanted eyes with their fingers. In spite of those references to her cultural heritage, she worked hard to convince herself that she was not, in fact, Chinese.*
>
> *I began drawing the genogram during this session. There was little for me to say or to ask. Gwen's story poured out in such a manner that I came to think she had long awaited the time and place to let it go. I empathized and listened in respectful silence as she continued.*

Victoria's brother died at age 17, and her stepsister died several years later at age 30, both of tuberculosis. The losses of her only two siblings were untenable for her. All her anchors were gone: her parents, her siblings, her husband. Within that sea of loss, her son Michael became her emotional partner, as dutiful sons will (Bowen, 1978; Haley, 1980). To maintain his loyalty to Victoria, Michael had to sacrifice his marriage and his autonomy (Boszormenyi-Nagy & Spark, 1973). The script was set after Michael's father died. Alcoholism was the symptom; abuse was the vehicle (Guttman, 1991; Stanton & Coleman, 1980; Stanton, Todd, & Associates, 1982). With Gwen gone, he was able to give his children to Victoria to soothe the pain of her multiple losses. It made sense that Victoria would attempt

to re-create her family of origin with her young grandchildren (Bowen, 1978; Kerr & Bowen, 1988). She had lost her siblings once and was not going to let that happen again.

> *Unresolved loss can create symptomatology. Symptoms and confusion keep people where they are "stuck"—while serving as a diversion from the pain of loss (Horwitz, 1997). Because these children were so precious to Victoria and Michael when they were alive, I felt a responsibility to help them maintain Anna and Stephen in the weave of the family's fabric by continuing to support the traditions and values Victoria and Michael held dear. At the same time, I needed to free Anna from her binds so she could move forward and move the family to a place of health and security.*

Michael died of cirrhosis of the liver in 1979 when Anna and Stephen were 12 and 9 years old, respectively. Suddenly, a new opportunity to unite the children and their mother emerged. Flooded with excitement and anticipation at finally having her children back in her care, Gwen flew to Sydney to bring them home to Hong Kong. Unfortunately for Gwen and her children, the reunion was never to come to pass.

> *I found myself literally on the edge of my chair, body bent forward. I had to consciously sit back and appear calm. I wanted to hear a "happy ending," but I knew these two women would not be in my office if the story ended as I wished. I was preparing myself to hear more pain.*

Gwen's mother warned her that the children might be emotionally bonded to their grandmother and that she should not take them away from Victoria and the home they knew in Australia. Despite this warning, Gwen arrived at Victoria's home to take the children after their father's funeral. The children were rude to their mother, crying, refusing to leave Victoria, and asking Gwen to leave "their home." Completely devastated by this rejection and wounded with the pain of loss a second time, Gwen went back to Hong Kong without her children. On her arrival, her father told her to go to bed and in the morning he would talk with her about her situation, perhaps to help her resolve her painful feelings. For the first time she felt a bit of closeness toward him and support for her role as her children's mother. He died that night, and the conversation never took place.

> Gwen reported thinking that she had lost her children forever. She hoped that her father would help her, give her guidance, perhaps have an answer. In the wake of grieving her father's death, she believed all hope was gone.
>
> Loss and grief, again and again. My challenge was overwhelming. But, then, look what I had to work with: two intelligent, courageous women, deeply loved by one another, and willing to take on the mantle of change. I was hopeful.
>
> I commented on the depth of love and fortitude Gwen must have experienced to make such a journey to Australia, only to be disappointed yet another time. Her strength, although not rewarded until many years later, was, in fact, an example on which Anna could draw during her own time of difficulty. Gwen looked at me in such a way that I knew she had never thought that her pain could become her daughter's strength.

Back in Australia, 12-year-old Anna cried through the night, wondering if she had done the "right thing." After all, her grandmother wanted them to stay with her. Being Chinese was not a "good" kind of person to be. Leaving Sydney, a city she knew, would be frightening. But still, Anna struggled with her decision and, at some level, never forgave herself for hurting her mother.

> This history was so important. The process unfolding before my eyes was rich as the two women dovetailed their experiences in their effort to educate me. Anna had felt guilty about her response to her mother for 18 years. Finally, there was a space and a place to work out all this pain.

Given these pressures and the confusion of her early childhood, it is not surprising that Anna grew into her adolescence and adulthood with considerable uncertainty about how to think of herself as a woman, an Australian, a Russian–European, a Chinese person, and the daughter of her mother. In addition to the clash of cultural values and norms, she received mixed messages from her grandmother and her mother as to how "competent" to become. Her grandmother raised her to be a caretaker to her brother and to herself. Anna was well schooled in Russian traditions, foods, and embroidery as well as how to put her brother's needs ahead of her own. Conversely, her mother encouraged her to be independent economically, psychologically, and emotionally, so she would never find herself trapped in a marital relationship like that of Gwen and Gwen's mother. Gwen learned that the price of staying in an unhappy marriage was too high. She did not want her daughter to repeat this transgenerational experience.

Gwen expected Anna to attend a university and recommended that she study economics, a field that would bring honor to Anna and the opportunity to attain financial security. Victoria had wanted Anna to get a job in a local bank as a teller, to build stability and live at home. Attempting to gain her mother's approval, Anna decided to attend the university. She struggled, but she lacked motivation and focus. While still an undergraduate, she left her studies to backpack around Europe on her own. On her return to Australia, Anna took a job in a bank. Her mother was disappointed; her grandmother was delighted. After a year at the bank, Anna decided she would not achieve the satisfaction for which she continuously searched in this job. In spite of her grandmother's fury, she left the bank and returned to the university to finish her degree.

It is interesting that both "mothers"—Gwen and Victoria—had at least two of the same goals for Anna: financial security and happiness. Because they had differed so much in regard to how to achieve these goals, it was difficult for Anna to recognize the commonality in their messages.

> I asked Gwen what she thought would be more important: for Anna to be happy and

unaccomplished academically and financially or to be unhappy and high achieving. Gwen struggled with this question, because her frame of reference was that being high achieving meant being happy, financially secure, and free to leave an unsatisfying marriage. She conceded that if Anna could be truly happy and not academically or financially accomplished, she would choose that. Would she consent to allowing Anna to make her own decision about both her happiness and her academic pursuit and be content with Anna's decision? Gwen spoke honestly and commented that it would be hard for her but that she was willing to work toward letting go of her expectations for Anna.

Perhaps for the first time, Anna chose to satisfy herself and pursued the area toward which she felt drawn, art history. During the second year Anna focused on her true passion: Asian art. She graduated with a degree in fine arts. In Australia, students are tested as to whether they are capable of accomplishing graduate-level work by completing an honors year (an optional fourth year of an undergraduate degree). This requires taking courses and writing a thesis. Anna's grades had been excellent, much to her surprise. Inspired by her own accomplishments, she committed to the honors year. A few months into her studies Anna found herself spiraling into depression. She became isolated, living alone in an apartment and rarely leaving, except when absolutely necessary. An old nemesis—bulimia—came back to haunt her. At various times in Anna's adolescence and early 20s she would starve herself and occasionally binge and purge. Now she forced herself to sleep for most of the day to avoid life in general as well as the temptation of yet another binge–purge session. When she was awake, she would look in the mirror and see a Chinese face together with a tall, medium-sized body frame and weight that fluctuated 20–30 lbs over the course of months. The image in the mirror confused her as to which culture even her body belonged. She was not petite, like most of the Chinese women she knew. Her face was not constructed like the pictures of

Russian girls her grandmother showed her. Her accent belied her place of birth. Just who was she supposed to be? To whom was she connected?

It was at this point that I most clearly saw the confluence of loss, as evidenced by Anna's symptoms of bulimia and her confusion about her multicultural identities. She couldn't decide which motherland to shove down and which one to throw up! If I could help her shed the guilt and shame, she would be free to pursue her strengths and identify her resources. Then, and only then, could she move toward her goals (Horwitz, 1997; Landau-Stanton, Clements, & Associates, 1993; Seaburn, Landau-Stanton, & Horwitz, 1995). The grief work and the treatment plan that would blend the cultures, honor the "mothers" and their respective missions, and offer a positive male influence was beginning to take shape in my thinking.

Anna made it through her honors year on sheer determination and applied for a master of philosophy degree in 1994. It was between these degree programs, in April 1994, that Anna met Paul Wong, an illegal immigrant from Hong Kong. He had been in Australia for 10 years and was about to be deported. During those 10 years he had managed to build up a reputable albeit small business and had also hired some employees. Anna was looking for a job. A mutual friend of Anna's and Paul's recommended that she seek employment at his shop. He hired her. They laughed together and began to date. He paid attention to her and treated her with respect. When it became clear that his deportation was imminent, Anna agreed to marry him that August. The marriage permitted Paul to remain in Australia and to continue on with his business. At first Anna was very happy. Living with Paul meant extinguishing the painful isolation she had known prior to meeting him. Because she had always been trained to take care of her brother, she merely transferred those skills to taking care of her husband. They prepared meals together, which gave her a schedule, a proper diet, and someone with whom to share the eating experience. The bulimia disappeared. It wasn't long, however, before Paul began to intimidate Anna by ostracizing her and then not speaking to her for weeks. She never knew what she had done wrong or what caused such a rejecting stance. He shamed her publicly by shouting at her in front of customers and inferring that she was stupid. He tried to control her time, made her feel guilty if she enjoyed herself with friends, mocked her family, and dismissed any ideas about her future growth, either personally or professionally. His idea of her role as his wife was that she always agree with him, make money for him, and stop thinking independently.

All of these messages were in direct opposition to Anna's ideas about herself, which she had learned from both her mother and, in a more contorted way, from her grandmother. Her confusion was understandable: Victoria had also taught her to take care of the men in her life. After all, Paul had a good business. He could offer Anna financial stability. Should she opt for security and give up any hopes of becoming the happy, independent woman her mother wanted her to become? It was easy to see how she had become depressed and confused.

Paul began graphically to describe his fantasies about killing people and how easy it would be for him to act on these homicidal feelings. Anna became fearful that she would inadvertently trigger his professed desire to kill. She became deeply saddened and, in spite of living with Paul, the old uncomfortable feelings of being alone and isolated re-emerged. Courageously, and despite her confusion and anxiety, she decided to travel to Taiwan to complete the research for her master's thesis. Although this trip was part of their premarital agreement, Paul never forgave her for disobeying him. He faxed her daily to ask where she was and what she was doing. The research effort was difficult and, coupled with the pressure from her husband, she returned to Australia before she had finished. Filled with guilt and frustration, she still hoped to save her marriage and stop the torment. On her return, Paul intensified the intimidation. Having given up the one area that gave her a sense of selfhood and pride, Anna became an easy target. She began to question her judgment, lost the bit of self-esteem she had begun to build,

and fell into depression. It was at this time that Gwen came to visit.

The multigenerational transmission of unhappy marriages, loss of dignity, feelings of powerlessness, gender issues, cross-cultural issues, and the unresolved issues of loss in Anna's story made me determined to facilitate the self-respect and feelings of competence that Anna and her mother so justly deserved. Now I understood how this rich history influenced the "here and now" of Anna's relationships with her mother and her husband. An important task would be to keep sight of the cultural transitions, rather than the differences among the cultural groups. Each of the family members were moving at different rates and directions along the cultural-transition pathway, creating asynchrony among them and their context (Landau, 1982; Landau-Stanton, 1985; Landau-Stanton et al., 1993). Armed with my appreciation for the power of unresolved grief and my understanding of the complexity of transition, I fashioned the following intervention.

TREATING GRIEF AND LOSS THROUGH A MULTICULTURAL LENS

Anna and Gwen were easy to engage during their portrayal of the family's history in those first two sessions. Anna in particular was eager to tell her story and to move toward health. However, it became clear to me early in the first session that each of them was busy protecting the other from the pain they both felt over their incredibly difficult past. Anna still suffered from the pain of rejection when Gwen first left her as well as the guilt of rejecting Gwen after Anna's father died. Her explanations of the past were filled with qualifications and excuses for her mother's absence as well as self-deprecating remarks. For example, Anna reported that "Of course Mom had to leave. It was unbearable for her. (Turning to her mother) I never blamed you, Mom, for leaving. I did wonder, however, what I had done to send you away." Even statements that were so carefully constructed with this much deference were painful and scary to share. Gwen was afraid to tell her daughter of her experience with Anna's father. She did not want to change Anna's image of her father or sabotage the father–daughter connection she only hoped they shared.

Each protected the other by nondisclosure. This modus operandus kept them emotionally apart. Thus, they maintained their tenuous connection by not alienating one another. Neither was willing to lose the other yet a third time. I knew I would have to create a safe space for anger and grief, because without expression of their hidden emotions Gwen and Anna could never truly be reunited.

The first two sessions had involved gathering the family's history and creating the family's transitional map. Gwen's discomfort in dealing with the pain of the past resulted in her suggesting that Anna continue treatment by attending the next few sessions alone. Gwen was straightforward in stating the difficulty she experienced in expressing her feelings openly, because her culture respects reserve and objectivity. Disclosure of emotions was discouraged; fortitude and perseverance were highly respected. Women were not in a position to advocate for what they needed or wanted. This cultural norm had played itself out in Anna's marriage as well. I knew I had to be cautious about how I dispelled this long-accepted position. Gwen shared with me that the therapeutic experience was scary for her. She did not believe she could keep from crying or maintaining the necessary emotional distance from the painful events of the past. She agreed to return to therapy after a few sessions. In the second session, with Gwen still present, we were able to celebrate her wisdom in recognizing that her daughter needed her now and that Gwen had finally taken her daughter home. I was able to integrate the techniques of here-and-now, historical, and ecosystemic approaches as I wove the pain of separations from the past together with the mother's strengths in the present. Celebrating Gwen's success at rescuing Anna substantiated the notion that change could occur. With the proof that these women could alter the course for the future, a new sense of energy entered the treatment.

The next three sessions constituted the middle phase of treatment and were held with Anna alone, exploring the meaning of her grandmother's influence on the many dimensions of her life experience. Family-of-origin work is one way of using a historical approach as the foundation for change in the here and now (Framo, 1992). Through this process of building on the genogram and constructing an in-

depth narrative of Anna's relationship with her grandmother Anna was able to view her childhood, her memories, and her feelings, past and present, from a multidimensional perspective. In an effort to work through her relationship with Victoria, I assigned Anna homework, asking her to create a list of "gifts" she had received from her grandmother (Landau-Stanton et al., 1993). Anna constructed an impressive list and developed in session the "lessons about life" that Victoria had taught her. She was able to express both her anger and the gratitude she felt toward her grandmother. Anna saw, for the first time, how important it was to her grandmother that she stayed close to her and cared for her in her aging years. As Anna and I explored Victoria's childhood, new understanding emerged regarding the connection between Victoria's brother's early death and her devotion to Anna's brother, Stephen. Anna also was able to see a connection between her own deeply felt zest for life and Victoria's "free-spirited" stepsister, who was a flamboyant personality and a dancer. The possibility that Victoria had re-created her family of origin (her siblings) in Anna and Stephen began to intrigue Anna.

During discussions about her parents' marriage, Anna came to appreciate how impossible it was for her mother to stay in Australia. Although she knew this at an intellectual level, an emotional clarity emerged: Her parents' divorce really did not have anything to do with her. She was able to stop wondering if there was something about her that her mother didn't want or love. She was able to understand that her father was an angry and depressed man, conflicted by his devotion to Victoria, who loved Anna, in spite of his difficulty in expressing affection.

Critical to the work of these three sessions was the exposure of Anna's split loyalties to the three cultures in which she was raised. Rather than continuing to see the cultures as being in opposition to one another, thereby forcing her to choose, Anna and I were able to identify ways in which each had contributed to her integration as a unique adult woman. What had been viewed as misfortune was reframed as a "special gift" that she had been given by having exposure to all three cultures and to two generations of parents. Now she had the opportunity to choose from among all those influences and select what she wished to carry forward. What she chose to leave behind could be honored, respected, and put to rest. Anna began to emerge from confusion, giving herself permission to select from a vast array of teachings, rituals, legacies, and expectations. Anna was free to be herself for the first time. Who better could speak to the multicultural influences on Asian art than Anna?

Anna's newly found selfhood helped her express her anger and frustration toward Gwen. She felt her mother was critical of her and that Anna could never please her. Anna knew she needed her mother, yet at the same time resented her for giving advice. Anna wanted to be independent and have her mother respect her opinions and choices.

Now the challenge for me was to bring Gwen back into the treatment and create a safe place for mother *and* daughter to speak openly and freely. Anna agreed that she would share with her mother how she felt frozen in time after Gwen had left her. Gwen agreed to attend the next session. I invited Gwen's husband John to attend and support his wife in what was surely going to be an emotionally laden session. Anna changed the rule of "protect your feelings at all cost" and risked self-disclosure. The session was fruitful in that Anna articulated her love for her mother and fear of losing her again if Anna lost her approval. She did not know how to negotiate being independent without being separated from her mother.

Gwen described in detail what she wanted for her daughter—to make her own decisions and move forward with her life. She gave Anna permission to "grow up" and not to be influenced by Gwen's expectations. Concerned that permission alone would not suffice, I assigned the following homework. Every day Gwen was to tell Anna, "You may leave me, but I will never leave you. Wherever you are, I will be with you, supporting you and loving you. I have faith in you and your decisions. Go forward without fear." In addition, if Gwen behaved critically toward Anna, Anna was to respectfully tell her mother how she wanted her mother to explain what Anna had done wrong (an opportunity Anna had never had with her mother or her husband). She also invited Gwen to tell her when she did well.

It is interesting that one of Gwen's disappointments was that her own mother was often critical of her and rarely made positive comments about Gwen. Now she was in a position to correct this problem for both herself and her daughter. The fifth session marked the end of the middle phase of treatment.

MOTHER AND DAUGHTER MOVE THROUGH THE GRIEF AND RENEGOTIATE THEIR RELATIONSHIP

The termination phase began in the sixth session and ended with the seventh session. Gwen and Anna continued to express their pain over their tumultuous yet strong connection to one another and to sort out the new ways in which they chose to relate. At the last session, Gwen and Anna reported that their relationship felt closer. Gwen was having some difficulty fulfilling the assignment given after the fifth session, because verbally expressing feelings of love and expectations created a kind of expressed intimacy that was new for her. However, she worked hard to give Anna what she needed. Gwen would have lots of time to practice, because she and John planned to retire in Australia and were already preparing to move. Anna was to return to Australia with her mother and stepfather.

In the last session Anna reported the warmth and positive feelings she experienced each time her mother told her she would never leave her. She reported feeling a little stronger and more self-assured. She looked brighter and stated, "I'm starting to know who I am." Four weeks later, and just before Anna left to return to Australia, she wrote me a note. She said, "For some reason, I suddenly find my eyes wide open and things making sense. I haven't felt that way for a long time. I guess you could call it 'growing'!"

EPILOGUE: BY ANNA, IN HER OWN WORDS

It has now been about 4 months since my return to Australia. I have to admit I was scared about coming back. The biggest fear was that I had to face a reality that may or may not be pleasant. That choice was ultimately my own and I chose the former.

I found employment as soon as I got back. I made contact with a lot of friends who had supported me with immediate responses to my letters and cards and messages of support while in the States. Sometimes it is still hard for me to accept that I was worthy of their care and concern. I am grateful to each and every one of them.

I've started dealing with the divorce proceedings. Slowly, I've exposed all those horrible secrets about my marriage as a way to be more honest with my friends and myself. One friend suggested I do a self-defense class in order to feel more empowered. I completed the class and obtained a certificate. I am really proud of that accomplishment. I found a place of my own and unpacked all my belongings, giving me a sense of stability and control over my own life. I decided to go back to graduate study, and although it is not the same course I had started during my marriage, I know it is something that will benefit me in my future. I can never go back!

Before I left for Rochester, I thought I could work everything out on my own—I just needed time. But time passed so quickly, and before I knew it, my life and mind spiraled out of control. Going to therapy in Rochester and working things out gave me a new lease on life. I was literally quite scattered and confused before I started therapy. I had so many unanswered questions wandering around in my mind that some days I thought I was actually going crazy. It's funny how those around me could see so clearly those things to which I was so blind. For once, I found answers that actually made sense. Now, every day, I stumble upon some insight that provides answers and illuminates strengths in me. It's not easy though. Some days are a real struggle, as it is tempting to fall into old patterns. But now, I have the awareness and tools to deal with these types of days. I would never have been able to get to this point without going to seek help and having such a great therapist who listened and understood.

When I first went into therapy, I assumed that I would be looking at the marriage itself and working with problems within that context. It was a shock to realise how much of my family history actually affected the person I am today. It was by going through my family history so meticulously; that is, by looking at not only my relationship with those in my family, but also looking at their relationships with each other, that I came to a greater under-

standing as to why certain behaviours existed within myself and them. By going back into my own history, I also discovered why certain tasks were so hard for me to accomplish. So as opposed to blaming myself for not being a "good" person, I realised I actually was OK. It was just that I had been hearing negative perceptions all through my childhood. I was then able to understand that I reacted to things in two ways; as a child and as an adult. This distinction further gave way to my ability to grow, and be aware of when I switch from one trait to the other, particularly in the relationship with my mother.

The exercise of Mum telling me that "she will always be with me" has been extremely strengthening. During the sessions and at home this was very important to me, because she had never verbalised anything of this nature to me before. Although, initially, it was quite uncomfortable (and I think it still is for her), I really needed to hear it. For once I felt that I had her support, no matter what. For some reason, I still need to hear it. Now it feels OK to ask to her to support me, as it gives me permission to be happy about the person I actually am.

Telling her what I need to hear from her when I get uptight has allowed me to act more like an adult with her. We've grown closer because she has begun to understand my needs. Although I still sometimes fear her criticism, I no longer fear telling her how I feel about it. By doing these exercises, I have found I can be myself, rather than trying to be the person I think my mother would like me to be.

I found addressing the issues with my grandmother quite difficult. It has only been recently that I feel I have been able to truly thank my grandmother for what she gave me. During therapy, I was still quite angry with her for trying to mold me into the person she wanted me to be and although I was asked to record the gifts she gave me, I felt this request was too hard to fulfill. Because my grandmother was dead, I could not elicit a response from her or actually tell her how I felt. I think this made it all the harder. Since I have had time to think, I realise I cannot lay blame on someone, who in her own way, loved me so much.

Because the therapy sessions were spread out over 2-week periods of time, I had a lot of time to think after each session. The sessions were full of so much information, particularly about my childhood, that I often left with a head full of unsorted thoughts. I wanted to find answers about my life. I realised that my family had so many secrets. It was the time between sessions that I think I found many of the answers I had been searching for. The sessions triggered these thoughts and then subsequent sessions consolidated them.

I would like to take this opportunity to thank my mother and stepfather for helping me during this period in my life. They let me have the essential time-out from the world that I desperately needed. Our 5 months together in Rochester was precious to me as I slowly grew and got back on my feet again. I learned so much about them and their love for me. I want to thank my brother, too, who has always been my best friend and confidant. He is there for me, no matter what happens.

Lastly, I thank Susan, for without her help, kindness, and generosity, I wouldn't be sitting here, able to tell this story as a strong woman and proud of who I am.

References

Boszormenyi-Nagy, I., & Spark, G. M. (1973). Loyalty. In I. Boszormenyi-Nagy & G. M. Spark (Eds.), *Invisible loyalties* (pp. 37–52). New York: Brunner/Mazel.

Bowen, M. (1978). *Family therapy in clinical practice.* New York: Aronson.

Framo, J. L. (1992). *Family of origin therapy: An intergenerational approach.* New York: Brunner/Mazel.

Gilman, C. P. (1979). *Herland: The lost utopian female society.* New York: Pantheon.

Guttman, H. A. (1991). Parental death as a precipitant of marital conflict in middle age. *Journal of Marital and Family Therapy, 17,* 81–87.

Haley, J. (1980). *Leaving home: The therapy of disturbed young people.* New York: McGraw-Hill.

Horwitz, S. H. (1997). Treating families with traumatic loss: Transitional family therapy. In C. R. Figley, B. E. Bride, & N. Mazza (Eds.), *Death and trauma: The traumatology of grieving* (pp. 211–230). Washington, DC: Taylor & Francis.

Kerr, M. E., & Bowen, M. (1988). *Family evaluation.* New York: Norton.

Landau, J. (1982). Therapy with families in cultural transition. In M. McGoldrick, J. K. Pearce, & J. Giordano (Eds.), *Ethnicity and family therapy* (pp. 552–578). New York: Guilford Press.

Landau-Stanton, J. (1985). Competence, impermanence, and transitional mapping: A model for systems consultation. In L. Wynne, T. Weber, & S. McDaniel (Eds.), *Systems consultation: A new perspective for family therapy* (pp. 253–269). New York: Guilford Press.

Landau-Stanton, J., Clements C. D., with Associates. (1993). *AIDS, health, and mental health: A primary sourcebook.* New York: Brunner/Mazel.

Seaburn, D., Landau-Stanton, J., & Horwitz, S. (1995). Core techniques in family therapy. In R. H. Mikesell, D-D. Lusterman, & S. H. McDaniel (Eds.), *Integrating family therapy: Handbook of family psychology and systems theory* (pp. 5–26). Washington, DC: American Psychological Association.

Stanton, M. D., & Coleman, S. B. (1980). The participatory aspects of indirect self-destructive behavior: The addict family as a model. In N. L. Farberow (Ed.), *The many faces of suicide: Indirect self-destructive behavior.* New York: McGraw-Hill.

Stanton, M. D., Todd, T. C., & Associates. (1982). *The family therapy of drug abuse and addiction.* New York: Guilford Press.

CHAPTER 17

RELIGIOUS AND CULTURAL ISSUES IN ECOSYSTEMIC THERAPY: A THERAPIST IN THE FLOW

Don-David Lusterman

As a psychology student in the late 1960s and early 1970s, nothing seemed more frustrating than having to end my involvement with a patient or a family merely because I had concluded a segment of my training. I felt that this arbitrary disruption was a disservice to patients and therapist alike. Moreover, it offended my sense of the esthetics of therapy. It seemed to me that one should treat a "case" from beginning to end—a perfect circle. This implied that, once the problem was identified, therapist and patients would strive together until the problem was resolved.

Yet another strand of my growth as a therapist had occurred in the late 1950s, long before I began the formal study of psychology. My first interest in the relation between helping people to change and perceiving their imbeddedness in their contexts developed when I was an itinerant tutor, working with children with learning problems. (For a fuller description, see Lusterman, 1990.) Working in their dining rooms, their kitchens, and the children's bedrooms, I became aware of how these troubled children affected their families and how their families affected them. It wasn't long before I reached out to their teachers, counselors, school principals, and other personnel. It struck me again how these children often became entwined with the adults who struggled to help them, and how these same adults had a great impact on them, for good or for bad. It wasn't long before I attempted to convene a meeting of the horde of professionals involved with the family of Janice, one of my clients. Janice, then 15 years of age, was being seen by a psychiatrist; her mother

was being seen by a social worker; and her father was being seen by a psychologist. In addition, many school personnel touched both Janice's life and the lives of her parents. Much to my surprise, when I suggested that we all meet, everyone agreed to come. By meeting's end, much had been communicated, including the sense that actions on the part of one professional often counteract those of another. We agreed to keep contact, in the hopes that more united action would be beneficial. We all left the meeting feeling hopeful. However, it was not long before it became clear that none of that hoped-for change was forthcoming. I became convinced that there was a need for some new process, one that took into account the way in which various systems interacted with, and sometimes impinged on, one another.

When I began my doctoral studies in the late 1960s, I expected to learn much about family development and treatment. My education as a psychologist, however, would take me far from my concerns about the treatment of families, let alone their larger contexts. My clinical professors saw family therapy as an esoteric and renegade discipline. As one professor said,

> It's hard enough to develop the skills to deal with the dangers and complexities of treating one person. There are no meaningful parameters to contain what might happen if you tried to treat a whole family at the same time.

I felt that the best I could do would be to extrapolate what I was learning about the various disciplines of psychology into my growing curiosity about families. Still another issue was the attitude (almost a taboo) on the part of my professors toward the possibility that religious identity might play a role in therapy. It seemed to spring from two sources: (a) a belief that science and religion did not mix and (b) a psychoanalytic worldview that carefully shielded the *person* of the therapist from the patient.

Two years into my studies, however, a great shift occurred. Many university students, responding to the social unrest unleashed by the Vietnam war, began a student strike. Some of them briefly established "alternative colleges." This provided an opportunity to study that which was "forbidden." The group I was involved with formed a study group to learn about the "dangerous fire" of family therapy. We read whatever we could find, and we watched the early films of Ackerman and Whitaker at work. We were impressed with the dramatic presence of these early giants. Unlike the impersonal analytic stance we were learning, these therapists made no secret of their own personalities. In fact, their use of their selves was an important factor in how they worked.

While I continued my doctoral studies, I was fortunate enough to undertake a parallel training with one of the pioneering systems-oriented groups: Roosevelt Hospital's Family Studies Program, which serves, among other districts, the Hell's Kitchen area of New York City. It was here that I began to work with Hispanic families, many of whom were so isolated that it took months of family work in their homes before we could even entice them to come to the hospital itself. Fresh from the academic critique of the reification of the concepts of ego, id, and superego, now I found myself embroiled in a new problem: Had we not, perhaps, despite the youth of our field, begun to reify "the family" as "the system?" It was the psychologist Bunny Duhl who said, in the early 1970s, "you can't kiss a system." It was in the late 1960s that I was instructed "If the whole family doesn't show for the appointment, don't see them—wait 'til they all come in." I was uncomfortable with the sense that within the still-young field of family therapy a new orthodoxy was already emerging. In

defining the "system" as the family, were we already somehow replicating an error that we could so easily see in more traditional approaches? This led to still more questions. What really defined a family system? If a grandparent, an uncle, a boyfriend, or a girlfriend were significant figures, were they part of the family? If only one person came, could we do "family therapy"? How did we picture the institutions and their impact on the family? Were they, too, part of the system? Were the therapist and those who observed the therapist's work also part of the system? Finally, and very much at odds with my earlier perfectionist belief that I would see the family through, I was now coming to a very different understanding. I began to think of the therapist as a collaborator with the family—a very much less hierarchized position.

While at Roosevelt Hospital, and over the next several years, I had the opportunity to watch the masters of family therapy at work, sometimes through videotape, and sometimes at conferences, working with families "live." There emerged from these observations an image of the therapist, with a mixture of charisma, skill, and sometimes even heroism, bringing the family from chaos to clarity, from failure to success. Beels and Ferber (1972) attempted to define "What Family Therapists Do." There was an unspoken assumption that by *system* one meant "family" (however that was defined) and that by *therapist* one meant an individual who was either, in Beels and Ferber's terminology, a "conductor" or a "reactor." Both conductors and reactors were seen as experts, at the top of the treatment hierarchy. With hindsight, it is easy to say that in neither instance was the therapist yet clearly defined as part of the system; rather, the emphasis was placed on the therapist's expertise, a position that placed him or her somewhat above the family. There was also an esthetic that seemed to accept the idea that the therapist, or in some instances the therapeutic team, would see the case from beginning to end, which seemed to confirm my earlier feelings. I found myself wondering if there were some therapeutic role that was not easily classified but that was neither conductor nor reactor. To add to my own confusion, I met the late Carolyn Attneave, who introduced me to the concept of "network therapy"

(Speck & Attneave, 1974). Drawing on her experience as a Native American, Attneave described the power of the tribe, the members of which would all meet together to aid a member in distress, and extrapolated this to the gathering together of a family's system under the leadership of a therapist who acted as a master of ceremonies and facilitator. Still another pioneer, E. H. Auerswald (1968), described an "ecological systems approach," which dealt with the interaction of patients, their families, and the agencies that provided services to them.

Later in my career, as I met the members of the Kapulsky family, I was drawn into a re-examination of much of what I had learned. I experienced an awakening sense of a different and more modest role for the therapist, a different understanding of who constitutes the "system," and a new understanding of the role played by the therapist's self—a role that was one of neither conductor nor reactor. Finally, I learned that a sincere therapeutic interest in a family's religious journey, combined with a willingness to share carefully the therapist's own religious and spiritual issues, could be a powerful force for change.

THE KAPULSKY FAMILY

Anya Kapulsky telephoned me and explained that she had been referred by a colleague at the university where I had for many years been a teacher. My colleague had recommended me in particular because I was known as a committed Jew. Anya explained to me that this would be a most important qualification, because she had many spiritual concerns. She also told me that my colleague had described me as a family therapist. This intrigued her. Until then, she knew only of therapists who saw one person at a time. I asked whom she was particularly concerned about in her family, and she replied that she worried most about Natalya, her 13-year-old daughter, who had a long history of school difficulty and was currently expelled from school. She explained that it was particularly important to her that Natalya receive Jewish schooling but that she was very disillusioned with the various Yeshivas (Jewish Orthodox day schools) and feared that they did not have the resources to handle "this difficult

child." She reported equal frustration with the various psychologists and the psychopharmacologist who had treated Natalya.

My first thought was that I felt entrapped by my colleague's ardent referral and by the intensity with which Anya described her feelings on receiving the referral. I imagined that she believed that I could be of special help because of my Jewish identity and also perhaps because I used what my colleague had described to her as this "new approach": working with the family. I envisioned myself as another in the long line of therapists who had, as Anya saw it, failed her child. Despite my trepidations, I finished this first telephone contact by making an appointment for the following week. I told her that I looked forward to meeting Anya's husband and the two children at that time. She said, "I will do my best to bring everyone." After I hung up the telephone, it occurred to me that there was something in her tone suggesting that I might meet only Anya the following week—that she still needed to check me out. I thought about calling her back and making it still clearer how important it would be to include all the family members. But something in her manner suggested that it would be wiser to let the meeting take its own course.

MEETING THE FAMILY THROUGH ANYA'S EYES

Forewarned by my hunch, it was no surprise when only Anya sat in the waiting room. She was a dark-haired woman, with a kind face that reflected years of worry, a pervasive sadness. Although it was a warm day, she wore the long skirt and long-sleeved blouse typical of Orthodox Jewish women. This garb not only symbolized the virtue of modesty but also, to the knowledgeable observer, declared her particular form of Jewish identity. She explained that the family would not be with her today. Yakov, her husband, had to work. Natalya, about whom she was consulting with me, had already seen so many therapists that Anya didn't wish to inflict another one on her unless she felt that the therapist could respect the family's needs. Because Avrum, her youngest, presented no particular problem, it seemed foolish to bring only him.

Then her tale poured out. Anya and Yakov had immigrated to the United States 15 years ago. It was a very stressful time and, toward the end of that first year, Natalya was born. She was a bright child, but even in infancy, the slightest stimulation made her very excited, and it was very hard to calm her down. A major reason for Anya's decision to leave Russia was her strong desire to become a good Jew. Although she had little opportunity to learn in Russia, she grabbed whatever she could. Yakov, by contrast, had no particular interest in rediscovering his Judaism. Anya herself became very interested in the study of *Kabbalah* (a mystical aspect of Judaism). Natalya had been an excellent student in the early grades of public school, although she was restless in class and a bit unruly. In the fifth grade, at Anya's insistence, and with little support from Yakov, she was enrolled in a Jewish day school. By this time her behavior seemed to have deteriorated. She had difficulty organizing herself and, in Anya's words, "got caught in her own mess." Anya felt that from that time forward, the school had scapegoated Natalya. She saw this as a great injustice and was doubly annoyed when Natalya was referred to a therapist who, after some months of therapy, reported seeing no emotional problems.

Anya reported that one day she had become very angry and hit Natalya with a hairbrush. Natalya told this to some classmates, who told her to speak to the principal, so that Anya could be charged with abuse. Natalya's therapist urged the principal not to call. Anya admitted that she often became very angry with Natalya, calling her bad names and sometimes hitting her. Often these outbreaks occurred when school would call to inform her of Natalya's misbehavior. Her reaction to the calls would lead to fights with Yakov, who saw her as overconcerned with Natalya and her problems. "I know that Natalya wants a close relationship with me, and I with her. But I have a problem. I am at first very patient, but then I lose it, and I am out of control."

Toward the end of our first meeting, I asked for permission to contact the various mental health people and schools who had been involved with Natalya. Anya readily consented but warned me that the mental health people wanted to put Natalya in public school because of the relative absence of pupil personnel services in the parochial schools. Anya was strongly opposed to this because of her religious convictions.

As we concluded, I told Anya that, for some reason, I found myself thinking about how Moses, when he arrived at the Jordan River, sent spies to spy out the Holy Land to see if it could be taken. She smiled at the analogy and admitted that, yes, in a way she had decided to "spy out the land." I told her that I hoped that she could be one of the spies who says that the land is filled with milk and honey and that it can be taken. My next task was to contact the various people with whom Anya had already consulted in order to begin to create an ecomap for myself that included these others.

MAKING CONTACT

Therapist 1: Dr. S, a Psychiatrist

Dr. S said she felt that when Anya had called seeking help that she was in fact dumping Natalya on Dr. S's doorstep. Dr. S believed that both Anya and Natalya were "very borderline." Dr. S reported that Anya fluctuated between an intrusive way of intervening in Natalya's affairs, often followed by a sudden and dramatic "dropping" of the youngster. She described Anya as the more educated and upwardly mobile of the two parents and indicated that Yakov seemed "somewhat boorish." Yakov, according to Dr. S, takes the position that Natalya is Anya's responsibility: "She spoiled her, and now, she must straighten her out." She also reported that Natalya had been removed from some of the schools because she was sexually provocative and that her Rorschach confirmed an unusual interest in sexuality.

Therapist 2: Dr. P, a Psychologist

Dr. P cautioned me, "I'm not a family therapist, but I know that would be the way to treat this girl. However," he added, "although this is a family problem, it will not be possible to treat it by seeing the family together—it just won't happen." He also indicated that the younger brother, Avrum, is considered to be a "perfect" child. He reported that he had tried to describe to Anya her enmeshment with Natalya and how Anya excluded Yakov, despite her anger at his lack of involvement: "She just doesn't get it." He diagnosed Natalya as having an oppositional disorder.

Therapist 3: Dr. Q, a Psychologist

Dr. Q told me that he had been referred after a hospital outpatient clinic had evaluated Natalya. The hospital team included a neurologist, a neuropsychologist, a child psychologist, a child psychiatrist, a social worker, and others. Their findings indicated that there was evidence of attention deficit hyperactivity disorder (ADHD) by parent report but not by school report. The hospital team saw evidence of oppositional defiant disorder. Probably the most impressive finding was a difference of 24 points between Natalya's Wechsler Intelligence Scale for Children's Verbal Score and her Performance Score. The school had also asked Dr. Q to examine Natalya for possible ADHD. His belief, however, was that her primary problem was her passive–dependent relationship with her mother. He had seen Natalya and Anya together a number of times. He reported that any time he attempted an intervention Anya would discount it, because, as she said, "you don't see things through our eyes." He described Anya as a great blamer but not a good assigner of responsibility.

The Referrer: Professor M

I also had gained permission to speak with the referrer. She told me that she was so happy that I had "come aboard," because my Jewish religious background and my interest in problems of immigration (about which she had heard me lecture) made me ideally suited to help the family. I thanked her for the referral.

Various School Personnel

I spoke with a number of rabbis who had been involved with Natalya. All reported that she was a likeable but difficult child and that they felt no longer able to serve her unless she made remarkable strides in her behavior.

MY MUDDLE

I felt burdened as I attempted to sort out the material and ideas presented by my various predecessors.

I felt that many judgments had been made about Natalya, her "possible" ADHD, her "enmeshment" with her mother, and her precocious sexuality. I had also been warned that Anya was a "blamer" and that none of the interventions that had been attempted succeeded for more than a week or two. The previous therapists attributed these failures to Anya's tendency to undermine therapeutic interventions. As I mused about each therapist's contribution I noted that none had mentioned the issue of religion or the disruption associated with immigration. I also found myself thinking how important it would be for me to both value and yet not be overly influenced by what I had learned. Now I felt ready for the next meeting, which I hoped would include all the family members.

MEETING THE FAMILY

I opened the door to the waiting room to find Yakov and Anya and their two children. Natalya, a sweet faced, fairly tall 13-year-old who appeared well into adolescence, wore a short-sleeved cutoff man's shirt and blue jeans. Her 11-year-old brother Avrum wore a *kippah*, the traditional headcovering of Orthodox Jewish males. The father Yakov was a tall man who shifted in his chair as I came out to the waiting room, leaving me with the sense that he was none too happy to be there. I noted that he was dressed in his working clothes, coverall jeans and a paint-stained shirt. I also noticed that, unlike Avrum, he wore no head covering. It was almost as if I were seeing two families, one consisting of Anya and Avrum, who identified themselves by their garb as Orthodox Jews, and Yakov and Natalya who, by their appearance, had chosen to enter the secular world. As I introduced myself and ushered the family into my office I found myself wondering what the power of this dichotomy might be.

Anya seated herself in a comfortable easy chair, directly facing me. Avrum chose the other easy chair, closest to his mother. This left several ordinary office chairs. Yakov chose a seat one distant from his son, so that I saw him basically in profile. Choosing to leave still another seat vacant, Natalya seated herself closest to me. I asked each what they liked most about their family. Anya spoke of how beautiful and gifted her children were, although she teared up as she sadly described how she saw Natalya as "wasting her talents." Yakov said that he thought that Anya's concerns about the children were a good thing but that it made him angry that that was all she ever seemed to think about. Natalya passed: "I have nothing that I can think of that's so good about my family. Maybe I'll think of something later." Avrum said that it was a nice family and that people cared about each other.

I then asked what each person thought might be improved in the family's life—what they hoped would come out of our work if we decided to work together. Anya said, "I want us to have a better life, less fighting, more spiritual life." When I questioned this, she said, "I wish we would have a real *Shabbos* (the Jewish word for Sabbath)—at least one day a week when we would all be together and have some peace, no fighting." Yakov said that all he wanted was, just like Anya, peace—no fighting. Then, looking down at the floor, he added, "But the person who makes the fights is Anya—she is always so angry at Natalya. I want the fighting to stop." Natalya said that she was growing up, so she wanted more freedom. Then she added, softly, "What really bothers me is about Avrum. I think he's a loser." Avrum, ignoring his sister's characterization of him, added, "It isn't only my mom and sister who fight. My mom and dad fight, too. I want it to stop."

As the session ended I commented on how important loyalty was in this family, how, in some way, they were so concerned about one another, and how important it was to find a way to stop the fighting, a wish they all shared. I asked whether they would like to make a next appointment. When Anya turned to Natalya to ask whether she would come back, Yakov gruffly countered, "Anya—this is a decision for *Natalya* to make? No—we should make it." Rather than permit this struggle about the hierarchy to continue in the office, I suggested that the family make its decision and call me the next day to schedule another appointment if they wished. I felt that it would have been unwise to continue the conversation in the office, because I could think of no intervention that would not appear to side either with Yakov or with Anya. I was also impressed with how Avrum, the youngest, revealed a crucial piece

of information: that it was not only his mother and sister who fought but also his mother and father. The next morning Anya called and said "We want to come back."

NATALYA'S TWO WORLDS

As we seated ourselves, Avrum said quietly, "They've been fighting again." Anya explained that Natalya was constantly borrowing money from her friends to buy all kinds of things and that she showed very poor judgment. "What kinds of things?" I inquired. "Jeans, rings, sweaters, all kinds of things." I sensed that this was Natalya's way of fitting in. Knowing how important the issue of Jewish identity was to Anya, I felt it would be premature to explore Natalya's "borrowing" as a way of costuming herself for the secular, "American" world. My fear was that this would only intensify the differences between Yakov and Anya. Instead, I asked Yakov what he thought about Anya's concern. I was pleasantly surprised to hear him agree: "No, it isn't right that she borrows like this. How can she ever pay it back?" Natalya retorted, "I have some money from them right now, and I'll do with it as I please. It's my money." Anya then began to beg Natalya to return the money. Yakov turned to me and said, "You see, this is what makes me crazy. She begs her. Then Natalya won't do it, and then things get very bad between them." Turning to Natalya he said, "If you don't give them back the money, I will find it, and I will keep it. You will have no money, and no new stuff." I commented that it was good to see Anya and Yakov agreeing on their goal, if not their method, although it must be hard for Natalya, because they were agreeing against her. Natalya sat quietly. As the session ended, I commented that I hoped a way could be found for Anya and Yakov together to help Natalya to return the borrowed money.

As they left, Natalya turned to me and said, "Nat—it's Nat—my friends don't call me Natalya." I found myself thinking, "So, she's telling me that maybe I *should* have gotten into the significance of her money as a way of becoming more like her friends." But I heard other echoes also—did Natalya want me to side with her being more "American" and less like her mother? Should I call her "Nat?" I felt quite torn. The issue of living in two worlds was important to me. As a strongly identified Jew living mostly in the United States but sometimes in Israel, I could understand Anya's need to hold "Nat" close to Jewish traditions of which she had been so deprived in Russia. From the day Anya arrived in the United States, she had struggled so hard to right this wrong. Her identity as a Jew, living now in a free country, was of paramount importance to her.

I could also empathize with Natalya's fierce need to fit in with her peers. This touched on still another struggle within me as I approached Anya. As much as I admired her attempt to regain her roots, I felt equally uncomfortable with her fascination with the *Kabbalah*, which the tradition sees as a mystical byway, far from normative Judaism. Could I respectfully accept where Anya was in her own struggle to define her identity? Could I be respectful of the path that Nat's apparent rebellion was taking—at least for now, to distance herself from Jewish education and Jewish life? Would my own predilections stand in the way? What of this should I share—and when, and with whom?

As I pondered these questions I found myself drawn to still another aspect of my personal belief system: a long-standing interest in Taoism. Although I am by no means a Taoist, I have for many years incorporated elements of Taoist thinking into my own values system. I found myself musing on how these beliefs might help me as I began to feel ever more at sea with the Kapulsky family. Briefly, the *Tao* is the Chinese word for *path*, or *way*. Watts (1975) describes the Tao as "the course, the flow, the drift, or the process of nature" (p. 41). One author says that the Tao may be best described as "the way the universe works." To understand the Tao one must abandon the Western notion that passivity and activity are opposites. Taoism prescribes a kind of inactivity, but its purpose is to help the Taoist to find his or her place in the flow of the universe. The expression "go with the flow," in this context, reminds us the Taoist does not so much seek the "way" but becomes sufficiently in the flow that the way emerges. I was becoming ever more aware that any attempt that I made to direct this diverse family, in the midst of its own growth, was doomed to fail.

I could be neither conductor nor reactor. Only "being" with them, finding their "flow," would permit me to be of some help.

THE POLICE ARE CALLED

It was not long before my acceptance of the Tao was put to the test. As I was closing up my office late one evening, I received a telephone call from a neighbor. She told me that she felt that, as a policewoman, she must ask me if the family that she saw getting into their car at a certain time that evening were my patients. I asked her why, and she replied,

> I had to intervene in a fight that the mother and the daughter were having. I saw the mother strike the daughter several times, quite hard, to the point that the young woman was pushed backwards. I took their names, asked them what they were doing in the neighborhood, and explained to the mother that it was my duty to report what I had observed to child protective services.

I was not surprised when Anya came alone to the following session. This permitted me to share with her my neighbor's report. "But," said Anya, "I came today alone to talk about the fight I had with Yakov. It came to blows, and I called the police." Then, out poured her own feelings of responsibility for the many acts of violence that had punctuated their marriage—violence involving Natalya and sometimes violence against Yakov. I told her that I had no alternative but to join with the policewoman in making my own report to child protective services (CPS). Anya told me that she felt somehow comforted, knowing that she would have to reveal to someone else this part of herself, which caused her such shame. Like many therapists, I had felt very threatened at the possibility that my role as therapist would be usurped by CPS and that perhaps my patient would be so angry that she herself would remove the family from therapy. Instead, Anya was reassuring me that perhaps this might help.

I explored Anya's belief that she had so little power in the family. She said that when she reached the point where she felt a desperate need to reach Natalya or Yakov and no words seemed to touch them she would resort to slapping. I told her that it was hard for me to see her as having so little power. She had come to a new country; mastered a new language; and was struggling, with some success, to find her own Jewish identity. Furthermore, she was creating a family environment in which Jewish identity could be explored and fought over. "These are no small accomplishments," I added.

"This may be so, but I feel that I am doing it alone," Anya replied.

> I know that Yakov is as concerned about Natalya's behavior as I am, but it's like he sits back, he doesn't say anything to me about it, or to her. So I always look like the bad one. He just seems to go on, like it was nothing. I get so angry at him, but I can't get him to hear me. Except sometimes when we fight. But even then, he says I started it, and in the end, I feel like the fool. Yet I am trying to make a Jewish home. Nothing is more important to me. But Yakov seems to do everything he can to undermine it. All he thinks about is success, work, money.

I suggested to Anya that she share her belief about Yakov's concern for Natalya with him and that she invite him to accompany her to the following session so that they could decide how best to care for Natalya in a manner on which they could both agree. It was most important, I told her, to begin by finding out what common ground they shared—in this case, their mutual worries. Only then, I said, would it be safe to talk about their differences. "Would you telephone him to invite him?" she asked. I replied that if she wanted him there, I believed that he would come.

MEETING WITH THE "EXECUTIVE TEAM"

"Since I have seen you only a few times, certainly fewer than Anya, I would appreciate it, Yakov, if you would tell me how you see things," I began. Yakov replied that he and Anya had many differences,

some about Natalya and some about, as he said, "just the way we see things." "Anya," he continued,

> worries about almost everything. It can be that I am not home exactly when Sabbath begins. It can be that she thinks that all I care about is work and money. It can be the littlest thing, like how Natalya dresses. I never know what will upset her next. And then, she gets very, very angry. Sometimes she is shouting, crying. Sometimes she is hitting. I believe in live and let live. I try to keep things calm, and let things go.

Anya sat quietly, eyes fixed on Yakov, listening attentively. I asked her how she felt about Yakov's description. "It is not untrue," she replied.

> I do get very angry. But Yakov, I feel so alone. I am so angry because you don't seem to see the things that are wrong. I feel like everything rests on my shoulders. If I try to tell you something is bothering me, you tell me it is nothing.

Yakov replied, "I'm just trying to calm you down."

"Yakov, do you think it's working?" I asked. Yakov shook his head.

"You know," he said,

> to listen to Anya, you would think I don't also try to help. For instance, if Natalya refuses to go on the school bus, I will wait and take her with me in the car in the morning. I do many things.

I wondered if either Anya or Yakov felt that what they were doing was working. For example, were they experiencing any great success in controlling Natalya's behavior? Both agreed that nothing was working. I wondered aloud what it must be like for Natalya, seeing how much her mother and father disagreed. "But we don't really disagree," Yakov interjected. "Maybe the way we try to get her to do things is different."

"So what is the effect?" I mused.

"I think we are canceling each other out," observed Anya, as Yakov nodded in agreement.

I asked what they could both agree on. Yakov

replied that he couldn't bear the terrible way that Natalya spoke to her mother, even using words like "bitch." He explained that, when he heard Natalya using such language he would take her aside and tell her it was a bad thing to do. Then Natalya would explain how bad her mother was making her feel, and he would tell Natalya that, even so, Natalya had to respect Anya. Anya said that she was surprised to hear that Yakov defended her, but still, maybe what Natalya got from that sort of exchange was the idea that Yakov was saying "Even if your mother is crazy, you still have to talk to her properly." Yakov also admitted, with a bit of pushing from me, that he was not always so happy with the way Natalya spoke to him or her brother either.

"So one thing you both agree on is that you want her to speak respectfully," I observed. I asked if they would be willing to learn some simple principles of psychology that could help them to change Natalya's behavior, adding with a smile that it would, of course, change theirs as well. We talked about very simple ideas, particularly about reinforcement and extinction. I described what a "time out" was and indicated that it was important that they understand that it was a time out for everyone, a chance to start over in a more positive way. They wanted to know how they could apply that to their daughter. Now, I thought to myself, they are thinking as a team, not competing, as they had before, about who was to blame. We agreed that their goal should be simple and easy to accomplish so that everyone could feel encouraged. They decided that the change for which they would work at first would be respectful speaking; Natalya's cursing and nasty tone would no longer be acceptable. I told them that I had forgotten one other important principle: modeling. If they wanted change in her communication, they would have to communicate with each other in a new way and with Natalya as well. Yakov and Anya agreed that they would tell Natalya that they were all going to work on this and that although they expected her to have trouble with it at first, she could talk to them about anything she wished to as long as she found respectful words. They were then to praise her warmly for improved communication. I suggested that all family members

attend the next session so that I could observe how they were applying their new ideas.

A FAMILY MEETING

As the next meeting opened, Natalya sat between her mother and father, and Avrum was at his father's side. Natalya opened the session saying, "My mother and I were just talking at home about a sad thing." Anya added,

> When Natalya was a little girl, I went to work, and my mother, who lived with us, took care of her, and also of Avrum, when he was very little. When Natalya was just entering fourth grade, my mother died, very suddenly. This was a terrible shock to Natalya, and this was when she began to have so much trouble in school. I tried to explain this to the teacher, but no one really listened. Up 'til then, everyone said that she was a good and a smart girl.

I turned to Natalya to ask her to tell me what she remembered of her grandmother. As I began to speak, I noticed that she was wiping away tears. As her mother stroked her hand, I commented, "So we know that you are a sensitive young woman, and the things that happen around you affect you very much."

"This is true," said Yakov.

> When there is fighting, if I am angry with Anya, or if she is scolding Avrum, this is when she is at her worst. Maybe you are right. Maybe it is because she feels so much. But we are all trying now, and none of us is getting as angry.

Avrum then added, "But don't think she is such an angel—just the other day she did something bad— she took money from me so that she could pay back some of what she owed one of her friends." I found myself thinking back to what I had learned about homeostasis. As I was considering some way of addressing this, Yakov turned to Avrum and said sternly, "Didn't we sit down with you to say that we didn't want you to tell on Natalya any more? Don't do it." Anya added, "Maybe we have misled you,

Avrum, but we don't want you to be a detective any more."

The following sessions continued to focus on the increased teamwork between Anya and Yakov. Some crises arose, mostly around school problems. The difference now was that the old alliances were broken. Avrum seemed more comfortable with his father, despite their differences about religion. Natalya, although still far from well behaved, was more responsive to her parents' concerns.

CPS CALLS

I received a call from CPS. The worker indicated that there was not enough evidence for a "finding" but that she thought on the basis of what the family had told her that family therapy should continue. I told her that I would reserve the right to contact her if I felt that the situation became volatile again, and I discussed this with Anya and Yakov, who told me that the one thing they were sure of was that there would be no more violence. Both agreed that it was so much easier to know that they could talk out what was bothering them and especially that they could do this with Natalya.

ANYA AND YAKOV

The summer was now approaching. Anya and Yakov knew that I would be away for almost 2 months. They called, indicating that they needed to see me alone, without the children. When they arrived, Anya was silent and tearful, and Yakov spoke gruffly. "I don't know what else I can do," he said.

> I am working so hard, to be better at
> home and to continue to make a living.
> But I still feel that Anya is always judging
> me. There is no appreciation. I can't go on
> this way. What is the point of all this?

Anya said, "It isn't about the children any more. It is about us. Maybe it always was. We came to you again, because you helped us with Natalya. Now you must help us."

"All I can do is to help you to look at what change would mean in your marriage," I said. "But it is dangerous. You may end up with a better marriage, but you may also be looking at a decent di-

vorce. What are the issues?" They began to list them:

- Yakov was bothered by Anya's increasing religiosity. She was not like this when they first married.
- Anya was concerned about Yakov's constant preoccupation with his work and his need to become a great financial success.
- Yakov felt that Anya had no interest in sex, even though she did not refuse him outright.
- Anya felt that Yakov showed little affection for her, so that she was always asking herself, "Does he really stay with me because he loves me, or just because we are married?"

There were only two sessions remaining. In these, we began by talking about Anya's increased interest in living a full Jewish life. Yakov was aware of my background and Jewish identification because he knew of my contacts with the various Jewish schools with which Natalya had been involved. At one point he asked me if I felt that there was anything "abnormal" about Anya'a concern with Jewish life. I asked him if he minded if I spoke personally, as my self even more than as a therapist. He agreed. With his permission, I spoke of how Judaism had always been a search for me, a constantly evolving part of my life. I told him that I myself had come from a home where one parent had a strong Jewish identity and the other had very little. I told them that I had found that in my own home, the rituals that we followed, especially those concerning the Sabbath, had provided us with at least one day a week that was guaranteed to increase family closeness. "So you do not think that her interest is out of line? " he asked. "On the contrary," I replied, "I think it is part of her attempt to regain what she felt was stolen from her in Russia." Yakov thanked me for my honesty. I suggested that they continue this conversation at home, thinking not about pathology but about what they could both agree on right now, as two Jewish parents.

In the final session we once again focused on what kind of life Yakov and Anya wanted to have together. They did not return to the Jewish issue but instead talked about their emotional relationship and how tried it had been by so many things. They spoke about the stress of immigrating and of the pressures that they suffered with the loss of Anya's mother, who had been a great help with the children. They shared their mutual pain about the problems they had encountered with Natalya and how their different approaches had made each feel so alone as they dealt with her many crises. I told them that I felt badly about leaving at such an important point in our work but that I would be returning at summer's end and that they should be free to call. Of course, I also left the name of my covering doctor in the event that there was an emergency.

EPILOGUE

I returned at summer's end, expecting a call from the Kapulskys, but heard nothing. I wondered whether this meant that things were going well or that they had gone badly and they sought another therapist. When I checked with my associate, I was relieved to find that there had been no call to him either. It left me with the hope that things were going well. I was tempted to call but felt that it would be experienced by them as a pressure to return to therapy.

A year had passed since the Kapulskys had ended therapy. I was preparing to write a chapter for this volume. I spoke with Anya, explaining to her that I would be writing a chapter that would include my work with her and her family and asking her how the family was doing.

She began by speaking about the changes she saw in Yakov as a parent. "When I first met you," she said,

> *I never thought that Yakov would really come to therapy. Somehow, you made it easier for me to get him to come. I think this broke the ice for him. I think it made him really begin to think about human relationships. He opened up and looked at his role in the problems our family was having, instead of just seeing everything as my fault. Even if I pushed him away because I felt that I knew better, after therapy he would challenge me in a better way, and then take a more effective role*

himself. This took some of the pressure off of me.

Then she spoke of changes in the marriage:

> *It took awhile, but we finally realized we had to look closely at our relationship as husband and wife. I think that seeing how we cooperated better with the children made it seem possible that we could change our marriage as well. Remember you used to ask us to rate things, 1 to 10? Now the marriage is between a 7 and a 9. When we started, it felt like it was a 1 or a 2.*

Concerning Natalya, she reported,

> *Natalya is now a 5 or 6. Her choice of friends is much healthier, and she is a much better friend. Sometimes her judgment is still not so good. She will still blow up sometimes, but I can stop myself if I feel that I am going to overreact. Often I wait until I can talk it over with Yakov if there is a problem, and he will take a role. This is such a nice change. Another important thing is that I think, underneath it all, she respects me for taking strong moral stands. Yakov and I have also been thinking a lot about all the talk about her having an attention problem (ADHD). We think that isn't true, and that's why therapy for that won't help. Yakov and I feel that we have the resources, as a family, to help her to improve. She is now having home tutoring and seems to be learning very much better. Avrum still does not have a very good relationship with her and sometimes still tries to tattle. We punish him for that, and it is happening less and less.*

"There is a big change in our religious life," she continued.

> *We are now Sabbath observers, all of us, and it comes from both me and Yakov. We can see the kids growing in their Jewish identity. You know, I came from next to*

nothing, everything was so hard, even to get a bit of matzo for Passover, and education was not available—but at least we knew we had a Jewish identity. For Yakov, it was even less. I respect him so much more now. He is a better man. Or maybe it is that I understand him better too, and I have changed.

"We wanted to tell you more about Natalya," she continued.

I realized that I was trying to push Judaism and Jewish education down her throat, and that this was making it poison for her. I realize now that she needs to learn for herself. All we can do is provide a good home. Even the protective service (CPS)— I am glad that you pushed this. It was very painful at the time, but it was a kind of alarm bell. We are a different kind of family now, a better family. There is a new respect.

"I want to say a little about the therapy," she concluded.

It is more than a year now, and we have had no more therapy, not for us, and not for Natalya. We learned that we could do much by ourselves, just as a good husband and wife, and as good parents. We learned that we can work with the school and the synagogue as partners, not as if they were the bosses, and we were just there to listen to what they said. Most important, because you let us know who you were and

reached out to us, to the school, to the other doctors, it helped a lot. We learned that therapy is a relationship of soul to soul.

As I pondered Anya's words, I found myself thinking about what I had learned from the Kapulsky family: There is no finished, perfect case. I was there to walk a piece of this family's journey with them. So many issues were touched: gender, immigration, ethnicity, religion, and how a family can find its own voice among the many other systems with which it must interact. With each issue, I realized, the outcome was unpredictable. The family continued its own development, long beyond therapy's end, still defining and redefining itself. I also learned that, to whatever degree I had touched the Kapulsky family, so too had they touched me.

References

Auerswald, E. (1968). Interdisciplinary versus ecological approach. *Family Process, 7,* 202–215.

Beels, C., & Ferber, A. (1972). What family therapists do. In A. Ferber, M. Mendelsohn, & A. Napier (Eds.), *The book of family therapy* (pp. 168–209). New York: Science House.

Imber-Black, E. (1988). *Families and larger systems.* New York: Guilford Press.

Lusterman, D-D. (1990). Ecosystemic intervention. In F. W. Kaslow (Ed.), *Voices in family psychology* (pp. 217–230). Newbury Park, CA: Sage.

Speck, R., & Attneave, C. (1974). *Family networks: Retribalization and healing.* New York: Pantheon.

Toropou, X. X., & Buckle, X. X. (1997). *The complete idiot's guide to the world's religions.* New York: Alpha.

Watts, A. (1975). *Tao: The Watts course way.* New York: Pantheon.

CHAPTER 18

STEPS TOWARD A CULTURE AND MIGRATION DIALOGUE: DEVELOPING A FRAMEWORK FOR THERAPY WITH IMMIGRANT FAMILIES

Jaime E. Inclan

ACT I: 1986

In 1986 I was a family therapy consultant for an agency in Brooklyn, New York, that served an urban poor population, including a good number of minority group clients. I worked with a small group of six therapists: two men and four women —two who were Latinos, four who were Jewish, two who were Catholic. At times, students in social work and psychology would join the group. The group met weekly and worked very intensively in a productivity-minded and highly monitored system, akin to the managed-care system of today. The group was cohesive and enjoyed good camaraderie. Discussions could be pretty frank, and presentations were relatively unguarded. The group had worked together for more than 1 year. Supervision included case discussions and live interviews during which I would frequently participate directly with the family.

A therapist expressed interest in presenting a case for consultation. The therapist, an eager, intellectually honest Jewish man, described the Gonzalez family as a two-parent Puerto Rican "blended" family that included three children from the mother's prior relationship and one on the father's side. In the current household were the two parents and the mother's three children, who were ages 9, 7, and 6 years. Carlos, age 9, was the product of Mrs. Gonzalez's prior relationship. Mr. Gonzalez also had a son, age 17, from a prior relationship. He lived in Puerto Rico with his birth mother. The spouses had been together as a couple for 9 years, exactly since the birth of the oldest child, Carlos, who was the identified patient.

Carlos, age 9, was getting poor grades, acting out in school, and being oppositional and uncooperative at home. This behavior had been evident for at least the last 6 months. The therapist had seen the family three times when he requested the consultation. The reason for the consultation was that the father was not fully engaged in the therapy and the therapist feared that he was getting ready to drop out of treatment.

The preconsultation discussion focused on two interrelated issues: (a) engagement in therapy, particularly, engagement of Latino men and (b) cultural change and value differences and how these affect family relationships. First, the group reviewed the notion of gender bias in the therapist–client alliance. This idea emphasizes that therapist bias—and, therefore, the tendency toward therapist–client alliances and collusion—would be expressed more commonly along gender lines; that is, male client–male therapist collusion, and female client–female therapist collusion, would be more prevalent than cross-gender alliances. In this case, however, the therapist had a closer working relationship with the mother than with the father, with whom he felt a sense of precariousness in the relationship. This alliance opened the way for a wide-ranging discussion.

The group quickly established that this type of therapy impasse, in which the father was at risk of dropping out of treatment, was common in the clinic's settings, regardless of the gender of the therapist. The group meandered through some important questions:

- What could this case teach us, as therapists, about therapeutic alliances with Latino and immigrant families?
- Are therapists in general less in tune with the needs and claims of Latino men? If so, why would this be so, and what can be done about it?

The group speculated about the different paces of acculturation in men and women and between children and parents of immigrants. The group questioned the extent to which family therapy includes cultural concerns in its developmental theories about the family and wondered about what room there is for culturally sensitive interventions in family therapy.

It became obvious that the conceptual lens would have to expand beyond the family if cultural concerns were to be fully integrated into our work. The appropriateness of an ecological systems approach, which is broader than the family systems view, began to surface as a framework more relevant to the understanding of family problems of poor people and immigrants. Intrinsic to the ecological framework, we argued, are questions related to the adaptation of families to their environments. Immediate therapy implications of this approach include the effects on couples and families of differences in the pace of acculturation. As a group, we considered further questions:

- Would not a focus on the stage of acculturation and adjustment to new environments be complementary to, and equally fundamental as, the life cycle stages perspective in regard to the understanding of family systems?
- Could it be that, in addition to narrowly defined gender affiliation tendencies in the therapist–family relationship, there are social and cultural value orientations (in which are embedded gender values and role attitudes) that have a profound impact on what one values and accepts as familiar, functional, and appropriate?
- How does patient–therapist collusion based on shared cultural assumptions influence the therapy process?

- What do these insights suggest for family therapy training?

Working with Carlos and his family allowed me to reflect on some personal issues about immigration that became clinically relevant to my work with Latino immigrants. In this chapter I include some segments of an interview with Carlos and his family, conducted in 1985, as a means of sharing how, in clinical practice, ideas about the role of culture and acculturation became more explicit for me. These issues are directly related to the known difficulty of engaging and retaining Latino and poor men in psychotherapy.

The group first addressed the therapist's concerns about the block that he was experiencing in reaching the father. Between the lines it was apparent that the therapist was taken by Ms. Gonzalez's position. His work with Mr. Gonzalez focused on exploring with him why he experienced difficulty accepting his wife's definition of the issues. Mr. Gonzalez's ideas about the problem were not granted the same priority.

Next, the group discussed the family's dilemma. The therapy had become a stalemated and sometimes heated debate between a vocal mother and a "resistant" father. The couple could not agree as to whether Carlos should be allowed to go to Puerto Rico to meet his birth father. Ms. Gonzalez argued for it, and Mr. Gonzalez demonstrated (mostly nonverbally) disapproval of the idea. She supported her position with opinions about the psychodynamics of Carlos's oppositionalism and rebelliousness. Mr. Gonzalez matched her arguments with stubborn resistance.

Because the first task was to re-engage Mr. Gonzalez in the therapy, I asked the therapist to begin the session by joining with him. I explained this orientation to the group by making reference to the French revolutionary Regey Debray, who in his manual for guerrillas stated that the first task of the guerrilla is to stay alive. Likewise, to help families, therapists must connect with family members such that they continue to endorse the process. I purposefully use language that suggests that social and political metaphors are as apt in describing the functioning of systems as those drawn from biology, cybernetics, literature, medicine, and so on.

The session started with the following sequence:

Therapist: Tell me, Mr. Gonzalez, how are things at home?

Mr. Gonzalez: Nothing has change [sic], same thing.

Therapist: Nothing has changed? What does that mean?

Mr. Gonzalez: It's the same thing, you know. It's the same thing. Don't change for nothing. It's the same problem and everything.

Therapist: How has the problem developed this past week . . . since I last saw you?

Mr. Gonzalez: Well, the problem is still there, it's the same. It's getting worse, I think.

Therapist: Getting well? [English not spoken clearly by father]

Mr. Gonzalez: Yeah, you know.

Therapist: What do you mean getting well?

Mr. Gonzalez: Worse. Saturday and Sunday, right, you know, Mother's Day. Me and my wife had an argument again because she wanted to take Joey to see his father, you know . . .

Ms. Gonzalez: But that's not his fault.

Mr. Gonzalez: I know it's not his fault, but you know . . .

Therapist: So what happened? So your wife wanted to take your son to see his natural father and . . .

Ms. Gonzalez: I wanted to try to set it up. Not that I wanted to go take him. I don't even know where he is. I know he is in Puerto Rico. I don't like the situation any better, but I think he has to know his father because sometimes I feel that all that hostility and things that he has is because he don't know his father. And, I think, in his mind, I don't know because I try to talk to him but he doesn't talk, you know. When he thinks, he just stays shut up, you know. And I think that maybe some of the problems he's having is that he thinks that his father is a wonderful person and is going to come and give him

everything that we can't. And [I] think that some of that hostility he takes it out on us because . . .

Therapist: So you raise that as a possibility. And, what is your opinion of that, Mr. Gonzalez?

Mr. Gonzalez: Really, really, I don't know . . .

Ms. Gonzalez: He's not handling the situation. I think he [son] handling it a lot better.

Therapist: What do you mean he is not handling it?

Ms. Gonzalez: Like he . . .

Therapist: Let me ask Mr. Gonzalez, how you did handle it?

Mr. Gonzalez: I raise with this guy. I grew with this boy.

The preceding segment includes some straightforward triangulation material in which Ms. Gonzalez on two occasions intervenes on behalf of Carlos and against Mr. Gonzalez ("It's not [Carlos's] fault"; "[Mr. Gonzalez] is not handling the situation, I think [Carlos] is handling it a lot better"). However, the cultural issues that were also present in this initial sequence were more prominent for me: questions regarding differences in acculturation within the couple, contradictions between gender role patterns that are founded on male leadership and power, the profound insecurities that so many immigrant men experience, and the huge struggle that immigrant women who struggle to change the future of their families face. The Gonzalezes became at that point, to me, prototypical of immigrant families.

This initial sequence in the session was delivered with different intonations: Mr. Gonzalez had his arms crossed over his chest, Ms. Gonzales had extended and open arms and legs; his English was poor, his accent heavy; her English was fluent, her accent very mild; he spoke in short, simple sentences, she was able to concatenate ideas in speech; she was assertive, he was stubborn; she was capable of and sought rhetorical debate; he looked for the therapist's alliance and support. This interpersonal communications pattern is demonstrated in the following sequence, in which Mr. Gonzalez presents his definition of the problem:

> The problem is still there ... me and my wife had an argument again because she wanted to take [Carlos] to see his father.
>
> Ms. Gonzalez interjects: "That's not [Carlos's] fault."
>
> The therapist asks Mr. Gonzalez to explain and, before he responds, Ms. Gonzalez speaks first and presents her understanding of the family dilemma.
>
> The therapist gives Mr. Gonzalez a second opportunity for assertiveness and asks him his opinion of his wife's position.
>
> Mr. Gonzalez concludes the sequence by backing out of a struggle for the definition of the problem: "Really, really I don't know."
>
> Ms. Gonzalez concludes the sequence by supporting Carlos over the father's position: "[Mr. Gonzalez is] not handling the situation. I think [Carlos is] handling it a lot better."

I was struck more by the underlying differences in their values than by the language differences between Mr. and Ms. Gonzalez. I thought about the earlier acceptance of women (relative to immigrant men) into the mainstream labor market, a known structural catalyst of this values change; about how the ecology of underdevelopment that supports single-wage-earner families and male domination of women gives way, through immigration, to the social necessity of dual-wage-earner families. The accompanying necessity of change in the couples power relationship involves great personal stress and significant turmoil in the relationship. It became clearer how, in a defensive response, men look back and hold more firmly to the "myth of the return"—the illusion that life will improve once the family returns to its country of origin—and how sad it is that so frequently the use of force becomes the pathetic instrument of male insecurity and resistance to change. Focusing on the process of macrosystemic changes and contradictions challenged and helped me as a therapist and consultant by making the struggles of couples

and families both more absurd and more manageable.

Ms. Gonzalez's presentation of the problem came first. It is framed in psychological understanding and the language of emotions. She uses words like hostility. She suggests that Carlos's problem might be viewed as one of an idealized birth-father image and displaced anger toward them as custodial parents. A few minutes later Ms. Gonzalez explains her views further:

> Sometimes [Carlos] gets mad because I can't give him nothing or something that he wants because there's no money, so we can't give it to him and then he gets an attitude and stuff like that and then he'll say, "Maybe I should call my father. Maybe I should go live with him." But he dosen't know who his father is.

Her suggested intervention follows: "It's just that sometimes I feel that if [Carlos] knew what kind of person his real father is, he'll stop coming down on us so much."

Mr. Gonzalez's presentation of the problem emerged subsequently:

> I grew with this boy, you know, since three days old ... I don't think that it's good that he's looking for his father now, you know what I mean? Let his father look for him.
>
> I believe that he meets his father, things are going to get worse and then he's going to fight more with you, the other boys, and then he's going to say, "I'm going to go with my father ..."

There was not much psychological language and sophisticated thinking in the rationale offered by Mr. Gonzalez. As a result, the therapist favored Ms. Gonzalez's positions and allowed her to advocate for her definition of the therapeutic situation. The therapist's values were, without question, more akin to those of Ms. Gonzalez than to those of Mr. Gonzalez, who presented as obstinate and defensive, not verbally fluid, and nonsupportive of modern views that emphasize involvement of birth parents in the lives of children.

Also, I was impressed with how the couple's dynamics were related to their different levels of acculturation. As the session progressed, I shifted from a structural to a more ecological (immigration–acculturation-oriented) approach. The initial structural approach that was taken had emphasized joining with Mr. Gonzalez, strengthening the therapist–father coalition in order to move toward detriangulating Carlos from the spousal conflicts and supporting resolution of the spousal conflict.

As I moved to a more ecological perspective I focused on the changes related to the Gonzalezes' immigration. I tried to visualize the family's current reality against the stereotype of their traditional culture, where the man is the sanctioned head of the household and the family spokesperson and the woman is complementary to him. As the session progressed, it became evident that the Gonzalez couple was not, in practice, a traditional one:

- Ms. Gonzalez is socially prominent and speaks over her husband and criticizes him.
- Ms. Gonzalez says [regarding her husband's lack of influence over her], "I am a strong-willed person and I don't let anybody lead me. I know the way I feel and I know what I want, and that's it. I don't care . . ."
- Ms. Gonzalez's use of language is not consistent with the traditional role: "Right now [Carlos's birth father] could walk in here and my son could tell him 'fuck you, motherfucker' or whatever and I would just sit here . . ."
- Ms. Gonzalez does not insist or even expect that Carlos respect his biological father or his stepfather.

Mr. Gonzalez's manifest anxiety in regard to his wife's lack of traditionalism reveals his own traditional internalized structures. For example:

Ms. Gonzalez: Everyday, I'm shopping, paying the bills, cooking, cleaning after somebody.

Mr. Gonzalez: You want to have a party every week. During the day, you want to be outside. Sometimes I come home at 6:00 p.m. in my house and she is not home yet. I don't know where she is at all day. "But I am working," she tells me . . .

The Gonzalezes were not aware that immigration is a catalytic agent for couples. Although they were not traditional in their relationship, they had not developed, as a couple, an alternative couple's framework that could guide the growth of their relationship and family. Their power struggle is also a search for sex role and relationship models. It is the struggle of immigrants attempting to cope within an environment that is new and different. Their shared dissatisfaction is evident in the following statement, which illustrates Ms. Gonzalez's explicit resentment about restricted activity and her husband's insecurity about her changing values: "I'm always with the kids. It's been two years since I went out alone. I went out for my birthday in February, a miracle. I went to Chippendales" (a women's bar where men strip for entertainment).

Changes were taking place that were not being facilitated by dialogue. In this supervisory session I began to think about ways in which therapist–client dialogue about cultural and immigration-driven changes can be of therapeutic benefit. Miguel Hernandez (1996), Hernandez and McGoldrick (1999), and Celia Falicov (1998), among others, have also found their own routes to very similar conclusions about the usefulness of reframing personal dilemmas in the context of acculturation change. Hernandez and I have further developed this perspective in a systematic way known as the *Culture and Migration Dialogue* (Inclan & Hernandez, 1992)

Toward the end of the session, after Mr. and Ms. Gonzalez's discussion of practical issues related to household chores and skewed responsibilities and privileges, I went into the room as a consultant, and the following sequence took place:

Consultant: This is difficult for them. It has nothing to do with him and her as persons. It has something to do with the fact that they . . . Are you Puerto Rican?

Mr. Gonzalez: Yeah.

Ms. Gonzalez: I was born and raised here [in the United States].

Mr. and Ms. Gonzalez established differences that they, at some level, understood as related to their differences in cultural experiences. He identifies himself as Puerto Rican, and she conditions and differentiates her identity: "I was born and raised here." *I repeated to myself the learning of the day: Socialization, to a very large extent, frames our expectations of self and other, our views of the world, and, therefore, a good understanding of cultural differences in socialization is a crucial part of couple's and family therapy.*

Next, there was follow-up on the theme of cultural differenes:

Consultant: They are victims of their cultures.

Ms. Gonzalez: He's too macho, and I am too modern!

Consultant: He grew up in one environment with one idea and she grew up here. So it's very difficult. I don't know if they understand that they are trying to do something that is very difficult ... to match [with each other] ... it [socialization differences] just really colors everything that you do. They are trying to find a common place, but it is tough. I think that you will be able to help them because it is not a fight that she is having with him or he with her. It is a bigger fight. And they are not fighters, they are puppets, its really one culture and another culture, and they are just little grains of sand.

The intervention was, at this time, only somewhat helpful to the family, who only later was able to work through some of its implications. As intended, it was immediately helpful for the therapist.

Therapist: Let's continue this Thursday because I think that was clarifying. I don't know if for you, ... but for me. I didn't realize you were born here. I thought you were both from Puerto Rico, so ...

Ms. Gonzalez: All my parents were raised here.

Therapist: Very different cultures.

Mr. Gonzalez: I don't think it has to be nothing that she was born here and I was born in Puerto Rico ...

Ms. Gonzalez: It is ... I keep telling him.

ACT II: 1967

The cultural reframing of personal dilemmas and the Culture and Migration Dialogue is a vehicle that Miguel Hernandez and I developed to facilitate the examination of changes that are consequent to immigration. It derives from the positive results that discussions about "untold stories," experiences, feelings, and ideas about their immigration have in the evolutionary and healing process of families with which we have worked. The insights that became apparent in the Gonzalez family interview provided some of the initial curiosity for the further development of this method of working.

Culture and Migration Dialogue is a personally challenging and rewarding method of working for Hernandez and me who, as immigrants, are fellow travelers and have our own set of experiences and feelings, some of which are more processed than others (as the reader is able to ascertain from the Act I: 1986 section). It is, at its best, as the title suggests, a shared process, a dialogue that includes the therapist in the sharing process. Thus, therapists who are preparing and willing to lead Culture and Migration Dialogue groups benefit from prior participation as group members. Although many therapists have had opportunity to explore and share information about ourselves as men and women, and as parents, according to our sexual preference, ethnicity, and so on, there has been little opportunity for therapists to share about ourselves as immigrants. This silence has also contributed to the relative inattention that immigration has received in the professional literature and in clinical practice.

The therapist's awareness of and manner of processing his or her immigration experience influences his or her ability to access this important realm of family dynamics. Key elements of family dynamics (relationship patterns in one's family of origin as well as in one's current family) open up when this domain of experience is considered. When this information is considered, therapists gain opportunities for reframing family dilemmas in culturally contextual ways. It has been my experience that the uncovering, validation, and reframing of immigration-catalyzed family conflict facilitates the healing process. It is in this spirit that I share my own experience of immigration.

I was born into a Puerto Rican family of relative affluence that provided me a somewhat sheltered and privileged upbringing. Family stories included those about my uncle's college experience at the University of Virginia law school and others about my parents' college years at Cornell University and Manhattanville College. In 1965, at age 15, I left Puerto Rico to spend my junior year of high school at a Benedictine school in Rhode Island. My social class background cushioned some of the potency of the culture shock I experienced. (I have since learned that social class privilege buffers but does not fully mitigate the impact of migration and cultural transition.)

My parents and I were surprised at the scope of the personal transformation that was initiated by my migration to Rhode Island. I did not foresee the magnitude of the change, or the direction that it would take. The most important fact about immigration is probably this one: It sets into motion unpredictable personal changes. Because past experiences play an important role in guiding people's expectations, and because immigration represents a profound change in the social context of families, the ambitions and expectations of many immigrants may be framed by values that were useful in another context and time but may not be atuned to the adaptive and normative expectations of the current environment. This discrepancy results in greater stress and conflict within and between loved ones. In this regard, the story of the Gonzalez family is not different from my own or from those of numerous others.

One thing of which my parents and I were certain, at the time, was that my immigration would be a temporary one. On completion of the task at hand (which typically was getting an education, for people of my social background), I would return. Thirty-three years later, I am still in the United States. I have frequently observed that many immigrants of today migrate with the idea of returning "home" in a not-so-distant future. This contrasts with the "traditional" immigrant outlook, in which "burning bridges" behind oneself is more prevalent. This expectation of returning home is the source of

other challenges for the immigrant, the family that sees him or her off, and the society that receives him or her. In me, such an outlook clearly had the effect of postponing and restricting an open experimentation with the new culture. Earl Shorris (1992) has documented this phenomenon in *Latinos*, in which he poignantly described how different types of social accommodations to the United States are consistent with the views and expectations that immigrants have about themselves.

My parents were looking to provide me with an opportunity to develop comfort with North American culture. As they saw it, such exposure would equip me with the skills to attain the greatest personal and economic success possible as Puerto Rico continued to develop. I had little idea of what I was seeking, although it was very clear to me that some change was necessary. I was underachieving academically and beginning to exhibit behavior that is born of boredom and lack of direction and purpose. For awhile I thought I should have been more purposeful about my coming to the United States. I have since learned that it is common for immigrants to believe that becoming more "North American" would be beneficial.

It is ironic that being away from Puerto Rico facilitated the reclaiming of my Puerto Rican-ness. I have learned that this process is common. I have also witnessed, with pain and anger, how uncomfortable large segments of society can be with this phenomenon. Political conservatives fear immigrants' search for and embrace of their roots and culture. It is their belief that embracing one's own culture will result in a closing of one's mind and heart to a different culture. My personal experience, as shared in this chapter, is that honoring one's history and culture is a necessary ingredient for becoming a full participant in a new society.

As "Jimmy," I arrived in Rhode Island, and immediately the transformation toward becoming "Jaime" again began. Reclaiming my birth name took 6 years, from my time in Rhode Island, through the development of political awareness and a love for the humanities, and through 4 years at Georgetown University. The definitive change moment occurred in New York's Washington Square Park when, in the beginning of our friendship, I told a very dear professor at New York University, George Kaufer, that he could call me either "Jimmy" or "Jaime." Kaufer, in his Socratic style, suggested repeatedly that I could choose my name.

At school in Rhode Island my first reaction was of culture shock and fear, which was great for my grades. I buried myself in my studies, shocked the school, and delighted my parents. At the conclusion of the first term I was the third highest ranking student in my class. Culture shock and fear are common among immigrants of varying social classes. In New York this is painfully observed in the many workers who drive taxis, clean offices, run elevators, or are submerged in blue-collar work, sometimes for years on end, before they stop to reflect on this initial stretch of the immigration run. Some see a future; others see unfulfilled dreams and promises. My reaction was one of confusion. I felt out of place. It took years for me to understand why I had become engrossed in the process of adaptation suffered by transplanted trees. First the new trees appear sad or wilted; most look as if they will not make it, and some do not make it. Others get help. Some are better suited for the challenge. Then I began to notice that the arrival of new trees also has an effect on the existing vegetation. Some plants benefit; some struggle with the new arrival for turf and nutrients; and some are negatively affected, temporarily or permanently. This became, for me, a metaphor for the process of immigration.

Those high grades additionally overburdened me with the feeling of being an impostor. I worried whether I could consistently hold that rank. The feeling made me hesitant. I finally understood that it does make a difference to play in one's home court. At an away game, one is not as confident, and the calls don't go one's way.

My grades went down every one of the next three terms at the school. My identity conflict was inversely correlated with academic performance. My depression and social withdrawal became intense. These feelings, and the influences of Mohammed Ali, Bob Dylan, Vietnam, and Cuba, in the ferment of the 1960s, brought about changes in my worldview. I began to understand fully how the environment—the social system—conditions the potential of individuals. Like so many others at that time, I

accepted the view that awareness is inextricably connected to social responsibility.

I participated in the social life of the school, but my major activity was internal, private. It was activity that I was unable to understand or describe until many years later. In conducting workshops on immigration, I have similarly observed the direct relation that exists between the level of trauma surrounding the immigration and one's freedom to connect emotionally and critically to this trauma. It has taught me patience in my work with immigrants.

I am very grateful to two people who shared every detail of my 2 years' experience in Rhode Island: Juan, who was a Venezuelan school veteran who had been at the school since the eighth grade, and my cousin, Jaime Luis, who had arrived from Puerto Rico only a year before I had. Together they provided the holding environment that I needed to survive and the contrast of style and character that would allow me to reflect and learn from our experience.

Juan had his *cuatro* (a Latin American string instrument) and, later, a guitar, on hand all the time. As opposed to Jaime Luis, Juan was more willing to be critical of what he experienced and to embrace his Latin American-ness. The transformation that began for Juan in Rhode Island continued as he passed through Massachusetts Institute of Technology and then found social meaning and affirmation in his work with the poor in his native Venezuela. Having found his social grounding, Juan is currently opening doors to new cultures. He, along with his wife and two children, moved to France for 2 years, where they adapted with great ease.

Jaime Luis died an early death 4 years ago. The doctors say he died of a heart attack. He had just arrived back in Puerto Rico from a business trip to England, called his mother, as he always did when traveling, and collapsed to his death. I believe Jaime Luis died because he was denied a way to find ease and comfort in himself and his Puerto Rican-ness. He was so purposeful and driven that he asked few questions and rarely raised doubts. I believe his style denied him the opportunity to experience the fullness of life. He felt he could not rest or deviate from his goal: success, which he approached through mainstream conformity. Jaime Luis was the guy who would resist wallowing in experience: "Don't think about it," he would say, "or you'll go crazy." Paradoxically, he died trying to avoid going crazy. He refused to see that the half-full glass was also half empty. I believe that a dose of "depression" and some room to reflect about his immigration and transformation processes would have saved his life. There are so many others like my cousin Jaime Luis, dying or living in an anxious chase.

In Rhode Island I began to develop a strong sense of difference between the "them" of the larger society and the Latin American "us": We played dominoes more than cards and played *futbol*, not football. Mostly, we were the guys who stayed back at the school when those painful short holidays came and all the other kids went to their homes, often with friends from the school. It became clear on those holidays that there are differences. In school we were all friends, played on the same teams, shared dormitory rooms and classes, and fooled around together. But when those holidays came, the dominoes players stayed back. Until late at night we sat in our dormitories, trying to make our guitars sing. Each of us, in different ways, learned to face the social realities of our new environment, its values, prejudices, rules, and expectations.

Now I am married and have three children. The youngest is 16. They have been raised in New York City. They attend(ed) the United Nations International School. They feel more at home in New York than I do. They feel Puerto Rican, each intensely, each in his or her own way. My wife and I are meeting their friends and their friends' parents. Some of them are beginning to visit with us when we take vacations from school and work. We usually have a great time. As is known, change takes time, usually generations. This chapter, however, is not about my children but about what I learned as a young immigrant and how it has affected my work with families.

In Act I and Act II in this chapter the reader is presented with two men at different stages of the acculturation process. In my case, it is evident that it was not until "Jimmy" was transformed to "Jaime" that I was able to participate and contribute to the society to which I had immigrated. It is a very straightforward process: a firm anchoring (through

validation and critical appraisal) in one's historical identity promotes integration and effective participation in new environments and relationship patterns, in family and society. Mr. Gonzalez, at the time of this interview, had not had opportunity to review and affirm his historical identity. His presentation of his self to his wife, children, and society was tentative, and his general posture was defensive. It is not surprising that his willingness to consider new alternatives (approaches to problems, shared power relationship) was limited.

ACT III: WORKING WITH IMMIGRANT FAMILIES: WHAT I KNOW NOW

Spurred by my early work with families such as the Gonzalezes and my participation in the Cultural and Migration Dialogue, I have learned much about the special problems that are part of the immigration experience and how these problems affect the couples and families who come to the clinic for help. Although it is beyond the scope of this chapter to review these in depth, I will attempt to outline the major issues family therapists must keep in mind when working with immigrant families. These themes are part of the work included in the Culture and Migration Dialogue (Hernandez & McGoldrick, 1999; Inclan & Hernandez, 1992) which is a method for developing a "cultural bridge" with immigrant families.

The Culture and Migration Dialogue is oriented by one's personal and clinical experience regarding the beneficial effect of connectedness and continuity (to one's historical, cultural, and familial roots) in the journey to evolve culturally and integrate into a different environment. Seamans and Fish (2000) summarized the background of this concept. They traced these insights to the work of Kurt Lewin (1948). Lewin studied the immigration and adaptation experiences of Jews and concluded that "a minority person's sense of security, stability, and self-esteem depended on the degree to which he identified with his own group." According to Lewin, when a minority group person attempts to leave his or her own group and form an identity affiliation with a "more powerful" group, he or she is usually rebuffed by the majority group. According to Lewin, the ensuing effect is one of social marginality, of nonbelongingness to either the former group or the new group. The psychological concomitant is increased vulnerability to feelings of insecurity, fear, and maladjustment. Others (e.g., Carter, 1991; McGoldrick, Pearce, & Giordano, 1982) have reached similar conclusions.

Immigration presents a challenge for ongoing connectedness and continuity. Discontinuity can develop with regard to the aspects of one's culture that are lost as the immigrant relocates. Immigration also involves significant changes in the personal network of relationships that sustain and support the social lives of individuals. Within the family, immigration generally serves as a catalyst for differences between the generations and the sexes. For example, it is very common for immigrant families to face the kind of sex role conflicts that are exacerbated by the different rates of acculturation in the spouses, as in the Gonzalez family. Similarly, the internalization by children of new and different values from their parents can result in increased intrafamily conflict. This conflict is especially difficult to negotiate when the parents and the children's generations are unaware of the values framework that organizes the beliefs of the other family members.

For example, in a recent therapy session an immigrant mother was arguing the "established norm" that she or her husband accompany their 15-year-old son to social gatherings and deny him permission to visit *casas ajenas* (foreign homes). The son, to my surprise, given the many instances when anger and rebellion were already manifest, pleaded for help from the therapist by looking at him with eyes full of despair. The therapist, informed by the Culture and Migration Dialogue, proceeded to frame the question as one that needed a "broader discussion" that facilitated the son's "understanding" of the mother's point of view. The therapist asked the son if he was aware of his parents' experience in growing up. The son made some general references to "old fashioned and religious adherence." The family had not had opportunity to dialogue about this issue in any depth, and discontinuity between the parents' experience in growing up and the current environment and *mores* of their son was obviously present. The therapist recommended that the parents

talk about their growing-up experience. He asked the mother to start the discussion by describing in detail the rural setting in which she grew up, including the home, the number of persons who lived there and their relationships to each, the daily routines for the father and for the mother, the meals they ate, and so on. As intended, it became very clear, especially to the mother, who was the principal target of the intervention, that the environment that served as a childhood frame of reference for her was very different from their current environment. It is routinely my experience that, for sharing in this way, a 1-hour session is insufficient. This need for more time to share suggests both the necessity of these reviews and the lack of openness that immigrants feel to share past experiences with their families in an open-ended descriptive way. Allowing enough time for the narrative to be told served the purpose of validating the mother's experience in the context of her time and place.

Immigrants, for the sake of their children's adaptation to the new society, or because of internalized inferiority feelings, frequently do not share their history and culture with their children. Some expressions of this are the imposition by parents of English as a language of preference and the overvaluation of North American products and methods over those of their native countries. This is one of several approaches that immigrants take to the mixing of cultures.

> Some immigrants may attempt to wall off the past, forcing their children to speak only English and never talking about the country they left behind. Or they may wall off the new culture, living and working in an ethnic enclave, never learning English or negotiating the U.S. system. Others assume a pattern of biculturality, passing to their children their stories and traditions while embracing the ways of the new culture. (Hernandez & McGoldrick, 1999, p. 173)

In my experience I have learned that there are especially serious consequences to becoming cut off from one's history or current environment, irrespective of the cutoff direction (culture of origin or current culture).

The method of the Culture and Migration Dialogue is a family-centered means of helping families prevent or work through culturally based cutoffs. It embraces the potentials of coevolution and individuation, as a family, through a process where "old world" experiences—for example, those of the parents' generation—are validated and legitimized as historically and contextually meaningful before "new culture" considerations are entertained. In therapy sessions I refer to the process as "building bridges." This concept is consistent with the notions of "starting where the patient is" (vs. starting at "you are now in North America"). It is also consistent with the therapeutic notion that benefit for the family can be obtained by re-experiencing incomplete or unsuccessfully processed changes associated with life cycle transitions. The therapeutic technique involves establishing with the family a point of bifurcation at which experiences were not shared or resolved and guiding the family through a conjoint process of understanding and renegotiating a new framework for continuity and differentiation. In the case described a few paragraphs earlier, what the therapist thought would be a two-session process ran over into the fifth session. Although the adolescent probed, and the mother made leading comments about discipline ("the strap," "respect," "parental authority") that could have moved the focus of attention away from the intended narrative, the therapist honored the Culture and Migration Dialogue method by allowing the parent time for a full explication of her experience. The sequence and timing of the explication and discussion parts of the dialogue are of essence. The potential for the derailment of the narrative about culture and values turning, early in the process, into polarized conflict is significant. It is valuable, then, at least in cases referred for therapy, that the process be held with therapeutic guidance. I have found that validation of the parental experience helps to increase the flexibility of both parents and children to consider new ways of relating to one another. Understanding that beliefs and expectations are conditioned by one's historical experience consistently helps individuals value the point of view of

the other, which is an important condition for successful family therapy. Learning to accept differences is especially important in work with immigrants, because cultural change and thus the possibility of differences in the values framework that shapes understanding is so prominent.

In the case just described, the young man became very curious about his mother's experience in growing up. He had had no idea of what life had been like for her. He developed a curiosity about visiting his country of origin and developed greater closeness with his mother. He saw her as a "victim" of an abusive (to women) and restrictive family system. This led to further interesting discussions. The idea of "victim" was, at first, clearer to him than to his mother, who described the experience with pride akin to the soldier who describes training camp as formative of moral strength and character. Through these discussions, the mother was able to reconsider her growing-up experience as both typical of the times and yet not fair to her. She did not move to consider her experience as an abusive one, which was her son's conceptualization of it. He, on the other hand, learned that his valuation of his mother's experience as abusive was dependent on his current, North American values framework. A critical element of the Culture and Migration Dialogue process is to attend to what family members feel. The ideas of use of narrative and the emphasis on validation of experiences address this part of the process. Therapy, however, also involves cognitive mastery and restructuring. One thing that I have found useful when working with parents and children in the processing of differences at the cognitive level is to present the children and parents with a model of cultural differences in the passage to adulthood (see Figure 18.1). Inclan and Herron (1989) described the traditional model as a two-stage model and the current model as a three-stage model. I ask the family to discuss the implications of having different models of what is normative and expected as a process of transition from childhood to adulthood. The family just described found that discussion of the differences they were experiencing at the level of cognitive models was helpful in further allowing the mother and son to understand and respect their differences.

Traditional Model

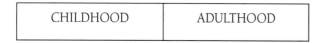

Current Model

CHILDHOOD	ADOLESCENCE	ADULTHOOD

Source: (Inclan and Herron, 1989)

FIGURE 18.1. Models of the passage to adulthood

In the process (the fourth and fifth sessions), the son was empowered to openly question his mother and the limits that she was imposing on his individuation and ability to establish independent relationships. The mother became more understanding of and sympathetic toward his requests. She did not, however, immediately commit to a change in approach. She went only as far as saying that she now understood that he was "very near that point." The son was subsequently allowed greater latitude in building social relationships. I believe that these discussions eased the way for the family changes that followed.

I recommend that therapists working with immigrant families consider use of the Culture and Migration Dialogue techniques as part of therapy. The aims are represented in the notion of making a "cultural bridge." To build the bridge the therapist first validates the old value or attitudes by crossing from the "here and now" side of the bridge into the historical past, which is the domain of the internalized values and cognitive structures of the historical and more traditional culture of the client(s). From within that territory the therapist evaluates when the couple or family is ready to face the challenge of crossing the bridge. This is a second-order migration. It represents accepting the notion of ecological health, that is, the emotional acceptance of the fact that a new environment demands a full new approach toward it. When the couple or family is comfortable with this notion, then they are ready for a further challenge. The couple or family can ad-

dress the reformulation of their network of interpersonal relationships. As a unit that addresses social demands, the family must adjust in form and function to remain ecologically healthy. Old customs and habits that were successful adaptations to a former social reality are at this point more open to review and change.

The review of culture and migration dynamics and the challenge that this poses for change includes, but is not limited to, a review of gender relationships. Many therapists directly focus on the review of gender role formation, function, and consequences. Because so much of my clinical experience is based on work with immigrants, I have used an immigration and acculturation framework to address the same issues. I attempt to develop a framework for the discussion of change that includes the broader orientation toward an ecologically healthy life. Cultural identity, class consciousness, race, gender relationships, and other forms of privilege all become subjects for review. When working with immigrant families I begin with the assumption that attending to the immigration experience will best enable me to enter into the world of the family with which I am consulting.

References

Carter, R. T. (1991). Racial identity attitudes and psychological functioning. *Journal of Multicultural Counseling and Development, 19,* 105–111.

Falicov, C. J. (1998). *Latino families in therapy: A guide to multicultural practice.* New York: Guilford Press.

Hernandez, M. (1996). Central American families. In M. McGoldrick, J. Giordano, & J. K. Pearce (Eds.), *Ethnicity & family therapy* (2nd ed., pp. 214–224). New York: Guilford Press.

Hernandez, M., & McGoldrick, M. (1999). Migration & family life cycle. In B. Carter & M. McGoldrick (Eds.), The expanded family life cycle: Individual, family and social perspectives (3rd ed., pp. 169–183).

Inclan, J., & Hernandez, M. (1992). Cross-cultural perspectives and co-dependence: The case of poor hispanics. *American Journal of Orthopsychiatry, 62*(2), 245–255.

Inclan, J., & Herron, G. (1989). Puerto Rican adolescents. In J. T. Gibbs & L. N. Huang

(Eds.), *Children of Color* (pp. 251–277). New York: Jossey-Bass.

Lewin, K. (1948). *Resolving social conflicts*. New York: Harper.

McGoldrick, M., Giordano, J., & Pearce, J. K. (Eds.). (1996). *Ethnicity and family therapy* (2nd ed.). New York: Guilford Press.

Shorris, E. (1992). *Latinos: A biography of the people*. New York: Norton.

Seamans, M. P., & Stone Fish, L. (2000). Dissecting life with a jewish scalpel: A qualitative analysis of jewish centered family life. *Family Process, 39*(1), 121–139.

Part IV
GENDER

INTEGRATING GENDER AND FAMILY SYSTEMS THEORIES: THE "BOTH/AND" APPROACH TO TREATING A POSTMODERN COUPLE

Ronald F. Levant and Louise B. Silverstein

This chapter arises out of an ongoing collaboration in which we are working to combine family systems theory and gender theory into an integrated approach to couples and family therapy. Family systems theory (Bowen, 1978; Kerr & Bowen, 1988) has emphasized the reciprocal nature of relationship processes, minimizing gender differences in communication styles and expectations about power and privilege. Feminist theory, in contrast, has made gender politics the focus of treatment and has minimized the systemic nature of relationships. Our efforts carry forward the pioneering "both/and" approach of Goldner (1988), who integrated feminist and family systems theory in her work with battering. However, we prefer to refer to *gender theory* rather than *feminist theory*, because our thinking also integrates the perspective of the new psychology of men (Levant & Pollack, 1995). Thus, we integrate what is known about gender differences (including masculine gender socialization and role strain) with a grasp of relationships as "emotional systems." Integrating these two theoretical paradigms provides couples with the tools for getting "unstuck" from even the most intractable relationship crises. To date, we have used this approach only with White, heterosexual, middle-class couples. In order for it to be useful for a wide range of couples, issues of immigration, ethnicity, racism, class bias, and homophobia would need to be incorporated in the same way that gender

ideology has been addressed in the current model.

THE BUILDING BLOCKS OF OUR INTEGRATED APPROACH

This is a multiphasic approach, and we outline it briefly below. Although we describe three phases of treatment, it is not a sequential or linear process. These phases can occur simultaneously and interact with each other in complex ways.

Phase 1: Learning to "Think Gender"
Educate the Couple Not to Take Things Personally. When the person we love most in the world does not respond in the way that we hoped he or she would, we might feel rejected, neglected, and even unloved. However, when we begin to see this person's behavior as the result of the past 3,000 years of gender socialization it is sometimes easier to feel less personally betrayed. Our approach teaches couples to view their partner's upsetting behaviors as "gender-based disappointments" that are the result of a historical and cultural framework. This reframing allows the injured partner to begin to feel less personally betrayed and can defuse relationship conflict.
Treat the Man's Normative Alexithymia. Levant and Kopecky (1995/1996) described how traditional masculine gender role socialization leads to the development of normative male *alexithymia,* that is, the

Correspondence concerning this chapter should be addressed to Ronald F. Levant, Office of the Dean, Center for Psychological Studies, Nova Southeastern University, 3301 College Avenue, Fort Lauderdale, FL 33314.

inability to discern one's own emotions and put them into words. We use a psychoeducational approach to help men overcome alexithymia and to develop emotional self-awareness (see Levant, 1997, 1998, for a more detailed description).

Help the Woman Let Go of the Responsibility for the Couple's Emotional Life. Traditional feminine gender role socialization trains women to feel that they are responsible for managing the emotions of the couple. Again, we use a psychoeducational approach to help women relinquish sole responsibility for the emotional life of the couple. Explaining the dynamics of pursuing and distancing in marital interaction can also be very helpful here.

Phase 2: Learning to "Think Systems"

Many people believe that if only they could find the "right man" or the "right woman," their marriage would work. People enter most relationships with an unrealistic expectation of how well a spouse should fit their ideal. As real life begins to interfere with one's fantasy of "the perfect marriage," a person tends to blame his or her spouse. The person assumes that he or she has simply married the "wrong" man or woman. Unless this misconception (which is based on what Bowen, 1978, described as "emotional fusion") is corrected, couples tend either to divorce or continue to live together in an atmosphere of blame and dissatisfaction.

Although it is easy to be clear about all the things one's partner does wrong, it is infinitely more difficult to focus on the part that one plays in beginning or maintaining negative relationship patterns. It is very easy to get caught in the "blame game." However, if a person does succeed in acknowledging what he or she contributes to the problem, he or she can then become empowered to change many of the unsatisfying aspects of the relationship.

A central construct in family systems theory is "differentiation of self," which is roughly equivalent to emotional maturity (Bowen, 1978). Individuals with emotional problems have lower degrees of differentiation of Self, which is reflected in their tendency to borrow or lend the Self to others. As a result, behavior for such individuals is *reciprocal*—that is, the behavior of each person in a relationship is dependent on and reinforced by the behavior of the

Other(s). Therefore, if one person in a relationship changes, those changes will be felt by the other person, and he or she also will change, automatically. Hence, if even one person in a relationship can increase the ability to focus on the Self, the total amount of conflict decreases. Our approach challenges each member of the couple to stop trying to change the Other and begin to take responsibility for changing the Self. This shift in gaze from Other to Self is a major component of our work.

Phase 3: Family-of-Origin Work

Most people can incorporate some of the principles of Phases 1 and 2 into our relationships. They then experience a dramatic decrease in conflict and a dramatic increase in the pleasure of their intimate relationships. However, some patterns of relating have developed over many generations and so are extremely difficult to change. For many people, understanding gender issues and the reciprocal nature of patterns of relating is not enough to achieve the kind of Self-focus that is necessary for enduring behavior change.

The ways in which people respond to their intimate partners have been established in their families during the very early years of life. Thus, the most effective way of changing those patterns is to return to one's early attachment figures and change the way in which one responds to family members. In Bowenian family systems theory it is necessary to rework the original relationships, that is, to practice being a Self in the presence of one's family. Work in the context of the therapeutic relationship is not sufficient.

We suggest that our clients undertake efforts to uncover the patterns of relating that have developed in their families of origin, including those based on gender role socialization. Most systems of therapy teach people to look back into their families to understand what happened to them as children. However, in some approaches one's understanding does not get beyond what one's parents did wrong. This way of thinking about families is not helpful, because it institutionalizes our tendency to blame our parents rather than helping one take responsibility for oneself. Unless one can achieve an empathic understanding of one's parents as children in their own families, one usually remains stuck in a pattern of blaming one's spouse. Maintaining a sense of one's self as an innocent victim of evil parents perpetuates a focus on the "sins" of one's partner.

A POSTMODERN COUPLE AT AN IMPASSE

The case we describe in this chapter was treated by Ronald F. Levant and is written from his point of view. Barbara, age 38, is a highly sought-after consultant in the financial services industry, and David, age 45, is a scientist who works for a major research university. Married in 1990, they had a true postmodern marriage: Both Barbara and David had high-powered careers and were committed to a role-sharing marriage. The couple graciously gave their consent to having their therapy described in this chapter, in which their identities have been disguised, and they have reviewed and commented on an earlier draft of the chapter.

The normative developmental stress of a first child transformed this role-sharing couple into a traditional marriage (see Silverstein, 1996, for a fuller description of this normative transformation). A baby, Jason, was born in November 1994. Barbara had originally planned to return to work full-time; however, after the baby was born, she panicked, feeling that she could not "abandon" Jason. She fired her child care helper and drastically cut back on the amount of time she spent at work in order to care for Jason. Barbara described this decision as "falling on her sword" in her career.

David, in contrast, remained in his demanding job. He made some accommodations to Jason's arrival, cutting back from 100 to 60 hours per week. However, his job requires that he be away often and for long stretches of time, traveling to major cities in the United States and Europe. His efforts to cut back have not been enough for Barbara, who feels utterly abandoned when he travels. His decision to take an extended series of trips when Jason was 6 weeks old hurt her "beyond the ability of words to convey." As a result, at the time therapy began, and for about a year afterward, Barbara was episodically furious at David. David, in response, felt very guilty and extremely anxious. The crisis intensified, and they entered couples therapy when Jason was 4 months old.

At the beginning of therapy the couple was clearly at an impasse. For example, at one of the first meetings Barbara said that she wanted David to be her partner. David responded that when he tries to be her partner, either in the form of suggesting plans, taking Jason, or talking to her about her life, she balks. Her rebuttal: His suggestions of plans irk her because they sound like he wants to escape from the responsibilities of parenthood, and that is the last thing she wants to hear because she feels so trapped; when he takes Jason he isn't sufficiently sensitive; and she is so furious with him she cannot talk to him about her life. As of this writing I had seen the couple for 40 sessions over a 14-month period.

Phase 1: Learning to "Think Gender"
Learning Not to Take Things Personally. From our perspective, this couple is experiencing a postmodern dilemma. They are part of the first generation to come of age in the postfeminist era. They were raised to expect that men and women can both have high-powered careers and assume equal responsibility for nurturing children.

However, traditional gender role norms remain strong in our culture. Thus, although Barbara had consciously planned to combine career and motherhood, her unexamined gut-level assumptions (resulting from her own socialization into traditional motherhood ideology) were that becoming a working mother would be the equivalent of "abandoning" her baby. Similarly, David had good intentions in terms of becoming a nurturing father. However, he became overwhelmed by his unexamined gut-level assumptions (resulting from his own socialization into traditional fatherhood ideology), which defined a good father as a "good provider." His anxiety about being able to provide adequate material resources for his family made it impossible for him to make significant changes in his commitment to work.

The first phase of work with this couple involved reframing their sense of personal betrayal and emotional abandonment as a "gender-based disappointment." Their behaviors were defined as a reversion to gender stereotyped roles, with Barbara becoming a full-time homemaker and David becoming the sole provider.

Barbara did not realize that it was her own internalization of traditional mothering ideology that led her to believe that, when push comes to shove, family responsibilities fall to the woman. Rather, she felt that she was forced to sacrifice her career because David could not or would not make a commitment to sharing child care on an equal basis. Similarly, David did not realize that his internalized vision of father as provider did not allow him to make a significant commitment to direct child care. Rather, he felt that Barbara did not appreciate his authentic attempts to assume half of the child care responsibilities.

It is not uncommon in states of high anxiety for people to regress to overlearned roles—in this case, those learned through traditional gender role socialization. However, most people do not realize that the birth of a child, in addition to being a positive developmental phase, is also a stressful event that generates anxiety in everyone. Without this perspective, each member of a couple often feels emotionally abandoned by his or her spouse. Learning to "think gender" helps to defuse some of the anger toward the Other.

Treating Normative Male Alexithymia and Normative Female Emotional Flooding.

(Although we have listed these two issues separately in the theoretical section above, we present them together here because of the reciprocal nature of their expression in therapy and real life.) At the beginning of therapy, David was literally shaking with anxiety in the session but had great difficulty identifying his emotions and putting them into words. He had been sleeping poorly and had lost 14 lbs. Barbara, in contrast, was flooded with emotions, particularly rage and fear of abandonment, and was fighting depression.

Barbara was fortuitously unable to make an early session due to child-care problems. This provided an opportunity to engage David in the psychoeducational program mentioned above in order to help increase his emotional self-awareness. As discussed elsewhere, men often find such a structured approach with clearly defined objectives very congenial to their learning styles (Levant, 1997, 1998). David took to this work and did quite well, which helped him take responsibility for his emotions. As the work progressed over the first few months, Barbara became better able to contain her emotions and deal

with them constructively, even though we were not focusing on her directly. Her progress was due in part to the fact that she felt comforted and relieved by the focus on David. His work in therapy relieved her of the responsibility of managing his emotional life as well as her own. David's increasing ability to discuss his emotions enabled him to take an active role in the problem-solving process. His increasing activity helped her to manage her anxiety so that she was then able to begin to approach him with less emotional intensity. This is a good example of how work with one member of a couple can help the other member to change as well.

Addressing the Pursuit–Distance Dynamic.

Prior to these improvements, Barbara and David's impasse was a classical gender-based "pursuit–distance" (Fogarty, 1979) or "demand–withdraw" (Christensen & Heavey, 1990) relationship. Barbara became overwhelmed with her emotions, that is, her sense of isolation and anxiety about mothering. She then pursued David, pouring out her feelings and demanding that he respond and comfort her with a sense of closeness. Unfortunately, David could respond only with distancing and withdrawal, which in turn increased Barbara's sense of desperation.

David felt terribly guilty about Barbara's unhappiness. However, because of his alexithymia he was helpless in the face of her demands for empathy. He thus withdrew emotionally. In an unconscious distancing maneuver, he often caved in to her demands about sharing child care arrangements without fully considering their consequences in terms of his need to modify work commitments. He then did not make the necessary arrangements at work (abetted by his difficulty in disappointing his colleagues) and ended up not meeting his commitments to Barbara, who felt doubly betrayed. Her despair about her situation was exacerbated by her rage at his inability to respond. She then became flooded with reactivity again, and the cycle would begin anew.

To help the couple emerge from this pursuit–distance impasse and improve their ability to resolve conflict, I taught them the standard marital communication and conflict resolution skills (empathic listening, nonreactive responding using "I" statements, and attempting to find solutions to conflicts that maximized both of their interests). They were able to use this method both in the session and at home and were moderately successful.

Initial Resolution of Reversion to Stereotyped Roles. As David's ability to discuss his feelings improved, he was able to say that he was getting mixed messages from Barbara that confused and frustrated him. On the one hand, Barbara said that she wanted him to participate more in caring for Jason. However, she also had trouble relinquishing control. Sometimes he felt shut out when she was nursing or putting the baby to sleep. At other times, she was critical of his way of managing Jason.

This is another typical gender-based conflict. In the traditional family, one of the only areas in which women have had power was in terms of child rearing. Thus, although they have felt burdened by child care, it has also been a source of power for them. Because Barbara had drastically cut back her job, child care had now become one of the few areas in which she had power and control.

From David's perspective, traditional masculine gender role socialization had not provided him with the skills for nurturing. Although he wanted to be an active caregiver, his sense of incompetence made him particularly sensitive to Barbara's criticism. This sensitivity predisposed him to withdraw from child care opportunities, leaving Barbara feeling abandoned. Again, gender socialization, rather than a lack of caring, was constructing their conflict.

After 4 months of therapy in which they were helped to understand much of their conflict as gender based, Barbara and David were able to negotiate a shared parenting arrangement. David was to care for Jason for 3-hour periods, allowing Barbara to have that time to do some professional work. Later in therapy the couple achieved a deeper and more significant resolution of this issue, which we discuss after a consideration of the work that the couple did in Phases 2 and 3.

Phase 2: Systems-Level Change

By helping David focus on what was going on inside him, I helped him begin to take responsibility for his feelings. Through this change, he reduced the amount of Self that he was borrowing from Barbara. Similarly, I helped Barbara realize her part in their failed negotiations. Barbara was able to gain better

control of her emotions and to feel less desperate. As her anxiety decreased, she had less need to pursue David in a demanding and blaming way, and he, reciprocally, felt less pressure to distance. Amelioration of the pursuing–distancing impasse allowed the couple to achieve a greater sense of closeness. From this position of greater intimacy, they were able to negotiate an arrangement that met both of their needs.

Understanding the reciprocal nature of their interaction helped each member of the couple begin to focus on the Self rather than blaming the Other. Barbara was able to understand that a part of her assuming sole responsibility for Jason emerged from her own definition of mothering, not simply because of David's failure to coparent more equitably. David was able to articulate his definition of father as provider, which helped him understand his reluctance to limit his commitment to paid work. This realization helped him become more responsible in following through on his commitments to Barbara.

Phase 3: Family-of-Origin Issues

As the couple continued to make progress in "shifting their gaze" from Other to Self, the treatment shifted to family-of-origin issues, based on Bowen's approach of encouraging clients to rework original family relationships by practicing being a Self in the context of the family of origin. Barbara is especially sensitive to abandonment. Her mother abandoned her to alcoholism, as she had been abandoned by her mother (Barbara's grandmother) to drug addiction. Barbara's father was a womanizer who had many affairs that were poorly hidden, including one with a maid who lived in the house. Barbara's brother is chronically depressed, and she has had bouts of depression herself. If she perceives even a subtle suggestion that Jason might be left alone, she is filled with images of the emptiness she sees in herself and her brother, and she reacts intensely. When David is gone on a business trip, she reexperiences the trauma of the early abandonment. Her attempt at mastering this trauma is to apply very high standards to caring for Jason. This need to protect Jason from her sense of abandonment is part of the reason that she finds child care so burdensome.

In her relationship with her mother, Barbara

learned to keep her feelings to herself, out of fear that if she were to say how unhappy she was she might lose her mother completely. This trait carried over to her relationship with David. She has difficulty asking directly for what she wants. She often keeps her feelings to herself, until she becomes emotionally flooded and the emotions spill out in a torrent of anger. This tendency not to share her feelings with David was abetted by David's need to distance himself from his own feelings. David's decision to travel when Jason was 6 weeks old was an example of his way of coping with his anxiety about new fatherhood. This decision was actually quite traumatic for Barbara, because she was abandoned at a time of high stress and anxiety. Subsequently, when the issue of travel came up she automatically assumed that he was going to abandon her and in that state of mind found it impossible to ask him for what she needed.

As therapy progressed, I made several suggestions for Barbara's family-of-origin work. After 6 months of therapy her mother came for a visit, and I suggested that Barbara work on trying not to lose her own voice (as is her custom with her mother) but rather try to be authentic, if only to herself. This helped her deal with her very complex set of feelings as her mother consumed alcohol on a steady basis during the visit. Working on being more authentic with her mother helped her in her relationship with David. She was able to move from assuming that he was going to abandon her, and getting furious, to being better able to calmly tell him what she needed. She thus shifted from a reactive–aggressive mode to a more proactive–assertive one. I also suggested that Barbara talk with her mother about her mother's experiences with her own mother growing up. To my knowledge this has not yet happened. As it now stands, Barbara sees her mother twice a year.

At the beginning David was out of touch with his issues regarding his family. As therapy progressed, David showed an increasing capacity to look at his family-of-origin issues. Early on, the couple discussed a conflict about keeping old magazines around. To Barbara, who wanted to get rid of them, they represented "death, decay,"–that is, her mother's neglect. To David, they represented his

mother's intrusiveness; for example, her getting rid of a collection of scientific magazines that he had cherished.

After a couple of months of therapy David began to experience sadness when he talked about his parents. He verbalized that he was sad because he felt that they had not made the most of their lives. In one session he commented that if his father had taken a job in management (rather than the blue-collar work that he did) he would not have been injured in late mid-life, and his parents might have had a better life. Similarly, after 6 months of therapy David was able to acknowledge that his mother's attempts to get close to him made him uncomfortable, so that has tended to keep her at a distance, much as he has done with his wife. A few sessions later he said to Barbara: "I have one for you. Don't ask me about my day. My mother used to do that, and it bugs the hell out of me." Exploring his reaction in the session, David could begin to see that more was at work than the fact that both his mother and his wife shared this "annoying trait." He began to realize that maybe if he could learn how to deal with his mother he might not have this problem with his wife.

Phase 1 Revisited: Fuller Resolution of Gender Role Strain

Letter-Writing Exercise. After 10 months of therapy David had learned to be articulate about his emotions. Barbara had improved her ability to hold onto her voice and to stay her tendency to assume the worst. She was better able to ask for what she needed calmly. Yet the couple remained at an impasse. It seemed to me that the impasse was being held in place by unresolved issues resulting from events in the first 6 weeks of their life as parents. Hence I suggested that they each write a letter to the other, to be shared in the session, wherein each expressed their own experiences in those first few weeks.

This exercise was designed both to help each of them focus on the Self by examining their unique experiences and to enable them to define the Self to each other. David was surprised to learn that Barbara's bottom line commitment was to Jason, not to her career. It was important to Barbara to articulate this definition of Self, even though she had also emphasized that she felt it was unfair that she had sacrificed her career whereas David was able to continue in his work. Barbara was surprised to learn about David's feelings about the importance of the provider role. He acknowledged that he had dealt with his anxiety and feelings of inadequacy as a father by digging down and coming up with his own father's model: Be a good provider and "put a cocoon around the family." He also revealed that his antagonism toward a particular child care provider had to do with his feelings about the fact that her salary, if prorated to full-time, would equal his take-home pay. Somehow, he felt that this financial arrangement trivialized his contribution to the family.

David's Growing Attachment to Jason. David began providing regular child care for Jason in the fourth month of therapy. Barbara soon felt quite comfortable with David's parenting abilities. As a direct result of this increased and regular contact, David became completely smitten with his son.

Rebalancing the Ledger Through a Structural Change. Although the letter-writing exercise was helpful in reducing some of Barbara's smoldering antagonism and David's anxiety, the couple still remained at impasse. It was not enough to revisit the painful period of their lives as new parents in order to find understanding and reconciliation, because the basic structure of their lives still remained unworkable from Barbara's point of view. This point was driven home after about a year of therapy, when David took a long series of business trips. His absence caused all of the old issues to resurface.

In one session David seemed finally to hear what Barbara had so desperately been trying to tell him: that if he wanted to hold onto his marriage, he simply had to give it a much higher priority. She made it clear that she was not going to stay in the marriage if he did not give it a higher priority. This brought several things to the fore. David had said earlier that he did not want to change his job just yet because he wanted to see things he had worked on for 20 years come to fruition. However, in response to Barbara's ultimatum, he backed down from this position, acknowledging that he has such a good record that he could do nothing for the next 5 years and it would not hurt his professional standing. In addition, he had by this time made some progress in overcoming his fear of being direct with colleagues when he could not tell them what he felt they wanted to hear—a behavior pattern that had previously resulted in his failing to meet some of his commitments to Barbara. Finally, as noted above, he had fallen in love with Jason. In response to these forces—Barbara's ability to find her voice and state her position forcefully, David's ability to state his position more directly, and David's positive attachment to Jason—David announced that he had decided to reorganize his position so as to drastically reduce both the travel and the time demands. This would free him up to share the child care more equally with Barbara. At first Barbara was skeptical about David's commitment but a few weeks later came to feel that a corner had been turned. The quality of their interaction in the last few sessions has been decidedly more relaxed and lighthearted, as if they have both gotten through a terrible ordeal.

This therapeutic event is extremely important for the treatment of postmodern couples. In past historical periods only men had the privilege of having high-powered careers and children. In the postfeminist era women have come to expect to enjoy the same privileges. However, the birth of the first child often stimulates a regression to a traditional gender-based division of labor. When this happens, both members of the couple experience stress, as documented by Arlie Hochschild (1989), who found that conflict over sharing family responsibilities was the most common source of marital discord among dual-earner couples.

Not all couples achieve this level of structural change. Most frequently, the impetus for change comes from the wife, as it did in Barbara's case. Now that women have the potential to provide for themselves and their children, some feel entitled to demand a more equitable sharing of child care and household responsibilities. However, traditional gender role norms are difficult to change, and many women do not find their voice on this issue. We believe that our emphasis on focusing on and defining the Self enhances the probability that both women and men will negotiate more successfully for the reciprocal benefits that postmodern marriage has to offer. Furthermore, we feel that without a serious attempt to find a more equitable gender role division of labor, resentments will continue to fester and eventually emerge as marital conflict.

Termination

I have recently taken a job that requires relocation out of state. This has imposed a time limit on the treatment of this case. Although the couple has made significant progress in resolving their marital impasse, work still remains to be done. Both members need to do more family-of-origin work. David needs to become better acquainted with how his family of origin has shaped his life and affected how he has functioned in his marriage. Barbara needs to continue her work on decreasing the emotional cutoff from her mother. The couple has agreed to continue their work with another family psychologist in order to maintain and consolidate their progress.

CONCLUSION

This chapter illustrates the integrated family systems–gender-based psychotherapy approach under construction by Levant and Silverstein (1996), with its multiphasic approach encompassing learning to think gender, learning to think systems, and family-of-origin work. In this chapter we paid specific attention to resolving both gender role strain and emotional fusion as cofactors in this couple's marital impasse. With regard to gender role strain, David improved his ability to be aware of and express his emotions, and Barbara was able to let go of, to some extent, the responsibilities for managing the emotional life of the couple. As David assumed more responsibility for his end, Barbara felt less emotionally flooded. With these gains under their belts, they negotiated conditions for David to provide significant blocks of child care, thereby giving Barbara time to attend to her professional responsibilities and providing David opportunities to get to know (and fall in love with) his son. The most consequential change occurred near the end of therapy, when David agreed to restructure his job so that he would travel less and spend more time with Jason.

With regard to resolving the emotional fusion, the first change was seen when David improved his ability to express his own emotions, thereby chang-

ing the overall emotional system of the couple and reducing the level of conflict. The next set of changes involved Barbara making some headway in being authentic with her mother, which helped her be more proactively assertive with David, and with David confronting his fears of letting his colleagues down.

I consider it a privilege to have been able to work with David and Barbara. I learned a great deal from working with them about being a couple in the postmodern era, about resolving relationship impasses, and about integrating feminist and family systems ideas.

References

Bowen, M. (1978). *Family therapy in clinical practice.* New York: Aronson.

Christensen, A., & Heavey, C. (1990). Gender and social structure in the demand/withdraw pattern of marital conflict. *Journal of Personality and Social Psychology, 59,* 73–81.

Fogarty, T. F. (1979). The distancer and the pursuer. *The Family, 7*(1), 11–16.

Goldner, V. (1988, March/April). Making room for both/and. *The Family Therapy Networker,* 55–61.

Hochschild, A. (1989). *The second shift.* New York: Viking.

Kerr, M. E., & Bowen, M. (1988). *Family evaluation.* New York: Norton.

Levant, R. F. (1997). *Men and emotions: A psychoeducational approach* [Video]. Hicksville, NY: Newbridge Professional Programs. [Out of print but available from Ronald F. Levant.]

Levant, R. (1998). Desperately seeking language: Understanding, assessing and treating normative male alexithymia. In W. Pollack & R. Levant (Eds.), *New psychotherapy for men* (pp. 35–56). New York: Wiley.

Levant, R. F., & Kopecky, G. (1995/1996). *Masculinity reconstructed: Changing the rules of manhood.* New York: Dutton/Plume. [Out of print but available from Ronald F. Levant.]

Levant, R. F., & Pollack, W. S. (Eds.). (1995). *A new psychology of men.* New York: Basic Books.

Levant, R. F., & Silverstein, L. (1996, August). *Bridging the gap from Mars to Venus: Treating couples' impasses.* Symposium conducted at the 104th Annual Convention of the American Psychological Association, Toronto, Ontario, Canada.

Silverstein, L. B. (1996). Fathering is a feminist issue. *Psychology of Women Quarterly, 20,* 3–37.

CHAPTER 20

SOMEDAY MY PRINCE WILL COME

Carol L. Philpot

In this chapter I tell the story of Carla and Steve, a couple who struggled with issues that appeared to be a direct result of the gender messages they had received while growing up. I first saw Carla alone, until it became clear that her concerns were related to her marriage. About the time we began couples therapy, I introduced a women's issues psychoeducational group for several of the women in my practice that served as an effective adjunct to couples therapy. The women in the group represented a variety of problems stemming from gender socialization: (a) the tendency of women to define themselves through marriage and children, (b) the importance for most women of intimate conversation in connecting with others, (c) the belief that women should defer to men and be financially supported by them, (d) the belief that women should be responsible for child care, (e) the struggle of men and women to understand one another because they have grown up in separate gender ecosystems, (f) the importance of beauty for women and financial success for men, and (g) the superwoman syndrome. The unconscious assumptions these women and men made about their roles resulted in dissatisfaction and conflict. Once they became conscious of the origins of their dissatisfaction, these couples were able to "break the rules" and thus create more satisfactory marriages.

SESSION 1

The attractive brunette lowered her head and blushed. "I'm really ashamed to admit this. It's so stupid. But I've fallen in love with my obstetrician, and I can't stop thinking about him." The young woman sat across from me on the couch, holding a rattle in front of her infant's flailing hands, alternately entertaining him and conversing with me. It was her first session, and she had spent the first half of her 50-minutes registering vague complaints, clearly tiptoeing around the real reason for her visit, until she felt she could trust me. She had been referred by another current client, also a woman with a young baby, a member of her play group. I could not suppress a half-smile.

"I know," Carla continued, smiling herself. "It's a cliche. I don't know how I can be so adolescent!"

"Oh, I suppose we can all get in touch with the part of us that's an adolescent without much difficulty," I mused with genuine empathy. "Tell me more about this obstetrician."

Carla brightened like a 16-year-old gossiping about her latest boyfriend with a classmate. She went on to describe a handsome, well-dressed, and clearly well-heeled physician whose touch was gentle, whose voice conveyed real warmth, and who listened to her concerns with rapt attention. She imagined that if she could somehow arrange to go to dinner with him, he would hold her hand, gaze into her eyes, and listen to her talk about her hopes and dreams in the candlelight.

"And what would those be?" I asked, referring to her hopes and dreams. She appeared startled by my question and paused before responding.

"I don't know anymore," she answered somewhat sadly. "I used to dream about getting married, having a baby, having a home of my own. I have all that and. . . ." Her voice trailed off, and she shrugged.

I waited a moment and then said, "A little like the Peggy Lee song, huh? 'Is That All There Is?'"

She sat upright, suddenly becoming animated. "Exactly! I feel so guilty, but I'm really not happy. I thought I would be, but I'm not. And it's not that I don't love my baby. I do. I'm glad he was born. I really don't want to go back to work right now. I want to be with him. I really didn't like my job that much anyway. It was so stressful. But this doesn't thrill me either! What's wrong with me, anyway?" The question was self-punitive, not really seeking an answer.

Despite what the reader may be thinking, this therapy session did not take place before 1963, when Betty Friedan published *The Feminine Mystique*, in which she described the problem with no name. In fact the client was a woman of the 1980s, a licensed practical nurse who had worked several years before marriage, who considered herself to be an equal partner in her relationship, and who believed (at least consciously) that she had choices about how she spent her life.

Although this case is more than 10 years old, I have chosen to share it because Carla (and the other women who made up the women's group I convened to serve as auxiliary therapy to their couples work) taught me a great deal about myself, my own gender role journey, and parallel process. At the time I was in a 25-year-old marriage to a physician. My three children were either in college or completing high school. I had been a psychologist and a professor for 10 years, having gone back to school to get my doctorate during my children's elementary school years. Although I had obtained a bachelor's degree and had taught high school for several years before the birth of my children, like most women of my generation I had dropped out of the workplace while my children were young, wanting to have a major influence on their values and early development. Now our children were fairly independent, into their own lives, and my husband and I were both busy practitioners who spent most of our time at work. Although we attended many social events together, and belonged to a group of couples who

were close friends, we basically lived parallel lives. Nonconflictual and smooth, our relationship was nevertheless devoid of intimacy and always had been. In the early years, I had found that very dissatisfying and had considered divorce when marital therapy had not changed our level of closeness. However, for a variety of reasons, not the least of which was the effect of divorce on children, I had opted to look elsewhere for the deeper connection I sought, finding it in colleagues who were psychologically minded and intellectually stimulating. By the time Carla walked into my office, my husband and I had slipped into a familiar and comfortable, if not very fulfilling, relationship.

As I conceptualized Carla's case, I thought about my own relationship. Carla had absorbed contradictory messages regarding her role as a woman in the 1980s. Her mother had been a homemaker whose husband had left her while Carla was still a young child. Her mother had obtained a job as a teller in a bank and had struggled to support her three daughters with a little help from her own mother and very small child support checks. Carla's mother had told her that she should always be able to support herself because "you can't trust a man to stay around" but had simultaneously conveyed the message that making a living was the man's job and that the woman was entitled to stay home and raise children. So Carla had gotten her education and job in the health care industry in hopes of finding herself a rich doctor to support her the rest of her life—not the best motivation for career selection, but not surprising given society's messages to women. Carla had not had a lot of success in the endeavor and, genuinely disliking her chosen profession, believed marriage to somebody, anybody, was her only way out. While at a fundraiser looking for a doctor to marry, Carla had met an electronics engineer who seemed to take an interest in her. He was shy and quiet but seemed to have financial potential. Carla described a rather lackluster courtship. Stan was nice, polite, and deferred to her preferences. He let her do most of the talking, although he didn't always seem to be listening, a precursor of things to come. Carla felt she could trust him; she believed that he was a responsible, steady man who would make a good husband and father. So when he proposed, she accepted. She had been more excited about leaving work and starting a new career as wife and mother than she was about Stan.

Now, 3 years into the marriage, she found herself fantasizing about having an affair with her gynecologist. Her marital complaints were few. Both she and her husband were overweight, and she found him physically unattractive. Their sex life was practically nonexistent but, only 3 months after the birth of their first child, they both found that acceptable and understandable. Stan was boring and frequently uncommunicative, but she had known that when she married him. He financially provided Carla and their baby a nice home and a good life; he helped with child care; they rarely argued because he usually gave in to her wishes; and in general he was a nice, cooperative, responsible man. Carla was busy with the baby all day, but she did not feel overwhelmed with the work or trapped in the home. She had frequent social interaction with other young mothers and their children. So why wasn't she happy? Because Carla had fallen for that centuries-old message that a woman's greatest fulfillment would come from marriage and children. She had expected that when Prince Charming swept her off her feet and rescued her from her life of drudgery she would live forever in a romantic haze of "happily ever after." The only explanation she had for not having achieved these results was that she had picked the wrong man, because only through the love and attention of the right man would she find happiness.

Carla's complaints in her first session somewhat reminded me of myself 20 years earlier. As I conceptualized Carla's case after the session, I also reflected on my own growth in the past two decades —with some sense of pride, I might add. I had let go of the notion that I needed a man to make me happy and had worked on making my own life productive, exciting, vital, and fulfilling. This shift in perspective had moved me away from the notion that my husband was deficient and needed changing and toward the idea that I had the power to change my own life within the relationship.

SESSION 2

As I prepared to help Carla set goals for therapy in the second session, I kept in mind the need to de-

bunk the myth of Prince Charming and empower Carla to take charge of her own happiness. Because a direct frontal assault on a deeply held myth seemed an unadvisable first step, I used a Minuchin "tracking" approach by going with Carla's fantasy. "So how do you think your life would be different if you were married to your obstetrician instead of Stan?" I asked speculatively. She needed some time to think about this, as her fantasy extended only through the early seduction stage of a relationship. I suggested she close her eyes, breathe deeply, relax, and then I took her through a guided fantasy. She was able to identify a few differences between her reality and fantasy but, not surprisingly, not very many. First of all, she would find her fantasy husband sexually attractive because he was trim, well dressed, and sophisticated. Second, her fantasy husband would be interested in her and what she had to say. Third, she would be more prominent in the community and would have an active adult-oriented social life in which she played a leadership role in volunteer organizations. Otherwise, she would continue to play the role of wife and mother and do the things she did every day. I pushed her to explore further.

I asked her to describe herself as she imagined this life. How was she different?

"Well, first of all, I am thin again and sexy like I used to be before the pregnancy. I would have to be, because no one as handsome as Dr. Allen would be interested in me the way I look now. And I imagine that I have an interesting career, something exciting to talk to him about when he does come home in the evening. Something besides diapers and feedings and laundry." (I filed away the issue of physical attractiveness being a woman's best asset for another time.)

"You mean like your nursing career?" I offered.

"No, I really hated that. It was a lot of cleaning up after people and waiting on them. I suppose if I were an RN—but no, not even that. Because, honestly, I don't like science and blood and guts and messing with people's bodies."

"Then what would it be? Remember this is a fantasy. You can be anything."

"Well, what I'd like to do is something that's fun —like a cruise director, or hotel concierge, or tour guide. Something where I work with the public in a recreational kind of job. I suppose while the baby is little I'd have to do something close to home. So, maybe in a hotel or something."

"And what would you talk about with your husband when he came home in the evening?"

"Oh, he'd tell me about his interesting cases, which I'd understand a little because I've worked in a hospital before. So we'd have something in common there. And I'd talk about the interesting people who came into the hotel and what I had to organize that day. Things like that."

"And how do you see him responding to you when you talk about those things?"

"Interested. Attentive. He'd be fascinated with my life and work, and I'd be fascinated with his. He'd be proud of me. See me as an equal. It would be a mutual thing."

We pursued this fantasy for a while. By the end of the session, Carla realized that many of the things she saw herself doing in the fantasy she could do in her present relationship. Others, such as the husband who listened attentively and was more slim, might require some couples work. But she could begin working on her fantasy by working on herself. I sent her home with homework—to draw up a list of things that she could do to bring herself more in line with her fantasy.

SESSION 3

The next week, Carla came in somewhat dejected. She had been thinking a lot about our session of the previous week, and she began to realize something that disturbed her.

"It's not really being married to Dr. Allen that would be great, " she said. "It's seducing him, it's getting him to tell me he loves me, it's the romance of the courtship that I want."

"I see," I responded, glad that she had this insight so quickly. "And once you've caught him?"

"Well, then we're back into this routine I have with Stan. Of course it could be better than what I have. I mean if I can make the changes I brought in on my list and Stan could just change a little bit, it would be better for us, too. But that still wouldn't fill that need for romance. Not even with Dr. Allen. Because marriage isn't like that. You get to know the other person, and they become predictable. There are no surprises. And you know they love you and so somehow you start to take them for granted. That would happen with anyone, I think. Unless it was someone totally untrustworthy, someone you were never sure of, someone who ran off and left you. And who would want that?"

The family-of-origin issue was looming its ugly head, without any prompting from me. I was conflicted. My agenda had been to explore the myth of perpetual romance, but I didn't want to lose the opportunity to deal with Carla's selection of Stan as a partner.

"Is that what happened to your mother, you think?" I ventured.

"Oh, certainly. She has told me many times that handsome, exciting men are dangerous. They just up and leave you when they get bored."

"They start to look elsewhere or what?"

"Well my father did. He had an affair and took off."

"Do you think he found happiness?"

"Well not with that one. He's been married three times. I think he finally just got too old to keep screwing around."

"Like bees and flowers, huh? Too many pretty flowers to stay put. But something made him stop. Do you keep in touch with him? Do you know if he's happy now?"

"No, I hardly ever see him. Mom was so mad at him, and we were just kids. We just didn't see him very often. And we certainly never talk about anything serious when we do see each other. It's—you know, kind of superficial."

"I see. I guess I was just thinking it might be interesting to get his point of view now that you're older and married yourself."

She stared at me for a moment and then said, "You don't think I'm like him, do you?"

"Why would I think that?"

"Well, I am fantasizing about having an affair. Geesh, I sure don't want to be like him."

"Rather be like your Mom?"

"No, I don't want to be like her, either. She got really screwed over."

"Certainly there must be other choices besides screwer and screwee," I mused.

Carla was very thoughtful for a moment. "God, if I thought I was doing to Stan what my dad did to my mom."

"As of yet, I don't see that you're doing anything to Stan."

"No, but I am bored and unhappy and think about someone else all the time. And Stan is not a bad guy, just boring as blazes. I always imagined that's how my dad saw my mom."

"That was your fantasy of their relationship?"

She nodded. "He was very handsome, and she said he was a charmer. And Mom—well, she was just Mom. I always thought that she just couldn't keep his attention. She just wasn't pretty enough or clever enough or something."

"It would be a lot of work to keep up with someone like that, I suppose."

"Yeah, I always thought so. That's what's good about being married to Stan. He's not handsome enough or smooth enough to attract other women. I don't need to worry about him."

"Except when he's not attractive or smooth enough to keep your attention."

"Aghhh!" she pulled her hair dramatically in frustration. "That's the problem. The smooth sexy guys turn you on but hurt you. The nice, boring guys treat you good, but just don't do it for you. Something is missing. You can't win!"

"And which would Dr. Allen be?"

"Well the sexy guy, of course."

"The one who'll hurt you."

"Well I don't think I really have to worry about that anyway because this whole fantasy is ridiculous. I'm only one of his patients. It's just that there's no romance in my marriage, never has been, and the fantasy fills that need."

"Which brings us back to the beginning. It's the chase that's fun, not the 'happily ever after'."

"Well that's what I started to tell you. When you think about that, it means you have to always be starting a relationship with someone new. You'd never really settle down with one because then you lose that uncertainty, that excitement of hearing them say they love you for the first time, the first sexual experience."

I raised an eyebrow.

"What?" she asked.

"Nothing, really. I was just thinking that research and personal experience tell me that most of the time you have better sex with someone you've come to know and trust. Someone you feel safe with, someone who really knows what you like and don't like. Knows your body and mind, so to speak."

Carla looked puzzled. "Yeah, I guess. But it's not just the sex. It's—"

I waited a long time. She finally said, "I just can't explain it."

"Well that might be good homework for you. Go home and think about this. Think about what makes the romantic phase of a relationship so wonderful. What do you get from it that you don't get in a long-term relationship? Then we'll discuss it next week. And if you get really stuck, read *Cinderella*, *Snow White*, or *Sleeping Beauty*, or even a Harlequin romance novel. It might give you some clues."

As Carla left, my mind wandered to Jennifer, another current client who had had an affair and for some of the same reasons Carla seemed to be raising. The affair had ended when her lover had left the area, and Jennifer had not revealed her transgression to her husband. But she was now struggling to get back the closeness she had lost in her marital relationship. I also thought about Leslie, who had many of the same complaints as Jennifer but had found a different solution, one that was equally disruptive to her marriage. Leslie, frustrated with the lack of intimate communication between herself and her husband of 30 years, had decided she felt closer to her female friends and no longer needed her husband. She had left him without warning, and he was devastated. And then there was Margie, who had referred Carla to me. Margie did not suffer from the romance myth but was stuck in her beliefs about male and female roles. Margie was a go-getter, assertive, ambitious, and career minded. But she was also the mother of a 3-year-old daughter. She assumed the duties of child care with frustration and resignation while goading her gentle husband to climb the ladder of success, something he was ill equipped to do. Finally, I thought of Janice, a lawyer with a 2-year-old son, whose life was exciting and fulfilling but exhausting. Janice and her husband Steve, a stockbroker, had come to me for marital therapy to resolve their arguments over housework and child care issues. Steve was more than happy to hire a maid to take care of both functions while he and Janice pursued their busy careers, but Janice suffered from feelings of guilt regarding leaving her toddler and resented the fact that Steve found the solution so simple. All of these women, although very different in most ways, were suffering because of their gender training. I wondered whether a women's psychoeducational/support group might be a nice adjunct to the individual and marital work I was doing and made a note to mention it as a possibility to each of these women.

SESSION 4

"They all end after you catch the man!" Carla exclaimed as she sank into the couch. "It's as if life stops after the wedding!"

"Funny how that happens, isn't it? Sounds like the way you describe yourself these days," I reflected. "Of course the stuff of daily life probably doesn't make for very interesting reading. There's not much romance in diaper changes, floor mopping, and carpooling, I suspect. What else did you notice about those old fairy tales?"

"Beauty is the highest value a woman has. That's what seduces the man to rescue her. That and purity. She has to be so good and innocent."

"If I remember correctly, in several of those stories the heroine takes a lot of abuse but doesn't fight back."

"Oh, heck no. She waits for a knight in shining armor to come rescue her."

"So another common element is women's passivity. They are helpless to change their lives. Only through the intervention of a man can life get better."

Carla gave me a sly smile and wagged her index finger. "I know what you're getting at. I'm waiting for Dr. Allen to rescue me."

"Now, would I suggest something like that?" I retorted.

She became somber again. "We've really been brainwashed, haven't we?"

"Some of us," I responded. "I happened to think *Nancy Drew* was the greatest series ever written when I was a kid. Of course, I don't spend my time

solving murder mysteries, but I certainly enjoyed the risk-taking, active way she jumped into things! Tell me, did you have a chance to read anything more modern or did you just stick to the fairy tales?"

"Well actually I was already reading a Danielle Steel novel, and after you gave me this assignment I started looking at it differently too."

"What did you discover?"

"Women use their beauty as power. It gets them the job, the rich guy, the promotion, whatever. But beauty is power, and if you're not beautiful you don't have much of a chance. Unless your daddy was rich and left you a bunch of money."

"The rescuing man again. Beauty gives you power over men, and men control the goodies. You know, Carla, the messages we have absorbed from our culture are often subtle, and they are all pervasive. Many times we are not even aware of how influenced we are by these things. And it affects all of us—men and women. Sometimes these gender messages are very detrimental. Not always, of course, but often enough that they are worth studying. I've been thinking that you might be interested in joining a women's issues group to learn more about how what we have been taught about womanhood has influenced your thinking and behavior and therefore your level of satisfaction with life. Any interest?"

THE WOMEN'S GROUP

And thus began a 12-week women's support group that had as much impact on the women with whom I was working as the individual and couples work I was doing. At the time, in the mid-1980s, the now-popular men's movement was unknown in Florida, but women's groups were quite common. The husbands of these women were very supportive of their participation in the group, especially as their wives became more sensitive to the effects of male gender training as well. They did not see the group as a threat or as a potential for a special bond to develop between the therapist and their wives. They were, I believe, pleased not to have to attend yet another psychotherapy session and still benefit from the information shared in the psychoeducational group. If I were to do this adjunctive support group today, I would have a male cotherapist whom I trust to present a gender-balanced perspective and counterbalance it with a similar men's group.

The women in the group—Carla, Jennifer, Leslie, Janice, and Margie—did not represent the whole gamut of women's issues that we could have explored, but they did present with a variety of problems that stemmed from gender training. Carla's belief that through marriage a woman would find her greatest fulfillment is still common in spite of the messages of the women's movement to the contrary (Dowling, 1982; Russianoff, 1981).

Jennifer, a special education school teacher with three adolescent boys and a marine biologist husband, suffered more directly from the fact that she was indoctrinated in a gender ecosystem that was very different from that of anyone else in her household. Her husband and boys had different value systems, different priorities, different communication styles, different problem-solving styles, and even different approaches to sexuality, because they were raised in a male gender ecosystem (Philpot, Brooks, Lusterman, & Nutt, 1997). Jennifer felt isolated and lonely, misunderstood, and unappreciated. When an old high school friend, a philosophical musician and artist who lived on his sailboat, came through town, he filled the emptiness Jennifer experienced. He had rejected the traditional male value of achievement in the establishment, he placed emphasis on personal fulfillment and artistic endeavor, he loved to read and discuss philosophy and spiritual matters, he enjoyed the process of getting reacquainted with Jennifer and inspired her to begin writing again. Jennifer frequently talked about her disagreements with her husband in terms of function versus form. Her husband was practical; his value system prioritized functionality. Jennifer, on the other hand, prioritized aesthetics: Does it look nice? Jennifer's artistic lover also valued form and encouraged her to continue to do so. It is easy to see how Jennifer became romantically involved with her artist, despite her respect for and friendship with her husband of 19 years. But the relationship came to an end when the itinerant sailor sailed on.

Leslie's unhappiness was more specifically connected to communication differences between the two gender ecosystems (Tannen, 1990). Leslie, a so-

cial worker, was married to Paul, an insurance agent. They had two grown children who no longer lived in the area. Paul came home from work every evening, plopped in front of the television set, and stayed there until he fell asleep. Leslie, who had not cared about this behavior when she had been busy raising children, now experienced extreme loneliness within her marriage. Paul would not talk to her, not because he was angry with her, but simply because he had nothing to say. Without talk, Leslie felt alone. She called her friends, spending hours on the telephone. She began to plan trips with her coworkers and her church group. Soon she found that she much preferred being with them than with Paul. With the children gone, she saw no point in staying married. She moved out. Paul was devastated and came to me for therapy. Paul suffered because he had learned the male style of communication—talk to impart information or to give advice—and his wife wanted to talk for connection. He was totally at a loss as to what Leslie wanted from him. He also had been lonely in the marriage but, not being able to identify his discontent, he had merely tried to distract himself from it by watching television or working. I worked with him on developing coping skills for his depression, taught him basic communication skills, (i.e., "I" statements, active listening, reflection, clarification), and helped him to partially overcome his alexythymia, all with the hope that Leslie might give him another chance. She did, mostly because she had invested more than 20 years with him and felt that he deserved better. Although I had shared a great deal with Paul about gender ecosystems and their effect on male–female relationships, when Leslie joined us for couples therapy I had not repeated myself. Therefore, the women's issues group seemed a perfect psychoeducational adjunct for her.

Margie's happiness was thwarted because she could not think outside the envelope. To me, as a therapist, the solution to the problem was simple: She and her husband Todd should simply switch gender roles. He was meek and mild; easily intimidated in a work situation; hated working outside the home; loved cooking, cleaning, and child care; was creative with woodworking and house repair; and preferred playing with his 3-year-old daughter to doing almost anything else. Margie was aggressive and assertive; had great ambitions for herself in the banking industry; enjoyed networking with other professionals; was bored by housework; and, although she loved her daughter, found being with children all day tedious. This seemed like a no-brainer, but there was a catch: Margie was absolutely convinced that a real woman would want to be with her child all day and that to do otherwise would make her deficient. Therefore, she tried to live out her ambitions through her husband. Her pressure merely made him very dysfunctional—depressed, anxious, disorganized. Then she had real reason to be angry. It was at this point that they had sought therapy. The women's group, I reasoned, would do more to change Margie's frame of reference than I could do alone.

Janice was only a step or two beyond Margie. Janice was a superwoman. She was attempting to do everything at once and found herself exhausted. Her husband Steve had suggested they hire someone to care for their child and to clean house because between them they made enough money to do so comfortably. At first Janice had thought that would be a great idea, but she found herself cleaning frantically so that the cleaning woman would not see her house messy. When she got over that, she became resentful that someone else was putting away her things and not always in the right place. She felt her privacy was being invaded. Furthermore she was really torn about leaving her little boy with someone else while she went off to the office. She realized that she wanted more time to watch her son grow up and to influence his development, but she feared taking time away from her career because she did not want to fall behind her colleagues. After awhile she became very angry with Steve, because he did not seem to have any of these conflicts. He simply accepted the fact that his career came first and someone else would have to handle home and hearth. To Steve her anger was irrational and a real departure from the logical, analytical woman he married. He began to speculate that her problem was hormonal, and then Janice really became infuriated. At this point they had entered therapy. Janice was a victim of superwoman syndrome and very appropriate for the women's group.

In the group the women participated in a number of structured exercises (see Exhibit 20.1) designed to help them identify the gender messages they had received from the larger culture that were preventing them from finding creative solutions to the problems they were facing at present. They identified common themes, commiserated with one another, and supported each other in defying gender norms in order to experiment with new ways of meeting their needs. They read books and articles, watched movies, listened to popular music, and discussed plays and television shows—all through a gender-sensitive lens. They became much more aware of the unconscious rules that kept them from making changes. They openly discussed what rules they wanted to pass down to their children and the importance of making changes themselves in order to provide healthy examples. A major focus of the group, however, was to maintain a balance regarding the effect of gender messages on men and women (Philpot, 1991; Philpot & Brooks, 1995; Philpot et al., 1997). Whenever a disadvantage for women was discovered I also alerted them to the disadvantage

---

EXHIBIT 20.1

Sample Exercises for the Women's Group

The Women's Room
Gender Survival Messages
Early Childhood Memories
Sex Stereotyping in Children's Literature
Sex Stereotyping in the Media
Sex Stereotyping in Music
Body Awareness
Power and Powerlessness
Marriage, Family, and Employment:
　Pros and Cons
Gender Messages—Systemic Questioning
Gender Inquiry
Role Reversal

Note. Most exercises were developed by Carol L. Philpot for her courses at Florida Institute of Technology, but several were borrowed and modified from Eberhardt (1987) and O'Neil (1985).

for men. The clear message was that both men and women are victims of their gender socialization and are merely following the rules they have been taught. In most cases, neither gender is deliberately attempting to hurt the other; they are simply behaving in an unconscious manner that serves to perpetuate the old patterns. Only sensitivity to the detrimental effects of gender socialization and a conscious effort to do something different will bring about change. Soon I began to see the results of the women's group in the couples sessions I was conducting.

COUPLES THERAPY

During the fourth session with Carla, I suggested that we might be ready to begin couples work to address the changes Carla had identified in her second session. I told Carla that because I had had several sessions with her, it would be important for me to have a few individual sessions with Stan—to balance the score, so to speak, and to get to know him. During my individual session with Stan, he revealed that he was aware of Carla's discontent but was too busy making a living to take her seriously. After all, his job as a man was to provide for his family, a task that took a great deal of energy and that he was performing well. He felt unappreciated by Carla because she expected too much. He indicated that he knew she was dissatisfied romantically but felt her expectations were very unrealistic.

"In real life you don't have a script writer providing you with the lines to say and the stage directions," he stated.

"No, and you don't have a wardrobe boy and a makeup man to make you look great, either," I answered.

Stan's take on the situation was that Carla lived in a fantasy world and that she needed to come down to earth. After all, he might not be Rhett Butler, but he was a decent guy who treated her right. It was hard to argue with that!

Couples therapy began with each partner sharing a list of strengths he or she could identify in the marriage and a list of the good qualities they saw in each other. Afterward they talked about areas in which a change would make their relationship more satisfying. These areas included (a) their physical health (i.e., their weight), (b) their communication, (c) the development of common interests, (d) their sex life, and (e) Carla's developing an interest in something outside the home. Although I proceeded with therapy using a cognitive–behavioral, social-learning approach as a framework (Stuart, 1980), I knew I would introduce gender issues whenever relevant and also look at family-of-origin and object-relations issues as they arose. During the 12 sessions I saw the couple we introduced a Caring Days exercise (i.e., they generated a list of nice little things they committed do for one another every day to show their love); worked on communication skills, particularly active listening and reflection for Stan; developed a contract for an exercise and diet program, which they followed together; and generated a list of enjoyable activities they could pursue on the weekly date night we instituted. Carla began to take computer classes, which simultaneously gave her a night away from home and gave her something in common with Stan. They actually began to play computer games at home. Carla also took on the role of social director for the play group and began to put her interest in social activities to good use, planning and implementing several creative activities for parents and children alike, for which she received many compliments. Both Carla and Stan began to lose weight as they supported and encouraged each other in this less appealing activity. Carla shared with Stan what she was learning about women's socialization in the women's group, and Stan began to share his experience as a man. Stan made the connection that he had rescued Carla from a job she hated and therefore served as her knight in shining armor but admitted that fighting dragons (i.e., working hard to support the family) got old after a while, particularly if it was not appreciated. He also became more in tune with the kinds of gender messages Carla had received regarding the fact that life ends after marriage, and he gained a better understanding of her dissatisfactions. As Stan took time to really hear his wife and reflect what he was hearing, Carla began to feel more affection for him. She began to tell him how much she appreciated the things he did and focused less on the things he did not do. The warmth in their relationship improved, and sex was reintroduced. I do not know if they ever did develop a passionate, exciting sex life, but both of them reported that their sex life had improved.

At one point, Carla's father came for a visit, and I encouraged her to talk with him more openly about what had happened to his marriage to her mother. By this time, Carla had a greater understanding of male gender socialization and more empathy for her father's struggle to find happiness, so the conversation was more productive than even I would have imagined. As it turned out, Carla's dad had a lot of empathy for her sense of something missing and her desire for romance but advised against following in his footsteps, essentially saying that it had not worked for him. Carla told him she was trying to put her energy into more productive channels, and he agreed that was a good idea, saying he should have done that much earlier in his life.

HAPPY ENDINGS

Between the women's group and the couples work I was doing with these families, many changes for the positive occurred. In the end Carla and Stan had a much more satisfying relationship, and Carla stopped fantasizing about her gynecologist. In fact, she began to fantasize about starting a catering business, which was a direct result of her social director activities with the play group.

Jennifer and her husband David rebuilt the closeness they had felt years earlier when they had first married and worked together as they traveled across country. David was a much more sensitive man than Jennifer had originally implied. He found the gender socialization material to be fascinating and began to contribute articles and books he ran across that addressed the issue. Because both were intellectualizers, using bibliotherapy was an acceptable way to introduce new material, which they soon began to apply to their relationship. They admitted that they had slipped into traditional roles and patterns over the years of their marriage and merely needed to be jarred back into being the open and creative people they both were when they met.

Leslie and Paul began to communicate at last. Paul now understood that, for Leslie, talk was connection, and he used the active-listening skills he

had learned to make sure she knew he was paying attention. He had a harder time telling her what he was thinking and feeling but eventually came to realize that he was not very happy with his life, either. He realized it had become a routine meant to distract him from looking at how empty he felt. Leslie, as a social worker, became very interested in helping him figure out what he needed to do to make his life more interesting and fulfilling. They developed a closeness for the first time they could remember. She had moved back in with him by the time therapy ended.

Margie finally let go of the notion that womanhood was defined by motherhood and went to work. She was much encouraged by Janice, who thought it was the right thing to do despite her own struggle with leaving her child. Margie was much less conflicted about leaving her child, once she made the decision, than Janice, because Todd quit work and stayed home to raise his daughter. It was not the same as leaving her child with a stranger. Todd absolutely blossomed in the role of stay-at-home father. His depression and anxiety lifted, and he became much more functional and trustworthy.

Steve finally began to understand Janice's struggle against the socialization that told her a good mother should stay home. He was able to share that his own message was that he could not stay home even if he wanted to and that sometimes that made him sad. As Janice and Steve shared more of their gender experiences they became more supportive and tolerant of one another. Although Janice had originally rejected Steve's suggestion that she do so, with Margie's support Janice decided to cut back on her hours so that she would have more time with her child in the growing-up years. The fact that Margie really understood the sacrifice made her more credible than Steve, who admitted to not understanding the conflict. The women's group helped her to come to terms with the career sacrifice she was making, not for the sake of her child but because she wanted the chance to participate more in raising her child. Some of this thinking rubbed off on Steve, who also cut back his work hours. Their lifestyle changed considerably, but they had more of a balance between family and home.

PARALLEL PROCESS AND PERSONAL GROWTH

I would be remiss if I were not to mention an important factor that took place in the middle of therapy. Sometime midway through the women's group, I became aware that although I had made great strides in taking charge of my own life and making it fulfilling, rather than expecting my husband to do that for me, I nevertheless was still in a passionless relationship which, although tolerable, prevented me from finding anything better. I realized, even as I was leading my clients in a different direction, that I still believed that without a man I am nothing. My marriage was important to me, not because of the relationship with my husband but because of what being married symbolized to society—that I was successful, not just as a professional but also as a woman. Why did I continue this charade? So, right in the middle of the women's group, at the age of 48, I left my husband of 27 years and began life on my own. The reason I must report this occurrence is that until I moved out, a repetitive topic in the group and in couples work was the dilemma raised by the wives of whether to stay in their marriages. They all seemed stuck. Progress was made in other areas, but none of them seemed to be able to commit to make the marriage work or to leave. Although none of them knew that I had left my husband, shortly after I did so they stopped the "to leave or not to leave" debate and got to work on their relationships. The parallel process was so dramatic that I cannot fail to mention it.

EPILOGUE

All of the marriages were intact and improved when the above cases were terminated, except mine. To my knowledge, the other women in the group are all still married, except Leslie and Paul. It seems he slipped back into old habits, and this time Leslie just kept walking. Perhaps this was more parallel process. I worry sometimes about Carla and Stan, because they did not start out with a strong physical or emotional connection. Maybe they have been able to create one—something I personally was not able to do in my first marriage. But Jennifer and David, Janice and Steve, and Margie and Todd all seemed to be happy and doing well when last contacted.

Within 2 years I had remarried and have been ecstatically happy in a much more passionate and vital relationship for 8 years. The risk I took in defying society's definition of a successful woman was well worth it. Now I am married because I love my husband and our life together, not because of the favorable impression being a married woman has on society.

References

Dowling, C. (1982). *The Cinderella complex*. New York: Pocketbooks.

Eberhardt, L. Y. (1987). *Working with women's groups* (Vols. 1 & 2). Duluth, MN: Whole Person Press.

Friedan, B. (1963). *The feminine mystique*. New York: Norton.

O'Neil, J. M. (1985). *A gender role workshop focused on sexism, gender role conflict and the gender role journey*. Storrs: University of Connecticut.

Philpot, C. L. (1991). Gender-sensitive couples' therapy: A systemic definition. *Journal of Family Psychotherapy, 2–3*, 19–40.

Philpot, C. L., & Brooks, G. (1995). Intergender communication and gender-sensitive family therapy. In R. Mikesell, D-D. Lusterman, & S. McDaniel (Eds.), *Integrating family therapy: Handbook of family psychology and systems theory* (pp. 303–325). Washington, DC: American Psychological Association.

Philpot, C. L., Brooks, G., Lusterman, D-D., & Nutt, R. (1997). *Bridging separate gender worlds: How men and women clash and how therapists can bring them together*. Washington, DC: American Psychological Association.

Russianoff, P. (1981). *Why do I think I am nothing without a man?* Toronto, Ontario, Canada: Bantam.

Stuart, R. (1980). *Helping couples change*. New York: Guilford Press.

Tannen, D. (1990). *You just don't understand: Women and men in conversation*. New York: Ballantine Books.

CHAPTER 21

DEVELOPING GENDER AWARENESS: WHEN THERAPIST GROWTH PROMOTES FAMILY GROWTH

Gary R. Brooks

By the time I first starting talking publicly about the Hiltons, I had already managed to neutralize some of the more painful memories. Nobody likes to remember the low points of his or her therapy career. Even less appealing is the prospect of sharing one's mistakes and blind spots with other professionals whom one would like to impress. But that embarrassment does not change certain realities of therapy life that are particularly well known to family therapists. Because of the nature of the work, therapists often fail to comprehend the full complexity of a situation as early as they would like. When a therapist joins with a family to create a new therapeutic system, he or she becomes subject to the pushes and pulls of so many forces that he or she often understands what has taken place only after he or she steps outside that system, reflects on what occurred, and consults with trusted colleagues. On certain fortunate occasions, the therapist gets a second chance.

With the Hiltons that stepping-outside process was accomplished just as it has been accomplished for many of my colleagues—through video replay, case consultation, reading, and intense self-reflection. In some important ways, however, this case consultation was different. The consultants were three other family therapists who had developed expertise in the intersection of gender issues and family systems. These other therapists (one man and two women) came to comprise a "gender consultation team" that allowed me to review the Hilton case with an intensely sensitive gender lens. I was dismayed by what I discovered in my therapy. Despite

my dismay, however, all was not lost. The consultation process was very valuable, because it helped me prepare for future work with the Hiltons, and it helped me crystallize some ideas that have become central to my work. I have come to believe very dearly that (a) gender is a major organizing variable in families, (b) all therapists must work diligently to understand how their personal gender socialization affects their therapy, and (c) a gender consultation group is an invaluable resource to improve one's family therapy interventions.

THE HILTONS: THE FIRST SESSION

Carolyn Hilton (age 41), a military wife of 22 years, made an appointment for herself and two of her children: Leah (age 16) and Tony (age 15). Carolyn was very concerned about Leah, because she had repeatedly been in conflict with school authorities over a variety of policy issues. She was much less clear about Tony, seeming to bring him along for unspecified reasons. When asked about other family members, Carolyn noted that her husband Walt (age 46), an Army colonel, was away on military maneuvers and certainly would not have come anyhow, because he had adamantly refused to participate in family therapy several years before. Rick (age 20) was living in another city, having left college to pursue work in clubs as a drummer. Buffy (age 11) was in school.

In trying to get an expanded version of the presenting issues, I learned that Leah was a very bright young woman, although a provocative and outspoken critic of almost every traditional institution. Carolyn described her daughter as "one of those radical feminist types." Since she had dropped out of individual therapy with a local psychiatrist ("he was a sexist pig, pill pusher"), Leah would enter therapy only if others also came ("to get to the bottom of this soap opera mess").

Tony had little to say, responding mostly with nods of his head or "yes, sirs". This prompted Carolyn to interject quickly with her motives for bringing him also—"he's too quiet and shut off . . . he needs to learn to open up more and be more in touch with his feelings."

Tony scowled at his mother's comment. In response to my questions he presented himself blandly as a "regular, normal, unweird" guy, who played football, studied, and participated in the Reserve Officers' Training Corps. He had never been in trouble, except for one "minor-in-possession" (alcohol) charge a few months earlier.

For the next 45 minutes, as I attempted to help Carolyn sharpen her concerns about what might help her feel better about her family, I had trouble getting a solid handle on the issues. Carolyn appeared to be very interested in her role as mother. Aside from Walt's generous financial support, she had been virtually a single parent for the entire marriage. Walt's military assignments had kept him out of the home for most months of the year, but Carolyn claimed this had ceased to be an issue many years ago. She had learned to occupy herself when he was away. She was very active with the Officers' Wives Club and was doing historical research on World War I Army nurses. She claimed to be reasonably happy, although worried about Leah and Tony. When asked about Buffy, she said little except that she was a bright and happy child who was loved by everyone. She had been voted fifth-grade class favorite and was considering entering the "Junior Miss" pageant.

The session continued at the same languid pace before I finally suggested a follow-up the next week. I urged Carolyn to invite Walt and Buffy to come also. Only after the session did I realize that I had completely neglected to get much information about Rick; this caused me to speculate about his role as a "forgotten" family member.

REFLECTIONS ON THE FIRST SESSION

I felt generally comfortable about the first session with the Hiltons, although I was not without some anxieties. Carolyn Hilton seemed easy for a therapist to like. She was motivated for therapy, had a positive attitude toward mental health professionals, and was eager to take responsibility for the family's well-being. Her expectations seemed modest enough—help her cope better with parenting issues posed by Leah and Tony.

Walt Hilton seemed to be more of a challenge. I knew I had to make an effort to engage him, but I anticipated a major struggle. Clearly, I thought, he had been minimally involved in the family, dismissive of Carolyn's concerns, and unlikely to value any therapy interventions.

Leah, I have to confess, was somewhat of an irritant to me, with what seemed to be an aggressively negativistic stance on nearly everything. There could be no doubt that she was intelligent and informed, but she also struck me as histrionic and more inclined to use her knowledge to attack others and righteously defend her own actions.

Although Carolyn voiced concern about Tony, I had a much more tepid reaction to him. He struck me as withdrawn and aloof, generally without opinions on anything beyond sports or outdoor activities. Even if I had extended great effort to join with him, I was not sure there was much to be gained.

Buffy sounded like a real charmer. Described by Carolyn as "cute and effervescent," she seemed a dramatic counterpoint to her gloomier and deadly serious older sister. Rick, as I learned quickly, was outside the mainstream—another forgotten family member.

In my reflections after the first session, I found myself conceptualizing the treatment issues in a manner that now seems sadly limited. I primarily felt the need to respond to Carolyn's concerns—help her find better ways to relate to Leah and Rick and quiet any exaggerated fears about them. Because the issues with Leah might have represented transitional family life cycle problems with her imminent departure as a young adult, I considered the need to get more help from Walt. Building a closer relationship with Walt seemed a logical strategy to help

Carolyn deal with the "empty nest" and shift her excessive attention away from her mothering role. As uncomfortable as I was with Leah, I pondered ancillary treatment to help her deal with her irrational anger and overdeveloped sense of responsibility. I was unimpressed with the need for intervention for Tony.

TREATMENT DERAILED

The day before the next appointment Carolyn called, saying that Walt was completely unwilling to come. When she mentioned to him that I had asked her to bring Buffy, Walt became enraged, wondering why she was always "dragging these kids off to head-shrinkers." Deflated by his response, Carolyn said she had decided to abandon therapy for the present time.

That plan seemed quite acceptable to me. I told myself that because Carolyn was the primary complainant—the "engine to drive the therapy"—her loss of interest would make therapy impossible. I thanked Carolyn for calling and made no serious effort to challenge this retreat from therapy.

CASE CONSULTATION AND RETROSPECTIVE ANALYSIS

Because of my involvement as a family therapy trainer, I spent more time reviewing the Hilton therapy than I might have otherwise. After all, it had been only a single session, and the system had seemed to right itself spontaneously after a brief period of disequilibrium. But the case review yielded far more material than I ever anticipated.

At the time of the case review, in addition to my role as leader of the family therapy training seminar I was also involved in a series of symposia on gender issues in family therapy. For these symposia, I was working closely with three other family therapists who came to comprise the gender consultation team noted previously. Together we uncovered a number of problematic issues in my initial session with the Hiltons.

First, I was disappointed to realize how readily I had accepted the traditional gender patterns in the Hilton family. Families, of course, are free to adopt whatever gender arrangements suit them. However,

when these arrangements become problematic therapists must be prepared to help families examine their gender patterns to determine whether they should be explored and renegotiated.

On many levels, Walt and Carolyn Hilton seemed to have a highly traditional marital relationship. The division of labor seemed consistent with traditional gender patterns, with Walt pursuing a career while Carolyn tended to the home and children. If Walt focused almost exclusively on his career, he would be impatient with the distractions of relationship problems. Because of her limited focus outside the home, Carolyn would take on disproportionate responsibility as caretaker and overseer of the family's emotional well-being.

Although this common gender pattern works for many couples for many years, it frequently poses major adaptive challenges. How were the Hiltons doing with this challenge? For example, for a traditional relationship to work, each partner must be able to appreciate the other partner's contributions, empathize with the other partner's unique problems and, when necessary, help shape alternative paths. It seemed quite possible that Walt had no clue about Carolyn's fears, just as she may have been insensitive to Walt's anxieties. Intergender communication seemed relatively absent. In addition, both Carolyn and Walt seemed to be responding to their stresses with "more of the same"—that is, rigidifying their commitment to traditional gender roles and intensifying traditional role demands on their partner (while simultaneously feeling shortchanged about what the partner was not providing).

The entire Hilton family seemed gender typed in terms of its style of managing stress. Walt and Tony seemed disposed toward repression, denial, and action; Carolyn and Leah seemed disposed toward direct confrontation of relational issues. Were Walt and Tony cutting themselves off from interpersonal relationships? Were Carolyn and Leah expected to overfunction as caretakers for the family? Questions immediately arose about Buffy. To what extent was her coquettishness an effort to distract and divert family members from their interpersonal tensions? What about Rick? Why was he not included? Could his absence represent more male avoidance and emotional flight?

As the gender consultation team and I continued to explore the role of gender in my work with the Hiltons, I began to question other possible areas of influence. Why was I so accepting of Carolyn's willingness to discontinue treatment? As a traditionally socialized man, was I susceptible to unrecognized collusion with Tony and Walt—with the "male" tendency to minimize relational problems? Was I sufficiently willing to challenge Walt and his tendency toward avoidance through intimidation? Was I myself so immersed in the male tendency to overwork that I was reluctant to challenge Walt's work obsession? Why was I so uneasy with Leah? Did her anger at men and patriarchy touch a nerve in my own life? Why was I so charmed by the descriptions of Buffy? Why did I forget Rick?

The interactions with my gender consultation team were invaluable in helping me recognize areas where I might have had gender "blind spots," that is, where I might have missed intervention needs and possibilities because of my own gender socialization. I was troubled to realize what I had missed and wished for a second opportunity. Fortunately, I got that chance slightly more than a year later. Before describing the second phase of therapy with the Hiltons. I detail how gender-informed case consultation prepared me to become a better therapist for this family.

ENHANCING THERAPY THROUGH GENDER ANALYSIS

Over the past 10 years, I have read the work of others who have called for "gender role psychotherapy" (Solomon, 1982), "gender-fair" therapy (Nutt, 1991), "gender-sensitive" therapy (Philpot, 1991), and "gender-aware" therapy (Good, Gilbert, & Scher, 1990). Several times I have tried to elaborate on my own ideas about this process (Brooks, 1990, 1991, 1992). It was not the Hilton family alone that stimulated my thinking about the promotion of gender-sensitive therapy for families but, from the standpoint of gender issues, they certainly were among the most challenging and most rewarding.

Because of the immediacy of gender issues in families like the Hiltons, I have developed a set of

gender-sensitivity questions I typically ask myself in my family work:

1. What meaningful messages has each family member received about "proper" conduct for his or her gender?
2. To what extent are each family member's problems consistent with traditional gender patterns?
3. How has each family member's participation (or nonparticipation) in therapy matched typical gender patterns?
4. How has my therapy work with this family been influenced by my own gender socialization?
5. Are there ways in which this family's larger context has affected each family member's gender role behavior?

Although my initial contacts with the Hiltons gave me only initial ideas about them in terms of these critical gender questions, subsequent therapy contacts (described later) provided abundant information to complete this analysis.

Meaningful Messages

The Hiltons, like many families, were struggling with how to negotiate traditional gender expectations in a number of critical areas. In most areas, Walt, Carolyn, Tony, and Buffy conformed closely to traditional expectations and seemed to form a gender-conservative subsystem. Rick and Leah rebelled against many traditional expectations and were initially exiled, although they ultimately united to form a gender-challenging subsystem.

Achievement and career emphasis. Walt and Carolyn had closely followed the traditional path, on which only men are to be career oriented. Leah challenged this expectation and, as a result, was in conflict with most other family members.

Autonomy and help-seeking. Carolyn was quick to seek professional help, whereas Walt, Tony, and Rick were true to the masculine code of rugged individualism and avoidance of help seeking.

Emotional expressiveness. In the Hilton family emotional expressiveness was "women's work." The men, particularly Walt and Tony, tended toward emotional stoicism at home, although Walt was prone to boorish outbursts in his work setting, and

Tony could be surprisingly aggressive in the athletic arena.

Interpersonal relationships.   Hilton men tended to isolate themselves, whereas Hilton women were highly concerned with interpersonal closeness and seeking interpersonal relationships.

Self-care and self-abuse.   Carolyn and Leah were prone to take on the traditional female responsibility of looking out for the emotional and physical well-being of all family members. Walt, Tony, and Rick tended to deny their problems and, as I would later learn, suppress their distress though substance abuse or emotional flight.

Gender Socialization and Family Members' Problematic Issues

In terms of their problematic issues and symptomatic distress, members of the Hilton family were highly traditional. In the most general terms, the men tended to flee, suppress, or act out, whereas the women tended to internalize or seek to placate and appease others. Walt Hilton submerged his affective distress in his work and in alcohol. Tony attempted to deny any emotional distress but, as I later learned, ultimately sought relief through alcohol. Rick tended to flee from most emotional intensity and sometimes sought relief through sexual acting out. Carolyn spent most of her life seeking to help others but was continually vulnerable to self-blame and depression. Leah sought to free herself from most traditional constraints but was subjected to intense criticism for her justified anger and labeled as pathological for her efforts to serve as a sentinel for family problems. Buffy was seemingly doing very well by following a traditional path as a "little princess" but might ultimately face enormous problems with an obsession to please others and become an emotional caretaker for her father.

Gender Socialization Effects on Therapy Participation

Once again, I witnessed the powerful organizing effect of gender as I studied how it had shaped the manner in which each family member participated in (or avoided) the therapy enterprise. Carolyn and Leah actively sought therapy help; Walt, Tony, and Rick resisted. In therapy sessions, Carolyn tended to be highly passive and dependent on therapist support before considering any comments or moves. She was quick to defer to Walt, initially relenting when he resisted therapy, later avoiding opinions that would counter his dogmatic assertions. Both Tony and Walt were highly resistant to therapy, and Rick's flight had made him unavailable. Tony was guarded and marginally participative. Walt was initially resistant and, when agreeing to come, was quick to seek to control the parameters of treatment. He tended to interact in a dominating, instrumental, and intellectually guarded manner, preferring tangible goals and minimizing emotional experience.

Reactivity of the Therapist

By and large, psychotherapy is a "feminine" activity; that is, the nature of the therapy process is more closely attuned to the stereotypical "female" experience than it is to the stereotypical "male" experience. This statement does not mean, of course, that all aspects of psychotherapy are more harmonious with women's experiences, or that men don't bring many "masculine" skills to the table. It simply represents my concurrence with Brown (1990), who argued that "the phenomenology of being female" provides female therapists with many advantages in terms of empathy, empowerment of others, and in the "capacity to comprehend the pain and alienation of others" (p. 229).

Because U.S. culture generally raises boys to avoid emotional sensitivity and to pay minimal attention to the subtleties of interpersonal relationships, many male therapists are complicated folks. The demands of their profession require them to process experiences and promote behaviors in a manner that runs counter to many aspects of their masculine socialization. Therefore, to become successful therapists they have to overcome many constraining aspects of their upbringing and behave in "unmanly" ways. This can usually be accomplished very well, but not without compromises and the occasional appearance of some "manly" behaviors that limit them as therapists.

In reflecting on the Hilton case, I have been able to identify a number of ways that my gender socialization affected my work. Although there were many areas of influence, I note only some of the more salient.

Conflict–avoidance. One problematic aspect of my male socialization has been my exaggerated need to accept a tenuous status quo and my occasional reluctance to push beyond superficial denial to uncover distress. In terms of relationships, I've learned to be somewhat conflict avoidant. Sometimes I reactively join with other male "repressors" against the concerns of female "sensitizers." Particularly powerful male figures are even more problematic for me. Obviously, an Army colonel like Walt Hilton could be quite intimidating. In general, I find it much easier to challenge the avoidant and denying defenses of a nonthreatening woman like Carolyn Hilton than an imposing man like Walt Hilton.

This tendency to align with conflict-avoidant and repressive men is not limited to powerful men, however. As an adolescent male I was keenly aware of the need to "fit in" and not "rock the boat." As a result, I find myself unusually reluctant to push adolescent males, uneasy with their scorn or rejection.

However, I can also be uncomfortable with certain women. I have never been particularly comfortable with women's anger or rage, so someone like Leah Hilton often makes me tense. Sometimes I have been overly charmed by traditionally pleasing young women like Buffy.

Women as caretakers, men as workers. Like many therapists, I often find myself overly accepting of traditional gender expectations about family roles: Women should be caretakers; men should be workers. This issue is more complicated than simply supporting women's interest in work outside the home, because it requires more dramatic shifts in gender roles. For women to become more free to pursue careers, men must also be encouraged and supported to become more broadly functional as caretakers, fathers, and domestic laborers.

In the Hilton family these traditional gender expectations had become especially burdensome. Hilton men struggled to find emotional meaning as they took on their worker roles, while Hilton women struggled with guilt over their need to meet their own needs as well as those of others. As a therapist I was too reticent to challenge this pattern. To me, the family had seemed so utterly dependent

on its traditional foundation of a workaholic husband/father and a caretaking wife/mother. To a large extent, they ultimately proved me wrong. They were far more capable of change than I had initially imagined.

Emotional intimacy among men. Because I have become so accustomed to instrumental and emotionally distant relationships among men, I have been slow to identify male emotional intimacy as an important therapeutic goal. As I saw with the Hiltons, the male family members suffered from their inability to break through the emotional constraints of their socialization.

Intertwined with the topic of male emotional intimacy is the problem of homophobia. As a male therapist it is especially vital that I overcome the homophobia endemic to my traditional male socialization. As I was to learn, this sometimes means that I must sometimes be prepared to lead the effort to help families cope with their irrational fears of gay and lesbian lifestyles.

Leadership and control. Like many other male therapists, I have come to prefer a therapy style in which I maintain clear direction and control of therapy sessions. I have found that I can be overly fond of passive and compliant family members, whereas I can be unduly threatened or uneasy with those who are prone to challenge my leadership. As a result, I need to monitor closely the degree to which my interventions are distorted by this stylistic preference.

Context Issues

As a career military family, the Hiltons were subjected to unusually intense pressures to conform to traditional gender roles. Although the numbers of military women are rising, the husband/father has typically been the member of the armed services. Families typically have been expected to accommodate to the man's career, perpetuating the potential for gender role strain. As a therapist, I found it critical that I fully appreciate this larger context if I were to have any hope of making culturally sensitive therapy interventions. That is, when helping a family strategize about change, I must remain aware of the realistic obstacles and penalties they might face if they act counter to the pressures inherent in their current social and political context. In working with this military family, my interventions might need to be different than they would have been if I were seeing them in a different cultural context—for example, a university campus, a rural community, a large city, an ethnic community, or a geriatric center.

MY SECOND CHANCE: GENDER-INFORMED TREATMENT

When Carolyn called me next, nearly a year later, she seemed to be on the verge of emotional collapse. She described a chaotic family situation with nearly every member in some state of severe emotional distress. Leah had run off to live with Rick and, while living there, had made a suicidal gesture. Tony had been kicked off the football team after getting a second alcohol-related arrest and a charge of driving without a license. Walt had increased his alcohol consumption to several drinks per night and been diagnosed with a bleeding ulcer.

The family clearly was in crisis. This crisis posed both a huge challenge and a second opportunity for me to help. Although alarmed by the chaotic state of affairs, I felt somewhat reassured that the many hours of consultation and case analysis had put me in a much better position to intervene.

Family therapy, now practiced under multiple theoretical rubrics, encompasses many types of therapeutic intervention. Like many family therapists I practice an eclectic version and adapt strategies and style to the specific family situation. Depending on what I encounter, I might place emphasis on the need to alter family structure, to reframe the family's understanding of each other's behavior, alter "solution behavior," increase individuation to lessen overreactivity, and teach alternative strategies to accomplish family goals.

To some extent, each of these strategies would have a role my long-term therapy with the Hiltons. Of greatest interest here, however, is my conviction that all of my interventions were immeasurably improved by the aforementioned gender consultation and case analysis. I will illustrate this by describing some of my interventions and highlight how they were enhanced by my enhanced gender awareness.

Joining: Creating a Therapeutic System

Regardless of theoretical orientation or strategic emphasis, a family therapist is unlikely to make progress unless there has been a successful initial engagement or "joining" with all family members. Minuchin and Fishman (1981) described *joining* as "the umbrella under which all therapeutic transactions occur . . . the glue that that holds the therapeutic system together" (1981, pp. 31–32).

In my initial interactions with the Hilton family I had found it exceptionally easy to join with Carolyn and Buffy. Carolyn was highly motivated and deeply appreciative of my efforts. Buffy was a delightful entertainer who charmed all who encountered her. On the other hand, I had considerable difficulty building a comfortable relationship with Walt and Leah. In the process of developing greater personal gender awareness I found ways to build bridges to Walt and Leah and, to the appropriate extent, distance myself from overinvolvement with Carolyn and Buffy.

My breakthrough with Walt came very early. Recognizing that his resistance had contributed substantially to the previous therapy termination, I felt the need for an immediate connection with him. I also realized that my failure to make to a better connection was, in part, a product of my irrational intimidation by men like him. With a better recognition of the fears and insecurities behind his aggressive façade, as well as improved insight into my own gender-based anxiety, I felt more compassionate and less fearful.

To reinforce the urgency of the situation, I told Carolyn that I felt it critical that she emphasize to Walt that I must speak with him as soon as possible. When he called me I described my concerns for his family and asked him if he would come visit with me to help me figure out how to help. Walt put up a mild resistance, noting they had "been down that road before," but relented to my pleas that I really needed him.

When Walt arrived, I made a special point of soliciting his views of the current situation, validating his beliefs whenever feasible. Without being overly solicitous, I made efforts to praise him for his successful military career and contributions to the well-being of his family. Less anxious, I felt more able to counter his dismissal of the family problems as inconsequential and of therapy as wasteful foolishness. "Colonel Hilton," I challenged, "you've done an incredible job of providing for your family and have been amazingly loyal in your responsibilities to them. That work is now in peril, and they desperately need your help, but they need it in a very different way. This time they don't need your labors or distant sacrifices. Instead, they need you to be involved and emotionally present to help them deal with their distress!"

Walt seemed shocked and unsettled, but he responded, "Doc, I'll tell you this right now, there isn't anything I wouldn't do for my family—when do you want to meet?"

In respectfully challenging Walt, I was able to overcome my personal intimidation as well as find a way to confront him in a manner respectful of his traditional male socialization. This was only a beginning, but it helped get him involved and seemed to initiate a far more productive series of therapy interactions.

My capacity to join with Leah was similarly improved by recognition of my personal reactivity to her and a more realistic appraisal of her irritation and frustrations. As I came to appreciate the difficulties she had experienced as an intelligent and assertive woman in a male-dominated family and military culture I came to see how she had been scapegoated by the family. Leah had challenged her parents to talk about the issues, but they had ignored her concerns as histrionic overreaction, perhaps related to excessive exposure to "feminist radical politics." To quell her constant emotional outbursts, they had sought psychiatric help and sedative medications for her.

With increased trust in my understanding of her, Leah became an invaluable therapeutic ally. She pointed out that Rick's "omission" from family discussion had not been coincidental. Rick and his father had been very close for the first few years but, as Rick's interests wandered to aesthetic and "girlish" activities, such as dance and music, Walt had rejected him. Although a straight-A student, Rick left high school in his junior year to play music in a nearby city and room with Mark, a "close friend." Walt and Carolyn had never broached the topic of Mark, choosing to distance themselves rather than deal with Walt's intense homophobia.

Because Leah had enjoyed an extremely close relationship with Rick and been devastated by his "exile" from the family, she helped me realize the importance of attending to this issue. Furthermore, she claimed that Tony was not the simple, well-adjusted guy he pretended to be. Although Tony harshly demeaned her efforts, Leah pleaded with him to open up and admit that several months before he had confided to her that he'd once considered suicide himself. Leah also insisted that even Buffy was heading for problems because of her obsession with beauty, charm, and popularity.

Reframing Symptoms and Realigning Subsystems

As is the case with all family systems, the Hiltons had relatively fixed ideas about who was the carrier of symptoms as well as about the qualities and characteristics of each family member. As a result, the Hiltons reacted to challenges in stereotyped ways and with overly restricted response repertoires. For example, Carolyn was seen as compassionate yet a poor decision maker. Walt was considered to be a tough leader but insensitive and crude. Even during relatively calm periods, predictable attributions would be made about each person's behavior on the basis of relatively rigid concepts about who that person was. In times of stress these attributions commonly took the form of attributions of pathology that polarized the family and isolated scapegoated members. To help the Hiltons move beyond their stalemated relationships I felt that I had to help them broaden their conceptual maps, stop thinking of each other in such limited ways.

Once again, improved gender awareness helped me re-evaluate family members so that I could help each family member think differently about his or her own behavior and the meaning of the actions of others. My improved recognition of Leah's actions helped me reframe her actions from those of an "angry and carping complainer" to those of a young woman courageously speaking out to save a family in trouble. Consistent with traditional female socialization, she was taking on responsibility for the welfare of others, even when it created discomfort in others.

In a critically poignant session Leah tearfully responded to taunts from Walt that she should be less reactive and more "even-tempered" like Tony. In a voice quaking with emotion, she said, "But Dad, how can you say that!? Tony is just running away from this family's problems. Everyone is freaked out and unhappy, but nobody dares to speak up. It kills me when you call me names when all I want to do is save this family before it falls apart!"

Once Leah's voice was reframed from that of a hysterical overreactor to that of a sensitive family loyalist, the family was challenged to confront its difficulties. Rather than expecting Leah to continue overfunctioning as monitor of family well-being, the family began to shift that responsibility. Tony confessed that at times he too had been concerned about his parents' relationship and sometimes avoided family contact. Buffy then broke into tears, admitting that she always felt tense and worried that she would not do well enough to please her parents. She wailed, "It tears me up when Leah is so critical of me and calls me 'the little princess'. She hates me, and I can't ever do anything right!"

With family tensions more open, I had a better chance of working with problem issues. Because it seemed clear to me that many family members felt isolated, I chose to focus on realigning relationships within subsystems.

Within the sibling subsystem I worked to help improve the quality of the interrelationships. The brother-and-sister relationships were highly problematic and sharply divergent in terms of differing standards of male and female conduct. Buffy and Tony were very traditional; Rick and Leah were more challenging of traditional roles. By openly addressing their estrangement and tensions as differences in value orientations, we were able to begin creating opportunities for communication and for improved understanding of each other. Leah was able to show Buffy that she actually cared for her and criticized her out of concern for her well-being. Rick was able to tell Tony about the pain he felt from Tony's homophobic rejection of him. Tony ultimately confessed to Rick that they shared a common anxiety about proving themselves in their father's eyes. In discussing the gender-based roots of their past differences, each sibling elevated his or her understanding of each other and came to feel a powerful unified commitment to overcoming family stresses.

The parental subsystem was equally benefited by improved gender awareness. Both Walt and Carolyn came to an improved appreciation of the factors leading to tensions with Leah and Rick. Furthermore, they realized how they had been prone to favor Buffy and Tony, sometimes pressuring them to live out their own unfulfilled gender-based role expectations.

My work with the marital subsystem was enhanced by my sensitivity to the role of traditional gender pressures in creating distress between Walt and Carolyn. In brief, I coached Walt and Carolyn to recognize the interconnection and reciprocity of their gender roles. The role choices of one partner shaped the role choices of the other. For example, as Walt began to see how his overwork and emotional isolation were creating burdens for himself he also began to realize how his extreme role behavior compromised Carolyn's life options. Likewise, Carolyn's behavior could limit Walt's options. For each to feel more fulfilled, they needed to consider new options —Walt as less work-focused and more involved with his family; Carolyn as more committed to a role beyond that of caretaker and mother. To enhance mutual empathy and "gender-coevolution," I helped Walt and Carolyn complete a process of "gender inquiry" (Philpot, Brooks, Lusterman, & Nutt, 1997). In this process, Walt and Carolyn explored the critical gender-based messages of their developmental history and speculated on creative paths to a new and more adaptive marital relationship.

Eventually, Carolyn herself admitted to periodic anxiety attacks and fears for the future "empty nest." She had become increasingly unfulfilled as an Army wife and had taken encouragement from some of Leah's feminist books (which she had covertly read). Eventually, through Carolyn's admission of unhappiness, we were also able to uncover many previously repressed issues in Walt's life. Walt admitted to periods of strange malaise and disinterest. He wasn't sure which had come first—his denial of promotion to General or his loss of interest in his Army career. He felt acutely apathetic and unappreciated. It seemed that both his family and his commanders had always taken him for granted.

In one particularly moving session, Carolyn pointed out that Walt had not been the same since a buddy's 9-year-old daughter had been killed in a car wreck. Walt was almost completely unable to shake the incident. In exploring the matter with Carolyn, they discovered the extreme investment they had made in Buffy as their last child. Walt, who had been emotionally absent during Rick's childhood, had wanted to compensate by holding tightly to his "little princess." Not surprisingly, this led very directly to an exploration of Walt's sense of loss from his rejection of Rick. In several intense sessions, Carolyn helped Walt confront his homophobia and finally reach out to Rick. With great difficulty, Walt made peace with Rick, only to discover unresolved issues with Tony, who had also longed for Walt's love and approval.

OVERVIEW AND CONCLUSION

In 2 years of family therapy, the Hilton family made immense progress in negotiating difficult transitions. Walt and Carolyn acknowledged their fears for the future and consciously applied themselves to a more rewarding couple relationship. Carolyn continued her interest in outstanding women in military history. Walt re-evaluated his extreme emphasis on his military career and developed long-repressed interests in music and theater. He made much better accommodation to his homophobia and began to re-establish his relationships with Rick and Tony. He spent considerable time with Leah, thanking her for her dedication to family but assuring her that he and her mother were now more committed to reassuming their proper parental roles. Finally, Walt and Carolyn began to "let go" of Buffy, who had decided she really preferred to be called by her given name, Gloria.

Thanks to families like the Hiltons, I have become intensely aware of the need to consider the critical role of gender in the lives of families. More and more family therapists are realizing that their past proclamations of "neutrality"—that is, the stance that they are value free and apolitical—have been not-so-harmless self-deceptions. Simply put, when therapists do not help women and men recognize (and deal with) the powerful gender messages of the larger culture they perpetuate the power and exacerbate the gender role strain of women and men. When they do

not point out the narrow and confining aspects of traditional gender ideology they participate in creation of a new generation of narrowly socialized children. More and more, family psychologists are realizing that, rather than being unwitting contributors to gender role strain, they must become educators and translators. Unlike few others, family psychologists can be gender brokers, agents who help families study their gender heritage; critique contemporary culture; and fabricate personal gender roles that are realistic, creative, and liberating.

References

Brooks, G. R. (1990). Psychotherapy with traditional role-oriented males. In P. A. Keller & L. G. Ritt (Eds.), *Innovations in clinical practice: A source book* (pp. 61–74). Sarasota, FL: Professional Resource Exchange.

Brooks, G. R. (1991). Traditional men in marital and family therapy. In M. Bograd (Ed.), *Feminist approaches for men in family therapy*. New York: Haworth.

Brooks, G. R. (1992). Gender-sensitive family therapy in a violent culture. *Topics in Family Psychology and Counseling, 1*, 24–36.

Brown, L. (1990). What female therapists have in common. In D. W. Cantor (Ed.), *Women as therapists* (pp. 227–242). Northvale, NJ: Aronson.

Good, G., Gilbert, L. A., & Scher, M. (1990). Gender aware therapy: A synthesis of feminist therapy and knowledge about gender. *Journal of Counseling and Development, 68*, 376–380.

Minuchin, S., & Fishman, H. C. (1981). *Family therapy techniques*. Cambridge, MA: Harvard University Press.

Nutt, R. (1991). Ethical principles for gender-fair family therapy. *The Family Psychologist, 7*, 32–33.

Philpot, C. L. (1991). Gender-sensitive couples therapy. *Journal of Family Psychotherapy, 2*, 19–40.

Philpot, C. L., Brooks, G. R., Lusterman, D-D., & Nutt, R. (1997). *Bridging separate gender worlds: How men and women clash and how therapists can bring them together*. Washington, DC: American Psychological Association.

Solomon, K. (1982). Individual psychotherapy and changing masculine roles: Dimensions of gender-role psychotherapy. In K. Solomon & N. B. Levy (Eds.), *Men in transition: Theory and therapy* (pp. 247–273). New York: Plenum.

CHAPTER 22

REDISCOVERY OF BELOVEDNESS

Becky Butler

There are particular clients I remember long after our work together has concluded. This seems to be true of clients whose experiences are more vivid or charged than those of others. It is also true of clients whose course in therapy inspires and teaches me. Working with Terri[1] provided many lasting lessons for me. One of those lessons was about providing therapy within a systemic framework. I was repeatedly reminded that a systemic lens is just that— a lens. It is not determined by the number of clients in the room. It is the lens through which clients are known and understood. Even when there is only one client present, the therapy room is implicitly populated by people who have had influence and impact on the life and self of that client. The larger context is always present. The impact of family structure and organization is always considered. The client is understood against a backdrop of influences, such as culture, race, gender, religion, and sexual orientation. Our clients bring both strengths and wounds from the very particular contexts of their lives. To deeply understand their lives, we must know and appreciate those contexts, both past and present.

There is a Hopi word, *hakomi*, that means "How do you stand in relation to these many realms?" I believe that healing from a systemic perspective carries that question in its belly. One of life's challenges and blessings is to live whole but not separate. Our clients are born not just from individuals, not just from families, but from cultures. The gifts they receive, and the ways in which they are challenged, occur in the context of community and, within that context of community, the journey to healing begins.

AN UNFOLDING NARRATIVE

My first meeting with Terri was brief. She came with a friend, Peg, a former client of mine. Peg had been encouraging Terri to enter therapy and had asked me if I would have an introductory session with her, so she could decide whether therapy was something she wanted to undertake. Terri was in her early 30s. She was tall and wiry, with short-cropped red hair. My principal impression was that she was tightly held, in every way. She would alternate between rhythmic tapping of a foot or hand or stillness so constrained that it seemed volcanic.

Ordinarily, I would have invited a new client to meet with me by herself, and I would have engaged her in a preliminary conversation about what had brought her to consider therapy at this time. But somehow this seemed like the wrong approach with Terri. My sense was that she was simply there to scout the level of safety in the room. My only consideration was to create that safety in whatever way necessary. Responding to her level of discomfort and to a fierce atmosphere of privacy about her, I met with Peg and Terri together. I spoke mostly to Peg,

---

[1] Names and identifying characteristics of clients have been changed.

inviting Terri into the conversation from time to time, but always allowing her to set the proximity. As the session drew to an end, I made the most direct contact, telling her that I would be happy to see her in therapy if she would like to schedule an appointment. Given the degree of her discomfort, the fact that she agreed to return indicated the extent of her desperation.

Terri returned a week later for a full session. The hypervigilant quality was diminished only slightly. She alternated between perching rigidly on the edge of the couch, pacing intently across the room, or excusing herself with stiff politeness to go out to the waiting room for water or air. She seemed painfully torn between her fierce privacy and a hungry desire for assistance. I was struck by how painful and difficult it appeared for her to be even remotely present —present in the room or present even in her body. She seemed engaged in a continuous effort to find flight from the sharp, intolerable edges of her inner experience.

In that session, Terri painted her current life as the culmination of a series of wretched failures, acts of cowardice, and repeated disappointments to those who had given much to her. She spoke mostly of her adult life, referring only briefly to her earlier years. She spoke of having once been a long-distance runner but having given that up against the recommendations of family and coach. In the process, she had also lost an athletic scholarship to college. She had tried several times to complete college, refusing any financial assistance from her family. She had, at various times, studied journalism, art history, and pre-med. Each time, she had dropped out before finishing her course of study. She had gone on to work as a security guard, a proofreader for a small publishing house and, most recently, a writer for a local newspaper. She described her writing as "crap" and her life as a "trash heap of unfinished careers."

Terri was forthcoming in identifying herself as a lesbian. She said that her sexual orientation was not something that caused her conflict, having come to peace with that many years prior. She reported having had a series of relationships with women who "didn't really communicate much." The relationships had been neither damaging nor particularly satisfying. The fact that none had been long lasting was, to her, yet another indication of her own deficits.

Terri made it clear that coming to a therapist was, to her, the final indication of utter failure. She was willing to do this only because her life had become intolerable. She did not know where else to turn. She described that several months prior she had contemplated suicide, once spending an afternoon holding a gun in her mouth. She railed at herself for her lack of courage to "do the deed."

I asked few questions during that session. What came through her presence, as much as through her words, was her utter self-loathing and her desire to exit. This included subtle ways of avoiding being present, or the more final version of suicide. I could feel how difficult and humiliating it was for her simply to be talking to me. My goals were twofold: to be free of judgment and to make the room large enough to hold that which seemed too difficult for her to contain within her own being. I wanted to create expansiveness and safety and to allow her whatever privacy she needed. I also asked her to abide by a contract of not harming herself, to which she agreed.

During the next several sessions, a picture of Terri's earlier life began to emerge. She seemed surprised that I would be interested in it. She saw her discontent as a result of current cowardice and failure and saw past experience as irrelevant. Nevertheless, she seemed willing to accommodate me. As she spoke, I heard the writer in her, and heard especially her love of the southern landscape. She had grown up in one of those small southern towns where life was languid and gentle. She described to me the stands of live oaks draped in Spanish moss, the hickory trees, the sweet gum and cypress. She talked about the spring, when the air was drenched with the heavy scent of honeysuckle. She described herself as spending most of her time among the trees, especially in a treehouse built in one of the live oaks behind her family's home. In detail, she described standing in the treehouse during a summer storm, feeling the swaying of the branches under her and listening to the howling of the wind. She described repeating her own name, mantralike, over and over. She described feeling as one with the oak, the wind, and the words. She spoke of knowing, in that moment, what it was that people referred to when they used words like *God* and *spirit*.

Terri's description seemed as entrancing as the initial experience. After describing it in a kind of reverie, she immediately became embarrassed, shaking herself out of the past, back into the present. Quickly, she re-guarded and diminished the experience: "I was a strange kid." I felt privileged to have heard her account, and I conveyed as much, saying something about the privilege of being allowed to share remembrances that seemed so sacred. She shot me a quick glance. Apparently, she had conveyed too much, and for the rest of the session, as well as several sessions thereafter, she retreated to an account of her childhood in which she appeared to be merely one of several players: descriptions not from inner remembrance but told as though from the point of view of an outsider.

Her father had been a physician, and her mother had been his nurse. A son, Winston, much adored, had excelled throughout school. Outgoing and charming, Winston had become the captain of the football team and high school valedictorian. Winston had gone on to The Citadel and was currently pursuing a successful career in the military. Seven years after Winston, Terri had been born, her arrival "a disappointment and a challenge." The accolades her parents had had for Winston turned into apologies for herself, an absentminded and mediocre student. She did fine in the trees, she said; it was coming down to earth that gave her trouble. She described a loving connection with her father. He was a bird watcher, and together they would go at dawn to the open fields outside of town, binoculars in hand. The one thing that Terri possessed that Winston had not was a patient presence. They would watch for hours, with few words spoken between them. These were her happiest times.

Terri described her father as having had some of the distracted quality that Terri saw in herself. It was Terri's mother who "kept everything together." She described her mother as competent and capable, rising to every challenge, carrying out multiple tasks efficiently. It was her mother who kept the medical practice operating; it was her mother who kept the family engaged in the community, who kept the household operating smoothly, who got first Win-

ston and later Terri to piano lessons and athletic practices on time. I began to picture the force of her mother's energy, in stark contrast to the languid and mysterious landscape surrounding them.

When I asked Terri whether her mother held any resentment about her many responsibilities, Terri replied sharply that her mother had carried burdens graciously, and an occasional sharpness was what anybody would expect. Terri described herself as her mother's greatest source of frustration and disappointment, perpetually late, meeting guests with mud on her clothes or tangled, untidy hair: "My mother put up with me always saying the wrong thing, doing the wrong thing."

I pictured Terri as living in a kind of congruence with the landscape, finding her greatest connection to self through the centuries-old trees, the gently arching branches, and the leaves stirring in late summer. Despite being a source of exasperation to her mother, Terri described how she had continued in her own unique way of moving through the world throughout grade school and into middle school. When she was at the end of middle school, however, two events coincided to dramatically alter the delicate balance with which she had maintained her own sense of wonder and still managed not to disrupt the family equilibrium. The first of these events was the unexpected death of her father.

When Terri described this period in her life, her affect changed significantly. It was as though she described it with a minute portion of herself. The heart and spirit present in her earlier descriptions were absent. The tight containment returned in full force. Face frozen, expression distant, she reported that she had been called home from school. An uncle, her mother's brother, was pacing in the front room. Her mother was locked in the bedroom. Her uncle told her that her father had died of a heart attack. He told her that Winston had been called back and would be there shortly. He said that she had to think of her mother now; she was a good woman, and she would need her very badly. He said that she must cry a little and then be strong for her mother.

As Terri described this, I could almost hear the keening that had never taken place. When I asked Terri what she had needed on that afternoon, she replied that her needs were irrelevant. I said that I was sure they had felt irrelevant but that I wondered what she would have needed if there had been space for her. She replied that she had needed to go up into her treehouse and never come down again. I asked if she felt as though a part of her had done just that. She snorted and looked away, then excused herself and left, once again, to pace outside the office.

When Terri returned, she asked if this were really necessary. All she wanted to do was to stop "lousing everything up." Her early years, and the lives of her mother and father, were irrelevant to her own failures. I replied that it must feel like a violation of privacy to be having these conversations. It made sense that they would seem unnecessarily painful. These were large events that had been placed, perforce, into small containers. I was sure it must be extremely painful to be sitting with them, even briefly. I offered her the ever-present option of engaging in a different level of conversation, focusing only on present-day events. I added, however, that seeing herself as a failure was so pervasive and long standing that it seemed wise to trace it back before returning to present events. I reminded her repeatedly that she could at any time slow this process down, or stop it entirely. I told her she was in charge of every step along the path. And I expressed my admiration for her courage in being willing to touch these feelings. She agreed to continue, grudgingly acknowledging that perhaps it made sense to discuss some of these events.

In between this session and the next, Terri called and said she wanted to tell me something over the telephone that was too difficult to say in person. She didn't want me to "make a big deal out of it," and asked me not to refer to it or bring it up during sessions. She told me, in quick, urgent sentences, about the second event that had dramatically altered her life. Her maternal grandfather had lived near them when she was little. They would take hikes together, although he rarely came to the house. She had been devoted to him, considering him her best friend. But on several occasions she had visited him and found him drunk. Usually, she left quickly when this happened, but on one occasion, not long after the death of her father, he had convinced her to stay. In the end, he had forced her to perform

oral sex. She had run home afterward, making herself vomit. Throughout the night that followed, she drank salt water to make herself throw up over and over again. After the urgent telling of the story, Terri hung up abruptly. I called her back to make sure she was not in danger of harming herself. She said she was thinking about it but was willing to contract that she would not.

At the next session, I asked Terri if she wanted me to bring up the telephone conversation. She didn't. I said that I would offer from time to time but that it would be up to her when or if she talked further about it. She seemed a little less tightly wound than before but mentioned that before the telephone call she had again been toying with her gun, thinking of suicide. Terri had a lock for the gun, and at my suggestion agreed that she would lock it and leave the keys with me until some future date. I knew that by entrusting the keys to me she was committing herself to this process at a much deeper level than she had previously.

When Terri talked about life after the death of her father, she continued to speak of it without affect. She described that she had had to "change her ways" after his death, because she "couldn't continue to be a pain in the butt" to her mother. She had started arriving at appointments on time, started keeping her room and clothing clean, started working harder in school. And she started running. She described beginning to run out of rage and desperation. Nothing could emerge in words or sounds, but she found release in great raw strides, gulps of air, and muscular exertion. She ran down the lanes, beneath the canopy of live oaks. In time, she ran on her school track team.

Terri described running with the same animation that had been evident in her description of her earlier childhood and the trees. She explained that as time went on, it became clear that she was a good athlete, the fastest cross-country runner at her school. She won at state competitions, and her coach encouraged her to compete nationally. She had found something at which she excelled. She also knew that it was a gift from God. She was too fast for this talent to originate within her. In our session, she talked of knowing beyond a shadow of a doubt that God had sent this gift to comfort her after the loss of her father, and she was very grateful. Running allowed her to keep all of her pain contained where it belonged. It allowed her to please her mother, and it allowed her to feel God's presence. Her deepening sense of God inspired her to become more involved with church. To her involvement in church and prayer she brought the same intensity of focus that she brought to running.

Terri described that in her senior year of high school, just when everything had found its place, she fell in love with a young woman on the track team. She described that she had been getting "crushes" on her female teachers for years, which had been easy to ignore. But this was different; she was becoming a young woman.

Terri immersed herself even more deeply in prayer and church activities. She began spending more time with a longtime male friend. They had been in grade school together and had stayed close through middle school. In retrospect, she recognized that he had been doing the same thing she was— trying desperately to convince himself of his own heterosexuality.

Despite her best efforts, Terri's feelings towards the young woman on the track team only intensified. Finally, after one track meet the two took a walk together, which ended in a kiss. Terri went to church every morning and every afternoon, praying for God to remove her desire. She knew that to pursue this attraction would mean losing all that was important to her: family, connection with the church and, ultimately, connection to God.

Terri showed little emotion as she spoke, although it seemed more difficult for her than usual to make eye contact. During our session, she described coming to the realization that because running had been God's gift to her, she would have to make a choice: renounce the thought of ever being involved with women or renounce God's gift to her. Emotionless, she described deciding to give up running. Her decision caused a general confusion, because she had just been granted an athletic scholarship. Her coach was baffled, and her mother was outraged and frustrated. She could answer none of their questions or help them understand. She knew she was again causing suffering to those around her,

but this was the only way she knew to "sin with integrity."

Terri had never run again. Neither had she experienced much in the way of spiritual connection. The description of her early life segued here into the description she had initially offered of her current life. She had begun college several times, resisting offers of financial help from her mother or brother. She maintained contact with them. She was cordial, involved in the life of her brother and his wife and children. But she described herself as "not really all there" when she was with them. Since giving up running, she had never really succeeded at anything, hence the "trash heap" of efforts. She described her mother as having "softened" in recent years but said that it was principally her own self-revulsion that made it difficult to be in her mother's presence.

I recalled that early in our sessions Terri had referred to having "made peace" with being gay. I asked her about that comment as it fit into these recollections. She insisted that she *had* made peace with it; she had recognized the cost and paid the price. She still believed that she had discarded a gift from God, and turned away God's plan for her, but she felt that in all likelihood she would make the same choice again. The choice, and the repercussions of that choice, were with her continually.

REFLECTIONS

This description of Terri's life did not unfold nearly as linearly as I have described above. It emerged in brush strokes, each addition adding depth and dimension to the preceding image. Throughout these initial sessions, I was aware that my task was to listen—not to interpret, not to build on what was being presented, not even to explore in any significant way, but simply to listen. My task was to bear witness to her pain as well as to the gifts and grace she had received. In simply telling her story, Terri was taking a great risk. I believe that she needed to know that the story could rest in the room and not destroy the sense of self that she seemed to have held in place through sheer force of will.

After the seventh or eighth session, when Terri's story had been conveyed in the depth described above, I was aware that a shift needed to occur; I needed to be present with Terri in a slightly different way. I also knew that the direction of that shift had much to do with the lens through which I saw her story. My training had included an emphasis on object relations and self psychology, as well as systems theory. I knew that those lenses provided useful frameworks for understanding Terri's history. Bowenian theory, for instance, seemed especially relevant to Terri's challenge of differentiating from her family. I had also been recently exploring constructivism. I had found myself relieved to hear the proposition that perhaps no one theoretical framework offers the "true" lens for all development of all clients. It resonated with my own experience at a Buddhist meditation retreat I had once attended. I had participated in an exercise in which we were asked a series of questions, such as "Where is your home?" and "Who is your family?" We were asked to answer the questions at progressively deeper levels of meaning. For every question, I found myself ultimately answering "I don't know." I had come to recognize the wisdom of acknowledging the limits of knowledge and was intrigued to hear that perspective applied to psychotherapy; perhaps all theories of development are merely lenses, rather than ultimate truth and, as such, may be equal in validity. One's task then becomes finding a lens that offers the client a vision of herself, and of her life, that offers hope and empowerment.

In thinking about Terri, I was aware of the damage that continued to be effected by the profoundly negative understanding she held of herself and of her choices. The lens through which she saw herself was condemnatory enough to have severed her connection with all that was good, capable, and loving in her, even severing her connection with her own deeply held spiritual experience. The lens was an internalization of how she had felt seen by others (family, society, church); there was little remnant of her early experience of herself as an innately good and spiritual being.

When I had first heard about facilitating in clients a new way of seeing their own narratives it had sounded essentially like a process of reframing, and I had been concerned that ultimately it would not be sufficient to create enduring change. However, this perspective interlocked easily and importantly with other frameworks, and the combination could be synergistically powerful. In working with Terri I knew that the therapeutic relationship we were building was of paramount importance. My work was about holding a vision of her as intelligent, creative, and spiritually vibrant. I needed to hold that vision with unwavering clarity and consistency (given her hypervigilance, she would be immediately aware of any crack in that lens). She was in the process of investing in the relationship we were building. Holding a systemic perspective, I needed to recognize that I myself was now part of the system within which she operated. Building upon the foundation of the relationship between us, I would need to begin to offer perspectives of Terri's life and choices that emerged from an understanding of her as worthy and capable. The process of arriving at a new narrative was inextricable from the painstaking creation of a safe and trusting therapeutic relationship. Although I assumed that this interlace between the cocreation of a new narrative and the safety of the relationship held true to some extent for all clients, I knew that it was especially important in working with Terri.

Terri also offered her own unique challenges in terms of the cocreation of a new way of understanding her story. Terri was fiercely loyal to her family. She also tended to see the world in black-and-white terms. Thus, she saw her family (especially her mother) as completely good. This vision was interwoven with her understanding of herself as primarily bad. Any perspective of herself as good threatened the position of her mother and family, because they were the ones who had conveyed to her the original negative image. Her loyalty to family was sufficiently strong, and her sense of self sufficiently fragile, that family easily outweighed preservation of self.

This challenged me to attend to several elements. One was the gradual introduction of shades of gray, including the possibility that the best of intentions can manifest in actions that are harmful to others. Terri needed to be reminded frequently that I recognized her mother's strengths and sacrifices. Had I not, Terri herself would have had to defend her. Terri would have sacrificed her own self in the defense of her mother rather than gain a sense of self through disloyalty.

I was also challenged to provide work that was vigorously systemic in nature, despite the fact that I was providing therapy for only one person from that system. I needed to operate from the understanding that systems theory is more of an ideology than a modality; how one *thinks* about clients is more important than the number of clients in the room. I knew I had to approach all of Terri's family members with equal compassion. I realized that in an effort to join with clients, I had in the past sometimes seen myself as an adversary of a larger system. For my work with Terri to be successful, I had to hold an understanding of myself as an ally to all those involved. Terri would not allow herself to be redefined (in her own eyes) if it in any way threatened the standing of her family. Although this became less rigid later in therapy, especially as we addressed the issue of abuse, it was at the forefront in this early stage. This challenge was an important point of learning for me. I had come to believe that when one individual heals in a system, the system itself always benefits, albeit not always comfortably. Terri challenged me to carry that belief steadfastly, always seeing the system as a whole with compassion.

In addition to this process of arriving at a new, more positive understanding of herself and her choices Terri also needed a place of safety in which initially to contain and later explore the overwhelming feelings that erupted in her. She needed to learn through experience that the feelings would not destroy her. I knew that she was somewhat dissociative, although I was unsure as to what extent. She was working hard, consciously much of the time, to keep her inner experience at a great distance. The cost of this was an acutely limited emotional range. Being with her, I felt as though she were operating within a fraction of the emotional area that should have been (and perhaps once had been) available to her. This was the tight, volcanic control that she evidenced.

Related to this were deep concerns about safety and self-harm. We needed to proceed slowly and with caution. I was aware of the importance of teaching Terri skills and tools for containment. We attended to practical tools, such as containment visualizations, diaphragmatic breathing, and other anxiety control techniques. I maintained ongoing attention to where Terri was in terms of potential self-harm, frequently using self-harm contracts and reviewing with her what she could do when suicidal feelings arose. My own task was to remain grounded and centered within myself. I knew that I was serving as her containment mechanism for the time being, and I needed to be a well-rooted one.

REVISIONING

During the next phase of therapy (roughly, Session 9 through Session 18), these various elements comprised our work together. As Terri described certain incidents, through a lens of herself as unworthy, I would gently offer an alternative understanding that was not so heroic as to be out of reach to her but compassionate enough to offer a slight shift in perspective. The series of "career disasters" she presented began to be seen less as a reflection of her inherent lack of competence and more as instances when she was not acting on inner direction and desire but rather responding to external expectation. Her path had been difficult to find not because of a lack of intelligence or competence but because she was so accustomed to overriding her own inner direction. We also spent time talking about the shades of gray between absolute success and absolute failure; success, at times, is achieved in ways that relate to internal experience, even survival, rather than ways measured by social standing or career advancement.

I also repeatedly differentiated between goodness of intent and skillful action. Terri needed me to know that her mother's intentions had been only positive. I suggested that sometimes, with the best of motives, our hopes for people can get in the way of allowing them to grow into the people they genuinely are. Drawing on her love of trees, I suggested the metaphor of a willow attempting to be a magnolia, an effort doomed to failure.

This seemed to be a metaphor with which Terri could live: one that managed to avoid criticism of her family and church as it offered a framework for the recovery of her own selfhood. The theme became a recurrent one. It did not produce an immediate or dramatic shift, but it did create small inroads through which she could acknowledge aspects of herself that were not wretched or deficient if judged by a different standard.

During this time, Terri's trust in me and in the process in which we were engaged was deepening. However, I also recognized that much of her hyper-vigilance was still in place. Being with her, I still felt as though I were sitting with a keg of dynamite. In retrospect, I believe that some of the potential explosiveness I felt was related to Terri's genuine potential for self-harm. I think that in some ways I was also feeling Terri's own fear of the size and intensity of her emotions. They seemed, to her, very dangerous. Whenever she felt herself becoming emotional or tearful in therapy, she would frequently leave the room, returning several minutes later. When I suggested that the therapy office was a safe place to allow the tearfulness, she responded with one word: "unacceptable."

During our next few months of working together, two important elements emerged, both related to what I have described above. The first was the extent of Terri's dissociation. She reported that there were frequently times when she would "check out" for several minutes at a time, even up to an hour. Sometimes when driving home she would suddenly find herself several miles off course, driving in a different direction. She described this with great embarrassment and admitted that it had been happening since middle school. These episodes were extremely shameful to her, and it seemed important to do some educating and some normalizing. We talked about responses to trauma, and that sometimes our psyches, in a self-protective effort, "check out." Rather than framing it as pathological, we recognized it as a coping mechanism that had been activated. Our discussions about this were always very practical, focusing on frequency, triggers, and addressing specific tools for containment that could be used in situations that might potentially lead to "checking out." I also continued to encourage her to set limits and boundaries around which topics we discussed.

The other important element that emerged during this period was Terri's alcohol use. Earlier in treatment, she had reported only occasional use. The reality initially emerged in relationship to her self-harm. There were during this period two occasions

when Terri had made emergency calls to me, both when she was feeling self-destructive. During the second of these calls, it was clear that she had been drinking. She came in for the session following the telephone call extremely embarrassed and confessed that she had been drinking heavily ever since high school, most recently drinking up to 12 beers a day, on a fairly frequent basis. She said that it helped keep her "numb." I offered the view that although sometimes it kept her numb, it also had the potential of pouring gasoline on the sparks of her self-destructiveness.

This session marked the beginning of the most difficult stage of therapy. Terri was extremely resistant to stopping her use of alcohol. I was absolutely clear that the continued dependence on alcohol would not only prevent genuine integration and healing but also that, in combination with the dissociation and self-destructiveness, it threatened her life. I also knew that she believed she would be destroyed by the feelings that she would have if she were to stop drinking. Terri knew that she had been progressing in therapy. I knew she had come to trust me and to recognize the extent of my commitment to her and to her healing. This process was providing the most viable opportunity for healing that she had had, and she knew it. Now, I was asking her to give up that which she believed had kept her alive.

The limits I set were clear but gradual. Terri initially was absolutely unwilling to stop drinking. We continued sessions for a short time, with the understanding that our focus would be solely on the alcohol use, the goal being for her to arrive at a point where she would be willing, with assistance, to stop drinking. We explored her history of alcohol use, the purposes it had served for her, the extent of her reliance on it, and various elements of her resistance to stopping. I stopped taking calls from her when she had been drinking. I then said that I would only see her if she would begin to attend 12-step meetings. By this time, she was willing to stop but insisted that she could stop on her own. I expressed concern that she was setting herself up for something too difficult to achieve without support. She insisted. We agreed that she would try and, if that proved too difficult, she would increase support as needed (12-step meetings, intensive outpatient treatment, inpatient treatment). It seemed likely to me that individual therapy would be insufficient as a form of intervention and support. This was an area in which support and feedback from a larger community were essential.

There followed a period of great struggle for Terri. The struggle included numerous attempts to stop drinking and numerous relapses. It included a period of 6 weeks when she refused to engage additional support, and I would not see her until she was willing to do so. She did return and began to attend initially 12-step meetings and eventually an intensive outpatient program. This was a period that also included one suicide attempt while intoxicated, followed by a hospitalization. This was a period that required, from me, confidence in the necessity of the limits I was setting. It was also one of the periods when I have been most aware that I can accompany clients up to a certain point, but that ultimately the work is theirs to do, as painful as it may be.

Terri did emerge from this period. It was not the end of her alcohol use—there were still a couple of relapses to come—but it was the beginning of her recovery. During the several subsequent months, the principal focus of our work was sobriety and the maintenance thereof. We both agreed that we would back away from discussing anything beyond daily coping. Much of this period was about helping Terri become rooted in daily life without alcohol. She initially hated the 12-step meetings, but she went and, after several lapses, she did stay sober.

This was also the last of the indications of self-harm. Our work together was increasingly cast in light of becoming present for life; Terri described it as "showing up." The episodes of dissociation were diminishing in frequency and in duration and, as difficult as it had been for Terri to stop drinking, her sobriety was allowing her to feel successful.

Toward the end of her first year in therapy Terri began to bring up issues from her earlier life that had been strictly off limits earlier. Her capacity to be present with feelings without being overwhelmed was much greater than before. There was more of a sense that emotions, although powerful, were not dangerous. She was increasingly able to see people and events in shades of gray rather than in black

and white. We talked about the loss of her father more than we had before. For the first time, she allowed herself to cry in front of me. She left the room less frequently.

Much of this time seemed to be about looking at Terri's childhood years with a compassionate lens rather than a lens that cast her as the eternal failure. She was able, at times, to feel anger about her mother's emotional unavailability without feeling as though the anger were disloyal.

There was one session in particular when she talked again about the abuse by her grandfather. Terri said that when she had been in her early 20s, her mother had discovered that Terri was gay. She described her mother, with a mixture of tears and anger, saying that she didn't want Terri to believe she was gay because of "what [her] grandfather had done." Terri's mother had gone on to say that the grandfather (her father) had sexually abused her when she was young, also, and that it had not made her homosexual. Terri described her anguish at discovering that her mother had known about the abuse, had been abused too, and had never intervened in any way.

Terri drank soon after the session but stopped the next day and, after 2 weeks of sobriety, she came in again. She seemed sad, but sad in a way that seemed tolerable for her. She expressed considerable anger, both at her mother and at her grandfather. She said, however, that she knew her mother "didn't have much to work with"; her mother's mother had committed suicide when she was 14.

Throughout the next year, Terri returned many times to these various parts of her life, each time with additional compassion for herself. She started to have a more genuine sense of family members' strengths and failings, and her fierce loyalty was replaced by a subtler blend of compassion, love, and realistic anger and regret.

We also returned many times to the issue of Terri's sexual orientation. Terri saw herself as having struck a bargain: She would acknowledge being a lesbian and, in so doing, would sacrifice her spiritual connection. I saw my task as assisting her to see that this did not have to be an either–or decision; as a lesbian, she could maintain, or recover, a deep and fulfilling spiritual connection. It had been such a central and formative decision for her that, even as other perceptions softened, this one was slower to yield. I was aware that this perception had considerable social and church sanction. There were several resources, however, on which she had to draw. Terri was extremely intelligent, well read, and well traveled. She had grown up in a provincial environment, but in adulthood she had lived in larger cities with vibrant lesbian and gay communities. She had models of lesbians and gay men who lived with pride, empowerment, and spiritual connection. Through these and other experiences it was possible to build on Terri's perceptions of other lesbians and gay men as good, even spiritual, beings. She was able to articulate that being gay was not sufficient to cut one off from God—and yet it had, for her. This created enough cognitive dissonance that the negative narrative was at least brought into question.

Ultimately, the best resource Terri had was her own early internal experience of herself as deeply spiritual. The memory was so strong in her, so easily evoked, that it eventually reasserted its reality. In tracing back messages about sexual orientation, and messages about religious connection, she was able to see that the belief that she had had to choose between God and self was not one that arose from her own experience. It was a belief that had been taught her. She had not *felt* disconnected from God as she began to love women. However, she did recall *thinking*, because of what she had been taught, that her attraction to women must lead to distance from God. There was a session in which she realized, vividly, that this belief had not arisen from her own inherent spiritual experience but had been imposed on her. Remembering her actual experience of spiritual connection, she saw that she had forced her experience to conform to her expectation. She believed that spiritual distance was the cost and thus she had forced her experience of spiritual connection to di-

minish. In addition to stopping running, which had been her principal means of connection, she had consciously chosen to stop all forms of prayer. She had stopped talking to God and had stopped listening for God's response.

Throughout much of this time I felt as though we were recovering the part of Terri that used to move among the trees, reaching for a sense of self not crafted by church and social order. That young child in the trees, and even the runner, had felt beloved by what she felt was sacred. Whether her sense of sacred was attached at the time to the word God, or to the names of the trees, or to her own name, a sense of spiritual belovedness had been present and, increasingly, I saw it return. This return of spiritual connection came interwoven with a sense of connection to others and to her own creative spirit.

EPILOGUE

At the time of this writing, Terri comes in for only occasional sessions. She has become increasingly involved in leading wilderness expeditions. In her descriptions of the breathtaking beauty of tropical rivers or the snow-covered silence of winter camping, I hear the same sense of sacredness that was present in her description of the swaying branches of the live oak in the summer storm.

With each remembrance of Terri, I also experience my own gratitude for the privilege of accompanying clients on such sacred journeys. I am also aware, both in my life and in my work, of the ways in which the negative narratives we have of ourselves keep us severed from a nourishing spiritual connection. I am reminded continually of the importance of finding our way back to experiencing ourselves as beloved by that which we hold as sacred.

PART V

FAMILIES COPING WITH PHYSICAL ILLNESS

"WE'RE AT THE BREAKING POINT": FAMILY DISTRESS AND COMPETENCE IN SERIOUS CHILDHOOD ILLNESS

Anne E. Kazak

The setting in which I work is a large pediatric cancer treatment center that sees 250–300 new patients annually. The staff includes more than 100 medical, nursing, and mental health professionals. Within the Division of Oncology, the Psychosocial Services Program is a multidisciplinary team of mental health professionals (psychologists, social workers, child life specialists) who provide comprehensive mental health services as integrated members of the treatment teams caring for patients and families. The family treatment I describe took place in the outpatient center of the Division of Oncology. It is a story about a family with a 2-year-old who was being treated for retinoblastoma, a form of childhood cancer. The course of family therapy for this family was relatively short term (4 months). I selected this family as an example of how research and intervention frameworks can work together.

My interests were likely shaped by childhood experiences. My father was a psychiatrist at a large state institution for people with mental retardation in upstate New York, and my family lived on the grounds of the institution throughout my childhood. I grew up in a community where mental and physical disabilities were a part of my daily world. The acceptance and normality of people with mental retardation was evident to me at a time when societal views were quite different. We had, for example, women with mental retardation in our home, assist-ing with childcare and housework, who became members of our extended family network.

Social ecology (Bronfenbrenner, 1979) informs my work as a way of understanding the natural order of individuals within systems (e.g., families, schools, communities, workplaces, cultures). With a social–ecological framework, therapists can shift between an individual focus and an emphasis on marital and other systems in the family. This approach has a strong developmental orientation, which is critical in interventions with children and adolescents. It encourages a competency-based approach, looking at normal child development in the face of serious illness. It also serves as a reminder that individuals and systems change over time and negotiate expected and unexpected transitions.

For some serious childhood illnesses, the transition from active treatment (e.g., chemotherapy for cancer) to ending treatment is important. Although many of the psychosocial resources provided to pediatric patients and their families focus on the period of active treatment, research shows that, for parents in particular, distressing psychological symptoms (including fears that their child could still die) are prevalent and disturbing for many years after treatment ends (Kazak et al., 1997). In the case presented in this chapter, the young child with cancer is preparing to resume normal development as her treatment ends. With the immediate demands of

The identity of the family described here has been altered to ensure their anonymity. I appreciate the thoughtful comments of Steve Simms and Abbie Segal-Andrews on an earlier draft of this chapter.

treatment lessened, some of these psychological issues may emerge for several family members.

BACKGROUND, REFERRAL, AND CANCER TREATMENT

Anthony is an 8-year-old boy whose sister Liana, age 2, was undergoing chemotherapy after an enucleation for retinoblastoma 6 weeks earlier. She was diagnosed with cancer at age 11 months. Anthony and Liana are the biological children of Louise, a physician, and Ray, a computer technician who worked primarily evenings and weekends. Louise is African American; Ray is White. Louise and Ray live close by Louise's parents. Ray's mother died suddenly about 1 year prior to Liana's diagnosis. His father and brother live in the region. Anthony's parents had asked that the school's psychologist see him because they were concerned about his anxious behavior (sleep disturbances, somatic complaints, tearfulness). The school psychologist's evaluation of Anthony indicated that it was likely that he was experiencing relatively normative, but nonetheless distressing, reactions to his sister's illness and treatment. She also learned that the family had raised these concerns with their oncologist at the Children's Hospital of Pennsylvania (CHOP), who had offered reassurance that this was probably normal and nothing to worry about. On the basis of the school psychologist's knowledge of families coping with serious illness and her awareness of the services available at CHOP, she called to discuss the potential usefulness of the family having a consultation with me, given their persistent questions.

Although it is atypical for my practice as a psychologist at the hospital that our patient and family were referred to me from outside the hospital, it appeared that the family's level of ongoing concerns warranted offering the family more help. The CHOP setting seemed ideal for this, given the staff's experience with treating children with cancer and their families and the opportunity to more fully integrate their medical and psychological treatment concerns. I also wondered if the school had a preventive outlook on behavior and a lower threshold for referral than our internal medical and nursing staff. That is, because CHOP staff work full-time with families

whose children are seriously ill, more normal developmental and behavioral concerns may not be targeted for referral. In contrast, the staff most often work with children, adolescents, and families whose symptoms accelerate to a psychological crisis at the time of referral.

Retinoblastoma is a malignant tumor of the retina that occurs in 1 of every 20,000 young children and comprises 3% of childhood cancers. More than 90% of affected children are cured, but some have limited vision after treatment. In 40% of cases the affected children carry a sporadically acquired new germline mutation. Most of these children with the genetic etiology have a negative family history, although their children are at 50% risk of developing retinoblastoma. The majority of patients with the genetic form of the cancer have tumors in both eyes. The usual treatment is removal of one eye (if only one eye is affected) or treatment with irradiation if both eyes are affected. When one eye is enucleated, the child receives a prosthesis and is able to see by adjusting to having one functional eye. When the tumors are in both eyes, as they were for Liana, radiation has generally been the standard treatment, with the goal of shrinking the tumors. Often an eye that has no hope for vision, even if the tumor is eradicated, will be removed. If there is extensive disease, the amount of radiation necessary to produce cure can cause sufficient damage to the retina so that after 3–5 years the scar tissue that develops can result in vision loss. In addition, the radiation affects the growth of normal bones and muscles, resulting in smaller facial bones. There is also a risk of the radiation causing later cancers, particularly in children with the genetic form of the disease (Meadows, 1995).

At diagnosis Liana was eligible for participation in a clinical trial, the goal of which was to determine whether two courses of chemotherapy would be successful in reducing the tumors. The hope was that by using chemotherapy it might be possible to avoid removal of Liana's eye and that radiation therapy would not be necessary. The treatment protocol was explained to Liana's parents during the discussion of the diagnostic evaluation. Her parents gave consent for Liana to be treated on the chemotherapy protocol.

Liana received her chemotherapy for 4 consecutive weeks in the outpatient clinic. With her parents present, she received intravenous injections of three chemotherapy drugs. The medications (carboplatinum, etoposide, and vincristine) were well established anticancer agents used frequently in pediatric oncology practice. Liana experienced the most common side effects from these medications, including hair loss, nausea and vomiting, anemia, and weakness. Other medical procedures that Liana received included physical examinations, venipunctures, and bone marrow aspirates and lumbar punctures. These last two procedures are particularly invasive and are generally associated with anxiety and distress for parents and patients alike. Our standard protocol for providing pharmacological intervention for procedures included an anesthetic cream whose numbing effects reduced the discomfort of the needle insertions and morphine and midazolam (a short-acting benzodiazapene) for pain and anxiety. Parents are viewed as partners and helped develop strategies for helping their child cope during the procedure. For a 2-year-old this often involves providing general comfort to the child (e.g., physical contact, soothing words, or use of music or toys to relax or distract the child). After a month of cancer treatment, it was determined that Liana's tumors had not shrunk sufficiently to control the tumor and continue with the chemotherapy-only protocol. Thus, it was decided that she would be treated with radiation therapy. She also had her left eye removed because of a detached retina and absence of vision in that eye.

THE FIRST SESSION

Louise and Ray were seen with both children for an initial family consultation, 2 weeks after Liana's prosthetic eye had been put into place. I introduced myself and explained that I would like to learn about how Liana's illness had affected them and their family and how I may be able to help them. Establishing a relationship with the family was of primary importance as we met and I began to formulate ideas of how we would work collaboratively. My impression of the family was that they were somewhat anxious, but open and eager to engage

with me. As would be expected from the referral question, the family directed the conversation toward Anthony's behaviors and their worries about them.

Anthony presented as a bright and articulate child who answered questions readily and seemed to enjoy being able to talk about his experiences at school and at home. He indicated having friends and doing well in school. He acknowledged having had stomachaches and, with parental encouragement, recalled some nights when he did not sleep well. In general, however, he reported little detail and showed minimal concern about these potential difficulties. When asked about his sister's illness, he said that "she had tumors" in her eye and that her eye had to be removed or it would "kill her or get really infected." With respect to the prosthesis, Anthony said that he called her prosthetic eye her "seashell eye." Asked what he called her other eye, he said her "eyeball." Anthony indicated that the ways in which things were different since Liana got sick included that his parents were often not at home and were busy taking Liana to doctors' appointments and that he spent more time with his grandmother. He also indicated awareness of Liana being physically ill and "cranky."

Liana, described by her parents as a very active child, was generally well behaved in the session and responded promptly to her parents' requests. She was, as might be expected, slow to build a relationship with me, reflecting the common apprehensiveness exhibited by our patients toward adults who might be performing an invasive exam or procedure. Liana drew pictures, played with toys, and seemed interested in the conversations that ensued around her.

As with virtually all families with children with cancer, Ray and Louise recounted detailed stories about how cancer has affected them and their family. They appeared glad to share their concerns and, for me, this provided an opportunity to connect with them by actively listening to their beliefs and how they viewed their circumstances. An overriding theme was that they felt that they were "at a breaking point"; that is, they had weathered Liana's diagnosis and treatment after a period in which they already felt exhausted from the death of Ray's mother and the completion of Louise's training, board certification, and decisions regarding employment.

Like many families coping with serious illness, the family had gone through a long diagnostic period, including initial visits to their pediatrician, who had felt that there was nothing wrong with Liana and urged them not to worry. As a physician, Louise felt particular guilt that she had not identified the problem earlier, that they had not persisted with further evaluations, and that they had not changed pediatricians when they felt dissatisfied. She acknowledged that reassurances that there was nothing else she could have done (e.g., the problem *was* identified early) helped somewhat but did not diminish the self-doubts that this experience had engendered. When Anthony began complaining about stomachaches, Ray and Louise felt quite confident that it was psychosomatic or attention-getting behavior. During a 3-day period when Anthony complained of leg pain and could not walk they became more alarmed. They assured themselves through pediatric exams that he had no organic basis for the complaints. Their concern then became that they do whatever was necessary to intervene with his psychological difficulties and to not allow them to become more problematic. I could feel the frustration that they felt in response to well-intended (and accurate) assessments that Anthony was exhibiting understandable behavior in response to Liana's illness. They, like most families in their situation, felt guilt over what they perceived as their lack of attention to him, especially given the stressors he experienced having an ill sister.

Interpreting family reactions to childhood cancer as a signal of derailment from individual and family development, I pursued an understanding of the family prior to Liana's diagnosis. I wanted to learn more of what their relationships were like previously and how their family functioned. From this, three important themes were identified that became critical in the treatment. First, Liana had been growing in a developmentally expected manner prior to her illness. However, her parents now struggled with what they saw to be immature behavior (e.g., reluctance to give up her bottle, resistance to toilet training, and refusal to sleep in her own room or bed). Second, Anthony appeared to have had separation

issues prior to his sister's illness. Of some concern, these included becoming very frightened on occasions when anticipating activities or going to new places. He was described in language consistent with that used with anxious children; he was a worrier. Third, discussion of worrying and who worries in the family precipitated knowing looks between Louise and Ray and nods of agreement that perhaps parental and marital concerns warranted further exploration. That is, the question of the extent to which anxiety was characteristic of the family system and how anxiety in one or both parents affected the marital and parental subsystems, as well as Anthony, was paramount in my mind.

Reinforcing my belief in the family's competence, I asked the family what they had already done to help Anthony. They indicated that, when he was upset, they would reassure him that he was fine and encouraged him to continue developmentally normal activities. The need to help get Liana back on track developmentally was a new concern for the family. They had not viewed her difficulties from this perspective. Ray and Louise indicated they had little time with each other and, although they knew that talking more would be desirable, had not done so.

At the conclusion of the first session I summarized our discussion by presenting the following synopsis of what I felt we could address:

- With regard to Anthony's behavior, I agreed with their oncologist and the school psychologist that his worries were not necessarily abnormal, given what he and his family have been through. I believed that he had many strengths and competencies.

- Louise and Ray remained concerned. Their instinctive sense that something was wrong was worth pursuing. I encouraged them to listen to their feelings and conveyed an understanding that their previous experiences in dealing with Liana's diagnosis could have increased their anxiety that Anthony's problems might go unrecognized.

- Anthony displayed symptoms of anxiety that would be best addressed now rather than risking that they become more pronounced. It appeared that he had been an anxious child prior to his sister's illness. Liana's illness may have sensitized him to somatic concerns and prompted fears and anxieties associated, for example, with her enucleation.

- The family had many strengths and had tried to help Anthony. However, they were stuck. There were other techniques that we could develop and implement together, such as cognitive–behavioral approaches, which may help Anthony develop coping skills.

- Helping Liana achieve developmental milestones was important. Her reluctance to do so was understood as part of the developmental derailment associated with serious childhood illness. The illness had affected the entire family, and the family may benefit from interventions in regard to this and other issues that will facilitate their struggle with how to move ahead with their lives.

- Dealing with the illness and attending to both children across a difficult year had affected their marriage and how their family functioned. I conveyed my sense that there were issues related to their marriage that Louise and Ray might want to discuss and offered this as a potentially important component of therapy.

I felt that the joining process with the family had gone smoothly. Louise and Ray nodded frequent agreement as I discussed the points above. I kept Anthony engaged in the conversation (e.g., telling him that he would feel better if he worried less). It was, however, the marital relationship that Louise and Ray appeared most eager to address.

The decision of how to focus family therapy thus presented itself in a not-uncommon manner. That is, should the emphasis be on the marital relationship or the child-focused symptoms, or should a broader family focus be maintained to understand family functioning? Louise and Ray's openness to discuss marital issues provided an opportunity to choose this last route. I felt that the family was open and able to identify that their marital stresses were important. I saw these as positive signs for a good outcome in therapy. They seemed to readily appreciate that helping themselves would help their children. I also felt that their natural inclinations to maintain parental boundaries were an asset. That is, they maintained a focus on their children and family in

the session while at the same time indicating to me that they felt marital concerns were a priority. We agreed to begin work focused on their marriage in the next session.

A few points related to the choice of starting treatment with marital therapy warrant further comment. First, in most pediatric settings a focus on the child-oriented problem is generally maintained. Indeed, a child-focused treatment could readily apply and be effective. Therapists working in pediatric settings may feel considerable pressure to ensure that the child's problem is addressed effectively. That is, although family-centered, hospital staff tend to focus most heavily on the child's behavior and symptoms. There is often concern that intervening at the level of the couple will contribute to a less immediate effect on the child. In this particular family I viewed the illness as a contributing stressor rather than as the focus of the referral question. With a problem more likely caused by the illness (e.g., distress during procedures or related to chemotherapy, withdrawal in adolescents, behavior problems), a more direct child-focused intervention was important. Furthermore, in the majority of families, explicit agreement to address marital issues first is not forthcoming in an initial interview.

This dovetails with the second point: My biases probably shaped the process of the session. That is, influenced by structural family therapy and systems theory, I tend to initially explore marital and other family relationships in some detail and look to identify how the parental subsystem functioned. Finally, guided by a social ecological framework, I felt confident that working with the couple would not detract from the referral concerns about Anthony; that is, the marital therapy could be complementary with intervening to help the children.

MARITAL THERAPY

Working with Ray and Louise provided the opportunity to learn about reciprocal relationships that affected how the family copes with their child's illness. They began by talking with me about their feelings of isolation and of how difficult it had been for them to spend time with each other. Anthony was born 3 weeks prior to the beginning of Louise's residency. Because Ray had flexibility in his schedule, he combined several part-time jobs in order to provide primary, in-home care for Anthony during Louise's residency. Ray indicated that he enjoyed the children and generally liked being a "Mr. Mom," although he felt isolated and as if he had no time to pursue his own interests. Indeed, Ray appeared somewhat depressed and overwhelmed as he talked. He also indicated that his family disapproved of his marriage to Louise because of her race. This had created substantial tension in their relationship and a tendency to rely on her family for childcare, further isolating him from his family. Although Ray's mother had formed a relationship with Anthony before her death, conflicts between her and Ray made it difficult for them to sustain these relationships. Ray expressed anger that he felt life was very difficult.

Louise felt that the demands of medical training left her with little time to spend with her family and that although she appreciated Ray's involvement with the children ("He is a *good* dad") she felt unable to shift the balance in their relationship. Her practice was in the midst of changes related to managed care, and she was resentful of the pressures to see more patients and spend less time with each. Louise exuded self-confidence and poise but noted that she handles stress well for a period of time and then "loses it," which she defined as spending an evening or a day often tearful and preferring to be alone.

When I asked how they coped, they showed me: Both were quiet. I asked how they helped each other during stressful times. They indicated that they did but, when I inquired as to whether this might be a strength (that they could support each other during difficult periods), they were unresponsive. Indeed, it became clear that their style was to retreat from each other. Over time, and under the pressures of Liana's illness and treatment, this had led to increasing feelings of isolation in the relationship. They indicated, for example, that they have different approaches to disciplining Liana. Ray tended to back off, whereas Louise preferred to intervene actively. They were aware that they disagreed but tended to become angry with one another and to walk away rather than pulling together to handle

situations jointly. Thus, it appeared that unresolved conflicts and avoidance of them were pertinent issues fueling their isolation. We also discussed that Louise and Ray had slept in separate bedrooms for over a year, beginning when Liana was ill. They had been unable to get her to sleep in her own bed and said that Liana's active sleeping style made it too uncomfortable for two adults to sleep in the same bed with her. Both agreed that they wanted things to change and that they "wanted their marriage back."

That Ray felt depressed became more evident in subsequent sessions. He described himself as a "perfectionist," "extremely competitive," and "never good enough." He seemed overwhelmed, withdrawn on occasions, and generally helpless with regard to what he felt that he could do to change his life. Both Ray and Louise agreed that Ray was depressed. We expanded this issue by examining how this affected family functioning and what treatment strategies could be considered. In general, Ray's depression affected his ability to be present and consistent with the children and led him to feel that, no matter what he did with them, that he was not a "good parent." Louise felt that she put additional effort into trying to bolster Ray's spirits but also became angry with him on occasion for his pessimism and difficulty in reaching out to her and the children.

Ray's depression was addressed within the couple's relationship and as an individual issue that might benefit from a cognitive–behavioral approach; that is, pessimism may reflect underlying feelings of helplessness that can be addressed successfully by coaching individuals to change the way they think (i.e., Seligman, 1990). Indeed, Ray showed symptoms of anxiety and depression and seemed to have little faith that his actions could make a difference. For example, his beliefs that he was not a good parent led him to withdraw or to evaluate relatively normal struggles in parenting as being his fault (e.g., "Other people can get their children to listen, but I can't."). The cognitive–behavioral approach helped Ray break interactions with his children down into smaller parts rather than react to the more overwhelming larger situation. We also identified ways in which he is a good parent and helped him see that his children do love and respect him. At most times, they also hear him, even when he felt that they did not comply with his request, or do so promptly and completely.

I introduced the idea that Ray might benefit from a consultation with a psychiatrist to determine whether medication would help him. Although I believed that psychotherapy was likely to be the most fruitful avenue for Ray and the family, I wondered if a pharmacologic intervention would also help energize him and complement this approach. I imagined that Louise and Ray might have already pursued this approach. Indeed, Louise had prescribed an antidepressant for Ray. Ray tried it and felt better but became concerned that it would make him feel too good. He worried that if he felt so much better that he might not be a responsible parent. While noting that Louise was trying to help by prescribing, I indicated that she should not be acting as Ray's physician. Again reinforcing the systems concept that Ray's feelings and behavior affected all members of the family and were influenced by them, I urged Louise to attend to her own feelings and asked how she felt stepping back from taking care of Ray in this regard. Already aware that giving her husband the prescription was not recommended, Louise seemed relieved to be given permission to attend to her own needs. She understood that therapy could be used to attend to her own feelings, which often seemed buried underneath the caregiving that she provided to her family.

Ray and Louise found the use of the cognitive–behavioral strategies helpful. They seemed to relieve some of Ray's distress, and he began a daily exercise regimen. As an athlete he found this satisfying and reflected on how it helped him relax and feel healthier. The intervention seemed to give Ray a different perspective, not only on his behavior but also on family interactions. He began to see, for example, how his worrying and preoccupations were similar to those that Anthony experienced. For example, Ray and Louise shared a story of a situation in which Anthony became anxious to the point of being nearly immobile in a crowded shopping mall. He was trembling and panicky about becoming separated from his parents in the crowd. They could readily see that his tendency to overreact made the situation worse (e.g., he could not focus or listen well). They learned to approach Anthony differently,

on the basis of the cognitive–behavioral model. For example, rather than saying "Don't worry, we won't let you get lost" or giving him solutions ("If you get lost, go to the security guard near the information booth."), they identified his beliefs ("You think you are going to become separated from us.") and helped him understand the situation as one in which he can take small steps to remedy the situation and calm himself by thinking about a good outcome (e.g., Question: "What would happen if we became separated?" Answer: "I would look for a security guard. I know that you will be looking for me, too. It might take awhile, but you will find me.").

After four couples sessions, Louise came to an appointment by herself, having told Ray that she wanted to have the chance to talk with me privately about herself. She was tearful throughout most of the session. My overall impression was one of great sadness, tinged with anger. Louise was most concerned that Ray had withdrawn from her, to a point where the process could not be reversed. She felt, for example, that he did not really want Liana to sleep in her own bed and that he had mixed feelings about their efforts to communicate and resolve conflicts. When Louise acknowledged her own feelings and role in the marriage, she stated that she did not tell Ray what she was feeling. She felt that he was very vulnerable and that there would be little that would come of it. Her anger and resentment over having to be the "strong one" in the relationship was evident, and she felt angry toward herself, noting that she saw that Ray was like this before they married but did not realize how difficult it would be. Neither, of course, could she have anticipated the stresses that they would experience related to Liana's cancer and its treatment. My interventions at this point were to support Louise's expression of her feelings and to encourage her to change some of her behaviors (e.g., speaking up for her feelings, speaking from her heart). I suggested that we do this in the course of the next couples therapy session so as to maintain the focus on marital therapy.

Seeing one member of a couple alone introduced possible complications in the treatment, and I was aware that I could be inducted into the family system in a way that could jeopardize the treatment at this point. Balancing Louise's level of upset and the positive effects of a compassionate response with the risk of alienating Ray and jeopardizing the couples work, I felt that it was possible to have one session with Louise in which our discussion would continue to be framed in terms of ongoing couples and family intervention. Although the optimal situation for seeing an individual would be after the couple had clearly agreed to it, I also recognized that both Louise and Ray had hinted during couples therapy that they would like some time to talk privately and that I had not explicitly discouraged this. Each was reaching out to reduce their isolation, although it was my hope that they would do so with each other rather than through me.

Louise started the next couples session by describing a time during the past week when she became extremely upset and was crying for 30 minutes. She said that afterward she tried to talk with Ray about her sadness that they were "growing more apart." Ray said that he didn't remember this discussion and seemed puzzled by her story. Linking this session with the individual session with Louise, I encouraged Ray to ask Louise questions to discover what she meant. He became defensive, crossed his arms across his chest, resisted the request, and said "I feel like she is saying that it is all my fault." This sequence illustrated the couple's conflict avoidance and demonstrated how they tended to isolate themselves. With encouragement, Louise responded that she wanted more support from Ray and more time to herself to read, go for a walk, and relax. Using Ray's interest in sports, I asked if he could be a coach and facilitate the resolution of their conflicts by listening to Louise in a different way. Although difficult, he identified ways that this might happen. However, his defensiveness persisted.

Prior to the next session I received a telephone call from Louise saying that Ray did not want to attend the next session because he was angry at me and felt that I too blamed him for problems. I asked her to encourage Ray to talk directly with me, either with a telephone call or by coming to the next session so that we could have a chance to discuss his important concerns. Both arrived for the session, and Ray appeared angry. With difficulty he told me that the last session had made him feel depressed,

angry, and worthless and that he saw no point in continuing therapy. Building on my relationship with them, and hoping to show him ways of resolving his conflict with me, I indicated that I was glad that he was able to tell me about this and labeled the feeling as helplessness. For example, he felt helpless when Louise expressed sadness and when she felt out of control. He also felt helpless when Louise brought the issues up in therapy, as this underscored his feeling of being unable to generate new solutions when overwhelmed. His helplessness made him want to run away or withdraw emotionally. He seemed relieved and accepted this as accurate.

Going back to the coaching analogy, I asked Ray what he would do with an athlete who felt overwhelmed by emotion and out of control. Ray said it would be different with a player, because you would "have their full attention, and they want you to help them solve the problem." With Louise, he felt that "things would never change." At this point Louise interrupted and said, "I just want you to be there for me. You don't have to solve the problem." Applying this concept to coaching, I asked if this was not always the first step in a relationship; that is, before you can help someone you need to establish that you are present for him or her. Sometimes this was very difficult, particularly when emotions were being expressed that may contribute to a feeling of being out of control. Ray cautiously agreed with this but noted that part of the problem was that Louise tended to be sarcastic with him and that this distracted him and made him angry. Louise agreed that she can be caustic, particularly when she feels that they are backing away from one another and not resolving conflicts. To reduce their isolation and foster conflict resolution we developed the following homework assignment together. Ray will identify a nonverbal signal to send to Louise when he perceived that she was not being supportive to him (e.g., if she is sarcastic). She will stop and come up with a different way of expressing herself to Ray. Ray, in turn, will note when Louise is feeling distressed and connect with her at these times without trying to problem solve.

In the next couples session there was a palpable sense of relief and more relaxed interactions between Louise and Ray. They indicated that, although they had not actually used the communication and conflict resolution system we developed, they were getting along better. It seemed that it was not always necessary for a discrete homework assignment to be completed in detail; that is, if an intervention tapped into the family process in a helpful manner, then the critical element may be the reframing of the problem itself. In this case, knowing that there was something (relatively unthreatening) that they could do that might enhance their interaction appeared to help punctuate their rigid and frustrating interaction patterns. We continued for the next several sessions to solidify these changes. At that point, Louise and Ray indicated that they handled conflict differently and more successfully and they could see how they were pulling for one another during stressful incidents rather than retreating from each other.

CHILD-FOCUSED ISSUES

While continuing to attend to their marital issues and interactions, Ray and Louise asked that we return to some of the concerns related to the children, specifically Liana's temper tantrums and general immaturity and Anthony's fearfulness. Our work together related to Liana focused on two general themes. The first was building on the stronger marital alliance to decide how to handle Liana's behavior and what expectations Ray and Louise had for her development. The second was coaching Ray and Louise to help Liana achieve developmentally appropriate goals and understand that, with their guidance, she would reclaim a normal developmental trajectory.

The treatment approach that was introduced at this point may be considered an isomorph of the couples work—that is, the approach centered on how to handle conflictual situations, read thoughts and behaviors differently, and support natural patterns of development. Specifically, we discussed ways of intervening earlier when one or both of them recognized a situation with Liana that was likely to escalate and redirected her to a more developmentally appropriate activity that was incompatible with a temper tantrum. For example, in preparing to leave the house for a family outing, Liana

might become impatient and then refuse to put on her coat. The couple developed strategies for recognizing early signs of irritability and redirected Liana to get her coat, gather the toys she would take with her, and so on. This was in contrast to previous incidents in which Liana's behavior escalated to the point at which they would carry her, screaming, to the car. They also generated activities that Liana could do to help them, building on her natural striving to be more mature and competent.

During these family sessions Anthony talked more about things that scared him, such as going through tunnels and over bridges. Whereas he had initially been reluctant to give much detail, I suspected that the changes in the marital relationship and other family dynamics may have contributed to helping Anthony express himself more freely. Both Anthony and his parents said that it was difficult to know when things would bother him and that his agitation and anxiety were seemingly unpredictable. Relying again on a cognitive–behavioral framework, I introduced and explained self-talk, or what people say to themselves about situations, and how it can affect the way that they feel. The emphasis was that the process of thinking and learning to think differently can help Anthony feel more in control. It was helpful in terms of encouraging him to identify ways to calm and comfort himself; that is, rather than being reassured by his parents ("Don't worry"), they prompted him to create ways of helping himself realize that he could handle a situation ("The bridge is tall and long. But, if I breathe deeply and count to myself, we'll be at the other side before I know it.")

TRANSITIONS IN TREATMENT

As with all therapy relationships, decisions about when to end treatment loomed unspoken in both the therapist's and family members' minds. My feelings were that the family had engaged well in therapy, worked hard, accomplished changes in their relationships, and thought about their behavior and relationships in ways that were empowering. They felt better. The question "Should we continue with treatment now to address further issues?" was in my mind. On the one hand, given the family's natural competencies, the changes they made, the fact that they were satisfied with therapy, and their limited resources (their insurance was unlikely to cover much, if any, of the cost of therapy), it was reasonable to end treatment. Alternatively, many of the issues identified (including marital strain, Anthony's anxiety, and the long-term impact of cancer on the family) would probably benefit from continued intervention. On the basis of my knowledge of the long-term psychological impact of cancer on families, I know that it is likely that cancer-related difficulties may emerge in the future.

The family's behavior suggested that they felt uncertain and may have wanted to terminate. Indeed, ending relationships is generally difficult and often not addressed explicitly. For a family that avoided conflict, I looked for clues that they could be circumventing the topic with me. After a family cancellation for a session that was not followed by a request to reschedule, I telephoned the family. During this call with Louise, I broached the idea that it might be time to stop. I presented ending as a positive option ("You have made many changes and seem to be feeling better.") while acknowledging that distress was still present ("The issues that we have worked on are likely to continue to be bothersome from time to time and will still need your attention."). Modeling an approach that includes closure, I asked that we have one more family session, irrespective of whether we continued treatment. Louise seemed eager to do so and agreed to an appointment a few weeks later, allowing her and Ray time to discuss whether they wanted to stop or continue treatment.

In my pediatric setting, the more traditional concept of termination is not necessarily realistic or helpful. Working with children and families over the course of treatment for a serious childhood illness lends itself to a model based on transitions. That is, there are many transitions in the course of treatment for childhood cancer, some expected (e.g., going home after an initial hospitalization with attendant adjustment to the diagnosis and returning to school, ending cancer treatment) and many unexpected (e.g., complications in treatment, relapse, other stressors impinging on the family). Returning for further help could be framed as an adaptive response to changing circumstances across the social

ecology rather than as a failure of family functioning, therapy, or both. As a therapist, the framework of transitions allowed me to reposition myself from being in the family as an active interventionist to being out and available as a consultant to the family if and when needed (Simms & Kazak, 1998). With respect to Liana's cancer and its impact on the family, the medical sequelae were evident. Although I hope she will be cured, the future will be colored by fears of radiation-related sequelae and second tumors. Her parents, and probably her brother, will remember the experience, although Liana is likely to recall little of it directly. These memories are likely to have a continued impact on the family's development and functioning.

In this family, I viewed cancer primarily as a stressor that magnified preexisting family struggles. This does not mean that the cancer and treatment experiences were not important. Indeed, it is likely to be the worst experience that the family had during their child-rearing period, and it shaped the course of the family indefinitely. At the point of seeking treatment, several members of this family appeared to be experiencing pain, and it was likely that the trauma of having had a child with cancer stirred up many underlying feelings and conflicts. It is not uncommon for families to pull together to get through acute crises but then feel as if they are falling apart later. It was a conscious choice in this therapy to keep the cancer active in the treatment but to not remain organized by it—that is, it was ever present, but the focus of the work was to build on family competencies and address the multiple areas of distress that the family brought to me.

One of my goals in discussing a change in treatment with the family was to assure them that psychosocial care will continue to be available to them in my setting. I discussed with them that physical and psychological sequelae of having had cancer are not necessarily the same but that both are important. It will be a challenge for them to find a way to integrate these experiences into their lives, in a way, I hope, in which cancer is not forgotten but so that it does not dominate their lives or cause significant distress. There is no clear roadmap for psychological adjustment after treatment for childhood cancer. In the course of therapy we identified some of the routes on their map that are challenging for them. They accomplished an excellent job of negotiating and generally overcoming the barriers that they encountered.

The final session went smoothly, with the family agreeing that they had made changes and saw clear improvements. They indicated that the individual and couples work had helped them develop strategies that could be applied across multiple family relationships. Most important, they understood that these issues were not fully resolved but could be addressed adaptively over time.

References

Bronfenbrenner, U. (1979). *The ecology of human development*. Cambridge, MA: Harvard University Press.

Kazak, A., Barakat, L., Meeske, K., Christakis, D., Meadows, A., Casey, R., Penati, B., & Stuber, M. (1997). Posttraumatic stress, family functioning and social support in survivors of childhood leukemia and their mothers and fathers. *Journal of Consulting and Clinical Psychology, 65*, 120–129.

Meadows, A. (1995). *CHP-571: A Phase II study of chemo-reduction for selected retinoblastoma patients* [treatment protocol]. Philadelphia: Children's Hospital.

Seligman, M. (1990). *Learned optimism*. New York: Simon & Schuster.

Simms, S., & Kazak, A. (1998). Family systems interventions in pediatric neuropsychiatric disorders. In C. E. Coffey & R. Brumback (Eds.), *Textbook of pediatric neuropsychiatry* (pp. 1449–1464). Washington, DC: American Psychiatric Press.

CHAPTER 24

A SNEAKY TEENAGER WITH DIABETES IN CONTEXT: STRETCHING MINUCHIN'S PSYCHOSOMATIC MODEL

Thomas C. Todd

When Sally came into the hospital, I jumped at the opportunity to work with her. After all, she had both the problems on which I had worked for 5 years with Minuchin's Psychosomatic Project (Minuchin et al., 1975; Minuchin, Rosman, & Baker, 1978): juvenile diabetes and an eating disorder. When I agreed to take the case, I had no idea how much she and her family would stretch my basic structural/strategic model, forcing me to draw on my full range of personal and clinical resources.

For me, this case supports Minuchin's contention that it is possible to approach a case with a clear conceptual model, expecting to see how the family represents an idiosyncratic variation of the model (Minuchin, 1981). Although that statement was true for me in regard to the present case, it in no way captures the anxiety and perspiration involved in getting a handle on an actual case, especially when the symptoms are life threatening. I am very grateful for the basic conceptualization, developed through years of collaboration in the Minuchin project, but I have learned never to become complacent, that there are never cases that one can be confident will be easy cases, straight out of the book.

CASE BACKGROUND

Referral Process

Sally, a 13-year-old with diabetes from a suburban, middle-class White family, was referred to a psychiatric hospital where I worked because the outpatient management of her diabetes had failed because of her secretive eating. Despite behaviorally oriented

management from an outpatient psychologist and psychiatrist and despite a wide variety of efforts on the part of her parents to keep her behavior under control, Sally frequently indulged heavily in candy and other forbidden snacks and then attempted to cover her actions by sneaking and self-administering insulin. Because her efforts at compensating were somewhat amateurish, her blood sugar level would take dramatic drops, which on several occasions brought her close to the point of coma.

Family Composition and Recent History

The family consists of four members. At the time of the inpatient treatment, her father, age 48, was a salesman in a discount appliance chain store. Her mother, age 42, held two jobs in the nursing field. Susie, age 14, was entering her sophomore year in the same high school where Sally would be a freshman.

The family acknowledged that events in the family over the previous few years seemed significant in understanding Sally's problems with diabetes, her secretive eating, and her lying. Her mother described her husband as a compulsive gambler. He resisted that label, believing that he was practically professional in his skill level and that he gambled only to make money.

At the time when Sally was initially diagnosed with diabetes at age 10, the family was living in a large house in an extremely wealthy suburb, and her father was a commodities speculator, investing his own funds and those of his wealthy friends. He believed, and her mother confirmed, that if a couple of transactions had been successful he would have been a multimillionaire. Unfortunately, however, he lost all of the family's money and significant sums belonging to his friends, and he ultimately had to declare bankruptcy and sell the house, moving to a much more modest neighborhood. After considerable nagging from his wife, the father took a poorly paid job as a salesman, although clearly his heart was not in it. He still spent long hours in the basement at home, working with his computer to devise new gambling formulas or new ways to speculate in the commodities market.

Sally's mother felt very locked into her two jobs. She held a highly responsible job in a national pharmaceutical corporation that required her to be out of town roughly 3 days every week. For economic reasons she moonlighted whenever possible as a nurse in a local obstetrician's office. Her total income was at least triple that of the husband's, and both conceded that they needed every penny of it.

Susie appeared to be everything that Sally was not. She was athletic and popular and an excellent student. Sally, in addition to having diabetes, was clumsy and socially inept. Although her grades were generally good, she was unable to involve her father in the ways that her sister was—by getting him to help with a sport, such as Susie's basketball, or with schoolwork, such as Susie's advanced math.

Sally's problems predated the onset of her diabetes and supported a diagnosis of an eating disorder. Her parents reported that she had always experienced significant social problems and had been "the butt of other kids' jokes" since early childhood. They described her as always having been "pudgy" and always wanting candy. She was always resentful toward her sister, to whom everything came easily; her only significant source of positive validation was in academic areas, where she consistently scored in the 99th percentile.

The parents described an increase in Sally's sneaky eating and what they called "insulin abuse" (stealing insulin to cover her sugar intake) over the year prior to the hospitalization. During this time she had gained 40 pounds. Her self-administered doses of insulin led to sharp drops in her blood sugar at night, resulting in grand mal seizures on three different occasions. The parents felt that they had little alternative but to wake her up and test her blood sugar in the middle of the night. They claimed that obvious remedies, such as locking up the insulin, were ineffective, and they sought treatment for Sally's self-destructive behavior.

Prior to her hospitalization, Sally had been seen in behaviorally oriented therapy for 5 months, with no change in her secretive eating and diabetic management problems. At the therapist's recommendation, Sally was hospitalized, but the parents withdrew her after 1 day because the hospital physicians "didn't understand diabetes."

The parents also reported long-standing marital difficulties, which the mother attributed to her husband's gambling, lying, and financial difficulties. They had been involved in marital counseling for 4 months without any impact. Shortly before Sally's hospitalization, her mother had insisted that her husband seek treatment for his depression, which she admitted that she had more difficulty tolerating than his irresponsibility.

INITIAL HOSPITAL CONTRACT

In addition to myself, other members of the treatment team included John Costigan, a child psychiatrist who also had a long-standing interest in juvenile diabetes, and Maggie Hahn, RN, the head nurse in the program, who was interested in diabetes and had considerable experience with eating disorders. Other specialists were also involved, including the hospital nutritionist and medical director and Sally's endocrinologist, who was unaffiliated with the hospital.

The initial treatment plan was straightforward and reflected a combination of standard hospital treatment and specialized treatment for Sally's eating disorder. Dr. Costigan and I would each see her two to three times per week in individual therapy. Maggie was her staff advisor, giving her assignments and monitoring her progress with the behavior modification program on the unit. Maggie and I, acting as cotherapists, saw various subsystems of the family for family therapy sessions. Initially Maggie and the other nurses tested Sally's blood sugar level and administered her insulin. Her diet was carefully selected and monitored on the unit, where she was initially confined. In addition to standard therapy groups on the unit, she was involved in nutritional counseling and in the various specialized groups that comprised the eating disorder program.

CASE FORMULATION

In terms of the problems around her diabetes, Sally's case does not qualify as a genuinely psychosomatic case, in contrast to the "brittle diabetics" of the Psychosomatic Project at the Philadelphia Child Guidance Clinic. Instead, she fits into what we labeled *behavioral diabetics*—people whose management problems are straightforward consequences of behavior such as eating sugar or lying about insulin. People with behavioral diabetes often show a different family pattern than true psychosomatic cases, but in Sally's case the similarities were more obvious than the differences, presumably because of the presence of an eating disorder.

Sally's family exhibited all of the family characteristics described in *Psychosomatic Families* (Minuchin et al., 1975):

- *Enmeshment:* There was clearly a weak boundary between the parental and child subsystems. Parental overinvolvement and lack of parent–child differentiation was present but complicated by strong cross-generational coalitions between the mother and Sally and between the father and Susie.
- *Overprotectiveness:* Both parents were overprotective in general, especially toward Sally. Neither girl was allowed to experience the consequences of her actions.
- *Rigidity:* All four family members locked into rigid rules that changed little from situation to situation.
- *Lack of conflict resolution:* Conflict, especially between the parents, never led to a productive resolution. Her mother would raise conflictual issues to some extent, but her father typically talked her into backing down. Conflicts with or criticism of Sally never went anywhere.

In the psychosomatic conceptual model one expects the symptomatic child to play a distinct role in family interaction. In some cases involving behav-

ioral diabetes, there is considerable scapegoating of the diabetic child by the parents, but this did not occur to any great extent with Sally. Instead, as mentioned above, she was treated in a much more protective fashion. Parental conflict was often detoured by the parents uniting in their benevolent concern for Sally.

Following Haley (1976) and Madanes (1980, 1981), I typically expect the specifics of symptom choice to be significant as a metaphor for other family problems. In this case, the parallels between Sally's lying and irresponsibility in regard to her diabetes and the behavior of her father were extremely striking. Neither she nor her father were held accountable by her mother (or in Sally's case, by her father, either).

Potential secondary gain from symptoms is always of concern and in Sally's case was extremely so. She had poor social skills and got little gratification from peer relationships or from her conflictual relationship with her sister. Both parents were preoccupied with their own problems and financial difficulties, yet neither would ignore Sally's life-threatening behavior in regard to her diabetes. Most of her diabetic crises occurred when her mother was out of town on business, pulling her father away from his computer and leading her mother to monitor her diabetes long distance. Finding new ways to help Sally connect with each parent and with her sister would clearly be an important goal.

COURSE OF HOSPITAL TREATMENT

The treatment team's case conceptualization was straightforward and seemed to promise a clear understanding of the case and blueprint for treatment. From the beginning of the hospitalization, however, it was obvious that the team members had their work cut out for them. Either her father or mother would spend literally 1 hour or more each day on the telephone with various members of the team. Both parents were heavily invested in their expertise concerning the management of Sally's diabetes and were quick to criticize decisions being made in the hospital. Sally's lack of compliance with parts of the program were repeatedly blamed on staff rather than Sally being held accountable.

Sally showed overt compliance with the program from the beginning and consistently completed assignments, obtained necessary signatures, and so on. Her lack of cooperation was much less obvious. She consistently played dumb and asked "what's the point?" of groups and other aspects of treatment, especially the eating disorder program. She tended to whine but rarely confronted either the staff or her parents directly. She seemed to use her diabetes to achieve other purposes, most notably to get out of groups early, citing physical complaints, or to obtain unscheduled snacks. The nutritionist worked closely with her but found that she "forgot" to record her snacks.

The parents were also pleasant and overtly compliant while presenting more subtle difficulties. On the surface they agreed that they needed some separate therapeutic time to work on marital issues. I increased their motivation to work on marital issues by noting that Sally found this a source of considerable anxiety. Somehow, however, her mother's business travel or other obstacles kept the parents from both being in the hospital at the same time. Her father came alone quite frequently, and at times the impression was unavoidable that her mother had "set him up" to come for help by himself. Both parents agreed that Sally needed a better relationship with her sister, yet they managed to get Susie to the hospital only once in the first month.

Early on, the plan was to give Sally increasing responsibility for her diabetes, as Sally and both parents wished. It was difficult, however, to get the parents to back off from their overconcern. Sally would often pout and become extremely passive when some aspect of the program was not going to her satisfaction. In doing so, she at times withheld information from staff that led to dangerous diabetic consequences.

Engaging the Father in Treatment

Balancing the roles of Sally's father and mother was one of my primary structural goals. This required me to be fairly strategic, because her mother had made a heavy-handed ultimatum that her husband must seek help for his depression. I found it difficult to push the father to become more involved without labeling him as defective and forcing him to lose face with his wife. The father unexpectedly provided the strategic key to involving him. He made it clear that he was using Sally's hospitalization as a vehicle for "sneaking" free therapy for himself. To some extent I became an open coconspirator in this process, minimizing the extent that he was playing into my own agenda. To make therapy less intimidating for him, I also made considerable strategic use of self-disclosure, playing on legitimate similarities between the two of us—that we were both gifted mathematicians, game players, and manipulative in interactions with others. This provided some tacit acknowledgment of the manipulative quality of our own interaction with each other, although I suspect that we each secretly were confident that we were getting the upper hand.

Parallel Process With the Team

Although it took the members awhile to realize it, the team became caught up in several dynamics that were similar to the family's process. Initially, the parents had impressed on us that Sally's diabetes management was extremely complex. Endless telephone calls to nursing staff and the nutritionist led us to become preoccupied with the minute details of insulin dosage and diet. For myself, the gravity of her symptoms and the fact that I was the only team member without a medical or nursing background made me feel extremely vulnerable, and I found myself doing uncharacteristic things, such as reading diabetic management handbooks. Ultimately Dr. Costigan realized that all of this preoccupation was keeping us, like the parents, from holding Sally accountable.

It also became obvious how easily the "team" could break down, particularly under conditions of high anxiety. Sally had an extremely serious diabetic crisis in the middle of the night that culminated in her being rushed to the emergency room. The parents were extremely upset and angry, and it became tempting for me and others on the core psychiatric team to blame night staff, poor communication between the doctors, and so on for this mishap. Like the parents, we found it easier to look for a medical or nursing scapegoat than to hold Sally (and ourselves) accountable. Rather than blaming staff or doctors or instituting a complicated diabetic regime for a single patient, I found myself fantasizing about insisting that one or the other parent would have to spend the night with Sally to chaperone her. This idea, which was not that far removed from what the parents were doing at home, was never seriously proposed, but I might have insisted had the parents persisted in attacking the night staff and medical director.

Another parallel to the parents' behavior was probably also fueled by our anxiety. In our eagerness to have Sally successfully out of danger, we were frequently misled by her apparent cooperation and were lulled into granting her freedom and diet-related privileges prematurely. We were also misled by the parents' superficial compliance, as well as their overinvolvement, and overlooked the ways in which they managed to avoid crucial components of the treatment plan.

Like the parents, we found ourselves oscillating between being gratified by Sally's "progress" and being frustrated and even infuriated by her. Our feelings toward the parents went through similar gyrations. We gradually began to realize what we had expected all along—that the treatment team was replicating the dynamics of the family. We clearly needed to take the initiative in making something different happen.

The "Credit" Program

Initially Sally was placed on the same point–level behavior modification system as all the other adolescents on the inpatient unit. As was true for all the patients on the unit, we were prepared to make necessary modifications to individualize her program and give her parents appropriate responsibility. In this regard the program was consistent with the use of behavioral programming for inpatient eating disorder cases at the program at Children's Hospital in Philadelphia (Liebman, Minuchin, & Baker, 1974) and to a Haley strategic model of inpatient treatment (see Fox, 1991).

The basic program was too easy for Sally and too complex for maximum effect with the parents. Sally was accumulating huge point totals for superficial compliance and for cooperation with the school program. The parents took little ownership of the program and instead became embroiled in Sally's complaints about lack of privileges.

Maggie suggested that we use a simple "credit" program that she had used successfully with other patients with eating disorders. Credits were used instead of points for promotion within the unit point–level system. In addition, privileges specific to Sally were added, such as unsupervised meals, checking her own blood sugar, and knowing her weight and blood sugar results.

We insisted that the parents become very involved in establishing individualized behaviors that would gain or lose credits. Positive behaviors specific to Sally included taking responsibility for her own behavior, expressing her feelings directly, and working on her own issues in group or with unit staff. She would lose credits for lying, blaming, splitting staff or parents, and for pouting or other forms of indirect communication (even including keeping her hair in her face when talking).

The credit system was introduced in the session that is highlighted below. Sally responded immediately to the clarity of the system by sitting up straight, taking her hair out of her face, and talking directly. We considered it just as important that the credit system allowed us to test the parents' behavior very directly, because each of them was required to find during the session a behavior of Sally's that earned a credit and one that lost a credit and to be direct with Sally about each. Both parents found it difficult to penalize her, but they recognized the need for their feedback to her, and they clearly wished to be seen as compliant with the team and the program

Creating a Crisis

I have highlighted the inpatient session that I regard as a major turning point in Sally's treatment. The team felt strongly that we had reached a crisis point in the treatment but that we had to mobilize this sense of crisis in the parents in order to break through their usual protectiveness of Sally. This followed the crisis indirection model of Minuchin and associates (Minuchin & Barcai, 1969). We began the session with a show of strength and solidarity by including the psychiatrist in the early part of the session.

Rather than continue the parents' preoccupation with the complexities of Sally's diabetes—based on our new realization that her diabetic management was not difficult given accurate information from Sally—we wanted to refocus the parents on simpler behavior from Sally, especially her lying and lack of responsiveness to the parents. During this phase of the session we had to combat a sense of being unfairly harsh with Sally until we began to see first her mother and then her father come around to confront Sally on this issue. Although this confrontation was definitely a channel for our aforementioned frustration with Sally, we never let our feelings dominate the interaction.

In the session, Sally responded well to the specificity of the new credit system, probably in part because of her increased motivation from being confronted from all sides. She began to show positive behavior in the session and received immediate praise for doing so.

Given considerable structuring from my cotherapist and me, the parents began to be much more specific in their feedback to Sally. It was still difficult for either of them to be critical without rushing in to undo their criticism in the next breath.

I became increasingly aware of the obvious connection between Sally's lying and her father's behavior and began to "seed" this issue without directly confronting the father at first. The mother responded to this issue but needed support not to back down or disqualify her position. What was surprising was how thoroughly Sally understood the connection and parallels between her behavior and that of her father, while her father continued to be extremely defensive. Sally received significant support for her perceptiveness and her lack of defensiveness about her own behavior, and she was given the task of reviewing the videotape with her father to show him the parallels.

By the end of the session we had achieved our goals with this unexpected bonus from Sally. Both parents had conveyed a clear message to her that it was time for a significant change in her behavior. They were clearly supportive of the new credit system, and all three of them had begun to implement it. Sally seemed positive about this new specificity and was already responding to it. Sally's mother had

begun to hold her ground with her husband around issues of chronic unresolved conflict between them, and Sally had tolerated their conflict without becoming symptomatic.

Subsequent Inpatient Interventions

During the remainder of the hospitalization we kept our promise to move slowly in giving Sally more responsibility rather than rushing to pronounce her "cured." Further diabetic crises occurred, but we were able to pursue a steady course and get the parents to do so also. Sally began to be much more direct, honest, and expressive and, as a fringe benefit, began to seem much more mature and be more popular with peers on the unit.

The parents continued to need work on two fronts. The new program made their overprotectiveness more obvious. Strategic assignments were given in secret to the parents that forced them to find justifications for taking credits away from Sally. Simultaneously Sally was given the secret assignment of deliberately creating situations of obvious negative behavior to provoke her parents to deduct credits.

Her father began to "get it" and be willing to look at his own irresponsible behavior, especially if it was linked to Sally's problem. Similarly, her mother became much more willing to insist on accountability from her husband, and both participated much more consistently in marital sessions. They also insisted on much more participation from Susie.

OUTPATIENT TREATMENT

Outpatient Family Therapy

Outpatient family sessions were definitely conducted on an as-needed basis, usually in response to some low level of crisis involving Sally. None of these had the life-threatening quality that had been characteristic of the period before Sally's hospitalization. Susie attended rarely.

I continued to support the father coming to many joint sessions without the mother as an ongoing effort to counteract their old pattern of overresponsibility on her part and underresponsibility on his. Unlike their earlier pattern, Sally's father seemed very involved with both girls and was definitely in charge when his wife was out of town on business. Sally appeared to obtain a good deal of support from her father and no longer seemed to need to have medical crises and symptoms to keep her mother involved.

Individual Sessions With Sally

Outpatient sessions with Sally began to take on the flavor of outpatient treatment of eating disorders, relatively uncomplicated by her diabetes. Her diabetes was a factor primarily as an ongoing temptation to "cheat" and hide her cheating, akin to a person with bulimia's vomiting. As Sally settled into outpatient therapy, she became more amenable to cognitive interventions about her weight and eating, interventions that had never had much impact during hospitalization.

The content of our sessions increasingly involved school, friends, and her developing interest in boys, all very normal teenage issues. Sally never became a steady consumer of therapy, which was fine with me, because it indicated that she was much more invested in real life as a teenager, compared to the regressive helplessness she had exhibited prior to her hospitalization. She derived considerable satisfaction from her life at school and with friends. Her relationship with her sister was the last area to blossom, and her sister was the last person in the family to acknowledge Sally's increasing maturity. Eventually they seemed to reach a mutually satisfactory balance point with little outside interference or mediation by either parent or myself.

Sessions With the Father

It seemed important to Sally's father that he never became an "official" patient, as was evident from the fact that he never scheduled even a single session that was to be specifically devoted to him. Somehow, however, circumstances conspired to have him end up in my office alone, ostensibly because Sally could not come or her mother was detained out of town. When I did have joint sessions with the father and Sally, her father often loitered at the end of the session to "steal" a few minutes to talk about himself. I both recognized and respected this process; although I rarely commented on it, I suspect that he knew that I knew what he was doing.

We had several man-to-man conversations, particularly about career issues. It gratified Father that I had some grasp of the mathematics of his nighttime efforts, and I was suitably impressed when he recruited a well-known mathematician at Northwestern University to review his ideas and formulas.

Marital Issues

My original expectation had been that marital sessions would provide an important key to the success of the case. Perhaps this was true symbolically, because I made a production out of scheduling separate sessions that Sally knew were intended to address marital problems; with the parents, I in turn insisted that we not spend the whole session talking about Sally. They seemed uncomfortable discussing parenting disagreements, let alone marital issues.

I did use my prerogative as Sally's therapist and their commitment to Sally's health and well-being to insist that they at least work on the issues that were so clearly parallel to Sally's problems, most notably Sally's and her father's sneakiness and lack of accountability. Her mother could not understand how Sally or her husband could lie so automatically and with little apparent guilt. Her husband was redefined as an expert on the subject who was instructed to teach his wife about the motivation for lying and how her behavior keyed into it.

As a predominantly structural/strategic therapist, I rarely spend much time with family-of-origin material. Following Pinsof (1995), I tend to seek family-of-origin material on a need-to-know basis only when my efforts at straightforward change are blocked. In the mother's case I had difficulty understanding how reluctant she was to hold her husband accountable. Some of this could be accounted for on the basis of her distaste for conflict; she also was poorly suited by background or temperament to deal with a skillful manipulator, as she and the father described her husband.

The mother went further than this in relating her marriage to that of her parents. She portrayed her mother as unsupportive of her father and unwilling to allow him to make any risky career decisions. According to her, this lack of support and stifling career decisions had left her father depressed and broken. She had sworn to herself never to do that to her husband. Unfortunately it meant that she had little tolerance for her husband's depression and that she did not counterbalance his risk-taking proclivities, even when they had resulted in bankruptcy and loss of the family home. I pursued this theme with the wife by constantly testing the limits with her, gradually persuading her that this legacy did not mean that she could not insist that she be able to count on her husband for some income. Similarly, his depression was not her fault and did not need to be her problem.

Considering the mother's background, it is probably not surprising that she was extremely relieved that her husband became so engaged in therapy. Because she and her husband believed that I understood him well, she was able to accept my assurances that some expectations and limit setting on her part would not push her husband into irreversible depression, like that of her father.

With very few formal marital sessions, the marital issues that had seemed so pressing before Sally's hospitalization seemed to dwindle in importance. The mother gave the father considerable validation for his increased role with Sally and was clearly relieved that she could go out of town on business without her previous worries. For my taste she still seemed amazingly tolerant of his taking financial risks and looking for the big score, but that was not my problem.

Susie's "Symptoms"

What proved to be the final chapter of the outpatient therapy concerned Susie instead of Sally. The father asked to come in alone to discuss some recent concerns he was having about Susie. Although she still seemed to be progressing toward college, her grades had slipped noticeably, and she seemed much less enthusiastic about sports. This created additional concern for him, because he had hoped that basketball could have provided scholarship funding for her to attend a prestigious out-of-state university. The father was quick to agree that most of what he was bringing up were really his issues rather than Susie's. He was able to acknowledge that he had been living somewhat vicariously through Susie's accomplishments and providing much of the energy behind her drive. This had been especially impor-

tant for him during the period in which he had been so demoralized and unhappy with what he saw as his own shortcomings. Even though his outward achievements were not significantly different, he was no longer so preoccupied with either his own or Susie's success. From a family systems point of view, it was also noteworthy that both Sally and Susie had moved to more moderate positions rather than either of them occupying the rigid and stereotypic roles they had filled at the beginning of therapy.

FOLLOW-UP

Sally and her family were not seen again in therapy following the 3 weeks in the hospital and 6 months of outpatient psychotherapy, which had included approximately 25 sessions with various individuals and combinations of family members. My primary contact during the 6-year follow-up period has been the mother, who on the surface appeared to be comparatively uninvolved in the outpatient treatment. She and the rest of the family view their experience, particularly the hospitalization, as being transformative for Sally and the rest of the family.

Most interesting to me was the fact that Sally wrote a play about her experience in the hospital (including a thinly disguised version of me), which was performed by the drama department of her high school. I learned this from the mother and do not know the details of the play. My distinct impression is that Sally considers her hospitalization a crucial event in her life and saw me as playing an important role. In keeping with the family systems focus of the treatment, Sally does not feel much specific gratitude to me and has not felt any need to stay in touch. Although I am definitely a "card-carrying" family therapist, and although the team and I were definitely proud of the changes in Sally's life-threatening problems and the family system, I admit occasional jealousy of colleagues who have more intense relationships with individual clients.

The parents are both significantly more grateful. They view both Sally's and Susie's college careers and subsequent development as normal and definitely healthy and generally see the hospitalization as a major turning point in the family's life. Both girls have done equally well, although neither was the spectacular success that the father had originally wanted. Most notably, Sally has definitely become a "normal" diabetic who handles her diabetes and related diet issues quietly and effectively, with no obvious limiting effect on her life.

In turn, I feel indebted to Sally and her family for their impact on my professional development. Although I definitely owe a debt of gratitude to Minuchin and his colleagues for the psychosomatic model and my structural/strategic approach in general, Sally and her family deserve credit for forcing me to enrich and add depth to the basic model. I suppose that, similar to Sally's play, this chapter represents an after-the-fact expression of my appreciation to them.

SUMMARY

I hope that I have been able to convey the extent to which my basic structural/strategic model was stretched by Sally and her family without my ever having to abandon it. My goals remained structural, whereas many of my initial moves were decidedly strategic in Haley's (1976) sense. Certainly I incorporated elements of other models, especially behavioral and cognitive–behavioral. In general I consider myself a shameless borrower, and there is little that I would consider off limits in achieving my structural goals and the goals negotiated with my clients.

In retrospect, I would never have anticipated that I would spend so much time in individual sessions, particularly with the father—the most resistant family member (other than Susie, who never developed a taste for therapy) became my most eager customer. We both recognized each other as skillful game players and manipulators, although never really ad-versaries. Although our early relationship was distinctly gamelike and manipulative, I would like to believe that I acknowledge my manipulation and that it was always in the service of helping him and the rest of the family find resources in unexpected places.

References

Fox, M. R. (1991). Strategic inpatient therapy with adolescent substance abusers: The Fox system. In T. C. Todd & M. D. Selekman (Eds.), *Family therapy approaches with adolescent substance abusers* (pp. 190–208). Needham Heights, MA: Allyn & Bacon.

Haley, J. (1976). *Problem-solving therapy*. San Francisco: Jossey-Bass.

Liebman, R., Minuchin, S., & Baker, L. (1974). An integrated treatment program for anorexia nervosa. *American Journal of Psychiatry, 131,* 432–436.

Madanes, C. (1980). Protection, paradox and pretending. *Family Process, 19,* 73–85.

Madanes, C. (1981). *Strategic family therapy*. San Francisco: Jossey-Bass.

Minuchin, S. (1981). *Anorexia is a Greek word* [Video]. Boston: Boston Family Institute.

Minuchin, S., Baker, L., Rosman, B., Liebman, R., Milman, L., & Todd, T. (1975). A conceptual model of psychosomatic illness in children: Family organization and family therapy. *Archives of General Psychiatry, 32,* 1031–1038.

Minuchin, S., & Barcai, A. (1969). Therapeutically induced family crisis. In *Science and psychoanalysis* (Vol. 14). New York: Grune & Stratton.

Minuchin, S., Rosman, B., & Baker, L. (1978). *Psychosomatic families*. Cambridge, MA: Harvard University Press.

Pinsof, W. M. (1995). *Integrative problem-centered therapy*. New York: Basic Books.

CHAPTER 25

HER RIGHT FOOT:
PAIN, INTEGRATION, AND THE
BIOPSYCHOSOCIAL MODEL

David B. Seaburn

In 1986 I accepted a joint clinical position at the University of Rochester School of Medicine and Dentistry, as a family therapist in the Strong Family Therapy Services of the Department of Psychiatry and in the Highland Family Medicine Residency Training Program. That change in my professional life marked the beginning of my efforts at integration.

Faculty in Strong Family Therapy Services have engaged in a lively discussion for well over a decade about what exactly they do as family-oriented therapists and trainers. That ongoing discussion has resulted in an evolving, integrative approach to family therapy and family therapy training that is called *transitional family therapy* (Seaburn, Landau-Stanton, & Horwitz, 1995). As an approach to treatment, transitional family therapy blends here-and-now, transgenerational, and ecosystemic factors when working with families, paying particular attention to how developmental and situational transitions or changes in the individual, family, and larger context may influence the presenting complaint.

At the same time that I was involved in these discussions I was also working in a primary-care medical setting where the reigning conceptual paradigm was the biopsychosocial model, as developed by George Engel (1977, 1980). In the residency program residents learned that the larger context of their patients' lives was just as important to their health as the complex systems within their patients' bodies. The obvious connections between the biopsychosocial model and transitional family therapy, both firmly grounded in general systems theory,

were not lost on those of us who worked in, and indeed bridged, both settings. We continue to build bridges between these two models, seeking an even broader integration on which to base clinical practice and teaching. Currently we conceptualize the biopsychosocial model as an assessment paradigm and transitional family therapy as a model for psychotherapy (see Figure 25.1).

In this chapter, though, I focus more on the biopsychosocial model than on transitional family therapy, because the biopsychosocial model has provided the greatest challenge to me regarding integrative practice. At the beginning of my work in family medicine the biopsychosocial model was just that: a model, a theory, a set of ideas that hovered above the ground of my experience but did not yet touch it; a theory that I learned but had not yet seen with my own eyes.

When I came to the Highland Family Medicine Center, a healthy conversation was beginning between some family therapists and some family physicians who shared a common interest in the role that the family plays in matters of illness and health. It was an exciting time of crossfertilization between disciplines. Engel (1977, 1980) critiqued the biomedical model as an inadequate way to approach many patient problems because it did not encompass enough of the patient's experience and suggested that physicians needed to know as much about the person of the patient, his or her relationships, and the social context as they did about the patient's organ systems, organs, and cells.

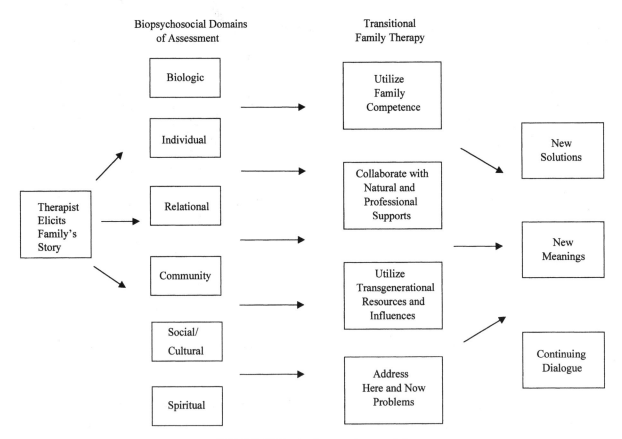

Biopsychosocial Domains
of Assessment

Transitional
Family Therapy

FIGURE 25.1. An integrative model.

I found it easy to embrace the biopsychosocial model at a theoretical level. I understood that family process was multiply determined and that everyone contributed in some way to how a family functions. It was easy to expand that notion to include all elements of experience, from cells to social systems, which were interrelated in a similar way.

In practice, however, I still focused on the family system, seldom integrating the patient's health issues adequately and certainly not recognizing the biology of experience as a system that is influential and fundamental. Without recognizing it, I embraced a "split biopsychosocial model" (Doherty, Baird, & Becker, 1987). I held the "bio" in one hand and the "psychosocial" in the other, trying to balance them but never quite integrating them. It wasn't until I worked with a variety of patients and families at the Highland Family Medicine Center that I was able to bring those hands together.

One of those patients was Mary (see Figure 25.2).

HER RIGHT FOOT

I first worked with Mary when her primary care physician referred her for treatment for depression. At the time, Mary, age 36, was single and working on her bachelor's degree at a local college. She had a long history of polysubstance abuse but had been in recovery for a few years. She was being treated with an antidepressant. I saw Mary for 2 years, during which time she worked on a painful history of sexual abuse at the hands of her sister and brother. She linked that experience with a tendency to be promiscuous in her relationships with men. Mary had one failed marriage that had produced a son. She saw her son regularly, but he lived with his father, with whom she had almost no contact. Gradually she made progress in therapy and continued to succeed in college.

During this time she also met Bob at her workplace. Their courtship was complicated, and therapy switched from an individual to a couples format. In

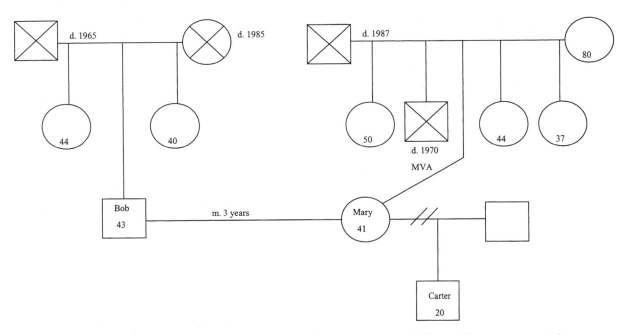

FIGURE 25.2. Family genogram. d. = deceased; MVA = motor vehicle accident; m. = married.

the process they decided to marry and continued in therapy as they adjusted to married life. After several months they left therapy. Mary was no longer suffering from depression, and the marriage had reached a comfortable balance.

I did not hear from Mary and Bob again for 3 years. When I did, I learned that things had changed dramatically. Mary's primary care physician, Dr. Chavez, explained that Mary was depressed again but this time for a different reason. Dr. Chavez asked if I could consult with her and Mary about the new problem that had emerged. I attended a medical visit in which Mary sat slumped and tearful as she talked about what had happened to her.

Two years earlier, Mary had developed problems with her right foot. She was diagnosed with a tumor that was damaging some bones. Surgery to remove the tumor was recommended. Mary agreed to the surgery, and the tumor was successfully removed. Unfortunately, as a result of the surgery Mary developed a new condition: reflex sympathetic dystrophy, a degenerative nerve disorder that manifests as extreme, constant pain; sweats; and swelling. As Mary explained, "I am 41, but the bones in my feet are 65."

Mary recounted all the treatment she had received in the last 2 years, including two additional surgeries for problems in the big toe of her right foot. A year later she had two surgeries on her left foot to correct some bone problems. Unfortunately, as a result, she developed reflex sympathetic dystrophy in that foot, as well.

To treat the reflex sympathetic dystrophy, Mary subsequently had 50 nerve blocks, wore surgical stockings, used crutches, went to physical therapy, and took pain medication and antidepressants. Nothing worked. Her primary care physician was concerned about Mary's escalating depression in the face of constant pain. Dr. Chavez, recognizing the biopsychosocial nature of the problem, hoped that I could help her in the overall management of the case and work with Mary regarding her depression.

THE IMPACT OF PAIN

I scheduled an appointment with Mary and Bob to discuss the problem in more detail and to assess what might be done to help. Mary again sat in tears, apologizing for not being able to stop. Bob sat beside her, his arm outstretched, simultaneously touching and pulling away from Mary's shoulder. His face was grim, but his voice was calm in an unsettling way. He said, "She's like this most of the time."

I started with the here and now, asking Mary to describe her pain so that I could understand it better. As she talked, she became more calm. What emerged was a complicated picture of a foot disorder that involved seven different forms of pain, something Bob had not known. Mary talked poignantly about each sensation and how her life was organized around them. She said there was no way to escape the pain. Nothing she did could take it away, to which Bob added that nothing he did made a difference, either.

The couple acknowledged that the physical pain had driven a wedge between them. Their communication was edgy, their sexual relationship was empty, but their commitment to the marriage was still strong. I suggested that it would take all of us—Dr. Chavez, Mary, Bob, and me—working together to make a difference in Mary's situation. I said that even though the pain may not dissipate, we might be able to develop ways to cope that helped Mary function better day to day. This would take psychotherapy, medication, and whatever other aids were available.

When I walked away from the session, I wondered how hollow my confidence had sounded to them. I did not feel as confident as my words. I wondered what we could actually do about the pain and its impact on Mary and Bob. I talked to Dr. Chavez, who acknowledged the same feelings. Only later did I recognize that I had quickly become biomedically fixated, placing Mary's feet at the center of the treatment universe, isolating the physical pain from other elements of her experience. Over the next 9 months, Mary and Bob would teach me that I was being simplistic, that this *was* a biopsychosocial dilemma. They would also point me toward a broader way to think, one that helped me understand the biopsychosocial model better.

THE TRANSGENERATIONAL CONTEXT OF PAIN

The next several months were marked by frequent conversations with Dr. Chavez about the frustration she was feeling over not being able to reduce Mary's pain as well as a series of individual, couple, and collaborative team appointments that included Dr.

Chavez. Dr. Chavez and I had known each other and worked on cases together before. The fact that we were located at the same facility made it easy for us to maintain ongoing, although oftentimes brief, communication. We provided support for each other. Together we resisted the temptation to order additional tests or procedures that were not medically indicated, and we tried to keep a balanced perspective on Mary's problem to avoid the twin problems of psychosocial or biomedical fixation.

In complicated biopsychosocial cases the most important early work often revolves around how the professionals will collaborate together to create a workable treatment context. Mary's case was no different in that regard. Unfortunately, the psychotherapy portion of the treatment plan was moving at a snail's pace. Mary, Bob, and I met weekly or biweekly but could focus only on their day-to-day coping. In that sense the work felt like crisis intervention. After 4 months we entered a 3-month period in which the case opened up.

The first turning point came when I shifted the focus to transgenerational issues and asked Mary and Bob to talk about the role that illness had played in their families of origin. Mary was still too distraught to discuss her family, so Bob talked about his. Bob grew up as the middle son in a family of five. He had two sisters. His father died when Bob was young. Bob was prematurely catapulted into the role of male head of the house, a role that included, among other things, providing ongoing emotional support for his mother. She was, in his view, alcoholic. She also had diabetes. Bob remembers his mother as having daily physical complaints that her doctors could neither diagnose nor treat. She turned to Bob repeatedly for understanding. He felt enormously burdened by her needs and also guilty that he could do nothing to help her. In the end he raged at her internally while presenting a mechanical façade of verbal support. Over time, he distanced himself from his mother, although the long arm of her needs was never far from him. He vowed never to be involved with a woman like his mother again.

Bob met Mary, who was intelligent and attractive and needed someone to lean on. Because she did not have any health problems, Bob did not have difficulty supporting her. When she became ill, though,

Bob felt like he was back in his mother's clutches, and he responded as he had with her. Bob said it was helpful when the physicians finally determined a diagnosis for Mary, because then he could accept that her pain was "real." But this did not alter Bob's interactions, which Mary experienced as contradictory. She felt Bob was nonverbally critical and distant while being verbally supportive.

Mary responded to this by trying to hide her pain. When Bob dutifully asked how she was feeling, Mary usually said "not bad" or "better." Bob could tell by her inability to ambulate and the sadness on her face that she was "not being honest," so he would press her further. Finally she would admit she felt awful, at which point he would blow up about her not telling him the truth to begin with.

In the next session I learned about health issues in Mary's family. She said that as a child she was not aware of her parents having any health problems but, as she got older, she learned that her mother had a long history of back pain. Interestingly enough, her mother had a history of foot pain dating from an automobile accident when her mother was 19. Mary's father, who was deceased, also suffered from chronic pain. He had had a degenerating hip and persistent abdominal pain. When I asked how her parents coped with the pain they suffered, Mary thought for a long moment and said "I don't know."

I suggested that Mary might learn something about coping with pain by talking to her mother, who lived out of state. Mary called her mother, and they talked at length about her mother's history of pain, how she coped, and what advice she might have for Mary. At the next session with the couple, Mary reported on her conversation:

> I told my mother I never heard her complain at all. So I asked her how she did that. She said, "You just don't talk about it. You pretend it's not there. Ignore it." My mother said it was important for me not to complain and that I should be sure not to burden my husband with it.

Later in the therapy, Mary would reflect back on that conversation with her mother:

> For me, trying to deny the pain, as I was taught to do, only made it more difficult to integrate the disease into my life. I didn't even realize that I was trying to do what my mother did. But we were taught to deal with all problems that way—smile and don't complain. The denial didn't work for me. It screwed me up totally. I had to accept the disease, which meant I had to accept the pain.

Mary's and Bob's family histories in regard to physical symptoms supported the notion that pain should be denied even when it is undeniable. This collision of family histories about the role of physical symptoms in intimate relationships created conflict in the marriage. Their marital conflict made the pain more difficult for them to cope with and added relational pain to their dilemma.

The couple worked on ways to recognize when their families were "in their household" influencing how they interacted as a couple. Gradually their communication around the pain improved, although their intimacy still lagged. Nevertheless, they were pleased to have less tension in their marriage.

THE COMPLEXITY OF PAIN

A month or so later, another turning point occurred during an individual session with Mary. Despite adjustments in Mary's antidepressant medication, she continued to sob, often uncontrollably, during therapy sessions. As I sat with her, I remember thinking that there must be more involved in the emotional response to her physical pain than I understood. So I asked her if she had ever felt emotional pain like this before. Without hesitation Mary said the only other time she had felt this depressed was when she was working through the sexual abuse.

I asked her how the pain she experienced from both situations was similar. She said that in both instances she had felt "vulnerable, needing to trust someone else and also I felt that people didn't believe me when I told them what was going on." As a child she wanted to trust her brother and sister but couldn't. She wanted help from her parents, but they withdrew and didn't believe her story. During the first 2 years of her foot problems, Mary experienced her doctors as authorities whom she needed to trust but who could not "fix it" or who did not believe she had the degree of pain that she described:

> It was the same as when I was a little girl and wanted someone to fix things, and it didn't happen. I felt alienated from the specialists about my feet. I felt like there was no one to turn to, just like when I was a kid.

This recognition helped Mary separate the emotional pain of abuse from the emotional pain related to the reflex sympathetic dystrophy. Being able to identify and differentiate the forms of emotional pain (to, in effect, name them herself) helped Mary gain greater agency over how emotional pain affected her (McDaniel, Hepworth, & Doherty, 1992). It also helped her current primary-care physician understand how the history of Mary's interactions with physicians shaped her interactions with Dr. Chavez in the present.

At this point in the therapy I recognized how complex the biopsychosocial model is and how impossible it is for any single provider to adequately treat certain problems without collaborating with professionals from other disciplines (Seaburn, Lorenz, Gunn, Gawinski, & Mauksch, 1996). I realized that the biopsychosocial model was not only a way to organize one's understanding of a patient's experience but also a paradigm for identifying who should be involved in the patient's care. If I had treated Mary and her husband without collaborating with Dr. Chavez, I would not have been nearly as effective; in fact, I might have been acting unethically in that I would have communicated to the patient and her husband that I was qualified to treat this complex problem on my own, which is the farthest thing from the truth. I learned that my work in primary care can never be done in a mental health vacuum; I am always part of a treatment team.

IMMERSION IN PAIN

The other concern I had at this point in the treatment was simple: Would Mary ever cope with her pain more effectively? A month later I got my an-

swer. Bob had planned a fishing trip with friends—an important step. The couple agreed that this would be good for Bob, and it would give Mary a chance to test her independence in dealing with the pain.

At the next appointment with Mary, she had a plan. She told me, through tears, that the only way she could get control of the pain was to immerse herself in it, let it "flow" over her. She needed to give herself to the pain completely, scream when she had to, lie on the couch as long as she needed to, and hurt without any denial.

This was not what I had in mind. As I listened, I became anxious. I was always afraid of Mary becoming suicidal, and the thought of her pursuing this experiment with her husband away gave me chills. I shared my concerns. She listened but was unswayed. We set up easy ways for her to contact her husband, me, or her physician in case she started "drowning" in the pain.

When Mary and Bob came back, Mary seemed like a different person, a fact to which Bob attested. She had followed her plan and found that it was the difference that made a difference. A few months after the completion of therapy Mary agreed to be videotaped discussing her experience with pain. During that conversation she reflected back on her week of immersion:

> For 2 years I believed the pain would go away. The change in my life was dramatic. One day I was living a full life, and the next day I couldn't walk. I was stopped. It affected my feelings, my thoughts, my relationship with my husband. I kept trying to make it go away. I refused to accept it as part of my being. I became very depressed. I just couldn't believe that I would have to spend the rest of my life like this. I didn't know how to deal with it, and I didn't want to. I tried to hide it from Bob. I would pretend things were okay when he asked me, but he knew that wasn't true. It would lead to arguments.
>
> The pain controlled my life. I had no way to live a normal life, because I couldn't be bigger than the pain. The pain

was bigger than me. Finally, I suspected the pain would be permanent. My doctor said that I was right.

About 6 months ago, I decided I needed to "allow" the pain, to be alone with it and let it surround me, and not deny it like my parents denied theirs. My husband went on a fishing trip, which allowed me to be alone for a week. So when he left I let the pain do whatever it needed to do. I cried. I screamed. When I went through that, it was like the beginning of the end of the pain controlling me. It was the beginning of my being able to be bigger than the pain and being able to control my thinking about it. The pain is still out of my control, but how I feel and act about the pain is different.

I couldn't help but notice the first time Mary told this story that Bob leaned toward her, his arm on hers, his face relaxed. She went on to discuss how she approached each day, recognizing that the pain needed to be accommodated but that accommodating the pain did not mean that she was totally limited.

I saw Mary and Bob for 3 more months. She continued on pain medication and antidepressants. She was still in daily pain but felt in charge of her daily living and less depressed. Bob and Mary continued to have some problems with intimacy, which, they acknowledged, had existed before the pain. We worked to help them get closer. Mary's primary care physician left the practice, and Mary entered a new practice with a different physician. He and I communicated about Mary several times before treatment ended. At termination Mary and Bob felt better about their relationship, and Mary felt she had a future despite her pain.

CONCLUSION

I have thought about Bob and Mary and have reviewed videotape of the case many times since I last saw them. The case is illustrative of transitional family therapy in that it called for work in the here and now, across generations, and within a particular ecosystem (medicine). In addition, Mary and Bob's problems made it easy for me to understand the interactional nature of the biopsychosocial model. I could see how biological processes influenced individual psychological processes, which in turn shaped relational interaction, which evolved in a larger family and medical–social context. I could also see that this process occurred simultaneously in reverse: Family and social interaction shaped relational interaction, which influenced individual psychological processes, which in turn affected biological processes (or at least one's perception of biological processes).

As a family therapist I learned the limits of family systems as an organizing way to approach such complex problems. Much as the biomedical model can reify biological processes, family systems theory can do the same to family processes. In a sense, it can limit my vision, blocking out other factors that may influence a family and its members. I realized how infrequently I asked patients about their health before I started working in family medicine and, when I did learn about health problems, I often thought of them as ancillary or as distractions. The "real stuff" had to do with what went on among family members. Patients like Mary and Bob helped me expand my conceptual and clinical perspective to include many more systems than I had before. They also helped me recognize that professional collaboration is essential to providing effective care in a vast majority of cases. Being a part of a treatment team is as essential for the therapist as being a part of a family is to a patient.

The final thing I have learned from the gradual process of embracing a more integrative paradigm is both simple and difficult. Engel (1977, 1980) was right: Integration starts with the clinical encounter. If one listens well, which is an art in itself, then the connectedness of all things will emerge. The challenge for me is never to marry my current paradigm, no matter how integrative it may appear to be, but to always be open to what patients and families may teach me next.

References

Doherty, W. J., Baird, M., & Becker, L. (1987). Family medicine and the biopsychosocial model: The road to integration. *Marriage and Family Review, 10,* 51–70.

Engel, G. L. (1977). The need for a new medical model: A challenge for biomedicine. *Science, 196*, 129–136.

Engel, G. L. (1980). The clinical application of the biopsychosocial model. *American Journal of Psychiatry, 137*, 535–544.

McDaniel, S. H., Hepworth, J., & Doherty, W. J. (1992). *Medical family therapy: A biopsychosocial approach to families with health problems.* New York: Basic Books.

Seaburn, D. B., Landau-Stanton, J., & Horwitz, S. (1995). Core techniques in family therapy. In R. H. Mikesell, D-D. Lusterman, & S. H. McDaniel (Eds.), *Integrating family therapy: Handbook of family psychology and systems theory* (pp. 5–26). Washington, DC: American Psychological Association.

Seaburn, D. B., Lorenz, A., Gunn, W., Gawinski, B. A., & Mauksch, L. (1996). *Models of collaboration: A guide for mental health professionals working with health care practitioners.* New York: Basic Books.

CHAPTER 26

HONORING THE INTEGRATION OF MIND AND BODY: A PATIENT WITH CHRONIC PAIN

Jeri Hepworth

It was not an auspicious first meeting. Much as I claimed to be comfortable working with people with chronic illnesses and pain, meeting Marian Brown was a downer. Marian, age 54 and African American with a history of fibromyalgia, was discouraged, complaining, and depressing, both to herself and to me. Marian's family physician, Dr. Lamoreux, had referred her to me, describing how she felt overwhelmed by Marian's pain complaints and decreasing activity level. Marian had never been to a therapist before, but Dr. Lamoreux had convinced her that she and I work together and that often patients who had a lot of pain were helped when they saw both of us. The physician had done a fine job of setting up the referral. Now I felt that I had to do something to help turn a woman who felt hopeless, discouraged, and angry into someone who could find a less painful life. Much as I initially tried to find what worked in Marian's life, all attempts were fruitless. Marian left the session looking as low as she had entered, and I left the session feeling that I was a sham, that I really didn't know how to help people who had really serious pain and discouragement. Who says pain isn't as contagious as depression?

This is a story of learning to practice what we preach. It is a story of integrating family and individual therapy, of integrating individual cognitive techniques with those of medical family therapy. It is a story of integrating mind and body, but mostly it is a story of integrating what one says one believes with what one really believes.

What I say I believe—that is, the necessity of in-tegrating mind and body, individuals and families—comes from my work as a family therapist within medical education and treatment settings. My colleagues and I (McDaniel, Hepworth, & Doherty, 1992, 1997) have organized our beliefs under the umbrella of *medical family therapy*, a biopsychosocial approach to psychotherapy with people with health problems that activates the families' strengths and personal choices as well as their connections with one another. These central concepts of agency and communion (Bakan, 1969) are facilitated when therapists and physicians actively collaborate with patients and families to incorporate their health beliefs into mutually derived treatment plans. I know how important these principles are, and yet I sometimes neglect what I know to be important. I think that was the case with my work with Marian, nearly 2 years ago, when I left the session not being clear about how to help.

Marian returned about 2 weeks later. Although I had regained most of my professional self-confidence, I was still somewhat surprised when she told me that she had found our session helpful and that she wanted to engage in regular sessions with me. I still didn't know what we were going to do, but I figured that it couldn't hurt to obtain a more complete history of her life and her illness. Marian was a small, frail-looking woman, whose arthritic hands shook when she talked. When she spoke about her family, however, she seemed to grow stronger in her voice and her certainty about how others didn't respect all of her pain. Marian had been married for 8 years to Spencer Brown, a tollbooth worker who generally worked second shift. At the time that Marian and Spencer married, Marian had been divorced from her first husband for nearly 20 years and had raised her daughter Coreen alone. Coreen, now age 34, was a happy single parent of Keesha, age 12. Keesha and Coreen, who worked as a secretary in a small office, lived within blocks of Marian and Spencer, and all the adults were very proud of Keesha's scholastic and athletic talents.

There were other important people in Marian's life. Her mother Evelyn, age 74, lived in another apartment in the same building as Marian and Spencer and suffered from severe diabetes and emphysema. Nearly fully home bound, Evelyn expected Marian and other family members to visit her daily and arrange for shopping, cleaning, and social contacts. Marian had two brothers, who also lived in town: an older brother, William, who worked and helped care for their mother, and a younger brother, Edgar, who abused alcohol and drugs and "couldn't be trusted." With the exception of attending Keesha's basketball games, Marian seldom was around people other than her family and had stopped attending church. Except for minor shopping trips, Marian's social contacts had decreased to her family and her doctors' visits.

Limited social activity was blamed on the fibromyalgia. Marian described how initially she had been diagnosed with arthritis and that, about the time of her marriage to Spencer, the arthritis seemed to worsen. Pain was all over her body, in joints and in muscles. Sometimes the pain was manageable; other times it was debilitating. Multiple medications had been tried, yet over the last 2 years Marian felt that she had fewer periods of relief and more periods of depression and severe pain. She was supposed to exercise, but she used a cane because it hurt to walk more than a block. The only activity that seemed to help was when she had been in a rehabilitative program and had enjoyed the water exercises in the pool.

Over the next couple of sessions I learned that Marian felt alone in her pain. She described herself as the one in the family who had always taken care of others—of her father during his terminal illness, of her mother during the past 10 years, of her daughter, and sometimes even of her granddaughter.

She described herself as always "having to be strong" for the others, handling family finances and decisions, arranging all holiday celebrations, and feeling that she had to initiate telephone calls and social contacts. She readily described her anger at other family members, who expected her to take care of them and seldom asked how she was feeling or if they could help.

In treatment, we focused on monitoring and increasing Marian's daily activity level and attempting to "put the illness in its place." The medical therapy principles of agency and communion (McDaniel et al., 1992) were salient in this work. Communion was enhanced as I encouraged Marian to become more effective in continuing with her life and increasing her social contacts while recognizing the difficulties her illness imposed. Agency was reflected as we celebrated minimal increases in functioning, particularly those that involved other people, such as visits to the school gymnasium to watch Keesha play on a sports team. However, it seemed that my attempts to recognize gains and strengths were equally met by Marian's constant examples of why increased activity was impossible or how such a visit to the school had increased her pain. The more we moved, the more we stayed the same.

Marian's complaints continued to annoy me. She complained about her pain, about how little she could do, and about how no one understood her. She usually described how her doctor seemed to understand her, but then she also complained about how no treatment worked. I assumed that she wanted to complain about me, but I wasn't successful in encouraging her to admit it. Occasionally I suggested that she bring in a family member to help us, but she said that no one would come. In retrospect I am amazed that I accepted her powerlessness about including other family members. Generally I would not so easily accept a patient's sense of hopelessness, but at that time I must have been feeling pretty helpless myself.

Marian expressed a peculiar combination of anger and smiles, of wanting to change and of fixed hopelessness. I found myself complaining about her to colleagues and to her physician but, similar to Marian's own behavior, I smiled to her face. Frequently during those sessions I found myself being very bored, even sleepy, and I often cut sessions short by encouraging her to keep on doing whatever she could. Because not much seemed to be changing, and yet she wanted to keep coming, we moved our sessions to every 3 or 4 weeks. I often felt relieved just to get through a session.

I imagine that we could have continued like this for a long time, and perhaps to many health care managers we continued too long as it was. But Marian claimed that talking about her pain was helpful, and I was only too happy not to think too much about this case or see her too often. Dr. Lamoreux gave me feedback that Marian appreciated our visits, but neither of us could identify overt changes. In many ways the sessions felt more like "visits" than therapy, but I had a busy life and was willing to put minimal energy into this case.

My busy life seemed to catch up with me one day when I experienced a frightening health event. I was sitting in a faculty meeting in our hospital when I felt a strong and sharp chest pain. Although it felt like the proverbial elephant sitting on my chest, I told myself that I was a healthy woman in her 40s, and of course nothing could be happening. I looked around at the physicians in the room and saw that none of them seemed alarmed, which further proved that I must be fine. But it hurt a lot, and soon I found myself leaving the room and standing against a hallway wall. A colleague saw me leave and came out to find me pale and fainting. I next remembered the lights in the emergency room, and me reassuring the doctors that I must be fine because I exercise frequently. Apparently, I received quick attention when I was wheeled into the emergency room in a desk chair by a couple of concerned physician colleagues.

My story was quite common and easily explained, but my acceptance did not come so easily. For about an hour, I stayed attached to the cardiac monitors in the emergency room, but my normal vital signs allowed for visits from my colleagues. We joked about how they had called my husband and then moved the faculty meeting into my room, around my bed. As a family therapist, I teach and collaborate with family physicians in a residency program, and a large part of what we teach is the

relation between stress and health. For my colleagues, this was an easily explained event of chest pain, probably due to stress or anxiety, compounded with my fear of the pain, which resulted in shock and short-term loss of consciousness. It was something they had seen, and it was something that, together, we had often explained to our patients. Yet I resisted this explanation for myself, just as our patients frequently resist our explanations.

It was true that my dear friend Sandra was dying from breast cancer, and it was true that I was spending huge amounts of time at her home as well as trying to keep up with all of my work and home responsibilities. It was also true that my father had died of a long illness the year before. But I wasn't like those patients of ours. I wasn't an anxious person, or one who somaticizes. I was different: I was a professional. I knew about stress and illness, and although I was under a huge amount of stress, I should be able to handle it.

Somehow hearing myself talk so irrationally to my friends and husband allowed me to listen to them. What I heard made me realize that many of them had experienced similar physical events when they were stressed. Others had seen physical symptoms in patients that were truly biopsychosocial events. During that morning, I realized that I had accepted the integration of mind and body only for other people. Certainly I was compassionate to my clients, but I think I had expected strong people (such as myself) either to have physical disease or to be able to handle their stresses without experiencing bodily symptoms. Lying in an emergency room bed, I began to accept that our bodies and our minds are integrated in ways that we certainly don't understand but in ways that are important to honor. Although I had said these things to colleagues, students, and patients for years, it took this dramatic personal event to help me believe them as well.

Insight doesn't always lead to profound change, and my insights didn't lead to a rapid decrease in Marian's complaints or a vast improvement in her symptoms. It may be just co-occurrence, or it may be that greater acceptance of my own complexity and uncertainty allowed me to be more accepting of Marian. Either way, I seemed to develop an increased interest in cases like Marian's after I had encountered firsthand the powerful connection between emotional and physical pain. I think that I began to accept that her pain was more real than I had initially believed. I began to respect Marian and the severe hurts that she experienced and did not try to quickly see her physical pain as a metaphor for emotional pain that she was unwilling to address. At the very least, I became more interested in her and more inquisitive.

First I became more inquisitive about Marian's pain. With all of our previous focus on pain management, I had never obtained the full story of how the pain affected her life. When asked, Marian described years of hoping that the pain would get better, and numerous visits to multiple doctors, all with disappointing results. Marian had tried exercise and pain management programs but could not stop the unpredictable cycles of lesser and greater pain. Each morning when she awoke, she had no idea whether her body would allow her to accomplish basic tasks or whether it would be almost too difficult to move from the bed, to the shower, to the chair. Her story was very painful to hear. Instead of someone who was always complaining, Marian changed for me and became someone who was enduring a fairly hellish existence. And yet she was still continuing to try to get relief. This was not a hopeless person but one who retained hope even when her experiences told her otherwise.

As I became more interested in Marian's symptoms, I began to ask Dr. Lamoreux more questions about her disease and their plans for management. As we discussed Marian's care, Dr. Lamoreux and I realized that we both had been maintaining a holding pattern. For example, Marian's psychoactive medications had not been assessed since she had come to our office 2 years earlier. Dr. Lamoreux recognized that Marian was on fairly high doses of Clonazepam to address her anxiety and relatively high doses of Nortriptyline to treat the pain and depression. Given the complexity of Marian's case, we obtained a consultation from a psychiatrist, who suggested that the Clonazepam be reduced and that the Nortriptyline was too sedating a drug for purposes of pain control.

Within a month, Marian had tapered herself from 3.5 mg of Clonazepam per day to 0.5 per day. At the same time, she moved from Nortriptyline to a less sedating and more effective drug. Marian's mood improved, and she claimed that she had more energy. The sleepiness that I had experienced in our sessions was no longer there, and Marian felt encouraged that we all were working together to decrease her pain. It seemed that those basic therapeutic principles of joining, history taking, and attending to the client's symptoms had benefits for all of us.

When Marian felt that we had more fully attended to her physical symptoms, she seemed more willing to discuss some of the other stressors in her life. With validation of her pain, Marian became more willing to talk about her family and her life stresses. I learned that Marian was angry that family members didn't ask about her pain, but she also was unwilling to let anyone know that she was hurting. In fact, if anyone asked how she was doing, she told them she was fine and changed the conversation. In our conversation, Marian began to see that she had a part in not letting others know of her feelings, and we joked about how she really wanted them to read her mind—to know what she needed without having to tell them. As Marian and I uncovered the frustrating interaction patterns in her family, I reassured her that they were quite common, and we began to use humor more as we played out fantasies of how others should read minds without us telling them what we're feeling.

It became clear that Marian wanted to share her life more with her family, particularly with her husband, Spencer. Perhaps with the protection of a little humor, she found it easier to describe how grumpy she was at home and how dismissive she was of her husband's attempts to help her. When Marian asked Spencer to come in, he readily agreed. In retrospect, this change to conjoint sessions may have been facilitated by my acceptance of Marian and our belief that involving others would make a difference.

The couple sessions were an exciting change from the individual sessions. Spencer was a kind, thoughtful, and articulate man who patiently supported his wife but welcomed the opportunity to be heard, by her and by me. Together they described how they tried to care for one another but that the pain was such a barrier, both physically and emotionally. They talked of their earlier zest for love-making and their joint frustration that touching Marian frequently produced pain instead of joy. They described a pattern in which Marian, when in pain, shot verbal daggers at Spencer, which made him want to avoid her completely.

Medical family therapy skills, particularly reassurance and psychoeducation, were helpful at this time. Both members of the couple enjoyed when I could describe a scene from one of their patterned encounters. I reminded them that the pattern was common, because illness affects couples in predictable ways. They were reassured to know that they were not "poor copers" but responded to the intrusion of illness as many couples do.

We noted how Marian and Spencer identified themselves as a couple coping with chronic pain rather than as a couple in mid-life with many opportunities and gifts. When I asked them to evaluate, on a scale from 1 to 10, how much the illness had affected their life together, both agreed that the illness was a 9, very powerful in their relationship. I talked with them about the possibility of putting the illness in its place, of recognizing that it was there and needed attention but also acknowledging that they had lives apart from the illness. When I asked each of them where on the scale the illness should reside, they selected 3 and 4. I suggested that moving from a 9 to a 3 was a fairly monumental task, and we all agreed that moving the impact of illness to a 7 would be a manageable goal.

Once we had a goal on which Marian and Spencer both agreed, we began to have fun thinking about how they could reach their goal. When asked about activities they both enjoyed, they mentioned car rides, lunches out, and attending their granddaughter's athletic and school events. Both agreed that Spencer's work schedule was difficult, because Marian felt strongest in the afternoon, just the time when he was preparing to leave for work. They considered what schedule changes might be helpful so they could take advantage of Marian's best times. Perhaps most significantly, they discussed how Marian could let Spencer know when the pain was really severe and she really didn't want to be pushed.

Marian and Spencer attended five couple sessions over 3 months. The family work documented how

the medical family therapy principles of agency and communion are mutually reinforced during treatment of somatic complaints (McDaniel, Hepworth, & Doherty, 1995). Communion was enhanced as Marian expanded her circle to include her husband and other family members. With inclusion, they all felt more empowered about their ability to cope with the pain and continue with life activities. Conversely, with increased agency, exemplified by Marian's enthusiasm about activities and decisions, she was also more welcoming to family members and neighbors.

As the couple worked together in therapy, Spencer changed his typical work hours to first shift. This allowed Marian to sleep later, take her time getting ready in the late morning, and then be most energetic when Spencer returned in the afternoon. Since they had talked about how comforting hot baths were for Marian, Spencer bought a portable spa for the tub, and Marian took long, soothing baths at least a couple of times each week.

They were proud that they had been getting out of the house frequently and described how Keesha's basketball coach had given them recognition for their frequent attendance. Marian described how it was still very difficult to get around, but she almost always felt better when she could say that she had done something active during a particular day. Even though Marian's level of pain had not significantly changed, she and Spencer were having a fuller social life and were much more satisfied with how they could talk with one another. They also shyly indicated that they had resumed more physical closeness and enjoyed touching one another again.

During the past year, I have seen Marian very infrequently. About 4 months ago, she came in to talk about the terminal illness of her mother Evelyn and how difficult it was for Marian to provide the care that Evelyn wanted. Marian, her brother, and Spencer had arranged for visiting nurses to provide most of the physical care, but Marian spent much of the day sitting and talking with her mother. She still was disappointed that her mother didn't recognize the severity of her pain, and although she understood that Evelyn was focused on herself, Marian still hoped that her mother would show more interest in her. We discussed how Evelyn's attention would become more inward at this time and considered how Marian might not get the attention she desired from her mother but could give herself credit for caring for her mother. Marian found pleasure in providing care for her mother and described how they were able to sit together and talk and watch television and how other family members visited and created a loving setting. Marian left feeling sad but also feeling that she was acting in the way that she wanted to during this time.

Two months ago, Marian came in to say that her mother had died 2 weeks earlier. Marian was bent over with pain and made deep sighs with every step to my office. Her brother had brought her in, and although he was worried about her he did not want to join us in the session. Marian sat heavily in her chair and told me how angry she was at her mother, not because she had died but because she had continued to be so demanding and unconcerned about Marian's welfare. Marian also said that it was time for her mother to die, that she had lived a full life, and that she had died feeling loved and accomplished. But as she neared death, Evelyn seemed to want more contact with Marian, and Marian felt that her attention to her mother had sapped her own energy and health.

It was relatively easy to help Marian again see how much easier it was to be angry than it was to be sad. She remembered our discussions of how we hold ourselves when we're angry: with tension and tightness that worsens muscle pain. We talked of how Evelyn had encouraged Marian to push herself to provide much care and in some ways ensured that Marian could always feel good about what she had done for her mother. Marian visibly let go of some of her muscle tension when she cried. She didn't sob in ways that hurt her body, but she sighed long and breathed deeply. She could see that holding herself back from being sad had contributed to making her feel tighter and having more pain.

Marian left my office walking as slowly as she had entered, but without the dramatic sighs at each step. Her brother stood up in the waiting room, relieved to see that she was smiling and visibly in less pain. Marian has real pain, and she knows that her husband, her family, and her doctors recognize it. Partly because of that, she also recognizes that she has some choice in how much she allows the pain to take over her life. I imagine that her physician and I will continue to serve as occasional reminders of this; we are willing to meet with her during those infrequent times when reminders from the "experts" are helpful. We hope, however, that Marian knows that the real expert on her health is not outside of herself.

As I look back over the months of treatment with Marian, I cannot help but think that my greater acceptance of the integration of physical and emotional health, made me more open to acceptance of Marian. I have never asked Marian whether she noticed a change in my response toward her, although she became very articulate about acknowledging the changes in herself. Even though we are fascinated by our own stories, our clients are generally most interested in what is occurring for them, and that is as it should be.

References

Bakan, D. (1969). *The duality of human existence.* Chicago: Rand McNally.

McDaniel, S., Hepworth, J., & Doherty, W. (1992). *Medical family therapy: A biopsychosocial approach to families with health problems.* New York: Basic Books.

McDaniel, S., Hepworth, J., & Doherty, W. (1995). Medical family therapy with somatizing patients: The co-creation of therapeutic stories. In R. H. Mikesell, D-D. Lusterman, & S. H. McDaniel (Eds.), *Integrating family therapy: Handbook of family psychology and systems theory* (pp. 377–388). Washington, DC: American Psychological Association.

McDaniel, S., Hepworth, J., & Doherty, W. (1997). *The shared experience of illness: Stories of patients, families, and their therapists.* New York: Basic Books.

CHAPTER 27

DIFFERENTIATION BEFORE DEATH: MEDICAL FAMILY THERAPY FOR A WOMAN WITH END-STAGE CROHN'S DISEASE AND HER SON

Susan H. McDaniel, Jennifer L. Harkness, and Ronald M. Epstein

Medical family therapy grew out of the experiences of family therapists working with other professionals to provide comprehensive, integrated health care for patients (McDaniel, Hepworth, & Doherty, 1995). This is the story of one such patient, her son, and those of us who were the three primary participants on her treatment team. To provide an account that comes closest to the experience itself, we have taken quotes from videotaped sessions and electronic mail communications that occurred throughout the course of therapy. Each provider tells part of the story in his or her own voice. The general commentary is provided by Susan McDaniel.

THE DEVELOPMENT OF BIOPSYCHOSOCIAL MEDICINE AND MEDICAL FAMILY THERAPY

Family Psychologist Dr. McDaniel

Every theory evolves in a particular context that is a fertile, determining environment for its development. Biopsychosocial medicine, an alternative to the reductionistic biomedical model, was developed at the University of Rochester School of Medicine out of the inspiration of one internist, George Engel (1977), working among a cluster of talented physicians interested in disease and the social aspects of the human condition (Epstein et al., in press). In 1980, I brought my family systems training to the psychosocially sensitive Department of Family Medicine. Family physician Thomas Campbell, having

just completed a fellowship with George Engel, joined me to develop a behavioral science curriculum for primary care physicians. This curriculum integrated family systems and biopsychosocial approaches, which evolved from a common root in general systems theory.

Once we had developed a curriculum (McDaniel, Campbell, & Seaburn, 1990), we realized that most mental health professionals did not communicate, much less collaborate, with the physicians we were teaching to provide family-oriented, biopsychosocial care. When lesser interventions (such as pleading with community therapists) did not rectify the situation, we decided to experiment with on-site family-oriented mental health services. The experiment succeeded beyond our expectations. Problems with communication decreased sharply and, even more important, the setting provided routine opportunities for innovation and collaboration with other health professionals. Of course, barriers to collaboration occurred daily, but my tolerance for working through them was high because I grew up in a medical family (my father was an obstetrician) and live in one now (my husband is a pediatrician and internist). This is a context that I understand.

We had brought family systems theory to the medical context, but what had we ourselves learned about family therapy in the process? With family therapists Jeri Hepworth in Connecticut and William Doherty in Minnesota also working in primary care

---

Some facts about the people involved in this case have been altered to protect the confidentiality of the patients.

settings, the development of medical family therapy seemed a natural next step in terms of developing a biopsychosocial approach for family therapy that recognizes the effect of physical issues on emotional processes (McDaniel, Hepworth, & Doherty, 1992, 1997). The treatment described in this chapter illustrates the importance of the overarching goals of medical family therapy: agency (or self-efficacy) and communion (or significant connection). As in every case, these goals were important for the patient, the family, and the health care team itself.

My first contact with this case was at a colloquium organized to bring together family therapists from Psychiatry and Family Medicine with biopsychosocially oriented physicians, including George Engel, Thomas Campbell, and Ronald Epstein, to watch a Public Broadcasting System video of the Arthur Miller play "Broken Glass." The father of psychoneuroimmunology, Robert Ader, also works at the University of Rochester Department of Psychiatry and had recommended the play to me as one that illustrates the interplay among sociocultural factors (World War II), interpersonal interaction (a married Jewish couple in Brooklyn), and symptomatology (conversion paralysis of the wife). We were all moved by the play and its importance to our work. In the discussion period Dr. Epstein mentioned that he had to leave early to see a patient who had many of the same issues represented in the play—sociocultural issues (she had immigrated from Czechoslovakia), interpersonal issues (she and her son struggled over her dependency on him), and symptomatology (hallucinations; depression; secrecy; and a diagnosis of severe inflammatory bowel disease, also called Crohn's Disease). In "Broken Glass" the family physician treated the couple without help from any other professionals. Dr. Epstein left the gathering saying that he realized he did not want to do the same, and he asked me if I would work with him to provide care for his patient. Still stimulated by the play and the discussion, I agreed.

I quickly recognized the complexity of the case and the likelihood that the systems work would include a mixture of individual and family sessions, in addition to close collaboration with the health care team. I was also convinced that there was an educational opportunity for all of us in the story Dr. Epstein told, so I asked our Medical Family Therapy Fellow, Jennifer Harkness, PhD, if she would like to work with me on the case. In the beginning, Dr. Harkness observed and assisted in the therapy. By the end, she functioned as a cotherapist with me for the family sessions and as an individual therapist for the identified patient while I took primary responsibility for the individual sessions with the patient's son. This example of medical family therapy occurred over a 10-month period and involved a total of 31 individual and family sessions (6 family sessions, 3 network sessions with the family and professional network, 10 individual sessions with the patient, and 12 individual sessions with her son) as well as multiple interactions with her primary care physician, Dr. Epstein, and various other members of the health care team.

Family Physician Dr. Epstein

In October 1996, I was asked by Vaclav Havlicek if I would take care of his mother, Lola. I had known the 53-year-old Vaclav as a patient for 3 years. His mother, age 82, was hospitalized with severe inflammatory bowel disease (Crohn's Disease), characterized by abdominal pain, diarrhea, and rectal bleeding, and was refusing surgery that might eradicate the disease. Mrs. Havlicek was on high doses of steroids, which made her legs swell and had long-term risks of osteoporosis and diabetes. Her care was further complicated by the fact that she was admitted to two different psychiatric wards at hospitals where I did not ordinarily admit. Trials of two antidepressants, an antipsychotic agent, and an anxiolytic appeared to reduce her emotional lability somewhat but clearly had not solved the problem. Communication with medical specialists and psychiatric staff was difficult, and neither time was there appropriate follow-up.

Mrs. Havlicek initially struck me as a bright, engaging woman who had endured much hardship; the death of her husband at age 30 of colon cancer, raising a 3-year-old in a repressive political environment in Czechoslovakia, a difficult emigration to the United States, and now this illness. Her son described her as "difficult," and this was initially manifested in the unrealistic hopes that she expressed in having me as her physician: "My son says that you are the best doctor in the world."

During this time, Vaclav was clearly struggling with his role as his mother's only living relative. Through prior psychotherapy he had come to the realization that he could not spend his entire life caring for his mother and that whatever was given would never be enough. As Mrs. Havlicek's medical situation worsened, she became more demanding of hospital nurses and her son. Vaclav had taken to occasionally contacting me by means of electronic mail; these communiqués increased, as did pages to me from the hospital nursing staff. The gastroenterologist, nutritionist, and colorectal surgeon involved in Mrs. Havlicek's care had few useful suggestions. The situation was beginning to seem hopeless.

Soon the risks of overinvolvement and my need to fix this situation crystallized. There were several elements of the case that were particularly cogent for me: First, the sense that no other physician had been successful in Mrs. Havlicek's care and that she did not like her previous doctor were warnings to watch out for unrealistic expectations—but they were also lures: Could I be the one to fix the unfixable patient? Second, I realized that I needed to place boundaries around my involvement with this patient for the treatment to be useful for her and manageable for me. I knew unrealistic expectations would be harmful to both of us. The request from her son, a patient of mine, to care for his mother, made the task even more onerous and inviting—could I not only fix the unfixable patient but also satisfy the needs and desires of her son to get his mother off his back? These mythical, heroic themes were balanced by the warning I took from "Broken Glass": Get help; you cannot do it all! Although I recognized that the need to accomplish the impossible was commonly part of physicians' own family expectations, asking for help was still difficult for me because of my interest in psychological aspects of illness and my training in family therapy. Fortunately, Mrs. Havlicek did consent to surgery, but she still harbored significant ambivalence and fear. Shouldn't I know how to manage this situation unassisted? My role was unclear—I am not an expert in management of severe Crohn's Disease, and I routinely refer patients who are suicidal to therapists. The recognition that help might be available brought me a sense of repose and relief. The question was, whom should I ask for help?

Because I felt the obligation to fix the unfixable, I also felt an obligation to find an excellent therapist. Experienced therapists willing to work with medically complex patients, and see patients outside their office settings, are rare. Also, I had fears of being criticized, as I had been by one psychiatrist, for having made the clinical "error" of caring for more than one person in the family. I chose a colleague, Susan McDaniel, PhD, with whom I had studied family therapy, who would recognize that the consultation might be as much to provide support for me as to provide direct assistance to the patient. Dr. McDaniel also involved a Medical Family Therapy Fellow, Jennifer Harkness, as a cotherapist. I explained my (not very modest) goals for the consultation:

1. to support Mrs. Havlicek during a difficult time before and after surgery and help her adjust to changes in her living situation, her physical functioning, and her self-image in order to live as independently as possible
2. to evaluate Mrs. Havlicek's mental state, which appeared to be labile
3. to share the care of a complex patient and thus relieve me of what seemed to be an overwhelming responsibility (or sense of responsibility)
4. to help Vaclav individuate—to be able to balance his needs with those of his mother and to help him prepare for a life without her.

Dr. McDaniel

A referral from Dr. Epstein is synonymous with the referral of a difficult (and usually fascinating) patient. Dr. Epstein is a very skilled family physician with training in both biopsychosocial medicine and family therapy. Once I read the reports from the patient's most recent psychiatric hospitalization, I could see why Dr. Epstein was worried. This patient had severe medical illness; the need for major surgery in the near future; and a history of suicidality, anxiety, and being difficult to manage medically and psychiatrically. I could sense from Dr. Epstein a feeling of being pulled into the case; it was a mixture of familiar connection, compassion, and feeling overwhelmed.

PRESURGERY SESSIONS: CRISIS INTERVENTION

The Initial Collaborative Session

The first session was attended by the patient, Mrs. Havlicek (Mrs. H); her son, Vaclav (V); Dr. McDaniel (Dr. M); Dr. Harkness (Dr. H); and Dr. Epstein (Dr. E). In medical family therapy we strive to conduct the first session with the referring physician, if possible, in order to hear the medical history and the physician's concerns and to gain his or her blessing for therapy with the family. Often this initial experience of collaboration by the treatment team is a powerful way to join and initiate treatment with the patient and family. For patients who define their problems as medical and not psychosocial, this beginning may be essential to making the referral "stick." Our first session took place in a hospital room established for family meetings. At that time, Mrs. Havlicek had been hospitalized for a week, receiving intravenous nutrition to regain enough strength and stability to withstand surgery on her colon. The patient quickly laid her cards on the table.

Mrs. H: I am an outspoken person. I don't know what this [meeting] has to do with my illness, and altogether I just don't know if it means some improvement for me. . . . I just don't know why [we're meeting].

Dr. M: Why are we here? Let's talk to Dr. Epstein about that and then we can each share our opinions.

Dr. E: I guess my concern . . . like we talked about before . . . is that your health is very fragile and you are going to be going through some pretty major surgery. You have had some problems with depression and also not wanting to live. And between the two of you, you have had some problems about how you can best help each other. So this is a time that I thought we could get together to help you and Vaclav optimize your health the best we can.

This is a high-risk time. I want you to get through the surgery not only alive, but living the way that you want to live. And without driving yourself crazy and driving Vaclav crazy.

Clearly this patient was not going to easily accept our services, although she had no reluctance to continue taking her psychotropic medications. Without Dr. Epstein at this session it is doubtful that this referral would have been successful. It was also clear at the outset that cultural issues were prominent. Fortunately, and coincidentally, Dr. Harkness's grandparents had emigrated to this country from Czechoslovakia. Searching for commonality, we silently agreed to use this as much as possible to put Mrs. Havlicek at ease so we could begin our initial assessment. It was also clear from the beginning that Vaclav was embarrassed by his mother's criticism of the United States and its health care system and by her attachment to the Old Country. Because of this, I worked to be especially respectful and understanding of the patient's history and values.

Mrs. H: [I] suffer so much, not for one person but for five persons.

Dr. M: Is your heart still back in Czechoslovakia?

Mrs. H: Yes. It wasn't [when I first came to this country] because I was healthy, I was happy. I had lots of friends here. Now in 2 years, five Czech people died: one a year. . . . Half of me is here and half is there, but I have to be reasonable. It is impossible to go there

Dr. M: Yes, right. So even though there is part of you that knows that your heart is there you have to accept that your life is here, and that is what is realistic.

Mrs. H: In Czechoslovakia they have everything. They make it easier. Here it seems to me [that you] scratch your ear this way [touching ears with arms crossed], when you can do it that way [touching ears with arms uncrossed].

Dr. E: She means that we do things here the hard way.

V: The wrong way.

Mrs. H: Yeah.

V: Mom, don't forget that every friend of yours from the Czech Republic writes to you and tells you how terrible medicine is there because everything is changing dramatically. Somebody told you that you should be glad to be in a hospital here and not in Prague.

Mrs. H: Yeah, that is true. Like I said, it means a lot of change.

V: The point is that we are not here trying to change America but [to see] what can be done for you and me.

Next I turned to evaluate her feelings regarding the upcoming surgery.

Mrs. H: [I'm] nervous like an old cat. Everyone is scared.

Dr. M: Are you scared?

Mrs. H: Yeah.

Dr. M: You are. Do you want to live?

Mrs. H: Yeah, of course I would like to, if it like [is a] little normal life. . . . I was never scared when I had another surgery, but this time I do.

Dr. M: And the difference is . . .

Mrs. H: You know, maybe because it will be close to the end. My husband had colon cancer so that is . . . (tearing up).

Dr. M: The similarity is upsetting . . .

Mrs. H: Yeah, when you are waiting, that is the worst time. Like when you go to the dentist and you know that he will pull out your tooth. That is similar. My friend's husband died a few years ago. I think that the older you are, you are more scared. . . . I don't have the discipline that I had before. Not any more: I changed.

Many patients' peculiar responses to medical interventions are rooted in past experiences. For Mrs. Havlicek, this hospitalization for bowel disease reminded her of the tragic experience over 50 years

before when her young husband, Vaclav's father, died at age 30 of colon cancer.

In addition to a life of loss and stress, Mrs. Havlicek also worried about mental illness. In an electronic mail note to Dr. Epstein, just before the referral, Vaclav said of his mother:

> She called yesterday and said that she is not sleeping anymore. That she has to go to urinate many times every night and she is certain it is nervous in origin. She also told me that she is very (or extremely) depressed, that she is very scared that she will end her life in a psychiatric ward, as her father did.

We learned that Mrs. Havlicek was critical and unhappy about almost everything, as well as paranoid about the hospital staff, the professionals on her health care team, her friends, and sometimes her son. She denied any history of psychiatric treatment in Czechoslovakia, although she had been hospitalized twice in this country for suicidality and once in the distant past for unknown reasons. Her father's experience in an old-fashioned asylum haunted her. She did take solace in the fact that medications currently used in psychiatry were a significant advance over anything available when her father was ill.

Trying to understand more about her recent psychiatric experience, we asked Mrs. Havlicek about the hospitalization that occurred several months before this session.

Mrs. H: This injury [pointing to her shoulder] happened at the end of January. I don't know why Dr. Epstein was so stubborn that I have to go on psychiatric [ward]. . . . I spend there 10 days. I could not eat the meal. They did not do absolutely anything. What will they do with my arm on psychiatry? I suffered and suffered, 10 days I was in hell for nothing.

Dr. M: It seems like over and over again you have the experience of wanting to be helped and somehow it is frustrating because you feel your needs aren't really being met. And it seems like it happens over and over again throughout life.

I began to understand that Mrs. Havlicek pulled for people to argue with her about the facts of her life, but what she really needed was for people to listen and respond to her emotional experience. Vaclav had a very hard time doing this; he fell into arguing with his mother again and again. I knew changing the way he listened and responded to his mother would be an important part of this therapy.

V: I feel that my mother sees many problems with America, with the world, with everybody. [To his mother] Sometimes I feel like you think everybody is against you, everybody is your enemy almost. I don't think it is true. [To providers] If something could be done about that in a sense, I think that would do a lot about her attitude toward surgery.

Given her history, I had my doubts that Mrs. Havlicek's negative, depressive attitude was situational; my guess was it was a long-standing, perhaps lifelong, pattern of coping, punctuated by periods of major depression. I suspected that Vaclav had an equally long-standing longing for his mother to be more positive and nurturing (toward him) but that this wish was unrealistic. If these theories proved to be true, we would need to treat Mrs. Havlicek's agitated depression, help her become more comfortable with the need for surgery, and help both mother and son support and differentiate from each other.

At the conclusion of the first session, Dr. Epstein expressed his own goals for the therapy.

Dr. E: For me, I have two concerns . . . taking care of you (to Vaclav) and taking care of you (to Mrs. Havlicek), because you are both my patients. I also want to talk about what we can do to help you get through this time (to Vaclav), because you are really the only family your mother has locally.

V: Right.

Dr. E: [To Vaclav] I know the past 6 months have certainly been challenging to you. What do you feel that you need either from me or from us collectively?

V: I would like for you to have a magic wand and change her attitude [laughing]. I would like her to feel better.

Dr. E: Is there a time that you could tell me about when she was actually feeling better, when she was the mom that you would like her to be now?

V: Actually, that would be difficult because I do not have much memories of that. I am concerned about how she feels, and does she want to live? Is she feeling well or not? I am concerned about this colostomy because, what sort of life will she have with it? I am concerned about her going to a nursing home too soon because she does not like people. The other thing I am concerned about is how she can accept help or not accept help. The fact is that I cannot be there every day.

It is evident from this exchange that Dr. Epstein is functioning as a cotherapist in this session. Also, Vaclav supported my hypothesis about his unrealistic expectations and demonstrated that he has insight into his own dynamics. It is interesting that Vaclav brought Dr. Harkness and me several articles during the course of treatment. The first was on mind–body integration, and the second was on attachment theory. An engineer, he clearly was well read on the psychological theories that might help explain his experience. Theories notwithstanding, he alternated between being worried about his mother and being furious about her demands on him.

Preparing for Surgery

At the end of the first session Dr. Harkness and I spoke about the case and realized that we would need to mix individual and family sessions to meet the goals established in this first session. Given Dr. Harkness's cultural connection, we agreed that she would conduct the individual sessions with Mrs. Havlicek and that I would take primary responsibility for the sessions with Vaclav. We would both attend the family sessions and attend to the collaborative relationship with Dr. Epstein. Because we frequently used electronic mail to communicate with Dr. Epstein, it was easy for both of us to be copied in on all contacts. Vaclav also initiated electronic mail contact with us, sent all messages to both Dr. Harkness and me, and often copied them to Dr. Epstein as well. He quickly caught on to the collaborative nature of our treatment and used the computer to facilitate communication.[1]

As it turned out, both Mrs. Havlicek and Dr. Epstein were skeptical after the first session; they both later acknowledged that they were unsure we could help. I was too busy trying to formulate a treatment plan that covered the many aspects of the case to think too much about whether it would work. Although the relational issues between Mrs. Havlicek and Vaclav were intriguing, the first priority in our biopsychosocial assessment was to clarify Mrs. Havlicek's mental status, lower the anxiety in the system, and help the patient prepare for surgery. Mrs. Havlicek denied any current suicidal ideation or plan and passed the mental status exam embedded in her first session, but some of her behavior reported by the staff outside this session seemed delusional or even halluncinatory. Dr. Harkness visited Mrs. Havlicek several times in the next week, and we discussed her mental functioning with Vaclav and the nurses, but the most helpful information came from her Dr. Epstein, who expressed in an electronic mail note his belief that the "hallucinoid" experiences were secondary to the hospitalization and the steroid medications needed to control her Crohn's Disease and would clear with time.

Dr. E: I've talked to her about some of those events, mostly last week. I think that she is not truly halluc-cinating, but having hallucinoid experiences at times, mostly relating to actual events in Czechoslovakia. She knows that they are not real. One such event was that a friend told her that the doctors knew that she really had cancer, and that the diagnosis was being kept from her. This actually did happen to her husband. . . . I would not entirely rule out some subtle cognitive impairment, but she does very well on a mental status exam. No sundowning noted by nurses. Most of her changes of topic are probably not because of distractibility or psychosis; it is avoidant and controlling, a coping mechanism when anxious.

We came to agree with this assessment, borne of

Dr. Epstein's longer term relationship with Mrs. Havlicek. Also, there were discussions about whether to change the dose or the medications she was taking. We decided to maintain the current regimen, wanting to keep from making a complex situation more complex. Fortunately, that was the right choice. Indeed, her hallucinoid experiences were transitory. We were all aware of the meaning of these symptoms to the patient.

V: The other thing that she is terrified of is that she will become crazy like her father. A couple of times I thought, well . . . it is coming . . . and now I am wondering if it is.

Dr. M: Definitely with older people who have been in the hospital for a long time, they can become delusional. It must be very upsetting to look at your mother and to see her so out of it. It sounds like, between the two of you, she has been difficult all along. She is so attached to you and has expectations of you that you do not share.

As we were gathering information to confirm a diagnosis about the delusional episodes we also held several family therapy sessions in the hospital with Vaclav and Mrs. Havlicek. These sessions followed the pattern established in the first session: treating Mrs. Havlicek with respect, encouraging her to become stronger as she moved closer to surgery, making sense out of her concerns given her history, talking about the differences between this country and Czechoslovakia, and helping Vaclav to hear the emotional realities embedded in what he experienced as provocative comments by his mother.

These themes were reinforced during individual sessions with Vaclav. Here is an exchange during one of the sessions in which we tried to connect Mrs. Havlicek's negativity with the anxiety that was understandable given her history.

Dr. H: I am curious. In a conversation with your mother, she mentioned having a friend who died of

---

[1] With regard to electronic mail communication among the providers and with Vaclav, care was taken to avoid identifying features of the case so that confidentiality was preserved.

cancer, and they did not tell the friend his diagnosis. Do you know about this?

V: She has a friend who did die of cancer about a year ago. That is something about this country: They do tell you if you are dying of cancer.

Dr. M: Yeah . . . but in a lot of other countries, they don't.

V: In Czechoslovakia, she probably did have some people . . .

Dr. M: Which is a horrible bind for her now because she does not trust our system. So when people tell her she doesn't have cancer, where does that leave her?

V: That is interesting! I was afraid that constant fear could not necessarily cause [cancer] to happen but . . . it may help it in some way.

Dr. M: Well, it could certainly cause anxiety, you know, if nothing else.

Vaclav took his mother's behavior at face value: To him, she was just a negative person. Over time, we appealed to Vaclav's considerable intellect to encourage him to look underneath the obvious to what emotions might be fueling her behavior. Later in therapy, we applied this same exercise to his own behavior. Vaclav was very invested in his spiritual development (especially Buddhism), but he maintained an engineer's exclusively cognitive view when it came to understanding the connection between emotions and behavior. It was this linear worldview that we slowly challenged in individual therapy.

It was unclear whether Mrs. Havlicek would survive this challenge to her health. Her mental health status also remained fragile. We knew that if she died before her relationship with her son improved Vaclav's attempts at differentiation would be extremely challenging. His mother's blessing for him to move on was very desirable. Their relationship had become very fused over the years, punctuated by Mrs. Havlicek's difficult emigration to the United States and Vaclav's series of failed relationships with women, including a marriage and a divorce. Together Vaclav and his mother spoke of wanting the other to be free and independent, but somewhere

inside each wondered about being able to survive on his or her own.

After several family sessions, Dr. Epstein sent us an electronic mail note: "Mrs. Havlicek really appreciated yesterday's family therapy session. She indicated that she was very suspicious of the whole process in the beginning, but now sees that it might be helpful." Meanwhile, after a slow start, Dr. Harkness was developing a strong relationship in individual therapy with Mrs. Havlicek, helping to lower her anxiety in the face of surgery.

Family Therapist Dr. Harkness

When we decided that I would meet with Mrs. Havlicek on an individual basis, I struggled with what therapy I could offer her. She had already been in the hospital for 3 weeks and made it perfectly clear to Dr. McDaniel, Dr. Epstein, and me that she did not want to work with us. At first I thought this attitude was strictly related to mental health services. I later learned it was generalizable to all health professionals.

The hospital staff described Mrs. Havlicek as unpleasant to care for, mostly because of her irritable mood and demanding demeanor. She complained about everything and everyone who entered her room. She was convinced that everyone around her either wanted her admitted to a psychiatric facility or secretly knew that she was dying. At that time, her mental health status was declining with her physical status; however, we constantly reassured her that we did not plan to admit her to a psychiatric facility. This gave her little comfort, and the medications she had to take for her Crohn's Disease complicated the situation with her mental status.

Mrs. Havlicek was on steroid medication to prevent her from bleeding profusely during her operation. Steroids often cause emotional lability and, sometimes, hallucinations and delusions. Also, she was on blood pressure medications, antidepressants, and anxiolytics, all of which can cause mental status changes. Part of her mental status changes included forgetting having met people the preceding day. This cognitive deficit made joining and building an established relationship with the hospital staff and me challenging. My hope was that she would survive the surgery, taper the numerous medications, and regain a functional mental status. Meanwhile, I provided empathy and reassurance as much as possible, trying to cut through her cantankerous presentation.

Dr. McDaniel

Individual sessions with Vaclav during this period were mostly focused on him expressing his anger about the ways in which his mother had been disappointing and difficult through the years. Letting out these negative emotions seemed to allow him to tend to her in this period of crisis. At the time of the referral, Vaclav vacillated between frequent, intense contact with his mother around crisis times and angry distance at others. We talked about more balance in the future, if she made it through the surgery, when he might be able to schedule regular visits with her several times a week, at times she knew she could count on. He then could count on having the rest of the time to himself. This plan operationalized an appropriate emotional distance for this pair who had had to pull together to survive in their early days in Czechoslovakia.

We were also aware that this issue of closeness and distance was important in the dynamics of the treatment team. Dr. Epstein initially felt overwhelmed with responsibility, much like Vaclav. By involving us with him and sharing the responsibility, we were all able to play our respective roles with enough—but not too much—involvement.

Through the family and individual sessions, we were seeing gradual improvement with the Havliceks in a psychosocial sense. (At this point, Vaclav brought us the article on mind–body integration, showing that we shared a similar outlook on the treatment.) However, Mrs. Havlicek's nutritional status was not improving, despite maximal intravenous therapy, and she remained physically weak. She alternated between being mildly optimistic, expressing a determination to live, and decidedly depressed, questioning her ability to survive all these biopsychosocial assaults. In an electronic–mail note to Dr. Epstein, Vaclav expressed his fear and concern:

> *Today my mother told me that she has no appetite and that she did not eat anything. Wonder if that is related to the increased*

> *IV nutrition. Also, she said that she was depressed and crying and does not know why. She is talking about slipping away painlessly, sounded a little bit like a wish she died when having the surgery.*

Worries about suicidality floated around during this period, but none were validated to us by Mrs. Havlicek. Finally, after weeks of delaying the surgery for fear that she would be too weak to recover from the operation, and recognizing that things were not going to improve any further, Dr. Epstein suggested to the colorectal surgeon to take Mrs. Havlicek to surgery despite the risks posed by her poor nutritional status. Fortunately, the surgery was technically successful, but it was impossible to reconnect her bowel, leaving her with a colostomy. When I ran into the surgeon soon thereafter, his comment was, "Now she needs you more than she needs me."

POSTSURGERY SESSIONS: ADAPTATION AND DIFFERENTIATION

For several days pre- and postoperatively Mrs. Havlicek was intermittently delusional, but her mood remained pleasant. This was a brief period that Vaclav much appreciated, saying that his mother was loving and positive (even if not totally competent) in a way that he had never experienced before.

V: One of the things that I was concerned about was that she would die and I would not have been able to remember a pleasant time with her. However, these past 2 days I have really enjoyed being around her. Obviously, I don't want her to be crazy, but I was glad it happened. Now she is back to complaining and saying her hallucinations and delusions.

Several days after the operation, Mrs. Havlicek's pain medication was discontinued, and her mood began to return to its more negative baseline. However, she never returned to the dark periods that were part of the months before the operation.

Dr. Harkness

The usefulness of my visits with Mrs. Havlicek was clear after her surgery. Postoperatively Mrs. Havlicek became less fragmented and delusional, especially after her morphine was discontinued and the steroids were tapered. She was able to recognize and trust me. I grew very fond of her, in spite of her occasional peevish presentation. Mrs. Havlicek reminded me of many things past and present. She reminded me of the work that I did as a volunteer in a nursing home facility. She reminded me of my 88-year-old great aunt, who struggles on a daily basis with chronic pain and depression. Mainly, she reminded me of my Czech heritage. This was a part of my own story about which I knew little, and I used this commonality to join with her and educate myself.

For Mrs. Havlicek, the cultural difference was the dominant story that organized her hospital and illness experience. Discussions about her homeland shed light on why she seemed so mistrustful of the American medical system. Complaining about and to the hospital staff was her only defense against the unknown. She was going to die fighting, if indeed she was going to die at all.

Mrs. Havlicek showed me pictures of her family, complete with stories of survival and loss. When her husband died of colon cancer at the age of 30, leaving her a single mother of their 3-year-old son, Mrs. Havlicek seemed to react to her loss by becoming enmeshed with her son and taking a job in a medical setting. Her son became her primary companion, her job an inoculation against illness. After her husband's death other family members and friends died, some more significant than others, but all carrying the same story of not knowing the truth about their illnesses. Her ability to connect past experiences of friends' and family members' deaths to present fears about her own condition was both impressive and oppressive. During this phase of therapy we also focused extensively on her considerable fears of institutionalization (related to her father), cancer (related to her husband), and perceived abandonment (related to her son).

Dr. McDaniel

Several weeks postsurgery, Mrs. Havlicek was discharged to rehabilitation at a nearby nursing home facility, where she slowly began to improve. During this time there were a few minicrises, like those before surgery, in which Mrs. Havlicek communicated

panic to her son. In an electronic mail note to Dr. Epstein, Vaclav described his ongoing struggle regarding his mother's negativity and his desire to differentiate:

> *I just had a call from her. It started very upbeat, but then she said that the next time I come in I can teach her how to "walk again," how to get up from the chair and get to the toilet. It was difficult for me. I told her I do not think that she needs to learn to walk, but that she needs to talk to you about it. She bitterly complained about some rehabilitation people, that they are not dependable, that they refused to work with her any more. I kept telling her to talk to you about it, and I think she was getting angry with me, telling me yes but meaning no. . . . Maybe she did not mean it, but what I heard was that she was giving me responsibility for her well-being in the hospital, and for her health, and I have a hard time accepting that. I do not think I can, I do not think I should.*

During this period of treatment we had weekly individual sessions punctuated with occasional family sessions. Dr. Harkness's conversations with Mrs. Havlicek focused on healing, gaining trust in the American medical system, and regaining her strength, as well as asking her about how she felt Vaclav was doing. Mrs. Havlicek clearly understood that her son was struggling, but she characterized her own behavior as out of her control: "[Vaclav] must be tired to have such problems with me, but what can I do? It is my destiny."

The sessions with Vaclav focused on helping him to accept his mother as she is, and had been, while grieving the mother he wanted but never had. We discussed her illness, its likely course, and its effect on her and on him. Vaclav continued to struggle with his mother's victimized stance. He particularly winced when his mother tried to show him her colostomy bag or talk to him about the details of her physical reality. During this period we also raised the issue that neither of them had discussed (although it had been a frequent topic of discussion by the treatment team): her eventual death, and whether it would be sooner or later. Mrs. Havlicek spoke about her death in a fatalistic (external-locus-of-control) way, whereas Vaclav struggled with his desire for her to take charge of her illness and her life (in an internal-locus-of-control way). I worked in individual sessions to introduce doubt and complexity into the stereotyped way in which he understood his mother's behavior.

V: When I say something to her like, "I am happy that the surgery helped and that you will have some sort of a decent life," or, "Maybe this will clear up?" she will say, "I do not know, maybe not." Not that she was ever a positive person.

Dr. M: Do you think your mother is dying?

V: No, because I believe that if she really wanted to die, she probably would have. I think that she is getting weaker and weaker, and it is getting more difficult for her to be on her own. Is she dying? My sense is that she could be like this for many years.

Dr. M: I am trying to understand what you make out of her saying ["I do not know, maybe not"]. Is it her accepting that perhaps she is dying, or is it something else?

V: I don't know. I think it could be that she really thinks that she is getting weaker and may be dying.

Dr. M: And is more accepting of that than she used to be?

We also asked about any business that Vaclav felt was unfinished with his mother. Vaclav reported that, after tending to her through this latest and most serious physical crisis, he did not feel that anything important was left unsaid or undone. This labor of love seemed to have fulfilled some debt.

In a family session they both were able to discuss Mrs. Havlicek's inevitable death. In a touching exchange, Vaclav agreed to take his mother's ashes back to Czechoslovakia. In individual sessions with Vaclav we continued to work on his understanding of his mother.

V: Right. The other thing that I just can't get out of my mind is the martyr, the victim.

Dr. M: Do you think she is just posturing for you to feel sorry for her?

V: It is for me more than for anybody else. We all have a focus for our life, and I think the focus of my mother's life is this martyrdom. This is "me against the world." It is like this colostomy thing. Some people can make it the center of their life, and others just keep going on living. My theory is that she almost needs this [approach] for living.

Dr. M: It organizes her life. So it is real hard to tell [whether she's saying] something meaningful about her coming to accept that perhaps she is in the waning months or years of her life, or whether she is in her victim/martyr stance?

V: Of course. Whenever she [complains about] something, I think, well maybe I should check into it. [The hospital nurse] says "Don't worry about it. In my opinion, you do more for your mother than most people that I have come across."

We discussed Vaclav's need to know that he was doing enough for his mother and asked what relatives and friends from Czechoslovakia would expect. Fairly quickly, Vaclav came to believe that he was doing a good job as a son caring for his ill and elderly mother.

During this time, discussion about whether Mrs. Havlicek would go home or to a nursing home were frequent. It was finally decided to give it a try at home.

The first victory was that Mrs. Havlicek accepted the aides who came to her house to help her. She did not like them but, unlike previous times, she accepted them. She tapered her anxiolytic medication on her own and continued to feel less anxious but remained on the antidepressant to help with insomnia. Vaclav was attentive, in person and by phone, but it soon became clear that his mother should not live alone. Mrs. Havlicek suffered several falls at home. One fall in particular landed her back in the hospital for observation. She also was experiencing rectal bleeding and was having trouble changing and maintaining her colostomy bag. Vaclav complained about not understanding the details of his mother's medical condition. When I reported Vaclav's questions to Dr. Epstein, he replied to me via electronic mail:

> I spent a while talking with [Vaclav] on the phone. I have explained the medical stuff to him repeatedly. It is not complex. She has residual disease, and he has trouble hearing this information.
>
> She is now requesting to go to a nursing home. She feels too frightened at home, with reason. She is really too frail to live alone safely. I take this as a good development for her. She will do well, I think—it is him that I worry about now. Keep me posted.

This kind of collaboration is invaluable when a patient like Mrs. Havlicek is in transition from independent to assisted living and when family members like Vaclav are anxious because of it. (Anxiety frequently prevents patients and family members from hearing the details of the illness the first, second, or even third time.) Although we on the treatment team work in the same facility and probably discussed this case in person at least briefly once every week or two, electronic mail afforded us new opportunities for timely communication. This convenience factor also occurred to Vaclav. He wrote the following to Dr. Epstein, and copied it to me and Dr. Harkness, about the possibility of his mother's referral to a nursing home facility:

> I just had a call from my mother, saying that she feels very poorly, that she shakes [because of her] nerves, that she is afraid of falling. . . . She is complaining all the time about the aides, even though I asked her to look at it from my point of view—that I feel much better when someone checks on her. When you listen to her, you would think the aides are definitely [making] the situation worse. I am realizing every day, more and more, that her stay in a nursing home is as much important for me as it is for her. I feel right now, a pronounced heartburn (pressure in the middle of my chest). I did have somewhat spicy

> breakfast, but wonder whether it is not more related to the phone call.

Dr. Epstein responded via electronic mail:

> Perhaps when you get phone calls like that, take a deep breath and think about prior emergencies that were able to be resolved with the passing of time. Your instincts are right, but both you and she suffer the consequences of overreacting.

Vaclav responded: "My message earlier may have sounded urgent. She is better now, there were no accidents, and she was just complaining about things as she has been for many years. My heartburn is gone too."

Soon after these electronic-mail exchanges, Mrs. Havlicek moved to a nursing home, where she made a surprisingly quick adjustment. The treatment team there agreed that Mrs. Havlicek was probably relieved (as was Vaclav) to be in a place that was safe and where she could interact with more people. Several weeks after her move to a nursing home, Dr. Epstein left town for a year's sabbatical. Mrs. Havlicek was able to make the transition easily to an internist on the nursing home staff. Dr. Harkness attended her first case conference at the nursing home, with Vaclav. She continued to visit Mrs. Havlicek for the first few months of her transfer, writing in her chart and communicating with the nursing home staff.

Dr. Harkness

Working with Mrs. Havlicek was logistically challenging at times but ultimately rewarding. Several staff members, including a nurse practitioner and a psychiatrist, kept me fully informed about any changes in her mental status, helping to keep me up to date during the time of her initial adjustment. Even though these collaborators were not on site with me, we were able to form a team whose members relied on each other to help construct a more complete story and a comprehensive treatment plan.

When Mrs. Havlicek initially established residence in the nursing home, my job moved toward helping her to adjust to her room, the staff, and the idea that she was beginning to lose more and more independence. The closed system that she tried to maintain with Vaclav was no longer possible. In fact, the more she tried to withdraw and reject providers, the more they were concerned and paid attention to her. Her depressive symptoms waxed and waned, but each succeeding episode lessened in severity. I attribute much of this to the collaborative efforts of the nursing home staff, her son, and our psychotherapy.

Through our work together, Mrs. Havlicek was able to write a different story about growing old: a story where she was not scripted to die in a mental institution, a story different from what she had observed with her father. Our sessions also involved discussions about her relationship with Vaclav and how they could improve their relationship. In the beginning, she did not trust that what she taught him would be enough to protect him. I think she felt if she stopped being protective and watching over him closely, he would make bad decisions and ruin his life.

Over time, Mrs. Havlicek was able to accept the supportive services from the nursing home providers, leaving Vaclav to feel less responsible for her caregiving needs. Mrs. Havlicek and I continued to work individually together with the idea that someday my services, too, would be transferred to a nursing home staff member.

About 7 months after we first met, I attended a second case conference for Mrs. Havlicek at which we planned for her mental health needs (like her physical health needs) to be met by a nursing home staff social worker. At that meeting, staff members shared their observations of Mrs. Havlicek's overall positive adjustment. She had become an advocate for many residents in the home, voicing complaints about food preparation and reporting any disrespectful treatment. The staff concurred that she was doing well but were concerned that her mental health status still remained fragile. The decision was made to supervise her medications and to continue her biweekly therapy sessions with the newly appointed staff social worker. Toward the end of the meeting, a chair opened up at the end of the conference table, and I moved down for a better view. I had been sitting next to Mrs. Havlicek up until that point. When she realized I was no longer next to her, she

looked nervously around to find me but relaxed when I caught her eye and smiled. She spontaneously told the staff that she enjoyed our sessions because they helped relieve her frustrations—this, coming from the person who refused mental health involvement in the beginning. I knew at that point that she would be fine. She understood how and why mental health services could help her. I negotiated to visit her once more before turning her care over entirely. I was comfortable that she had successfully made the transition through surgery to the nursing home, improving her relationship with her son and even widening her social network.

Dr. McDaniel

Individual sessions with Vaclav took a new turn during this period. Each session began with an update on his mother and their relationship, about which he had increasing insight. In an electronic–mail note from this period, he wrote us about her complaints about nursing home staff:

> I try to listen and acknowledge the difficulties and encourage her to ask/tell people there. I know this whole thing sounds like a call for attention, something that happened many times in the past. I will call the social worker today and tell her this. I thought you should know too. It is interesting to realize that some characteristics of my writing to you are similar to my mother calling me.

And, like his mother, a little support and reassurance went a long way in these exchanges.

The balance of the sessions during this time did not focus on managing Vaclav's relationship with his mother; rather, we spent most of the time discussing the ways in which his relationship with his mother affected his relationships with other women. We learned that Vaclav was either attracted to a woman physically or emotionally and spiritually, but not both. As his view of his mother came into more realistic focus, he began to believe that perhaps he could find a female partner who more fully met his needs. As Dr. Harkness terminated her relationship with Mrs. Havlicek, we agreed that our work with Vaclav was also coming to an end. A family therapist functions like the mental health version of a family physician; Vaclav and his mother both know that we would remain available should the need arise.

TEAMWORK IN POSTMODERN HEALTH CARE

Returning to the goals of the consultation, we all feel satisfied about the work we did. The three of us provided support and information to each other in what was a very complex, multiproblem case. As a team we were able to support Mrs. Havlicek through her difficult surgery (which she initially vowed not to have), her adjustment to a nursing home (which she consistently stated she would refuse), her improved physical functioning (although her survival was in serious doubt prior to surgery), her improved mental status (although her paranoia and depression are never entirely absent), and her improved social functioning (which also seemed in serious doubt prior to surgery).

An important part of every medical consultation is providing information that will shape or change the referring physician's view of the patient, especially when that patient is viewed as problematic. In this case, Dr. Epstein progressed in his view of Mrs. Havlicek from describing her as "difficult and noncompliant" to "a person traumatized and confused by cultural transition" to "someone with an inadequate support system" to, finally, "an intelligent person faced with difficult choices."

In addition, the relationship between Vaclav and his mother matured. He no longer seems resentful of the care he provides for his mother; he sees her twice a week at regular times, and he calls her in the interim. For her part, Mrs. Havlicek expresses confidence in her son's ability to have a successful life, although of course she reserves the right to evaluate any major decisions. Perhaps one of the most telling signs of differentiation at this point is Vaclav's increasing desire to have a serious, committed relationship with a woman ("I want a life partner."). It is as if his mother has assumed her rightful place in his life, and now there is room for a full relationship with a peer.

We now have terminated family therapy with both Vaclav and Mrs. Havlicek, with the understanding that they (or their health care team) are welcome to consult again. Two points in time may make this likely: when Vaclav does become serious with a woman and wants to work on intimacy directly, and perhaps when Mrs. Havlicek dies. Although the former seems likely, the latter may be unnecessary as both Vaclav and Mrs. Havlicek have confronted this issue, which was so threatening when we began our work together.

So many patients, like Mrs. Havlicek and Vaclav, have complex biopsychosocial problems that demand a team approach. Medical family therapy requires flexibility and collaboration with the patient, the family, and the other providers, whether they be a primary-care physician, a surgeon, or the head nurse at a nursing home. A fully systemic approach conforms to a particular patient's and family's needs. More time and energy early in treatment often mean briefer and more comprehensive therapy in the long term. It also means increased agency and communion for the patient, the family and, not incidentally for us, the health care team itself.

References

Engel, G. (1977). The need for a new medical model: A challenge for biomedicine. *Science, 196,* 129–136.

Epstein, R. M., Morse, D. S., Williams, G. C., le Roux, P., Suchman, A. L., & Quill, T. (in press). Clinical practice and the biopsychosocial model. In R. M. Frankel, R. E. Quill, & S. H. McDaniel (Eds.), *The biopsychosocial model.* Rochester, NY: University of Rochester Press.

McDaniel, S. H., Campbell, T. L., & Seaburn, D. M. (1990). *Family-oriented primary care: A manual for medical providers.* New York: Springer-Verlag.

McDaniel, S. H., Hepworth, J., & Doherty, W. J. (1992). *Medical family therapy: A biopsychosocial approach to families with health problems.* New York: Basic Books.

McDaniel, S. H., Hepworth, J., & Doherty, W. J. (1995). Medical family therapy with somatizing families. In R. H. Mikesell, D-D. Lusterman, & S. H. McDaniel (Eds.), *Integrating family therapy: Handbook of family psychology and systems theory* (pp. 377–388). Washington, DC: American Psychological Association.

McDaniel, S. H., Hepworth, J., & Doherty, W. J. (1997). *The shared experience of illness: Stories of patients, families and their therapists.* New York: Basic Books.

CHAPTER 28

HIV/AIDS, FAMILIES, AND THE WIDER CAREGIVING SYSTEM

Robert Bor and Riva Miller

How does a therapist respond to the presentation of an entirely new problem? HIV provides an interesting contemporary example of how therapists have come to define and redefine their role when working with chronically ill people, their families, and other professional caregivers. The problem associated with HIV infection, however, places therapists in double jeopardy. Not only do they have to work with a disease, but also issues that arise in therapy sessions may be as personally relevant for the therapists as they are for the patients. These include issues about sex and sexuality, drug use, secrecy, death, loss, and personal risk taking, among others. A therapist's professionalism may not offer immunity or solace from these sometimes-painful issues. In this chapter we describe how, as therapists, we have applied systemic thinking to the development of a hospital-based therapy service and have attempted to respond to some of the complex psychological issues of patients and how this work has affected our relationship. It also describes how working in this field has changed our practice.

The most obvious initial problem when a therapist is faced with an unfamiliar clinical problem is whether to use an established and well-documented approach to therapy and the problem or to improvise and try different approaches. The dilemma is most often resolved by combining both in a unique blend of established theory and idiosyncratic and innovative practice. The advent of HIV infection in the early 1980s is no exception. Therapists working in both medical and nonmedical settings are at the forefront of caregiving and patient management. HIV

infection provides an interesting contemporary example of how therapists have come to define and redefine their role when working with chronically ill people, their families, and with other professional caregivers.

Our clinical practice and research in this area over the past 15 years have focused on how HIV infection affects families and the impact of HIV infection in the therapeutic practice. The term *AIDS* was used in the early years to describe a stage of illness when the immune system was compromised and illnesses such as pneumonia developed. The main focus of this chapter is on the social context in which HIV infection emerged and the developments in therapy at the time when AIDS first became a medical and social problem. We have also examined the challenges faced by therapists, which include dilemmas about (a) patient confidentiality in the light of public health concerns; (b) whether and how to give information about risk-taking behavior, HIV tests, and treatment; (c) how to work effectively with gay men and with same-sex couples, a community that historically has had a difficult relationship with mental health services and that may not easily recognize how "family" therapy can benefit them; and (d) an increasing number of areas in which there is underdeveloped training, such as helping parents cope with the loss of a child, examining cultural factors that affect beliefs as well as both medical and psychological care, working with families and within systems in which significant secrets prevail, and responding to the "roller coaster effect" on patients who are encouraged by the advent of new medical treatments but who then later lose hope and expectation in the face of new setbacks.

OUR BACKGROUND, TRAINING, AND WORK CONTEXT

Our respective specialist trainings in family therapy in the late 1970s and early 1980s reflect the dominant approaches and style of practice at the time. Family therapy in the United Kingdom at the time was taught according to the grand models or theories (structural, strategic, or systemic), and the range of family issues with which we worked in live supervision mostly related to the standard mental health problems that affected individual members. Family therapists at that time also worked almost exclusively in mental health settings. It was no coincidence, therefore, that when AIDS was first described in the medical literature in 1981 few family therapists were well placed to work with affected families and their professional and nonprofessional caregivers. However, family therapists did not necessarily shun professional work with people with HIV infection in the 1980s because of apparent homophobia. Our articles were readily published in peer-reviewed journals; many colleagues came to train with us, enhancing our ideas and skills; and we were invited to workshops by family therapists in the United Kingdom and abroad to share our experience with seasoned practitioners, suggesting strong interest in the problem. However, because family therapists had done little until then to develop links within the gay and lesbian community and to develop collaborative approaches to therapy in health care settings, it was another 10 years before family therapists worked more intensively with families affected by HIV infection and in health care settings.

There are many different and complex strands to our own professional relationship that have enhanced our work with the problems and issues brought about by HIV/AIDS. As two therapists, we were an "unlikely couple" to come together because of the differences in our ages, gender, professional backgrounds, and career stages. At the time we came together, Riva Miller was a social worker and family therapist working at the Royal Free Hospital Haemophilia Unit, and Robert Bor was a clinical psychologist who had recently completed his family therapy training. We recognized in one another an ability to deal with high levels of uncertainty and unpredictability as well as a willingness to take risks and seize opportunities.

The Milan systemic approach was especially relevant to our practice in the early 1980s because we were required in our work setting—a London teaching hospital—to be able to teach other health care workers an approach to therapy that had a clear structure. Most approaches to therapy in health care settings at that time focused on the issues for individuals. However, it was no coincidence that we were both attracted to the Milan systemic approach, because we are both inherently curious about how people cope with problems and adversity; how beliefs inform people's actions, and therefore their relationships; and we do not have a drive to actively rescue people and solve their problems. Second-order cybernetics and the narrative approach seemed natural and fitting conceptual frameworks for our own ideas about therapy and clinical practice. Riva had worked for many years introducing systemic ideas into a traditional doctor-led health care system. Robert came from a medical family background and felt compelled to apply systemic ideas to a health care setting. The stage was set for a creative and industrious partnership, and we quickly set about establishing a hospital-based systemic therapy service for people affected by HIV infection.

We drew extensively on systemic theory and techniques when planning and developing the service. There were many challenges and potential obstacles from clinicians and health service managers that forced us to think beyond our training and experience. Health service managers were afraid that a comprehensive HIV infection service might draw resources away from other high-cost specialties, such as the liver transplant unit, nephrology, and hemophilia, at a time when budgets in the health service industry were being cut. We took a "one down" position and visited every medical team and specialty in the hospital to learn about their needs and expectations of an HIV counseling and therapy service. In so doing we were also able to identify other colleagues who might help and support our work. Above all, we learned to be patient and to wait until the hospital system was ready for the service to start.

It was a clear choice not to have our HIV service as part of the existing psychology, social work, or sexually transmitted diseases clinics, although this also meant that we were more vulnerable and had to contend with a level of interprofessional rivalry. We made a policy that everyone referred to us had to be under the care of a doctor, which also meant that we were required to collaborate and consult with practically every medical specialty and unit in the hospital. This had clear advantages in terms of securing our position in the hospital. We rapidly developed an approach to joint patient consultations that included one of us and usually a doctor or nurse working with the patient. This was a rare departure from the more traditional and dominant medical model of practice in the United Kingdom, which tended to be hierarchical and doctor led. However, it proved to be a highly significant intervention and helped demystify the therapeutic process and share responsibility and knowledge of therapeutic skills, and it also taught us an enormous amount about the medical aspects of HIV and the process of medical consultations.

The development of a same-day HIV test and result service was a further innovation that we pioneered, and an evaluation of it was published in the *British Medical Journal* and was to set a benchmark against which other HIV testing services in the United Kingdom could be evaluated. On the basis of this testing service, a specialist HIV physician and, subsequently, a comprehensive multidisciplinary team, was appointed to work with the infected patient. As systemic thinkers and therapists, and having knowledge of some of the complex psychological, social, and ethical issues surrounding HIV care, we also participated in lively and sometimes fiery debates about patient confidentiality, public health concerns, HIV testing policies, and care protocols. Sometimes we were challenging; at other times we were curious, or played devil's advocate (we were also silent at times) and posed circular, hypothetical, and future-oriented questions to one another, to our colleagues, and to ourselves about these issues. On occasion we would reflect the difference in views by each taking opposing positions in meetings, as one

might do when faced with a couple who disagree but have equally tenable positions. We also had to step back and let events happen that we might have wanted to prevent. For example, when a physician decided to carry out an HIV test on a patient without first obtaining the patient's consent we helped him to give the result to the patient and hoped that the demands of the experience would lead to better practice with other patients in the future. It was through working together, consulting with one another, debating, and sometimes disagreeing that helped us to think about such situations and to support one another's decisions.

We have worked with more than 1,000 individuals and families affected by HIV over the past 15 years. Because each patient or family has presented with unique and specific issues, we have always sought to avoid working with families in a predictable way or relying on a limited range of ideas and skills. Readers who are interested in learning more about our application of systemic ideas to the problem of HIV might read some of our work that has been published elsewhere (e.g., Bor & Elford, 1994, 1998; Bor & Miller, 1991; Bor, Miller, & Goldman, 1992; Miller & Bor, 1988).

CASE STUDY

The case that follows is not necessarily typical of those we see in practice, because there does not appear to be a "typical case" in this field. However, it does illustrate a number of applications of our ideas and raises issues about therapy, which are certainly debatable and possibly contentious. The patient and his family described in this case might have never come for therapy if HIV had not become a problem for them. Events and processes challenged the dynamics of relationships in the family at different stages of the patient's illness. Themes of protection and control of one family member by another emerged in therapy sessions. The perturbations caused in this family system by HIV included coping with a child dying before his parents, accepting the consequences and conflicts of an alternative lifestyle in a conventional family, managing the disruptions caused by entrenched patterns of communication, and dealing with secrets. The main feature of our approach is to respond to the main concerns and needs of the patient in the face of illness rather than responding to predetermined ideas about helping people who confront serious health problems. This may be an elementary point for most readers, but experience has taught us to acknowledge and identify at an early stage beliefs in ourselves, our patients, their families, and professional caregivers that may constrain progress in therapy (Wright, Watson, & Bell, 1996). This case was enormously complex, and at times personally distressing. Consultation with one another helped us to maintain clarity, direction, and confidence.

Conrad's Diagnosis With HIV

Conrad, age 33 and gay, sought an HIV test through our hospital because he suspected that he was infected with HIV. Over the previous year he had noticed symptoms that he connected with HIV. Conrad recognized his risk for HIV as being high because he had been a sex worker who had had unprotected anal intercourse with other men in the past. The problem that first brought him into contact with a psychologist (Robert) was a needle phobia that had to be overcome in order to have a blood sample taken for an HIV test. Because he had a background in clinical psychology and expertise in cognitive–behavioral therapy, his doctor referred him for counseling to help reduce his anxiety in order for testing to proceed. The test result confirmed that Conrad had indeed been infected with HIV, a result he had anticipated.

The next few months were characterized by a period of adjustment. Conrad was determined to look on the bright side and to be optimistic about his prognosis, and he declined professional support or therapy from us. This presented us with our first significant problem, because one of the doctors with whom we worked was insistent that newly diagnosed patients require intensive psychological support. She was concerned that Conrad might lapse into a depression and might be inclined to have unprotected sex with clients or other sexual partners. The dilemma for us as therapists was that the patient had not asked for help, neither had he identified a problem for himself, and yet one part of his professional care system felt that he ought to be in

therapy. We partly resolved this dilemma by working closely with the doctor and sharing our own concerns about working with a patient who probably did not want to enter therapy and who might prove resistant. We also recognized the doctor's legitimate public health concerns and were able to "downgrade" our therapy to brief counseling. We told Conrad that, as a routine, all newly diagnosed patients were offered health-promoting counseling that covered issues as diverse as stress management and relaxation, diet, financial and life insurance advice, as well as information about safe sex and the free provision of condoms. The effect of Conrad's attendance at several counseling sessions was that the doctor felt reassured that we were "keeping an eye on him." It also enabled Conrad to meet with a counselor without him feeling pathologized because he was seeing a therapist, which is a central tenet of our therapeutic approach.

Conrad's Admission to the Hospital

Six months after his diagnosis, on Christmas Eve, Conrad was admitted to the hospital with an acute lung infection. His original therapist was on leave at the time. Consequently, when Conrad asked to see a therapist because of his anxiety about what to tell his elderly parents about his hospital admission, he was seen by Riva, who was on call to the inpatient team. Until his admission to the hospital, Conrad had chosen not to tell his parents about his diagnosis of HIV because he believed that the news might "kill" them. They knew he was gay and that he was running a successful male escort agency, but he had never discussed HIV with them. He told Riva that his need to preserve a secret about his health was that he did not want to be viewed by his parents as the son who let them down. To compensate for this, he had provided them with financial assistance to give them the lifestyle they would not have had without his support. The family was expecting to spend Christmas Day together. After his bedside therapy session, Conrad decided to keep the secret of HIV from his parents, but he told his younger brother Thomas so that Thomas could attend to Conrad's business affairs. Conrad also informed his married sister Anne.

Conrad enlisted Thomas's support in corroborating a story for his parents that Conrad was going on a vacation. Thomas's concern about the immediate crisis over Conrad's health forced him to respect Conrad's wishes about keeping information from their parents. Riva recognized the attendant problems brought about by secrets at times of serious illness and anticipated that Thomas may become stressed by having to maintain secrets within the family. Use of hypothetical and circular questions about disclosure in the session helped Conrad to consider the consequences of secrecy within the family, and on Thomas in particular, especially in view of Conrad's deteriorating health (see Bor et al., 1992). For example,

- What effect do you think it will have on Thomas that he knows something about you that he cannot tell your parents?
- What might help Thomas keep the secret?
- What would have to happen to you for you to tell your parents?
- How long would you want Thomas to keep the secret?
- What reaction from your parents would you fear the most if they were to find out?

The intention behind the last two questions was to help Conrad think about when and how he might disclose his HIV infection to his parents and to identify his main concerns for himself and his parents if they were to know about his diagnosis. Conrad decided to disclose his HIV status to his parents 2 weeks after being discharged from hospital, although he chose not to tell them that the doctors had started to use the term *AIDS* in view of his lung infection. He was determined not to let them see him in poor health or vulnerable and, consequently, he waited until he was over this opportunistic infection.

Conrad's Parents Become Involved

Soon after disclosure of his infection to his parents, Conrad again sought help through therapy. His opening statement to Riva was "HIV is not a problem for me, but supporting and counseling my parents is a burden I can do without." He maintained that he was coping well and wanted Riva to see his parents without him. He sought to protect his

mother, in particular, from the reality of his situation—that of declining health and early death. He wanted Riva to inform his parents about his AIDS diagnosis but to keep them optimistic and hopeful. He feared that increasing his mother's worry about his health would escalate the number of telephone calls she made inquiring about him. He viewed these calls as intrusive and disturbing because they increased his feelings of impotence about placating her worries.

The diagnosis of AIDS, made at the end of his recent hospital admission, compelled Conrad to ask for help, threatening his view of himself as coping with HIV and controlling communication between himself and his parents. Conrad found a way to resume control by arranging the appointment, bringing his parents to the hospital, and introducing them to Riva. He then left his parents with her.

The initial dilemmas for Riva were twofold. The first dilemma was how to respond realistically to questions about Conrad's prognosis without giving his parents the "bad news." The second dilemma was whether to encourage Conrad to attend sessions with his parents or to comply with his wish for them to be seen separately. Seeing the family together would enable everyone to express and hear each others' views, which might not be possible in conversation outside session. However, allowing Conrad to feel he could control the closeness and distance of relationships was deemed at that time to be more important than seeing him with his family. A considered decision was made to see the "family" as they presented. By using a systemic approach, some interventions could be made that helped prepare the family for Conrad's death without breaching confidentiality.

On the first occasion when Conrad brought his parents to the session, Riva clarified with Conrad, his parents, and his siblings that no medical or other details about Conrad would be given without him being present. Details of separate meetings with Conrad or the family would remain confidential, although HIV infection in general could be discussed. This statement helped to engage the family members and preserved some neutrality. It was possible to elicit from the parents what they considered to be Conrad's main concerns or worries and how their concerns might affect their relationship with him and with their other children.

Conrad's parents were seen on their own four times, twice with Conrad's sister and brother and twice with Conrad. Like Conrad, his parents were ambivalent. They wanted to know about his prognosis while at the same time not wanting to know the reality, thereby protecting themselves and each other from the full implications of Conrad's rapidly deteriorating health. The main task for Riva was identified as helping Conrad and his family keep the fine balance between maintaining hope and living as well as possible within the realities of his life-threatening condition.

Despite describing themselves as a "close family," they had communication difficulties, because each tried to protect himself or herself and others from the reality of AIDS by not talking about it. An aim of therapy was to help the different members of the family talk to each other about painful and seemingly unspeakable issues about loss and even where Conrad wanted to be buried.

After a few sessions alone with the parents, the fine balance of family interactions had been upset. As Conrad's parents appeared to become closer to Riva, or perhaps as Conrad felt excluded from the therapy sessions, he conveyed that there was "nothing more" that Riva could do for his parents. In this way he controlled the interaction between Riva and his parents. The previous patterns of control were resumed by Conrad also restricting his parents' telephone calls and visits to him. They acquiesced to these requests, which in turn protected Conrad from having to face his mother's disapproval of his lifestyle and disappointment that he would not fulfill her wish for grandchildren. Conrad's father kept control of his emotions to protect himself and Conrad from getting too close and risking discussions about his sexuality that might have implications for both of them. Conrad also wanted his father to accept the reality of his being gay by acknowledging that his partner James was his lover and not just a friend.

As Conrad's health deteriorated, he asked for support for himself for the first time. He was seen on one occasion, and he clearly stated that his main concern was that he could become physically and mentally dependent on others. This was very hard for him, as he had been successfully independent since age 13. Ways that he could still manage to keep control were discussed.

Soon after this session, Conrad was admitted to hospital with a serious eye condition that was a precursor to losing his sight. Once again he was quite clear that the help he wanted was for Riva to deal with his parents' panic. It was more difficult to help him to discuss his own anxiety about becoming blind; throughout his main concern was his parents and the threat of dependency on others. Some hypothetical future-oriented questions were used to help him address these two issues:

- Which things would be easiest, and which most difficult, for you if you had to depend on your partner James?
- How might you deal with those that are the most difficult?
- What images would you want to remember of your relationship with your parents and siblings?
- What, if any, issues do you feel need to be dealt with for you to feel more settled?

During this hospital admission, after this meeting, Conrad arranged to meet his parents in Riva's office rather than in the ward. This was to protect them from seeing other patients who were dying of AIDS. Riva, in turn, took the opportunity to suggest to Conrad that he join her in a meeting with his parents for a brief time to enable them to discuss issues of concern to all of them. The challenges for Riva again were twofold. The first dilemma was how to balance the realities of Conrad's situation with some hope for the future of the family; the second was how to allow Conrad and the family to control how they wanted to be seen and how much they wanted to talk to each other. Themes of protection and control emerged early in the session. Conrad's injunctions to keep his parents "informed" about his health were a protection for himself and his parents. Riva took her clues from this and always aimed to find a way to enable them to say what they wanted but not to push them to confront issues they did not wish to confront. Conrad was able to say in this session what he wanted for his funeral and that he wanted his partner James there and involved. He also said he wanted no tears. His parents, although initially upset, were able to say what their difficulties were. One was which priest to approach. Conrad helped by indicating the one he wanted. His father was able to say how difficult he found it to view James as Conrad's partner and always referred to him as his "friend."

These were the only issues discussed in the presence of Riva, who decided at that point to leave the family together and to be without her. This was the last contact as a family with Riva.

Conrad's death some days later presented an opportunity for ongoing bereavement therapy for the family, which took place over 6 months. Conrad's death marked not the end of the problem but rather a new stage in the process.

The family already trusted and had a relationship with Riva. It was especially important to them in the early days after Conrad's death to be able to talk freely to her. They lived in a small village and were very concerned that neither of them could talk freely to anyone in the community about the cause of his death. Some of the sessions were spent discussing how Conrad's death affected each of them individually and the family as a whole. The challenge once again was to help them have hope for the future and to be able to express their thoughts. They all said that Conrad's death had brought them closer together. Once they had been able to say that his death, after all the months of suffering, was a relief, the space between sessions became longer, and Riva knew it was time to help them to cut off from the hospital and that part of their experience.

The role of Riva in working with the medical and nursing staff was particularly important. Riva initially took the extreme stress about needles away from the team and dealt with Conrad, enabling him to have his blood test and to be helped into a position of receiving the monitoring and treatment he needed. Conrad's self-confident, optimistic attitude made it difficult for the medical and nursing staff to address the more difficult issues about his deteriorating health and eyesight. Regular meetings with the HIV team reporting on how issues were raised and addressed with Conrad helped to relieve some anxiety for the medical team. Dealing with the family meant that when they visited the nurses knew

that some of their concerns were being addressed and avoided the problems they had about tensions that might occur among Conrad, his parents, and James. Another dilemma raised was how best to maintain patient confidentiality as the team members were unsure who knew what about Conrad. Riva helped the medical and nursing staff to respond in a general way to information sought about Conrad and to enable them to ask of Conrad the questions that could not be answered by other health care workers.

A theme throughout the case was how to deal with Conrad's requests for Riva to deal with his parents' questions about his HIV and prognosis. Once the hypothesis had been made that control was an important theme in the family, interventions were made accordingly. Riva was clear that she would respond in a general way and help the parents ask Conrad the questions to which they wanted answers. Because they rarely did ask him, it was assumed that they did not really want to know. Riva was quite clear that because Conrad was going to die at some point, she was willing to deal with the family as they presented, always knowing that the bereavement work would start from the first contact. Being triangled by the wishes of Conrad and those of the parents was not an issue, because the aim was clear from the start. HIV at that time (i.e., in the 1980s) was a life-threatening condition, and the treatments had not yet affected prognoses as they do now, in 2001.

HOW OUR EXPERIENCE HAS CHANGED OUR PRACTICE

This case illustrates how new problems are revealed at different stages of illness and how the wider system (family and health care providers) is directly involved in therapy, even if they are not physically present in sessions. At some stage, our work included sessions with the patient on his own, with him and his brother, with his parents, and with the whole family. Sometimes, other professional caregivers also were present in sessions, to promote collaboration and share skills. This more flexible approach to working with the patient system is a significant departure from, and expectation in, some family therapy (and psychotherapy) approaches to remain inflexible about who attends sessions and the frequency with which sessions are held. It also points to the need for improvisation on the part of the therapist, who might inadvertently fail to address and respond to the patient's needs by indicating to the patient what he or she should do to solve his or her problems. A related issue is that in this case, at the beginning of contact with the patient, therapy was relabeled "counseling" in order to engage the patient and to acknowledge that he might not have had a psychological problem requiring specialist help.

How has our work with people affected by HIV infection influenced our therapeutic style and our view of therapy? It is difficult to separate the influence of clinical work from the influence of changes in our work setting on the delivery of health care and the dynamics within our own work relationship. The theory and repertoire of skills conveyed to us in our initial training as a psychologist, a medical social worker, and as family therapists are now infinitely broader and probably less tightly constrained than within the single unifying Milan systemic conceptual framework. HIV infection is a problem of great complexity, and we cannot afford to offer a single "labeled brand" of therapy for every problem, although applying a systemic framework through which to view our practice has proved invaluable.

Some readers may feel that Conrad's drive to control relationships and therefore distressing feelings that accompany loss resulted in Riva's being triangled in by him. This problem was extensively discussed between the therapists and presented us with an ongoing dilemma. On the one hand, we recognized that, as an individual facing a terminal disease, Conrad needed to find ways to cope and maintain a sense of control over his life. On the other hand, the extent to which Conrad used this coping strategy interfered with the caring and grieving process for all involved. Our response to the dilemma was to acknowledge that, providing we were not asked to deceive or cause harm to anyone, we would have to respect the wishes of the patient. At the same time, we had a duty to point out to him the potential consequences of some of his actions. We also shared with Conrad our concerns that we

sometimes felt triangled in by him. We pointed out that if his relatives had inaccurate information about the stage of his illness, they might not be able to provide care in a way that they might choose and that this in turn may influence their feelings and relationship with him. One consequence of Conrad's need to exercise control, we acknowledged, was that he may have wanted to protect himself from painful feelings, although he was certainly aware that the effect of his death on his relatives may have led to a complicated grief reaction. As therapists, we acknowledged to ourselves that in most situations we can only highlight dilemmas or illuminate specific problems; we cannot coerce patients into arriving at what we believe to be the "right" or "better" solutions.

So much that is published in the psychotherapy literature describes what therapists "do" to their patients to treat them. The loop is seldom closed, and we hear little about how therapists' experience changes their practice. Working with multiple systems, at different levels within systems, and with the range of problems highlighted in this chapter has significantly broadened and enriched our approach and reflects the dialectical relationship that exists (or should exist) between theory and practice. Our practice has recently shifted from a model of therapeutic intervention to one of consultation and collaboration. Although second-order cybernetics continues to underpin our current approach in therapy, we address many other concepts and dimensions within our framework. In particular, these include issues about attachment, context, attending to biopsychosocial processes, illness benefits, the typology of illness, gender, sexuality, and time and timing in therapy, among many others (see Bor, Miller, Latz, & Salt, 1998). The emphasis in session is on narrative and storytelling, although we have not lost sight of some useful skills in cognitive–behavioral interventions. This suggests a more integrative approach, which is a pragmatic response to our context and specialist problems. Our approach is less technique driven and more democratic. Patients are invited to play an active part in treatment and care. We invite feedback about progress, openly display our uncertainties and, where relevant, our ignorance. We even share feelings we may have about issues, although we take care not to reverse the role in session by imposing onto the client our own needs.

The consultative approach can be unsettling for people who are more accustomed to traditional forms of therapy. However, it reduces our stress by sharing responsibility with the patient and others. Having to confront the deaths of many of our patients (and sometimes, too, multiple members of a family) has necessitated our finding of emotional space and rituals for coping with these losses. Our own relationship has been sustaining at these times because we were able to express feelings about loss and feel supported by a combination of both a personal and sometimes a professional response from one another. This has helped us to cope with loss and to reach a more balanced perspective of the patients and work we have done with them. It has also helped us to prepare for grief work with the surviving family members when this has been requested.

Engaging in teaching and research has helped reflect on our approach and methods and mitigated against feelings of burnout when the emotional pressure of the work has been intense. At times, the activities or rituals enabled us to reflect on some of the intense emotional situations that confronted us. The activity of writing and teaching also served to clarify and develop our ideas about therapy. Our teaching approach was mostly systemic; it involved both of us, and we used process to convey many of the issues we wanted to teach rather than presenting material in a linear and didactic fashion. We did not always agree on ideas, but our differences in viewpoint were a challenge rather than a threat to our relationship.

Three dominant ideas stand out most when we look back at some of what we have practiced and written about. These include our approach to talking to patients about "dreaded issues" or their greatest fears, reframing and rebalancing problems and situations that might appear hopeless, and developing a collaborative and contextually sensitive approach to therapy that could be applied to most health care problems and in most health care settings (see Bor et al., 1998).

Encountering blocks or periods of "stuckness" in our work has encouraged us to be creative, to use humor, and even to dabble in the absurd. We recognize that we have been a resource for one another; our collaborative approach with Conrad, his family, and his health care team is but one example. Our work within the wider hospital system to develop the therapy service was equally important and certainly no less challenging. Even though we now work in different settings and are at different stages of our careers, we still come together over difficult or challenging problems and help to refresh one another with ideas when work takes it toll. We share a belief that opportunities are created out of obstacles.

The experience of working with families facing a life-threatening illness in a hospital setting has enriched us in a number of ways. The first is the recognition that we all have the potential to convey a message of hope through therapy and a conviction that everyone can find a positive aspect to his or her life even when facing illness and death. The second has been the application of our approach and ideas to other health care problems and in other systems, because our work with families affected by HIV/AIDS has been adapted to helping people with other chronic health conditions. Last, our own work relationship has not only endured but been strengthened after 15 years of collaboration. The old adage of "two heads are better than one" was a fitting one for our work. It is now difficult to imagine safe, challenging, creative, and effective practice without the relationship of a close colleague at work. We maintain balance between our individual interests and situations for which we feel a need to collaborate or consult with one another. The experience of working with people affected by HIV infection reminds us not only of the fragility of life but also of the strength we gain from relationships. This in turn helps all of us to cope with and adjust to the unexpected.

References

Bor, R., & Elford, J. (Eds.). (1994). *The family and HIV*. London: Cassell.

Bor, R., & Elford, J. (Eds.). (1998). *The family and HIV today*. London: Cassell.

Bor, R., & Miller, R. (1991). *Internal consultations in health care settings*. London: Karnac Books.

Bor, R., Miller, R., & Goldman, E. (1992). *Theory and practice of HIV counselling*. London: Cassell.

Bor, R., Miller, R., Latz, M., & Salt, H. (1998). *Counseling in health care settings*. London: Cassell.

Miller, R., & Bor, R. (1988). *AIDS: A guide to clinical counselling*. London: Science Press.

Wright, L., Watson, W., & Bell, J. (1996). *Beliefs: The heart of healing in families and illness*. New York: Basic Books.

PART VI

FAMILIES COPING WITH SERIOUS MENTAL ILLNESS

FROM THREE LANGUAGES TO ONE: INTEGRATING INDIVIDUAL, FAMILY, AND BIOLOGICAL PERSPECTIVES IN THE TREATMENT OF AFFECTIVE DISORDERS

David A. Moltz

It may be, for instance, that professionals change more than patients or families when using these techniques. (Anderson et al., 1986, p. 201)

It is only in retrospect that change is experienced as occurring at a particular moment; in reality, it happens slowly, incrementally, and obscurely. However, as we look back and construct a coherent story of our development, certain events stand out as milestones along the way.

THE PROJECT

I was very fortunate in the circumstances of my psychiatric training. Although my residency program was known for its strong psychoanalytic orientation, the founding director had just retired. While the program's psychodynamic orientation remained and I got a strong grounding in individual psychotherapy, other possibilities became available as well. At the time (the early 1970s), psychiatry was at the beginning of its return to medicine and biology. As residents we read R. D. Laing, but we also learned psychopharmacology, and the third edition of the *Diagnostic and Statistical Manual of Mental Disorders* was on the horizon. At the same time, family therapy was in the early stages of development and had all the fervor, excitement, and promise of a revolutionary approach to change. My training occurred at the convergence of these three approaches to understanding human behavior and change: the individ-

ual, the biological, and the family. I was offered three different lenses to look through and three different languages to describe what I saw. I spent years trying to integrate these languages, to develop a model for working that would allow me to use all three.

Six years after finishing my residency I pursued formal training in structural family therapy at the Philadelphia Child Guidance Clinic, under Salvador Minuchin. This training was helpful to me in my project of integration. Family therapy provided a way to look at problems from a perspective larger than the individual and allowed more options for facilitating change. It was a powerful and exciting expansion of possibility. However, this widening of view was at the expense of the individual perspective. Individual issues were seen as the expression of problems in family structure, and change occurred through identifying, and intervening to correct, these structural issues. And if the perspective of the individual was downplayed, biology was not addressed at all.

In 1981, fresh from this training, I went to a conference organized by William McFarlane, a colleague and friend.[1] He brought together a group of researchers who were developing what together became known as "psychoeducational" approaches to the treatment of schizophrenia. These approaches were of interest to me because they started from an understanding of mental illness as biologically based and then used this model to join with the family

---

[1] The proceedings of that conference can be found in McFarlane's (1983) book, *Family Therapy in Schizophrenia.*

and the individual as allies against the illness. The goal was not to fix the family but to help them in their efforts to cope more effectively with the illness. In what to me was a startling innovation, the conference program also included representatives of families from the newly formed National Alliance for the Mentally Ill. Agnes Hatfield, one of the leaders of the family advocacy movement, spoke about the family's perspective on schizophrenia and its treatment. She described how family members consistently felt blamed by mental health professionals, how they were made to feel responsible for the illness. Then she said that of all therapists, family therapists were the worst in this regard. This was a clarifying moment for me. I saw family therapy as the way to the future, a radical redefinition of ideas of causation and of change. It was shocking to hear that family approaches were guilty of the same sins as individual therapy, only more so; but as soon as she said it I knew that she was right. Family therapy as generally practiced removed the blame for the problem from the individual and placed it squarely on the family.

Psychoeducation seemed a promising direction for my interest in integrating biological, individual, and family approaches. It offered a way to accommodate multiple realities: A biological illness affected an individual who was part of a family, which was affected as well. Also, there was room in the model for intervening at all those levels. Most important, there was an absence of blame: The illness, not the individual or the family, was responsible for the problems.

There was a refreshing modesty to these approaches: After watching the videotapes of master therapists transforming families with their interventions and learning the strategic and paradoxical family approaches, with their metaphors of struggle and battle, the idea of approaching families as a consultant, an ally, was very refreshing. Compared to the structural approach, this was a boring therapy, without fireworks, actually not "therapy" at all, but more

and more evidence showed that it worked. People with schizophrenia had significantly fewer relapses and hospitalizations when they and their families were engaged in these ways (Anderson, 1983; Falloon & Liberman, 1983; Kopeikin, Marshall, & Goldstein, 1983).

In the past few years I had become interested in bipolar illness and had already done some work with families with this condition (Moltz, 1991). Affective disorders seemed to be especially perplexing to families and to pose particular challenges that were different from those of schizophrenia. Soon after this conference I saw a notice for a course being given at the local medical school on psychoeducational approaches to bipolar disorder. A psychiatrist named Demitri Papolos had developed a five-session psychoeducational model that focused on discussing the family's and the individual's experience of the illness and teaching them about medical aspects of the condition.[2] As part of the course, participants were expected to videotape their work with a family, using this model.

THE FAMILY

I signed up for the course, and I decided to ask the Ferrer[3] family to participate in my "demonstration" interviews. Lydia Ferrer was a 42-year-old woman in the middle of a severe depression, who was being treated at the mental health center where I worked. As the psychiatrist on her treatment team, I knew that she had four adult children and a sister who were all very involved with her, and I thought that the family could benefit from this approach. In addition, there were aspects of Lydia's case that were puzzling to me that I wanted to explore.

For one thing, there was the question of etiology. Many aspects of Lydia's depression pointed to a biological illness. She experienced the depression, her second serious one, as having come out of nowhere, with no apparent precipitant. She had classic symptoms, such as insomnia, anorexia, loss of interest in

---

[2] Dr. Papolos has since coauthored a book on affective disorders that is an excellent resource for individuals and their families (Papolos & Papolos, 1997).

[3] The names and identifying characteristics of family members have been changed. Aspects of my work with this family have previously been published (Moltz, 1993).

her usual activities, social withdrawal, and suicidal impulses, and these were very different from her usual functioning. Both of her severe depressions, and the many milder depressions that preceded them, occurred at the same time of year, from December to March, suggesting a biologically based seasonal cycling.

However, there were psychosocial factors that complicated this view. The first serious episode, 2 years before, occurred soon after Lydia separated from her husband of 24 years because of his alcoholism and physical abuse. It was tempting to hypothesize that the depression was a reaction to her separation and to the stresses of life on her own. Even the seasonal occurrence was not so straightforward: As in many families with alcoholism, the Christmas season had often been a time of intense stress and difficulty for Lydia and her family, and the winter depressions might be part of a learned response to that stress.

Some members of the treatment team were also concerned about Lydia's relationship to her children. Robert, 23, had moved away from home 7 months earlier, and Mary, 21, had moved out 2 months ago. Celia, 19, also had moved recently, to get married, and was now pregnant. Only Patricia, 22, remained at home. During Lydia's initial evaluation the social worker raised the possibility that she was "overly close and too dependent on her children. She needs to prepare for them leaving home and her aloneness." The evaluating psychiatrist noted that "family issues and deep psychodynamic conflicts support her condition." These concerns seemed to be supported by her children's response to her depression. They, and her sister Elsie, were very involved in caring for her and monitoring her condition. Robert was especially involved and called me frequently, at one point reporting on the shape and consistency of her stools.

However, this formulation of problematic family dynamics did not explain why Lydia did so well when she was not depressed. She described herself as active, social, and happy, with many interests and pursuits. Three years earlier she had obtained her high school equivalency degree and was now taking education courses at the local community college. For the last 12 years she had worked as an aide in a daycare center, a job that she referred to as "medicine" because she enjoyed it so much. Why were these family issues not affecting her except when she was depressed?

However, the biggest difficulty with this formulation of problematic family relationships was that it wasn't helpful. After a course of antidepressants Lydia recovered from the depression, and her therapist held a series of family sessions to explore and address these issues. In these sessions it was noted that Lydia did not let her children know when she was angry or upset; that the family spoke for her; that she was sensitive and easily hurt; that the family worried about her when she was away from home and "appear to infantilize her"; that she needed to speak up for herself, and her children needed to allow her to stand on her own; that she had difficulty expressing anger, and her family had difficulty hearing it; and that the family was "very protective of one another." Family members listened dutifully to these formulations, but they clearly did not like the view of themselves that was being offered. Celia did not return after the first of these sessions, and other family members surmised that she "felt dumped on." Furthermore, there was no sign of any positive change in the family or in Lydia as a result of the meetings.

Seven months after antidepressants were started, the medicine was tapered and discontinued. Lydia was doing well at the time, without symptoms of depression, but 3 months later she again became seriously depressed. Again it was possible to understand this depression in several different ways. It started while Lydia was in Puerto Rico visiting her father, who was quite ill. Lydia's parents divorced when she was 13, and she and her siblings lived with their father until they left home. It was easy to imagine that her recent visit, and his illness, upset her equilibrium. However, from the medical perspective, she had stopped antidepressants not long before, and the onset of the depression was in the middle of winter, when her depressions had always occurred.

Antidepressants were started again, and the distraught telephone calls from her family resumed. One month later, at Lydia's request, she was admitted to the psychiatric unit of a local general hospital. She did not particularly benefit from the hospitalization, and when she was discharged after 1 month (when her insurance coverage ran out), she was still depressed. However, several weeks later she was significantly improved, and we began to discuss plans for ongoing treatment. I was concerned by how rapidly the depression had returned after antidepressants were discontinued and thought that an extended trial of medication was indicated. Because of the recurrent, episodic nature of the depressions, and because of evidence of brief periods of hypomania following the depressions, I recommended a trial of the mood stabilizer lithium. It was at this time, following the hospitalization, soon after Lydia's recovery from the most recent depression, and just as lithium was being started, that I invited the Ferrer family to participate in a series of meetings to discuss Lydia's illness.

INITIAL FAMILY MEETINGS

These sessions were remarkable and were the heart of my work with Lydia. The structure, which followed the psychoeducational model, was simple. All sessions were framed by a focus on recurrent depression as a biological condition. The family was given a pamphlet about recurrent affective disorders, both to provide information and to stimulate questions. We talked about symptoms, episodes, course, treatment, and prognosis. However, in addition to presenting information, there was an emphasis on talking about the experience of the illness: What was the family's experience of Lydia's episodes? How did they understand what she was going through? What were their theories of causation? What frightened or frustrated them; what did they not understand? How did they each react, and what did they find was helpful or not helpful? What was Lydia's experience of their reactions? What was helpful, or not helpful, from her perspective? What made her better, and what made her feel worse?

These were fascinating meetings for me. For one thing, my role was completely different from what I was used to as a family therapist. My job was to ask questions, to facilitate discussion, to provide information, to learn from the family and help them learn from each other. I wasn't trying to figure out

what they were doing wrong, so I could fix it; I was more interested in learning what they did that worked and in helping them to figure that out together. The dominant tone was one of interest, curiosity; it was more like a series of interviews than therapy sessions. When I shared information about recurrent affective disorders, I was the "expert," but my expertise was about the disorder, not about them. They were the experts about their own experience, and I learned from them.

Another difference from my family therapy experiences was what I would now call "transparency." My position was not strategic or paradoxical; I had no tricks up my sleeve. I asked the family members about their experience, I told them what I knew about the illness, and I answered their questions as best I could. Of course I had a position, but it was one about which I could be open with them: that they all were doing the best they could in coping with an illness that was baffling, frustrating, and immensely challenging and that the more information they could get from me, and from each other, the more effective they would be in fighting it.

Lydia was fully involved in these discussions, as were her children and her sister. That there was a different tone was confirmed by the family's attendance. Celia, who had dropped out of the previous family therapy after the first visit, didn't come to the first of these sessions. But she clearly heard that these meetings were different; she came to three of the four remaining sessions. Lydia and Elsie came to every meeting, and Robert and Patricia missed only one each.

This was not a dramatic, interventionist approach; what drama there was came from the family, not from me. Simply talking together about the illness in a neutral, low-intensity setting had very powerful effects. For example, Lydia said that she had experienced Patricia, the daughter who still lived with her, as distanced and uninvolved during her recent depression. She felt that Patricia spent as little time as possible with her and "didn't seem to care." Patricia was not present for this discussion, but Elsie responded by telling Lydia how devastated Patricia had been by her illness. She said that Patricia would call her before coming home to find out how Lydia was doing, to prepare herself. "There were times when I was more worried about her than you." Celia told of intense discussions with Patricia, when Patricia talked about how hard it was to see her mother like that and despaired of "being a perfect daughter" like Celia was. As a result of this discussion with her family, Lydia's understanding of Patricia and her behavior changed; she understood that Patricia had stayed distant because of how much she cared, not how little, and a potentially serious breach between them was resolved.

In these sessions Lydia and her family had the chance to go over their experiences together, to compare reactions and ask each other for clarification. For instance, during the depression there were times during visits from her children when Lydia would jump out of bed with her blankets and run into another room, without explanation. Now she described how hard it was to hear everyone visiting and chatting with each other while she felt outside and excluded. Elsie responded that Lydia made it clear at other times that she didn't want to be the focus of attention, so no one knew how to act. At another point Elsie described all the efforts she and the others had made to get Lydia out of bed and asked if it had helped at all; Lydia said it had not and that if she got up it was "only to get you off my back." Robert talked about what it was like to walk into his mother's bedroom and find her staring at a handful of pills and how helpless and frustrated he felt when she expressed her hopelessness and despair. Lydia told him what it was like for her to feel that way; and somehow this exchange, as painful as it was for both of them, helped.

As the sessions progressed, the medical information that was part of the model also had an impact on the family's experience. For example, Robert described his intense frustration during the worst of the depression, when he and his siblings would spend all morning trying to get Lydia out of bed. They were convinced that she would feel better if she got up, but she refused. Finally, sometime in the afternoon, she would get up and shower, and in fact did seem to do better for the rest of the day; but the next morning she would be back in the depths of depression, and the struggle would start anew. Robert was angered and demoralized by this repeated experience. I was able to explain to him that depression typically has a diurnal variation, being worse in the morning and improving as the day goes on. It was likely that Lydia's getting out of bed in the afternoon was the result, rather than the cause, of her improvement and that her retreat the following morning was an expression of the illness rather than of her will. This information about the biology of depression relieved Robert's frustration and confirmed Lydia's experience that her family's pushing and prodding had not been helpful.

Other medical information was more disquieting. We discussed the genetics of affective disorders and the possible familial association of mania and hypomania as well as depression. Elsie realized that her (and Lydia's) mother probably had undiagnosed depression, and she expressed concerns about her own experiences of depression. Robert talked about times when he "spurted out ideas," "overbooked myself," and tried to function beyond his capacities and wondered whether those might have been episodes of hypomania and therefore cause for concern. I told him that hypomania did not necessarily predict full-blown affective episodes, and at the same time we talked about how to monitor his behavior, and others' reactions to him, in order to prevent escalation at those times.

It was remarkable to me that the focus on diagnosis and biology facilitated change in the family, rather than inhibiting it as I might have feared. Focusing on the depression as an illness allowed aspects of Lydia's behavior, and of her family's reactions, to be addressed in a nonblaming way. For example, her apathy and lack of motivation during the illness, which her son saw as unnecessary "giving in," could be understood as a typical symptom of depression rather than a weakness of character. Robert's "overinvolvement" in his mother's care took on a different meaning as he described how her helplessness and despair during episodes made it necessary for him to "become the parent for my mother," and he talked of what that was like for him. Lydia's children could acknowledge the level of conflict and bickering into which they fell when their mother was ill and understand it as an expectable reaction to the stress and frustration of her condition. As each of these issues was discussed as a function of the illness, it was detoxified and neutralized. By the end of these meetings, Lydia could say that her depression had brought them all closer together as a family.

I learned a great deal from the Ferrers in these meetings. They were extremely articulate in speaking about their experiences and taught me many things about the issues confronting families with affective disorders. Approaching their experience through the language of illness, which might have been distancing and objectifying, had the opposite effect. We were allies in the struggle against the illness, and because I was not trying to uncover their problems as a family I could be open to listening and learning from them.

In addition to hearing their frustrations and struggles, I learned about their successes. Partly because they were a closely knit family, highly interdependent and supportive of each other (the very qualities that had been pathologized in the earlier family work), they had developed some highly effective solutions to the problems created by the depression. Although the hospitalization had done very little for Lydia's depression, it had provided a model on which her family could draw for their own use. Robert and his sisters realized that Lydia didn't like the socializing that went on around her when the family came to visit, "when we were ourselves, and she couldn't join in," and when she came home from the hospital they set up a system to address this problem. They organized themselves into shifts, with one person on duty at a time. "It was like a hospital situation; one person was the head nurse for the house." That person controlled traffic, limiting the number of visitors at any one time. He or she made sure that Lydia was comfortable and was available to her for conversation as she wished but without pressing it. The family stopped trying to force her out of bed; instead they let her rest. "She responded to a tranquil environment, and we stopped pushing her." This solution worked for everyone. Lydia liked knowing that there was always someone available, and she was very comfortable with just one person being present: "When there were two, it excluded me." The family members responded to the structure as well; Patricia and Mary, who had previously had difficulty helping, were more comfortable with a well-defined role. At the

change of shift, information was passed on, "like a report." Those who were not on duty could go about their lives, knowing that someone was there and that they could call in at any time to see how things were going.

According to Robert, once they came up with this structure "things started clicking," and Lydia was better within a week. The improvement also fit with the time course of antidepressants, so it was difficult to know for sure which factors were responsible. But it was clear that Lydia's family had developed a very creative solution to a problem posed by the depression and that both Lydia and her family thought this was very helpful. It was also clear to me that this solution came out of the family's particular needs and drew on their particular resources and that I could not have "intervened" to create it. In fact, without these family meetings I probably would never even have known about it.

Toward the end of these meetings we all talked together about the possibility of recurrence. This was a difficult discussion, because no one wanted to consider the possibility that the depression could happen again. Was it not possible that now that they understood about the illness they could prevent it? Lydia, especially, did not want to think that she would ever have to go through it again. I suggested that lithium and other medications might prevent future episodes, or make them milder, shorter, or less frequent but that, with a history of three severe depressions within 3 years, there was a good chance that at some point it would recur. In spite of the intense anxiety raised by this idea, there was general agreement that "we'll do what we have to do." It was also clear to everyone that these discussions would make it easier for the family to work together in the future.

The structure and goals of these sessions changed my relationship with the family: Lydia, her family, and I were now joined as partners in her care. Although I did not meet with the family regularly or frequently after the initial meetings, they were available to participate as needed, and they knew that I was available to them and that, at important choice points in Lydia's treatment, we would reconvene.

THE LONG TERM

Over the next several months Lydia's lithium dose was stabilized, and antidepressants were again tapered and discontinued. She again went to Puerto Rico to visit her father, and this time her mood remained stable. However, 6 months after starting lithium she developed a disturbing set of symptoms: lethargy, weakness, bloating, poor coordination, and hoarseness. Two weeks later she was again depressed. This time laboratory tests confirmed that the depression was a consequence of treatment: lithium had interfered with the functioning of her thyroid gland, and Lydia had medication-induced hypothyroidism, accompanied by depression.

As these symptoms developed, Elsie joined my meetings with Lydia, and she kept the family informed about our discussions. When the diagnosis of hypothyroidism was clear, we had another family meeting, to discuss this complication of treatment. Her children hoped that the depressions might have been caused by hypothyroidism all along. However, because prelithium thyroid studies had been normal, I told them that this was unlikely. They were disappointed, but because they were included in the discussion they were able to support Lydia as, in consultation with an endocrinologist, thyroid hormone was added to her regimen, and the lithium was continued.

With this treatment Lydia's symptoms gradually improved, and she did well on maintenance lithium and thyroid hormone until the following January. At this time, approximately 1 year from the beginning of the last, hypothyroidism-related depression, she again became depressed. The onset was sudden, with her typical symptoms of insomnia, anorexia, loss of interest, crying, and withdrawal. However, this time the depression was less intense; she was able to continue working and, without adding antidepressants, she began to improve within a month.

At this time another family meeting was held, to assess family members' experience of this episode. Everyone agreed that Lydia was depressed, but because it was not as intense as the previous depressions, they were not as frightened and, because their anxiety was less, they were better able to be available to Lydia without overwhelming her with their concern.

I met again with the family 1 month later, when the depression had resolved and Lydia was doing well again. The purpose of this meeting was to answer any questions that they might have and to discuss the next steps in the treatment. This discussion was purposely postponed until the depression was over; during an acute episode it is difficult for the depressed person to fully participate in decision making.

One question concerned the lithium. Lydia felt that it had been helpful in ameliorating the depression, but she had concerns about taking it indefinitely. There were side effects, such as weight gain and fatigue, and she didn't like the idea of taking any medicine if it wasn't absolutely necessary. Her family, especially Robert, shared this concern. I reviewed what we had previously discussed in terms of lithium's effectiveness. Although it had not prevented this episode, it did appear to have lessened the depression's intensity and duration. However, because of Lydia's concerns about side effects and about long-term drug use, I suggested a possible alternative. Because there was a strong seasonal component to her depressions, I raised the possibility of intermittent lithium prophylaxis, starting every fall and continuing through the winter. This would lessen the period of side effects and allow for a drug-free interval but would probably involve a greater risk of episodes. After extensive discussion of the risks and benefits of the various options, Lydia, with her family's support, decided to continue lithium on a regular basis.

For the next 2½ years Lydia stayed well. She continued taking lithium and thyroid hormone, she had no complaints about side effects or symptoms, and she lived her life. I saw her approximately monthly, for "check-ins" to monitor her mood and her medication. She was busy with work, with her grandchildren (she now had three), and with helping her sister Elsie, who was having troubles in her marriage. Patricia moved out, and Lydia said that she very much enjoyed living on her own, but a short time later Robert, between jobs, moved back home. For some months Lydia and I had again been discussing the possibility of discontinuing lithium, as a trial. She had gone through two winters without depression, her life was going well, and she wanted to see whether she still needed the lithium. Because this decision could affect her family as well as herself, and because of their strong involvement in treatment up to this time, we agreed that it was important to include them in this decision. So, 3 years after our first family meetings, we all met again to discuss the next steps in treatment.

This meeting was another remarkable experience for me. The tone was of a family reunion. Mary brought her 2-year-old son, who had been born since our last meeting, and I felt like a distant but valued uncle at a family gathering. Everyone but Celia was present, and initially there was much chatting and catching up. When we got down to business the first topic was whether, after 2½ years without an episode, family members still worried about Lydia becoming depressed. Each in turn said that he or she was not worried, but when I asked Lydia who she thought worried about her the most, she said, "All of them! They would all jump if I said that something was coming on."

We then talked about the decision to stop lithium. Even after I emphasized the increased risk of a depressive episode, everyone supported Lydia's decision to try herself off of the drug. She herself expressed anxiety about stopping, because of fear of another depression; but she was tired of taking pills and wanted to know for sure whether she needed them, so she decided to "go for it."

The next task was to negotiate the issue of monitoring for prodromal signs. If Lydia stopped lithium, it would be important to watch for the earliest signs of depression so that treatment could be initiated as early as possible in the course of the episode. However, Lydia felt that her family was already too concerned about her well-being, and she did not want them observing her any more closely than they were already. There was general laughter when we agreed that with her family, the goal was less caring, not more.

In further discussion we identified a pattern of increased vigilance by the family leading to withdrawal by Lydia, which led to heightened vigilance. We agreed that if her family believed that Lydia

would alert them if she was becoming depressed, they would worry less about monitoring her. The family also agreed that since our original meetings Lydia had become more open about her moods, and Elsie noted that at the beginning of the last depression, 2½ years ago, Lydia had told her when the first signs appeared. This was reassuring to the other family members and gave credence to the idea that they did not have to be overly vigilant.

How was it that we were now able to discuss family patterns that had been identified at the beginning of treatment and that had been raised unsuccessfully in the initial family therapy sessions? For one thing, these patterns were now understood as reactions to Lydia's illness rather than as family pathology. There was no blame in the discussion; rather, we were able to approach the behavior from the perspective of whether it was helpful in coping with the illness. If family vigilance and monitoring made Lydia more uncomfortable and caused her to withdraw, it was not useful and needed to be modified. If Lydia's withdrawal made her family more vigilant, she would have to address their legitimate concerns about her safety and well-being if she wanted them to back off.

The other difference was my relationship with the family. Because of the initial psychoeducational meetings and our contacts since, we were strongly connected. They knew and trusted me, and I them. There was a sense that we were working together toward a common goal.

The last task of the meeting was for Lydia to identify the symptoms that were characteristic prodromal signs of her depressions. This was important to clarify so there could be agreement on what would and would not be cause for alarm. It was also important to demonstrate to her family that Lydia was taking the possibility of recurrence seriously. Her list of first signs of onset included trouble sleeping, decreased appetite, and loss of interest in usually enjoyable activities, such as listening to music or playing with her grandsons. One night of insomnia would not necessarily be cause for concern, whereas two nights would be. Any of these symptoms would be more worrisome if it occurred in the winter, when her depressions usually started. We reached explicit agreement that Lydia would alert her family if she had any concerns and that they would do their best not to monitor her behavior.

This process was closest to what I did as a family therapist: negotiating differences, working with complementarity, changing patterns of behavior. The focus, however, remained on the illness and coping with it; any changes in the family were to facilitate this.

After this meeting Lydia tapered and discontinued the lithium. The only change that she noticed as a result was increased energy. She told me that her family continued to be very concerned, but she was able to take this more in stride. She continued to do well and to remain stable for over a year and went through another winter without depression. She did, however, have significant family stresses during this time.

A few months after stopping lithium, Lydia came for a routine follow-up visit accompanied by Robert. She told me that she had just discovered that he had been snorting heroin regularly for over a year. Robert was now living at home and was about to start a job, and he said that he wanted to stop. Lydia had brought him along so that we could discuss options for treatment.

I referred Robert to an outpatient detoxification program, and 2 weeks later we had another family meeting; Lydia, Celia, and Mary came to talk about Robert and how to deal with his addiction. Her daughters were primarily concerned about the effects on Lydia of Robert's addiction, but she seemed to be handling it well; she was appropriately angry, frustrated, and worried about Robert, but she showed no signs of depression. Robert had not gone to the detoxification program, and we talked about setting limits on his behavior. Three weeks later, after he stole money from her, Lydia asked him to leave, and he did so. She and her daughters maintained friendly contact with him but did not support his drug use.

Fifteen months after stopping lithium and a year after the crisis with Robert, Lydia again became depressed. She called me as soon as she identified prodromal signs, which were just as she had predicted: insomnia, anorexia, and loss of interest, occurring in December. In some ways the course of this episode was the same as previous ones: Lithium was re-

started, followed by antidepressants, and over the next several months Lydia's condition slowly improved. However, there were also important differences. For one thing, Lydia reported that she was not agitated or suicidal as she had been in previous episodes; she knew that she was depressed, and it would pass, and she was not panicking. She said that her family wasn't panicking, either. They were available to her but were not overwhelming her; they kept an attentive distance. "Now they call and ask how I am, but then we talk about other things." Lydia attributed the difference in her own state to these changes in her family. When I commented that this depression didn't seem as bad as previous ones, she said that it was just as bad, "but my family is responding differently. Before, they were more desperate, so I was more desperate."

For me, this was a confirmation of what I had come to believe about the etiology and treatment of affective disorders: that individual, family, and biological factors converged and interacted. There was no doubt that Lydia's depressions were biologically based and that lithium had been very effective in minimizing recurrences, but that was not the whole story. Off lithium, she was having a recurrence, but it was different; the expression of the biological illness, her experience of it, was modified in important ways by changes in her family's behavior.

During this period Lydia brought Mary to one session, and Mary and Celia joined Lydia for another. When the episode resolved, we had another family meeting, with Lydia and all four children attending, to discuss their experiences of the episode that had just ended. It had not been easy for any of them, perhaps especially for Robert, who was in a residential drug program at the time and could not take charge of his mother's care as he had done during previous episodes. However, it was clear that, overall, everyone had been more accepting, less panicked, and less responsible for "curing" the depression; it was also clear that this had been very helpful to Lydia.

REFLECTIONS

That was the last family meeting I had with the Ferrers. After the episode, Lydia and I agreed that she would continue taking lithium. Antidepressants were again tapered and discontinued, and she continued to do well. Six months later I moved to another state, and I lost contact with Lydia and her family. Now, 7 years later, I cannot provide follow-up on the course of Lydia's illness. I can, however, offer some thoughts about the effects that the work we did together had on me.

It would be inaccurate to suggest that my experience with Lydia and her family was in itself transforming for me. It was one step in a long process that began with my psychiatric training and continues today. However, it was an important step, an organized and conscious change in my approach to families.

My experience with the Ferrers confirmed my belief in the importance of a "three-dimensional" systems view, one that encompasses individual, interpersonal, and biological systems. I saw the powerful effect that such a perspective had on my practice. I learned to join with the family and with the individual through the biology, and I found that this integrated approach could facilitate change rather than inhibit it. In the 8 years that I worked with Lydia and her family, we had only six family meetings in addition to the initial sequence of five psychoeducational sessions. Yet the family was involved in her treatment at every step, and their understanding of the illness, and their role in coping with it, changed in important ways over that time.

I found unexpected resonances between "traditional" family therapy and these new techniques. Fundamental concepts of family therapy, such as joining and reframing, took on new meaning in my work with the Ferrers. The educational approach offered an extremely effective way to join with the family, and the biological, "illness" perspective was a powerful form of reframing. As my experience increased I found that my practice was simultaneously informed by family therapy and by psychoeducation: I could choose from either approach as appropriate, but both were present in all my work. I learned a great deal about families and affective disorders from the Ferrers, and I continue to explore that area in my work with individuals and with families. I also

learned a great deal about respecting the family's motivations, strengths, and talents.

In the most fundamental sense, my experience with the Ferrers marked a change in how I relate to families. It marked a shift from a model of therapeutic intervention with the goal of changing the family to one of consultation to help family members achieve their own goals. This change is not just in the words; these are two very different models of the helping relationship, and especially of the distribution of power in that relationship. In my work with the Ferrers I learned that I could be helpful without being directive, that I could stand next to them rather than above them, and that I could learn from them as well as teach.

References

Anderson, C. M. (1983). A psychoeducational program for families of patients with schizophrenia. In W. R. McFarlane (Ed.), *Family therapy in schizophrenia* (pp. 99–116). New York: Guilford Press.

Anderson, C. M., Griffin, S., Rossi, A., Pagonis, I., Holder, D. P., & Treiber, R. (1986). A comparative study of the impact of education vs. process groups for families of patients with affective disorders. *Family Process, 25,* 185–205.

Falloon I. R. H., & Liberman, R. P. (1983). Behavioral family interventions in the management of chronic schizophrenia. In W. R. McFarlane (Ed.), *Family therapy in schizophrenia* (pp. 117–137). New York: Guilford Press.

Kopeikin, H. S., Marshall, V., & Goldstein, M. J. (1983). Stages and impact of crisis-oriented family therapy in the aftercare of acute schizophrenia. In W. R. McFarlane (Ed.), *Family therapy in schizophrenia* (pp. 69–97). New York: Guilford Press.

McFarlane, W. R. (1983). *Family therapy in schizophrenia.* New York: Guilford Press.

Moltz, D. A. (1991). Families with affective disorders. In F. Herz (Ed.), *Reweaving the family tapestry: A multigenerational approach to families* (pp. 286–308). New York: Norton.

Moltz, D. A. (1993). Bipolar disorder and the family: An integrative model. *Family Process, 32,* 409–423.

Papolos, D., & Papolos, J. (1997). *Overcoming depression* (3rd ed.). New York: HarperPerennial.

CHAPTER 30

INTEGRATING PSYCHIATRIC ILLNESS INTO HEALTHY FAMILY FUNCTIONING: THE FAMILY PSYCHOEDUCATIONAL TREATMENT OF A PATIENT WITH BIPOLAR DISORDER

Teresa L. Simoneau and David J. Miklowitz

Alan, a 27-year-old single man, was recovering from a manic episode on the psychiatric unit of a private hospital when I first met him.[1] This was Alan's second hospitalization for bipolar disorder; the first was 2 years earlier, shortly after he graduated from law school. He was prescribed lithium after his first episode of mania, but he stopped taking it shortly after he was discharged from the hospital because of bothersome side effects and disbelief over his diagnosis. His mood remained fairly stable for 2 years until a few weeks before his most recent hospitalization.

I was a graduate student in clinical psychology working as a project therapist on a randomized clinical trial, the University of Colorado Family Project (CFP), in which family-focused psychoeducational treatment (FFT; Miklowitz & Goldstein, 1997) was being compared with individual crisis management with naturalistic follow-up (CMNF) in patients with bipolar disorder (Miklowitz, Frank, & George, 1996). I had been working on the project for 4 years when I was assigned to meet Alan, discuss the clinical trial with him, and conduct a diagnostic interview to assess his appropriateness for the study.

During our initial meeting I learned that, until recently, Alan had worked for a large law firm. Shortly before his latest manic episode, he was assigned some difficult and time-consuming cases. As the stress of his job increased, his mood became more and more unstable. He was irritable and would frequently argue with his supervisor. He wasted long hours on tangential issues and dead ends.

He also became obsessed with a high-profile legal case. He was convinced he could do a better job defending the case than the assigned lawyer could. After sleepless nights working on the case, he would come into the office energized about his ideas and feeling pressured to share his theories with coworkers. When his supervisor approached him about not getting his work done, he was argumentative and accused his supervisor of "nagging." He was hospitalized after disrupting the courtroom proceedings in one of the firm's cases.

I described the clinical trial to Alan during our first meeting. He wanted to participate, but he requested that only his mother be involved with the study. He doubted whether his father would agree to be involved in family treatment. Because Alan was going to be living with his parents after discharge from the hospital, I felt it was important to include Alan's father, if he would agree to participate. When I contacted Alan's parents, Betty and George, I was surprised to hear that they both agreed to participate in the study. However, Alan's reading of his father proved to be diagnostic of struggles in their relationship, which frequently surfaced during family treatment.

FAMILY-FOCUSED PSYCHOEDUCATION: RESEARCH BACKGROUND

The use of family psychoeducational interventions for the treatment of people with a major psychiatric

---

[1] This chapter is written from the point of view of Teresa L. Simoneau (TLS).

illness is a fairly recent development in the treatment strategy for these disorders. Psychoeducational family treatment interventions were originally tested in controlled clinical trials with families of patients with schizophrenia after the climate of the family environment was found to be an important predictor of the course of schizophrenia. Specifically, familial attitudes toward patients with a psychiatric illness (expressed emotion [EE]) were related to the course of schizophrenia and other psychiatric illnesses. Relatives rated high on EE hold more critical, hostile, or overinvolved attitudes toward the family member with psychiatric illness and display more negative behavior when interacting with that family member (Hooley, 1986; Miklowitz et al., 1989; Miklowitz, Goldstein, Falloon, & Doane, 1984; Simoneau, Miklowitz, & Saleem, 1998). Patients in families with relatives who are high in EE have more frequent relapses of their illness than patients in families who do not have high-EE relatives (for reviews, see Hooley, Rosen, & Richters, 1996; Miklowitz, 1994; Parker & Hadzi-Pavlovic, 1990).

Family interventions, designed to modify these stressful family environments, have been applied to families of schizophrenic patients to improve their course of the illness. Several controlled studies have shown that the addition of a family intervention to standard medication management of schizophrenic illness decreases the rate of relapse when compared with medications alone, or in combination with individual therapy, over 6 to 24 months of follow-up (Falloon et al., 1982, 1985; Goldstein, Rodnick, Evans, May, & Steinberg, 1978; Hogarty et al., 1986; Leff, Kuipers, Berkowitz, Eberlein-Vries, & Sturgeon, 1982; Leff, Kuipers, Berkowitz, & Sturgeon, 1985; Tarrier et al., 1988). These interventions have been successful in decreasing negative attitudes of parents toward their offspring who has schizophrenia (Hogarty et al., 1986; Leff et al., 1985; Tarrier et al., 1988) and improving patients' functional status (Falloon et al., 1985; Goldstein et al., 1978). The design of the treatment interventions varied, but all of them included family education on the nature of schizophrenic illness and an intervention to improve family coping (for a review, see Goldstein & Miklowitz, 1995).

The effectiveness of psychoeducational family treatments for reducing the symptomatology of patients with bipolar disorder is currently being studied in controlled clinical trials (Goldstein & Miklowitz, 1994; Miklowitz et al., 1996). Similar to studies of patients with schizophrenia, results are showing a benefit of family treatment in the course of bipolar disorder. Specifically, patients with bipolar disorder who received FFT with their family members had fewer relapses and had longer periods between relapses than patients who did not receive family treatment (Miklowitz et al., 2000).

APPLICATION OF FAMILY-FOCUSED PSYCHOEDUCATIONAL TREATMENT

Alan and his family were randomly assigned to receive FFT along with standard mood-regulating medications for Alan's bipolar disorder. FFT is based on Falloon's behavioral family management (Falloon, Boyd, & McGill, 1984) and consists of 21 family sessions (12 weekly sessions, 6 biweekly sessions, and 3 monthly sessions) conducted in the clinic or in the family's home. The components of the therapy include a behavioral analysis to assess family strengths and weaknesses and three major treatment modules: (a) psychoeducation about the illness, (b) communication-enhancement training, and (c) problem-solving skills training. FFT focuses on helping the family to (a) process and integrate the most recent episode, (b) recognize the patient's vulnerability to future episodes, (c) accept psychotropic medications as necessary for mood stability, (d) distinguish personality-based behaviors from symptoms of mood instability, (e) see the impact of life stress on the course of the illness, and (f) re-establish functional family relationships after the episode. The overall goal of FFT is to help the family re-establish a state of equilibrium after the stress and disruption to the family from an episode of the patient's illness.

As a therapist trained in the FFT model, I conducted the treatment of Alan and his family with a therapist in training (a first-year graduate student in clinical psychology). Cotherapy offers the benefit of having more than one person available to monitor the therapy process and of having the ability to ally with different subsystems of the family at different points in time. My cotherapist and I also attended weekly group supervision sessions with the principal investigator of the study, David J. Miklowitz, PhD, and other project therapists. The purpose of the supervision was to process difficulties that arose during the treatment and to monitor compliance with the treatment model. These sessions were invaluable to me in working with Alan and his parents. I received useful insights, practical suggestions when I was feeling "stuck," and support when I was struggling with my own feelings and reactions in working with Alan and his family.

Although the family intervention was the major form of treatment provided to Alan through the CFP study, individual issues surrounding his illness also needed to be integrated into the treatment. A balance needed to be achieved between focusing on the illness and symptoms Alan presented and focusing on family treatment issues. In this chapter I describe Alan's treatment through each of the phases of FFT and some of the challenges I experienced as a therapist using this model.

Assessment Phase

Individual and family assessments were used during the assessment phase of FFT. I wanted to understand how Alan and his parents were coping with his illness and how their coping styles may have affected the family's functioning. Family treatment would then build on the identified coping strengths of the family. Ineffective coping strategies or negative interactional styles are not a major focus of the assessment or the treatment with FFT. However, it was sometimes difficult to ignore negative interactional processes in Alan's family, such as during the family assessment.

Individual Assessments.   Individual assessments of Alan and his parents were conducted while Alan was still in the hospital. I met with Alan twice while he was hospitalized for his manic episode: first, to introduce him to the study and build rapport, and later, to conduct a diagnostic interview to confirm the diagnosis of bipolar disorder. Alan was still in a hypomanic state during those initial meetings. As with many bipolar patients in that state, he was very interpersonally engaging. He was open, talkative, and had a good sense of humor. Alan impressed

me with his intelligence, insightfulness, and articulateness.

Alan described a long history of mood swings, which had been very disruptive to his life. As a teenager, he remembered being depressed "most of the time." He felt isolated and rejected by his peers, so he spent much of his time alone. His first episode of mania came just after his law school graduation. Several late nights of "cramming" for his final exams followed by sleepless nights of celebration after finishing law school probably contributed to the onset of his manic episode. Frank and colleagues (Frank et al., 1994; Malkoff-Schwartz et al., 1998) have hypothesized that an interruption in social routines and circadian rhythms can contribute to the onset of manic episodes.

Alan's illness was very debilitating for him. Although he was able to finish law school and hold down a job for a couple of years, the illness had clearly affected his interpersonal relationships and was currently affecting his ability to function at a job.

When I met with Alan's parents for individual interviews I was surprised at the differences between them and their son. Alan's parents were both working-class people: Betty was a secretary, and George was a welder. Although they were both pleasant and cooperative, they were not as articulate or as interpersonally skilled as Alan. Betty was a somewhat anxious woman who became more talkative as her anxiety rose. George was an "Archie Bunker" type who had strong opinions about politics, sports, and other topics, including Alan's illness. Consistent with Alan's initial concern, George voiced skepticism about how family treatment was going to help his son, but he agreed to participate for Alan's sake. Although George was at times difficult to interact with and opinionated, overall he was a likable gentleman, and he clearly cared about his son. I worked hard to establish a rapport with George, because I felt it was important for him to be involved in Alan's treatment. Alan was currently living at home, so he had a lot of contact with his father. The tension in George and Alan's relationship was an ongoing source of stress for Alan that could potentially influence his bipolar illness.

Alan's parents both expressed pride in Alan's

achievements through law school, but they were also critical of him and his behaviors. George felt that Alan could be doing better regarding his illness if he tried harder. Betty resented the fact that Alan and his father did not get along better. She blamed Alan, because she felt he should be more understanding and respectful of his father. In addition to the criticism, Betty also seemed "emotionally overinvolved" with her son's life. She would call him several times a day from work to check on how he was doing, and she did not want to go away for the weekend and leave him alone. At the time, I thought that reaction was reasonable given the stress of Alan's recent episode and her concern for his emotional well-being.

Family Assessments.   About 1 month after Alan was discharged from the hospital, he and his parents came to the University of Colorado at Boulder for a laboratory-based family assessment. Whereas the individual assessments allowed Alan and his parents to tell their stories of his illness, the family assessment allowed me to observe their family interactional styles and communication patterns. During this assessment, the family first engaged in a playful task, after which they discussed two conflict issues. My cotherapist and I observed these interactions from behind a one-way mirror.

During the playful task, the family discussed and tried to come to an agreement about what a Rorschach card looked like to them. Alan and his parents seemed to thoroughly enjoy the task. All three of them came up with several ideas about the card, and they laughed and joked with each other about the ideas that were presented. While observing Alan and his parents during this task, I was drawn in by their laughter and was impressed by their ability to have fun together. Everyone participated equally, and they listened to each other's ideas. I felt this was definitely a strength of their family—their ability to "play" together.

The emotional climate of the family changed dramatically during the problem-solving discussions. I asked the family to discuss two conflictual topics identified by family members during individual interviews. They were given 10 minutes to discuss each topic. During the first interaction, the family discussed Alan's irritation at his father for not talk-

ing more with him. Alan and George began discussing this issue together, but Betty interrupted and gave excuses for George's behavior (e.g., "Your dad's tired when he comes home."). Later, she criticized Alan for the way he approached his father (Betty, in a scolding tone: "You treat him like a child. Your father is an adult."). Thus, Betty blamed Alan for this issue.

The second issue focused on Betty's desire for Alan to be more independent and resume some activities outside the home. However, Betty revealed during the discussion that she herself was reluctant to do activities outside the home because she feared for Alan's safety if she left him alone, which is why she would call him two or three times a day from work. This left her feeling angry and resentful toward him for interfering with her life and with plans she had made with George to travel in their motor home. Alan expressed feelings of being a burden to the family after his latest episode when he needed to move back into his parents' home. However, he also felt very vulnerable with his unstable moods and wanted his parents to be with him as much as possible.

Whereas Alan was active and expressive during the family Rorschach task, he was withdrawn, submissive, and apologetic during the problem-solving interactions. Critical expressions by his mother seemed to shut him down. His regression made me feel protective toward him, and I was angry at Betty for shutting down the more engaging parts of his personality.

The conclusion of the family assessment required my cotherapist and I to give feedback to the family. Consistent with the FFT model, we wanted to focus on the strengths of the family. However, it was difficult for me to be objective after observing their negative family interactions. I was focused on the way Alan's parents interacted with him. I realized that I overidentified with Alan, perhaps because we were close in terms of age and education or because he had been so engaging in our prior meetings, and I resented the repressive effect his parents had on him. Fortunately, my cotherapist had a different perspective of the family and their interactions, having met Alan and his parents for the first time during the family assessment. She felt Alan's parents displayed a sense of helplessness and were perhaps feeling protective toward him because they did not want him to experience further emotional pain as a result of his bipolar disorder. They were understandably angry at the disruption to their lives and routine, but they showed a lot of care and concern toward their son. In that context, the responses of Alan's parents seemed normal given the grief, disappointment, and anxiety the family experienced relative to Alan's diagnosis. My cotherapist's perspective helped me take a more systemic view in which Alan's behavior was part of the interaction that occurred with his parents. These insights helped me be more neutral and objective when giving feedback to Alan and his family.

My cotherapist and I, by reframing some of the negativity as positive traits of the family, identified and shared four strengths with the family during the feedback session: (a) they were willing to identify and openly discuss the problems they were having with each other, (b) they expressed a desire not only to improve family relationships but also to pursue individual interests (which was an appropriate goal given the developmental stage of the family), (c) they clearly cared for each other and wanted to work through these problems together, and (d) they enjoyed each others' company. The family responded very positively to this feedback. Alan's parents seemed relieved that we did not blame them for his problems, and they seemed pleased with the family strengths we identified. This session helped my cotherapist and I to build some credibility with the family and to create the beginnings of an alliance with the family as a system.

Treatment Phase

My cotherapist and I conducted FFT in Alan's parents' home. Although the treatment can be conducted in a clinic setting, we chose to meet with this family in their own home to increase their level of comfort during the therapy and, we hoped, to improve compliance by making it more convenient for them.

The family treatment intervention consisted of three parts: (a) education about bipolar disorder, (b) communication-enhancement training, and (c) problem-solving skills training. Moving from the

assessment phase to the treatment phase was a major change in focus from what I had done with Alan and his parents up to this point. The individual and family assessments, which gave me information about Alan's illness and the family's functioning, generally is viewed as nonthreatening to the family system. The family treatment would test the family's flexibility and openness to change.

Psychoeducation. The main goals of the psychoeducational phase were to educate the family about bipolar disorder and to provide a rationale for the family's involvement in Alan's treatment. The five to six sessions of education tend to be more didactic in nature, and less threatening to the family system, than are the communication skills training sessions. Thus, it gave my cotherapist and I a chance to strengthen our alliance with the family before beginning communication skills training. During the education module we reviewed Alan's manic and depressive symptoms; we had him identify the prodromal symptoms leading up to his latest episode; and we discussed the etiology, treatment, and management of the illness. To make the sessions more relevant to Alan and his parents, we asked them to give examples from their own experience and encouraged them to express their reactions to the educational material.

The symptom review directly addressed the first goal of FFT: helping the family to integrate their experience of Alan's latest episode. Although the family was fairly knowledgeable about the illness, they had never discussed it together or heard directly from Alan how he experienced his symptoms. I asked Alan to describe the symptoms he experienced during episodes of mania and depression and empowered him by labeling him as the "expert" about his illness. He seemed to enjoy his elevated role as an expert in the family, a position that was new for him.

Although I knew from Alan's individual interviews how debilitating his symptoms were to him, I had not realized the power they had in the family system. He was basically a prisoner in his home because he and his parents were fearful of him having "uncontrollable symptoms" while he was away from home. In addition, when he was symptomatic his parents altered their plans and normal activities to be with him. Because Alan had been depressed since the time of his discharge from the hospital, his parents had been spending most of the last 2 months at home with him during their time off from work.

Alan's parents expressed frustration and anger at his failure to improve. They believed that he had more control over his moods than he exerted.

George: I'm trying to understand his problem. I'm realizing there is a problem. Part of it, I believe, is a willpower to handle it. You have to be strong.

Alan: It's hard for me to have people say you should have the willpower to control this when I feel like these moods leave me with very little control. It makes me feel like I'm not doing something that I should be doing. But, when I'm in a depression it's hard to figure it all out, and it just makes you feel worse when someone thinks you aren't trying to help yourself.

George: The reason I said that is when I get a headache, I don't take an aspirin. When I had surgery, they said I wouldn't go back to work right away, but I did. I think that's my makeup. I just go on and do what I need to do, regardless of what's going on with my body.

Betty: I think a lot of it is psychological. I think a lot of times people psyche themselves up. They say, "I'm not going to get sick, I'm not going to let this happen." I think the mind is pretty powerful.

Hooley and Licht (1997) found that high-EE relatives (i.e., relatives holding critical, hostile, or over-involved attitudes toward the family member with a psychiatric illness) were more likely than low-EE relatives to make these internal-controllability attributions, blaming the patient for negative behaviors that may actually be symptoms of the illness. I could understand how Alan's parents could hold these internal-controllability beliefs. I was frustrated with Alan as well during those weeks when he was continually symptomatic. When he was depressed, he was very passive and would allow the slightest change in his mood to disrupt his entire day, including our sessions. He would refuse to verbally engage in the didactic material, stating that his symptoms

were interfering with his ability to participate. However, he would readily talk at length about the symptoms he had experienced during the week. When he was hypomanic, I was overwhelmed by his incessant talking. He would frequently interrupt people who were speaking, and he was hard to direct. I was irritated with what I perceived to be his sense of entitlement.

Dealing With Subsyndromal Symptoms. An ongoing dilemma in conducting therapy with people with bipolar disorder is how to handle subsyndromal symptomatology, such as what Alan presented. Although FFT focuses on what to do in the case of a relapse or florid symptomatology, Alan was having milder depressive and manic symptoms that did not require aggressive treatment or hospitalization. However, his symptoms were severe enough to affect our sessions and his relationships. Alan's medications were being altered by his psychiatrist to help him stabilize his mood, but during those early sessions he was showing no signs of significant improvement.

When I processed my feelings regarding Alan's behavior and symptoms in the weekly supervision group and asked for suggestions, several issues became clear. First, I realized that part of my frustration came from the fact that I had let Alan's symptoms have power over our sessions, similar to how Alan and his family allowed his symptoms to have power in their family system. I allowed Alan to monopolize sessions by talking at length about his symptoms. This process left me feeling helpless and frustrated, similar to the feelings Alan's parents expressed. Although I wanted to acknowledge his difficulties, I could see that spending the whole session focusing on his moods was not helpful. Thus, I decided to let him talk briefly about his "terrible week" with his symptoms at the beginning of each session, but then I focused the family on the session's goals (e.g., "I can see it has been a difficult week for you. But I think it would be most helpful at this juncture to move on to our agenda. What we will be covering today is . . ."). I let Alan and his family know my rationale for this structure (i.e., that families seem to benefit more from a predictable structure than an open-ended treatment contract). Although Alan initially admitted feeling criticized, he began to expect me to provide that structure to the sessions. The structure also helped me feel more in control of the sessions and allowed me to progress through the treatment protocol.

The second issue that became clear from supervision was that Alan and his parents did not make a distinction between behaviors that represented normal mood fluctuations or personality traits and behaviors that represented symptoms of his bipolar illness. I felt it was important for them to begin to make those distinctions so that they were not held hostage by every change in his mood. To do this, I normalized the process of having mood fluctuations. I discussed how stressful situations can influence a person's moods and how moods can influence one's reactions to stressful situations. George and Betty gave examples of how their own behavior changed with their moods. Then I asked Alan to talk about his moods and whether he could distinguish when he was having symptoms of his illness versus when he was "just in a bad mood." Initially, he was unable to see much distinction between his mood states, but gradually he began to connect some mood states with provoking agents (e.g., arguments with his parents).

Third, I used Alan's continuing symptoms as a way to highlight the chronicity of his illness and his vulnerability to future episodes. Alan had returned to his baseline functioning fairly quickly after his first manic episode; however, he was having more difficulty stabilizing his mood after his most recent episode. The vulnerability–stress model maintains that people with bipolar disorder have a biological vulnerability that is expressed as an episode of illness when that person is under a significant amount of stress. This model provided a rationale for involvement of Alan's parents in managing the illness; the family could create a less stressful environment by improving communication and managing their problems more effectively. Alan and his parents embraced the vulnerability–stress model, perhaps because it decreased some of the family's sense of helplessness in regard to Alan's mood swings.

Finally, in the supervision group someone raised the possibility that some of Alan's symptoms and corresponding refusals to participate in the sessions were a manifestation of resistance. I decided to ap-

proach this problem by aligning with Alan's expressed desire to return to better functioning. I required him to participate during each session, but he could assess the severity of his symptoms and participate in accordance with what could reasonably be expected of him given his level of symptoms. By keeping his symptoms from totally interfering with therapy I gave him the message that he should engage in the treatment process even though he was symptomatic. In essence, I was modeling what I expected him to do with his life: take control to the extent possible and not let the illness dominate his life.

Dealing With Issues of Loss.   A theme that continued to emerge throughout the education phase was the losses that Alan and his family felt as a result of his illness. Although this issue was not a particular focus of FFT, I felt it was important to discuss these themes with the family. Similar to what people describe with a physical illness, Alan felt he had lost his "healthy self." Because of his illness, he had lost his job, his independence, and much of his social life. He also felt he had lost his identity:

> *You lose yourself when the illness starts. You become the illness, and it's hard to regain a sense of yourself after going through something like this. I don't think of myself as just bipolar, but other people see me like that.*

His parents also expressed their grief and disappointment that Alan had to deal with this illness when he was just starting his career in law. These issues of loss seemed to be keeping Alan and his family from moving on with their lives. Empathizing with their feelings of loss seemed to provide some validation for their experiences and helped the family to proceed with the grief process. These discussions with Alan and his parents taught me about the importance of acknowledging for families the deep sense of loss they experience as a result of having a family member with a psychiatric illness.

The "Relapse Drill."   The education sessions ended with a "relapse drill" (Marlatt & Gordon, 1985). Specific strategies were to be used if Alan showed symptoms of an impending relapse: Betty was to contact Alan's psychiatrist if Alan was unable to do so, George and Betty were to reduce stress in the family by avoiding discussing conflictual topics with Alan, and Alan was to stick to a regular sleep–wake schedule. The family identified behavioral symptoms that would alert them to changes in Alan's mood: sleeping fewer hours, being overly talkative, and being more irritable were signs of an incipient manic relapse, and sleeping more hours, withdrawing, and being more tearful were signs of an incipient depressive relapse. The relapse drill helped the family to consolidate what they had learned during the education sessions. Unfortunately, the family soon had to use these skills.

Communication Enhancement Training

Communication skills training builds a foundation for effective coping and problem-solving within families. Enhanced communication is therefore seen as a means to decrease stress within families. FFT focuses on three main skills: (a) active empathic listening, (b) effective ways of giving positive and negative feedback, and (c) constructive requests for behavior change.

My cotherapist and I had established a strong alliance with Alan and his family during the education sessions, and Alan's mood was beginning to be more stable. Both of these factors proved to be important during the communication training, because this training confronts the family's self-styled patterns of interacting. Alan and his parents reacted to this treatment module with more resistance.

Dealing With Resistance to Role Plays. Role plays (the core technique for learning new communication skills) are used iteratively in FFT to coach people in how to listen without reacting and how to give feedback and make requests that are more likely to generate positive responses. Feedback on the role plays, elicited from other family members and given by the therapists, help to solidify the process. Role playing is often met with resistance by families because the role plays frequently unbalance a system's hierarchical structure.

Alan and his parents had rigid rules around who interacted with whom in the family, and they resisted changes to their established communication patterns. Alan and his mother had a close, somewhat enmeshed relationship, whereas Alan and his

father had a more distant relationship. This family structure was apparent with their seating arrangement: Alan and Betty sat next to each other on the couch, and George was on the other side of the living room in a chair. George and Alan resisted changing the distance in their relationship.

TLS: George and Alan, why don't you sit next to each other during this role play?

George: I can hear him okay from here.

Alan: Yeah, we don't need to move.

TLS: I know, but when doing this speaking and listening exercise, sitting next to each other is another way of showing interest.

George: He knows I'm interested, don't you, Alan?

Alan: Yeah, I know you care.

TLS: Well, why don't we try it both ways. Do the role play first from where you are sitting and then do the role play again sitting next to each other. We'll see whether they feel different, okay?

Betty often helped to maintain the distance between George and Alan. The following interaction was typical of attempts to get George and Alan to talk with each other and shows Betty's role in rescuing them:

Alan: We don't talk very much. Maybe every once in a while we get together and talk.

George: I'm not a big talker.

TLS: Are you a good listener?

Cotherapist: Perhaps you could be in the listener role with Alan in the speaking role?

Betty: [interrupting] Do you want to hear about my trip to Florida?

TLS: Maybe later. Right now, I would like to have George and Alan speak with each other.

George: It's a good story. Why don't you tell them.

Betty: [starts telling her story to no one in particular].

I tried being "supportive but persistent" in dealing with their resistances, making my expectations clear:

TLS: I can see how difficult it is for you both (George and Alan) to speak with each other. But, I would like you both to practice talking with each other by doing this role play. Maybe with practice it will become easier! You can talk about anything you want, like the football game last night.

The strong alliance I had built up with George and Alan allowed me to push them to interact in ways in which they were not accustomed. At times I felt as if I was pushing George and Alan too hard, but I think part of that feeling came from how difficult it was to watch George and Alan interact. They were very uncomfortable with each other and often were at a loss for words. My instinct was to rescue them and not have them do role plays with each other. However, I continued to request their participation in role plays together because I wanted them to generalize these skills to increase the probability that they would engage in more positive interactions together outside the sessions. Their negative interactions were a major source of stress for Alan and thus a major risk factor for his illness.

Dealing With Resistance to Homework. The family was given assignments to practice the communication skills in between sessions. For example, they were asked to give positive feedback to each family member or to be a "listener" with each family member at some point between sessions. Because homework assignments are seen as an integral component to the generalization of the communication skills outside of the therapy sessions, I felt it was important for them to do the assignments. However, Alan and his parents rarely followed through with their assigned homework. They provided a number of excuses: they were too busy to practice the skills, they forgot, or Alan was too symptomatic.

When dealing with the resistance to the homework, I preferred not to challenge them but instead tried several other approaches. I would take responsibility for not explaining the assignment clearly enough and reiterate the rationale for the homework exercise. I explored their reasons for not doing the

homework, thinking that we might uncover some underlying issue that interfered with completing the task. Because the homework was rarely done, I always gave positive feedback for whatever portions they completed.

Despite all of my efforts, the family's compliance with the homework continued to be poor throughout the treatment. It was frustrating for me, because I felt a lot of responsibility as their therapist to get them to do the homework. Being part of a research study, I felt pressure to have the family follow through with the expectations of the therapy. In addition, in the supervision group the importance of the homework was often stressed. To my surprise and relief, however, there was evidence that Alan and his parents were generalizing the skills taught during the sessions even though they did not do specific assignments. They would talk about using specific skills with each other or with people outside the family. Thus, although I continued to assign homework, I did not feel I needed to be rigid about them doing the assignment in the specific way I had asked them. Perhaps this family was learning the skills by means of a different mechanism.

Dealing With Deeper Family Issues. Core individual and family issues (e.g., Alan's insecurities and George and Betty's marital conflict) surfaced during the communication-enhancement training. FFT, because it uses a skills training model, does not usually focus on exploring these issues in depth. However, when these issues interfered with skills training I felt I needed to explore them enough to understand how to proceed with teaching the skills. For example, Alan resisted doing a role play in which he was required to make positive requests of his parents. I explored Alan's resistance and found that he felt vulnerable and insecure when he asked others for help. He feared rejection. I knew that family treatment was not going to fully resolve that issue for him, but I felt that making requests of others was an important skill for Alan to have. Therefore, I spent time problem-solving with Alan how he could make requests of others without feeling so vulnerable.

The negative-feedback exercise uncovered several long-standing conflicts and old resentments that the family had difficulty putting aside to learn the skills, even when asked to focus on more neutral topics. In particular, Betty and George revealed long-standing conflicts in their marriage. Betty expressed resentment at George's instability in holding jobs over the years, and George expressed anger at Betty's overprotective behaviors with their children. The structure of the negative-feedback exercise (i.e., stating exactly what the person did that was upsetting, telling the person how it made you feel, and suggesting how the person could do it differently in the future) provided a format to give feedback in a noncritical manner. However, because of the underlying emotional conflict in their marriage, George and Betty's expression of negative feedback often sounded critical and judgmental, even with several rehearsals. This pattern is seen in Betty's attempts to give negative feedback to George:

Betty: You always leave your dishes laying around after you've eaten. I don't know why you won't pick them up. I always have to go around picking up after you and Alan.

Betty then received feedback from me on how to express her feedback in a different, more constructive manner. I asked her to repeat the negative feedback to George.

Betty: When I come home there are always dishes laying around. I'm tired, and I don't see why I should have to pick up after you. Can't you pick up after yourself?

Betty again received feedback from me on her role play, and I modeled how she might give George the feedback she wanted to express. Betty was able to describe the differences between my feedback and her own, but she was unable to incorporate this insight into her negative feedback to George. I acknowledged how hard it is to change ways of communicating and let Betty and the family know that they would have more opportunities to practice these skills.

Alan's family never fully mastered the skill of giving negative feedback; however, I observed an interesting process. When family members were able to

discuss how it felt being on the receiving end of the negative feedback, it seemed to take some of the power of the criticisms and negative judgments away. Especially for Alan, the criticisms no longer "shut him down." He was able to respond to the criticisms and problem solve about how to change the situation. Although studies have shown an association between relatives' critical attitudes toward patients with a mental illness and relapse (Hooley et al., 1996; Miklowitz, 1994; Parker & Hadzi-Pavlovic, 1990), I wondered whether Alan's growing ability not to internalize the criticisms acted as a protective mechanism for him against the stress of the criticism.

Dealing With Relapse. Bipolar disorder is a cyclic illness, and relapse is common (e.g., Gitlin, Swendsen, Heller, & Hammen, 1995). About 4 months after starting FFT, Alan experienced a relapse. He had a major depressive episode, which greatly affected his functioning. Although the episode resolved much faster than his prior depressive episodes, the relapse brought back his feelings of helplessness about managing the illness.

During the first session after resolution of the episode, the family questioned whether the treatment was effective, because it had not prevented the episode. That session was difficult for me. Alan's mood had not been consistently stable since we started treatment, and now he had had a full-blown episode. Perhaps his illness was too severe to be treated with family treatment. Perhaps he needed some intensive individual treatment.

I acknowledged how frustrating and discouraging a relapse can be and explored their feelings about the episode. We discussed how they handled the relapse, that is, what symptoms they were able to recognize, what efforts were effective in managing the symptoms, and what they would do differently in the future. This review helped the family recognize what they had done differently with this episode and helped them feel more control over their situation in regard to Alan's illness. They felt positive about the way they handled the relapse and felt the relapse drill helped them know what to do when faced with Alan's increased symptoms. Although it was not clear to the family (or to me) what effect the family treatment was having, by the end of the session the family felt better about the treatment.

Dealing with my own reactions to Alan's relapse was more difficult. Although Alan's bipolar illness was not as severe as that of other clients with whom I had worked, I questioned my ability to manage the treatment of Alan and his parents. When I expressed these doubts to the supervision group I realized that I felt a sense of failure because of Alan's relapse. I was measuring my success as a therapist in terms of Alan's course of illness. Although the theory is that FFT will improve the course of bipolar illness, the mechanism whereby treatment may affect the course of illness or the pace at which change may occur is not well defined. Therefore, even though my questions remained, I decided to be more patient with the treatment process and evaluate the effects of treatment after Alan and his parents had completed FFT. I also entertained the disturbing possibility that, with or without changes in the family, Alan's illness may not improve.

Problem-Solving Skills Training

The final portion of the family intervention focused on teaching an approach to solving problems. Without effective problem-solving strategies, family problems can go unresolved and can become a source of stress. The goal of the problem-solving module is to teach a structured problem-solving approach that families can use to see problems through to resolution. This approach involved six steps: (a) identifying a specific problem, (b) listing alternative solutions to the problem, (c) discussing the merits of each solution, (d) choosing an optimal solution or set of solutions, (e) planning how to implement these solutions, and (f) reviewing the effectiveness of the solutions chosen. As with the communication skills, I encouraged Alan and his parents to begin with simple problems and then to move to more emotionally laden or complex conflicts.

Often, by the time a family has reached the problem-solving module they have incorporated some of the communication skills, and they are able to progress through the problem-solving exercise with minimal direction from the therapists. However, Alan and his family had difficulty getting beyond the first step of the problem-solving: defining

the problem. They quickly reverted to their pattern of judging and criticizing, as shown in this interaction, during which they discussed how to decide what to watch on television in the evening:

TLS: The first thing is to agree on the problem. Why don't the three of you talk about the issue and use your speaking and listening skills to come up with an agreement on what the problem is.

Alan: The problem is what kind of a schedule to have for watching television.

George: Right. I've got a solution.

TLS: Hold onto your idea for the solution. We're not at that step yet. We're still trying to define the problem.

Cotherapist: It sounds like you need to define more explicitly why it's a problem because you've come up with some solutions in the past, but none of them have worked. So, what is the problem?

Betty: All George ever wants to watch is sports. [All laugh]

Betty and George begin to argue about what he watches on television while Alan writes down his definition of the problem.

TLS: It looks like you've written down the problem. Do you want to check out your definition of the problem with your parents?

Alan: What to do about the television schedule so that everybody is comfortable with the arrangement.

George: But I have to watch the sports review following the 5 o'clock news, all right?

Betty: No. I think everybody should vote on it.

Alan: [sounding irritated] We're supposed to be deciding if this is an accurate statement of the problem; we're not supposed to be solving the problem yet.

The family continued to discuss the definition for a few more minutes and was eventually able to come up with a definition of the problem on which all three of them agreed. After the problem was defined, Alan and his parents were able to progress through the problem-solving steps with little coaching from me and my cotherapist. In the problem-solving module I saw growth in the family's ability to handle difficult issues. For example, Alan was able to raise the issue of his parents being too overprotective, and they were able to use the problem-solving exercise to come up with ways to give him more space.

CONCLUSION

The integration of family-focused psychoeducational treatment with the individual treatment of Alan's bipolar illness seemed to positively affect the management of his illness in several ways. At the beginning of the family treatment, Alan and his parents were very discouraged about his prognosis and felt helpless in the face of the illness because his mood was so unstable after his latest manic episode. They were beginning to understand the cyclical nature of bipolar disorder, Alan's vulnerability to future episodes of mania or depression, and his lifelong need for treatment. Thus, they were motivated to know what they could do to get control of the illness and prevent further episodes. FFT helped them understand how they could influence the course of Alan's illness through effective management of stress within the family and helped Alan understand the importance of maintaining regular sleep–wake rhythms and adhering to medication regimens.

The education sessions, with Alan sharing his experience of his symptoms, helped Alan and his parents to be more understanding and accepting of his illness. At the beginning of FFT, Betty and George believed that Alan had more control over illness-related behaviors than he exerted. They had high expectations of him and were left angry and frustrated when he was unable to follow through with those expectations. With a better understanding of the illness, and an increased ability to distinguish Alan's normal moodiness from symptoms of his illness, Alan's parents were more realistic in what they expected of Alan and were more supportive of him. In addition, Alan was better at giving his parents clear messages about when he needed their help and

intervention. Thus, his parents did not need to be as involved with Alan's illness, because he was taking more responsibility in managing it. Together, these changes seemed to decrease the stress within the family and the stress on Alan, which possibly acted as a protective mechanism for him.

Communication and problem-solving skills training created more functional relationships among family members. Betty and George encouraged and supported Alan in engaging in more age-appropriate behavior. By the termination of treatment, Alan was pursuing activities outside the home, such as taking a real estate class and developing friendships outside the family, and Betty and George were making plans to travel. The illness was no longer the major focus in their lives. In general, the family was more involved with each other in a healthier way, and communication was more open, especially between Alan and his father. Alan seemed to be more confident in himself and his ability to manage his life and his illness.

Negative communication patterns were still apparent at the termination of therapy; Alan's parents continued to express criticism and blame toward Alan. Although the expression of critical statements by Alan's parents might have signified the presence of detrimental high-EE attitudes, qualitatively there was an important change in the family's interactional patterns. When Alan's parents were critical of him he would now stand up for himself instead of withdrawing and shutting down. He did not seem as sensitive to the criticisms. In addition, the negative interactions did not continue on for as long as they did at the beginning of therapy; someone would restate his or her negative comment in a different way or would refocus the family on the task at hand, breaking the negative cycle. Simoneau et al. (1998) found that the continuation of "point–counterpoint" negative interactions were more typical of high-EE families than of low-EE ones. Thus, even though Alan's parents continued to make negative statements, by the termination of treatment Alan's family appeared to be interacting more like a low-EE than a high-EE family, because the negativity did not persist.

Alan and his parents taught me about how families cope with the losses associated with having a family member with a psychiatric illness and how families can positively influence the patient in his or her struggle for control over the illness. The chronicity of bipolar disorder is an issue I had discussed with many families before treating Alan and his parents. However, this issue had new meaning for me with Alan and his family, perhaps because of my identification with Alan or his eloquent way of expressing his losses. I had a new appreciation for the devastation an illness such as bipolar disorder can cause in the life of the person with the illness and in the lives of his or her family members.

Given the challenges facing Alan and his parents, I was impressed by the strength, determination, and resiliency they showed in dealing with his illness. Although they were understandably frustrated at times with the instability of his illness, Alan's parents continued to be hopeful and supportive of him. That support was very meaningful to Alan and seemed to provide him with a base from which to fight his illness. The family's "fighting spirit" was certainly an inspiration to me during times when I questioned whether FFT was going to be helpful to Alan.

The treatment of Alan's bipolar disorder by integrating family-focused psychoeducation with the individual management of Alan's illness seemed to be an effective treatment modality for him. FFT increased the support and understanding Alan received from his parents and enhanced communication within the family. During the year following completion of FFT, Alan continued to be followed every 6 months to assess for symptoms of his illness. About 7 months following termination of FFT, Alan's psychiatrist tried to take him off of lithium. Alan experienced a rebound depression that lasted for about 2 months. This episode resolved when he was placed back on lithium. His mood was otherwise stable during the year following treatment. Thus, the episode seemed to be related to withdrawal of his mood-stabilizing medication. By the end of the second year of follow-up, Alan had started some part-time work out of his parents' home and was beginning to make plans to move out on his own.

Results from the CFP have shown a benefit of FFT over CMNF (Miklowitz et al., 2000). Patients who received family treatment showed greater improvements in depressive symptomatology over the year of treatment than patients who received crisis management with no family treatment. In addition, patients assigned to FFT had fewer relapses and longer periods between relapses than patients assigned to CMNF did. No significant differences were shown between groups in manic symptomatology. The mechanism by which FFT may be effective has yet to be understood, but there is evidence that changes in patients' positive interactional behavior mediates the relation between family treatment and changes in patients' symptomatology over the course of treatment (Simoneau, Miklowitz, Richards, Saleem, & George, 1999). Thus, family therapy may serve as a mechanism to re-engage bipolar patients with their families so they can benefit from the support of their relatives during a time of transition and crisis. It is clear that the family can play an important role in enhancing mood stability in the lives of bipolar patients.

References

Falloon, I .R. H., Boyd, J. L., & McGill, C. W. (1984). *Family care of schizophrenia*. New York: Guilford Press.

Falloon, I. R. H., Boyd, J. L., McGill, C. W., Razani, J., Moss, H. B., & Gilderman, A. M. (1982). Family management in the prevention of exacerbations of schizophrenia. *New England Journal of Medicine, 306*, 1437–1440.

Falloon, I. R. H., Boyd, J. L., McGill, C. W., Williamson, M., Razani, J., Moss, H. B., Gilderman, A. M., & Simpson, G. M. (1985). Family management in the prevention of morbidity of schizophrenia: Clinical outcome of a two-year longitudinal study. *Archives of General Psychiatry, 42*, 887–896.

Frank, E., Kupfer, J. J., Ehlers, C. L., Monk, T. H., Cornes, C., Carter, S., & Frankel, D. (1994). Interpersonal and social rhythm therapy for bipolar disorder: Integrating interpersonal and behavioral approaches. *The Behavior Therapist, 17*, 143–149.

Gitlin, M. J., Swendsen, J., Heller, T. L., & Hammen, C. (1995). Relapse and impairment in bipolar disorder. *American Journal of Psychiatry, 152*, 1635–1640.

Goldstein, M. J., & Miklowitz, D. J. (1994). Family intervention for persons with bipolar disorder.

In A. B. Hatfield (Ed.), *Family intervention in mental illness* (pp. 23–35). San Francisco: Jossey-Bass.

Goldstein, M. J., & Miklowitz, D. J. (1995). The effectiveness of psychoeducational family therapy in the treatment of schizophrenic disorders. *Journal of Marital and Family Therapy, 21,* 361–376.

Goldstein, M. J., Rodnick, E. H., Evans, J. R., May, P. R. A., & Steinberg, M. R. (1978). Drug and family therapy in the aftercare treatment of acute schizophrenia. *Archives of General Psychiatry, 35,* 169–177.

Hogarty, G. E., Anderson, C. M., Reiss, D. J., Kornblith, S. J., Greenwald, D. P., Javna, C. D., & Madonia, M. J. (1986). Family psychoeducation, social skills training, and maintenance chemotherapy in the aftercare treatment of schizophrenia: I. One-year effects of a controlled study on relapse and expressed emotion. *Archives of General Psychiatry, 43,* 633–642.

Hooley, J. M. (1986). Expressed emotion and depression: Interactions between patients and high- versus low-expressed-emotion spouses. *Journal of Abnormal Psychology, 95,* 237–246.

Hooley, J. M., & Licht, D. M. (1997). Expressed emotion and causal attribution in the spouses of depressed patients. *Journal of Abnormal Psychology, 106,* 298–306.

Hooley, J. M., Rosen, L. R., & Richters, J. E. (1996). Expressed emotion: Toward clarification of a critical construct. In G. Miller (Ed.), *The behavioral high-risk paradigm in psychopathology* (pp. 88–120). New York: Springer.

Leff, J., Kuipers, L., Berkowitz, R., Eberlein-Vries, R., & Sturgeon, D. (1982). A controlled trial of social intervention in the families of schizophrenic patients. *British Journal of Psychiatry, 141,* 121–134.

Leff, J., Kuipers, L., Berkowitz, R., & Sturgeon, D. (1985). A controlled trial of social intervention in the families of schizophrenic patients: Two year follow-up. *British Journal of Psychiatry, 146,* 594–600.

Malkoff-Schwartz, S., Frank, E., Anderson, B., Sherill, J. T., Siegel, L., Patterson, D., & Kupfer, D. J. (1998). Stressful life events and social rhythm disruption in the onset of manic and depressive bipolar episodes: A preliminary

investigation. *Archives of General Psychiatry, 55,* 702–707.

Marlatt, G. A., & Gordon, J. R. (Eds.). (1985). *Relapse prevention.* New York: Guilford Press.

Miklowitz, D. J. (1994). Family risk indicators in schizophrenia. *Schizophrenia Bulletin, 20,* 137–149.

Miklowitz, D. J., Frank, E., & George, E. L. (1996). New psychosocial treatments for the outpatient management of bipolar disorder. *Psychopharmacology Bulletin, 32,* 613–621.

Miklowitz, D. J., & Goldstein, M. J. (1997). *Bipolar disorder: A family-focused treatment approach.* New York: Guilford Press.

Miklowitz, D. J., Goldstein, M. J., Doane, J. A., Nuechterlein, K. H., Strachan, A. M., Snyder, K. S., & Magana-Amato, A. (1989). Is expressed emotion an index of a transactional process? I. Parents' affective style. *Family Process, 28,* 153–167.

Miklowitz, D. J., Goldstein, M. J., Falloon, I. R. H., & Doane, J. A. (1984). Interactional correlates of expressed emotion in the families of schizophrenics. *British Journal of Psychiatry, 144,* 482–487.

Miklowitz, D. J., Simoneau, T. L., George, E. A., Richards, J. A., Kalbag, A., Sachs-Ericsson, N., & Suddath, R. (2000). Family-focused treatment of bipolar disorder: One-year effects of a psychoeducational program in conjunction with pharmacotherapy. *Biological Psychiatry, 48,* 582–592.

Parker, G., & Hadzi-Pavlovic, D. (1990). Expressed emotion as a predictor of schizophrenia relapse: An analysis of aggregated data. *Psychological Medicine, 20,* 961–965.

Simoneau, T. L., Miklowitz, D. J., Richards, J. A., Saleem, R., & George, E. L. (1999). Bipolar disorder and family communication: Effects of a psychoeducational treatment program. *Journal of Abnormal Psychology, 108,* 588–597.

Simoneau, T. L., Miklowitz, D. J., & Saleem, R. (1998). Expressed emotion and interactional patterns in the families of bipolar patients. *Journal of Abnormal Psychology, 107,* 497–507.

Tarrier, N., Barrowclough, C., Vaughn, C., Bamrah, J. S., Porceddu, K., Watts, S., & Freeman, H. (1988). The community management of schizophrenia: A controlled trial of a behavioural intervention with families to reduce relapse. *British Journal of Psychiatry, 153,* 532–542.

CHAPTER 31

THE CONSEQUENCES OF CARING: MUTUAL HEALING OF FAMILY AND THERAPISTS FOLLOWING A SUICIDE

Nadine J. Kaslow and Sari Gilman Aronson

October 23, 1984—By the time you receive this, I shall have joined the ranks of the deceased. The time for regrets and amends has passed; and it is time for me to take definitive action before I lose my sanity. I am truly frightened at times; for what I am about to do is not reversible. However, I believe that taking my life is the only option left.

—Lea's suicide letter

Her problems were so terrible, we couldn't imagine how she could live with them. She seemed to try everything, and nothing helped her suffering.

—Lea's mother

We knew she would kill herself, we just didn't know when.

—Lea's father

In reflecting on the diverse families from whom we have learned, I realized that one of the most poignant and powerful family contacts that we have had was with the family of a patient who killed herself. In preparing this chapter, we experienced again the long-term overt and subtle professional and personal reverberations of our work with this patient and family.

We saw Lea in individual therapy in a cotherapy model for 2 years while we were in training. Two years after starting therapy, Lea killed herself. Lea's

treatment with us was characterized by a flexible integration of a variety of individually oriented therapeutic techniques (e.g., biological psychiatry, psychodynamic psychotherapy, cognitive–behavioral therapy, community interventions). Although family dynamics were a central focus, with the exception of one occasion we were unable to integrate family therapy into Lea's overall treatment during Lea's lifetime. However, 2 years after her death we spent a therapeutic afternoon with her parents. Working through Lea's suicide forced us to examine the biological, psychological, and social factors leading to her death. As a result of our experience we came to appreciate the need to involve the family in all individual cases of adults with serious psychiatric disorders.

We begin by describing Lea's life and suicide. Then we discuss our postintervention work (interventions following a suicide) with the family. Finally, we articulate how our involvement with Lea's family indelibly influenced our development as clinicians.

TREATMENT STRUCTURE

It was common in our training milieu for people with a severe mental illness to be treated in individual therapy in a cotherapy model as well as to receive community-based and family interventions. The cotherapy approach facilitated our sharing of the burden of treatment and the provision of a holding environment. We treated Lea together from

---

This chapter was written to honor the memory of our patient, Lea, and is dedicated to her parents.

October 1982 to June 1984; Sari was a psychiatry resident, and Nadine was a psychology intern. Following Nadine's move to a new city for a faculty job, Sari treated Lea alone until Lea's suicide in October 1984. Because of the intensity of Lea's suicidal ideation, self-destructive behavior, and her social isolation, we devised a daily telephone plan, with each therapist responsible for alternating weeks of calls. Medication management was ongoing. We had contact with Lea's roommate, ex-lover, work supervisor, Alcoholics Anonymous sponsor, and mother.

We were supervised by a supportive and experienced community-oriented psychiatrist, with additional consultations by psychiatrists, clinical psychologists, and psychoanalysts. For the most part, supervision and consultations did not focus on engaging the family.

LEA'S LIFE

When we met Lea, she was 29, divorced, and working as a nurse's aide at a state psychiatric hospital for children and adolescents. She had been hospitalized for depression, suicidality, and alcohol and drug use following an argument with her lesbian lover (Sue) over their breakup. Lea was referred to us, because no private therapist was willing to care for her; "she is too difficult to treat and a high suicide risk."

In our first few meetings, we learned that Lea was born in a medium-size Midwestern city, the only child of an intact marriage. Her father was a manager in a large corporation, and her mother was an administrative assistant. Lea told us her mother had alcohol and depression problems; her mother denied this. Lea also let us know that she had had numerous childhood hospitalizations for pneumonia and had sustained a head injury at age 4 following a car accident. Her mother described her as the "neatest little kid," who was intelligent (Lea's IQ was reportedly 160) and curious, although her school performance was average, and she often skipped school. Lea described herself as "friendly but shy and a loner." Lea depicted her parents' marriage as "tense and unsatisfactory, and I had serious problems with both my parents."

Lea married a coworker in her hometown at age 20:

Sam was kind, so I felt really bad about abusing drugs and alcohol and sleeping around, and so I divorced him. Then, I became involved with Sue, and we moved here together. I wanted to leave my parents, but not be too far away, and I needed a better job. . . . My attendance at school was erratic, but I did complete my junior year in college, and received an [Associate's] degree as a nurse's aide. I have been an aide and an emergency medical technician, and I've done okay. But, I stole medications from each job. . . . I've been on a softball team and in a bowling league. . . . I was afraid to get close to anyone.

When asked about her psychiatric history, Lea told us that she had been depressed and had heard voices since age 4.

The voices became hostile and critical when in my early 20s and around the same time, I started losing it. I was hospitalized five times for trying to kill myself, and three of those times I almost died. Most times I tried to kill myself was after I broke up with somebody. I have also had tons of inpatient and outpatient substance abuse treatment.

On the basis of Lea's history and presentation, we diagnosed her as having schizoaffective disorder, depressive type; alcohol and polysubstance dependence, in partial remission; borderline personality disorder; and temporal lobe epilepsy.

OUR THERAPY WITH LEA

When we met Lea, she was friendly, motivated, afraid, and guarded. "I don't want so many extremes. I am tired of being at the edge of the cliff with depression. It's been a roller coaster, and I want to have something to live for." She was reluctant to describe her day-to-day life or her past. Concerning her family, Lea said,

My parents looked like a nice couple to others, but they fought a lot. I was the

peacemaker and the battleground. Dad
was closer to me and defended me, which
made my mom jealous. But Dad also hit
me until I turned 16. I remember when he
was so angry he said he was going to
kill me.

Working with Lea quickly became challenging, as she failed to answer her telephone at the appointed times, canceled sessions, slashed her wrists, threatened to stab or shoot herself with her roommate's loaded gun, and drank.

Lea: When I do these things, it's like I am watching myself in a movie. I am not sure I want to give up my escape hatches.

Nadine: You give mixed messages. You come for help and tell us how scared you are, and yet you refuse our help.

Lea: I don't believe anybody cares about me.

Sari: Well, we are here because we are interested in helping you.

Lea: Ever since I was a child, it's been hopeless.

Following our initial and intense roller coaster ride with Lea, and after she attended her grandfather's funeral with her parents, we began to feel more warmly toward Lea as she became more engaged in therapy and less symptomatic. We appreciated the courage it took for her to begin to share childhood memories of hurt, abandonment, and punishment.

> *My mother was unpredictable and reject-*
> *ing. She'd be nice and then she would at-*
> *tack me and tell me she didn't love me*
> *anymore. I hate myself because my mother*
> *hated me and I bet that's why I want*
> *to die.*

Lea became preoccupied with the possibility that her father was dying and that neither parent would discuss it with her. "My father is the most important person in my life, and I don't want him to die before I do. I can't live without him." One of her poems, "Parents," captured some of her feelings.

> *As you lie sleeping miles away*
> *I am awake and thinking of you*
> *Here I am, the child of your dreams*
> *Your link in the chain of immortality*
> *I am in pain and I cannot tell you*
> *For I have seen you hurt too much already*
> *To see your faces would mean the world*
> *But enable me to hurt myself even more*
> *You have always loved me and wished me*
> * well*
> *And tonight I will do the same for you*
> *For tomorrow I may no longer be here*
> *To carry on your hopes and your*
> *validation of life.*

Another poem, "Returning Home," written prior to a visit home, captured her struggle to differentiate from her parents and her desire to bond more positively with them.

> *And so we are to become acquainted again*
> *After many years of emotional absence.*
> *The love has always existed*
> *But has worn many faces*
> *And the faces were not always gentle.*
> *I come to you with different ways*
> *Because I am learning all over again.*
> *Some of those ways undo what you have*
> * taught*
> *And substitute emotional honesty.*
> *I am afraid of the retrograde anger I feel*
> *For I do not wish to blame or accuse*
> *Merely to understand that some things*
> * were not right.*
> *You may find my honesty cause of discom-*
> * fort*
> *For I will tell you that I do love you*
> *But that your power over me has lessened*
> *And I do not stand in awe anymore.*

After discussing this poem and Lea's destabilizing reactions to her visit home, we more actively encouraged her to consider family sessions.

Nadine: We could help you have a more honest relationship with your parents if they joined us for family sessions or if you and your parents saw other therapists for family meetings.

Lea: I am not interested.

Sari: This could be really helpful, why are you reluctant to consider this?

Lea: It would be too hard.

Sari: Is there anything we could do to help you feel more able to talk with them?

Lea: I can tell what you guys are doing, and I'm not interested. End of discussion.

In addition to these direct discussions with Lea about the value of family therapy, we explored her differential feelings to us and how these related to feelings about her parents. We hoped such interchanges would shed light on Lea's reluctance to have family meetings and that resolution of the issues raised would set the stage for future family meetings.

> *Nadine, I can't live without you. You are the only person I trust. You are empathic and understand me even when I don't. I think we are soulmates. Sari, I know you care about me and have my best interests in mind. I just can't feel as comfortable with you. You must dislike me or get sick of me, even though you don't act that way.*

Lea would say that her reactions to us were "not anything like how I feel toward my parents." When we discussed the splitting, overidealization, and devaluation, Lea would say (happily) "That's just how I feel." Over time, she began to acknowledge some similarities between her negative feelings toward both parents and her reactions toward Sari. "Neither of my parents are like you, Nadine. The closest thing is anything that was good with my father."

Finally, and after a number of months, Lea requested that we meet with her and her parents to improve their communication. We spent considerable time preparing for this session.

Lea: I am very concerned about my parents' visit. I don't know how the session is going to go. I am not sure my mother really cares about me. She can't support me when I'm different from her.

Sari: You've come a long way to be willing to have this session.

Lea: That's true. I'm interested in what they are going to say.

Nadine: Your parents' willingness to come for a session indicates that they want to help you out.

In July 1983, we met with Lea and her mother. Her father canceled at the last minute. We used a model for the session developed for female patients with borderline personality disorder and their mothers (Teitelman, Glass, Blyn, & Jennings, 1979) to help Lea and her mother express their positive feelings toward each other. We suggested that they not focus on the negative aspects of their relationship until they felt a more positive connection.

Lea: I'm glad you came, Mother.

Mother: I am really glad that you asked me. I've never done this before, but I really hope it can improve our relationship.

Lea: I am nervous, too, but they convinced me it was worth a try.

Mother: Lea, I haven't been very good at telling you how often I think of you and how much I care about you. That's probably because my parents didn't really know how to do that with me. Having you was one of the best things that ever happened to me, and I have loved you from the moment I laid eyes on you. It just seems like everything went wrong.

Nadine: How things went wrong is a concern to both of you, but what we are trying to focus on now is the positives that are obviously there. And Mom, you did a good job getting us started with that.

Lea: It means a lot to me to hear you say you have always loved me. I have always loved you, too. I have always appreciated your intelligence, and you encouraged me to develop my own.

Mother: I have always thought that you are brilliant and you are gifted, too. You are imaginative, creative, and good with words.

Lea: Right now my words are failing me.

Both Lea and her mother told us the session was helpful, and we felt they had made some progress. At the end of the session, Lea said "this was better than I expected." The following conversation later ensued.

Lea: I expressed positive feelings toward my mother, and she listened. I am really disappointed my father didn't come.

Sari: How could you talk with him about how much his presence would mean to you?

Lea: There's no point to this.

Nadine: We won't know until you try.

Lea: Sari, are you ganging up on me, too?

Sari: This is really painful, but it might be helpful.

Lea: It's just the story of my life, and I'm ready to drop it.

Shortly after this session, Lea had more urges to drink and thoughts of dying. We listened as she described hallucinations of people coming toward her, laughing, and criticizing her. She told us daily that she was not doing well at work or school and that she wanted to stop therapy. At times she told us that her mind was blank, and at other times she indicated that she felt overwhelmed by her sadness and hopelessness. She shared her confusion about her bisexuality. When we suggested more family work, Lea replied, "If we do that, my voices will get worse, the apparitions will haunt me, and I'll have to kill myself."

In 1984 Nadine accepted a faculty position at another university that would begin in July. Sari had one year of residency left. We both talked with Lea about treatment options, and she decided to continue with Sari. As termination with Nadine approached (June 20, 1984), Lea became more psychotic and dissociated. After termination, Lea sent Nadine a warm and loving letter and gift, and spoke with her twice on the telephone. Nadine and Sari communicated each time Lea contacted Nadine.

Lea continued to worsen, despite taking antide-pressant, antipsychotic, and anti-epileptic medications. Her suicidality intensified after Nadine left, leading to a hospitalization the day Nadine moved. Following discharge, Lea deteriorated further.

Lea: My mother never phoned me when I was discharged. I don't think she gives a shit. Would you believe that my father offered to pay for me to go to school? For the first time in my life, he wants to send money to help me. I don't think there is any point to this therapy.

Lea persistently wanted Sari to sanction her death and considered her refusal a serious breach of empathy. She decided not to visit her family as planned and continued to talk of her desire to "end it all . . . give in, and kill myself." She denied a specific suicide plan: "I can't kill myself yet, it would devastate my parents. And, if I want to kill myself, you can't stop me."

Over the next few months, Lea stopped all involvement with others, including her family. Her work attendance became spotty, and her coworkers and supervisor were concerned about her talk of suicide. This led to meetings and three-way telephone calls among Sari, Lea, and Lea's supervisor to help preserve her job.

Three weeks prior to her death, Lea reported the following.

Lea: I am more into my psychosis, my private world, which is peaceful and kind. I want to leave town and start over.

Sari: I think we should talk about how things are going.

Lea: No, that would be too much effort for me.

Sari: I'm concerned that you broke off contact with three friends.

Lea: I'm also not talking to my parents. I'm angry with everybody. At least when I am angry, I do better on my tests in school.

Prior to her suicide, she called in sick for 1 week and then worked the night preceding her death. On this evening, she told Sari on the telephone, "I hit my favorite patient tonight. My behavior horrifies me. This is something I just can't live with."

On October 23, 1984, Lea wrote separate suicide notes to each of us but did not mail them until the day she committed suicide. The next day, she brought in her diary and photograph album for Sari to "read and toss." Lea was so upset when leaving that the session was extended, and she agreed to return the next day. The next day Lea said she wouldn't kill herself, but Sari remained concerned. On October 26 a session was held with Lea, Sari, and Sari's supervisor. Lea refused all interventions and was not committable. On October 29 Lea failed to keep her appointment, Sari received Lea's suicide letter and notified the police. Over the weekend, when Lea did not come to work, her ex-lover, Sue, telephoned the police. Sue and the police entered Lea's apartment and found her dead. The death was classified a suicide; the date of death was estimated as October 26, 1984.

The Suicide Letters

We were informed of Lea's death by means of the only two suicide letters that she wrote. These letters highlight the interpersonal dynamics that are critical to appreciating Lea and her family dynamics.

> *Dearest Nadine,*
>
> *By the time you receive this, I shall have joined the ranks of the deceased. The time for regrets and amends has passed; and it is time for me to take definitive action before I lose my sanity. I am truly frightened at times; for what I am about to do is not reversible. However, I believe that taking my life is the only option left. Perhaps in eternal rest, I could finally sleep; and I would welcome that wholeheartedly. As Odette had Von Rothbart, I have the voices—however, I cannot escape the curse. These past few weeks have been hell. The voices are calling me from far away—and now, I must join them. After all I've tried for two years, seems like twenty . . . seems like twenty. I would like to [make] clear at the outset that the closeness that existed between us was not a*

mistake on the part of the therapist. Rather, getting to know you and becoming attached to you has been one of the warmest, richest experiences in my life. Before I threw my journal away, it gave me great pleasure to relive the building of a trust relationship, to respect, to affection. You taught me and gave me a great deal; and no matter what type of hell I end up in, I will always remember and be comforted. From my vantage point, you and Sari gave me two years that I would not otherwise have had. That can only attest to your expertise as therapists. I am saddened by thoughts of my kitties—my father will have them put to sleep, as was my other cat. Maybe we will reunite at another time and place. So, Nadine, I will bid you farewell—bereft of dignity, funds, friends, and my sanity. I have remembered things lately that are driving me over the cliff's edge; and so, I shall plunge into the abyss. Do not mourn my passing—remember the humor instead. I shall miss you, Nadine.

> *Fondly, Lea*

And to Sari . . .

> *Dearest Sari,*
>
> *By the time you receive this, I shall be dead—no melodrama to it; just a simple statement of fact. Your words keep ringing in my ears, "we'll probably get over it"—and I know that you will—and quickly—your anger at me will supplant emotionality and caring; and will hasten the healing process. The quotation from the Apology of Socrates that I was trying to recall is "For this fear of death is indeed the pretense of wisdom, and not real wisdom, being the appearance of knowing the unknown; since no one knows whether death, which they in their fear apprehend to be the greatest evil, may not be the greatest good" and, for me, I feel that it is the most humane thing to do. To conquer death, you only have to die. To conquer living, I must not*

only contend with my world around me; I must also struggle with myself. And, as I've been telling you these past few weeks, I am very tired. There is a touch of irony to this—I was born on a Wednesday, and shall die on a Wednesday—"Wednesday's child is full of woe" as the rhyme goes. . . . I read my journal before I threw it out—I felt amusement and affection as I read my entries about never becoming as comfortable with you as I became with Dr. K.— and the steady progression from liking, to trusting, to genuine affection and attachment—. I shall cherish the memories. And, so, Sari, I shall leave you—I am emotionally bankrupt and tired of fighting for nothing. I will do as the voices have been bidding me for the last few weeks; and join the motley assemblage—the cacophony that robs me of even sleep. I hope you have learned from me as I have from you [then] I would know that my life amounted to something. . . . I know that I shall languish in eternal torment for what I am about to do—but, perhaps a different kind of hell will be more palatable. I only know that the voices and apparitions double-teamed me the other night until I finally fainted. I hope that God bestows his blessing on you; and I know from my own observations that you will do extremely well in your field—you are excellent at what you do. Goodbye, Sari—and take good care of yourself—I have an investment in you.

Fondly, Lea

From early on, Lea had different transferences to us, which were reflected in the two suicide notes. For the most part, she idealized Nadine and devalued Sari. However, at times, she became rageful toward Nadine and felt warmly toward Sari. She developed an unhealthy symbiotic attachment to Nadine and thus felt threatened when that relationship was disrupted. Lea reported falling in love with Nadine but felt too ashamed to discuss these feelings. Her suicide note to Nadine was warmer and

more loving than the one sent to Sari, yet embedded in it was Lea's disappointment and hostility. We believe that Lea's reactions toward Nadine reflected her experience in her family in which attachment was associated with symbiosis leading to either a lack of a true self or total self-annihilation when the attachment is disrupted. Lea more openly expressed hostility and ambivalence to Sari. She projected her anger onto Sari and distorted Sari's behavior toward her. For example, Lea took out of context the phrase, "we'll probably get over it" and used this phrase to blame Sari, much like she blamed her parents, for her death. She believed that the anger she had projected onto Sari would overpower Sari's positive attachment to her, which would minimize the effects of her suicide. Similarly, she believed that her parents would not be affected if she died.

Despite a focus on the transference, we, our supervisors, and Lea were unable to discern the roots of many of her reactions. We assume this was related to Lea's difficulty discussing past experiences and memories. Lea felt bereft and hopeless following the loss of her perceived fusion with Nadine. She was flooded with painful memories, which she felt unable to discuss: "I have remembered things lately that are driving me over the cliff's edge; and, so, I shall plunge into the abyss." Throughout the treatment, questions regarding sexual abuse were raised with Lea; however, she denied memories of any such experiences.

Course of Events Following Lea's Suicide

On learning of Lea's death, each of us had brief telephone contact with Lea's parents. We offered support, answered questions, and left the door open for further contact. Our next 1½ years were characterized by soul searching, emotional pain, and a distance in our close friendship that only Lea's suicide could explain. On Mothers Day—not coincidentally, 18 months after Lea's suicide—we talked about how Lea's family dynamics had permeated our responses to her death and our friendship. It was clear that we needed to visit her grave.

This visit, which occurred in a distant state, took place following a series of telephone calls between ourselves and Lea's parents. Although we only asked for the location of Lea's grave, her mother invited us to their home. She later telephoned us, reiterating her invitation and stressing how much such a visit would mean to her and her husband.

Nadine: We really appreciate your inviting us to your home.

Mother: We know you both went to a lot of trouble to come here, and we are surprised and grateful. We realize that this may be difficult for you.

Sari: This is difficult for all of us. I was touched by your openness and desire to talk with us.

Nadine: Are there ways we can be helpful to you?

Father: We don't understand why she was so troubled. We were surprised you kept her alive as long as you did. We distanced from her because we knew it would be painful when she died.

Sari: I think all of us wished things had gone differently, and are left with questions. What's been your way of understanding what happened?

Father: [Turns to his wife and says quietly] I don't know.

Mother: Lea was the most creative and fun child, but she started having lots of trouble when she turned 12. We never understood if it was the head injury, or her epilepsy, or something we did wrong, or something we knew nothing about. As she got older, she pulled away so far, it was impossible to reach her. She didn't think we loved her.

Nadine: What's clear is that you both loved her very much and are very pained by her death.

Mother: [Silence] You know, we haven't been able to talk about her death, except for right after she died. It's still very hard for us.

Father: I think it was my fault; I remember hitting her when she was little.

Mother: No, that's not it. You know she always adored you. I was the one who she felt was so cold and rejecting and who she hated.

Father: You did the best you could.

Mother: But it wasn't good enough. [begins crying]

Nadine: This makes you really sad and [it] seems like you each feel guilty. Those are normal feelings that most families have when someone they love commits suicide. People also feel anger or shame or lonely or rejected when there's a suicide.

Mother: That sounds familiar. It's hard for us to talk about those things. Did the two of you have those feelings. Can you talk about them?

Sari: Yes, we each have felt all of those feelings at different times.

Nadine: Initially, it was really hard for us to talk about our reactions. We have worked very hard to talk about this with each other, and coming here today is part of that process.

Mother: How did you learn to talk about it?

Sari: It hasn't been easy, but we just kept trying. Maybe our talking about this today will help the two of you be able to continue to talk about it.

Mother: I can't believe Lea never thought her death would really hurt us.

Father: We haven't known what to do, so we just go on.

We talked with Lea's parents for a few more hours, and they shared more of their pain. The four of us tried to put together the pieces of Lea's life and death. We used discretion in what we shared but did offer useful insights to her parents. They painted a picture of Lea before her major difficulties began, provided more information about her medical and psychiatric history, and shared her autopsy report. We all discussed the possibility that traumas had occurred in Lea's life that she was unable to disclose. Her parents were curious to know if she had told us anything that would help them better understand her. We gained a richer sense of the warmth that had existed in her family. We all came to a mutual understanding that Lea's difficulties were a result of biological, psychological, and social factors that interacted in a lethal manner. At the end of our meeting, her parents thanked us for coming, expressed a desire for future contact, and said they would be more able to talk with one another. Lea's father suggested we follow them to the graveyard, a place he visited frequently.

WAYS THIS FAMILY CHANGED OUR THINKING AND PRACTICE

Our involvement with Lea and her family helped us grow personally and professionally as we struggled to recover from an early psychotherapy trauma. No therapist can lose a patient to suicide and not ask "What did I do wrong, and what should I have done differently?" We were fortunate that Lea's parents were helpful in our efforts to address these questions. The major ways our involvement with Lea and her family influenced us as psychotherapists; family therapists; supervisors and, in Sari's case, as a physician are the realizations that (a) we acknowledge the need to involve the family in the treatment of adults with serious psychiatric disorders, (b) we know the value of family therapy even when only an individual is present, (c) we appreciate the importance and power of postintervention for families whose loved one has committed suicide, and (d) we are committed to the belief that families and therapists can provide mutual healing.

Family Involvement for Adults With Serious Psychiatric Disorders

We will never know if Lea's death could have been avoided if family therapy had occurred. Although research underscores the importance of family involvement for individuals with character problems or psychotic disorders, and for suicidal people, the literature does not address ways to engage the family when the adult patient is adamantly against any family involvement. We never thought of terminating the treatment because of her refusal, and we believe that such an action would have been irresponsible and unwise.

As a consequence of our failure to involve Lea's family actively in her therapy, we have become assertive with adult patients in encouraging and addressing concerns about family therapy. However, we are sensitive to family members' fears that such an approach would destabilize the family in a harmful way and that specific parameters may need to be applied when these concerns seem potentially warranted. In addition, when working with families who are geographically separated, and where there are concerns that periodic sessions would destabilize the family's homeostasis without offering the requisite support for the family to address the issues elicited during sessions, we have implemented more regularly scheduled conference calls.

Family Therapy With an Individual

Lea taught us that it is helpful to conduct family therapy with an individual, even those with serious psychiatric disorders, for whom family-of-origin exploration cannot be primary. The treatment may be facilitated by two therapists, as the triad may elicit key family interactional patterns. Such a structure increases the possibility that the adult patient can experience a more positive family-type environment that enables her or him to develop a more positive sense of self, a higher degree of autonomy, and more adaptive interpersonal skills. Such changes can set the stage for the patient to engage with her or his family in a more differentiated manner.

For such a process to occur, and for splitting to be addressed, the cotherapists need to examine their interactions with the patient and one another and ascertain how these interactions reflect their own personal psychologies and the patient's family dynamics. When the latter is the case, and the therapists discuss these interactions with each other and with the patient, illuminating information about family dynamics may emerge. Our work with Lea helped us to appreciate the importance of sharing information without blurring the therapeutic boundaries. Our contacts with Lea and her parents underscored that there may be a large discrepancy between one family member's perceptions of the family and the full nature of the family relationships and that this discrepancy should be a focus of the therapy.

Postintervention

We wish such books as *Suicide and Its Aftermath: Understanding and Counseling the Survivors* (Dunne, McIntosh, & Dunne-Maxim, 1987) or *Silent Grief: Living in the Wake of Suicide* (Lukas & Seiden, 1997) had been available when Lea died or even when we went to visit her family. The strategies described for working with survivors of suicide could have guided our interventions, and we may have been able to communicate with Lea's family sooner and in more depth. In addition, we could have recommended to the family that they read these books, because the stories shared and information provided would have enabled them to feel less alone in their grief and pain.

In preparing for our postintervention meeting with Lea's parents, we had to work through much of our sadness, anger, guilt, shame, and fear. Addressing our reactions with one another was a complicated and painful undertaking. We tried to help each other, each wishing that our reactions were more similar and that the other could just comfort us. That our distance from each other paralleled that of Lea's parents was confirmed when we met with them. When conducting postinterventions now, we emphasize the importance of each individual coming to terms with her or his reactions and with family members learning to accept differential reactions within the family unit.

We each felt very sad about Lea's death, and both of us felt guilty and responsible for her suicide. Nadine believed her leaving killed Lea because of the intensity of their attachment. Sari felt she was unable to influence Lea's self-destructiveness because of Lea's rejection of her efforts to help. Both of us feared being blamed by the family; this concern was more prominent for Sari. We debated about the amount of contact to have with Lea's family when we went to visit her grave. Because we were professionally young, our healing may have taken longer and delayed any major outreach to the family. Once we engaged in a healing process within the cotherapy dyad we were able to help Lea's parents work through some of their grief, sadness, anger, shame, guilt, fear, helplessness, rejection, and blame. To help families through this difficult process, it may be useful for the family therapist to

- underscore that the individual who committed suicide saw no other alternative and chose the only pathway that would alleviate her or his suffering;
- communicate the acceptability of grieving;
- highlight the importance of the survivors not be-

coming self-destructive and of obtaining emotional and physical support;
- explore and monitor family members' own suicidality;
- educate the family about suicide, the grief process, and the value of mutual support groups;
- teach effective coping strategies for managing painful feelings and loss; and
- examine family members' prior experiences with loss.

Mutual Healing of Therapists and Families

On the basis of our socialization as family therapists, we had assumed that it was our job to be a healer, coach, or conductor, depending on the theoretical orientation that guided our interventions. It was not until we met with Lea's family that we came to appreciate the extent to which the families with which we work can help us to examine and work through our own unresolved emotions and conflicts. The fact that our meeting with Lea's parents led to mutual healing for all concerned has resulted in our being more receptive to the ways in which families in therapy can and do serve as supervisors and family therapists for their therapists.

There was much that we learned and were able to address during and following our meeting with Lea's parents that may not have been possible otherwise. First, on the basis of their feedback during the postintervention session, our perspectives on families' reactions to suicide were broadened. What we had not anticipated was their lack of surprise about Lea's suicide, their appreciation for our efforts, their empathy for our pain, and their understanding of the challenge that Lea's life and death posed for us as therapists. These reactions enabled us to be more accepting of Lea's death and more compassionate toward ourselves. Second, we were able to see how creating a context in which all four of us could share our particular voices about Lea enabled us to better understand her, her suicide, and our reactions to her death. The emotional gifts we received from Lea's family were unexpected. Our experience with Lea's family and many families since then has highlighted the possibilities for growth for therapists and families when they work together in a manner that is mutually healing.

CONCLUDING COMMENTS

Our writing of this chapter has been another important step in healing and growth. Prior steps included extensive discussions with one another, conversations with trusted colleagues, meeting with Lea's family, and presenting Lea's case in detail to the American Foundation for Suicide Prevention. Each of our careers was influenced in major ways by Lea's life and death. Nadine initially treated many borderline and psychotic women with serious histories of self-mutilation and suicidal behavior. She later conducted clinical research on suicidal behavior in women and developed expertise in postintervention work with families. Sari continued to work with severely ill suicidal and violent patients and has trained others to work with patients with psychiatric illness and character pathology who are prone to violence. For both of us, these professional trajectories reflect an effort to gain mastery over Lea's suicide.

The most challenging aspect of writing this chapter was deciding how self-disclosing to be. How much was it advisable or safe for us to honestly share our profound feelings of guilt, failure, incompetence, loss, and shame regarding our treatment of Lea; our lack of treatment of Lea's family; and our differential reactions to Lea during her life and her death? A major factor in our sharing of this situation was that Lea's family was open with us, respectful of our process, and appreciative of our personal and professional efforts. As a result of our good fortune at being able to achieve a positive connection with Lea's parents, we have been able to come to terms with Lea's death.

References

Dunne, E. J., McIntosh, J. L., & Dunne-Maxim, K. (1987). *Suicide and its aftermath: Understanding and counseling the survivors*. New York: Norton.

Lukas, C., & Seiden, H. (1997). *Silent grief: Living in the wake of suicide*. Northvale, NJ: Aronson.

Teitelman, E., Glass, J. B., Blyn, C., & Jennings, D. (1979). The treatment of female borderlines. *Schizophrenia Bulletin, 5*, 111–117.

PART VII
SUPERVISION

CHAPTER 32

INTEGRATIVE SUPERVISION: A METAFRAMEWORKS PERSPECTIVE

Catherine Weigel Foy and Douglas C. Breunlin

In the autumn of 1997 we both attended a conference to commemorate the 25th anniversary of the first family therapy training conference sponsored by the Institute for Juvenile Research (IJR) in 1972. A group of distinguished presenters gathered to reflect on the evolution of the field. The legacy of the pioneers and the models they spawned were lauded, but presentations about contemporary family therapy clearly signaled that today the field is evolving toward integration. Having taught and practiced family therapy in Chicago for decades, we felt it fitting that such a conference would occur in the Midwest, which has served as an intellectual meeting place to synthesize the pure and sometimes controversial theories put forth by the East and West coast traditions of family therapy (Breunlin, Rampage, & Eovaldi, 1995). For example, Pinsof and his colleagues at The Family Institute developed "integrative problem-centered therapy" (e.g., Pinsof, 1995), and Breunlin, Schwartz, and Karrer (1997) at IJR developed "the metaframeworks perspective."

However, the conference offered no specific workshop on how to supervise from an integrative perspective. This follows the pattern in the field, where supervisory practices arrive on the coattails of theory development in family therapy. During the 1980s much effort was devoted to the development and articulation of supervisory practices (Liddle, Breunlin, & Schwartz, 1988). It is not surprising that we now struggle to articulate exactly what an integrative supervision would look like (Breunlin et al., 1995), and we offer this chapter as an example of our work.

This case study illustrates integrative supervision grounded in the following theoretical principles. First, because integrative supervision holds everything about a case to be potentially relevant, being problem focused helps manage the complexity of supervision. The guiding principle is: If a theory isn't relevant to solving the problem at hand, then it isn't relevant. What are relevant are the constraints that keep the family from finding and implementing an adaptive solution to the problem (Breunlin, 1999). Bateson (1972) called this *negative explanation*. Constraints can be uncovered in many ways, but a straightforward way is to ask the question "What keeps you from . . . ?" Families and their therapists solve problems by collaboratively identifying and lifting constraints. Once the constraints are lifted, the family will find its own solution. Constraints occur in the human domains of action, meaning, and emotion and can exist anywhere in a biopsychosocial system. We encourage therapists, therefore, to hypothesize and access all necessary levels, including the levels of biology, person, relationship, family, community, and society. Whatever the level, we use the six metaframeworks proposed by Breunlin et al. (1997) to identify and name the constraints: organization, sequences, development, mind, culture, and gender. For example, if polarization of parental leadership keeps a child from being respectful, we would say that an organizational constraint exists at the level of the family.

The same theory of constraints applies to supervision. As supervisors, we want to know what a particular supervisee needs to learn to become a better therapist and what keeps him or her from learning it. By addressing the supervisee's constraints to learning we are providing effective supervision that addresses both the needs of the supervisee and the case. To illustrate the process of integrative supervision, we have selected one case from which we present four vignettes.

Our therapist in training, Elaine, entered a postgraduate training program to learn systemic therapy. An African American in her late 30s, Elaine was married and had three children. She had recently completed her master's degree in counseling psychology, during which she had received training primarily in individual therapy. Before beginning graduate studies, she had worked in a variety of settings within the human services field with direct service responsibilities. In this capacity, Elaine had provided parent training to court-ordered clients in a mental health center. In her current work she met only briefly with individual adult clients for solution-focused assessment and intervention before referring them for further treatment. This professional background created the initial expectations Elaine held about the practice of therapy and its relation to what she was about to learn.

Elaine's first training case was the Cancia family, consisting of a father, Michael (age 39, an ironworker), a mother, Sylvia (age 34, an insurance clerk), Zachary (age 10), and Anna (age 6). Sylvia stated that the presenting problem was Zach's anger, which frequently erupted both at home and at school. She believed that his angry attitude conveyed a lack of respect for his elders, including herself. He disobeyed her, defied his aunt, and hit a female teacher. Before the first session, we discussed these symptoms and wondered how they might be construed as a presenting problem. Elaine suggested that Zach sounded like a pretty disrespectful little boy. We agreed that in the initial session Elaine would organize her conversation around the constraint question: What kept Zach from being respectful?

The entire therapy occurred over a 9-month period and included 14 sessions. During this time the constraints that kept Zach from being respectful were addressed successfully. The work included changing the way Sylvia dealt with Zach when he

was angry, addressing a coalition between Sylvia and Anna against Zach, working with Sylvia around marital conflict that eventually led to a separation, improving the sibling relationship between Zach and Anna, and addressing some academic and behavioral problems Zach had at school. The following four vignettes highlight the integrative nature of supervision. The supervision occurred as part of a clinical externship in family therapy conducted at IJR. Catherine Weigel Foy was the supervisor for Elaine's group, and all references to the supervisor in the vignettes refer to her.

VIGNETTE 1: MAKING CONNECTIONS

As an integrative supervisor, I enjoy the excitement and challenge of the initial session. As a beginning family therapist, Elaine would be challenged to enter the session with a few preliminary hypotheses and would have to read the feedback of the session to identify the constraints to Zach's ability to behave respectfully. How Elaine read, engaged with, and hypothesized about this feedback would constitute a baseline of her systemic skills. How she and I, her supervisor, interacted around this feedback would set the tone for the supervision of this case. In this initial supervision experience I attempted to validate some aspect of Elaine's competence and find at least one sequence in the therapy that piqued her curiosity about systemic therapy.

Only Sylvia, Zach, and Anna attended the first session, and Sylvia curtly noted that she hadn't told Michael about it, asserting that he worked nights and couldn't attend anyway. Elaine conducted a solid first interview, addressing the problem and establishing a consensus with Sylvia that disrespect constituted a good description of the problem. Elaine's attention, however, centered primarily on Sylvia, with occasional questions directed toward the children. Her questions suggested that she was thinking systemically, but there was little evidence that she could engage the whole family system in the therapy. As the family talked with Elaine, one sequence occurred repeatedly: Each time Elaine inquired about the problem, the mother complained about Zach's lack of respect and, when asked to comment on his mother's concerns, Zach complained about the behavior of his sister, Anna, who then sought and received attention from Sylvia. This sequence was of interest to me, because it included the three present family members and, I thought, could elicit a constraint that kept Zach from being respectful. From this sequence I inferred that Sylvia and Zach couldn't connect around the issue of anger and respect, that Zach was preoccupied with Anna's lack of respect for him, and that Anna and her mother might have a coalition that further angered Zach.

Because the feedback from this sequence was so rich with hypotheses about constraints, I wondered what kept Elaine from commenting on it. I had several hypotheses in this regard: As a novice family therapist, Elaine had not yet seen enough "in session" sequences to be able to read the feedback offered by it; her attention was focused on some other constraint; her first live supervision session had created performance anxiety that kept Elaine from seeing these in-session opportunities; or she could read the sequence but didn't know how to address it. I asked one of the team members to make a note of the VCR counter numbers so we could go directly to one occurrence of this sequence after the session.

After the session the team convened, and Elaine was invited to offer her observations and ideas about the session. She said she liked the family but was frustrated by Sylvia's passivity. I then asked her what hypotheses she had about the presenting problem and the constraints to solve it. She noted that Zach defied only women in positions of authority and wondered about Michael's absence from this session. Elaine hypothesized that Zach may be fighting "in his father's place" to maintain a male position in the family. She also hypothesized that the apparent distance in Sylvia and Michael's relationship was caused by conflict and wondered how this affected Zach's behavior. She wondered how much of Sylvia's feelings about her husband were "transferred" in her dealings with her son.

Like most beginning family therapists trained in traditional psychological theories, Elaine's initial hypotheses were grounded more in positive explanations—that is, theories about what caused the problem of disrespect—rather than negative explanation—that is, what kept Zach from being respectful. I

complimented Elaine, noting that she had evoked the gender, organization, and mind metaframeworks to understand the presenting problem and then invited her to consider how to convert her hypotheses from positive to negative explanations.

Elaine had a hard time doing this, so I suggested that we review a bit of tape, and played the segment that showed the sequence noted earlier. After the first viewing, Elaine saw the segment as an illustration of Sylvia's description of the problem and Zach's refusal to deal with it. Elaine's response confirmed for me that what kept her from noting and working with this sequence in the session was lack of experience. I told her that her description fit the data but suggested we play it again, and this time I asked her to consider what kept Zach from responding to his mother's statement of the problem. This time Elaine noted that perhaps Zach did hear his mother but that his sense of justice about her preference for Anna kept him from responding to her as if his anger occurred in isolation. She also noted that Sylvia also didn't hear Zach, as she ignored his concerns about Anna. I asked Elaine what metaframework might help explain these events, and she chose organization, noting that Zach and his mother seemed to have a polarized relationship and that this polarization might be exacerbated by a coalition that Sylvia and Anna might have against Zach, further keeping Sylvia from being able to address Zach's concerns.

Whereas a traditionally trained structural family therapist might be content with this hypothesis (Minuchin & Fishman, 1981), I pushed for other hypotheses, particularly one that would address the sibling subsystem. Elaine wondered if Sylvia's expectations of Zach and Anna were different and, if so, how this might make Zach himself feel disrespected. I suggested that another metaframework might be necessary to understand this issue, and Elaine selected development and gender, noting that perhaps the expectations for Zach and Anna were not age appropriate and were rigidly grounded in gender expectations.

Elaine and I now had a more complete, albeit complex, understanding of the sequence. But this complexity only becomes cumbersome if it contributes nothing to planning therapy. Fortunately, this simple sequence formed the basis for an important part of the treatment planning over the next four sessions. First, Elaine resolved that in the next session she would look for the sequence and, if it occurred, to comment on it. To do so would automatically make Elaine hypothesize and interact more systemically. She would balance her involvement with Sylvia and the children.

When the sequence did occur in the second session, Zach again complained about Anna. When Elaine took him seriously and gave him permission to elaborate, he said that his mother never corrected his sister's misbehavior, only his, and that his sister often provoked and then tattled on him. Sylvia initially disagreed but, when pressed by Elaine, she admitted that Zach had a point, but then added that, being older, Zach could be expected to behave more maturely. Already prepared with the development metaframework, Elaine hypothesized that Sylvia was expecting Zach to act older than his age. Elaine and Sylvia discussed what would be age appropriate for a 10-year-old boy, and for a moment it appeared that cultural expectations separated the two women, but Sylvia agreed to observe the children's interactions between sessions. Over the next few weeks Sylvia noticed the children's interactions at home and confirmed that Zach was correct. Validating Zach strengthened his relationship with Sylvia, began to correct the coalition between Sylvia and Anna, and gave Zach and Anna opportunity to work out their own relationship. Elaine helped Sylvia draw a boundary around the sibling subsystem so that Zach and Anna could work out their squabbles on their own and worked out some ways that Zach could be given greater privileges as the older sibling; for example, his bedtime was made later than Anna's. These changes greatly reduced the conflicts at home, and Sylvia reported that Zach was being more respectful.

VIGNETTE 2: WHAT TO DO ABOUT MICHAEL

Integrative therapy presupposes that the client system is the entire biopsychosocial system in which the problem is embedded. The entire system, however, need not be present for every session. Deciding who should be present and why is an important

question for integrative supervision. Pinsof (1995) suggested that individuals present in the sessions constitute the direct system and that those absent constitute the indirect system. In the Cancia family, Sylvia and the children initially constituted the direct system, whereas Michael, the extended families, and the school formed the indirect system. A key decision for Elaine was whether to include Michael, and the initial constraint question was: What kept Michael from coming to the sessions?

Although Elaine clearly took into account Michael's possible contribution to the presenting problem, she seemed too ready, at times, to accept Sylvia's definition of the therapeutic system: "me and the kids." In the sessions with the children present, Sylvia was uncomfortable talking about Michael and showed her displeasure with him by disagreeing with anything positive that Zach said about him. Elaine's attempts to address Michael in the family therapy provided no clarity about his role in the family, so I suggested that Elaine meet alone with Sylvia for part of a session to discuss Michael. This change of session format did not mean I intended to have Elaine abandon family therapy but rather that having Sylvia alone in the direct system would increase Elaine's chances of understanding Michael's role in the family.

Elaine liked this idea and stated that she felt Sylvia needed that time with the therapist. Elaine's response suggested that she might believe Sylvia needed individual therapy in order to solve the presenting problem. I suggested to Elaine that meeting with Sylvia to discuss Michael was not equivalent to embarking on individual therapy but rather a plan to address who should be in the direct and indirect systems. I felt it vital to draw this distinction for Elaine lest she conduct her time alone with Sylvia as if she were initiating individual therapy.

When Elaine met alone with Sylvia she learned that the couple had separated on many occasions (an ebb-and-flow sequence) and that, although Michael currently lived at home, the couple had what Sylvia called a "companion arrangement" in which Michael provided financial support and Sylvia kept house. Sylvia also said that Michael drank heavily on weekends and sometimes had angry outbursts when he was drunk. Elaine did not question the nature of the drinking or of the outbursts, so I telephoned and asked her to clarify both. I was concerned that Michael might be an alcoholic, that domestic violence might be occurring, or both.

Such moments when a therapist fails to attend to important feedback occur for beginning and, sometimes, experienced therapists, and it is the responsibility of the supervisor to ensure that the therapist addresses them. The constraints to addressing such material can range from failure to grasp the significance of the feedback to blocking on it because it triggers an interface issue for the therapist. Asking Elaine what kept her from addressing the drinking and the outbursts was a way to test these supervisory hypotheses.

Sylvia assured Elaine that Michael was not abusive toward her or the children but rather that "outburst" meant that, when angry, he broke things in the house. Elaine clarified that Sylvia did not believe that she or the children were in danger. Although I remained concerned about these developments, it seemed that Sylvia herself was not intimidated by Michael, neither did she seem to be asking for help to deal with his behavior. She seemed, rather, to prefer to continue the focus on Zach's disrespect. I was concerned that a shift to a different problem could jeopardize Elaine's alliance with Sylvia; therefore, I suggested to Elaine that she monitor the situation but not make it the primary presenting problem.

A similar opinion was rendered about Michael's drinking. Michael's drinking undoubtedly constituted a constraint to the couple's relationship, but to address the drinking would necessitate Michael's involvement in the therapy, and Sylvia remained opposed to including him.

Given this opportunity to ponder Michael's role in the family, Sylvia was able to expand her understanding of Zach's constraints to being respectful. She speculated that her and Michael's frequent separations and angry fights probably affected Zach. She seemed pensive about this but then added that it was she who had intentionally excluded Michael from the session and preferred that he not be invited. It seemed clear that Sylvia was struggling to decide whether to stay married to Michael, but she did not reach out to Elaine and ask for help with this decision.

After this session, Elaine and I discussed Michael. Elaine initially wondered why Sylvia put up with Michael at all and suggested that she would do well just to get rid of him immediately. I asked Elaine what might keep Sylvia from making such a decision. When we examined Sylvia's Filipino culture, her religious beliefs about marriage, and her possible financial dependency on Michael, Elaine was able to back away from this position.

I asked Elaine why we might want to bring Michael into the direct system, and Elaine correctly noted that he should be involved if his presence were needed to lift constraints to the problem. We both agreed that Michael was part of the web of constraints, but I also pointed out to Elaine that integrative therapy prioritizes protection of alliances among family members and the therapist and that one important principle of application is that Elaine should do nothing to jeopardize her alliance with the most important person in the system—that is, Sylvia—because if this alliance is broken Sylvia might withdraw the family from treatment (Pinsof, 1995). We decided, therefore, that Elaine would continue to spend part of each session alone with Sylvia to monitor Sylvia's feeling about the marriage.

I was relatively certain that the ebb-and-flow sequence of angry outbursts and separation would probably recur but also felt that Sylvia could not be forced to address this sequence. Several weeks later, the sequence did occur again, and Sylvia asked Michael to leave. He did, and in subsequent weeks Zach seemed to be calmer. Later in therapy, Sylvia acknowledged that not long after the start of therapy she had resolved to permanently separate from Michael and that the latest outburst was confirmation to her of her need to do so. I felt some regret that I had not pushed Elaine to include Michael in therapy.

VIGNETTE 3: A CHANGE AT CHRISTMAS

At one point there was a 2-week break from therapy for Christmas. At the next session Sylvia reported that she had decided to deviate from the Cancia family tradition and had not invited her family of origin to share the holiday, neither had she decorated in the usual fashion or purchased gifts. At the last minute, under pressure from Michael and Zach, she "threw together" a small celebration for the four of them.

During the mid-session break, Elaine hypothesized that Sylvia was depressed during the holidays, and she thought it best to address this with Sylvia during their time alone. I agreed that the manner in which Sylvia handled Christmas should be broached but suggested that depression was but one of several constraints that may have kept Sylvia from "doing" Christmas in the customary way. I suggested that Elaine explore this with Sylvia and to be particularly open to the notion that Sylvia's response to the holidays could be either a show of strength or of weakness.

Sylvia disclosed that over the holidays she felt herself becoming angry both with Michael and her culture's expectations of women as "tenders of the hearth." She stated that Christmas exacerbated these expectations, and were she to have done "Christmas as usual" she would have been expected to host Christmas dinner for her sisters and their families and that that would only mean another holiday when her sisters and Michael got drunk while she did all of the work. Elaine told Sylvia that she seemed to have made a conscious choice not to have a traditional Christmas.

Behind the mirror, I hoped that Elaine was reading this feedback using the gender and culture metaframeworks. Sylvia proceeded to describe herself as "more American" than Michael and that she wanted a "50/50" deal with him but said he resisted such a marital arrangement, believing that bringing home the bacon was enough. Elaine seemed to hear Sylvia but did not seem to know how to encourage her to elaborate these cultural and gender constraints.

I wondered whether Elaine would read this feedback about the holiday as a sign of strength, signaling a shift in Sylvia's identity, rather than a sign of weakness and evidence of the paralyzing effects of depression. In the postsession discussion, Elaine said she understood what Sylvia had said about culture and gender but was concerned that these views were

Sylvia's rationalizations to deny a depression. After all, she noted, Sylvia hadn't even been able to buy her children presents. I countered that perhaps the only way Sylvia could get herself out of one part of the holiday tradition was to have no part of any of it, including gift buying. Elaine agreed this could be the case but seemed annoyed that I wouldn't concur with the diagnosis of depression. I reminded Elaine that in integrative systemic therapy we are always willing to consider intrapsychic constraints but that there must be evidence to support this hypothesis. I asked what other signs of depression Sylvia manifested and whether Sylvia herself was signaling a need to work on depression. Elaine backed off and agreed to spend time alone with Sylvia, thus affording her an opportunity to address individual concerns should she have them.

Another question raised by the Christmas episode is what kept Elaine from using the opportunity to discuss a change in the couple's marital rules. Had Elaine considered what had kept Sylvia from approaching Michael and saying: "Let's do Christmas differently this year?" One hypothesis was that Elaine wanted to do this, but didn't know how or was afraid to do so given her concern about Sylvia's depression; another hypothesis was that Elaine had given up on the marriage and thought that Sylvia had used the holiday as garnering another reason to leave. Our later discussion revealed that Elaine had been so focused on her own hypothesis about depression that she had not thought about other possible meanings of the behavior. After reflecting on my hypotheses, Elaine said she thought Sylvia was withdrawing further from the marriage. She then said she planned to explore this more during her time alone with Sylvia. I hoped these discussions would create an opening to invite Sylvia to work with Michael on the marriage. Elaine remarked that although she didn't see this happening, she, too, wanted to offer Sylvia this opportunity.

VIGNETTE 4: THE ISOMORPHISM OF SYLVIA, ELAINE, AND THE SUPERVISOR

Integrative supervision explores and uses the relationship between the supervisor and therapist as a context for therapist development. This is often done by working with the isomorphic nature of the therapist–family and therapist–supervisor relationships (Liddle & Saba, 1983).

Gender was an omnipresent reality in this supervision. I was very aware that the supervisory system (supervisor and trainees) as well as the therapeutic system (therapist and family) was primarily female. Zach was the lone male in the direct system, and he was the identified patient. Michael was an absent male who posed significant problems for Sylvia. How the three powerful females would keep from overwhelming the males in this system was often on my mind. I posed the question to Elaine to consider how the dynamics of the therapy might be different if the therapist were male. She allowed that Sylvia might defer more to a male, whether African American or White, and that more in-session conflict between Zach and Anna might occur as they vied for the attention of a male. Elaine, very thoughtful after making this statement about the children's response to a male therapist, stated she was struck with how important men, and particularly their father, might be to the children.

When I asked how the dynamics in supervision might be different if I were male, she immediately retorted that if the supervisor were an African American man she would be faced with more dilemmas. She went on to proudly share her family history of strong, dominant women and remarked how our particularly gendered therapeutic and supervisory systems suited her just fine. I told Elaine that such strength in women is to be celebrated but that we must also figure out how to nurture and support real strength in men. Zach, as well as Sylvia and Anna, needed this from us. Elaine's level of comfort in the supervisory system provided a good medium through which learning could take place, but I was concerned that our relationship might be too comfortable and not challenging enough of her beliefs about men as well as women. Both Elaine and I left this conversation more thoughtful.

Gender also interacted with race and ethnicity in both supervision and therapy. As a White woman, I held membership in the dominant culture, whereas Elaine, an African American woman, was a member of minority culture, as was Sylvia, a Filipino woman. During the early phases of supervision, to build my

relationship with Elaine, I sought to underscore areas of similarity between Elaine and me: gender, profession, marital status, sibling position in a large family. But this attempt to draw on our similarities seemed insufficient to counterbalance the difference of race, as informed by profoundly different religious, economic, and political experiences. In subsequent discussions about gender and culture, I noted that, although Elaine seemed to consider the hypotheses offered by others, she was not very forthcoming with her own ideas. It is not surprising, then, that Elaine had difficulty initiating a substantive, in-session discussion about Sylvia's cultural background. She accepted Sylvia's explanations about her differing level of acculturation from Michael's, but she did little to build on this.

It seemed that Elaine was struggling with how to integrate her identity and experiences as an African American woman into the therapy with a Filipino woman and her family, under the supervision of a White woman of Irish–German descent. I wondered how muddled and disempowered Elaine felt. Elaine met my attempts to address our own cultural differences by focusing on the case—on similarities and differences between herself and Sylvia—and although she made a plan to expand such discussions with Sylvia in session, she never followed through with this. When I asked what had happened to her plan, she said that the timing of this discussion didn't seem appropriate.

I chose to respect Elaine's boundary with regard to culture and race for two reasons. First, I thought that the therapy was progressing well and didn't seem at an impasse because of this constraint. I also understood Elaine to be telling me, even if indirectly, that she wasn't ready for this discussion. I wasn't sure our supervisory alliance could withstand the pressure required to force such a discussion. The effort would require a willingness to reach into the depths of one's struggles, of one's pain, fear, or shame, to look into the face of the cost of privilege. I wanted Elaine to define her own reality, and it seemed prudent at the time to wait.

In retrospect, it occurred to me that meeting alone with Elaine outside group supervision to address these constraints may have been helpful. I hold many hypotheses about our difficulty. Was there a comfortable fit between Elaine's growing professional identity and her personal identity as an African American woman? How did my membership in both the profession of Elaine's choice and in the majority culture affect Elaine and her developing professional identity? How did the role of supervisor, and any power attached to that, influence Elaine? Most important, had I conveyed enough of a comfort level with my own racial identity to invite an exploration in supervision? Exploring differences can minimize potential constraints. Had Elaine and I been able to do this, the supervision would have been a far richer experience for both of us.

CONCLUSION

I believe that Elaine learned from her work with the Cancia family, and I believe the family was helped enormously. Sylvia had a greater understanding of and empathy for her son's struggle with anger. She had learned how to deal with him more effectively in those moments. The sibling relationship between Zach and Anna improved as Sylvia shifted out of the coalition with Anna and focused more on the marital conflict. Zach's academic performance and behavior at school had improved with mother's nurturance, support, and effective limit setting.

The supervisory process had provided fertile ground for the important changes the family made. Elaine was enabled to entertain more hypotheses about the family's constraints, which in turn influenced how she planned for and intervened in session. And, most important, through the continual return to the theory of constraints, Elaine learned focus in family therapy. Trainees new to systems work can easily be muddled by the complexity of a case and turn to working individually with clients. I attempted to highlight for Elaine the important decision points in the therapy—who should be included in the direct and indirect system of treatment, when the modality of treatment should be changed, and how to use the self of the therapist in the therapy. These decision points can be easily missed without

the focus that constraint theory provides. As Elaine expanded her hypotheses while maintaining her focus, she enabled the Cancia family to consider other options to resolving the presenting problem.

Each experience conducting integrative therapy and receiving integrative supervision enriches the therapist's template. The clinical decisions that are sometimes haltingly made with the aid of supervision become more spontaneous as familiarity with the theory of constraints increases and the therapist is exposed to classes of cases with similar profiles. One never reaches a point at which the "I have seen it all" attitude sets in. Therein lies one of the real treasures of integrative work: Each case is uniquely defined by the subtle interaction of the family and the therapist and by the many decisions they address to make therapy successful.

References

Bateson, G. (1972). *Steps to an ecology of mind*. New York: Ballantine Books.

Breunlin, D. C. (1999). Toward a theory of constraints. *Journal of Marital and Family Therapy, 25*, 365–382.

Breunlin, D. C., Rampage, C., & Eovaldi, M. (1995). Family therapy supervision: Toward an integrative perspective. In R. H. Mikesell, D-D. Lusterman, & S. H. McDaniel (Eds.), *Integrating family therapy: Handbook of family psychology and systems theory* (pp. 547–560). Washington, DC: American Psychological Association.

Breunlin, D. C., Schwartz, R. C., & Karrer, B. M. (1997). *Metaframeworks: Transcending the models of family therapy*. San Francisco: Jossey-Bass.

Liddle, H. A., Breunlin, D. C., & Schwartz, R. C. (Eds.). (1988). *Handbook of family therapy training and supervision*. New York: Guilford Press.

Liddle, H. A., & Saba, G. W. (1983). On context replication: The isomorphic relationship of training and therapy. *Journal of Strategic and Systemic Therapies, 2*, 3–11.

Minuchin, S., & Fishman, C. (1981). *Family therapy techniques*. Cambridge, MA: Harvard University Press.

Pinsof, W. M. (1995). *Integrative problem-centered therapy*. New York: Basic Books.

CHAPTER 33

USING THE MULTISYSTEMS MODEL WITH AN AFRICAN AMERICAN FAMILY: CROSS-RACIAL THERAPY AND SUPERVISION

Nancy Boyd-Franklin

The process of working with poor, inner-city families who present with many problems is often a major challenge for family therapists (Aponte, 1994). This can be especially difficult for young therapists starting their careers, who are involved with cross-racial or cross-cultural treatment and are struggling to understand the complex cultural issues that their clients present. In addition, older family members may challenge beginning therapists because of their youth and lack of life experience, further adding to young therapists' feelings of incompetence.

Many family therapists are confronted for the first time with the realities of poverty and inner-city life, which may include homelessness; poor living conditions; substandard housing; a lack of basic resources such as food, clothing, furniture, books, and school supplies; crime; gangs; violence; death; drugs; AIDS, and so on. It is often very challenging and even painful for therapists to approach these issues.

The presenting problem may be only the tip of the iceberg; therapists may find that families are grappling with multiple problems involving various family members. When this is the case, families are likely to feel overwhelmed, and the therapists working with them are susceptible to adoption of such feelings themselves. These families also may be involved with multiple agencies that they experience as extremely intrusive, such as the police, courts, schools, hospitals, juvenile authorities, child protective services, probation, and mental health services.

To best treat African American families, it is necessary to recognize their strengths and to conceptualize and intervene at multiple levels and in multiple

systems (Hill, 1999). The Multisystems Model (Boyd-Franklin, 1989) provides family therapists with a sound theoretical model and intervention approach that can lead to the empowerment of therapists and families alike. This approach includes, as necessary, the individual, a subsystem of a few family members, the nuclear family unit, the extended family, significant others, and nonblood family members. Church, community resources, and, particularly with poor African American families, the social services system, must all be taken into account. Individuals who are untrained in a multisystemic approach are at a serious disadvantage when working with such families. Without the ability to prioritize problems, understand the families' real-life issues, understand the culture of diverse families, and work effectively with other systems, therapists often feel incompetent and overwhelmed.

In addition to training, this type of multisystems work requires a special approach to supervision. There is often a multisystemic parallel process between the therapist and the supervisor that will mirror the process between the therapist and the family. This is more markedly evident in cross-racial treatment and supervision. The case example presented in this chapter was a turning point for me as an African American supervisor. It crystallized the interrelationship between treatment and supervision and indicated firmly the parallel process of empowering therapists to empower families. The honest exploration of cross-racial dynamics in the supervisory process allowed the therapist to openly explore these issues with the grandmother during the family's treatment. Recognition and praise of the therapist's strengths allowed him to offer a similar validation to family members.

CASE EXAMPLE

Background

The following case example[1] illustrates the Multisystems Model of family therapy with a poor African American inner-city family. Although the first sessions were office based, much of the subsequent work was home and community based. The importance of a home- and community-based family systems approach in reaching important extended family members cannot be overemphasized (Boyd-Franklin & Bry, 2000). This case offers a clear example of family resiliency and interdependence and demonstrates the many strengths common to poor African American families: survival skills, strong extended family bonds, spirituality, and religion.

In addition, this case was a challenge for me as an African American supervisor. I helped a young, relatively inexperienced, and somewhat fearful White male therapist join effectively with an African American family in which there was a great deal of conflict. It served as a "turning point" case for me, because it encapsulated all of the complex influences of my own training as a family therapist as well as the challenges of supervision in a multisystems case.

Mark Brown

Mark was a 14-year-old African American boy referred for family therapy by his school guidance counselor. His behavior had been deteriorating in school for the past year as he had become increasingly involved in gang activity and fighting with his peers. His family consisted of his grandmother, Mary Brown; his sister, Paula (age 15); and his cousins, Robert (age 20), Craig (age 10), and Robin (age 2). Mrs. Brown had legal custody of the children and supported them through public assistance. She reported that she was determined to keep this family together.

Jonathan, a young, White male therapist, was assigned to this case. He learned in the first session that Mark's behavior had become very problematic at home and in school following the death of his mother 6 months earlier. She had been an intravenous drug user who, through the shared use of contaminated needles, had contracted AIDS, the cause of her death.

Mark's grandmother was very religious and attended a Church of God in Christ. Initially, Mark was very involved in the church but began to pull away as a teenager. This had greatly concerned his grandmother, who was afraid that he would be "led astray" by his peers into further gang activity.

Mrs. Brown was an extremely strong woman—very verbal, articulate, and forceful. The therapist, as a young White man, initially struggled with the process of connecting with her. In contrast, Mark was relatively easy to talk with and to connect with. Therefore, Jonathan initially found himself drawn to Mark and intimidated by Mrs. Brown. He became overwhelmed and frustrated in sessions, particularly when Mrs. Brown, who could be very blaming of Mark, talked of little but Mark's problems, unwilling to focus on his strengths.

As the supervisor, I realized that if Jonathan joined only with Mark and antagonized his grandmother, the opportunity for change would be lost. I realized that a parallel process was occurring for the therapist and for Mrs. Brown; that is, both were feeling frustrated. Therefore, I worked very hard with Jonathan in supervision to see Mrs. Brown in a more positive light: to understand the burdens she felt over her grief at the loss of her daughter, her challenges in raising five grandchildren, and her own health concerns. We also discussed Jonathan's concerns about how he would be perceived as a White male therapist.

I encouraged Jonathan to spend a few sessions joining with the grandmother individually, praising her efforts and empathizing with her burdens. It is interesting that as the grandmother felt more understood, she was able to form a therapeutic relationship with Jonathan and to work together to help

---

[1] To protect the confidentiality of this family, all names and important identifying information have been changed.

Mark. Also, as she felt that her burden was eased through support, she became less blaming of Mark. In one session Jonathan explored with Mrs. Brown how it felt for her to work with a White male therapist. Mrs. Brown reported that she had not been troubled by his race or gender; what had concerned her more was the fact that the therapist was young and might not understand how difficult it was to parent. She responded that after this session, she felt more reassured that he understood her.

Initially, Mrs. Brown had been reluctant to involve the rest of her family in treatment. She was very invested in seeing Mark as *the* problem. After the therapist succeeded in joining with Mrs. Brown, she was able to allow him to meet with the rest of the family. Because a number of the grandchildren were resistant, an office visit was not possible. A home visit was arranged for later in the month when all of her grandchildren would be at home.

Approximately 1 week later, Jonathan received a call from a very angry and panicked Mrs. Brown, who reported that Mark had gotten involved in a "gang fight" in school and had been suspended. She was both "worried sick" and furious at him. The therapist met with Mrs. Brown, the school principal, the police officer, and Mark at the school that afternoon. They explored the details of the fight and the terms of his suspension.

Mrs. Brown was initially overwhelmed by the charges and the involvement of so many systems. She reported to Jonathan that she couldn't even think clearly about which questions to ask, or how to best understand what was happening with her grandson. The therapist helped her to calm down and supported her as she prepared a list of questions for each agency. He then accompanied her to the school, the police department, and the court.

Mrs. Brown, with the therapist's coaching, was able to intervene effectively in the school and the court systems and to advocate for Mark. As each week's family therapy session began, Jonathan and Mrs. Brown reviewed what she had accomplished in the preceding week. This also empowered her to set better limits for Mark. Without being overly punitive or blaming, she was able to make clear to Mark that there would be consequences for his actions. These

consequences also were reviewed with Jonathan at subsequent sessions.

The police officer recommended to the judge that Mark be given probation rather than time in a juvenile detention center. His school suspension lasted a week, during which Mrs. Brown imposed the punishment that he must remain at home and do extra chores, including cleaning the bathroom and the kitchen. With the therapist's help, she was able to stick to these consequences. Mark's behavior began to improve at home.

On Mark's first day back in school, the therapist, Mrs. Brown, and Mark met with the principal. Mark's guidance counselor, who also attended, suggested an "alternative school" placement for Mark for the remainder of the year that would offer smaller classes, less contact with rival gang members, and one teacher who would communicate regularly with Mrs. Brown. Mark and Mrs. Brown agreed to these conditions. The therapist supported Mrs. Brown in her efforts to remain in touch with Mark's teacher and probation officer. Mark's behavior and grades improved.

The home visit finally occurred approximately 2 weeks later. During it, a genogram was constructed with the family. It became clear that the entire family had experienced multiple losses and deaths and that all were grieving in their own way. The therapist learned that, in addition to the death of Mark's mother, his Aunt Carla, Mrs. Brown's other daughter and the mother of his three cousins, was an active drug user who was homeless and "living on the streets." Mrs. Brown expressed concern during the session that this daughter might also have HIV or AIDS. She rarely visited the family, and all were constantly worried about her safety and well-being. Jonathan encouraged family members to talk about their losses and concerns. For the next three family sessions, grief work was done with the family. Jonathan encouraged each family member to share memories of Mark's mother. The entire family, including even the youngest members, joined together in creating a family drawing of their memories of her on a large sheet of brown paper. This was then hung in a special place in the family's living room.

When Jonathan explored how family members coped with grief, all members, including Mark, reported that they prayed often for his mother and his aunt. Jonathan was surprised that Mark shared this, because in a previous session Mark had been adamantly opposed to attending church with his grandmother. When this was explored, Mark clarified that he believed in God but did not want to be forced to go to church. Mrs. Brown was surprised and somewhat relieved to hear this. To her further surprise, Mark's cousin Robert indicated that he felt similarly. Jonathan was able to use this opportunity to help Mrs. Brown to explore this issue with all of her grandchildren. It became clear that one reason that they had not mourned together was that Mrs. Brown and the three other grandchildren attended church together, but Mark and Robert had not been a part of this ritual and were in rebellion against what they perceived as the "strict rules" of the church.

In supervision, Jonathan and I explored the cutoff that had occurred in this family based on religion. I encouraged him to explore with Mrs. Brown whether she would accept the "beginning step" of having a family prayer ritual to mourn the family's losses with her grandchildren. She agreed. The grandsons Mark and Robert were seen alone together for part of that session to see if they would be willing to participate. It is interesting that they were eager to take part in this family ritual. They seemed ironically to miss the presence of prayer in their lives, despite their remaining adamant about wanting "no part of church."

The therapist was able to help Mrs. Brown, Mark, and Robert negotiate this impasse. They all agreed that Mrs. Brown would lead them in prayer at home for Mark's mother, who had died, and for Robert's mother, who was characterized as "lost to drugs." The therapist suggested that this could take place in the next home-based session. In that session, Mrs. Brown gathered all of her grandchildren and the therapist in a circle and prayed for both of her daughters. It was a very moving ceremony, and all of the children, including Mark, cried. After the service, Mark put his arm around Mrs. Brown and hugged her as she cried. This session had gone a long way to repair Mark and Mrs. Brown's relationship and was a major turning point in treatment. Mark's behavior at home and in school continued to improve. The family was seen for four more

monthly sessions to monitor their progress. These home-based visits provided an opportunity to share information about Mark's and the other children's continuing progress and to provide Mrs. Brown with continued support as her autonomy increased. Therapy was completed in June after the children successfully completed the school year. There were no more fighting incidents with Mark, and his probation was lifted by the court.

Supervisory Process

As an African American supervisor doing cross-racial supervision with a White male family therapist, I faced distinct challenges in the supervisory process. Jonathan was an eager, dedicated young man who felt overwhelmed by Mrs. Brown—afraid of her anger and worried that he might inadvertently offend her in treatment. Although his psychology doctoral training included a course in multicultural treatment issues, it had been rather superficial and had not addressed the complex and subtle issues inherent in cross-racial therapy. Jonathan's experience was typical of what many young White therapists encounter as they work with strong, assertive, angry African American parents for the first time.

I also sensed that Jonathan was afraid to raise these concerns with me, as we had just begun working together and he was anxious that I might question his cultural competence. As his supervisor, I had to help him to relax and feel comfortable enough with me so that these issues could be discussed. I tried to normalize his concerns by telling him that other supervisees had reported to me that, because I am African American, it was often hard to talk with me about their fears and concerns in working with African American families. I then asked him if he had had similar concerns. At that point, he relaxed visibly. He told me that he was afraid I would see him as incompetent, and he was embarrassed by his fears—of me and of the grandmother in the family he was treating.

Once again, I normalized Jonathan's fears and discussed with him the parallel process that was occurring. I emphasized that this was the most important work we would do in supervision together. Jonathan then shared with me that he had been working in his own therapy on his issues with his father, whom he had experienced as very angry and judgmental. We talked about how experiences in our families act as "buttons" for all of us and can influence our work as family therapists. This led to a very important discussion of the therapist's use of self and some ways in which Jonathan could use his own feelings in the treatment process.

Jonathan also reported that he felt incompetent because he was young and had not been a parent—a point that had been repeatedly stressed by Mrs. Brown in an accusatory manner. I began what turned out to be a number of discussions on these issues by talking with him about how parents and grandparents of children and adolescents who present with serious problems often anticipate blame from family therapists and other mental health professionals. This expectation is often more prominent with African Americans, who often bring a large degree of "healthy cultural suspicion" to the process (Boyd-Franklin, 1989; Grier & Cobbs, 1968). Many parents and grandparents in this situation will accuse therapists in anticipation of receiving blame. With this foundation established, Jonathan and I talked about the process of starting to praise Mrs. Brown for her love of her grandson and her determination to get help for him. We role played a number of important reframes that he used with Mrs. Brown, which included praising her strength—"You are a very strong woman"—her survival skills —"You are a survivor"—and her love—"You love your grandson and you are determined to get help for him." He learned to reframe her anger in a number of ways. He would acknowledge her anger and the reframe that she was "a fighter for her grandson."

In a parallel process, I began to actively praise Jonathan during supervision when he was able to successfully reframe Mrs. Brown's anger. We also explored his own initial feelings of inadequacy in his work with Mrs. Brown. He talked about feelings of being rejected by her. We worked hard to help him to not take her rejection personally but to see it as an indication of how judged she felt.

Discussion

This case illustrates many of the aspects of African American cultural strengths that are described in the beginning of this chapter. The role of the grandmother, Mrs. Brown, is typical in an African American extended family, in which older generations often intervene to take in children after the death of the children's parents or the parents' incapacitation due to illness, drugs, or incarceration. The cultural values of collective unity and interdependence are evident in Mrs. Brown's determination to "keep her family together." Evident in this family's life are the values of spirituality and religion as well as the multigenerational conflict that can often result when parents or grandparents with strong and strict religious values conflict with adolescents in rebellion against them.

Another interesting aspect of this case is the continued spiritual beliefs of the young men in the family, despite their lack of adherence to formal religion. The therapist was able to use their spirituality in order to help Mrs. Brown, Mark, and his cousin Robert join together as a family to pray for the boys' mothers without getting into a power struggle about church attendance.

In keeping with the structural family model (Haley, 1976; Minuchin, 1974), every opportunity was taken to empower the grandmother (the family executive) and to put her in charge: She was asked to lead the prayer; the therapist accompanied her to school and court, rather than going himself; and she set clear consequences for Mark's school behavior and suspension.

The Multisystems Model was applied throughout treatment. Jonathan, with my help as his supervisor, was able to join effectively with all of the subsystems in the family—grandmother, Mark, Robert, and the other children—and to bring them together. This led to a facilitation of the family's mourning process. Within this model it became clear to Jonathan and myself that Mark's role was to get help for his family members who all had unresolved grief and mourning issues. He was acting out their collective sadness and depression.

The Multisystems Model was also helpful in empowering Mrs. Brown and Mark to successfully navigate the complex interactions with the school system, the police, the courts, and the probation department. Once again, it was extremely important that the therapist empower the grandmother to take charge and to intervene effectively with these systems herself on her grandson's behalf. It would not have been as effective if the therapist had done this himself.

Finally, this case illustrates the challenges and importance of good supervision in training therapists to work effectively within the Multisystems Model. The supervisory process was a very "active, hands-on approach" (Boyd-Franklin, 1995, p. 369). As the supervisor, it was important that I be available to the therapist and provide a supportive environment within the supervision where he could process the difficult aspects of this work. The supervisory process provided him with an opportunity to further his own understanding of the therapist's use of self in the cross-racial treatment process. This is particularly important in supervision of therapists working with African American families who may initially be resistant to treatment. As Jonathan felt validated and had his own frustration acknowledged, he paradoxically was able to successfully reframe the grandmother's concerns and to join more effectively with her. Searching for the positives and the strengths in this family, particularly in the grandmother, who was angry and frustrated, allowed him to reframe her love and concern for her grandson. This led to the development of a therapeutic alliance with her that contributed greatly to the positive treatment outcome.

References

Aponte, H. (1994). *Bread and spirit: Therapy with the new poor*. New York: Morton Press.

Boyd-Franklin, N. (1989). *Black families in therapy: A multisystems approach*. New York: Guilford Press.

Boyd-Franklin, N. (1995). Therapy with African American inner city families. In R. Mikesell, D-D. Lusterman, & S. McDaniel (Eds.), *Integrating family therapy: Handbook of family psychology and systems theory* (pp. 357–371). Washington, DC: American Psychological Association.

Boyd-Franklin, N., & Bry, B. H. (2000). *Reaching out in family therapy: Home-based, school and community interventions*. New York: Guilford Press

Grier, W., & Cobbs, P. (1968). *Black rage*. New York: Basic Books.

Haley, J. (1976). *Problem-solving therapy*. San Francisco: Jossey-Bass.

Hill, R. (1999). *The strengths of African American families: Twenty-five years later*. Lanham, MD: University Press of America.

Minuchin, S. (1974). *Families and family therapy*. Cambridge, MA: Harvard University Press.

Author Index

Numbers in italics refer to listings in reference sections

Subject Index

About the Editors

SUSAN H. MCDANIEL, PHD, is Professor of Psychiatry and Family Medicine and Director of the Family Programs and the Wynne Center for Family Research in Psychiatry at the University of Rochester School of Medicine. She is known for her publications in the areas of medical family psychology, family systems medicine, and family therapy supervision and consultation. Her special areas of interest are assisted reproductive technologies, somatization, genetic testing, and gender and health. She is a frequent speaker at meetings of both health and mental health professionals.

Dr. McDaniel is coeditor, with Thomas Campbell, MD, of the multidisciplinary journal, *Families, Systems & Health*, and serves on several other journal boards. She coauthored or coedited the following books: *Systems Consultation* (1986), *Family-Oriented Primary Care* (1990), *Medical Family Therapy* (1992), *Integrating Family Therapy* (1995), *Counseling Families with Chronic Illness* (1995), and *The Shared Experience of Illness* (1997), two of which have been translated into several languages.

Dr. McDaniel was Chair of the Commission on Accreditation for Marriage and Family Therapy Education in 1998, and President of the Division of Family Psychology of the American Psychological Association (APA) in 1999. APA recognized her as the 1995 Family Psychologist of the Year. In 1998 she was the first psychologist to be a Fellow in the Public Health Service Primary Care Policy Fellowship, and in 2000 she will receive the award for Innovative Contributions to Family Therapy from the American Family Therapy Academy.

DON-DAVID LUSTERMAN, PHD, is in private practice in Baldwin, New York. He founded the Program in Family Counseling at Hofstra University (1973). Dr. Lusterman was the founding Executive Director of the American Board of Family Psychology (now part of ABPP). He is an ABPP Diplomate in Family Psychology, a Fellow of the APA and of the American Association for Marriage and Family Therapy, and he was named APA Family Psychologist of the Year (1987). Coauthor (with the late Jay Smith) of *The Teacher as Learing Facilitator: Psychology and the Educational Process* (1979), coeditor of *Integrating Family Therapy* (1995), and author of numerous articles and book chapters, he is also a consulting editor for the *Journal of Family Psychology* and is on the editorial board of the *American Journal of Family Therapy*.

CAROL L. PHILPOT, PSYD, is Dean and Professor of Psychology at the School of Psychology, Florida Institute of Technology, where she directs the marriage and family track and teaches psychology of gender. She was the founder of Community Psychological Services of Florida Tech, a training clinic for upper-level doctoral students. She is a Fellow of the APA, a past president of APA's Division of Family Psychology, a member of the American Family Therapy Academy (AFTA), and an American Association for Marriage and Family Therapy (AAMFT) Approved Supervisor. Dr. Philpot is on the editorial boards of the *Journal of Family Psychology* and *The Family Psychology and Counseling Series,* has authored numerous articles and book chapters in the areas of gender-sensitive psychotherapy, clinical training, family assessment, and therapy and divorce and has presented nationally. She has been quoted in *Bridal Guide, Bride, New Woman, Ladies Home Journal* and *Redbook* magazines and is a regular contributor to the *Sexy Seniors* column in *Florida Today's Generation Plus.* Dr. Philpot is a licensed psychologist and a licensed marriage and family therapist. Her book titled *Bridging Separate Gender Worlds: Why Men and Women Clash and How Therapists Can Bring Them Together* was published by APA in 1997.